The Coopers & Lybrand Guide to Growing Your Business

The Coopers & Lybrand Guide to Growing Your Business

SEYMOUR JONES
M. BRUCE COHEN
VICTOR V. COPPOLA

Coopers & Lybrand
New York, New York
Albany, New York
Philadelphia, Pennsylvania

John Wiley & Sons
New York / Chichester / Brisbane / Toronto / Singapore

Library of Congress Cataloging in Publication Data
Jones, Seymour, 1931-
    The Coopers and Lybrand guide to growing your business

    Bibliography: p.
    1. Industrial management. 2. Business enterprises—
Finance. I. Cohen, M. Bruce. II. Coppola, Victor V.
III. Coopers and Lybrand WD Scott. IV. Title.
HD31.J627 1987   658   87-21688
ISBN 0-471-85941-9
ISBN 0-471-85940-0 (Paperback)

Printed in the United States of America

10 9 8 7 6 5

CONTRIBUTORS

The contributors to this book are experienced, dedicated Coopers & Lybrand professionals with a depth of experience and involvement working with businesspeople in the "middle market"—those organizations operated by owners rather than by professional managers. The middle market includes most closely held and many small-to-medium-size companies—probably over 90% of U.S. businesses—and encompasses almost every type of enterprise, including service-oriented, technology-based, and manufacturing.

The vast resources of Coopers & Lybrand enabled us to call on these contributors from a variety of business areas, disciplines, and locations across the country.

Michael L. Borsuk, Melville, New York

Glenn C. Davis, Newark

Robert E. Engle, Indianapolis

Edmund B. Galvin, Chicago

David A. Gaston, Columbus

Daniel A. Giannini, Baltimore

Frederick W. Haas, III, Baltimore

vi

Joel F. Levy, New York

Richard S. Lough, Los Angeles

Norman R. Milefsky, New York

Daniel J. O'Brien, New York

John M. Ryan, Springfield, Massachusetts

Thomas A. Sherman, Minneapolis

Robert H. Stavers, San Jose

Michael J. Tashjian, San Diego

In addition, the following Coopers & Lybrand professionals contributed noteworthy insights and assistance: Charles F. Bodo, Philadelphia; Gordon E. Budke, Spokane; David A. Carpenter, Philadelphia; Richard M. Cummins, New York; Louis A. Donnini, Philadelphia; Richard M. Kaye, Detroit; James F. Lafond, New York; and Charles N. Porter, Atlanta.

People who devoted much time and effort to helping us clarify a number of technical areas are: Edward J. Abahoonie, New York; Ronald W. Banasz, Baltimore; Richard W. Genetelli, New York; Bruce Goldberg, Philadelphia; Edward R. Hansen, New York; Anne H. Maher, New York; Cleghorn D. Penn, Atlanta; Loren G. Peterson, New York; Joseph J. Nugent, Philadelphia; and Samuel Starr, Washington, D.C.

Finally we thank John R. Weigand in New York, our editor, whose demands for clarity and consistency kept the book on the right track.

S.J., M.B.C., V.V.C.

PREFACE

This book grew from a need that we at Coopers & Lybrand, the international accounting and business advisory firm, have perceived in working with growing businesses for many years: Entrepreneurs require business information to deal with the financial pressures of our changing economic environment, an environment that can encroach on profitability as well as on the very potential of U.S. enterprise. We, the undersigned writers of *The Coopers & Lybrand Guide to Growing Your Business*, believe that the potential for growth in business is now as great as ever. The marketplace is not only viable but also dynamic.

Any business—whether it is relatively young, or rich in tradition; whether it is owner–manager operated, or has a full financial staff—must accept the challenge of dealing with our complex economic environment. By scanning the table of contents or the overview section in Chapter 1, readers will find a range of financial topics to help in meeting this challenge. The *Coopers & Lybrand Guide to Growing Your Business* offers—to both new entrepreneurs and those with business experience—ideas, systems, suggestions, and plans to enhance profitability, growth, and prosperity.

SEYMOUR JONES
M. BRUCE COHEN
VICTOR V. COPPOLA

New York, New York
Albany, New York
Philadelphia, Pennsylvania

January 1988

CONTENTS

The Coopers & Lybrand Guide to Growing Your Business

intense competition by specializing in small-dollar leases that competitors didn't want. He learned how to market his service effectively through direct-mail solicitation while he continued to devote most of his time to developing and marketing the product. Meanwhile, he hired lawyers to collect past-due lease contracts, a controller to maintain the financial records and accountants to prepare financial statements. Thus, he was able to develop technical knowledge while effectively utilizing the talents of others.

This example illustrates that you don't have to master every skill to conduct your business. You must know your weaknesses, however, and make sure that you have effective backup in partners, employees or consultants. It may be a question of taking in a partner to get investment capital, personal contacts or a needed talent (a "mister inside and mister outside" arrangement), or of hiring an experienced plant manager to compensate for your lack of production expertise.

WOMEN IN BUSINESS

Since World War II, women have played an increasingly significant role in business, as indicated by these revealing statistics:

- ☐ Women fill an estimated one-third of all management positions in the corporate world, up from less than 20% in 1972.
- ☐ About 25% of all small businesses are owned by women, and the Small Business Administration predicts that percentage will increase to about 50% by the year 2000.
- ☐ Women now earn one-half or more of the undergraduate degrees granted in accounting, advertising, pharmacy and personnel management. They earn more than one-third of the degrees in law, business and management, computer science and data processing.
- ☐ A recent survey by Baylor University revealed that 47% of the male executives surveyed were comfortable working for a woman. That percentage is up from 27% just 10 years ago.
- ☐ Numerous advice books have appeared on the market, offer-

ing women tips on how to succeed in business. They discuss dress, gamesmanship and a better understanding of "cultural conditioning."

All of the entrepreneurial characteristics described in this chapter apply equally to men and women. Women entrepreneurs, however, sometimes face additional challenges. Our experience with many women entrepreneurs and those who have become partners at Coopers & Lybrand indicates that women entrepreneurs need to focus on three additional issues: networking, balancing priorities and finding role models.

Networking

Because their emergence as a significant and integral part of American business is relatively recent, women need to focus on making the right contacts. Meeting the right banker, finding other sources of capital or gaining access to a potential major customer may require greater effort. In our experience, advisers (accountants and lawyers) take on a more significant role—and must understand the need to provide introductions and networking opportunities.

Most cities have women's networking organizations—including several national organizations and ones dedicated to specific industries. The efficacy of these organizations varies widely. Most women report there is no substitute for calling on people—using long-standing contacts, calling friends of friends and soliciting referrals.

Balancing Priorities

Women must often balance a career, children and husband. Some women have suggested that they sacrificed a family life to achieve success in business. (In fact, many men have done the same.)

But women clearly have a greater challenge in balancing personal and business demands. They must find creative ways to satisfy the rigorous demands of a business career and maintain a satisfying personal life. Day-care centers, "flex time," a home office and a spouse who shares the child-rearing responsibilities are options that allow women to balance their lives successfully.

Many women have fixed times during each week for family contact and communication. Others have deferred having children or have chosen not to have children or to get married. Whatever decisions she makes, success is more easily achievable if the woman (and presumably any others affected) is comfortable with her choices.

Role Models

Women business owners who have had female role models report that they were better able to cope with the challenges of their business life.

Males can find numerous role models in every industry and at every level of achievement. They can identify those they can relate to and emulate them. Women also have role models in every industry, but they're not as evident. Some are well known, such as Liz Claiborne, president of the Fortune 500 company of the same name. There are many others. In fact, five of Fortune Magazine's 50 most fascinating businesspeople of 1986 are women, including Ms. Claiborne.

USING OUTSIDE PROFESSIONALS

Before operations begin, you'll probably have to rely on outside professionals for legal, tax and accounting advice. Later, when your business gets off the ground, you'll need the services of an independent accountant and, possibly, of management consultants. Few small and medium-sized companies find it practical to hire staff lawyers, tax specialists or management consultants. Those that do can seldom furnish adequate backup in support staff and research facilities.

The Certified Public Accountant (CPA)

The independent accountant's basic function is, of course, to report on financial statements. A CPA's knowledge of your business and of business in general makes this person an indispensable adviser on a wide range of matters. Your accountant can evaluate the financial implications of major business decisions, such as whether to buy or lease, build or purchase, acquire or be acquired. Your accountant can also identify weaknesses in internal controls and render vital assistance in tax planning, financial forecasting and choosing sources and types of financing, among other services. Few businesspersons will, or should, take a significant financial step without consulting their CPA.

In selecting the CPA, you'll probably do best by preparing a list of likely candidates and narrowing it down by process of elimination. You should be able to get several names from your business acquaintances without any trouble. Each firm should be interviewed and asked pointed questions about its approach to service, experience in the industry, range of services offered, personnel and fees. In evaluating the answers, think in terms of your future as well as current needs. Outgrowing advisers in a short time can be costly.

You should not ignore your reaction to personalities in evaluating a professional consultant, as it's important to be comfortable with the person. An atmosphere of cordiality and mutual trust makes for the most productive relationship.

The Lawyer

A lawyer should play an integral role in any of your decisions with legal implications. Thus, such items as contracts, leases and notes should be prepared or at least reviewed by counsel. Like accountants, lawyers often have a competence in general business matters that goes far beyond their primary professional discipline. For example, a corporate lawyer experienced in acquisitions is also likely to be skilled in negotiations.

Range of Services. Corporate reorganizations, real estate and estates and trusts are generally within the competence of most law firms. You would not, however, presume that a firm is experienced in, say, pension plans without confirming that fact. Accounting firms also may offer services in many areas of business management besides financial reporting. Examples include: acquisitions and reorganizations, international taxation, data processing, accounting systems, production planning and materials management. Some accounting firms offer specialized consultation in such areas as employee benefits planning, business valuation and computer services.

The roles of lawyer and CPA can overlap and, in fact, some practitioners are members of both professions. It's inadvisable, however, to use one professional to satisfy both roles. Few individuals can attain, even fewer can maintain, a high level of expertise in two demanding professions. The ideal arrangement is one where the CPA and attorney work together to consider financial, tax and legal effects of all significant business transactions.

Fees and Other Factors

Professional fees are usually based on time and the level of personnel used. For defined tasks, such as reporting on financial statements or preparing tax returns, a fee can usually be estimated in advance. For other services, you can ask for a range of hourly rates. Fees should not be an overriding concern. They are often recovered many times over as a result of professional advice. Considerations such as firm location, size and possible conflicts of interest may also influence your choice of professionals.

SUMMARY

A successful business can provide the satisfaction of being your own master and substantial financial rewards.

Success as an entrepreneur requires:

☐ A great deal of energy
☐ The ability to make decisions
☐ Self-knowledge, including knowing what you don't know
☐ Dealing effectively with a variety of people—employees, customers, suppliers and lenders
☐ Making yourself understood
☐ Knowledge of the product and the market
☐ Balancing the conflict between business and personal goals
☐ A lot of luck

3

Business Planning

A meaningful business plan and financial forecast are vital to the growing business, both as management tools and as instruments to raise the necessary capital and financing.

For the entrepreneur, the plan helps to define objectives and keep the business on target. For investors, the plan provides a framework to tell them who you are and why you need what you need. The forecast answers such critical questions as when you'll need the money, how it will be used and how it will be repaid.

The plan demonstrates the viability and potential of your business, as well as your knowledge and understanding of the variables necessary for successfully attaining your objectives. It also provides the financier with a basis upon which to evaluate both the potential for return on investment and the individuals who will manage the business.

Since your business plan is the first manifestation of your capabilities that the investor sees, it's important that it be carefully prepared. The planning process also can serve as a valuable exercise that should increase the chances of success in your venture.

WHAT IS BUSINESS PLANNING?

Business planning is contemplating: where your business is today; what the key market, technological, management, finance and other conditions are; what your goals for the business are, and, most importantly, how you realistically expect to get there. The course of action is spelled out in a business plan, and budgeting and financial forecasting are part of business planning.

Successful entrepreneurs and business managers must deal effectively with constant change. Good planning helps guide your company more steadily through our rapidly changing environment. In most companies, large and small, real planning is not accomplished. Either management, particularly of many entrepreneurial companies, believe they can effectively "fly by the seat of their pants" as they did when they were smaller, or the planning process becomes mired in a bureaucratic morass. The fact is that few entrepreneurs or corporate managers are really interested in being intimately involved in planning, because they recognize that planning is a time-consuming function for which they believe they are poorly qualified. But, as the founder or executive management of your company, why leave the consideration of a plan affecting the viability of the company to anyone but yourself?

Planning in a large company is different from the planning needed in a smaller company. For example, a smaller company's planning is much more susceptible to the impact of marketing and manufacturing variations. On the other hand, the smaller company is probably more flexible and can be more responsive to shifts in customer needs, the economy and other variables. Smaller companies usually should strive to excel in short-term planning.

Each company should identify its abilities and plan to capitalize on its advantages. The planning should be unique to the company. It must be based on careful analysis of all aspects of the business and aimed at creating, rather than stopping, something. The objectives of the company should be stated in terms of specific results, and plans must be measured and reviewed against timely and accurate management information, such as operating results, product and customers' profitability and inventory and receivable positions.

THE BUSINESS PLAN

Typically, business plans are prepared as a necessary part of raising capital from potential investors, bankers and other lenders, "going public" or a private sale of all or part of the company. Business plans also are prepared regularly by well-managed companies as a management tool.

In raising capital from third parties, such as venture capitalists or an investment firm, who may have had little or no previous contact with your company, a formal business plan is your calling card. Usually you will not get in the door without one. A principal purpose of a business plan when raising capital is to get your proposal read, so that you can take the next step.

The following are certain "do's" and "don'ts" to consider when preparing your plan:

- ☐ Be brief, but include everything important to the business. A proposal of seven to ten typewritten pages, double-spaced, is often ideal. Leave secondary issues and information for discussion at a later meeting.

- ☐ Avoid highly technical descriptions of your products, processes and operations. Use layman's terms. Keep it simple and complete.

- ☐ Be realistic in making estimates and assessing market and other potentials.

- ☐ Discuss your company's business risks. Your credibility can be seriously damaged if existing risks and problems are discovered by outside parties on their own.

- ☐ Don't make vague or unsubstantiated statements. For example, don't just say that sales will double in the next two years or that you are adding new product lines. Be specific. Substantiate your statements with underlying data and market information.

- ☐ Internal business plans and budgets normally are more detailed than those presented to external users. Accordingly, internal documents should be summarized and properly structured to facilitate review by outside parties.

☐ Enclose your proposal/business plan with an attractive but not overdone cover.

☐ Provide extra copies of your plan to speed the review process.

A business plan is unique to the company and, accordingly, the approach used and structure of plans varies considerably. Regardless of form, however, certain basic questions should be addressed concisely and closely in considering your plan:

☐ What is the company's business? While this may seem obvious, many plans tell the reader on page 20 what business it's in, and with some plans you're never certain.

☐ What are the company's objectives?

☐ What are the strategy and tactics that will enable the company to reach those objectives?

☐ How much money will the company need, over what period and how will the funds be used?

☐ When and how will the money be paid back?

The business plan shows investors and lenders the quality and depth of your corporate leadership and indicates management's ability to reach their stated goal. These factors lie at the heart of the decision to invest in your company.

Begin with a Summary

Every financier has more business plans and related material to read than he or she can possibly digest. To make it easier, therefore, we recommend that a summary of what you are trying to accomplish appear on the first one or two pages of your plan.

Your summary should clearly address the reasons why someone should invest in your company and should include a brief discussion of:

☐ The market potential

☐ The product and technology you expect to capitalize on

☐ The track record and depth of your management team

☐ Abbreviated financial forecasts

☐ The desired financing.

Describe Your Business. Briefly describe your company, its products and industry, including:

☐ Your company's operating history, present ownership and future objectives

☐ Your product's function and uniqueness

☐ The technology involved

☐ Your company's role within your industry and the trends in that industry.

Assess Your Market Potential. Market potential is where financiers separate the investors from the entrepreneurs. Many good products are never successfully commercialized because their inventors don't stop to analyze the market potential or assemble the management team necessary to capitalize on the opportunity.

This section of your plan will be scrutinized carefully. Your market analysis should therefore be as specific as possible, focusing on believable, reasonable and obtainable projections, including:

☐ The size of the potential market and market niche you are pursuing

☐ The market share you anticipate achieving

☐ The competition—who and what

☐ The marketing channels you expect to use

☐ The potential customers—who, where, how many

☐ The pricing of your product, compared with competitive products.

We recommend that you use independent studies to verify the

potential of various markets or market niches. These studies, in addition to being highly credible, can be very helpful in demonstrating both to you and to the financier the size and scope of the opportunity.

Specify Your Marketing Strategy. The ability to market your product successfully is just as important as your product's development. In presenting your marketing strategy, therefore, be sure to include a discussion of:

- ☐ The specific marketing techniques you plan to use—that is, how you plan to identify, contact and sell to potential customers
- ☐ Your pricing plans—demonstrating the value added to the customer, versus the price paid
- ☐ Your planned sales force and selling strategies for various accounts, areas and markets
- ☐ Your customers—how many there are and where they are located
- ☐ Your customer service—which markets will be covered by the direct sales force, which by distributors, representatives or resellers
- ☐ Your specific approaches for capitalizing on each channel and how they compare with other practices within your industry
- ☐ Your advertising and promotional plans.

Present Your Product Development. In broad, fairly nontechnical terms, present the status of your product development, to allow someone reasonably familiar with the technology or industry to conclude whether you are dealing with a concept, prototype or product ready for market. Points to cover in this section include:

- ☐ The extent of invention or development required to complete your projects successfully
- ☐ The track record of key people in developing similar products
- ☐ The proprietary aspects of your technology

☐ The reasons why your product is more advanced or better than the existing technology, products or services.

Outline Your Operations. Outline your plans for operations within various time frames. For instance, development, early manufacture, market development and first product installation—as well as facilities, work force by job category, extent of subcontracting, sources of supply and warranty and service strategy.

Your work-force analysis should represent a head count by function or department (or both) for a specified time period. This analysis not only will allow you to better plan your hiring, but also will demonstrate to potential investors the sensitivity of your plans to the hiring of key personnel.

Describe Your Management Team. Financiers invest in people—people who have run or are likely to run successful operations. So potential investors will look closely at the members of your management team. Your team should have experience and talents in the most important management disciplines, such as research and development, marketing and sales, manufacturing and finance. This section of the business plan should, therefore, introduce the members of your management team, highlighting their track records. Detailed resumes should be included in an appendix.

Provide a Financial Summary. Detailed financial forecasts also should appear in an appendix, but within your business plan— condensed to about a page—you should include a financial summary of your company, income statement, cash-flow analysis and balance sheet. Be sure this information addresses the extent of investment you'll need and provides the basis for a financier to decide on the potential future value of the investment made. The following is an illustrative outline of a business plan:

1. *Introduction and Summary of Business Plan*
   - Purpose of the plan
   - Business and history of the company
   - Major customers

- Summary of comparative income statement results
- Address and telephone number.

2. *The Company: Its Industry and Objectives*
    - Industry background
    - Corporate short- and long-term objectives
    - Company size; market share
    - Expected rate of profitability goals
    - Strategies to reach objectives.

3. *Products and Services*
    - Principal products or services
    - Proprietary position and potential
    - Product development
    - Trademarks and royalty agreements.

4. *Market*
    - Assess market size, history, market segments and product position in the market
    - Costs/benefits of the product
    - Market pricing: company's strategy
    - Evaluation of competition, type of competition, customer service, lead time, price, terms, location, product quality
    - Marketing strategy defined; how and why will sales be made
    - Describe type and size of customer base; relationship and percent of total sales with major customers; stability; special terms
    - Product distribution and sales force
    - Advertising and promotion approach
    - Product or product-line profitability and markups.

5. *Manufacturing*
    - Plant locations and description of facilities
    - Describe manufacturing process if unique
    - Capital equipment requirements

- Labor force
- Cost and quality control
- Back-up sources of supply.

6. *R&D and Engineering*
   - Status of product line; what remains to be done, how, time required, at what cost
   - Product life cycle, technical obsolescence
   - Plans to meet competition and/or obsolescence
   - Needs for manufacturing and applications engineering
   - Proprietary and patent position.

7. *Management*
   - Management team, responsibilities, skills
   - Identify principal owner-managers
   - Human-resource projections and plans
   - Supporting external advisors and relationships, attorneys, accountants, investors and lenders
   - Board of directors.

8. *Historical Financials*
   - Latest balance sheet plus income statements for past two to three years
   - Provide brief explanation of major operating variances
   - Consider sales and cost of sales data by product line if significant.

9. *Financial Plan and Forecast*
   - Profit and loss/cash flow forecast, by month or quarter for first year, and by year for years two and three
   - Forecasted balance sheets at year-ends
   - Provide summary of all significant assumptions used in forecasts considering sales plan, changes in customer base, selling-price increases, margin improvements, material and labor and other operating-cost increases, capital expenditures required, changes in receivable collection patterns, inventory lead time and turnover,

trade credit terms and availability and the effects of
income taxes.

10. *Proposed Financing*

- Desired financing
- Use of proceeds
- Securities or debt instruments offered, terms
- Payback and collateral.

11. *The Future*

- Commentary and summary on where the company is
  going.

In planning for "start-ups," new ventures, new product lines and
additional plants, the following should be considered:

☐ Identify the critical events or actions that must occur in order
for you to achieve your objectives; for example, opening of a
pilot operation to test a new product or service or approval on
a patent application

☐ Identify and assess the key assumptions on which the new
venture's success depends

☐ Set out events which must take place in a necessary sequence;
for example, the sequence may be:

—. Completion of concept

—. Product testing

—. Prototype developed

—. Pilot operation opened

—. Market tests

—. Production start-up

—. Initial key sales

☐ Develop a graphic presentation of the aforementioned sequence of key events by dates and by expenditures, if appropriate.

The Plan as Management Tool

Entrepreneurs and others who sit down to prepare an initial business plan are surprised to discover that the process is really a corporate self-appraisal and sometimes a personal self-appraisal. Certainly it is not an easy self-appraisal. It is this assessment aspect of business planning that makes the process so important for any ongoing operation to perform on a regular basis, even when additional financing is not a factor.

The corporate self-appraisal may be performed in conjunction with establishing an operations budget for the coming year. In conducting your corporate self-appraisal, ask yourself the following questions:

- ☐ What business am I really in?
- ☐ What skills in our organization are valuable or unique?
- ☐ What is my position in the industry?
- ☐ What is the nature of our markets?
- ☐ What customers am I serving? Where is my market?
- ☐ How do major customers view us?
- ☐ What image do we have in the marketplace?
- ☐ What image changes would we consider desirable?
- ☐ What market share do I want? When?
- ☐ What major changes are likely:
  - —. In our present services and projects?
  - —. In the technology of our industry?
  - —. In the nature of our competition?
- ☐ What, if any, plans should I have for product improvement?
- ☐ What are my five greatest strengths?
- ☐ What are my greatest weaknesses?
- ☐ What are my objectives for profit improvement?
- ☐ What business do I want to be in, in three to five years?
- ☐ How can I finance growth?

☐ Will my objective require capital expenditures?

☐ What specific steps do I need to take if the organization is to achieve my objectives?

As a result of your management assessment, the objectives of your company may be more clearly defined and stated. Also, the appraisal and planning process should put you in a position to better summarize strategies and tactics that will enable you to reach those objectives.

In determining your operating strategies, consider the following with respect to your stated or reevaluated objectives:

☐ What will be the effect on my current organization? Do I have the proper management, or must I recruit?

☐ What is the likely impact—short-range and long-range—on my financial statements? Can I afford this course of action?

☐ Can I raise the necessary funds for implementation? How much will I need? When?

☐ Does this strategy utilize my strengths and minimize my weaknesses?

☐ What will be the reaction of my bankers, stockholders, customers and community?

☐ What is the probability of success, and what must I do to improve my chances?

☐ What is the risk of doing nothing?

☐ How long will implementation of my plan require, and what will be the results?

☐ In what ways can I minimize the risks?

☐ When will I break even?

☐ What would be the impact of outside forces such as changing customer demand, recession, government regulation, labor unrest and competition?

☐ When should the plan be reevaluated for possible revision?

The Plan as a Road Map

The business plan should be used to guide and evaluate the direction and actual operating results of the company, as against those planned. If, after completing the business plan, it is popped in a drawer because it's out-of-date the day after it was prepared, you've missed the point of the process and you're throwing away good work and a useful tool.

The plan should be updated regularly to act as the real road map of the company. Variance from the plan should be understood and evaluated and factored into management's understanding of its marketplace.

In order to do this, you need an effective information system. Many entrepreneurial businesses suffer from a lack of management information. For example:

☐ Timely operating statements and balance sheets are often lacking

☐ Inventory records can be lacking or inaccurate

☐ Tracking of waste, product shrinkage and inventory losses may not be in place

☐ Product-cost accounting may not exist or may be out-of-date

☐ Aging of receivables may be prepared late and not reviewed by corporate management; old charges and credits based on such agings may hinder clear analysis of receivables and potential losses

☐ Profitability by plant, office, key customer and product may need to be determined and tracked.

Financial Forecasting

Most forms of business financing require forecasts. These forecasts serve to demonstrate not only the need for funds but also the potential future value of equity investments or debt repayment. Developing the proper financial forecasts is therefore a critical factor in obtaining capital for your business. It is important that your forecasts clearly:

☐ Establish the need for funds in the amount requested

☐ Demonstrate your ability to either realize the investment or repay the loan

☐ Indicate your understanding of the financial implications of your business's growth plans

☐ Portray a realistic measurement of your planned business activity—that is, integrate your financial plan with your business plan.

Content. The forecasts, including income statement, cash-flow and balance sheet, should cover a minimum of three years—a period in which realistic assumptions can be made without projecting too far into the future. The forecasts should be designed monthly, at least until you achieve positive cash flow. This is particularly significant because a positive annual cash flow may mask certain monthly cash deficiencies that must be provided for in the financing plan.

Sales. Sales forecasts should be based on prices that adequately consider the market for the product and its value to the customer versus competitive products in the marketplace.

Investors sense a serious danger signal when an entrepreneur suggests there's no competition for his or her product or service. The product may be unique but there are probably other products that do the same function. If so, the pricing has to be evaluated in light of those products.

Your pricing also should reflect cost considerations. The price should produce a return sufficient to cover the level of expenses typical for a company in your industry. In high-technology businesses, for example, higher gross margins generally are required to cover the higher costs of research and development, as well as marketing and distribution.

Cost of Sales. Since cost of sales is usually a company's largest expenditure, it's important to forecast it realistically. Costs should be divided among materials, labor and overhead, with the greatest attention paid to the most important cost components (for instance, materials in a high-tech company). Here are some points to keep in mind:

☐ Identify the significant materials components, together with cost estimates

☐ Integrate labor and overhead costs with your business plan

☐ Demonstrate that employment levels are adequate to meet production schedules

☐ Measure your cost of sales information against some industry norm, and explain any variances from that norm.

Expenses. All expense categories should be reflected in your financial forecasts. Although they are subjective determinations, they should be tied to actual forecasts, such as head count by department, space estimates, trade shows you plan to participate in and advertising programs. Expenses also should be compared to industry norms.

Balance Sheet. Because your balance-sheet performance has an impact on your cash flow, it will be a key concern to potential investors. The balance sheet should be integrated with the assumptions in the income statement. Important factors to keep in mind are:

☐ Levels of inventory must be considered in relation to the expected availability of products and service levels you plan to provide your customers

☐ Estimates of the capital equipment necessary to support your operation should identify types of equipment required in the manufacturing, engineering, sales and administrative processes

☐ As a start-up, or even growing, company, you'll need to keep your accounts payable fairly current if you want to keep sources of supply open.

Cash Flow. Cash-flow analysis is critical to any capital investment and the survival of the enterprise, because businesses can't operate without adequate cash.

This is a difficult area for most entrepreneurs and one we always review in our financial forecasts, to ensure that the analysis has been done and that it correlates with the other statements. The cash-flow statement will highlight cash receipts and disbursements from operations, financing activities and capital expenditures. Projected on a monthly basis, it will enable you and the investor to quickly assess the venture's cash-flow sensitivities.

If financial forecasts are prepared properly, they can substantially increase the probability of obtaining capital and can act as a tool to measure and evaluate actual performance. Prepared improperly, they substantially diminish your chances of obtaining financing and increase your risk of not managing the business properly from a financial perspective.

Financial Forecast or Budget? There is a distinction between a budget and a financial forecast. A budget is a company's planned course of operating during a period and generally is structured to motivate performance as well as communicate planning strategy. Budgets may or may not factor in the negative effects of all significant contingencies and uncertainties. The budget is prepared as part of the planning process, but normally is not an item for outside consumption.

A financial forecast, on the other hand, is management's best estimate of the company's most likely results of operations and financial position in the forecast period. The financial forecast should be realistic and both consider achievable opportunities and give recognition to all cost factors and contingencies. It is this more conservative and more realistic forecast that is used in a business plan, not the company's operating budget.

Developing a Forecast

A financial forecast and budgets should be based on three key items: an operating profit and loss statement, a forecasted cash-flow statement and a forecasted balance sheet.

A financial forecast that has been prepared without one of these three elements has a major blind spot.

A financial forecast is as good as the assumptions that underlie it. Assumptions must be carefully considered, using the best available information. Forecast assumptions must take into account both external and internal conditions.

All key assumptions used should be clearly stated in notes accompanying your financial forecasts.

External conditions include the inflation rate, market conditions in your industry, availability of supplies and labor and changes in income-tax and other laws.

Internal conditions are those sales, marketing and other assumptions that can be influenced by company plans or actions.

The following are examples of factors that must be considered in developing assumptions for internal conditions:

Sales

☐ Based on specific sales and marketing plans and studies, what are forecasted sales by period?

☐ What are sales by unit by period?

☐ What price changes are reflected in which periods?

☐ What are sales by period by major customer?

Cost of Sales

☐ What is the lead time to build inventory to service the forecasted sales level?

☐ What are the cost components (materials, labor, overhead) of cost of sales and what were cost factors based on?

Selling Expenses

☐ Relate selling and commission expense to sales levels

☐ Relate sales and marketing expense to promotion plans.

General, Administrative and Other Expenses

☐ Be specific; relate to specific plans, employee head counts, lease agreements and other planned commitments.

Receivables

☐ Forecast buildup of receivable levels based on expected average days sales outstanding and industry receivable turnover statistics

☐ Factor assumptions for sales returns, allowances, discounts and bad debts.

Inventory

☐ Forecast buildup of inventory levels based on lead times required for production and expected inventory turnover statistics.

☐ Factor assumptions for waste, shrinkage, obsolescence and slow-moving inventory.

Capital Expenditures

☐ Forecast capital expenditures based on production and other plans using contracted amounts or respectable estimates

☐ Consider forecast of major repair and maintenance items.

Financing

☐ Factor in assumptions about draw-down (funds taken as needed) of financing, including related interest cost and/or dividend requirements

☐ Determine that financial ratio and other debt covenants can be met on the basis of forecasted financial statements.

Anyone who has ever prepared a simple financial forecast or budget manually knows well the frustration of changing even a minor assumption and then re-doing the entire package. Now, with microcomputers and their electronic spreadsheets, the "number crunching" drudgery of preparing financial forecasting is greatly eliminated.

Easy-to-use microcomputer software applications make it possible to project the financial impact of forecasted changes in sales,

4

Sources of Finance

A common characteristic that one sees in a profile of all successful enterprises is adequate capital. In fact, adequate capital may well be the single most critical factor in determining whether a business will survive. By adequate capital we mean *available* capital, that is, not only money or liquid assets but also capital you can raise from outside sources *when you need it*. All other factors—cost, restrictions, reporting requirements, and so on—are secondary to this single consideration.

Volumes have been written about financial presentations, cost of capital, sources of money, types of collateral, negotiating terms, and so on. In this discussion, we will touch on most of these points, but our emphasis will always be on maintaining liquidity and funding growth through access to capital. The discussion is presented in three sections. In the first, we deal with the basic information demanded by lenders or investors, including your personal character, the nature of your business, your financial needs, and the guarantees you intend to offer for payment of interest or dividends and, in the case of loans, redemption of principal. In the second section, we cover the technicalities of business finance, including:

☐ The debt-versus-equity decision, with the relative advantages and disadvantages of each method

☐ Leverage, its upside potential, and downside risk
☐ Cost considerations
☐ Evaluating sources
☐ Acquisition financing
☐ Retaining your present capital through effective tax and financial planning

The third section deals with negotiating loan agreements, the provisions you want and those you want to avoid.

THE BASIC THREE QUESTIONS

All vendors and investors, however diverse their needs and objectives, will demand satisfactory answers to the following questions:

☐ Who are you?
☐ How much do you need, over what period, and how will the money be used?
☐ When and how will you pay the money back?

Who Are You?

This question is concerned with certain of your basic characteristics and those of your business; notably, what are your qualifications and aspirations, the management structure of your business, and your strategic position.

Personal Characteristics. Your prospective financing sources will want to know about your background, education, experience and business goals. Naturally, you will highlight whatever demonstrated capabilities you have for developing and managing a company. In describing your business goals, refer to specific time periods, ideally one year, three years and five years.

Management Structure. Lenders know that good management can succeed despite bad balance sheets, and bad management can easily destroy the best of financial positions. They will want answers to the following questions:

- ☐ Do you have a management team, or are you a one-person show?
- ☐ If you are in it alone, do you intend to keep things that way?
- ☐ If something happens to you, how will the business continue?
- ☐ If your goal is growth and physical expansion, is there enough depth of talent to manage those expanding operations?
- ☐ What provision have you made for ensuring the continuity of your business, that is, by grooming an associate or an employee to take over?

Your business may well represent your most significant asset, and its success may depend on the quality and continuity of management. If your ultimate goal is a sale, continuity may be less of an issue, but even here there are financial implications best faced up front. Certainly, when they know that the entrepreneur will eventually sell the business, lenders or investors will look more closely at the collateral or assets of the company than they would otherwise. Assuming the worst case, that is, that you become ill or disabled and other management is weak, they may be forced to liquidate their position.

Strategic Position. The next fundamental "identity question" concerns your strategic position, a concept that takes in the nature of your market as well as what stage of the economic cycle you are in. This last point refers to the developmental stages through which all entrepreneurial-managed businesses evolve:

- ☐ Start-up
- ☐ Initial growth
- ☐ Physical growth
- ☐ Possibility of going public or sale.

You should be prepared not only to identify the stage you are in but also to describe how you hope to develop through later phases. Your position in the economic cycle has a bearing on appropriateness of the kind of financing you have in mind, and possibly that of the prospective lender as well. For example, most new businesses start up or receive "seed" capital from the owner, his or her family, or other sources not in the business of making loans. On the other hand, many successful high-technology companies were started by owners who convinced venture capitalists to support them from the beginning. These entrepreneurs understood their particular products and their niche in the marketplace.

Always try to understand the investor's or lender's viewpoint. If you have a unique technology or marketing idea, be explicit about it. You cannot assume that the new investor or lender will know that fact. For example, even though the chemical industry is a basic industry, many specialized chemical companies are recognized as high-technology operations. Their access to capital is greater, in terms of sources and amounts, than many comparable companies in other industries. You, the entrepreneur, know your product and market best and can best identify its technological potential.

How Much, for How Long, and for What Purpose?

The basic tool for answering these questions is a set of financial projections. With your accountant and financial advisers, work out the most realistic forecast of your profit, cash flow and balance sheet position for the coming year on a monthly basis, and for four years thereafter, on an overview basis.

Let's look at some basic principles for developing these plans:

☐ Spell out your assumptions carefully. This will go a long way toward answering many questions that might ultimately be raised.

☐ Be realistic. An overly optimistic forecast will understate your real cash needs. Take into account the probability of reverses. If you do not, you will lose credibility with lenders when you approach them for emergency funds. Loss of credibility with lenders is to be avoided at all costs.

☐ Present only an overview, but have plenty of supporting data available. Most lenders or investors do not have the time or inclination to spend hours poring over a detailed forecast. When they do dip into detail, they do it selectively, so that you must have a great deal of information readily available that ultimately may not be asked for. Very likely, however, the prospective lender will compare your data to industry averages, evaluate your own historical patterns, and ask questions about margins, trade credit, customer terms, and so on. Your answers should not be more than a telephone call away.

☐ Know the sensitive factors in your forecast and plan adequately for any downside risks in those factors. This is sometimes called cushion financing. It involves analyzing such critical factors as sales, costs, and margins to determine what would be the capital impact if performance in these areas were at the worst levels foreseeable and arranging backup financing with a line of credit or alternative source for that contingency. Investors and lenders tend to consider "worst-case" planning as evidence of creditable realism on the part of management.

☐ Work closely with your financial advisers in developing your plans. We all have a tendency to fix upon our goals and develop a kind of tunnel vision, centered on those goals. By working with advisers and reviewing plans carefully as you progress, your logic can be subjected to the critique of those whose opinions you respect. Business is too complex today for any one individual to spot all of the problems, let alone resolve them.

☐ Arrange your financing when you do not need it! From a tactical point of view, this is probably the single most important piece of advise we can give. Commonly, companies seek to arrange financing or borrow money when faced with a crisis such as the inability to meet a payroll or the sudden need for the acquisition of expensive new facilities. These are precisely the situations in which lenders tend to be toughest. They see your position as weak, and they are reluctant to lend. Remember, most financiers are basically merchants whose stock and trade is money. They want to put their commodity to work with people who they feel confident can earn them a good return. To them, a successful entrepreneur, planning well ahead for long-term needs, will typically offer the most favorable prospects.

☐ Be sure to consider trade credit adequately in your plans. Are you stretching the trade as far as you safely can (without jeopardizing deliveries)?

☐ Identify the collateral you can offer. Forecasted balance sheets will reflect potential assets that would support greater capital levels. As your business grows, receivable and inventory levels will also expand with two vital implications; capital will be needed to finance their expansion, and the higher asset levels themselves will provide collateral to support greater amounts of financing.

When and How Will You Repay?

All financial sources, equity or debt, need some reasonable assurance that their original investment will be returned to them. Any plan that you present must indicate the how and the when of the payback.

Debt Financing. When you are seeking debt financing, make sure your presentation contains the following items:

☐ A cash forecast that shows you plan to repay. If the forecast indicates the need for further debt to refinance what you are presently borrowing (which should not in itself be prejudicial to most lenders), you and the lender should evaluate whether you are structuring the loan appropriately. If your forecast indicates a continuous need for differing levels of funds over the forecast period, your loan request should probably be for revolving credit arrangement. These arrangements typically provide for a maximum loan amount and permit borrowings up to a stated percentage of accounts receivable and inventories, so that borrowings fluctuate through the maturity date. At maturity, some automatically convert to term notes.

☐ A balance sheet forecast that provides the lender some indication of what values will be available to him or her for collateralizing the loan. If the projected values are in the form of receivables and inventories, you should probably be dealing with a commercial bank or commercial finance company, using a revolver or some form of secured-asset-based financing designed to vary with the level of assets. Such financing has provided an excellent source of capital to many growing companies because their access to capital increases in proportion to their volume of business and their working capital needs.

In addition, note the following basic guidelines for preparing a presentation for debt financing.

☐ Base your loans for facilities and equipment on the life cycle of those facilities. Many small and growing companies have made the mistake of trying to finance major expansions over too short a period, with the result that they deprived themselves of sufficient cash flow. Remember that when the new facilities come on-stream, your demands for current types of financing will probably also increase with expansion of sales volume, receivables, and inventory levels. If one looks back over the past few years, the value of establishing long-term loans for expansion of facilities is readily apparent. Later, when we talk about some overlooked sources of financing, we will discuss some possible low-cost methods of obtaining such capital.

☐ Identify the term over which you actually need the financing. Too often entrepreneurs try to start with short-term or other loans requiring a fixed payback, failing to recognize that increased volume as they grow creates greater financing demands. As a result, the entrepreneur spends too much time worrying about financing matters, specifically in arranging new financing instead of concentrating on the basic problems of the business. It is good to follow the principle, "Do not finance long-term needs with short-term money."

OUTLINE OF OPERATIONS

For best effect, your presentation should be organized around a business or operating plan. An outline of this plan should be a part of your presentation.

Preparing the Outline

The outline should be brief—8-10 pages at most. If prospective lenders want more detail, they will ask for it. One mistake of many entrepreneurs is to present voluminous plans, which may discourage potential sources that have neither the time nor the inclination to wade through them.

First, break down the plan by major topics:

☐ *Objectives.*
☐ *Specific Goals.* These are benchmarks for achievement of objectives.
☐ *Strategic Position,* including:
—. History of business
—. Products
—. Marketing and competitive posture
—. Sources of materials and labor supply
—. Facilities and capital expenditure forecast
—. Current and prospective capitalization.
☐ *Management,* including: ·
—. Organization
—. Resumes of key people
—. Plans for growth.
☐ *Pro Forma Financial Statements,* including critical assumptions.

Then identify the key factors that determine whether the investor or lender will become involved. Each case is different. In light of the issues discussed earlier, focus on the five or six areas that, for your particular business, make the ultimate difference for your successful operation. Explain your plans to your advisers; tell them what you are doing and why. They will probably have input that can help you and greatly increase your chances of success.

Prepare a one-page loan request indicating what funds you want, in what form you want them, and how you plan to pay them back. Close the outline by indicating the three best reasons for the financier to invest. Attach your brief plan to the request. Expect to be challenged. When meeting with lenders or investors, do not be defensive. Be prepared for a critical attitude, and for questions in reply to your answers. Some of the questions may seem almost provocative, reflecting an unsparing scrutiny of your motives and capabilities. You should remain cool and calm, replying in a manner that reflects confidence in your product and company. This composure will greatly increase your chances of success. Too many entrepreneurs become agitated, unable to understand why others question their obvious talent. Many financing opportunities have been lost, even at the closing, because of the entrepreneur's hypersensitivity.

An example of a corporate plan outline is shown in the Appendix to this chapter.

TECHNICAL POINTS

Having dealt with the basic questions of the financier, let us look at a few more technical aspects the entrepreneur should be familiar with.

The Debt-versus-Equity Decision

Two major considerations in financing are the type of arrangements to be used—that is, debt or equity—and the amount of indebtedness to be incurred. In the choice of financial arrangements, the entrepreneur may be able to use one of a variety of hybrid instruments, reflecting both debt and equity, such as debt issued with equity kickers—warrants, options, or other stock rights—designed to provide investors with additional incentives. In determining the amount of indebtedness to be incurred, the owner-manager's objectives as well as what the market will accept are of prime importance.

Advantages and Disadvantages of Each. Essentially, all types of debt have a commonality in respect to advantages and disadvantages, as do the various sources of equity. There are some meaningful differences, however, such as preferred versus common stock, and these differences must of course be considered.

Debt. Consider these factors in a debt arrangement:

Advantages

☐ Interest is typically a known cost. (Although rates are typically related to the lender's prime rate, it is reasonably estimatable.)

☐ Normally debt confers no claim on the future earnings of the company.

☐ Indebtedness may be used as a tool for increasing returns on equity, such as through leverage (discussed later).

☐ Interest is tax deductible; therefore, in a profitable and growing company, debt typically has a lower effective cost to the borrower.

☐ Debt involves no dilution of the owner's interest.

Disadvantages

☐ Interest is a fixed cost and increases the break-even point for the company. If the business experiences difficult times, debt will augment financial problems.

☐ Repayment schedules increase the cash outflow of a company and must be considered in future plans. Even in a revolving situation, where debt increases or decreases with asset levels, provision must be made for refinancing at the end of the agreement.

☐ Debt is not permanent capital with an unlimited life; provision must be made to refinance or repay.

☐ Debt instruments typically include substantive covenants or restrictions affecting control of the business by the entrepreneur and management. These will be discussed in greater depth later.

Equity. Consider these factors in an equity arrangement:

Advantages

☐ Equity financing has no fixed cost; typically, its cost depends on the future value of the company. (Where the equity is in the form of preferred stock with required dividends, this advantage may disappear.)

☐ A higher equity base provides leveraging capacity to gain more capital through debt financing. If, for example, for every dollar invested in equity capital, your financiers provide two dollars of debt, you can effectively increase availability of capital by three dollars.

☐ Stock and other forms of equity can provide permanent capital with no required payback. (In fact, however, most equity financings for small and medium-sized enterprises do contain some provision for payback. One device commonly stipulated is a put, under which the investor can require the company to repurchase his or her stock at a predetermined price or based on a formula.)

☐ If the new equity is preferred stock, dilution of the current owner's equity and value does not occur. (Admittedly, it can be difficult for a growing entrepreneurial-type business to finance on this basis without providing for convertibility to common stock.)

Disadvantages

☐ Dilution can be significant. Each case is different, but whatever percentage of equity you give up, you are sacrificing that percentage of all future growth. This sacrifice represents the true cost of the amount of capital received.

☐ Because of dilution, equity—not being tax deductible when

repaid in the form of either dividends or liquidation—typically has a higher cost than does debt. When you consider the potential dilution of future value against money received up front, the cost can be substantial. Equity provides the investor with an element of control over your business. How much control depends on the terms you obtain but, in many cases, even a less than 50 percent interest can convey substantial powers, such as the right to elect board members or veto major transactions. Significantly, there is a definite trend toward recognizing the rights of minority interests. The holder of a majority interest may have a fiduciary responsibility to minority shareholders. Finally, the investor may request similar restrictions to those found in loan agreements, if certain unfavorable events occur.

Note on Hybrid Instruments. Hybrid instruments present a special problem. Here it is necessary to determine if a reduced fixed-cost disadvantage of debt is offset by an unknown future cost of the equity kicker.

The Decision-Making Procedure. Once you understand thoroughly the implications of the various financing arrangements, you can make your choice. From a purely financial point of view, the key factors in your decision will be:

☐ *Cost.* Calculated and based upon projections of the company
☐ *Cash Flow.* Reviewed against projects of the company over the short run
☐ *Risk.* Determined by amount involved and method of repayment.

Also consider carefully how much loss of control you will be able to live with. Businesspersons often realize later that they cannot continue in business under conditions they accepted at the start.

Leverage

The concept of leverage is critical to most financing decisions and strategies for growing companies. Simply stated, leverage is the ability of the company to use a lender's money (debt) to increase the return on a company's equity base. Figure 4.1 illustrates in a simplified way how financial leverage works. Company A and Company B are identical, with one important distinction: Company B has borrowed an additional $100,000 of long-term debt on the same terms as an earlier $100,000. Company B earns the same rate of return (15 percent) on the additional funds as it would have on only $100,000 and pays the same tax deductible fixed interest on the debt (10 percent). By borrowing the extra $100,000, Company B has increased its net earnings from $21,000 to $24,000 and its rate of return on equity from 10.5 percent to 12 percent.

Company A	
Long-term debt 10%	$100,000
Stockholders' equity	200,000
Total capitalization	$300,000
Earnings before interest and taxes (15%)	45,000
Interest expense (10% × $100,000)	10,000
Earnings before taxes	35,000
Taxes (40%)	14,000
Net earnings	$ 21,000
Rate of return on equity ($21,000 ÷ $200,000) =	10.5%
Company B	
Long-term debt, $10%	$200,000
Stockholders' equity	200,000
Total capitalization	$400,000
Earnings before interest and taxes (15%)	60,000
Interest expense (10% × $200,000)	20,000
Earnings before taxes	40,000
Taxes (40%)	16,000
Net earnings	$ 24,000
Rate of return on equity ($24,000 ÷ $200,000) =	12%

Figure 4.1: Example of Financial Leverage

We can summarize the advantages of leverage as follows:

☐ If an investment opportunity exists to provide a rate of return higher than the fixed rate of the indebtedness, leverage will operate as indicated in Figure 4.1.

☐ Higher amounts of debt or equity capital at work open up more opportunities. Acquisitions of companies or expansion of facilities become more realistic with more money at work.

☐ Debt used for leverage does not provide any direct control over the business to the lender.

All this looks great, but it's not the whole story. Leverage has its negative as well as its positive side. For example:

☐ If invested funds do not earn as high a rate as the debt, or if you have a loss, the interest on the debt must still be paid. Interest is a fixed cost that increases your break-even point and exaggerates the effect of downturns in your operation. This is the exact reverse of what leverage was intended to do.

☐ Debt has a maturity and repayment schedule, affecting your future cash flow.

☐ Restrictions in loan agreements affect operations of your business.

You must consider all these pros and cons and analyze investment opportunities as well before putting funds to use. Empires have been built upon leverage, not only in real estate (a good example) but in all types of business. Conversely, some of our greatest bankruptcies resulted when bad situations were aggravated and the process of decay accelerated because of substantial debt.

Cost Considerations

The entrepreneur should be able to assess the full cost of the capital he or she is seeking. In the case of borrowed capital, the ultimate cost is determined on the basis of various factors, many difficult to anticipate, of which the current interest rate is only one. The ultimate cost of equity capital is reckoned in terms of dilution of equity and value.

Interest Cost

Commonly, the true or effective interest cost is much higher than the nominal (stated) interest rate. This is due to certain factors that can be grouped into three categories: those that reduce the amount of capital available, those that raise overall cost, and those of a hybrid nature.

Factors That Reduce Available Capital

Compensating Balance Requirements. These are funds that must be left on deposit with the lender. The following example illustrates the cost impact that compensating balance requirements may have:

Loan amount	$100,000
Less compensating balance requirement (10%)	10,000
Available capital	$ 90,000
Annual interest at a stated 14% rate	$ 14,000
Effective interest rate ($14,000 ÷ 90,000) =	15.56%

If you have a "float"—that is, a difference between book and bank balances reflecting uncleared checks—and that float maintains a consistent level, you can apply it to fulfilling your compensating balance requirement, thereby reducing, to the extent of the float, the amount of available capital you must segregate in these balances.

Up-Front Loan Discounts. The lender takes the finance charges or interest in advance.

Lags in Clearing Checks Received from Customers by Lenders on Accounts Receivable. In essence, the bank or finance company is delaying your collection of the receivables, effectively increasing your cost of capital.

Factors That Increase Overall Cost. These factors may operate up front or over the loan term:

☐ Points or other fees charged at the closing of the financing, which represent current dollars to be amortized over the life of the loan and determine the effective interest rate;

☐ Commitment fees for committed lines not used

☐ Prepayment penalties if a loan is paid off before maturity.

Hybrid Factors. "Equity kickers" such as warrants, options, or convertible features; or "puts", which allow the financier to require the borrower to buy back the equity kicker, thereby establishing a minimum additional cost.

Calculating the Cost. The preceding factors must be quantified to determine the average amount of capital available during the loan term together with the total costs on a year-by-year basis. Then, by discounting the annual costs back to present-day dollars at an appropriate interest rate, you can determine the current effective cost of capital. The interest rate must be adjusted for inflation, since a dollar today is worth more than it will be 5, 7, or 10 years from now. Present value tables are available to help you compute these amounts.

Equity Cost

Determining the true cost of equity capital—whether in the form of common stock, convertibles, warrants, or options—is a somewhat more difficult exercise than determining the cost of borrowed capital. The key factors are:

☐ The percentage of common stock ownership that the investor ultimately receives

☐ The company's projections of future growth in earnings and value (typically investors are skeptical of forecasts and will discount them by as much as 50 percent)

☐ An appropriate multiplier for earnings in the industry

When you compute the cost of an equity financing, you will typically find the rate of return or effective cost very high. Whether you should consummate the transaction will depend on two main considerations: first, your evaluation of investment opportunities exceeding the computed cost rate; and second, your ability to use the funds as a leverage base for further financing.

Equity Financing

In securing funds from any outside equity investor, it is useful to have, at the time of investment, a buy-out formula to establish clearly the cost to you of regaining the entire value of your company. If you and the investor can agree on an equitable formula based upon anticipated growth and establish an appropriate put (where the investor can require the company to buy his or her stock back) *and* a call (where the company or entrepreneur can repurchase the investor's stock), you will greatly reduce the potential for future stress.

Here again, consider the investor's position. If your goal is ultimately to create a public company, the investor will probably resist any formula that would allow you to buy him or her out at a price substantially lower than a future public offering might entail. Therefore, in any financing agreement, some clauses will give the investor rights to share in any public offering with you, to prevent dilution of his or her equity interest on a percentage basis, and to seek "piggyback" rights on any stock registration you file. Such rights allow the investor to sell his or her stock at the same time as yours, with the company bearing all or a portion of the registration cost. All of these terms and conditions are common and should be expected as a normal part of negotiations by the entrepreneur. However, the terms should be negotiated carefully. The key point is to agree clearly and definitively on a buy-back formula or approach up front, in order to reduce the possibility of friction with lenders and financial strain.

Choosing Financing Sources

An important factor, perhaps the principal factor, in your choice for the type and source of financing should be your business objective. For example, if your ultimate goal is to build a professionally managed technology company, you should probably talk, in the very early stages, to groups specializing in venture capital and in other forms of equity finance. Why? Because these groups understand and are comfortable with the financing of technology and growth and can provide wide access to capital for technological ventures. They can also help you secure a professional management team.

Alternatively, if you are building a growing and profitable family enterprise with a basic product or service, your concern may well be to maintain a certain market niche in the foreseeable future. In this case, your focus should be on building contacts with banks, finance companies, and other traditional debt sources. The entrepreneur's ultimate goal here is to ensure access to capital without creating any future calls on the equity position of the business.

For emerging businesses, the chief sources of funds are banks, institutional investors (which may, of course, include banks), and all levels of government. These institutions generally follow clear-cut criteria in selecting their borrowers and investments, and they generally provide printed information on the types of loans and investments they make. You should not assume, however, that these institutions, even those in the same class, will respond identically to your proposals. At any one time, a bank or investing body may be more or less conservative than other organizations of its kind, may be interested in a specific industry, or may offer unique financing arrangements—unique not so much in respect to rates but as to term and other conditions of repayment and amounts offered.

Commercial banks and commercial finance companies are the chief sources of commercial credit. The finance companies, however, are willing to deal with higher risk operations, often providing credit to new or expanding smaller companies that cannot secure adequate lines from banks. The finance companies rely to a greater degree on collateral values than the banks do, but the cost of funds from these companies generally reflect the greater degree of risk they assume.

Some Tips on Approaching Lenders. It is best to approach your source when your need for funds is not acute. At other times, your negotiating strength may not be as great. Ask a number of banks or investing groups—three or four will normally be ample—to evaluate your business plan (see Appendix) and propose a financial package to meet your needs. They should respond readily; this type of project is very much in their line.

Tell all parties what you're doing at the outset. Give the fullest and most objective consideration to the proposals, and then make your selection. The process of selection and the implementation of the proposal must be reasonably expeditious. If you fail to act on the proposal, you may give the impression that your intentions are not serious, that is, that you are just dabbling. The financial community is close-knit, and a reputation for insincerity could close doors to your company.

Government Sources. Government agencies often provide financing on more favorable terms in respect to amount, interest rates, and conditions of payment than do private sources. If you are in an area of high unemployment, for example, the local Economic Development Authority may give priority to your loan request. If you are building a plant in a rural area, the Farmers Home Administration may guarantee a term loan to your business to support physical expansion or increased working capital needs. To entice you to a particular community, a local development company (quasi-governmental or private) may, in combination with the Small Business Administration and local banks, provide capital for expansion at average rates lower than those of most banks. In many urban or depressed areas, grants such as Urban Development Area Grants (UDAG) may be available to reduce the financial impact of your expansion. Many federal and state agencies even make outright grants in certain cases.

Your bank or financial adviser should be able to supply you with information on this kind of financial assistance. In addition, you can consult your local chamber of commerce, the appropriate office of your state or local government or of the federal government, and your trade association. Once you have a lead on a particular opportunity, do not hesitate to ask the agency involved for further information and assistance in applying for financing. That is what they are there for.

Some Financing Vehicles

Financial analysts distinguish a number of stages in the development of business. The first two stages are initial growth and physical expansion. In the first stage, the financing picture is dominated by three borrowing vehicles; in the second stage, more specialized types of financing are also feasible.

The Initial Growth Stage. A new business usually has a tremendous need for funds. Typically, its accounts receivable and inventories are growing rapidly, and even though profits may be good, the maintenance of cash flow, through credit lines, is critical to support higher levels of working assets.

Three types of financing vehicles commonly available to support this growth are:

☐ *Revolving Lines of Credit.* Revolving credit is a continuous arrangement whereby the funds available to the borrower at any time represent the difference between a maximum established at the outset and the amount of loans outstanding. Typically, commercial revolving credit is collateralized by accounts receivable.

☐ *Accounts Receivable Financing.* Funds are advanced as goods are shipped, on the basis of a defined proportion—typically 80 percent—of eligible accounts receivable. Normally, the lender has some say in the matter of which customer accounts it must accept as collateral. Usually invoices are financed only for a specific period, normally 90 days from shipment. A variant of accounts receivable financing is factoring. Here the receivables are sold rather than used as collateral. This technique costs more than borrowing on receivables, but it eliminates some of the cost inherent in maintaining the accounts on the books and also the burden of assuming the credit risk.

☐ *Inventory Financing.* Normally this kind of financing is provided in tandem with accounts receivable financing. Because of the comparative illiquidity or inventory (which is seldom valued at more than 50 percent of the value for finished goods, lower for raw materials, and even less for work in progress), the advance rate on this form of asset is characteristically below that for receivables.

In negotiating any of these three financing vehicles, there are a number of features that you can stipulate to maximize the amount you receive. In the case of credit line, for example, the maximum granted might be tied to some growth factor in your business.

Other features that could be advantageous to you in connection with these vehicles are:

☐ Maximized advance rate on receivables and inventories based on *quality of your assets*

☐ Maximized time period for eligible invoices

☐ Provision for periodic temporary overadvances as an emergency capital source

☐ An inventory value defined for advance purposes as sales value or current costs [never last-in, first-out (LIFO) costs].

Physical Expansion Stage. Typically, physical expansion involves creation of new employment, which is an advantage in securing certain specialized financing vehicles, among which are:

☐ *Industrial Revenue Bonds (IRB).* Many states have programs to facilitate construction of new or expanded manufacturing facilities, essentially plant and equipment. The manufacturing company issues bonds, but the state underwrites them. The interest paid on IRB's is tax exempt and therefore bears a lower interest cost (typically about 70 percent of normal long-term rates). Often it can be used to provide 100 percent of new capital needs. Under current legislation, this interest exemption will not be available after December 31, 1989.

☐ *Leasing.* Assets, or more properly, the use of assets, may be acquired by leasing. This method may, in certain circumstances, be less costly than direct purchase.

The advantages of leasing are:

☐ 100 percent financing of asset cost, often including installation, is available

☐ Current loan agreement covenants may not be affected

☐ Payments are level over the term

☐ The terms may be longer than those available under other types of financing and are inherently more flexible.

The disadvantages of leasing are:

☐ Costs are usually higher than they are for debt; that is, the implicit interest rate is higher

☐ When the operation is profitable, property ownership provides an acceleration of tax benefits due to the offset of accelerated depreciation versus level rental payments

☐ Residual value may not revert to lessee unless stipulated in purchase option or renewal clauses.

Acquisition Financing

The acquisition of another business is a major event. Before embarking on this venture, you should carefully analyze the business and tax implications of the move (see Chapter 6). Do not try to go it alone; consult with your financial and legal advisers and with your key managers.

Some Guidelines. It would be difficult to furnish a complete syllabus of acquisition procedure because no two acquisitions are exactly alike. The following recommendations, however, are widely applicable to asset acquisitions (rather than acquisitions of stock).

Assets of the Acquired Operation. Look closely at financing potential in the assets of the proposed acquisition. Often you will be able to generate considerable cash from these assets, through either borrowing or outright sale of excess capacity. Acqusitions funded in this way are referred to as leveraged buyouts.

The following example illustrates this kind of acquisition; in this case, the acquired company is a consumer goods manufacturer.

	Capital Provided	Source
Real estate loan	$ 750,000	Savings bank

Equipment loan	800,000	Commercial banks
Working capital (receivables and inventory)	500,000	Commercial finance company
Subordinated acquisition debt	350,000	Seller
Equity	25,000	Entrepreneur
Total	$2,425,000	

The company in this example was able to consummate this highly leveraged deal because the business was basically sound, producing adequate cash flows to carry the debt and liquidate the principal; the assets had significant financing value; and the seller was willing to take a portion of the sales price over a period of years.

Intangibles. Where the seller seeks a significant amount for goodwill or intangible assets, negotiate for a deferred payout over several years, subordination to the other creditors, and either lower-than-market interest rates on the payment or a balloon payment or both. The amounts finally agreed on should be discounted to current dollars at an appropriate interest rate. These recommendations are designed to protect you from overpaying for intangibles.

Allocation of Price. The greater the percentage of the purchase price that is allocated to tax-deductible items, more is the advantage to you. If you can pay less for goodwill, which is not tax deductible, and more for a covenant-not-to-compete or consulting agreement, the tax benefits can reduce your net cost substantially. If these items are paid out over several years, the current cost (or present value) is reduced even further. Frequently, sellers are willing to trade tax benefits, deferred payouts, or low interest rates in return for receiving a price at or close to the asked price.

Tax Implications. Federal and state income taxes cen be substantial; tax savings or deferrals, therefore, can be significant sources of future cash flow (thereby reducing financing needs). In the case of marginally attractive acquisitions, the net tax result may be the determining factor in whether to go ahead.

Minority Shareholders. If there are minority shareholders or key management people who want to stay in or invest, consider offering them equity at a fair price. They provide equity financing and reduce the cash you need to acquire the company.

Contingent Payouts. Where possible, avoid payments hinged on future earnings without a dollar limit. These arrangements may well involve you in legal complications. There is, furthermore, a real possibility that the seller will gain legal rights at your expense or even substantial control of your business. If necessary, concede the seller a higher fixed price in return for a long-term payout. The present value may be within both the seller's and your acceptable range. Generally speaking, you should travel the contingent payout route only where the present value of expected future payments is clearly lower or the inherent risk of achieving projected returns demands a sharing by the seller. The seller should not be rewarded with additional amounts that result from your innovativeness and creativity.

Ownership of Real Estate. Evaluate with care ownership of any real estate to be acquired. Usually it is best to own real estate separate from the operating company. This ensures maximum flexibility in the selling of either the company or the real estate and provides an avenue (rent) to secure funds from the operating company.

Retaining Capital in the Business

No matter how much capital you obtain from outside sources, you will not get far in your business if you let that capital leak away without being put to effective use. The most common cause of capital leakage is poor cost control, especially the failure to give priority to more urgent expenses over less urgent ones. A probable second in rank is poor asset management, as evidenced by insufficient turnover of accounts and the presence of idle facilities and equipment that could be either put to use or sold. Other deficiencies that waste capital are:

☐ *Unprofitable Product Lines.* This defect is usually a direct result of unrealistic sale policies.

☐ *Failure to Utilize Internal Capital Sources.* Examples are failure to secure appropriate trade credit terms so that deliveries balance cash flow, overly liberal sales terms and collection policies; and neglect of cash sources such as life insurance policies.

☐ *Excessive Tax Payments.* This usually results from failing to adopt tax methods initially that will minimize income and other taxes in the long term.

Tax Planning. Tax rates are high; for every dollar your company earns before taxes, federal and state government could take more than 40 cents. They are, in effect, partners in your business without sharing the risks. Remember that every tax dollar saved goes directly to increasing profitability. The benefits of deferring taxes are also important; in certain cases the fiscal consequences of deferring a tax can be practically the same as those of not paying the tax at all. If the deferral lasts long enough, the amount of the tax will be defrayed in reduced interest expense.

In an inflationary period, the dollar return from tax planning tends to increase significantly for several reasons. First, both current-year taxes and estimated tax payments for the coming year are reduced. In a growth company, estimated taxes are typically based on the prior year's taxes. Thus a *double cash-flow benefit* can be achieved. Using the interest rates prevailing today, the present value of taxes (and other obligations) deferred for long periods is significantly reduced.

Consider the following tax-saving techniques:

☐ *LIFO Inventory.* If the cost of materials is rising, the use of the LIFO method for inventory increases cost of sales to reflect current and latest costs, resulting in a deferral of tax. There are ways of maximizing the benefits of LIFO with a minimum of disruption to your business. In fact, with recent relaxation of IRS restrictions, it is now possible to report results of operations simultaneously on both a LIFO and a FIFO basis to meet banking, credit, and investor needs.

☐ *Depreciation.* Try to deduct the cost of fixed assets, including property, plant, and equipment, over as short a period as possible.

☐ *Installment Sales.* You may be able to defer the tax on the gross profit on sales reflected in your year-end accounts receivable. You can do this if you are on the installment method of accounting for tax purposes. You can elect this method if your sales terms require or contemplate more than one payment— for example, 10 percent, either at point of shipment or point of order, with the remaining 90 percent payable in one or two installments due on normal terms. This requirement is flexible, not absolute. If credit or marketing considerations dictate that the installment terms should not be extended to all customers, you can still implement the installment method on sales to specific customers. You can also limit installment sales to late in the year (say, the last quarter) when collection by year end is unlikely. If you elect the installment method for tax purposes, you are not bound to use it for financial statements. Therefore, there will be no adverse effect on reporting results of operations; all profits are reported on a normal accrual basis.

☐ *Export Sales.* If you have significant amounts of export sales, consider the benefits of establishing a Foreign Sales Corporation (FSC). Essentially, an FSC will allow you to defer tax on a portion of the income produced by export sales. The period of deferral is maximized if you establish an FSC corporation having a fiscal year ending one month later than that of the existing operating corporation.

☐ *Utilization of Losses.* Be sure that any loss operations are either in a branch or a subsidiary corporation that may be included in a consolidated return. This ensures that any losses will be converted into current tax savings through offsetting taxes on profitable operations.

☐ *Separate Tax Treatments for Component Operations.* Examine all areas of your business to determine if any particular components can be treated as a separate entity and accounted for on a cash basis. In that way you will pay taxes on the income from that operation only when cash is received. This articulation is usually feasible if inventories are not a major component of your business. For example, any service operations involving extensive repair or maintenance work, especially under warranty, might qualify.

Do not wait until the end of the year to formulate strategies with your tax advisers. If you do, you will always find that the opportunity for effective action has been lost. In fact, the later in the year you act, the harder it will be to implement most of these opportunities.

NEGOTIATING LOAN AGREEMENTS

Most entrepreneurs approach negotiations involving money with intense anxiety. Too often they are either defensive to the point of belligerence, or they are too meek and get less than they should have gotten in respect to both amounts and terms. If you adhere to a few basic principles, you should be able to keep to the path of moderation between the two extremes.

Some Guidelines

First, make full use of your advisers, particularly your lawyer and your accountant. They may help you understand the significance of some of the points raised and determine which points are worth fighting for. Second, never suppress any of your objections to or misgivings about any point. Remember that all terms are negotiable—until the agreement is signed. Third, remember that you are dealing essentially with an institution and not an individual. A loan officer or financier may use reassuring formulas such as, "Don't worry; if anything goes wrong, I'll be here to help you, and give you a waiver"; but in the long run it is the written word that will bind. You have no way of knowing whom you will be dealing with in the future or what will be your negotiating position. Finally, look at everything from a long-range point of view. Restrictive clauses and covenants may not seem burdensome now, but four or five years from now they may be serious impediments. If you are apprehensive about the effect of any restrictive provision over the long term, try to build in a cushion. One way to do this is to link the restriction—by percentages, formulas, and ratios—to factors that can be expected to grow with the growth of the company.

The preceding guidelines deal with general principles. The following suggestions focus on more specific points:

- [ ] Try to establish a ceiling on the interest rate demanded. If necessary, offer a floor to fix your financing cost within a certain range. The more severe inflationary conditions are, the harder it will be to obtain this concession.

- [ ] Try to maximize the average use of capital. Among the possibilities you might propose are moratoriums on principal and/or interest for 1-2 years, balloon payments (for example, a 10-year loan with a 20-year payoff schedule), or any other expedient that would increase average capital and reduce payments in the early years.

- [ ] Seek a right of prepayment without penalty to allow you to refinance if rates go down.

If financial statements are required from independent accountants, it may be possible to arrange for limited reviews, as opposed to full audits. Limited reviews cost less but still provide the financier with a certain level of comfort.

Evaluate personal liability provisions very carefully. Try to set a limit on personal liability and also exempt specific assets, such as your home.

Covenants and other tests should not be too restrictive; otherwise, growth may be hampered. Severe limitations on capital expenditures are particularly burdensome. Restrictions on other borrowings should not preclude future financing.

Consider eliminating debt-to-net-worth ratios from the debt test, if possible, or alternatively exempting such items as deferred taxes and accrued salaries and wages, to allow more room for tax planning alternatives.

Ask for 30 days to cure a default, if default provisions trigger. Further, suggest the provision not trigger until notification is received from the financier.

Do not make too much of limits on dividends. The IRS, under certain provisions of the Internal Revenue code, can assess a stiff tax on the company for unreasonably accumulating retained earnings. A limit or barrier on dividends in a loan agreement is one argument for not paying dividends and thereby avoiding the tax.

Define clearly and in writing all unusual or subjective terms utilized in the agreement. Both parties should be able to look to the agreement for a clear definition of terms used.

Minimize collateral to maintain flexibility for possible future financings.

Consider carefully the nature of the collateral you are pledging in the light of future dealings with vendors and other third parties. In your industry it may be unusual for companies to collateralize debt with inventory or receivables. If so, point this out to the lender or investor. If this policy could put you at a competitive disadvantage, you have a strong argument against it.

If your pledge your stock, take a close look at provisions triggering default. They may allow the financier effectively to take control of your company.

APPENDIX: ANALYSIS OF A CORPORATE PLAN OUTLINE

The following report was prepared by a client of Coopers & Lybrand (name, product data, and dates have been changed). It outlines the company's present status—in terms of strategic position, sources of materials and labor, capital expenditures, capitalization, and management. A series of forecasts in the form of pro forma financial statements cover income, manufacturing overhead, marketing and administrative expenses, cash flows and balance sheets for a five-year period.

Outlines of this sort have proven to be useful tools in:

☐ Formulating long-range goals
☐ Determining financial needs
☐ Securing equity and debt financing.

The company in this example is a manufacturer of heavy equipment. The basic concepts underlying the plan and the approach, however, would be the same if we were dealing with a supplier of audiovisual aids or a foodstore chain. The development of this outline follows the standard format for any type of organization (as described in this chapter), although this plan outline, like any other, has its own special emphases.

Allied Engineering Corporation

Allied Engineering Corporation (hereinafter referred to as the "company") is a Massachusetts corporation organized on June 30, 1982. Its offices are located at 100 Industry Avenue, Springfield, Massachusetts. The company was founded by John Anderson, a graduate mechanical engineer with a BSME from the University of Massachusetts. Prior to founding the company, Anderson worked for manufacturers in the machine tool field for a 10-year period, holding various positions involving the design, manufacture, sales, and service of machine tools.

The company began as a manufacturer's representative in the field of machine tool accessories, handling product lines such as power chucks, power work rests, feed drives, and various grinding wheel dressing devices.

This activity became profitable after nine months, at which time the company acquired a distributorship for the power chuck and power work rest lines. Territorial coverage, at first restricted to New England, was expanded into upstate New York, New Jersey and Eastern Pennsylvania by the appointment of subagents. At approximately the same time, the company began to design and manufacture, through subcontractors, complete hardware packages, including electrical controls for use with the power work rests. This activity proved profitable and helped stimulate further territorial expansion, this time into Ohio. In Ohio, the company established business relations with a whole new group of important machine tool builders.

In mid-1984, the company became an importer and U.S. agent for the machine tool products of an English company. This line has been very successful, and the company has acquired a similar position vis-á-vis two other English firms.

In late 1984, the company became aware of certain problems associated with the manufacture of lathes, specifically with the feeding of bar and tube stock into various turning machines.

Foreseeing a substantial market for lathes of advanced design (in light of the rapid expansion in the use of numerically controlled turning equipment), the company began to investigate several design concepts. After a three-month effort, a simple, realistic solution to bar feed problems was found. The concept and design criteria are known as "the Guide."

To date, the company has received two firm written orders for the Guide and has built, shipped, and received payment for the first of these orders. Six additional machines have been manufactured and are available for shipment.

On September 1, 1985, a patent application for the Guide was made at the U.S. Patent Office in Washington, D.C.

The Product

Thousands of products in many industries begin their existence when a long bar of steel is fed into the spindle of a screw machine of an automatic lathe. One end of the bar is held in a chucking device and rotated at high speed. At this point, various cutting, drilling, and threading tools perform a sequence of machining operations. When the multiple machining is complete, the newly machined piece is cut off the end of the bar, which must then be moved further through the spindle, exposing another length of bar stock, and the machining cycle is repeated. The entire process is fully automated. The feeding of bar stock is itself nonproductive and, therefore, manufacturers want to accomplish it with maximum efficiency. The concept of efficiency takes into account such factors as safe operation, low noise levels, efficient loading of multiple bars, smooth control of bars as they are fed, minimum floor space consumption, rapid changeover from one stock diameter to another, simplicity of electrical interconnection between the bar feeder and the machine tool to which it is coupled, and the ability to handle a wide range of stock diameters.

The Guide resolves these problems and provides solutions that are presently not available to machine tool builders and users. Today's manufacturing machines are becoming more efficient and are operating at higher rotational speeds. To handle this requirement, the Guide utilizes supports that retain the bar stock every 36 inches between three rollers. In addition to promoting safety, these rollers operate at a lower noise level than other feeds that allow the stock to whip inside a steel tube in a V-trough. The Guide handles multiple bar stock with a simple loader mechanism. The bars are fed into the front of the machine instead of into the rear, as is done in much of the equipment presently in use. The Guide translates the bar stock by rotating the bar and simultaneously skewing rollers in the triroll supports.

This approach provides smooth, easily adjusted feed control, eliminating the stock bounce that is unavoidable with pneumatic rams and chain drives utilized in other designs. The absence of rams makes the Guide a very compact machine. Other feeders must be longer than the bar stock to provide room for the ram to push on the end of the bar; some feeders are as much as eight feet longer than the Guide's. The Guide provides extremely simple adjustments from one stock size to another via a hand wheel at each station. From this one adjustment, the support and loader mechanism are set to any bar size in the range of the Guide. Changeover of the four-station Guide is accomplished in a comfortable five minutes, a time unmatched by other feeders. The control package supplied with the Guide provides manual control as well as operation by today's most sophisticated numerical control systems. Interconnection to a turning machine is accomplished with as few as four wires.

The Guide utilizes modular construction, which costs less to manufacture and makes possible the simple conversion of the basic machine to several models. The first model handles various lengths of stock from one-half inch to two-and-three-quarter inches in diameter. At present, the company is developing a feeder utilizing the same principles that will be designed for use with multispindle turning equipment.

The Guide is the most universal and versatile stock feeder available today and provides effective engineering solutions to various problems associated with all other similar equipment.

Marketing

The Guide in its present form has a market price of approximately $10,000 per unit. The company intends to market it in the United States through machinery distributors and manufacturer's representatives, which will handle sales to the user. The company has concluded agreements with several such organizations, which have been in their field for many years. Sales to original equipment manufacturers (O.E.M.) will be handled by the company. In previous years, O.E.M. lathe manufacturers have designed and built most of the stock feeding equipment supplied with their machinery. Newer turning equipment designs have substantially changed the stock feeder capability requirements, particularly in terms of very high rotational speeds. In addition, stringent regulations imposed by the Occupational Safety and Health Administration concerning safety and noise pollution have further served to make existing stock feeder equipment obsolete. Today's lathe manufacturers are extremely busy and in this position have little or no surplus engineering hours to devote to the development of new accessories such as stock feeders, a fact that may account for the high interest manufacturers are currently showing in the Guide. The company feels that the O.E.M. potential constitutes a significant new market and will contribute as much as 85 percent of the company's early business and average approximately 50 percent over extended periods of time. A considerable number of contracts have been established with some of the more prominent lathe manufacturers. These contracts have generated requests for quotations in the amount of $400,000. A substantial portion of this equipment, if ordered, will eventually be shipped to a division of an automobile manufacturer. The company envisions an annual U.S. sale in excess of 400 machines by 1991.

The company is presently involved in negotiations with a large British corporation which specializes in automotive components and stock feeding equipment. In late 1987, Mr. Anderson visited the British company at its invitation and inspected its machinery division. Subsequent to this meeting, the British company expressed in writing its interest in becoming the company's agent for distributing the Guide in Common Market countries and also raised the possibility of eventually becoming a licensee for manufacturing the Guide. The company is presently negotiating specific terms.

Competition

There are few manufacturers of stock feeding equipment in the United States, and only one manufacturer whose sole product is stock feeding equipment. Other manufacturers of stock feeding equipment are typically very small entities operating within larger companies, and their sales represent an extremely small percentage of the parent company's overall sales. Investigation of all known stock feeding equipment, both inside and outside the United States, has not uncovered any model that utilizes the principles of the Guide or that is comparable to it, particularly in regard to rotational speeds, safety, and noise levels.

Sources of Material and Labor Supply

The company subcontracts the manufacturing of the producer's components and subassemblies, performing only the assembly function in-house. In the building of the first seven machines, approximately five subcontractors were used. There are a substantial number of other subcontractors within easy access that are capable of fulfilling the same requirements. The company plans to absorb most of the operations presently subcontracted during the next three years.

At present the company has 10 employees. It is not anticipated that the acquisition of additional personnel will present any problems.

Manufacturing Facilities and Capital Expenditures

The company occupies premises at 100 Industry Avenue, Springfield, Massachusetts, pursuant to an oral agreement; rental is $2,500 per month. These facilities encompass approximately 15,000 square feet, of 5,000 square feet are taken up by the company's office and manufacturing activities and 10,000 square feet are left unoccupied. Management believes that its facilities are presently adequate for the company's requirements but will not be for long. On the basis of business projections, management has planned a tentative 5,000-square-foot expansion in the third year of operation and believes that this expansion will provide adequate facilities for the ensuing five years. The premises are leased from Mr. Anderson, their sole owner.

The following is a schedule of estimated capital expenditures for the next five years:

First Year, Early

Item	Condition	Quantity	Price
Bridgeport miller	Used	1	$ 1,700.00
Surface grinder	Used	1	3,000.00
Engine lathe	Used	1	4,000.00
Brand saw	New	1	1,200.00
Cutoff saw	New	1	1,200.00
Drill press	New	1	500.00
Sunnen hone	New	1	4,000.00
Belt sander	New	1	500.00
Bench grinder	New	1	200.00
Arbor press	New	1	300.00

First Year, Early

Item	Condition	Quantity	Price
Flame cutting equipment	New	1	3,000.00
Black oxide equipment	New	1	3,000.00
Fork lift truck	New or used	1	4,000.00
			26,600.00
Tooling and inspection equipment			7,400.00
Shop storage and warehouse equipment			25,000.00
Office equipment and furniture			2,000.00
Truck	New	1	4,000.00
Research and development: electrical and pneumatic test equipment and experimental hardware			10,000.00
Total			$75,000.00

Equipment prices include cost of freight and installation in all years.

First Year, Late

Item	Condition	Quantity	Price
Numerical control drill	New	1	$35,000.00
Plain miller	Used	1	7,000.00
Multispindle drill (4)	New	1	2,000.00
O.D. grinder	Used	1	3,000.00
Bridgeport with optics	New	2	8,000.00
Bridgeport	Used	2	4,000.00
Hardinge lathe	Used	1	5,000.00
Compressor	New	1	2,000.00
Jigs, fixtures, and perishable tools			9,000.00
Total			$75,000.00

Second Year

Item	Condition	Quantity	Price
Bridgeport	Used	2	$ 7,000.00
Machining center	New or used	1	125,000.00
Surface grinder	New	1	7,000.00
Engine lathe	New	1	9,000.00
			148,000.00
Jigs, fixtures, and perishable tools			12,000.00
Shop storage and warehouse equipment			25,000.00
Office equipment and furniture			2,000.00
Total			$187,000.00

Third Year

Item	Price
Capital equipment	$100,000.00
Office equipment and furniture	3,000.00
Trade truck	3,000.00
Total	$106,000.00

Fourth Year

Item	Price
Capital equipment	$100,000.00
Office equipment and furniture	3,000.00
Research and development equipment and hardware	20,000.00
Total	$123,000.00

Fifth Year

Item	Price
Additional capital equipment and replacement of earlier used equipment	$100,000.00
Office equipment and furniture	5,000.00
Trade truck	4,000.00
Total	$109,000.00

Management and Directors

The names and addresses of the officers and directors of the company are as follows:

Name and Address	Position
John Anderson Springfield, Mass.[1]	President, treasurer, and director
Phyllis Anderson Springfield, Mass.	Director
Robert W. Clark Springfield, Mass.[1]	Director, secretary
David Anderson Boston, Mass.	Director
Ralph Davis Longmeadow, Mass.[1]	Director
Paul Johnson Suffield, Conn.[1]	Director

[1]Denotes members of the Executive Committee scheduled to meet weekly. Meetings of the full Board of Directors are scheduled quarterly.

The company is actively involved with outside counseling. The Massachusetts chapter of SCORE (Service Corps of Retired Executives), sponsored by S.B.A., is providing substantial guidance in the areas of planning, marketing, and manufacturing. Financial service is being obtained through a coordinated effort with SCORE and the international accounting firm of Coopers & Lybrand. Corporate counsel is being provided by the law firm of Lyons and Kennedy.

Capitalization

The authorized capital stock of the company consists of 80,000 shares of common stock, without par value. The company is presently involved in a private intrastate offering of its common stock. Prior to the offering, stockholders owned 45,000 shares. The offering to the public is 20,000 shares at an offering price of $10 per share. This price was arbitrarily set by the company; it was not based on earnings, and the company does not represent that the stock has a market value of $10 or could be sold at that price. No dealer, salesperson, or other person has been authorized to give any information or make any representation of the offering. All proceeds will go to the company. To date, 3,400 shares have been purchased by the public, leaving 16,600 shares available. If the offering is completed, the purchasers will own 20,000 shares, or approximately 30.7 percent of the shares that will be outstanding.

Long-Range Plans

The long-range plans of the company encompass expansion of the existing equipment designs, extension of marketing efforts into foreign countries, development of additional feeder equipment, and introduction of new machine tool products.

The present Guide designs have been created particularly for applications with single-spindle lathes. This covers adaptations from simple engine lathes to sophisticated, numerically controlled turning centers. With additional engineering, the present design will be adaptable for use with other types of equipment requiring stock feeders, such as single-spindle automatic screw machines, cutoff saws and presses.

As discussed in the "Marketing" section, considerable efforts have been made toward expanding business into the European Common Market countries through association with a British company. There are other markets of comparable importance, such as Japan. To date, however, no contacts have been made.

The company has given considerable thought to applying the Guide principles to other feeder designs. Currently, interest is focused on developing units capable of adapting to multiple-spindle turning equipment. At least three additional feeder models are envisioned, compatible with four, six, and eight-spindle equipment, respectively. In the five-year forecast, funds have been allocated for use in the development of this new feeder equipment. New product development is also basic to the company's long-range plan. Concepts have been formulated toward the development of a turning machine, and some preliminary engineering work has been done. Management believes there is a tremendous need for such a machine of proper design and price. There is no question that the company's personnel are capable of designing such a machine and producing a prototype. As presently conceived, the turning machine could sell at the rate of several thousand per year, at a unit sales price in the vicinity of $15,000. Should the turning machine concepts prove sound, the company expects that additional capitalization will be required to pursue this effort. (Potential revenues from the sale of these turning machines have not been included in the five-year forecast.)

The following financial statements represent management's best forecasts of financial position and the results of operations during the five-year period ending June 30, 1993.

Basic Assumptions

Operating

Sales. Sales terms are net 30 days. Two-thirds of the sales volume during 1989 and 1990 will be handled through distribution to the user market. In 1991 and thereafter, one-half of the sales volume will be to the O.E.M. market and one-half to the user market. Sales to the O.E.M. market will be the net of a 10 percent discount to the O.E.M., while sales through distributors will be at full list price but will result in a 10 percent commission to the distributor.

Management estimates that average selling prices and volume during the forecast period will be as follows:

	1989	1990	1991	1992	1993
Volume in units	50	150	240	310	420
Average gross selling price	$10,000	$10,500	$11,000	$12,000	$13,000

The higher selling prices after 1990 are primarily the result of more advanced phases with more capabilities than the initial model. Management intends to pursue a vigorous program of cost reduction in order to maintain the sales price of the Guide at competitive levels. Thus it is expected that, while the sales prices of the present models may decrease in later years, more advanced models will account for a greater percentage of sales volume, with a resulting higher average selling price in future years.

Cost of Sales. Materials and subcontracting costs are based on actual costs to date of constructing bar feeders, adjusted after 1989 to reflect:

☐ A gradual transition over the period from purchase of all parts to full manufacture by the company of its own parts

☐ Increased costs resulting from the manufacture of a more advanced model

☐ The expected results of management's cost reduction program and economies resulting from higher volume levels.

Manufacturing labor will increase over the period as more manufacturing activity is performed to replace subcontracting. At the same time, labor rates are expected to increase at rates ranging from 6 to 10 percent per year. Fringe benefits have been included for all types of labor at 28 percent gross payroll.

Anticipated increases in assembly labor are based on management's estimate of the manpower required to handle expected volume levels and expected increases in labor rates. Management expects to increase the number of assembly employees by 2 each year.

Manufacturing overhead as shown in the detailed schedule is based on management's estimate of the amount and type of costs required for the volume levels projected. Rent is raised in 1991 to reflect additional space used. Engineering salaries are based on the salary and fringe benefit costs of the following number of people:

1989	1
1990	1
1991	2
1992	3
1993	4

Anticipated research and development costs for new and improved products and new product lines have been included. Rapid depreciation is used for tax purposes, while book depreciation is based on the straight-line method using the estimated useful life.

Marketing Expenses. Marketing expenses are based on management's estimate of the effort required to achieve the forecast volume levels. Commissions reflect 10 percent of the sales volume forecast to be handled by distributors. Sales salaries are based on the following staff, including, in the later years, a full-time sales executive:

1989	2
1990	3
1991	3
1992	5
1993	5

Advertising consists primarily of trade advertising, and provision has been made for one trade show in 1989 and two shows in all other years.

Administrative Expenses. Administrative salaries increase significantly after 1990 to reflect the addition of an officer to assist the president on a full-time basis and to provide for continuity of management. Office salaries are based on the following number of people, including an office manager or controller in the later years:

1989	2 (part-time)
1990	3
1991	4
1992	5
1993	5

Provision has been made for legal costs expected in connection with the company's patent activities. Key man insurance is carried on the president and, for the first two years, on the company's consulting engineer. These policies build cash value approximately equal to their yearly cost. Bad debts have been provided for at 1 percent of sales as the company expects to pursue an aggressive sales policy.

Federal and State Income Taxes. Income taxes reflect both federal and Massachusetts taxes. Tax credits for research and development are expected to remain unchanged. The timing of cash payments for income taxes and related estimates is based on current provisions of the laws.

Accounts Receivable. Projections are based on an average of 40 days sales in receivables at all times. This average provides for possible payment delays by customers. Customer deposits and prepayments have not been considered for projection purposes.

Inventories. Management estimates that one month's supply of raw material and purchased parts will be required to be on hand at all times. The projections reflect this estimate. The projections reflect an inventory of three months' sales as in process and finished at an average of 50 percent complete. This is consistent with the 12-week manufacturing cycle estimated by management.

Accounts Payable and Accrued Expenses. Projections are based on an average of one month's raw materials and purchased parts carried in inventory plus a comparable amount for the material and parts content of the in-process and finished inventory.

Financing Assumptions

Management is presently seeking sources of equity and debt capital. The ratios of equity and debt financing cannot be determined at this time. For purposes of the projections, however, the following have been assumed:

☐ The company will raise $100,000 of equity capital during 1989

☐ The company will secure debt capital of $250,000 during 1989 and 1990. The assumed terms of such debt include interest at 9 percent and principal payback at an equal rate on each August 1 beginning in 1990.

Capital Expenditures

The projections include capital expenditures in the amounts estimated by management and during the periods management believes necessary. Such amounts and periods are as follows:

1989	$150,000
1990	$187,000
1991	$106,000
1992	$123,000
1993	$109,000

5

Forms of Doing Business

One of the most important decisions to make when going into business is on the appropriate form of business ownership. This decision will have far-reaching tax, financial, legal and business implications.

There is generally no one recommended form for carrying on a particular business activity. The decision must be based on the specific facts and circumstances of each individual situation. As changes occur or different needs arise, the form of doing business may need to be reexamined and the alternatives reevaluated. In this chapter we will explore the principal forms of doing business, with special emphasis on the advantages and disadvantages of each form (for a tabular comparison of various forms of doing business, see the appendix to this chapter).

PROPRIETORSHIP

A proprietorship is an unincorporated business owned by one individual. It can be undertaken without the formalities associated with other forms of business, and in some states you may not have to register. A key disadvantage of doing business as a proprietorship or as a partnership is personal liability for the obligations of the business. But both partnerships and proprietorships afford their owners the ability to exercise exclusive control.

Taxation

Since a proprietorship is not a separate entity for tax purposes, it does not pay a separate income tax. The taxable transactions of the proprietorship are attributed to the proprietor, who combines them with his or her income, if any, and pays a tax based on total taxable income. The net profits of the business are taxed to the proprietor regardless of actual distributions. The individual income tax rates range from 11% to 38.5% in 1987, and either 15% or 28% in 1988 and thereafter.

Self-Employment Tax. In lieu of Social Security taxes paid equally by an employer and employee, the net earnings of a proprietorship are subject to a special self-employment tax, shown in the following table. The table assumes an annual increase in maximum taxable income of approximately 4%.

Year	Tax Rate	Maximum Income	Maximum Tax
1988	13.02%	$45,700	$5,950
1989	13.02	47,600	6,198
1990	15.30	49,700	7,604

Nondeductible Expenses. Generally, a proprietor cannot deduct as a business expense any payments for personal coverage under group hospitalization, life insurance or medical plans. Payments for employee coverage are deductible.

A retirement plan may be established and contributions deducted as an adjustment to total gross income, but not as a deduction from proprietorship income. Currently, the defined contribution limit is the lesser of $30,000 or 15% of net self-employment income for profit-sharing plans, and 25% for money-purchase pension plans (for further detail, see Chapter 10). For defined-benefit plans, the contribution limitation must be actuarially determined.

Unlike a corporation or partnership, which is allowed to amortize organizational expenditures over a period of not less than 60 months, a proprietorship is not permitted to deduct amortized organization costs as a business expense.

Tax Year. The tax year of a proprietorship is a calendar year, unless the proprietor can demonstrate to the IRS that a fiscal year conforms more closely to the proprietor's business cycle. It is the authors' understanding that the IRS will only allow a proprietorship to report its income on a fiscal-year basis if the proprietorship was the taxpayer's sole source of income. If a fiscal year is granted, all income and expenses must be reported on a fiscal-year basis.

Liquidation of Business. A proprietorship may be liquidated by sale or incorporation. A partial liquidation may be effected by sale of part of the business, with the remaining interest operating as a proprietorship or continuation of the business in partnership with the buyer or buyers.

Partial or total disposition of the proprietorship is viewed as the sale of its individual assets. Whether gains or losses are recognized, and whether they are deemed capital or ordinary, will depend on the basis and nature of the assets sold (see Chapter 6).

For example, if a business consisted only of accounts receivable, inventory and plant and equipment, the sales price would be allocated to the assets sold before determination of the nature of gain or loss. Gain or loss recognized on the sale of receivables and inventory would be ordinary, since they are not capital assets. Gain recognized on the sale of plant and equipment would be subject to applicable depreciation recapture laws (i.e., ordinary income must be recognized to the extent that depreciation or cost recovery was claimed in the past, since depreciation is used to offset ordinary income) and, accordingly, would be ordinary or a combination of ordinary and capital. Capital gain will be recognized if the sales proceeds can be allocated to intangible assets, such as goodwill. The sales agreements should specify allocation of the sales proceeds to various assets or the IRS may try to impose a different allocation.

On termination of a business, recognition of gain or loss on assets will not occur until actual disposition of the assets. The death of the proprietor has an income tax significance for the proprietorship, and the value of the business is included in the proprietor's estate for estate-tax purposes. The proprietor should provide in writing for the disposition or continuance of the business after his or her death.

State Taxation. Similar to federal law, a proprietorship is not a separate taxable entity for most state and local income tax purposes. Generally, the income or net profits are included within the individual taxable income of the proprietor and subject to the state or local individual income tax. Currently, 43 states and the District of Columbia impose some form of individual income tax on net profits. In addition, many jurisdictions, particularly local taxing authorities, will impose unincorporated business taxes on the net profits of the business separate and distinct from the individual. If the proprietorship transacts business in more than one state or locality, the individual proprietor may be liable for income tax in both jurisdictions. In such cases, however, the income subject to tax is usually divided between the jurisdictions, or the proprietor may claim a credit on his resident state or local income tax return. These apportionment or credit provisions are established as an attempt to eliminate the potential for double taxation inherent in a multijurisdictional business.

Aside from income taxes, a proprietorship will typically find itself subject to a wide variety of other state or local taxes imposed on business entities. Sales and use taxes, for example, may be imposed on the purchase of materials, supplies or equipment by the proprietorship or may be required to be collected on sales to retail customers. Other general types of taxes that may be encountered include gross receipts taxes, payroll taxes, real or personal property taxes, net worth taxes and mercantile license taxes. Certain industries, such as trucking, insurance or energy, may be subject to a variety of specialized taxes as well.

PARTNERSHIP

The tax definition of a partnership is a syndicate, group, pool, joint venture or other unincorporated organization, through or by means of which any business, financial operation or venture is carried on, and which is not, within the meaning of the (Internal Revenue) Code, a corporation or a trust or estate. Classification as a corporation under tax law requires an organization to assume more corporate than noncorporate characteristics.

Generally speaking, there are two types of partnerships: general and limited partnerships.

General Partnership

The legal definition of a general partnership is "an association of two or more persons to carry on as co-owners a business for profit." General partnerships are typically found in professions that are service-oriented and not capital-intensive, such as law, accounting and medicine. A capital-intensive business may operate as a general partnership if the prospective partners are able to provide the required capital and willing to accept the additional risk.

The most serious disadvantage of a general partnership is the unlimited legal liability of its partners. Creditors may attach personal assets to satisfy partnership debts after all assets have been sold. However, even owners of corporations sometimes may have to accept personal liability to guarantee the debts of the corporation, especially when the corporation is new or deemed to be speculative by creditors.

Limited Partnership

A limited partnership includes not only the general partner or partners but also one or more partners not bound by the obligations of the partnership. Limited partners are only liable for the debts of the partnership in the amount of their respective capital contributions, provided they do not participate in the management of the partnership.

A limited partnership is usually formed by the general partners to secure additional capital or to spread the risk of the venture without forming a corporation. A limited partnership is common in real estate development, oil and gas exploration and motion picture ventures.

A limited partnership is taxed as a general partnership. The danger of acquiring too many corporate characteristics, and thus being classified as a corporation under tax law, is somewhat greater with limited than with general partnerships.

Taxation of Partnerships

A partnership does not pay federal income taxes, although it is required to file an informational income tax return. The partnership functions as a conduit through which the various tax attributes flow to the partners. Partners combine their respective shares of partnership income and loss items with other income and losses for the year.

The federal income tax rate assessed on the partners' taxable income is a function of their marginal tax rate. Partnership income is taxed regardless of actual distribution. All or part of the income may be subject to the self-employment tax. Income of a limited partner generally is not self-employment income. If the partner is a corporation, corporate tax rates apply.

The partner's share of the tax attributes of the partnership, such as income and losses, capital gains and losses and credits, may differ from his or her interest in the capital of the partnership, provided there is economic justification for the difference. Gains, losses and credits cannot be allocated among partners solely to avoid taxes.

Losses from partnership operations recognized by each partner are limited to the adjusted basis in his or her partnership interest. The adjusted basis is the total contributions of the partner:

☐ Increased or decreased by his or her allocated share of profits and losses from operations in prior years

☐ Increased by his or her share of certain partnership liabilities

☐ Reduced by withdrawals.

If the loss is in excess of the allowable limit for any one year, it may be carried forward to be used in a year in which the partner's basis exceeds losses.

Deductibility of Personal Items. Personal items, such as the cost of membership in qualified retirement plans, life insurance or coverage for hospitalization or medical reimbursement paid by the partnership on behalf of any or all partners are generally not deductible from the partnership's taxable income. The payments are treated as nontaxable distributions that reduce the recipient's basis in the partnership. Guaranteed payments to a partner as compensation for services are taxable income to the recipients and deductible by the partnership. Costs of participation in qualified retirement, medical and hospital plans are deductible by the individual partners on their respective personal returns, subject to the usual limitations. The partnership may deduct as an expense the cost of the benefits paid on behalf of its employees. Generally, partners cannot be employees.

Contributions by Partners. When a partner contributes property, including cash, to the partnership, the partner's basis in the partnership increases by the adjusted basis in the property contributed. Generally, the adjusted basis is the cost of the partner less depreciation allowed. The partnership receives the property at the basis of the partner on the date of transfer. Since the partner receives partnership interest or increased partnership interest in return for the property, neither the partner nor the partnership recognize gain or loss on the exchange in most instances.

When a partner gives property in exchange for cash, the transaction is treated as a sale rather than as a contribution. If the partner renders services in exchange for a partnership interest, the transaction is treated as compensation in an amount equal to the value of the interest received.

Treatment of Liabilities. The partner's basis in the partnership is increased by his or her share of partnership liabilities. Conversely, if the partner contributes property subject to a liability and the partnership assumes the liability, the partner is deemed to have received a cash distribution equal to the aggregate liability assumed by the other partners.

For example, consider a partner who contributes property with a value and basis to him or her of $100,000, on which there is a $40,000 mortgage, to a partnership with three other equal members. The partner is deemed to have received a cash distribution of $30,000, and his or her basis in the partnership is reduced by the same amount. The partner's basis in the partnership is $100,000 (basis in the property contributed) less $30,000 (liability assumed by the other partners), or $70,000.

If no stated agreement dictates which partner is personally responsible for a particular liability of the partnership, the liability is allocated among the partners based on each partner's share of partnership capital.

Distributions to Partners. A distribution to a partner during the life of the partnership is not taxable, unless the partnership distributes money in excess of the partner's basis in his or her partnership interest. The excess amount is recognized as a gain to the partner. The sale or distribution of unrealized receivables and substantially appreciated inventory by the partnership are subject to special rules.

Partners as Outsiders. When the partner deals with the partnership in a capacity other than as a partner, he or she must be treated as an outsider. For example, if the partner sells an asset to the partnership for an amount in excess of his or her basis, gain must be recognized on the sale. Loss from a sale may be recognized, unless the partner has a direct or indirect interest subject to certain attribution rules in the partnership's capital or profits of more than 50%.

Termination of Partner's Interest. There are two methods by which partners may terminate partnership interests. First, some or all of the partnership interest may be terminated by sale to other partners or a new partner. Most partnership agreements provide for the approval of a new partner by the remaining partners and detail the procedure for liquidation of a partnership interest.

A selling partner's ratable share of income or loss from operations is proportionate to the number of days the partner held an interest during the taxable year. As a result, the seller must wait until the end of the partnership's taxable year to determine his or her share of income or loss, because few partnerships would find it feasible to close their books at an interim date.

Tax Aspects of the Termination of a Partnership Interest. Generally, a capital gain or loss is realized on the sale or liquidation of a partnership interest, except when the sales price or amount received in liquidation is attributable to unrealized receivables or inventory items that have substantially appreciated in value; this is treated as ordinary income. Whether the capital gain or loss is long- or short-term depends on the length of time the interest has been held. The partner may exchange his or her partnership interest tax free for shares of a corporation as long as the transaction meets certain control requirements.

Numerous arrangements exist for handling a deceased partner's interest. A partnership agreement should address these matters, and a prospective partner should review them with a tax adviser.

Sale of a partner's interest will not terminate the partnership unless: (1) the remaining partners cease to continue operations in the partnership form or (2) the sale, combined with other sales and exchanges in the preceding 12 months, transfers 50% or more of the total interest in partnership capital and profits.

Taxable Year. Generally, a partnership must adopt the taxable year of the partners who collectively own a majority interest in partnership profits and capital (subject to a three-year look-back rule). Failure to satisfy the majority interest rule means the tax year of the principal partners (i.e., partners who separately own a 5% or more interest in partnership profits and capital) is to be used. If neither rule is fulfilled, a calendar year becomes the taxable year.

It is possible to adopt a fiscal year for a partnership if an adequate business purpose can be demonstrated to the IRS. Generally, if the partnership has received 25% or more of its gross receipts within the last two months of the proposed fiscal year for three consecutive years, it can meet this exception.

Registration To Do Business. Partnerships usually are required to register with the state in which they are organized. Normally, they don't have to be registered with the federal government. Partnerships need an employer identification number to file income tax returns and, if there are employees, for remittance of income and Social Security taxes withheld from salaries. It is imperative to apply for the number as soon as the partnership is formed.

State Taxation. While state and local taxation of partnerships generally follows the federal treatment, there are certain specific peculiarities that require review of the jurisdiction in question. For income tax purposes, the partnership is normally not a taxable entity. There may, however, be certain jurisdictions that impose an income tax on partnerships, such as New York City, the District of Columbia and Illinois. As with a sole proprietorship, most state and local jurisdictions will impose other taxes, such as sales and use, gross receipts tax, business and occupation, and property or unincorporated business taxes, on the partnership entity itself. Regardless of any business taxes directly on the partnership, states with a personal income tax generally will tax the individual partners in their separate capacity on their distributive share of the partnership items of income, deductions, gain, loss and credits. In most states the character of these items remains constant using the partnership merely as a "conduit" to pass the items through to the partners. In those circumstances, the partnership will be required to file, with the state or local jurisdiction, an informational return similar in content to the federal return.

A partnership is liable for informational returns when it has contacts with a state. The necessary contact generally exists whenever the partnership either does business in a state or has a resident partner within the state. If the partnership engages in activity or has resident partners in more than one taxing jurisdiction, informational returns typically must be filed with each jurisdiction and the income or net profits of the partnership divided among the jurisdictions. The partnership must then provide each partner with information not only as to the partner's total distributive share of the partnership income or loss items but also of the division of these items between the various taxing jurisdictions. The partners in turn may then be required to file returns and pay tax on their own behalf in each jurisdiction. Some jurisdictions may also require the partnership to withhold tax on behalf of nonresident partners.

CORPORATION

For federal income tax purposes, the distinguishing characteristics of a corporation are:

☐ *Continuity of Life.* The death, bankruptcy or retirement of, or the divestiture of interest by, any shareholder or group of shareholders does not cause a dissolution of the corporation.

☐ *Limited Liability.* A shareholder is not personally liable for the indebtedness of or claims against the corporation, except in very special circumstances.

☐ *Free Transferability of Interest.* Generally, shareholders may sell all or part of their interest to any buyer without the consent of the other shareholders.

☐ *Centralization of Management.* The board of directors is the authoritative body elected by the shareholders to make independent business decisions on behalf of the corporation.

Organization

The organization of a corporation requires attention to administration and capitalization. Administrative tasks include drafting the charter and the bylaws; filing the certificate of incorporation and paying filing fees in the state of central business operations, and following other state statutory procedures, such as the election of a board of directors. Legal consultation is essential when establishing a corporation.

Capitalizing a corporation is achieved through contributions of cash or other assets by investors to the corporation in exchange for equity. The tax implications of debt versus equity financing are discussed below, under "Pitfalls."

Taxation

The corporate income tax rates for taxable years beginning in 1987 and thereafter are as follows:

Taxable Income	1987 Blended Rate	1988 and Thereafter
Up to $25,000	15.0%	15%
$25,000 to $50,000	16.5	15
$50,001 to $75,000	27.5	25
$75,001 to $100,000	37.0	34
Over $100,000	40.0	34

The special blended rates apply to corporations with fiscal tax years that include July 1, 1987.

The Tax Reform Act of 1986 eliminates the 28% alternative capital gains rate for corporations. Accordingly, a corporation's net capital gains and gains on the sales of business property will be taxed at the regular corporate rates.

The repeal of preferential treatment for capital gains is effective for any taxable year beginning on or after July 1, 1987. For a taxable year that begins before July 1, 1987, present law will apply, but the alternative capital gains rate will increase to 34% for capital gains recognized after December 31, 1986.

With the passage of the Tax Reform Act of 1986, corporations (other than those corporations making an S Corporation election) will still be able to elect or remain on a fiscal year for reporting purposes.

Double Taxation. A corporation cannot deduct dividend payments, so the corporation and the shareholders pay taxes on the same income. The Tax Reform Act of 1986 repeals the individual's annual exclusion for qualifying dividends for taxable years beginning after 1986. A shareholder-employee with a controlling interest in a corporation may designate his or her share of the corporate earnings as compensation in lieu of a dividend. The IRS will permit the compensation deduction only for amounts it deems reasonable in relation to services performed. If the IRS deems the compensation deduction excessive, it will reclassify the excessive amount as a dividend (see Chapter 11).

Recognition of Gain or Loss. A corporation may be acquired or formed without recognition of gain or loss at the shareholder level. The transfer of property, including cash, by one or more persons to a corporation is a nontaxable event to the transferers if only stock and certain securities of the corporation are received in return, and the transferers own 80% or more of the value of the outstanding stock of the corporation immediately after the transfer. If they receive other property, such as cash or short-term debt, they may have to recognize gains on the cash or the fair market value of the property received. In addition, the acquisition of one corporation by another may be effected by the exchange of the shares of the acquiring corporation for the shares of the acquired corporation. The exchange is tax-free, because the shareholders are considered to be in the same economic position before and after the exchange (see Chapter 6).

Consolidated Tax Returns. A corporation that owns a minimum of 80% of one or more corporations may elect to file a consolidated federal tax return. As a result, the loss from one company may be offset against the income of another.

Favorable Treatment of Recognized Gains and Losses (Shareholder). On liquidation of a corporation, a shareholder may receive capital gains treatment on the transaction. Individuals who own stock in companies that qualified as "small business corporations" at the time of issuance, and that issued the stock in accordance with specific requirements, may be entitled to ordinary loss treatment on sale of the stock at a loss.

Fringe Benefits. Certain benefits are not taxable to employees of partnerships or corporations. A proven shareholder-employee of the corporation may be able to receive nontaxable benefits even though the costs are deductible to the corporation. In a partnership, this is not possible if the recipient is a partner, because a partner may not be an employee.

Many benefits, such as qualified retirement plans and noninsured medical reimbursement plans, must be provided on a nondiscriminatory basis to all eligible employees in order to receive the favorable treatment allowed under the law. A detailed discussion of fringe benefit plans may be found in Chapter 10.

Pitfalls

Accumulated Earnings Tax. This tax is imposed on accumulations of income considered to exceed the reasonable needs of the corporation. The additional tax is assessed by the IRS and does not reduce the regular corporate levy. The rate is 27.5% of the first $100,000 of accumulated taxable income plus 38.5% of the amount of excess of $100,000.

The law permits corporations to accumulate at least $250,000 of earnings before the imposition of a penalty tax ($150,000 for certain personal service corporations). For techniques to minimize exposure to this tax, see Chapter 11.

Equity versus Debt. Debt may be more advantageous than common or preferred stock as a corporate capitalization vehicle. The corporation may deduct interest paid on debt securities, but not dividends paid on stock. The repayment of debt principal is not taxed to the debt holder, but the redemption of stock may be treated as a dividend unless special redemption provisions are satisfied.

Minimal and/or proportionate equity capitalization in relation to indebtedness could mean that all or part of the debt will be deemed equity. That means interest payments would be considered dividends, and therefore would not be a deductible corporate expense (see Chapter 11).

Personal Holding Company. The personal holding company will be assessed an additional tax of 38.5% in 1987 and 28% thereafter on undistributed income. The personal holding company is not subject to the accumulated earnings tax. The tax is calculated on undistributed corporate earnings and may be avoided by paying sufficient dividends.

The corporation is subject to the personal holding company rules if (1) 60% or more of the adjusted gross income consists of personal holding company income, such as dividends, interest, royalties, gains from securities transactions and personal service income, and (2) at any time during the last half of the taxable year, more than 50% of the outstanding stock was directly or indirectly owned by not more than five individuals (see Chapters 6 and 11).

State Taxation. State taxation of corporations can take different forms. The most prevalent form is an income tax; currently 44 states impose some type of income tax. Other taxes imposed directly on the corporation depending on the particular state are gross receipts tax, franchise tax, net worth tax and property tax. In order for a state to impose any tax on a corporation it must first demonstrate a "minimum contact" with the corporation or its business activity. Generally, the requisite contact always exists for a state to tax a domestic corporation (a corporation incorporated in that state) regardless of the activity in that state. In order to tax a foreign corporation (a corporation incorporated in a state other than the state seeking to impose a tax), a state must prove a connection or presence between the foreign corporation and the state. That connection is most commonly evidenced through a foreign corporation's "doing business" in the taxing state. Doing business is most easily described as having property or people employed in a particular state.

If a corporation transacts all of its business in one state, that state will then tax 100% of the business activity. If a corporation engages in multistate activity, this entails allocating and apportioning the business activity based on a mathematical formula that separates the business activity based on location of property, payroll and gross receipts.

The second most prevalent state tax on corporations is one measured by net worth. Generally, such a tax is based on the value of the capital stock, surplus and retained earnings. In order for a state to impose a net worth tax, it must still demonstrate a minimum contact by the taxpayer and the state. Net worth taxes are imposed either in addition to or as an alternative to net income taxes.

Another common state tax is one based on gross receipts. Normally, this type of tax is measured by total revenues of the business without any deduction for costs of goods sold. The gross receipts tax is utilized most by local tax authorities because it is easy to enforce and administer. More important, a gross receipts tax will generate a tax cost to the business regardless of the results of operations.

S CORPORATION

The S Corporation has tax attributes of the corporation and the partnership as well as certain features of its own. The S Corporation is designed to function as a conduit and allow taxation of corporate earned income only at the individual shareholder level. The shareholder realizes the income and deductions.

Requirements for Qualification

An S Corporation must:

☐ Be a domestic corporation
☐ Not be a member of an affiliated group of corporations
☐ Have only one class of stock
☐ Have no more than 35 shareholders
☐ Have only individuals, estates or certain types of trusts as shareholders
☐ Not have a nonresident alien as a shareholder.

A corporation that meets all of the above requirements may elect S Corporation status. The election requires shareholders' unanimous consent. If the election is made within the corporation's first taxable year that the election is effective, each person who was a shareholder (or was treated as a shareholder) at any time during the pre-election portion of the taxable year also must consent to the election. The pre-election period rule has been instituted to prevent allocations of income or loss to ineligible or nonconsenting shareholders. If the election is made after the fifteenth day of the third month of the taxable year, it will not become effective until the following taxable year.

Termination of Status

S Corporation status may be forfeited if (1) any of the conditions for qualifications are no longer satisfied, (2) shareholders owning more than 50% of the stock of the corporation, including nonvoting stock, consent to revoke the election or (3) for three consecutive years, the corporation has accumulated earnings and profits from taxable years in which an S Corporation election was not in effect and receives passive investment income that exceeds 25% of gross receipts.

Taxation of Shareholders

Shareholders report their respective shares of the taxable income or loss of the S Corporation on their individual returns for the current taxable year. Shareholders must report taxable income even if it is not distributed during the current taxable year.

The tax treatment of distributions depends on the source of the distribution. Generally, distributions from the accumulated adjustments account are not taxable. The accumulated adjustments account consists of income earned after 1982 and previously taxed to shareholders, but held by the S Corporation. After the accumulated adjustments account has been exhausted, distributions are made in the following order:

☐ Undistributed previously taxed income from years prior to 1983 retained at corporate year-end. This is not taxable.

☐ A distribution of accumulated earnings and profits, which is taxable as a dividend.

☐ A nontaxable return of capital equal to the shareholder's remaining stock basis.

☐ Any distribution exceeding a return of capital. This is treated as a long- or short-term capital gain.

Advantages and Disadvantages

The principal advantages of the S Corporation over the regular corporate form are:

☐ There is no regular corporate tax, so double taxation is avoided.

☐ Corporate long-term capital gain, with limited exceptions, is taxed directly to shareholders, which allows shareholders to offset other capital losses on their personal returns.

☐ Corporate net operating losses are deductible directly by shareholders, subject to limitations, and therefore shelter other income from taxes.

☐ The tax on unreasonable accumulations of earnings does not apply to S Corporations.

☐ The accumulated adjustments account and previously taxed earnings may be removed in cash from the corporation without incurring individual tax.

☐ An S Corporation may issue small business corporation stock. This allows shareholders to receive an ordinary loss deduction on the sale of worthless stock.

☐ An S Corporation may transfer stock to children 14 years of age or over and thus shift taxable income to lower tax brackets. A transfer must be bona fide or it may be disregarded by the IRS.

☐ The S Corporation is not subject to the minimum tax, as is a C Corporation.

☐ The S Corporation may continue to use the cash method of accounting.

The major disadvantages of the S Corporation are:

☐ Stringent requirements for qualification

☐ Vulnerability to termination or revocation

☐ Elaborate nature of the rules of governing the amount, form and timing of income distributions

☐ Imposition of the built-in gains tax or capital gains tax on disposal of certain assets owned prior to the S Corporation election

☐ S Corporations and partnerships only offset passive losses against passive income

☐ S Corporations and partnerships are generally required to adopt a calendar year

☐ Generally, an S Corporation may not deduct fringe benefits attributable to a more-than-2% shareholder

☐ The imposition of the passive income tax on S Corporations with C Corporation earnings and profits. The tax is imposed when passive investment income exceeds 25% of gross receipts

☐ The S Corporation must allocate income and loss according to the shareholder's percentage of ownership. Partnerships are not necessarily required to allocate income and loss according to ownership percentages. These special allocations must be codified in the partnership agreement

☐ The basis of a shareholder in an S Corporation is limited to capital contributions plus any qualified loans made by the shareholder to the S Corporation. In a partnership, a partner's basis equals capital contributions plus a respective share of recourse and nonrecourse loans.

The Tax Reform Act of 1986 provides that for corporations making an S Corporation election after December 31, 1986, an additional tax approximating the existing double tax will be imposed on the disposal of assets existing on the date of selection but sold within a 10-year period after the date of election. This is effective for tax years beginning in or after 1987.

When Should an S Corporation Be Considered?

The following conditions are favorable to the establishment of or conversion to an S Corporation. No one condition should be regarded as determinative by itself.

☐ The corporation can reasonably anticipate a loss in the next taxable year for which there will be no immediate benefit available from a net operating loss carryback. This situation is typical in the early years of a company's operations.

☐ The corporation has a problem with excessive accumulated

earnings (i.e., sizable taxable income and cash available for distribution).

☐ The shareholder or prospective shareholder has children who are in a lower tax bracket, so there would be a tax advantage in transferring shares to them. The Tax Reform Act of 1986 mandates that children under the age of 14 who receive more than $1,000 of unearned income from the S Corporation be taxed at their parents' top marginal rate. If the shareholder is, or anticipates becoming, an employee of the corporation, he or she might consider a salary reduction to increase the undistributed income to which the children would be entitled. The shareholder would be required to demonstrate that the reduced salary is adequate compensation for his or her services. Otherwise, the IRS may claim that some or all of the transferred amount should be taxed as compensation followed by a gift to the children.

The following highly simplified illustration demonstrates the tax advantages of electing S Corporation status for an existing C Corporation. This example ignores the additional advantages on liquidation.

Tax Year 1986

S Corporation earnings taxed at top individual tax rate $500,000 × .50	$250,000
C Corporation earnings taxed at top corporate rate $500,000 × .46	230,000
Tax savings for a C Corporation	$ 20,000

Tax year 1988

S Corporation earnings taxed at top individual tax rate $500,000 × .28	140,000

C Corporation earnings taxed
   at top corporate rate
   $500,000 × .34   170,000

Tax savings by electing to be taxed
   as an S Corporation $ 30,000

As shown above, in 1986 and preceding years, electing to be taxed as an S Corporation could result in the payment of more tax than if the entity was a regular corporation and no distributions were made. With the passage of the Tax Reform Act of 1986, the top individual tax rate is now lower than the top corporate rate. As a result, switching to S Corporation status can mean saving substantial tax dollars in 1988 and future years.

State Taxation

The state taxation of S Corporations has no general set of rules; instead, it is characterized by inconsistency and complexity in the respective states. When considering the election for federal purposes, care must be given to review all states where the enterprise may be liable for state taxes.

In some states, the S Corporation status is disregarded entirely. In that instance the corporation is taxed as a regular corporation. In other states the federal election automatically controls the state election. And finally, some states require the shareholders to specifically make a state election regardless of the federal election. Where the election is allowable in a state, the taxation of items may still differ from federal treatment.

The areas of greatest disparity of tax treatment are capital gains, excess net passive investment income and tax preference income. The states also differ on the types of income items that are taxed at the shareholder level depending on whether the shareholder is a resident or nonresident of the taxing state. Currently, there is no clear and uniform method for resolving state issues in this area of state taxation. Therefore, the best advice is to exert care in reviewing the state tax consequences of an S Corporation election.

SUMMARY

A proprietorship lacks the formalities associated with other forms of business. Proprietorship income or loss is combined with other sources of income or loss on the proprietor's personal return.

A partnership is formed when two or more persons elect to share profits, losses and credits without the structural formalities of a corporation. A partnership agreement may provide for reasonable income, loss and credit apportionments in different percentages than the partners' capital ownership percentages.

A corporation is a statutory entity that affords protection from personal liability. Fringe benefits paid to corporate officers are deductible at the corporate level as business expenses and the payments made on behalf of the employee are excludable from the employee's income.

S Corporations shareholders must include income or loss from operations on their personal returns. An S Corporation may continue to use the cash method of accounting while regular corporations, with exceptions, must use the accrual method of accounting. The S Corporation is not subject to the accumulated earnings tax, as is a corporation. Similar to a regular corporation, the shareholders of an S Corporation are protected from personal liability.

Appendix: Comparison of Various Forms of Doing Business

Treatment of Income and Expenses	Proprietorship	Partnership	Regular Corporation	S Corporation
Character of Income and deductions	Tax attributes are reflected in the individual's return and, as such, maintain their character.	Conduit—no tax to partnership	Taxed at corporate level.	Conduit—could be passive income. Potential corporate built-in or capital gains taxes.
Capital gain	Capital gains are taxed as ordinary income.	Conduit—taxed as ordinary income at the partner level.	The 28% alternative tax rate for net capital gains is repealed for taxable years when the new corporate tax rates are fully effective.	Possible corporate capital gains or built-in gains tax; conduit—taxed as ordinary income at the shareholder level.
Capital loss	Limited to $3,000 per year; excess is carried forward indefinitely. Losses offset ordinary income on a dollar-for-dollar basis.	Conduit—limitations apply at the partner level.	Carry back three years and carry over five years as short-term capital loss offsetting only capital gains.	Conduit—limitations apply at the shareholder level.
Section 1231 gains and losses	Taxed at individual level, combined with other Section 1231 gains or losses of individual; net gains are capital; net losses are ordinary.	Conduit—limitations apply at the partner level; taxed as ordinary income.	Taxable or deductible at the corporate level.	Possible corporate capital gains or built-in gains tax; conduit—limitations apply at the shareholder level; taxed as ordinary income.

Treatment of Income and Expenses	Proprietorship	Partnership	Regular Corporation	S Corporation
Expensing of depreciable business assets	Election to expense is allowed up to $10,000 a year. Expensing allowance phases out dollar for dollar when the cost of qualified property placed in service during the taxable year is between $200,000–$210,000.	Same	Same	Same
Organization costs	Not amortizable.	Amortizable over 60 months.	Amortizable over 60 months.	Amortizable over 60 months.
Charitable contributions	Subject to limits for individual. Generally, gifts to public charity: cash, 50% of AGI; appreciated property, 30% of AGI. Other limitations for specific items contributed. Unused portion may be carried forward five years.	Conduit—limitations apply at the partner level.	Deduction is limited to 10% of modified taxable income. Unused portion may be carried forward five years.	Conduit—limitations apply at the shareholder level.

Treatment of Income and Expenses	Proprietorship	Partnership	Regular Corporation	S Corporation
Dividends received	Treated as ordinary income; no exclusion or deduction. Treated as portfolio income.	Treated as portfolio income.	80% to 100% dividend-received deduction. Special rules on portfolio income for closely held corporations.	Treated as portfolio income.
Alternative minimum tax	For individuals, the alternative minimum tax rate is 21%. The exemption amount is determined by filing status and alternative minimum taxable income.	Conduit for preference items. The alternative minimum tax is calculated at the partner level.	For corporate taxpayers, the alternative minimum tax rate is 20%. The alternative minimum tax is imposed on alternative minimum taxable income in excess of $40,000, but only if the amount is more than the regular corporate tax. Portion of AMT tax may be applied as a credit against future regular tax.	Conduit for preference items. The alternative minimum tax is calculated at the shareholder level.
Tax preferences	Depletion, accelerated depreciation, excess drilling costs, passive losses, net unrealized gain on certain charitable contributions, among others.	Conduit—preference items separately stated and reflected in the calculation of AMT at the partner level. No book-tax preference.	Book-tax difference, depletion, accelerated depreciation, net unrealized gain on certain charitable contributions, among others.	Conduit—preference items separately stated and reflected in the calculation of AMT at the partner level. No book-tax preference.

Treatment of Income and Expenses	Proprietorship	Partnership	Regular Corporation	S Corporation
Accounting methods	Cash or accrual.	Cash or accrual, but partnership with C Corporation partners with more than $5 million gross receipts and tax-shelter partnerships cannot use cash method.	Accrual, but cash available to C Corporations with $5 million or less gross receipts.	Cash or accrual.

Treatment of Compensation and Benefits	Proprietorship	Partnership	Regular Corporation	S Corporation
Partner's or shareholder's "reasonable" salary	Not applicable.	Can be deducted by partnership or treated as an allocation of partnership profits.	Deductible by the corporation and taxable to the shareholder-employee.	Deductible by the corporation and taxable to the shareholder-employee.
Group hospitalization and life insurance premiums and medical reimbursement plans	Medical expenses are an itemized deduction. Only medical expenses exceeding 7.5% of adjusted gross income will be deductible. Self-employed individuals can deduct up to 25% of their medical insurance premiums through 1989 unless they are covered by a qualified plan. No deduction is allowed for life insurance premiums.	Cost of partner's benefits generally not deductible by partnership. May be treated as a distribution to individual partners, eligible for possible deduction at partner level. Partners can deduct up to 25% of their medical insurance premiums through 1989, unless they are covered by a qualified plan.	Cost of shareholder-employee's coverage is generally deductible as a business expense if the plan is a qualified plan "for the benefit of employees."	Same as partnership for more-than-2% shareholders, including eligibility to deduct up to 25% of their medical insurance premiums through 1989.

Treatment of Compensation and Benefits	Proprietorship	Partnership	Regular Corporation	S Corporation
Retirement benefits	Limitations and restrictions basically same as regular corporation.	Limitations and restrictions basically same as regular corporation.	Limitations on benefits from defined benefit plans—lesser of $90,000 or 100% of compensation.	Limitation on contributions basically the same as a regular corporation.

Allocations, Distributions and Loss Limitations	Proprietorship	Partnership	Regular Corporation	S Corporation
Basis of allocating operating income or loss to owners	All income or loss picked up on owner's return.	Partnership profit and loss agreement (may have "special allocations" of income and deductions if they reflect economic reality).	No income allocated to stockholders.	Pro rata portion of income or loss and separately stated items, based on per share, per-day allocation.
Distributions to owners	Drawings from the business are not taxable; net profits are taxable, and the proprietorship is subject to the tax on self-employment income.	Generally not taxable.	Payments of salaries are deductible by corporation and taxable to recipient; payments of dividends are not deductible by corporation and generally are taxable to recipient shareholders.	Payments of salaries deductible by corporation and taxable to recipient; distributions generally not taxable.

Allocations, Distributions and Loss Limitations	Proprietorship	Partnership	Regular Corporation	S Corporation
Limitations on losses deductible by owners • basis • at-risk • passive loss	• Not applicable • Limited to amount at risk • Passive loss limitations apply to owner.	• Limited to partner's basis (including entity level debt) • Limited to amount at risk • Passive loss limitations apply at the partner level.	• No losses allowed to individual, except on sale of stock or liquidation of the corporation • Certain closely held corporations subject to the at-risk rules • Certain closely held corporations subject to passive loss limitations.	• Limited to shareholder's basis (contributions to capital plus loans to corporation) • Limited to amount at-risk • Passive loss limitations apply at the shareholder level.

	Proprietorship	Partnership	Regular Corporation	S Corporation
Structure of Ownership				
Formal election required	No	No, but a partnership agreement should be drafted.	Must incorporate under state law.	Yes
Qualified owners	Individual ownership.	No limitation.	No limitation.	Individual citizens, resident aliens, estates and certain trusts may be shareholders. Number of shareholders limited to 35.

Structure of Ownership	Proprietorship	Partnership	Regular Corporation	S Corporation
Type of ownership interest	Individual ownership.	More than one class of partner permitted.	More than one class of stock permitted.	Only one class of stock permitted.
Transfer of ownership	Assets of business transferable rather than business itself.	Consent of other partners often required if partnership interest is to be transferred, depending on partnership agreement. New partnership may be created.	Ready transfer of ownership through the use of stock certificates; restrictions may be imposed by shareholder's agreement.	Shares can be transferred only to certain individuals, certain types of trusts or estates. No consent is needed by a new shareholder for S election.
Taxable year	Usually calendar year.	Must have a calendar year unless there is a business purpose, such as a natural business year.	Any year is permissible on adoption; changes require business reasons. Special rules apply to personal service corporations.	Must have a calendar year unless there is a business purpose, such as a natural business year.
Flexibility	No restrictions.	Partnership is contractual arrangement, within which members can do in business what individuals can, subject to the partnership agreement and applicable state laws.	Corporation is a creature of the state, functioning with powers granted explicitly or necessarily implied, subject to judicial construction and decisions.	Same as regular corporation.

Structure of Ownership	Proprietorship	Partnership	Regular Corporation	S Corporation
Capital requirements	Capital raised only by loan or increased contribution by proprietor.	Loans or contributions from partners (original or newly created by remaking partnership).	Met by sale of stock, issuance of bonds or by taking on other corporate debt.	Met by sale of stock or issuance of debt, but corporation can issue only one class of stock and is limited to 35 shareholders.
General	Proprietorship	Partnership	Regular Corporation	S Corporation
Liability	Individual is liable for all business liabilities.	General partners individually liable for partnership liabilities. Limited partners liable only up to amount of his or her unpaid capital contributions, plus distributions in the last year (in many states).	Shareholder's liability limited to capital contributions.	Same as regular.
Business action	Sole proprietor makes decisions and can act immediately.	Action dependent on the agreement of partners or general partners, as defined in the partnership agreement.	Unity of action based on authority or board of directors.	Same as regular corporation, except unanimous consent is required to elect S Corporation status, more than 50% of shareholders needed to revoke. S status, however, can be revoked by failure to meet requirements.

General	Proprietorship	Partnership	Regular Corporation	S Corporation
Management	Proprietor is responsible and recognizes all profits or losses.	Except for limited or silent partners, investment in partnership involves responsibility for management decisions.	Shareholder can receive dividends without sharing in responsibility for management.	Shareholders entitled to allocable shares of income and income items without responsibility for management decisions.

6

Buying or Selling a Business

A buyer of a business should know:

☐ What type of business am I interested in and how will I find it?

☐ How much should I pay for a particular business?

☐ How should the transaction be structured?

☐ Will the new business meet my objectives?

☐ Am I familiar with the company's industry, its products or services, its people and its facilities?

☐ What postacquisition action needs to be taken?

A seller of a business should know:

☐ How much is my company really worth?

☐ What are my financial objectives?

☐ What are my options?

☐ How will the transaction be structured?

☐ How do I package my company for sale?

FINDING A MERGER PARTNER

Perhaps no aspect of mergers and acquisitions is more misunderstood than how the buyer and seller find each other. To begin with, let's look at three key questions helpful in identifying a buyer or seller:

- ☐ Why do people generally look to acquire or sell a business?
- ☐ How would I go about identifying a buyer or seller?
- ☐ What pitfalls should I look for along the way?

The following are a few reasons business people decide to buy a business:

- ☐ To acquire technology, either to complement or to replace their own.
- ☐ To acquire management to supplement their own skills, to replace aging or inadequate managers in their own business or sometimes even to replace themselves.
- ☐ To acquire complementary products, to broaden their own product lines, to sell more items through the same distribution channels or to sell more items to the same customers.
- ☐ To acquire new markets or new distribution channels, either for their own products, to hedge against their own market or to enter a faster growing segment of the market.
- ☐ To acquire production facilities to update, modernize, expand or consolidate, or to locate in a geographic area better suited for the business.
- ☐ For growth. Growth can be achieved with new products, new markets or new channels, and can create a more viable entity.
- ☐ For diversification.
- ☐ To manage risk or provide a second outlet if the present business is susceptible to quick product or market breakthroughs.
- ☐ As a defensive strategy to prevent the original business from being acquired. Your cash and borrowing power can be used to make your business a less appetizing acquisition.

☐ To satisfy their egos.

☐ For other personal reasons, such as providing something for children or other relatives to operate without being consistently under your control—a way of letting them grow into your shoes.

Similarly, there are good and valid reasons for selling a company. We've listed seven:

☐ Lack of management continuity—no heir to take over the business.

☐ Inadequate resources to realize full potential. Someone else could make the business grow faster by infusing it with more capital, better management or new products and technology.

☐ Convert investment to cash for personal or estate-planning reasons, for retirement, etc.

☐ Business doesn't fit long-range plans. A division, say, is not going in the same direction as the rest of the company.

☐ Doesn't fit financial objectives, is not making expected returns or requires significant investment that would better be made elsewhere.

☐ More valuable to others—fits into the product, market or long-range planning of another firm.

☐ Third-party pressures from regulators, banks, investment houses, shareholders, etc.

How do you match your needs to a seller's needs? How do you identify a company to buy or a buyer for your company?

You must have a well-thought-out plan of what you want your business to be. You should have focused personal goals, such as wealth, fame, leisure, "business as usual," income level and competitive stance. You should assess your business strengths and weaknesses and your personal resources, strengths and weaknesses.

After evaluating goals and resources, the two should be compared. Can you do what you want to do with what you have? Do you need to change goals? Can you acquire necessary resources? Can you do this internally? Or do you have to acquire?

The key elements involved in finding an acquisition candidate are:

- ☐ Identification of goals
- ☐ Resource assessment
- ☐ Setting acquisition criteria
- ☐ Industry screen
- ☐ Company screen
- ☐ Contact strategy

You must first list and analyze your goals. Ask yourself:

- ☐ How big do I want to be?
- ☐ How profitable?
- ☐ When?
- ☐ Whom do I want to serve?
- ☐ With what product or service?
- ☐ What market niche do I want?
- ☐ What will be my reputation?
- ☐ Why will I survive?
- ☐ What are my strengths? List them.
- ☐ What are my weaknesses? List them.
- ☐ What opportunities do I see? List them.
- ☐ What threats, both internally and externally, do I see to my business? List them.
- ☐ How do I manage my business? One-man show, leader, overseer, etc.

Establishing Criteria

If you have decided to consider acquiring a company, and if you are up to it in terms of time, effort, cost (financial and psychic) and risk, then the next step is to establish the acquisition criteria.

It is important for both buyers and sellers to narrow their choices. The specific criteria used will depend on the reasons for buying or selling. Those often used are:

- ☐ Products, markets or facilities
- ☐ Location
- ☐ Size and cost
- ☐ Health of company (turnaround or not)
- ☐ Growth prospects
- ☐ Financial measurements (e.g., profitability, ratios, cash flow)
- ☐ Financing structure—will you pay in cash, stock, be highly leveraged, etc.
- ☐ Control—should the target be close enough that you can control operations?

The Corporate Culture

It is important to find a compatible corporate culture. Who can you live with? Factors to consider include:

- ☐ Risk tolerance
- ☐ Management tenure
- ☐ Age of company and management
- ☐ Management's education level
- ☐ Facilities environment
- ☐ Capitalization structure
- ☐ Work ethic
- ☐ Religious or geographic differences.

Finding the Kind of Buyer or Seller You Want

- ☐ Within the targeted industry, talk to contacts, suppliers, customers, competitors, distributors and users.
- ☐ Go to brokers and finders; talk to industry specialists, investment bankers, venture capitalists, business brokers.

☐ Contact other professionals who know the industry, including local businesspeople, accountants, attorneys and bankers.

Many business directories are available to help identify candidates. They include:

☐ Dun & Bradstreet
☐ Standard & Poor's
☐ Moody's Industrial
☐ Compustat and Merger Data Bases
☐ Industry directories
☐ Trade publications

Develop an active portfolio of potential candidates who most clearly meet your acquisition criteria. The network should be as broad as discretion permits. Acquirers should have exposure to as many targets as possible, but divesting usually requires limited exposure and significant discretion.

A Highly Interactive Process

It is not unusual to start with a list of hundreds of companies that on the surface meet one or more of the acquisition criteria. To narrow them down:

☐ Start with the targeted industry
☐ Match firms with criteria
☐ Narrow down to 50 or so
☐ Look more closely at target and criteria
☐ Narrow down to 10-15 for more in-depth paper and contact review

This becomes the first group of realistic candidates. Narrow these down to five candidates for solid, detailed acquisition review, finding out as much as you can about:

- ☐ Owners
- ☐ Managers
- ☐ Reputation
- ☐ Track record
- ☐ Financial status
- ☐ Banking relationships
- ☐ Product/market status.

This brings you to contacting the company. Contact strategy is important, from the initial contact through maintenance of the relationships and closing the deal. Key issues include:

- ☐ Who makes the initial contact, how, and where? Wherever possible, the contact should be principal to principal to establish individual credibility and chemistry.
- ☐ What is communicated at that time? Generally, a description of your business, your desire to expand (or sell), your reasons and your present exploration or expansion possibilities (joint agreements, joint working management, etc.).
- ☐ How should the principal be contacted? A mutual friend or acquaintance, a direct telephone call or a short, friendly letter can provide the introduction. If the target is represented by a broker, contact with the broker is appropriate.

Certain pitfalls must be avoided if the acquisition is to succeed. We listed six typical problem areas we've encountered that tend to be overlooked:

- ☐ Management compatibility
- ☐ Patience
- ☐ Ego on both sides
- ☐ Not enough homework
- ☐ Time constraints
- ☐ Misreading your own strengths and weaknesses.

The safest acquisition is one with similar products selling to similar markets, where your strengths and knowledge are greatest. The toughest, riskiest type of acquisition is one that involves both new products and new markets, making you heavily dependent on existing management at the acquired company.

The Business Investigation

Once you find a company that *appears* to be the right fit, how do you determine if it is right for you? How do you avoid the disaster of a company that is dressed up for sale, and sold hard, based on an unrealistic history and potential?

What do the numbers really mean? Is the cash flow there, or will you need an injection of working capital to achieve the forecast?

What are the hidden values and where are the inherent weaknesses and problems—like high customer turnover; the possible loss of major customers due to poor customer service; technological obsolescence of the product a few years down the road; and shifts in the marketplace away from the seller's product or service.

Buying someone's business is a lot like buying a used car. You are looking at a used company, buying used property, plant and equipment, used inventory, used technology, a used customer base and tax positions. What shape is the company really in?

Many businesses for sale should never have been started in the first place. Some have been terribly mismanaged. Some have been victims of the economy or market. Many will limp along year after year in a state of bare survival.

These bad situations can nearly always be avoided by good business planning, patience and doing your homework on the investigation.

If you do not have the experience in a particular area—marketing, technology, law, finance or taxes—round out your team with the right professional help. A business investigation generally covers the company; management; products and services; the market; operations; financial data; and the forecast.

But before you examine data, you have to know the seller's business, its market and its operations. There is no substitute approach.

What You Need to Know. In general, the more background information you gather in this first stage of your investigation on a
particular target company and its management, the better position
you are in to propose a transaction, anticipate crucial issues and
determine a seller's willingness to negotiate.

Most of what you need is available from the credit community,
industry sources, customers and public information.

Issues to be addressed here are:

☐ Do you know the industry?

☐ What type of company succeeds and fails in the industry?

☐ What is the image of the company and its products or services
compared to the competition?

☐ What is the company's niche in the industry?

☐ Where is the industry going?

☐ What seasonal factors affect the industry?

☐ What is the specific history of the company? Ownership
changes? Major customer gains or losses?

☐ What is the company's overall business strategy, motivation
and direction? Is it aggressive in product development? In sales
strategy?

☐ Is its market share increasing or decreasing?

Take a hard look at management. What is their reputation in the
marketplace? If key management or former owners are staying on
as employees, how would the company be affected if they were to
leave?

What does the company's credit rating look like?

Do you know the real reason the company is being offered for
sale? This is often difficult to determine, but it is usually worth the
attempt. Have their been recent attempts to sell the company? What
happened to those deals?

What are the broad terms of the acquisition likely to be? Do you
really have a deal? For those of you who have attempted to buy
companies before, you know quite well that many times when there
is a stated desire to sell the owner's head and heart are not neces-

sarily set on a deal. You can—and probably will often—waste valuable time talking to people who are really not interested in selling. They may have such conversations with you solely to determine the value of their business in the marketplace or to cater to their own egos.

Products and Services. A basic objective of many acquisitions is to expand product lines. The decision to proceed with such a deal depends on the type of product information you gather from the seller.

In addition to obtaining the expected product line information, you should be concerned with the rate of product change in the industry. Does the company have significant product liability concerns? Review the warranty terms offered in the industry. How does the company stack up against the industry in terms of warranty terms and experience?

Finally, does the company have adequate patent and trademark protection? How much patent and trademark litigation has been experienced in the industry?

The Market. The decision to pay a purchase price over that indicated by historical results, and how high that premium will be, is usually based on your assessment of the seller's market. Market conditions will be an important factor in your forecasts for the company and in the rate-of-return forecast you make for your investment.

What's the market size? Is the market growing or does the company operate in a "mature" market? What factors affect demand?

You have to evaluate the competition. Who is the competition? How do companies in the industry compete? On customer service? Lead time? Price? Terms? Location? Product quality?

What is the type and size of the company's customer base? Are there special terms for certain customers? What is the degree of customer turnover? What is the sales volume of major customers?

What is the nature and importance of the field sales force? How are sales people compensated?

What are the channels of distribution? Are there any changing patterns in the distribution process?

What is the advertising and promotion approach? You should review advertising programs, media and other sales promotion programs for cost and effectiveness.

Finally, you'll want to review product-line profitability and mark-ups.

Operations. Information gathered on operations must be as reliable as practically possible to ensure the seller's production capability fits your needs.

You must figure in the cost of replacing any outdated or worn-out equipment; these costs can be high, given inflation and advances in technology.

The information you gather will also be important in reevaluation of assets for tax and financial reporting purposes after the deal is closed.

In obtaining information on the location and description of plants and property you should ask:

- ☐ Are the facilities close to good transportation, material sources and labor supply?
- ☐ What is the plant capacity and its current utilization?
- ☐ Do building codes, zoning laws, energy supply or real estate taxes pose a problem?
- ☐ Is machinery and equipment in good working order? Up-to-date? Are there any OSHA and EPA problems? Are maintenance expenses in line?
- ☐ What are future capital equipment needs? Do the projections make sense? How do future capital needs compare to past experience?
- ☐ How satisfactory are production method, efficiency and lay-out; warehouse requirements; and quality control?
- ☐ What has been the trend over the past few years on downtime, waste and scrap? Absenteeism? Accidents? Grievances? Over-time?
- ☐ How is the labor turnover? What is the extent of unionization?
- ☐ What has been the experience with delays and delivery time?

Evaluate other measures of customer service, including returned goods.

☐ How satisfactory are the principal suppliers? Are there alternative sources of supply?

☐ Finally, what type of data processing functions does the company have? Does it own software or hardware? Is the system relatively new? Do the systems produce timely and reliable management information?

Financial Data. Competent financial analysis is also crucial to structuring and valuing the transaction. You should supplement your review of the basic financial statements with detailed breakdowns, analyses and statistics from internal operating statements.

Examine operating results of at least the past three to five years. What's the compound growth rate? What have been the effects of new product or business segment additions and deletions?

How do the results, including the relative significance of cost of sales and general selling and administrative expenses, compare year to year and with industry experience? What are the reasons for the differences?

A category of expense called "private company expenses"—personal expenses that are really a return on investment to the individual owner and may be a dubious tax deduction—must be looked at pretty hard in evaluating the business. Indeed, overall profitability may be enhanced by eliminating or reducing such expenses on an ongoing basis.

What is the extent of total compensation paid to key officers and owner managers? Review:

☐ The extent of travel and entertainment reimbursements

☐ Company cars for personal use

☐ No- or low-cost company loans to key people

☐ Consulting services to related parties

☐ Relatives on the payroll

☐ Rental of facilities from the owners and other dealings between the company and its owners.

How does the aging of accounts receivable look? Is it improving or deteriorating? What are the credit policies, collection period and bad debt experience?

What has been the trend in inventory level by component (materials, in process, finished)? Seasonal needs?

What is inventory turnover experience? Is the inventory out of balance (i.e., fast-moving, high-profit items out of stock while slow-moving, low-profit items are in oversupply)? What is the extent of excess and obsolete inventory? What is the experience with inventory write-downs?

What is the basis of inventory valuation (fifo, lifo, etc.)? Are inventories marked down to market as required, or is the owner holding on to old inventory waiting for the market to come back?

Are there proper inventory records? Adequate cost systems? Many companies are managed by the "seat of the pants." If you are buying a company without much in the way of basic management tools, you could be running a company with no style of management after you assume control.

Here are some key financial questions:

- [ ] Are maintenance and repair expenses reasonable? Does it appear that capital items have been charged off?

- [ ] What amounts are due from officers, owners and other non-trade sources? If you are buying a company with these types of receivable, what you are looking at might really be adjustments to the net worth.

- [ ] Are liabilities current? Have all the payables and statutory taxes been filed and paid when due?

- [ ] Do vacations and sick pay accrue? Are there severance pay liabilities?

- [ ] Have product warranty and service been taken into account as liabilities?

- [ ] Are there pension plans with unfunded past service costs? What vested pension liabilities exist? What happens if the plans are terminated? Can the sale of the company automatically trigger a termination? Has the company complied with the ERISA requirements?

☐ What outstanding litigation exists and how will legal matters be dealt with in the acquisition agreement?

☐ What is the nature and extent of the loan and credit agreements with lenders? Are the credits guaranteed by the owners? What assets are pledged? Will the credit agreements terminate on sale of the company?

☐ Have you reviewed carefully the principal taxes to which the company is subject and the amounts paid for the past three to five years.

☐ If you are buying stock of a company, rather than assets, you succeed and inherit all the tax positions, both good and bad, of the prior owners. "Private company expenses" can become a mine field of exposures for you as the new owner. The IRS can disallow those prior expenditures. You pick up the tab, unless you are adequately protected by the purchase agreement, backed by escrow funds or other security arrangements.

☐ What accounts for any difference between the company's effective tax rate on its financial statements and statutory rates?

☐ What years are still subject to IRS audit? What has been the nature and extent of prior tax audit adjustments?

☐ Is the company really reporting income in all the states in which it conducts business—that is, states in which it has inventory, salespeople, offices or leased property?

The Financial Forecast. The evaluation or preparation of a forecast of the seller's company is the most critical part of the investigation, and in many ways, analysis of the forecast is the end result of all the other steps performed—the reason for doing all the other analyses.

Since the forecast presents your eventual payback on your investment, it discloses the value of the company and should relate directly to the purchase price and other terms of the deal. Some points to consider in the review of financial forecasts include:

☐ Forecast of profit and loss/cash flow should be by month or quarter of the first year and by year for the next three to five years.

☐ Do the significant assumptions used in the forecasts adequately consider:

—. the sales plan

—. current sales backlog

—. changes in customer base

—. selling price increases

—. margin improvements

—. material, labor and other operating cost increases

—. the effects of income taxes

—. capital expenditures required?

☐ Forecasted balance sheets should be prepared for each year end. Do the forecasted balance sheets properly reflect receivable collection, inventory turnover and trade payable patterns? How do they compare to past experiences?

☐ Are the projections consistent with industry and overall business expectations?

☐ Finally, the present value of the forecasted cash flow should be calculated at an appropriate expected rate of return to determine company value. For a discussion of valuation, see the section on valuing a business later in this chapter.

As a rule, new businesses carry a higher risk of failure than established companies. Business acquisitions need not be unusually risky, since the business that has already proved its ability to survive has a track record that can be analyzed, measured and evaluated with a reasonable degree of accuracy. However, the buyer has to beware and make a serious investment of time up front.

PACKAGING YOUR COMPANY FOR SALE

Owners are sometimes more concerned with tax savings than with reporting earnings and financial condition until they are financing, going public or structuring their company for sale. Their accounting practices historically may be designed solely to minimize income taxes. Their financial statements may not have been audited or even prepared in accordance with generally accepted accounting principles. If you are in this position, you must be prepared to put your "accounting house" in order to package your company for sale.

Conformity of financial statements to prescribed rules and generally accepted accounting principles is required by the acquiring company, particularly if it is public, because of SEC requirements. These requirements apply whether there is to be a pooling (exchange of shares) or an acquisition of your company for cash and/ or stock. Poolings require that certified or financial statements be available for consolidation with the acquiring company on an historical basis. Under purchase accounting, the SEC requires that the historical financial statements of the acquired company are presented in certain filings under certain conditions.

Even if statutory requirements are not a factor for the acquiring company, for the seller there is no way to demonstrate true financial condition or results of operations except by having financial statements prepared in accordance with generally accepted accounting principles.

Since most purchase acquisitions are highly leveraged (that is, accomplished by borrowing and pledging the assets to be acquired), it is necessary to demonstrate to the acquirer's financiers that the underlying acquisition has the assets and earning power required for leveraging.

The basic price for your company will be determined by a number of factors, all relating, of course, to its demonstrated earning power. Other vital considerations include whether the deal can be leveraged and the necessary tax benefits derived from the underlying acquisition, whether the purchase is of stock or of underlying assets. The acquired company's past tax practice may influence whether or not the deal can even be consummated and the price.

It is not necessary that the financial statements of your company be audited, but rather that they be auditable by your own auditors or the acquiring company's auditors, since the acquirer will always review the underlying financial presentations using its own auditors and financial consultants.

If you have engaged in practices that aren't acceptable from a tax or accounting point of view, these issues must be addressed or corrected where possible. Companies that have used unacceptable practices have been prohibited from either selling the companies or going public (which is another way of selling your company).

Tax issues that may have to be addressed by some companies include treatment of cash sales, personal expenses, comingling of the owner's personal expenditures with company expenses and inventory "cushions" or understatements. The existence of such tax and accounting problems may impair a company's ability to demonstrate earning power and may require significant documentation in order to establish pro forma results of operations to the satisfaction of the buyer. Finally, accountant's reports bearing significant qualifications or disclaimers prevent an acquiring company from including the seller's financial statements in statutory filings with the SEC.

Related party transactions also need to be reviewed and perhaps restructured, particularly when a company is going public or when part of a group of related companies is being sold as an economic unit. If certain related companies are being sold, they must firm up their financial position by creating a discrete unit not dependent on other affiliated economic units. For example, if real estate is owned by the seller personally, he or she must decide whether to include that in the sale or arrange for long-term leases so that the economic viability of the unit being sold can be determined.

POSTACQUISITION INTEGRATION

Why do so many acquisitions fail to meet the buyer's expectations? Commonly, business combinations are arranged by a small group of senior executives of the acquiring company without the involvement of operating personnel. The integration of the acquired company into its new parent is rarely well planned in advance because of the tendency to deal with more immediate priorities. Operational aspects tend to be addressed only after the legal combination has been achieved. This frequently causes serious disruptions, high management turnover and failure to achieve business objectives. A well-planned and executed integration process is critical to all acquisitions.

Some areas for consideration in the integration plan are:

☐ Will operations be consolidated, partially modified or remain autonomous? What does operating autonomously really mean to you and the company acquired? What are the ground rules? What are the benchmarks for performance and responsibility?

☐ How will budgets and operating plans change in the short and long term after the acquisition?

☐ How are employee benefit plans to be integrated? Will some plans be terminated and others implemented?

☐ What about data processing operations? Can systems be integrated or consolidated?

☐ What management and accounting control systems must be established or changed?

☐ What tax policies and elections need to be considered and made?

Obviously there are many questions that must be addressed specifically in the integration of an acquired company, whether it is to be consolidated into your existing business or operated autonomously. A well-thought-out plan of action is critical to the realization of your investment.

VALUING YOUR COMPANY

Valuing a business is not an exact science, but a complex process that requires sophisticated techniques and considers many factors to evaluate the underlying economic substance of the proposed transaction.

When Valuation Is Needed

There can be several reasons for valuing a business or part of a business. Valuations are commonly done when:

☐ A business or a business segment is to be bought or sold

☐ A value must be placed on a minority interest in a business

☐ Business owners must agree on a value for a "buy-sell" agreement

☐ A value is needed for employees receiving options or warrants to purchase stock in a business

☐ The value of a majority or minority ownership position must be determined for estimate tax purposes or for a gift of stock to family and others

☐ A business owner needs to make the business part of the financing process.

Ways To Value a Business

There are many ways to assess the value of a business. In some cases, book value may be the best indicator of the company's value to an investor. If a company has a regularly traded stock or if comparable companies have traded stock, a value based upon the estimated, freely traded value may be appropriate. A third method estimates the value of future income or cash that can be extracted from the enterprise.

A determination of the economic value of a company requires consideration and judgment of all significant factors affecting its operations, including:

☐ The nature and history of the business

☐ The capability and depth of management

☐ The outlook for the business in light of general economic conditions

☐ Historical operating results and the potential for future profitability

☐ The current financial condition of the company

☐ Cash needs and projected cash flows

☐ The record of past dividend payouts and potential future dividends

☐ Contractual arrangements

☐ Investors' attitudes as reflected in market prices and price-earnings ratios of comparable publicly held companies.

While all these factors must be considered in the appraisal value of any company, primary emphasis should be placed on estimated ability to generate future cash flows.

Valuation Based on Adjusted Net Worth. Businesses are often valued by determining their net worth or net assets (also known as book value or stockholder's equity).

But this book value, as determined by generally accepted accounting principles, is not ordinarily the best indication of the value of an operating enterprise. Traditionally determined book value does not reflect either the earning power of the company or the replacement value of the company's assets, particularly where the company has a large investment in fixed assets, has developed a particular expertise or has other intangible assets not reflected in its accounts. Accordingly, book value based on historical cost is usually an inappropriate measure of the going-concern value of a company, except to temper a value placed on the company by other methods of valuation.

However, if book value is used for valuation, reported company net worth should be adjusted to a net worth at market value.

Some balance sheet values that should be examined for possible adjustments are:

☐ Over- and underestimated receivable reserves

☐ Market valuation of investments carried on a cost basis

☐ Net realizable value of inventories

☐ Current values for property, plant and equipment

☐ Values attributable to patents, trademarks, favorable contracts, license and other agreements

☐ Low-interest loans and securities that should be adjusted to market rate

☐ Liabilities that may be understated or not recorded, such as:

—. Pension and other employee benefit plans and arrangements

—. Reserves for income and other taxes, including possible penalties and interest attributable to prior understatement of income taxes for a variety of reasons

—. Reserves to be established if certain operations are curtailed or terminated

—. Reserves to settle outstanding legal matters, including governmental proceedings

—. Reserves for warranties or uninsured product liabilities

Price-Earnings Valuation. The most common way to value publicly held companies is the price-earnings method. This is simply the price of a share of a company's common stock in the public market (e.g., $10) divided by its earnings per share (e.g., $1) for a p/e ratio of 10. If this publicly held company had 1,000,000 common shares outstanding, the market valuation of the company would be $10 million ($10 market value per share times the number of shares outstanding).

A closely held business can be valued by the p/e method by multiplying net income by an appropriate multiple, determined by examining multiples for similar publicly traded companies. The primary advantage of the price-earnings valuation method is its simplicity.

There are, however, serious limitations in determining a proper multiple. The stock of a closely held corporation is not publicly traded. A below-market multiple should be used because the stock is not as liquid as those traded on the public market. There are exceptions, such as when the public market does not reflect real values or is not itself an active market.

Finally, it is very difficult to find a truly comparable publicly held company, even in the same industry. To do so, you should focus on the nature of the companies' business, the location of the businesses, the relative audit of revenues derived by the companies, their financial structure and corporate form and all other relevant factors, particularly unique items that might differentiate the companies. The company to be valued should have similar resources and face similar economic opportunities. Visits should be made to the companies it's being compared to.

Valuation Based on Future Cash Flow. The ultimate measure of a company's value is the level of profitability an investor can achieve from an investment. The rate of return to an investor is ultimately measured not by the accounting profits from the investment, but by the cash flow potentially available. Cash flow is truly the only means for providing a recovery of the investment and a return on the investment. Only cash can be used for reinvestment or for the payment of dividends.

To use the cash-flow method, the following information must be obtained:

- [ ] Projected operating results (income statements) for the next five years, converted to a cash-flow analysis (*see following illustration*).
- [ ] Estimate of the company's net tangible assets at the end of five years
- [ ] An appropriate rate of return (also known as a capitalization rate) to be used to determine present value or discount the cash flow over the projected period and the value of the net assets expected at the end of the projected period. The present-value rate gives the value in today's dollars of the future stream of income or cash flow.

Determination of an appropriate rate of return is of primary importance. You will note in your valuation calculations that small changes in the rate of return or discount rate produce significant changes in valuation. Stated simply, the rate of return is defined as that percentage return that an investment must earn each year, taking into account competing investments and risks to be assumed. Higher returns are expected for investments in closely held companies whereas a lower rate is acceptable on published rates for costs of borrowed funds.

There is no restriction on the number of years used to project cash flows. Many times the projected period is based on the estimated average remaining life of the assets, a principal lease term or a major agreement such as a license or royalty agreement key to the continuation of the business as presently constituted. Additional cash flows added by projecting additional years will be offset, in part, by reduction in the present value of net assets available at the end of the projection period, since the discount factor decreases over time.

Illustrative Case

Valuation of XYZ Company, Inc.
(000s omitted)
Adjustment of Projected Operating Results to Projected Cash Flow

	Years Projected					Value Today
	1	2	3	4	5	
Net Income	$100	$130	$165	$205	$250	
Add: Non-cash charges						
Depreciation and Amortization	15	18	20	22	25	
Deferred Income Taxes	10	12	10	13	10	
Less:						
Capital Expenditures	(30)	(20)	(20)	(30)	(20)	
Projected Cash FLow	95	140	175	210	265	$606
Net assets at end of fifth year					1,300	737
	95	140	175	210	1,565	
At a present-value factor of 12%	0.893	0.797	0.712	0.636	0.567	
Present value of cash flow	$ 85	$112	$125	$134	$887	$1,343

Presently, XYZ, Inc. has an estimated value of $1,343,000, assuming a 12% expected rate of return.

ADJUSTING HISTORICAL FINANCIAL STATEMENTS

A key source of information in analyzing and investigating a business is a company's historical financial statements. Comparison of forecasted amounts to historical operating results is important to an understanding and an evaluation of projected cash flow from operations.

Adjusting Operating Results

The following are a few examples of the kind of income-statement adjustments that may be necessary to produce a more accurate view of historical or projected results of operations:

- ☐ Portions of business not to be acquired or that will be discounted or otherwise excluded for the valuation.

- ☐ Owner's compensation and fringe benefits not to be paid in the future should be subtracted. Also, consider the effect of benefit plans to be terminated or expanded.

- ☐ Unusual bad debt and inventory write-offs. However, make sure that such write-offs are indeed "unusual" and are not the kind that usually occur.

- ☐ Additional depreciation and amortization of property, plant and equipment and intangibles through a planned valuation of these assets following the acquisition.

- ☐ Addition or reduction of financing costs as a result of changed circumstances.

- ☐ Changes in the company's tax position as a result of changes in tax laws or the company's circumstances. Will it be able to use available carryforward losses and credits?

Table of present values for $1

Rate of Return

Yr	10%	11%	12%	13%	14%	15%	16%	17%	18%	20%	22%	24%	26%	28%	30%	32%
1	0.909	0.901	0.893	0.885	0.877	0.870	0.862	0.855	0.847	0.833	0.820	0.806	0.794	0.781	0.769	0.758
2	0.826	0.812	0.797	0.783	0.769	0.756	0.743	0.731	0.718	0.694	0.672	0.650	0.630	0.610	0.592	0.574
3	0.751	0.731	0.712	0.693	0.675	0.658	0.641	0.624	0.609	0.579	0.551	0.524	0.500	0.477	0.455	0.435
4	0.683	0.659	0.636	0.613	0.592	0.572	0.552	0.534	0.516	0.482	0.451	0.423	0.397	0.373	0.350	0.329
5	0.621	0.593	0.567	0.543	0.519	0.497	0.476	0.456	0.437	0.402	0.370	0.341	0.315	0.291	0.269	0.250
6	0.564	0.535	0.507	0.480	0.456	0.432	0.410	0.390	0.370	0.335	0.303	0.275	0.250	0.227	0.207	0.189
7	0.513	0.482	0.452	0.425	0.400	0.376	0.354	0.333	0.314	0.279	0.249	0.222	0.198	0.178	0.159	0.143
8	0.467	0.434	0.404	0.376	0.351	0.327	0.305	0.285	0.266	0.233	0.204	0.179	0.157	0.139	0.123	0.108
9	0.424	0.391	0.361	0.333	0.308	0.284	0.263	0.243	0.226	0.194	0.167	0.144	0.125	0.108	0.094	0.082
10	0.386	0.352	0.322	0.295	0.270	0.247	0.227	0.208	0.191	0.162	0.137	0.116	0.099	0.085	0.073	0.062

TAX ASPECTS

The structure of a transaction will influence how the transfer of ownership is taxed. Transactions may be taxable or nontaxable to the seller; normally, the parties can determine which by agreement. If the seller will realize a loss on the transaction, nontaxability is generally not advantageous.

Prior to 1987, the favorable long-term capital rate was a primary consideration in determining whether the seller sold stock or assets. Since the Tax Reform Act of 1986, capital gain and ordinary income are taxed at same rate. Sellers are now more concerned about avoiding or minimizing double taxation, first at the corporate level and then on the shareholder level.

Nontaxable Transactions

If the transaction is to be nontaxable, the seller must receive stock only. If money or nonmonetary assets are received, any gain realized would be taxable.

If the selling corporation exchanges assets for stock, it must distribute the stock received to its shareholders and liquidate if the exchange is to be tax-free.

If the acquiring corporation is not publicly held, a noticeable transaction is generally not desirable to the seller, unless shareholders can arrange beforehand (possibly with the acquiring company) to dispose of the buyer's shares at a reasonable price. This might be done with a buy-sell or redemption agreement.

Basis to Seller

Assuming the buyer gives only stock, the seller's tax basis in that stock will be the same as its basis in the property surrendered. (Holding periods will also be the same.) The seller will be taxed only on subsequent sale of the stock (in a taxable transaction) and only if the amount received exceeds that basis. If the seller is an individual and holds the stock for life, his or her estate will not be taxed on the gain realized during his or her lifetime.

Basis and Attributes to Buyer

The acquiring corporation will take over the acquired corporation's basis in the property received. In addition, the new owner will acquire important tax attributes of the selling corporation (unless the principal purpose of the transaction was avoidance of federal income taxes)—net operating loss (NOL) carryforwards are an example.

For acquisitions after 1986, however, loss carryforwards have been limited whenever there is an *equity structure change* or *owner shift* by more than 50 percentage points in three years or less. An equity structure change is an ownership change in a nontaxable acquisition. An owner shift is any change in the holdings of a 5% (or greater) shareholder of a corporation. All less-than-5% shareholders are treated as a single 5% (or greater) shareholder.

The Tax Reform Act of 1986 limits the amount of postacquisition income that can be offset by a preacquisition NOL to a specified rate of return on the value of the acquired company. The rate applied is the "long-term tax-exempt rate," which is the highest federal long-term rate adjusted to reflect an equivalent rate on tax-exempt bonds. Although this rate is intended to ensure that the value of the NOL will not be greater to the acquiring company than to the selling company, it is much lower than the return that most buyers would require in an acquisition. Loss utilization will be stretched over a long period and may not cover operating income of the acquired company.

In determining the value of a company with losses, any capital contributions made within two years before the change of ownership are excluded. Certain capital contributions are exempt from this rule, including those made when the company was formed, before the first year for which there is an NOL carryforward and to continue basic operations of the company's business (e.g., meeting the payroll). This rule may cause problems, however, when shareholders of a loss corporation have made large capital contributions in an effort to revitalize the company. Also, the stock value of a company whose assets consist one-third or more of investment assets must be reduced by the value of these assets (net of their share of liabilities).

In addition, NOL carryforwards would be totally disallowed if during the two years following an ownership change the new owner fails to continue the operations or assets of the old corporation in a manner that satisfies the "continuity of business enterprise" requirement. Also, consolidated return limitations and the business purpose requirement remain.

Other tax attributes that are affected by this new limitation rule include built-in losses, net capital loss carryovers and credit carryovers, such as investment tax credit and foreign tax credit. A built-in loss is generally a loss economically accrued before acquisition but recognized on disposition during any of the five taxable years following the ownership change.

Taxable Transactions

The interests of the buyer and the seller may conflict when it comes to deciding on whether the buyer will receive stock or assets. From the seller's standpoint, sale of stock is the simplest way to sell ownership of a corporate business in a taxable transaction. Once taxable gain is realized, the seller is relieved of all contingencies attached to the corporation (other than those stipulated in the sales agreement with the buyer), and does not bear additional costs and expenses if the selling corporation is liquidated. Also, in this transaction, the seller generally avoids double taxation.

Buyer Purchases Assets

Usually it is to the buyer's advantage to acquire assets rather than stock. The buyer avoids the problems of contingent liabilities, paying for unwanted items and incurring additional costs if the acquired company is liquidated. If the purchase price of the assets is higher than the seller's basis in them, the buyer will receive a higher basis. Finally, outright ownership of assets may make it possible to allocate basis advantageously—that is, more to items such as inventory and depreciable property and less to nondeductibles such as goodwill.

Generally, a purchaser will achieve a more favorable tax position by acquiring assets rather than stock. On the other hand, the economics of many taxable stock purchases hinge on the ability to create additional depreciation deductions by electing to step up the basis of assets to the cost of the stock (a "338 election"). Prior to 1987, the one-time cost of obtaining the step-up was a tax payable on recapture items, chiefly the seller's previously taken depreciation and investment tax credit. Since 1986, the entire amount of the step-up for the buyer has become taxable at the full 34% rate, and investment tax credit is recaptured as before. Since the present value of future deductions could never exceed this cost, stepping up assets is no longer a viable option.

However, there is also an exception to this rule if the acquired company has NOL carryovers that can offset the one-time gain.

The 338 election can be beneficial, especially with the new restrictions on NOLs discussed previously.

An additional transition rule for eligible closely held corporations allows favorable prior law treatment for liquidation sales and distributions before January 1, 1989, provided the liquidation is completed before that date. A corporation is eligible if its value does not exceed $5 million and more than 50% of its stock is owned by 10 or fewer individuals who have held their stock for five years or longer. Relief under this rule is phased out for corporations with values between $5 million and $10 million.

If buyer and seller are corporations, an asset sales treatment can be accomplished in a stock transaction if a Section 338(h)(10) election is made. The election allows the buyer a stepped-up basis in the assets and permits the seller to retain attributes of the company being sold. The seller's concern will be the basis differential between stock and net assets. (Note that this election does not avoid double taxation, but, if used effectively, can substantially reduce tax liability.)

The *mirror-image* planning structure has been used recently by acquirers interested in breaking up the target and making selective sales of unwanted assets or subsidiaries. The mirror-image structure does not provide an asset basis step-up; rather, by liquidating the acquired corporation into one of several newly formed acquisition subsidiaries, the purchaser can dispose of a portion of the recently acquired business at a stepped-up basis tax-free by selling the stock of one or more of these newly formed subsidiaries.

In a mirror-image acquisition a holding company and various subsidiaries are formed. The capitalization of each subsidiary is based on the fair market value (or purchase price) of the assets to be acquired. The parent and subsidiaries purchase all of the seller's stock. The acquired corporation is then liquidated tax-free into the parent and its subsidiaries. While each receives the mirrored assets that are not stepped up, the parent has a higher basis for each subsidiary; individual sales of the unwanted subsidiaries' stock can then be achieved without a taxable gain. Because of the complexity of tax strategies involving the method of acquisition of assets or stock of a company, they should be reviewed by your tax adviser before the acquisition is completed.

Sales of Assets

Sometimes it is desirable to sell assets without liquidating the corporation. Continued existence of the corporation may be advantageous if it has substantial net operating loss carryovers. These carryovers may be used to offset any gain realized on the sale of business assets and also to offset future income from the reinvested proceeds of the sale. The personal holding company provisions of the code discussed below may be applicable.

Whenever the stockholder's taxable gain on a sale of stock is substantially greater than the corporation's gain from the sale of its assets, continued existence will mean tax savings. Apart from this consideration, an elderly stockholder may find it desirable to keep the corporation alive so that the stock may pass through his or her estate, thereby acquiring an increased basis without giving rise to a liquidation tax. The personal holding company can be an effective tool for this purpose.

Personal Holding Companies

A personal holding company (PHC) is a closely held corporation that derives its income primarily from investments. The technical requirements that a corporation must meet to qualify as a personal holding company are:

☐ At any time during the second half of the taxable year, more than 50% of the outstanding stock must be owned by (or on behalf of) five or fewer individuals.

☐ At least 60% of the adjusted ordinary gross income must fall into one or more of several defined classes of income. Adjusted ordinary gross income is gross income less gains from the sale of capital assets and from a sale of property used in trade or business.

Income items considered in determining if the 60% requirement is met include most forms of passive income, including—with certain limitations—dividends, interest, royalties and rented income earned under a personal service contract.

A personal holding company is subject to taxation on its undistributed income. The PHC is also subject to double taxation on the appreciation of its assets: once when the corporation sells them and again when the shareholder receives the proceeds or other property as dividend or on liquidation. Despite these tax drawbacks, the personal holding company can be a valuable financial planning tool.

Valuation of Shares. Most PHCs are unlisted and have comparatively few shareholders. Their stock is not readily marketable and is therefore generally valued by shareholders at below the level of the underlying assets. For example, a gift of a 10% interest in a typical PHC whose only asset is 1,000 shares of General Motors would be worth considerably less than a gift of 1,000 GM Shares.

The IRS has allowed discounts of as high as 20% on assets; the courts have been more generous, granting allowances as high as 55%. If the shares convey the right to force a voluntary liquidation (as opposed to dissolution in bankruptcy) under state law, the total value of personal holding company shares may then be equal to its net asset value.

Tax Advantages. PHCs offer important tax advantages that can minimize, and in some cases virtually eliminate, double taxation.

Deductions. The combination of the standard 80% dividend-received deduction and deductions for owner-manager compensation and operating expenses can easily exceed ordinary income, thereby generating a net operating loss. Note that for the alternative income tax computation, the 80% dividend-received deduction is not allowed; however, this should only be a problem if the deduction exceeds $80,000. This net operating loss can be applied against capital gains, reducing them to the point where the effective corporate tax rate is less than the individual rate. Thus, the tax cost to a PHC when it disposes of assets at a gain may, in some cases, be substantially lower than the tax would have been to the former outright owner of these assets, had the owner sold them and realized the same gain. Finally, a PHC's capital loss can be carried back three years, but there is no such provision for individuals.

Fringe Benefits. The PHC may maintain fringe benefits such as a qualified pension or profit-sharing plan, a qualified medical reimbursement plan or life insurance on behalf of one or more employee-shareholders. The cost of these plans is an operating expense.

Gift Giving. Since PHC shares are difficult to market, they have been used to make direct gifts where a trust otherwise would have been necessary. Because of the formalities and petty expenses associated with setting up a trust, you should consider this alternative if you are contemplating a restricted donation of any kind.

7

Asset Management

Effective asset management is critical to the successful operation of a business. A unique product or service may enable a business to be profitable despite a certain amount of laxity, but in periods of inflation or recession or both, protecting your balance sheet is just as important as maximizing the bottom-line figure on your next year's income statement. In fact, especially in high interest rate conditions, next year's profit might depend on how well you "turn" your assets.

In this chapter, we deal with three basic kinds of assets: cash, inventory and capital items. Cash management is essentially a question of maintaining liquidity and maximizing the return on working capital. Inventory management involves balancing delivery and manufacturing costs against carrying costs to identify and maintain optimal levels for thousands of separate items. Capital budgeting is an approach to controlling investment in capital assets by evaluating the profitability of each asset, both prospectively and on the basis of demonstrated performance.

The rules of asset management make sense for enterprises of any size. For emerging businesses, however, especially in times of economic adversity, they are vital to survival.

CASH MANAGEMENT

A company's cash flow is the indicator of its economic health. Having cash to meet obligations as they fall due is the primary requirement for continued business existence. Handsome profits are not meaningful if all your cash is tied up in excess inventory, machinery or other noncash assets. A certain degree of liquidity is essential in any business.

Next to judgment error, lack of effective control over cash resources is the most common cause of business failure. The casualty rate from this defect is particularly high for smaller businesses in their formative early years. Paradoxically, prosperity itself is often the problem. Flourishing sales entail heavy expenditures for raw materials and payrolls to meet increases in volume, and the company finds itself with an unbridgeable gap between accounts payable and accounts receivable.

No business can be completely insured against adverse circumstances, but with a well-designed financial management system you are at least in a position to minimize the adverse financial consequences. Cash management involves:

- ☐ Knowing how much cash you will need, when you will need it and where you can get it
- ☐ Adjusting spending plans realistically to meet changes in financial expectations
- ☐ Maintaining an appropriate balance of cash — neither so little as to constrict operations nor so much as to forfeit significant earnings from putting the cash to productive use.

Cash-Conserving Techniques

Cash management employs a wide variety of techniques, ranging from the simple to the sophisticated.

Accelerating Collections. From the time you deliver to the customer to the time their payment is received and credited to your account, there is a chain of procedures, many of which you can expedite. For example, you can:

☐ Streamline banking arrangements by shortening the time lag between customer payments and the deposit of those funds to the company's bank account. If your company has more than one logical collection point for remittances, consider having all remittances sent to a single address, such as a postal box number. You can give a bank with a branch near that post office the authority to collect remittances from the postal lockbox and send you daily a list of receipts. Many banks will grant you a zero-balance account, whereby you can borrow based on the average balances of remittances in the lockbox account with them.

☐ Factor accounts receivable or, alternatively, honor bank credit cards. Your choice would depend on which option offers the lower cost and your assessment of impact, if any, on your image. Allow discounts or modification of other terms on accounts receivable to promote quicker customer payment. Here, the validity of a particular rate offered would depend largely on how the effective annual rate of the discount compares with the highest available bank interest. Expedite the transmittal of invoices and statements to customers; a delay of even one day is costly. Invoices should be issued at the time of shipment.

☐ Review accounts receivable continuously for delinquencies and step up collection procedures. If an amount is due 30 days after shipment, call for payment on the thirty-first day if the cash is not received. Do not wait another 30 days.

Credit Policies. One way to avoid a collection problem is to ship only cash on delivery (C.O.D.). In most businesses, however, this kind of stringency would seriously reduce volume. The chances are, therefore, that you will have to grant credit to most of your customers. This means you will have to evaluate all your customers' financial strengths and their reputations. There is no shortcut to this evaluation process; poor credit management is a major factor in many small business failures.

Centralization is essential to an effective credit program. Credit policies should be explicit, put into writing and circulated to all concerned, including salespeople. All orders should be subject to confirmation by a credit officer.

It is possible to obtain credit insurance as blanket protection against bad debts. The cost of insurance can be worthwhile if some or all of your customers are in businesses that are vulnerable to adverse economic or technological developments.

Delaying Disbursements. With disbursements, you are at the opposite end of the chain of procedure between delivery and final transfer of funds. Nevertheless, the same principle applies, only instead of "expedite" you "delay." Thus, you can:

☐ Make sure bills are not paid before their due dates.

☐ Take advantage of any latitude in payment terms. For example, with various forms of insurance — notably, workmen's compensation insurance — it is often possible to pay premiums in installments without finance charges.

☐ Make it a policy to release checks at the latest acceptable time, and impose the policy throughout your organization. Mail checks at the end of the day and, where possible, at the end of the week.

☐ Give full consideration in your choice of bank to the factors of mailing and clearing time.

Taking Advantage of Discounts. The standard 2% discount for payment within the first 10 days is equivalent to interest at an annual rate of about 36%. If your cash position is so weak that you are unable to take advantage of discounts you may be able to borrow the necessary funds from a bank for the purchase. The cost of borrowing may be well below the annualized savings from the discount. On the other hand, if you can delay paying a bill for 60 days without alienating the vendor, the effective rate for the discount drops to less than 15%.

Temporary Cash Investments. The essential function of cash management is maximizing the productive use of cash. This means ensuring that cash not needed for operations is invested. The following discussion covers common short-term cash investment possibilities

Table 7.1
SOME SHORT-TERM INVESTMENT VEHICLES[a]

Type of Investment	Usual Maturity	Minimum Investment	Liquidity	Interest Paid	Description
Money Market Funds	7 days average	$1,000	Marketable	Daily	Mutual funds concept of diversified investments with portfolio management
Certificates of Deposit	30 days–1 year	100,000	Marketable	At maturity	Bank time instrument issued for a specified period earning interest at a stated rate
Bankers' Acceptances	30–270 days	10,000	Marketable	At maturity	Time draft drawn on and guaranteed by a bank
Repurchase Agreements	1–29 days	25,000	—	At maturity	Sale of securities with agreement to repurchase at maturity at a stated price and rate
Commercial Paper	5–270 days 30–270 days 90–270 days	100,000 50,000 25,000	Nonmarketable	At maturity	Unsecured promissory note issued by a corporation to meet short-term cash needs
U.S. Treasury Bills	To 1 year	10,000	Marketable	At maturity	Short-term U.S. government obligation

[a]Due to rapid changes in investment vehicles, check with your investment adviser for the most up-to-date information.

(also summarized in Table 7-1). Note that many instruments can mature in as little as one day.

Money Market Funds.

☐ These are pooled investments in the short-term money market. They operate on the same principle as mutual funds and offer much the same advantages of diversified risk and professional management. Unlike some mutual funds, money market funds can be redeemed anytime; most permit withdrawals by check. Before investing in this kind of fund, ascertain the priorities and historical performance of the management in regard to safety, yield and growth.

Certificates of Deposit.

☐ These are time loans to banks collateralized by savings accounts in the lender's name. The term is anywhere from 30 days to one year and interest is at a set rate. Certificates of deposit are backed by the full faith and credit of the issuing bank and in most instances are insured by the FDIC up to $100,000. Liquidation of the account before term is subject to heavy penalty.

Commercial Paper.

☐ This term takes in a variety of unsecured, interest-bearing promissory notes generally issued by major corporations or their captive finance subsidiaries. Maturities begin at 1 day; more than 270 days is unusual. You can obtain commercial paper directly in return for a loan, or you can buy it through a broker. Here, too, the risk factor depends on the creditworthiness of the lender; higher risks should be reflected in higher interest rates.

Bankers' Acceptances.

☐ A banker's acceptance is a draft drawn on a bank and accepted by it. The life of these drafts is usually somewhere between 30 and 270 days. For the most part, acceptances are used to finance transactions involving merchandise, where the drawer of the draft is the seller. A small fee is charged to the drawer. Bankers' acceptances are considered somewhat more secure than promissory notes issued by a bank.

Bank Repurchase Agreements.

☐ In this case you lend to a bank, taking money market securities as collateral. The bank agrees to buy back your loan at a set price in anywhere from 1 to 29 days. Your interest is the difference between the repurchase price and the amount you advanced.

Treasury Bills.

☐ These are short-term obligations of the U.S. government, non-interest-bearing and issued at a discount. The minimum purchase is generally $10,000, and maturities range from one week to one year. Treasury bills are considered to be one of the safest short-term investments; they are liquid and can be bought or sold through banks and stock and bond brokers.

Hints for Short-Term Investing

Shop around before you choose an investment. Yields, even on comparable instruments, vary considerably. Also, since yields may be quoted on the face amount or current market price, make sure the yields you are evaluating are expressed in the same terms.

Try to link your investing activities to financial forecasting so you can establish a schedule of maturities designed to give you cash when the forecast indicates you will need it. (Make sure the repayment date is fixed for every investment.) Do not permit too wide a spread between maturity dates, regardless of forecast indications. Allow for the unexpected.

The Cash Budget

The cash budget, as distinguished from the operating budget

(Chapter 3), is a forecast of expected cash receipts and cash disbursements within the budget period. The receipts and expenditures are estimated on the basis of expected levels of activity, the anticipated rate of accounts receivable turnover and any seasonal factors likely to affect cash flow.

Estimating Cash Receipts. A company's cash receipts typically depend on the collection of accounts receivable — an activity fundamental to every business. Estimating collections is more involved for some firms than for others, but in all cases the method used is essentially the same, because estimates must be based on budgeted sales and past collection experience. To project collections, you need the following information:

☐ The budgeted sales figure for each month

☐ The collection pattern; that is, the proportion of billings for which payment is received in successive time categories, such as the first month, the second month, the third month

☐ The proportion of uncollectible accounts.

Some companies sell on discount, others offer 90-day credit and still others sell to prime accounts that almost invariably remit payment within 30 days. Although every business requires a slightly different approach, collections can be estimated with reasonable accuracy, provided they are constantly revised to reflect changes as they occur.

Generally, the relationship of collections to sales does not vary significantly from month to month. To illustrate this point, assume the following relationships between the collections and sales of a company, as determined by analysis of its records:

☐ 70.0% are paid within the discount period

☐ 24.0% are paid within one month of the sale

☐ 4.5% are paid within two months of the sale

☐ 0.6% are uncollectible

On the basis of this information, the estimate of collections for January 19XX is computed as follows:

Month of Sale	Sales	Collection in January	
		Percentage	Amount
October 19XX	$60,000[a]	0.9	$ 540
November 19XX	70,000[a]	4.5	3,150
December 19XX	90,000[a]	24.0	21,600
January 19XX	60,000[b]	70.0(98.0)[c]	41,160
Estimated collections for January 19XX			$66,450

[a]Actual.
[b]Budgeted.
[c]After discount of 2%.

Your company may experience variations in collections for different months during the year. If so, you must analyze collection experience separately for each month and apply these percentages to the budgeted sales data. Take care to avoid distortions due to unusual situations in past years, such as strikes and fires. Simply eliminate the affected period in determining the percentages to be used.

If your company has investments, schedule the anticipated income from them by months or by quarters. Do not forget to allow for the cash resulting from sale or redemption as well. Anticipate receipts from miscellaneous sources. Admittedly, this kind of income is difficult to predict and not often significant. But where experience indicates that there will be such income, a conservative estimate is appropriate.

Estimating Cash Payments. The major portion of cash disbursements consists of payments for materials, labor, other expenses, capital improvements and retirement of indebtedness.

Materials.

☐ Systematize your policies, item by item, for time of payment and utilization of trade discounts. Your past practices should be applied to the appropriate items in the operating budget and to other cash requirements of the business. If you have been taking trade discounts whenever possible, your cash planning will be simplified because discounts are generally taken within 10 days and the operating budget is probably stated at net cash figures rather than at invoice cost.

Labor Costs.

☐ Labor costs are usually a large portion of a manufacturing company's cash requirements. Because the payroll must be met at specific times, the timing of labor costs is simplified. The figure to use in planning cash requirements is the net cash payroll, since taxes and other items withheld from the gross payroll are not usually paid in the same period.

Other Expenses.

☐ Projected cash requirements for noncash items, such as depreciation, should not be in operating budget schedules. For this purpose, expenses on the accrual basis, such as insurance and property taxes, are treated as noncash items. Instead, you should provide for these expenses in the cash budget in the period in which they are paid. If, for example, all bills are paid on the tenth of the following month, there is a month's lag between incurring and paying expenses.

Items Not Under Profit and Loss.

☐ In addition to payments for materials, labor and other expenses, you should provide for expenditures not included in the profit and loss accounts, such as payments of indebtedness, dividends, capital improvements and all accrued items. Most of the large payments have specific dates of payment and can be determined easily.

The Three-Way Budget. Coopers & Lybrand has developed a cash budget that has been in use for many years. Known as the Three-

Way Budget, Coopers & Lybrand's system is designed to enable small and mid-sized businesses to focus on liquidity problems and to plan and control month-to-month operations without great expenditures of time and money. The budget is built around the three basic aspects of cash management: operations, cash flow and financial condition. Experience has shown that these items are interdependent and must be treated simultaneously.

Benefits. To the businessperson, the system is valuable because monthly they can:

- ☐ Match actual operating results against forecasts and act on warning signals by taking corrective measures
- ☐ Determine with reasonable accuracy when to borrow and how much
- ☐ Monitor the company's financial strength on a regular basis.

The system is also valuable to the banker, who can:

- ☐ Compare anticipated income with prior years and, when actual results are available, with current performance as well
- ☐ See when cash will be derived from company operations and when from credit grantors; when the cost of major projects will be paid; and when long-term loans, operating costs and bank loans will be repaid
- ☐ Determine, on a monthly basis, the company's financial position, including the value of the asset security pledged as collateral for loans and advances.

Structure of the Budget. The Three-Way Budget consists of:

- ☐ A statement of objectives
- ☐ A statement of assumptions on which the forecasts are based, covering such matters as:
  - —. Expected line of credit available
  - —. Gross profits and expense levels and trends

—. Market share

—. Major developments anticipated during the budget year, featuring projections of monthly:

Cost of sales

Earnings

Flow

Profit and loss

☐ Statements covering the same subjects as the above four projections, but comparing the monthly results of actual operations for the elapsed portion of the current year with the previous year's projections.

Preparing the Three-Way Budget. Start with an opening balance sheet and reports on the prior year's results in as much detail as you can reasonably achieve. Estimate the expected sales level for the coming year and identify any anticipated changes from the previous year's levels. Now you are in a position to pinpoint revenues and expenses to specific months of the coming year. On the basis of anticipated sales, and allowing appropriate lead time between sales and cash collections and between commitments ˙and their eventual payment, you can determine the outlays needed to meet that level of sales.

You should scrutinize last year's results for unusual factors that may affect projections. For example, seasonal fluctuations in volume and product mix, personnel changes and additional output at new facilities can affect expenses, as can increases in raw material costs and new capital expenditures, such as added equipment or plant facilities.

Examine the characteristics of different expenses. For example, net income and balance sheet items are accounted for with the accrual method of accounting, but in determining cash flow for items such as insurance, professional fees, licenses, commissions and property, business and income taxes, the cash basis is used. Expenses for sales promotions, production, utilities, advertising campaigns, maintenance and vacation costs are subject to seasonal fluctuations. Interest and income taxes must be developed monthly because of their direct relationship to bank advances and earnings.

The procedures for preparing the Three-Way Budget are relatively simple. We summarize some principal points in the following sections. Although the finished statements are separate, they are closely related and are prepared in tandem.

Everything flows from the basic sales projection and the assumptions of how these sales will be met. Accordingly, by completing the cost-of-sales and earnings statements, you obtain major elements needed for the cash-flow statement and balance-sheet projection.

Monitoring Performance. Once you have completed the Three-Way Budget, you have a series of monthly projections for revenues, expenses and account balances covering a 12-month period that will keep you informed of your company's financial and operational condition. The statements will be sufficiently detailed to permit meaningful comparison with actual performance on a day-to-day basis, so that where disparities occur you can take prompt corrective action.

Taking Corrective Action. Since a budget is no more than a statement of what will happen if observed trends continue and new plans materialize, you must expect variances and deal with them promptly when they arise.

Variations from the financial plan may be caused by any one of a number of unexpected factors, external or internal. External factors include market conditions, increases in property taxes, strikes and plant shutdowns. Among the countless internal factors are abnormal maintenance and repairs, idle time, defective production, returned sales and customer and supplier defaults. Whether they are favorable or unfavorable, controllable or uncontrollable, variations from plan demand immediate attention.

Unfavorable developments that cannot be controlled can be met by protective measures or by adverse revision of the plan. Favorable developments, on the other hand, can result in positive revisions in long-term plans, as well as allocation of surplus cash to loan repayments, increased advertising expenditures, temporary investments or even a totally new and ambitious program.

Reviewing and Revising the Budget. The same principles apply to reviewing and revising cash budgets and to the operating budget (see Capital Budgeting in this chapter).

Case Study Illustrating the Three-Way Budget

The following case study illustrates, step by step, the preparation of a cash budget on the three-way principle. Though the subject, which we call the Relentless Pursuits Company, is fictitious, the facts, figures and events are a composite taken from client situations. You may want to use a computerized model to duplicate the process illustrated in this study (see Chapter 3).

Objectives. The Relentless Pursuits budget is based on an explicit set of objectives that anticipate a requirement for financing during a period of inadequate cash flow. These objectives, formulated with some care and summarized in a written statement, are as follows:

☐ To continue increased market penetration

☐ To expand physical facilities to meet increased product demand

☐ To improve product quality without increasing unit cost.

Assumptions. Relentless Pursuits establishes a series of fundamental assumptions as a basis for assigning revenues, expenses, cash receipts and expenditures to the appropriate periods. This process is highly deliberative and results from the owner-manager's evaluations and judgments in all areas including economic conditions, competition, employee relations and banking relationships. The guiding principle is that a budget is only as good as the assumptions on which it is based. For purposes of this illustration, we will make the following assumptions:

☐ A $120,000 mortgage loan commitment from a government development agency collateralized by a new building facility, payable $5,000 a month beginning in October

☐ Construction costs to be paid in four equal monthly installments

☐ A 30% sales increase on an annual basis

☐ A 12.5% gross profit margin on sales on an annual basis

☐ A 10% increase over prior year in total expenses, including interest expense

☐ First-quarter inventory buildup for peak summer sales season

☐ Collection of accounts receivable anticipated to be 40% in month following sale, 50% in subsequent month, and 10% in third month (for purposes of illustration there are no uncollectable accounts)

☐ Payments for raw material purchases in January through September anticipated to be 75% in the first month following purchase and 25% in the subsequent months of that period; payments in October through December anticipated at 100% in the months following purchase

☐ Labor costs and interest expense paid as incurred

☐ Most other expenses paid in the month after they are incurred

☐ $1,200 a month set aside for estimated income tax payments.

Preparing the Budget. By applying all these assumptions to the basic sales expectations, Relentless Pursuits is able to complete the Three-Way Budget as three separate projected monthly financial statements in the three basic categories: cost of sales, earnings and cash flow. These categories are shown in Figures 7.1a, b and c, respectively. In addition, Relentless Pursuits can use the information provided to produce a balance sheet, also broken down monthly. The balance sheet is shown in Figure 7.1d. The total presentation can be given to the bank to obtain and maintain assured financing.

To prepare these four exhibits develop and record:

☐ Statement of business objectives

☐ Assumptions upon which the forecast is based.

Now project cost of sales and operating statements as follows:

☐ Estimate net sales by month (Figure 7.1b, line 1; in computerized models, this can be done by specific dollar or unit estimates or an initial estimate and a growth percentage for each subsequent period).

☐ Apply lead-time assumptions to establish monthly estimate of:

— . Inventory levels required to service projected sales

— . Production required to meet projected sales and inventory needs

— . Raw material purchases needed to meet projected production needs.

☐ Estimate monthly inventory levels, considering the period of inventory buildup to meet peak season sales (Figure 7.1a, lines 1 and 14).

☐ Estimate overhead items and direct labor costs based on the projected production schedule (Figure 7.1a, lines 3–12; note assumptions made for payment of expenses).

☐ Compute the monthly cost of sales figure (Figure 7.1a, line 15) using the most recent gross profit information available. If gross profit tends to fluctuate by season due to the sales mix, then a monthly figure will be needed.

☐ In Figure 7.1a, add line 14 to line 15 to arrive at line 13. This permits computation of line 2, monthly material purchases, thereby completing Figure 7.1a (line 13 minus lines 1, 3 and 12).

☐ Review Figure 7.1a, noting the reasonableness of expense allocations and the material content of cost of sales compared with prior experience and in light of current projection.

☐ Giving consideration to the timing of payments, transfer the appropriate information on Figure 7.1 from a to c and d as follows:

Item	Line	Figure 7.1c	Figure 7.1d
Inventory	14	—	Line 3
Direct labor	3	Line 6	—
Insurance	5	Line 7	—

(a) PROJECTED STATEMENT OF MONTHLY COST OF SALES FOR THE YEAR ENDING DECEMBER 31 (IN DOLLARS)

	January	February	March	April	May	June	July	August	September	October	November	December	Annual Budget	
1 Inventory at beginning of month	68,000	110,000	157,000	189,000	210,000	195,400	178,200	148,600	120,200	99,300	92,800	85,400	68,000	1
2 Material purchases	78,500	86,400	72,200	62,300	38,100	49,900	49,600	41,500	32,600	42,800	37,100	36,200	627,200	2
3 Direct labor	3,600	3,600	3,600	3,600	3,000	1,100	1,100	1,100	1,100	3,000	3,600	3,600	32,000	3
Factory overhead														
4 Fuel	800	800	800	600	400	200	200	200	400	600	800	800	6,600	4
5 Insurance	400	400	400	400	400	400	400	400	400	400	400	400	4,800	5
6 Utilities	1,500	1,500	1,500	1,500	1,000	900	900	900	900	1,000	1,500	1,500	14,600	6
7 Maintenance and repairs	300	300	300	300	1,500	2,000	2,000	2,000	1,500	600	300	300	11,400	7
8 Property taxes	633	633	633	633	633	633	633	633	633	633	633	637	7,600	8
9 Trucks	400	400	400	400	200	50	50	50	150	300	400	400	3,200	9
10 Employee benefits	50	50	50	950	50	50	50	50	50	950	50	50	2,400	10
11 Depreciation	1,350	1,350	1,350	1,350	1,800	1,800	1,800	1,800	1,850	1,850	1,850	1,850	20,000	11
12	5,433	5,433	5,433	6,133	5,983	6,033	6,033	6,033	5,883	6,333	5,933	5,937	70,600	12
13	155,533	205,433	238,233	261,033	257,083	252,433	234,933	197,233	159,783	151,433	139,433	131,137	797,800	13
14 Inventory at end of month	110,000	157,000	189,000	210,000	195,400	178,200	148,600	120,200	99,300	92,800	85,400	80,200	80,200	14
15 Cost of sales	45,533	48,433	49,233	51,033	61,683	74,233	86,333	77,033	60,483	58,633	54,033	50,937	717,600	15

Figure 7.1. Relentless Pursuits Company: Key Reports in the Three-Way Budget

(b) PROJECTED STATEMENT OF MONTHLY EARNINGS OF SALES FOR THE YEAR ENDING DECEMBER 31 (IN DOLLARS)

	January	February	March	April	May	June	July	August	September	October	November	December	Total	
1 Sales	48,700	52,500	53,600	55,100	70,200	89,400	105,600	93,200	71,400	65,800	59,300	55,200	820,000	1
2 Cost of sale	45,533	48,433	49,233	51,033	61,683	74,233	86,333	77,033	60,483	58,633	54,033	50,937	717,600	2
3 Gross profit	3,167	4,067	4,367	4,067	8,517	15,167	19,267	16,167	10,917	7,167	5,267	4,263	102,400	3
Selling expenses														
4 Salaries and commissions	900	900	900	900	1,200	1,600	1,800	1,600	1,200	1,200	900	900	14,000	4
5 Advertising	100	100	100	100	300	600	800	600	300	200	100	100	3,400	5
6 Delivery and freight	150	150	150	150	300	650	850	650	350	200	150	150	3,900	6
7 Automobile	150	150	150	150	150	150	150	150	150	150	150	150	1,800	7
8 Depreciation	100	100	100	100	100	100	100	100	100	100	100	100	1,200	8
9	1,400	1,400	1,400	1,400	2,050	3,100	3,700	3,100	2,100	1,850	1,400	1,400	24,300	9
Administrative expenses														
10 Salaries	900	900	900	900	900	900	900	900	900	900	900	900	10,800	10

Line	Item													Total	
11	Professional fees	125	125	125	125	125	125	125	125	125	125	125	125	1,500	11
12	Printing, postage, and so on	100	100	100	100	100	100	100	100	100	100	100	100	1,200	12
13	Telephone and telegraph	100	100	100	100	100	100	100	100	100	100	100	100	1,200	13
14	Business taxes and licenses	150	150	150	150	150	150	150	150	150	150	150	150	1,800	14
15	Sundry	50	50	50	50	150	150	150	150	150	150	50	50	1,200	15
16	Interest	200	575	1,090	1,555	1,705	1,665	1,620	1,400	1,080	860	750	700	13,200	16
17		1,625	2,000	2,515	2,980	3,230	3,190	3,145	2,925	2,605	2,385	2,175	2,125	30,900	17
18		3,025	3,400	3,915	4,380	5,280	6,290	6,845	6,025	4,705	4,235	3,575	3,525	55,200	18
19	Net profit before taxes	142	667	452	(313)	3,237	8,887	12,422	10,142	6,212	2,932	1,692	738	47,200	19
20	Income taxes	50	233	158	(109)	1,133	3,107	4,348	3,550	2,174	1,026	592	258	16,520	20
21	Net profit	92	434	294	(204)	2,104	5,770	8,074	6,592	4,038	1,906	1,100	480	30,680	21

Figure 7.1 *(continued)*

(c) PROJECTED STATEMENT OF MONTHLY CASH FLOW FOR THE YEAR ENDING DECEMBER 31 (IN DOLLARS)

	January	February	March	April	May	June	July	August	September	October	November	December	Total	
Cash receipts														
1 Receivable	47,350	47,580	50,000	52,560	54,090	60,990	76,370	93,960	99,020	85,720	71,340	63,760	802,740	1
2 Mortgage loan	30,000	30,000	30,000	30,000	—	—	—	—	—	—	—	—	120,000	2
3 Bank loans	—	26,000	48,000	36,000	23,000	—	—	—	—	—	—	—	133,000	3
4	77,350	103,580	128,000	118,560	77,090	60,990	76,370	93,960	99,020	85,720	71,340	63,760	1,055,740	4
Cash disbursements														
5 Raw material purchases	30,000	68,875	84,425	75,750	64,775	44,150	46,950	49,675	43,525	42,975	42,800	37,100	631,000	5
6 Direct labor	3,600	3,600	3,600	3,600	3,000	1,100	1,100	1,100	1,100	3,000	3,600	3,600	32,000	6
Factory overhead:														
7 insurance	—	—	—	—	—	—	4,800	—	—	—	—	—	4,800	7
8 property taxes	—	—	—	—	—	—	7,600	—	—	—	—	—	7,600	8
9 other, excluding depreciation	3,050	3,050	3,050	3,050	3,750	3,150	3,200	3,200	3,200	3,000	3,450	3,050	38,200	9
Selling expenses:														
10 salaries and commissions	900	900	900	900	1,200	1,600	1,800	1,600	1,200	1,200	900	900	14,000	10
11 other, excluding depreciation	400	400	400	400	400	750	1,400	1,800	1,400	800	550	400	9,100	11
Administrative expenses:														
12 professional fees	—	—	1,500	—	—	—	—	—	—	—	—	—	1,500	12

#	Item	1	2	3	4	5	6	7	8	9	10	11	12	Total / End
13	business taxes and licenses				1,800									1,800
14	salaries	900	900	900	900	900	900	900	900	900	900	900	900	10,800
15	interest	200	575	1,090	1,555	1,705	1,665	1,620	1,400	1,080	860	750	700	13,200
16	other	250	250	250	250	250	250	350	350	350	350	350	350	3,600
17	Income taxes	1,200	1,200	1,200	1,200	1,200	1,200	1,200	1,200	1,200	1,200	1,200	1,200	14,400
18	Plant addition	30,000	30,000	30,000	30,000									120,000
19	Long-term debt repayment				5,000				5,000				5,000	15,000
20	Bank repayment						6,000	6,000	32,000	45,000	27,000	12,000	5,000	133,000
21		70,500	109,750	127,315	119,405	77,180	60,865	76,920	93,225	98,955	86,285	71,500	58,100	1,050,000
22	Cash over (short)	(6,170)	685	(845)	(90)	125	(550)	735	65	(565)	(150)	5,660		5,740
23	Cash balance at beginning	—	6,850	680	1,365	520	430	555	5	740	805	240	80	12,270
24	Cash balance at end	6,850	680	1,365	520	430	555	5	740	805	240	80		18,010
25	Bank loan at beginning	—	—	26,000	74,000	110,000	133,000	127,000	121,000	89,000	44,000	17,000	5,000	
26	Loans (repayments)	—	26,000	48,000	36,000	23,000	(6,000)	(6,000)	(32,000)	(45,000)	(27,000)	(12,000)	(5,000)	
27	Bank loan at end	—	26,000	74,000	110,000	133,000	127,000	121,000	89,000	44,000	17,000	5,000	—	—
28	Accounts receivable	58,350	63,270	66,870	69,410	85,520	113,930	143,160	142,400	114,780	94,860	82,820	74,260	74,260
29	Inventories	110,000	157,000	189,000	210,000	195,400	178,200	148,600	120,200	99,300	92,800	85,400	80,200	80,200
30	Bank security	168,350	220,370	255,870	279,410	280,920	292,130	291,760	262,600	214,080	187,660	168,220	154,460	154,460

Figure 7.1 (continued)

(d) PROJECTED MONTHLY BALANCE SHEETS FOR THE YEAR ENDING DECEMBER 31 (IN DOLLARS)

	Opening	January	February	March	April	May	June	July	August	September	October	November	December	
Current assets														
1 Cash	—	6,850	680	1,365	520	430	555	5	740	805	240	80	5,740	1
2 Accounts receivable	57,000	58,350	63,270	66,870	69,410	85,520	113,930	143,160	142,400	114,780	94,860	82,820	74,260	2
3 Inventories	68,000	110,000	157,000	189,000	210,000	195,400	178,200	148,600	120,200	99,300	92,800	85,400	80,200	3
4 Prepaid expenses	—	—	—	1,125	2,200	1,925	1,650	6,544	5,236	3,928	2,620	1,312	—	4
5	125,000	175,200	220,950	258,360	282,130	283,275	294,335	298,309	268,576	218,813	190,520	169,612	160,200	5
Fixed assets														
6 Cost	158,700	188,700	218,700	248,700	278,700	278,700	278,700	278,700	278,700	278,700	278,700	278,700	278,700	6
7 Accumulated depreciation	40,000	41,450	42,900	44,350	45,800	47,700	49,600	51,500	53,400	55,350	57,300	59,250	61,200	7
8	118,700	147,250	175,800	204,350	232,900	231,000	229,100	227,200	225,300	223,350	221,400	219,450	217,500	8
9	243,700	322,450	396,750	462,710	515,030	514,275	523,435	525,509	493,876	442,163	411,920	389,062	377,700	9

Current liabilities														
10 Bank loans	—	—	26,000	74,000	110,000	133,000	127,000	121,000	89,000	44,000	17,000	5,000	—	10
11 Accounts payable	40,000	88,500	106,025	93,800	80,350	53,675	59,425	62,075	53,900	42,975	42,800	37,100	36,200	11
12 Accrued liabilities	3,700	5,008	6,316	7,249	8,532	9,415	11,148	5,350	4,950	4,150	4,350	3,700	3,700	12
13 Income taxes	—	(1,150)	(2,117)	(3,159)	(4,468)	(4,535)	(2,628)	520	2,870	3,844	3,670	3,062	2,120	13
14	43,700	92,358	136,224	171,890	194,414	191,555	194,945	188,945	150,720	94,969	67,820	48,862	42,020	14
15 Long-term debt	—	30,000	60,000	90,000	120,000	120,000	120,000	120,000	120,000	120,000	115,000	110,000	105,000	15
16 Shareholders' advances	45,000	45,000	45,000	45,000	45,000	45,000	45,000	45,000	45,000	45,000	45,000	45,000	45,000	16
17 Capital stock	5,000	5,000	5,000	5,000	5,000	5,000	5,000	5,000	5,000	5,000	5,000	5,000	5,000	17
18 Retained earnings	150,000	150,092	150,526	150,820	150,616	152,720	158,490	166,564	173,156	177,194	179,100	180,200	180,680	18
19	243,700	322,450	396,750	462,710	515,030	514,275	523,435	525,509	493,876	442,163	411,920	389,062	377,700	19

Figure 7.1 *(continued)*

Property taxes	8	Line 8	—
Fuel, utilities, main-	4, 6,	Line 9	
tenance and re-	7, 9		
pairs, trucks, and	and 10		
employee bene-			
fits			

☐ Complete lines 4-15 of Figure 7.1b by estimating selling and administrative expenses.

☐ Prepare the first month's estimate for the following items:

    Figure 7.1b
      Line 16 Interest expense
      Line 20 Income taxes

    Figure 7.1c
      Line 15 Interest payments
      Line 17 Income taxes

☐ Again, considering the timing of payments, transfer the appropriate information on Figure 7.1 from b to c as follows:

Item	Line	Figure 7.1c
Salaries (selling)	4	Line 10
Salaries (administrative)	10	Line 14
Professional fees	11	Line 12
Business taxes and licenses	14	Line 13
Printing and postage, telephone and telegraph, and sundry	12, 13, 15	Line 16
Interest	16	Line 15

☐ Applying the appropriate assumptions for receipts and disbursements (Figure 7.1c), allocate information for lines 1, 2, 5, 10, 11, 18, and 19.

☐ Complete Figure 7.1b for the month, and determine if it appears realistic in light of all assumptions. Then complete Figure 7.1c, estimating either bank loans (line 3) or bank repayments (line 20).

☐ Complete the first month of the schedule and include the following items:

Line 1 Cash
Line 2 Accounts receivable
Line 10 Bank loans
Line 13 Income taxes
Line 16 Shareholders' advances
Line 17 Capital stock

Then perform the remaining steps for the balance sheet, Figure 7.1d, as follows:

☐ Net fixed assets, line 8, should agree with beginning amount, less depreciation expense (Figure 7.1a, line 11, and Figure 7.1b, line 8), plus plant additions, if any (Figure 7.1c, line 18).

☐ Accounts payable, line 11, should agree with the beginning balance plus liabilities incurred (Figure 7.1a and b) less cash payments (Figure 7.1c).

☐ Long-term debt balances, line 15, should change in accordance with Figure 7.1c, the net of lines 2 and 19.

☐ Retained earnings, line 18, should change by the income of Figure 7.1b.

☐ Apply accrual accounting techniques used in cost-of-sales and earning statements to expense payments of Figure 7.1c to compute lines 4 and 12.

☐ Complete Figure 7.1d for the first month, and determine if it is reasonable in light of all assumptions.

☐ Adjust first-month statements as necessary.

☐ Repeat the procedure for each of the remaining 11 months of the year.

Cost-of-Sales Statement (Figure 7.1a). The cost-of-sales statement clearly reflects the seasonal factors inherent in the changing sales pattern and the company's productivity and vacation cycle.

Insurance and property taxes (lines 5 and 8) are level throughout the year. Material purchases clearly reflect the inventory buildup during the first four months of the year, and the seasonal factor clearly shows up in the summer months (lines 3, 4, 6, and 9). Direct labor (line 3) and related factory overhead costs (line 12) are substantially lower, and maintenance and repair costs (line 7) are definitely higher during the same period when maintenance will least interfere with production.

Cost of sales per month is one of the principal factors in projecting monthly earnings. The amount of detailed support needed for this projection depends on the extent of product lines and the product mix implicit in the sales projections.

Earnings Statement (Figure 7.1b). The earnings statement shows the rising and falling curve of monthly sales expected for the year with the heaviest month, July, more than twice the lightest month, January. By staggering the cost of sales, the gross profit spread is even larger, ranging from $3,167 in January to $19,267 in July.

As would be expected, selling expenses rise dramatically for the May-October period, and administrative expenses are highest during the March-September period because of heavy interest charges.

Earnings for the year show a healthy overall picture, with gross profit running at the targeted 12.5% and net profit before and after taxes running about 6% and 3.5%, respectively.

Cash-Flow Statement (Figure 7.1c). In calculating the timing of a bank loan, the cash-flow statement is critical. This statement shows that because of the heavy expenses entailed in the inventory buildup to meet summer sales, Relentless Pursuits would be in serious trouble without the bank loans (line 3). Even with the advances, the company will be cash poor in February and very tight through November. The statement thus serves as both an indicator of the right timing for the bank loan and as an early warning to management that if actual performance were to fall below the expected level, the company might have problems.

The importance of the cash-flow statement as a tool for monitoring operations can be shown in several examples. If sales for a given month — or cumulative sales through that month — are significantly below budget, management is forewarned that receivables for the following months will be lower than anticipated and that liquidity problems may develop unless action is taken. Management has adequate lead time because the customer-payments assumption realistically provides for a pattern of staggered payment ranging from 30 to 90 days. Similarly, any substantial departure from the anticipated pattern of cash collections can be a warning. The modest cash balances anticipated for the April-November period indicate that the company would be wise to review its collections and the collectibility of outstanding balances for possible follow-up each month.

Balance Sheet (Figure 7.1d). Breaking down the balance sheet for each month rounds out the picture for both management and lending agencies. By itself, the balance sheet shows an increase in total assets from the opening balance of $243,700 to the closing December balance of $377,700. In conjunction with the other statements, it provides both a broad and a detailed profile of projected company operations for the year, enabling both management and lending agencies to assess the year's prospects clearly and confidently.

Monthly Reporting of Actual Performance. Up to July, monthly reports show a reasonable relationship between budget and actual results, but in that month, significant differences develop, suggesting the need for operational changes. To illustrate this, the accompanying Figures 7.1e, f, g and h present the results of operations for seven months of the period ending in July.

The exhibits show that sales were 3% higher than anticipated prior to July but that July sales themselves were considerably under forecast. The deficiency resulted from external factors, primarily a number of strikes in a highly industrialized area, which reduced consumer purchasing power.

Although raw material purchases declined in July, when sales decreases became apparent, the purchase slowdown did not match the sales decrease. As a result, Relentless Pursuits's management must consider action to deal with the effects of decreased accounts receivable, increased inventories, increased bank loans and decreased payables. With inventories already excessive, purchasing according to projections would aggravate the imbalance further. A prolonged strike would make it difficult for the company to main-

(e) STATEMENT OF COST OF SALES FOR THE SEVEN MONTHS ENDED JULY 31 (IN DOLLARS)

	Month				Year to Date			
	Projected	Actual	Difference Over (Under)	Comments	Projected	Actual	Difference Over (Under)	Comments
Inventory at beginning of period	178,200	181,700	3,500		68,000	68,000	—	
Material purchases	49,600	38,400	(11,200)	Down due to sales decrease.	437,000	440,900	3,900	Increased purchases due to increased sales; offset by July decrease.
Direct labor	1,100	900	(200)	Production down due to decreased sales and inventory buildup.	19,600	19,900	300	Increased production to meet increased sales prior to July.
Factory Fuel	200	200	—		3,800	3,650	(150)	Mild winter.
Insurance	400	450	50	Rate adjustment for new addition.	2,800	3,150	350	Rate adjustment for new addition.

Utilities	900	1,000	100	Increased power consumption because of heavy repairs.	8,800	9,050	250	Increased production to June plus July repairs.
Maintenance and repairs	2,000	2,600	600	Employee carelessness caused equipment burnout.	6,700	7,100	400	Fewer repairs during increased production to June.
Property taxes	633	667	34	Increased mill rate.	4,431	4,669	238	Increased mill rate.
Trucks	50	50	—		1,900	1,940	40	
Employee benefits	50	50	—		1,250	1,300	50	
Depreciation	1,800	1,800	—		10,800	10,800	—	
	6,033	6,817	784		40,481	41,659	1,178	
	234,933	227,817	(7,116)		565,081	570,459	5,378	
Inventory at end of period	148,600	165,950	17,350	Sales volume down.	148,600	165,950	17,350	
Cost of sales	86,333	61,867	(24,466)		416,481	404,509	(11,972)	

Figure 7.1 (continued)

(f) STATEMENT OF EARNINGS FOR THE SEVEN MONTHS ENDED JULY 31 (IN DOLLARS)

	Month				Year to Date			
	Projected	Actual	Difference Over (Under)	Comments	Projected	Actual	Difference Over (Under)	Comments
Sales	105,600	72,200	(33,400)	Industrial community riddled	475,100	452,850	(22,250)	Sales volume up approximately
Cost of sales	86,333	61,867	(24,466)	with strikes; consumers have decreased buying power.	416,481	404,509	(11,972)	3% over projections prior to July.
Gross profit	19,267	10,333	(8,934)		58,619	48,341	(10,278)	
Selling expenses								
Salaries and commissions	1,800	1,600	(200)	Decrease in sales.	8,200	8,190	(10)	Varies with sales.
Advertising	800	800	—		2,100	2,150	50	
Delivery and freight	850	750	(100)	Decrease in sales.	2,400	2,350	(50)	Varies with sales.
Automobile	150	150	—		1,050	1,075	25	
Depreciation	100	100	—		700	700	—	
	3,700	3,400	(300)		14,450	14,465	15	

Administrative expenses						
Salaries	900	900	—	6,300	6,300	—
Professional fees	125	125	—	875	875	—
Printing, postage and so on	100	145	45 Increased postal rates.	700	845	145 Increased postal rates.
Telephone and telegraph	100	120	20	700	770	70
Business taxes and licenses	150	150	—	1,050	1,050	—
Sundry	150	180	30	650	730	80
Interest	1,620	1,635	15 Higher loan balance.	8,410	8,460	50 Higher loan balance.
	3,145	3,255	110	18,685	19,030	345
	6,845	6,655	(190)	33,135	33,495	360
Net profit before taxes	12,422	3,678	(8,744)	25,484	14,846	(10,638)
Income taxes	4,348	1,287	(3,061)	8,920	5,196	(3,724)
Net profit	8,074	2,391	(5,683)	16,564	9,650	(6,914)

Figure 7.1 (continued)

185

(g) STATEMENT OF CASH FLOW FOR THE SEVEN MONTHS ENDED JULY 31 (IN DOLLARS)

	Month				Year to Date			
	Projected	Actual	Difference Over (Under)	Comments	Projected	Actual	Difference Over (Under)	Comments
Cash receipts								
Receivables	76,370	77,840	1,470	Increased sales to June.	388,940	397,380	8,440	Increased sales to June. July
Mortgage loan	—	—	—		120,000	120,000	—	decrease will reflect in
Bank loans	—	—	—		133,000	133,000	—	decreased collections in
	76,370	77,840	1,470		641,940	650,380	8,440	August and September.
Cash disbursements								
Raw material purchases	46,950	48,360	1,410	Increased purchases to June.	414,925	428,795	13,870	Increased purchases to June.
Direct labor	1,100	900	(200)		19,600	19,900	300	Refer to cost of sales.
Factory overhead:								
Insurance	4,800	5,400	600		4,800	5,400	600	Refer to cost of sales.
Property taxes	7,600	8,000	400		7,600	8,000	400	Refer to cost of sales.
Other, excluding depreciation	3,200	3,200	—		22,300	22,190	(110)	
Selling expenses:								
Salaries and commissions	1,800	1,600	(200)		8,200	8,190	(10)	
Other, excluding depreciation	1,400	1,400	—		4,150	4,275	125	

Administrative expenses:			Increased purchases.				Increased purchases.
Professional fees	—	—	—	1,500	1,500	—
Business taxes and licenses	—	900	—	1,800	1,800	—
Salaries	900	—	—	6,300	6,300	—
Interest	1,620	1,635	15	8,410	8,460	50
Other	350	350	—	1,950	2,150	200
Income taxes	1,200	1,200	—	8,400	8,400	—
Plant addition	—	—	—	120,000	120,000	—
Long-term repayment	—	—	—	—	—	—
Bank repayment	6,000	4,000	(2,000)	12,000	5,000	(7,000)
	76,920	76,945	25	641,935	650,360	8,425
Cash over (short)	(550)	895	1,445	5	20	15
Cash balance at beginning	555	(875)	(1,430)	—	—	—
Cash balance at end	5	20	15	5	20	15
Bank loan at beginning	127,000	132,000	5,000	121,000	128,000	—
Loans (repayments)	(6,000)	(4,000)	2,000	—	—	—
Bank loan at end	121,000	128,000	7,000	121,000	128,000	7,000

Figure 7.1 (continued)

(h) BALANCE SHEET FOR THE SEVEN MONTHS ENDED JULY 31 (IN DOLLARS)

	Projected	Actual	Difference Over (Under)	Comments
Current assets				
Cash	5	20	15	
Accounts receivable	143,160	112,470	(30,690)	July sales down.
Inventories	148,600	165,950	17,350	Purchases slowdown did not match sales decrease.
Prepaid expenses	6,544	6,956	412	
	298,309	285,396	(12,913)	
Fixed assets				
Cost	278,700	278,700	—	
Accumulated depreciation	51,500	51,500	—	
	227,200	227,200	—	
	525,509	512,596	(12,913)	
Current liabilities				
Bank loans	121,000	128,000	7,000	
Accounts payable	62,075	52,105	(9,970)	Purchases slowed because of sales decrease.
Accrued liabilities	5,350	6,045	695	
Income taxes	520	(3,204)	(3,724)	Decreased earnings.
	188,945	182,946	(5,999)	
Long-term debt	120,000	120,000	—	
Shareholders' advances	45,000	45,000	—	
Capital stock	5,000	5,000	—	
Retained earnings	166,564	159,650	(6,914)	
	525,509	512,596	(12,913)	

tain the market that would justify projected buying and payment levels. Furthermore, cash collections in August and September will be automatically lower because of the reduced sales level already experienced.

Although cash flow for the year to date has been in step with the budget, the company must expect problems during August and September unless remedial action is taken. The ending cash balances for these months in the original budget (Figure 7.1c) were small and, thus, to avoid significant deficits for both, the company must cut back cash outlays. This cutback may include cancellation of all purchases for raw materials for August, thereby reducing inventories and payables by $41,500 (see Figure 7.1a, August, line 2). Peak collections on receivables previously anticipated for August will not be realized. The cancellation of August purchases combined with moderate cutbacks of purchases in July, however, would reduce payments on raw material purchases by $8,400 in August and $33,925 in September.

Although the company may have some minor cash problems in August, prompt action should restore stability by September. It should be noted here that, in the absence of a budgeting system, Relentless Pursuits might well have observed the sales decline and considered some kind of remedial action. Nonetheless, the owner-manager probably could not have acted on a timely basis and might have had to resort to a more drastic move — such as drawing up an emergency analysis of his financial position, evaluating it and then weighing what action might be required. The company could be enmeshed in serious financial problems before corrective measures could be taken.

Reviewing the actual results of operations, as shown (Figures 7.1e to h), we can see that other variances are not material (aside from the departure from the sales budget). Also, the reasons for being off course are not related to any chronic condition likely to influence future sales or cost expectations. Accordingly, preserving the basic budget and taking appropriate precautions for the summer months would be preferable to making budget revisions. The budget must be seen for what it is — a practical guide to cash control.

Key Information Generated. From the completed budget, the company obtains four critical items of information:

☐ The year's profit is expected to be $30,680 (Figure 7.1b, line 21).

☐ Cash-flow deficits call for a loan of up to $133,000 during the period February-May (Figure 7.1c, line 3).

☐ The loan can be repaid during the year, with all suppliers paid and sufficient cash left to retire the balance of estimated income tax liability (Figure 7.1c).

☐ Adequate security to justify loans, such as a first mortgage on the new building from the government development agency, and accounts receivable and inventories.

Summary

A cash budget furnishes management the key tool for control of a company's cash position. When properly prepared and maintained, the budget serves as a frame of reference for evaluating the financial consequences of operating decisions and provides advance indication of financial weaknesses. Coopers & Lybrand's Three-Way Budget is based on operations, cash flow and financial condition. The system is designed to facilitate revision of assumptions in light of changing conditions. It is readily adaptable to computerized projection modeling.

INVENTORY MANAGEMENT

Maintaining the appropriate level of inventory is a critical success factor. Few operations can produce entirely to order. Typically, customers expect quick delivery; inability to oblige them means loss of orders. Even if you can do almost entirely without an inventory of finished products, you will probably need to maintain stocks of parts and materials. If you stock any item unnecessarily, you will suffer a drain on your resources through the interest on the capital invested plus carrying charges, which together can often run more than 25%. On the other hand, insufficient stock can mean reduced customer services or, with materials and parts, curtailment of production with consequent impairment of customer service.

Underlying Principles

The appropriate level for an inventory item is a function of numerous factors, such as rate of turnover, time needed for replacement and purchase price as a proportion of total inventory investment, including carrying cost. As a consequence, you cannot expand or contract inventory as a unit; you must apply different multiples to each distinct item or group of items.

For example, if you decide to reduce your inventory to raise cash and cut all items by the same percentage, the faster-moving items would be depleted first. Since these items account for a high proportion of total volume, pressure on customer service would be disproportionately high for this items. Faced with mounting customer complaints, you would have little choice but to put through a series of rush orders. This action could not fail to have some disruptive effect on existing production schedules. Before you could get the situation back under control, your production would probably have dipped sharply and your customer service with it.

Even if you avoid this kind of across-the-board manipulation, your inventory will develop imbalances unless there is an adequate assessment of the factors that influence inventory. These factors are constantly changing quantitatively. For example, sales of a particular item may be rising, or its cost may be falling.

Danger Signs

The following conditions are symptomatic inventory problems:

- [ ] Inventories are climbing faster than sales
- [ ] There is noticeable shifting in inventory mix
- [ ] There are sharp disparities between actual stock and accounting records
- [ ] Write-offs for obsolete materials are increasing in proportion to inventory investments
- [ ] Established reorder points and order quantities are more than a year old
- [ ] Back orders and lead times are increasing significantly

☐ There are frequent customer complaints about back orders and missed deliveries

☐ Interruption of production schedules is frequently required to expedite specific orders

☐ Interruption or cessation of production is frequently required because of lack of materials

☐ Machine setup costs are increasing significantly

☐ Machine downtime exceeds past experience

☐ Inventory turnover rates are generally below average for the industry

☐ Scrap costs are higher than past averages

☐ Material costs are rising at rates faster than overall product costs. The portion of cost of sales attributable to materials exceeds that of the industry in general

☐ Distribution costs exceed industry norms and are rising at a faster rate than overall product costs

Analysis and Control

Strictly speaking, inventory control should be continuous. It is possible, however, to achieve a degree of control through periodic analysis.

Control Based on Periodic Analysis. In the periodic approach, a diagnostic analysis is carried out and certain routine controls are applied. Under the Coopers & Lybrand method, the analysis is constructed around two parameters: usage distribution and turnover. Usage distribution relates inventory movement (in terms of dollar value) to inventory investment, annually and cumulatively. Turnover shows the supply of each item on hand in terms of weeks or months available, calculated at the current annual rate of usage. For each of these parameters, four tabular reports are prepared: two dealing with maintenance and spare parts or raw materials and the other two with finished goods.

Inventory Analysis. The results of a typical Coopers & Lybrand inventory analysis are shown in Figures 7.2 and 7.3, which deal with finished goods. In the turnover report (Figure 7.2), the various coded items are ranked in descending order of coverage, defined as the number of months' supply on hand (column 6). Coverage is computed by dividing inventory on hand in units or dollars (columns 7a and 7b) by monthly usage, either units into units or dollars into dollars. (Allowance must be made for rounding off in the figures.) Monthly usage (in units or dollars) is computed by dividing annual usage in units or dollars (columns 4a and 4b) by 12. Notice that annual usage is shown as a cumulative percentage of dollar usage (column 5) as well as item by item (columns 4a and 4b).

The segment covered in this report demonstrates a clear need for a drastic overhaul of inventory management practices. For many items, the supply is excessive. The quantity of the item in entry 4, for example, will suffice at the present usage rate for 472 months — almost 40 years! To compute that excess in monetary terms, we begin with the cost of the item, which is 11.8 cents (19 in column 4b divided by 161 in column 4a). There are 6,339 units on hand (column 7), which when multiplied by cost per unit works out to a dollar value of $748. We can evaluate the excess amounts for future periods by subtracting from $748 the number of months' usage we need to maintain for customer service. The results for four points in the future are shown in columns 9a-9d.

Other imbalances are pointed out in the report itself. Column 8 shows the percentage of total inventory that each item, plus all preceding items, accounts for.

The turnover report highlights the slow-moving or stationary items. The usage distribution report (Figure 7.3) is designed to emphasize the faster-moving items, which may also account for considerable excess inventory. The breakdown in this report is the same as in the turnover report, but the items are ranked in descending order of dollar usage.

In the usage distribution report, we find that slightly more than 4% of the items account for 41% of the annual dollar usages. This statistic is not unusual, especially with diversified manufacturers. Those fast-moving items are supported by less than 11% of the inventory investment, indicating a very poor balance. In general, the cumulative investment for the fast-moving items should be much

(1) ITEM CODE	(2) CUM % ITEMS	(3)† S C	(4a) ANNUAL USAGE UNITS	(4b) USAGE DOLLARS	(5) CUM % $ USAGE	(6) MOS COV	(7a) INVENTORY UNITS	(7b) DOLLARS	(8) CUM % $ INV	(9a) 3 MONTHS	(9b) 6 MONTHS	(9c) 12 MONTHS	(9d) 24 MONTHS
										DOLLAR COVERAGE IN EXCESS OF			
1 1863	0.55		7667	30668	7.97	2	136	544	0.85				
2 976	1.10		2515	29628	15.67	4	70	896	2.25				
3 1175	1.65		19501	21451	21.23	1	172	189	2.55				
4 423	2.20		1385	20082	26.45	.6	66	963	4.06				
5 542	2.75		24234	16964	30.86	.7	1341	939	5.53				
6 874	3.30		3371	16260	35.08	2.1	670	2812	9.93				
7 645	3.85		2951	11688	38.12				9.93				
8 659	4.40		1175	11041	41.00	.9	91	853	11.26				
9 1831	16.50		446	2673	70.85	1.2	46	274	33.53				
10 2314	17.05		202	2610	71.53	2.0	33	425	34.19				
11 798	17.60		192	2560	72.19	2.5	40	542	35.04				
12 1089	18.15	1	912	2553	72.86	5.1	386	1082	36.74				
13 484	18.70		792	2534	73.52	5.1	334	1068	38.41				
14 1162	19.25		365	2338	74.12	.6	17	108	38.58				
15 518	19.80		2417	2175	74.69				38.58				
16 882	20.35	1	152	2116	75.24	.2	3	45	38.65				
17 163	20.90		689	2068	75.78	20.3	1165	3495	44.12	2978	2461	1427	
18 554	21.45		573	2064	76.31	3.3	156	560	45.00	44			
19 365	22.00		144	1993	76.83	.9	12	153	46.00				
20 969	22.55		152	1921	77.31				45.23				
21 3073	54.45		90	604	94.36	6.9	52	349	80.84	198	47		
22 828	55.00		602	602	94.51	2.6	129	129	81.05				
23 2254	55.55		45	602	94.67	2.1	8	107	81.21				
24 839	56.10	1	36	600	94.83	7.7	23	383	81.81	233	83		
25 847	56.65		62	590	94.98	1.4	7	67	81.92				
26 113	57.20		88	575	95.13	6.9	43	326	81.92				
27 905	57.75		75	568	95.28				82.43	184	42		
28 1447	58.30		161	564	95.42	17.5	235	824	83.72	683	542	260	
29 721	58.85		262	550	95.56	2.9	64	135	83.93				
30 1359	59.40	2	147	543	95.71	1.8	22	82	84.06				
31 178	96.70		27	21	99.99	18.7	42	33	97.52	28	23	12	47
32 516	97.25		44					89	97.66	84	79	68	710
33 4248	97.80		161					748	98.83	743	739	729	
34 477	98.35		84						98.96	82	80	75	66
35 655	98.90		000						99.29	212	212	212	212
36 574	99.45		324						60.80	324	324	324	324
37 637	100.00 TOTAL			384,966			128	63,886	100.00	128	128	128	128
										24424	12121	5904	1919

Callout notes:

> Eight items account for 41 percent of the dollar usage but this is covered by only 11 percent of the inventory investment.

> 75 percent of the usage supported by 38 percent of the inventory.

> An aging of the total inventory category. $24,424 of the total $63,886 is in excess of 3 months supply; $12,121 is in excess of 6 months...

*Column numbers and left-hand numbers added.
†Special code.

Figure 7.3. Inventory analysis, finished goods usage distribution report.

(1) ITEM CODE	(2) CUM % S	(3)† ITEMS C	(4a) ANNUAL USAGE UNITS	(4b) DOLLARS	(5) CUM % USAGE	(6) MOS COV	(7a) INVENTORY UNITS	(7b) INVENTORY DOLLARS	(8) CUM % INV $ INV	(9a) 3 MONTHS	(9b) 6 MONTHS	(9c) 12 MONTHS	(9d) 24 MONTHS
574	0.54				0.00	999.9‡	20			324	324	324	324
637	1.00				0.00	999.9	8	128	0.71	128	128	128	128
655	1.65			16	0.00	999.9	22	000	1.04	212	212	212	212
4248	2.20				0.01	472.5	6339	748	2.21	743	739	729	710
477	2.75		4	9	0.01	117.6	49	84	2.34	82	80	75	66
2205	3.30			64	0.02	66.0	22	356	2.90	340	324	292	228
516	3.85		44	21	0.03	50.5	185	89	3.04	84			47
471	4.40		2	32	0.04	42.0	7	117	3.22	234			53
6035	4.95		5	72	0.06	36.0	15	253	3.62	168			99
1372	5.50		153	71	0.08	31.4	400	186	3.91				44
278	6.05		1680	84	0.10	25.7	3500	180	4.19	159	538	523	12
281	6.60		154	446	0.21	21.4	275	597	5.44	686			
725	7.15		31	430	0.33	20.9	54	753	6.61	646			
925	25.85		1442	1874	5.59	6.4	764	993	35.72	525	56		
138	26.40		1526	1221	5.91	6.3	805	644	36.73	300			
552	26.95	1	6341	790	6.11	6.3	3309	407	37.36				
585	27.50		69	798	6.32	6.1	35	405	38.00				
898	28.05		135	1569	6.73	6.0	68	791	39.24				
858	28.60		671	322	6.81	5.9	329	158	39.48				
1896	29.15		153	165	6.85	5.7	73	79	39.61				
131	29.70		7800	156	6.89	5.5	3550	71	39.72	42			
864	30.25	2	270	213	6.95	5.3	120	95	39.87	87			
379	30.80		75	448	7.06	5.3	33	199	40.18				
1175	89.00		19501	21451	89.49	1	172	189	99.98				
383	89.55		839	277	89.57	.1	6	2	99.98				
536	90.10		670	201	89.62	.1	3	1	99.98				
413	91.65		210	42	89.63	.1	1		99.98				
794	91.20		841	10096	92.25			12	100.00				
2004	91.75		1702	117	92.28		1	1	100.00				
648	92.30	3	56	162	92.32				100.00				
502	92.85		210	167	92.37				100.00				
188	93.40		44	221	92.42				100.00				
592	93.95		101	246	92.49				100.00				
113	94.50		88	575	92.64				100.00				
158	95.05		314	640	92.80				100.00				
3232	95.60	1	571	842	93.02				100.00				
1529	96.15		616	1439	93.40				100.00				
742	96.70		193	1741	93.85				100.00				
365	97.25		144	1993	94.37				100.00				
518	97.80		2417	2175	94.93				100.00				
2589	98.35		519	3027	95.72				100.00				
1293	98.90		1374	4724	96.95				100.00				
645	99.45		2851	11688	99.98				100.00				
331	100.00		146	73	100.00				100.00				
TOTAL	100.00			384,966				63,886		24424	12121	5904	1919

Annotation boxes within the figure:
- "Special identification of overstocked items, degree of overstock, and aging of items"
- "100 4 percent of the cumulative inventory investment is..."
- "Almost 40 percent of the inventory items with 6 or more months supply on hand"
- "account for 7.2% of usage value (100–92.28)"

*Column numbers and left-hand numbers added.
†Special code.
‡Printout symbol for infinity.

Figure 7.2. Inventory analysis, finished goods turnover report.

closer to their cumulative dollar usage. Moving down to the slower-moving items, we see (in entry 16) that 38% of the total investment supports 75% of the total usage; the other 62% of the investment supports only 25%. Clearly, this is the area of inventory investment to focus on for potential reduction.

Corrective Measures. The information from the diagnostic analysis can be applied to realize immediate inventory reduction caused by overages and excess quantities. Also, it can help you plan to institute routine controls such as the following:

☐ On slow-moving items: (1) purchasing controls to prevent unnecessary buildup and (2) disposing of obsolete items

☐ On fast-moving items, manual controls to ensure timely purchasing of items in economic quantities.

Continuous Inventory Control. Continuous control monitors inventory on a daily basis. The same historical usage information used in the diagnostic surveys is used prognostically to arrive at demand projections for each item. (The accuracy of the projections can be monitored by comparing levels of both inventory and inventory investment actually realized over a period with the levels predicted for the period.) In relation to projected demand, the factors relevant to optimal inventory levels are mathematically processed to determine the size of individual orders (taking into account quantity discounts), reordering schedules and stock levels — levels that provide maximum defense against depletion of stock in relation to cost of funds tied up.

The information and control systems associated with the continuous approach can be independent of preexisting control systems or linked to them. One sophisticated feature of continuous inventory control is that it generates data with which it is possible to evaluate the effect of alternative methods of control on inventory investment.

Liquidating Inventory

Essentially, there are four methods to liquidate inventory. The first of these is sale. If you sell to a regular customer, the chances are that you will get a better price than if you attempt to unload goods in bulk on the market.

Bulk sales should be a last resort, used when it is doubtful the item can be disposed of by any other means. You should induce customers to buy and stock items that they previously relied on you to stock. In essence, you try to get them to take earlier delivery. Special incentives can also be offered. One effective device is the spare parts package: the customer is offered the right to purchase a number of constituent parts together with the completed product at reasonable markup over the price of the product alone.

A second method of disposition is returning stock to the original vendor. You may be surprised to discover how often this is possible. Even when suppliers will not grant full credit, they may be willing to take back merchandise in return for an allowance or on a restocking fee or other arrangement.

The remaining two basic methods of disposal are conversion and trade. Some of your surplus items may be convertible into other more important items at little cost. Often a surplus part can be used in the same way as an out-of-stock item of lower quality. If this is so, overall savings might be achieved by using the surplus part before reordering the standard one.

Trading as a method of disposition has increased in recent years with the appearance of companies that offer various services in return for inventory items. They often take items at full value. The range of services these companies offer is broad, and chances are you will be able to find something you can use. Their usefulness may be limited, however, because they tend to prefer consumer or standard industrial products.

Administering an Inventory Reduction Program. If your periodic analysis or continuous control process determines excess inventory levels, you might need an inventory reduction program. It is important to exercise firm control over a planned disposal program for inventory. The most effective approach is to designate a manager or a team of managers to serve as liquidation supervisors.

Each member of the team is responsible for categorizing items according to the method or methods of disposal as well as negotiating with company salespersons or outside contacts. Make sure the supervisors keep careful records, and require them to report regularly on their progress. In addition, it is advisable to establish targets to evaluate the performance of individual managers in disposing of inventory.

If inventory is limited in volume and variety, these arrangements can be more or less informal. Otherwise, a formal approach is preferable to ensure effective reduction of inventory levels. Your assignments to supervisors should be in writing, and their reports to you should be written and follow a prescribed format. If you have more than three or four supervisors, you would be well-advised to hold regular scheduled meetings to monitor progress.

Remember that each dollar of inventory reduced (without reduced sales levels) cuts carrying costs by 25 cents or more.

Just-in-Time Operating Philosophy

Manufacturers have been forced to improve performance and productivity or lose a competitive position in the domestic and international marketplaces.

Faced with growing competition from abroad, demands for improved quality and service and the need to maximize resource productivity and minimize costs, many manufacturing companies are realizing that change is necessary for their survival. But even when the problem is acknowledged, it may be difficult to find nuts and bolts solutions to these challenges.

Just-in-Time (JIT) is a companywide operating philosophy that has as its basic objective the elimination of waste. It is not a program to replace continuous inventory control. Under JIT, waste is considered anything other than the minimum amount of equipment, materials, parts, space and workers' time absolutely essential to add value to a product. Your key operational phrase thus becomes adding value. JIT strives to identify activities that do not add value to your products and eliminate them.

The simplest way to identify unnecessary activity is to apply a few tests to each step of a routing:

☐ Does an activity (for example, inspection, transport, receiving, purchase ordering and expediting) add cost without changing the physical or chemical characteristics of an item?

☐ Does an item stop or pause at any point during its journey through your manufacturing site?

☐ Is an operation performed to compensate for something that was not done properly the first time?

If your answer to any of these questions is "yes," then the activity becomes a candidate for creative problem solving and elimination. This philosophy points to two basic tenets of JIT:

☐ Identify and eliminate the cause for pause.
☐ If you can't use it now, don't make it now.

You should be aware of the following basic concepts in a JIT program:

Housekeeping. This means more than keeping a clean workplace. It means that each person is responsible for his or her equipment, ensuring that necessary tools are in the right place and that everything is clearly accessible and visible for all employees to see. It would not be unusual to realize a 10% productivity improvement by applying the simple principles of housekeeping.

Operation Training. Training management, staff and the labor force to work harmoniously and effectively to become an efficient, problem-solving team.

Quality Improvement. In JIT, the emphasis is on continuously reducing variance for improved manufacturability. Staying within accepted or engineered tolerance limits is not JIT's goal; rather, JIT strives for elimination of variance. The operator, not the inspector, becomes responsible for "zero defects." It is vital to provide the necessary tools to enable the operator to manage the quality process. Your long-range goal is to eliminate inspectors because they add no value to the product and cause delays.

Uniform Plant Load (UPL). This concept is simple: if you sell daily, then make it daily. This means that every model is manufactured in small lots on a daily basis. Whenever possible, the end items are manufactured to demand and not to stock. In order to foster a make-to-demand environment, you have to reduce manufacturing lead time dramatically. UPL is not how fast a machine or process can operate; it is a production rate for all components and assemblies that matches your demand rate. The primary benefit of UPL is to eliminate indirect labor costs for managing or transporting excess inventory.

Redesign Process Flow. To achieve rapid throughput and the productivity opportunities afforded by UPL, your process flow or functional layout usually requires redesign. The objective is to eliminate any operations that don't add value and group dissimilar but dedicated equipment together in a cell configuration. Wherever possible, these cells should be dedicated to a product group (focused facility) so that maximum flexibility to your UPL demand cycle time can be achieved. Your UPL rate will vary as demand varies. Once the cell has been set up to maximize the efficiency of labor ("keep your man busy, not the machine"), your UPL rate determines the operation's rate in the cell; the higher the demand, the shorter the cycle time and the higher the number of operators assigned to the cell. The goal of a good cell is to pay the same labor hours per unit, regardless of demand rate. This also implies moving from fixed to variable or assignable burdens.

Setup Reduction. By dedicating your equipment to product groups, some setups or changeovers are completely eliminated. Where multiple components must be shared by the same manufacturing resource, you must significantly reduce changeover time in order economically to make only enough for each day's demand. Companies that try to "engineer" improvement through technical or capital-intensive solutions usually do not achieve their goals. The most effective setup task groups are those that have the actual operators as members. The operator knows the problems, and makes the improvements work by participating in the solution.

Full-System Scheduling. Once the UPL has been established and the cells put in place, it is usually time to establish the pull system. Pull-system scheduling coordinates production with actual demand, rather than launching orders based on a predetermined schedule for short-term parts requirements.

Supplier Networks. The last activity in the JIT cycle is getting the supply pipeline involved in delivery only when needed. Quality improvement starts at the beginning of the JIT program, but the pull system is not implemented until flow and demand have been sufficiently smoothed out. Supplier networks analyze and redefine your supplier policies and standards to minimize supply lead times and inventory investment and to move to a more cooperative relationship. To adjust to your demand, your supplier must aggressively implement JIT also. You play a significant role in your supplier's JIT implementation.

In summary, the core of the JIT philosophy is the elimination of waste in all forms, especially in material, labor and plant capacity. JIT works for you through:

☐ Increased awareness of potential problems in areas such as quality, throughput and service

☐ Synchronization of output with demand

☐ Simplification of all aspects of the process

☐ Incorporation of a philosophy of continuous improvement throughout the company

☐ Elimination of variances in all aspects of the manufacturing process.

Computer Integrated Manufacturing (CIM). CIM is the process of taking current manufacturing technologies and techniques one step further by linking them all to work in harmony to serve a common corporate goal. Such technologies and techniques include computer-aided design and manufacturing, group-technology coding and classification, just-in-time scheduling and inventory planning, robotics and automated materials handling, manufacturing planning and control software and computer-based technologies (hard-

ware, software, database systems and communications networks).
You can no longer expect improved labor productivity alone to offset overseas producers' significantly lower wage rates and protection in their home markets. You must look elsewhere for competitive
gain, and CIM is an alternative. Its advantages range from improving factory flow and time-to-market for new products to increasing
the range of product choices and the level of product quality — not
just labor productivity.

CAPITAL BUDGETING

Capital budgeting is essentially a matching of available sources
of funds with the most beneficial utilization of those funds. The
concept gives us a common basis on which to evaluate alternatives.

A capital expenditure is an outlay intended to benefit more than
one fiscal year. The value received for the outlay may be tangible,
such as equipment or even a complete facility, or the replacement
or repair of a facility, or for production, distribution or provision of
a service. It may also be an intangible such as research and development, public relations or a patent.

The starting point for capital budgeting is the gathering of proposals for capital expenditures. You should encourage all employees to contribute any idea they think worthwhile. The use of a basic
format for proposals ensures that the person initiating the request
has at least considered such key factors as estimated costs, operating cost benefits and timing.

Evaluating Budget Proposals

Evaluation of proposed capital expenditures should cover such
factors as the relationship between anticipated returns or benefits
and costs for a specific project and the relative net effect of various
alternatives. Methods of cost-benefit analysis are described in the
following subsections.

Cost-Benefit Analysis. A cost-benefit analysis is an integral part
of the evaluation process. You may dispense with it only when the

proposed expenditure is for an item needed to maintain production (for example, replacing the burned-out motor that operates several essential machines or replacing a leaking roof) or to stay in business (e.g., installing equipment to satisfy a pollution abatement order). The analysis is based on a standard economic model where benefits minus cost equals cash flow. Two factors are compared: one is external — the cost of capital — and one internal — anticipated return on the investment. The return should exceed the cost or the investment is not worthwhile.

Cost of Capital.

☐ The cost of capital may be calculated in different ways, always on the basis of the interest rate. In a practical sense, for most small businesses, the cost of capital is the marginal cost of borrowing through the best available vehicle, often the cost of borrowing from a bank. For a closely held company, the effective capital cost might also be viewed as "opportunity cost" — what the funds might earn (or save) if management used them elsewhere.

Return on Investment.

☐ Return on investment is calculated from the anticipated annual net aftertax savings that will result from capital expenditures. These net savings, also termed net cash flows, are the net benefits connected with the acquisition and its subsequent use. In the case of a machine bought to replace an outdated model, the initial cash flows would be the purchase outlay less any proceeds from sale or disposition of the old model. Over the life of the machine, there would be additional outlays and costs.

The outlays could take the form of building modifications necessary to install and use the machine or the cost of inventory or repair parts required to keep it running efficiently. Likely benefits would be cash savings realized from the increased efficiency or the production process, income tax saved by additional depreciation deductions throughout the life of the machine and the expected salvage value of the machine at the end of its useful life. Figure 7.4 shows the derivation of net aftertax savings (or losses) for a particular item. For simplicity, only the more important cash flows are used.

Type of Cash Flow	Year:	1	2	3	4	5	6–10	11–15
1. Incremental sales								
2. Incremental cash savings								
or expenditures								
a. Maintenance								
b. Operation								
Labor								
Materials								
Equipment downtime								
3. Other incremental cash savings								
or expenditures								
4. Total beforetax effect								
5. Tax effect								
6. Subtotal								
7. Tax effect—depreciation								
8. Salvage value								
Net aftertax cash savings								

Figure 7.4 Work Sheet for Estimating Aftertax Savings

Only incremental cash flows related to the investment are considered in the capital budgeting process. Overhead costs are not considered unless they are specifically attributable to the project and different from those that would be experienced if the project were not undertaken. For an example of an includable overhead cost, consider the impact of purchasing a device that would modify a machine currently in use and raise annual output from 100,000 to 125,000 units but would also raise direct costs from $0.90 to $1.00. Assume also that the product sells for $1.50, that no other costs are affected and that the machine could continue to be used without alteration. The benefits to be considered in the cash-flow analysis would be computed as follows.

	Current Equipment	Current Equipment with Device
Units produced	100,000	125,000
Sales value of units produced	$150,000	$187,500
Direct cost of units produced	$90,000	$125,000
Gross margin	$60,000	$62,500
Annual benefit (expected effect on gross margin		$2,500

In this case, installation of the device would result in an incremental annual benefit of $2,500 over the machine's remaining life. Because there is a risk in every cash-flow projection, you might wish to discount the aftertax savings accordingly. This exercise is illustrated in Table 7.2. The discount factor, expressed by a multiple, is subject to your judgment.

Two Methods of Comparison. There are two methods for comparing cost of capital and return on investment. Under the internal method, the two rates are computed separately; under the present-value method, the rates are computed together. With both methods, return on investment is calculated on the principle that money received in the future has less value than money received now. Money has a time value in terms of its opportunity cost (cost at which it could be invested elsewhere). The discounted or present values of future aftertax savings are obtained from tables that give, for any rate and any number of years, a factor or multiple based on one dollar.

The application of these two methods is illustrated in Tables 7.3 and 7.4. These tables are based on an investment of $100,000 covering the cost of a hypothetical facility and of establishing an inventory in connection with it. This $100,000 is net of the salvage value of discarded equipment that the new facility replaces. The anticipated net aftertax savings resulting from the investment are as follows:

Table 7.2
DISCOUNTING OF CASH FLOWS TO ADJUST FOR RISK

	Project A—Fairly Certain			Project B—Moderately Risky			Project C—Very Risky		
Year	Cash flow	Risk discount factor	Risk adjusted cash flow	Cash flow	Risk discount factor	Risk-adjusted cash flow	Cash flow	Risk discount factor	Risk-adjusted cash flow
1	$40,000	1.00	$ 40,000	$50,000	1.00	$ 50,000	$ 50,000	0.90	$ 45,000
2	50,000	1.00	50,000	70,000	0.90	63,000	80,000	0.75	60,000
3	50,000	1.00	50,000	60,000	0.80	48,000	90,000	0.60	54,000
4	30,000	1.00	30,000	40,000	0.70	28,000	100,000	0.35	35,000
5	20,000	1.00	20,000	40,000	0.60	24,000	70,000	0.20	14,000
			$190,000			$213,000			$208,000

End of Year	Savings
1	$ 50,000
2	60,000
3	30,000
4	20,000
5	20,000
6	30,000
	$210,000

The cash savings for the sixth year include the proceeds from liquidating inventories and scrapping the equipment.

The internal method is illustrated in Table 7.3. It involves determining the rate of compound interest required to discount future earnings — net aftertax savings — from the purchase so that they equal the investment required now, $100,000. Compounded at that rate, the present discounted values of future savings could be invested today for periods corresponding to the number of years before each saving is realized, and the aggregate result would be equal to the total projected future savings, $210,000.

The rate is found through *intrapolation*: the net aftertax savings are discounted at different rates until a close approximation of the true rate is arrived at. In Table 7.3, the rate of 33% is found after successive trials with four other rates. If this percentage is higher than the cost of capital, the expenditure is evaluated in comparison with other investment opportunities. If you have alternative investment possibilities, you can rank them by applying the internal-rate-of-return method to each. Those ranked highest receive priority.

In the present-value method (Table 7.4), you discount future earnings by the amount of your estimated cost of capital and compare the result with the expenditure called for. If the total discounted future earnings surpass expenditures, cost of capital of the investment is justifiable. The rate used is often called a cut-off rate because it eliminates projects below the rate. To rank projects, divide the present value of future earnings by the initial investment.

Table 7.3
ESTIMATING THE INTERNAL RATE OF RETURN

Year	Cash Flow	i = 20%		i = 40%		i = 30%		i = 35%		i = 33%	
		Factor	Present Value	Factor	Present Value	Factor	Present Value	Factor	Present Value	Factor	Present Value
1	$50,000	0.83333	$ 41,667	0.71429	$35,715	0.76923	$ 38,462	0.74074	$37,037	0.75188	$ 37,594
2	60,000	0.69444	41,666	0.51020	30,612	0.59172	35,503	0.54870	32,922	0.56532	33,919
3	30,000	0.57870	17,361	0.36443	10,933	0.45517	13,655	0.40644	12,193	0.42505	12,752
4	20,000	0.48225	9,645	0.26031	5,206	0.35013	7,003	0.30107	6,021	0.31959	6,392
5	20,000	0.40188	8,038	0.18592	3,719	0.26933	5,387	0.22301	4,806	0.24029	4,608
6	30,000	0.33480	10,047	0.13281	3,984	0.20718	6,215	0.16520	4,956	0.18067	5,420
Total present value			$128,424		$90,169		$106,225		$97,589		$100,883

Table 7.4
COMPUTATION OF PRESENT VALUE (BASED ON INVESTMENT OF 15%)

Year	Flow	Discount Factor	Present Value
1	50,000	0.86957	$ 43,479
2	60,000	0.75614	$ 45,368
3	30,000	0.65752	$ 19,726
4	20,000	0.57175	$ 11,435
5	20,000	0.49718	$ 9,944
6	30,000	0.43233	$ 12,970
	Total present value		$142,922

The higher the resulting ratio is (1.43 in Table 7.4), the more secure the proposed expenditure is as an investment.

Do not forget that future cash flows are uncertain and risks are involved. For very risky projects (such as a new product line), consider using a cut-off rate of two or three times your cost of capital.

Evaluating Your Capital Budget Practices. The following conditions indicate a deficiency in capital budgeting, either in the process itself or in the basic management information system.

☐ Assets acquired without knowledge of top management

☐ High incidence of budgetary oversights, especially failure to allow for significant costs

☐ Estimated income not realized

☐ Estimated cost savings not realized

☐ Status of approved expenditures not reported to top management

☐ Permanent decline rate in level of return on assets after capital expenditures

☐ Continuing need to refine cost data

☐ Serviceable plan or equipment not in use (especially recently acquired items)

☐ Poor feedback from company personnel on ideas for improvements or changes

☐ Chronic lag behind competition in introducing new ideas.

Monitoring

Once you have made a capital investment, it is essential that you keep track of how that investment is performing. If an item is not fulfilling expectations, the sooner you know it the better. It is a question not only of taking remedial steps, which in drastic cases could consist of reversing the investment by withdrawing it from service and trying to recoup costs, but also of being able to apply the knowledge gained to future investments.

Tracking and Postaudits. There are two ways of monitoring the performance of capital items: keeping track of operating costs and holding periodic audits. The documentary basis for tracking costs is a series of reports produced at scheduled intervals showing the operating costs connected with individual items. These reports permit item-by-item analysis of variances between budgeted and actual costs.

The Postaudit. The periodic operating cost analysis will not give you all the information you need to evaluate the performance of the capital item. The total performance picture, including certain factors that cannot be computed readily in dollars, can be presented only in a broad evaluation or audit. The frame of reference for the audit is your original scheme of estimates covering every aspect of performance, such as operating and other costs and effect on sales volume, unit output and labor costs. The audit should consider changes in such key factors as sales prices, labor rates and fuel costs.

Postaudits may be held several times during the life of the capital item. A preferred time for the first audit is the year beginning 90 days after either the completion of the installation or the time at which the asset was predicted to become significantly productive.

8

Accounting Systems and Internal Controls

Businesses have life cycles that affect the way they are managed and how their information is processed. Something common to all stages of a business's life cycle is the need for an accounting system and controls over such a system.

Accounting has been defined as the process of identifying, measuring and communicating economic information. Each business has a system for this process. The system can be as basic as checkbook records (cash basis of accounting) used by a beginning entrepreneur or as complex as an on-line (state-of-the-art) computer network supporting the activities of a mature multilocation corporation.

The procedures and policies in place safeguarding assets and generating reliable records reflect the business's internal controls. They can be as basic as two authorized signatures on the (cash-basis) checking account or as complex as policy manuals and internal audit departments.

BASIC CONCEPTS OF ACCOUNTING

In its broadest sense, accounting is the "language of business." In this chapter, our intention is not to equip you to be an accountant but rather to introduce you to the language of business and to the need to implement controls to protect your investment. Every business needs strong financial management. Companies need a combination of the owner-manager's talent, a competent financial officer, such as a controller or chief financial officer, and an independent accountant. The outside accountant, especially one from a recognized firm, lends credibility to financial statements, serves as a "sounding board" for ideas and provides creative advice.

An enterprise's accounting system encompasses procedures and policies to protect assets against loss (caused by intentional and unintentional errors) in processing transactions and provides reliable financial records.

The most obvious function of accounting is to keep track of assets and liabilities through continuous recording of changes in items such as cash, accounts receivable, inventory, capital equipment, accounts payable and debt. Accounting generates information for assessing a business's financial position and performance through the balance sheet and statements of profit and loss and cash flow; for meeting operational requirements, such as maintaining desired inventory levels or preserving the continuity of customer service or production, and for systematic assessment of performance in many key areas.

The following three premises are inherent in the concept of accountancy as understood today:

The Entity.. A business undertaking is treated for accounting purposes as a separate entity distinct from the parties that provide funds or capital for the operation. (In business operations, planning and formulating goals, however, the owner-manager and the business are inseparable.)

The Going Concern.. In the absence of evidence to the contrary, a business is treated as continuing in operation indefinitely. (Otherwise, assets would be valued at liquidation value rather than cost.)

The Matching of Revenues and Costs.. Depending on the accounting principles in effect, income must be recognized when earned or collected. (Accounting principles used for managing a business need not always be the same as those for income tax purposes.)

ACCOUNTING SYSTEMS

Accounting is a concept; an accounting system is the body of records and procedures that implement that concept. The basic records for a manual or computerized accounting system include journals, ledgers and registers. Automated accounting systems need not be exceptionally complex. Computerization can range from the simplest electronic spreadsheets on a microcomputer to very complex proprietary accounting packages on large mainframe computers with actual computer operations performed by the end user. Putting the operations in the hands of the user is referred to as "end-user computing." From these records are compiled operating financial statements as well as specialized reports such as sales by region or by person, profitability by product or division, backlog, production variances and other important data.

Standard Procedures

Accounting is usually thought of as a record-keeping activity; as such, it is distinct from the activities it records. The modern concept of an accounting system, however, tends to override this distinction. Thus, for example, ordering merchandise and dispensing funds are considered accounting system procedures even though these activities are not of a record-keeping nature.

The following record-keeping procedures are standard in both manual and computerized systems.

- ☐ Preparing, checking and processing forms, such as sales orders and invoices, in connection with business transactions
- ☐ Recording transactions in books of original entry, such as voucher register, sales journal and payroll register
- ☐ Posting to the general ledger
- ☐ Conforming general ledger balances to subsidiary ledgers or registers
- ☐ Preparing a trial balance of the general ledger
- ☐ Preparing statements from the trial balance that reflect the results of operations for the period and the financial position of the enterprise

☐ Preparing special management reports using statistics or other specific data.

In a computerized system these events can be integrated, so that a single entry at the appropriate time initiates several of the steps which would normally be done as individual manual steps.

Accounting Cycles

To understand accounting systems, think in terms of groups of related functions that are basic to the operation of a business. Among these are purchasing goods or services, selling to and collecting from customers, controlling production and inventory and paying salaries. Such fractions are often termed cycles because they are carried out continuously and each depends on a particular set of procedures that must be performed in a certain sequence.

Three typical cycles, common to most business entities, are:

☐ *Revenue Cycle.* Sale of goods, billing and cash collections
☐ *Buying Cycle.* Payroll, purchasing and cash disbursements
☐ *Production Cycle.* Production of goods or services, labor and overhead charges.

These cycles include several types of transactions that can vary within the operation of the business entity. These transactions may have additional subdivisions; for example, sales can be divided into cash and credit sales, domestic sales and foreign sales. All these cycles and transactions reflect the natural business process for each entity.

The accounting system should generate a series of financial reports, schedules and statements. The basic requirements for financial information reporting apply equally to hand-posted accounting systems and to computer-processed data; they should be timely and accurate and include the data necessary to manage the business.

A sample monthly manufacturer's operating statement is presented in the appendix to this chapter (Exhibit 8.1). It must, of course, be tailored for each specific circumstance. All of the data for these reports should come directly from accounting records or should be easily obtainable. Comparisons should be made with planned (or budgeted) amounts to indicate the direction of business activity. The key indicator report at the outset of the exhibit and the two graphs at the end show the direction in which the business is going.

Specialized Reports

The monthly three-part financial reporting package — balance sheet, income statement and statement of cash flow — is necessarily broad in scope. For a close-up view of specific aspects of your business, you must rely on specialized reports. These reports need not be lengthy or costly. For the most part, you will find the data you need in the records of your basic accounting system. The following subsections describe the subjects most often covered in these important management aids.

Profitability. An analysis by individual products or lines of business can shed light on "off-target" areas that need attention. For example, a product may be less profitable because of obsolescence, softness in demand, price competition or manufacturing inefficiency. Pinpointing the cause permits evaluation of changes in order to improve profitability or may indicate a need to terminate the product.

Accounts Receivable. Accounts receivable is a critical barometer, not only of cash flow but also of satisfaction with the company's products. Behind every disputed account may be a more serious problem. Simple aging analysis, combined with systematized response to and resolution of disputed accounts, can keep a debt from going bad and avert customer dissatisfaction.

Inventory. Understanding inventory position is not easy. Overall balance sheet amounts should be broken into segments. The inventories can then be aged, permitting a review of slow-moving items. They can be balanced, tested and reported to protect against out-of-stock conditions (stock-outs); subsequently, meaningful decisions on stock disposition and overall inventory management can be made.

Cash. Daily, weekly and monthly monitoring is essential. A forecast of cash inflow and anticipated needs must be available. One major element of this forecast would be a purchase commitment report — that is, a detailed record of commitments to suppliers for future purchases, including the contract prices. (Cash should never be left unproductive; any excess should be invested.)

Payroll, Production, and Cost Variances. Weekly payroll analyses, production reports or variance analysis of standard versus actual costs are all important to business efficiency. If job costs are used as the basis of the analysis, progress reports on unfinished jobs may provide other critical data.

Sales Backlogs. A sales backlog report can be used to monitor purchase and production staffing schedules. A schedule of shipments showing promised or order-received dates compared to actual shipping dates is a measure of customer service.

Labor Turnover. A high labor turnover may be related to low shop morale; it may also explain excessive operating costs. Remember that a new employee costs a good deal before he or she approaches normal efficiency.

Projections. It is possible to construct a hypothetical series for each report extending several months into the future based on monthly financial reports from the past six months. Using these projections, management can identify potential problems. A shortfall revealed in a cash-flow forecast for which the necessary funds might have to be raised by additional borrowing or improvements in inventory turnover or receivable collections is one example.

Checklist for System Performance

Examples of questions you can ask yourself to test the efficiency of your accounting system:

☐ Is financial data available on a timely basis?

☐ In your experience, has this data been reasonably accurate?

☐ Does this system ensure that orders are approved and processed on a timely basis?

☐ Are shipments billed on a timely basis, and is data generated to ensure an adequate collection follow-up effort?

☐ Do records provide you with production information, especially regarding:

—. Slow-moving or obsolete items?

—. Movement of goods through the production process?

—. Shipments?

—. Backlog?

—. Performance of individual salespersons?

—. Sales by location, region, bureau, or division?

—. Product profitability and relationship to sales commissions?

—. Sales forecasts?

☐ Does the system ensure that vendor discounts are taken, and is the priority of a payable readily established?

☐ Is cash information readily available?

☐ Do the reports generated by the system answer more questions than they raise?

If the answer to any of these questions is no, corrective actions are probably necessary.

INTERNAL CONTROLS

Internal controls monitor compliance with established policies and procedures. They are used within an enterprise to reduce unintended exposure to business, financial and accounting risks.

Two different aspects of internal control are included in this broad definition: *internal accounting controls* and *administrative controls*. (Administrative controls are sometimes referred to as "operational controls" because they deal with the operations of the business rather than with the accounting for those operations.) There is some overlap between these two classes of controls; the same control can affect accounting and operations, but for most purposes they are distinct.

Internal Accounting Control

There are five general objectives that provide a business entity with good internal accounting control:

1. *Completeness.* All transactions are recorded in the accounting records.

2. *Validity.* All recorded transactions represent economic events that actually occurred and were executed in accordance with prescribed procedures. (Example — All recorded sales represent actual shipment of goods to valid customers authorized by responsible personnel.)

3. *Accuracy.* Transactions are recorded at the correct amount, in the right account and on a timely basis at each stage of their processing. (Example — Sales amounts, quantities, dates and customers are correctly recorded in subsidiary records and summarized in the general ledger.)

4. *Maintenance.* Accounting records, after the entry of transactions, are properly controlled so that they continue to reflect accurately the operations of the business.

5. *Physical Security.* Access to assets and the documents that control their movement is restricted to authorized personnel. (Example: Physical controls over finished goods shipments do not permit shipment until sale documents are initiated and approved.)

Reliable records and safeguarded assets are necessary to the effective functioning of any business. The management of the smallest business must record transactions accurately, avoid accounts errors and quickly locate errors that do occur. Depending on the size of the business and transaction volume, double-entry bookkeeping, control accounts for receivables and payables and periodic trial balances may be appropriate. Wherever possible, routines are divided between individuals so that one individual reviews another, documents are numbered and accounted for to safeguard against omissions and standards are established to draw attention to unusual transactions.

Computers have mechanized much of the accounting process and have permitted controls to be systematized.

Internal Control in a Computer Environment

The form of controls or the manner in which they are applied may be different in a computerized system. Some manual controls are unchanged such as the physical controls over assets, documents and records. Other controls are accomplished by a combination of computer and manual operations. For example, the computer may be used to generate a report of suppliers' invoices for which no goods have been recorded as received, but the investigation and follow-up of these items are done manually.

Internal controls in a computer environment include additional procedures that ensure continued and proper operation of programmed accounting procedures. Programmed accounting procedures are those that would normally be carried out manually by the staff but have been converted to automated procedures. Additional procedures include general controls over the data-processing function, broadly categorized into five areas:

Implementation Controls. These are the policies and procedures that ensure that systems and programs are correct at the time of initial implementation and subsequently when modified for changes in the business entity. The scope of these controls include approval by management of the system's specifications prior to development or selection, the scope of testing, completion of technical documentation and end-user documentation and proper training of system users.

Program Security Controls. Properly designed, these control procedures protect programs from unauthorized changes. These controls should protect not only the machine language or executable code but also the human readable, or source code, from which the machine language is derived.

Data File Security Controls. Data files may contain not only financial information but also trade secrets vital to continued operation. In today's business environment, this confidential information should be considered an asset, afforded the same protection as the business's other assets. Likewise, there are legal considerations for the protection of information. Proper controls protect data from unauthorized modification, whether malicious or accidental. The protection of data files may be physical retention in a secure environment, computerized protection for on-line data files or a combination of these procedures. In any event the information on data files should be afforded the same protection it would receive if records were totally manual.

Computer Operations Controls. These controls ensure that only authorized programs are executed and that all executions of programs are for authorized purposes. In the simplest of environments this may be accomplished by physical retention of programs when they are not needed for operation of a particular process. In the more complex environments, automated security packages may protect the programs from unauthorized execution.

System Software Controls. System software is the collection of programs used in the computer operation. The most commonly known is the computer operating system which manages the hardware resources and controls the reading and writing of data to various media. Other software includes generalized programs such as sort programs, print utilities and file space managers. These programs and systems should be subjected to the same management approval process as application programs to ensure that the proper options are selected, tested and implemented.

Computer systems use computer programs that require specific definitions of tasks and precise instructions for accomplishing them. Those programs and their use can be controlled so that the instructions are consistently followed. This combination of precise instructions and consistent operation affects the way controls are applied.

Usually, the effective and consistent application of instructions can be ensured by controlling the design, security and use of computer programs and data files.

Representative Control System

Let us examine how accounting controls work in just one accounting cycle: the buying cycle (see "Accounting Cycles" in this chapter).

Placing Orders. The initial procedure deals with placing an order for goods or services. The order may come through department managers or corporate officers, or under blanket purchase orders. An important control on the ordering and receiving process is centralization. Only certain designated employees should be permitted to authorize a purchase.

Other controls cover either the purchasing or receiving process. Controls on purchasing include:

- ☐ Imposition of order criteria; that is, ensuring that the price is the lowest available for the quality or type of goods purchased, that the quantity ordered is economical (a three-year supply of paper clips at a bargain price may be no bargain) and that the purchase is within the company's budget. To implement these controls, a purchase order form that specifies the quantity, price and all other relevant data should be used.

- ☐ Systems for ensuring that purchases of components or subassemblies for a product do not significantly exceed the sales forecast for that product. These systems should be sophisticated enough to consider lead times for delivery and alternative sources of supply.

- ☐ A special function (for which a single person might be held responsible) for following up orders not received.

The most important control on receipt is checking goods for conformity with the purchase order (quantity, quality, type, etc.). This control is generally implemented by requiring a prenumbered receiving report with provision for the data to be completed and signed by a designated employee. Copies of the packing slip can sometimes be used as receiving reports if they are numerically controlled.

Purchase and Expense Distribution; Vouchers and Accounts Payable. The second and third procedures in the buying cycle involve:

☐ Vouching (recording) and processing vendor invoices

☐ Entering the vouchers in a payable system, verifying the arithmetic on the invoice or voucher and then checking them for approvals

☐ Entering the vouchers in a summary or register for distribution in the general ledger.

Processing a vendor invoice requires procedures to ensure that payment is in the correct amount, is made only once and not before the preplanned date (considering invoice terms, cash discounts and cash availability) and is for goods and services actually received and authorized. Such procedures might involve comparing the invoice with the receiving report, noting that prices and quantities agree with those on the authorized purchase order and verifying the arithmetic. The paid invoice should be canceled, preferably by a perforating stamp to prevent duplicate payment. Payments should not be made on duplicate invoices.

When entering vouchers in the payable system, there must be controls to ensure that all items were recorded. Vouchers can be prenumbered sequentially and a designated employee made responsible for periodically accounting for missing numbers.

Distributing vouchers for summarization in the general ledger means assigning account numbers to each transaction. This procedure should ensure that a salesperson's credit-card bill is included in travel and entertainment expenses and in accounts payable, rather than in some inappropriate account.

Cash Disbursements. The final procedure in the buying cycle is the issuance of a payment check. The signature on the check is itself a control, but it is a good idea to have the voucher package attached to the check for review by the check signer. Once in a while, you might catch an error or defalcation that has slipped by prior controls. Discrepancies might include duplicate payments, payments for the wrong amount, absence of regular payments and excessive payments to one vendor — the last a possible indication of fraud covered by false invoices.

Instituting and Evaluating Controls

In many cases, putting in an internal control is a routine matter, involving simple adaptation to a sequence of activities. In some cases, however, the required adaptation is more complicated. There may be several possible approaches that vary in cost and in their effect on other operations.

To cite a simple example, selling for cash only would eliminate the risk of credit losses, but it would also restrict sales potential and perhaps increase the risk of cash misappropriation as well. Before resorting to this extreme form of protection, you should consider establishing credit evaluation policies, requiring accountability for credit decisions and establishing follow-up collection procedures. Similarly, you could reduce the risk of failing to bill for goods shipped or services provided by hiring an employee whose sole responsibility is to monitor and document all shipments, match them against invoices and compare the invoice price with catalogues or a published price list. A less expensive but equally effective procedure would be to match prenumbered shipping documents and production forms, as well as freight bills, with invoices, making sure that all discrepancies are investigated on a timely basis.

Sources of Assistance

If your company's financial statements are audited by an outside accounting firm, the firm will provide comments and suggestions on your company's system of internal accounting controls. In addition, we suggest some basic reading on the subject. Particularly useful is the book *Evaluating Internal Controls: Concepts, Guidelines, Procedures Documentation* by Kenneth P. Johnson and Henry R. Jaenicke (New York, John Wiley & Sons, 1980).

Questionnaire for Evaluation

Exhibit 8.2 in the Appendix to this chapter is a portion of a questionnaire designed to help evaluate a company's system of internal accounting controls. The complete questionnaire was developed by Coopers & Lybrand and is reproduced in its entirety in *Evaluating Internal Controls*. Questions relate to specific control objectives listed at the head of each sequence. The flowchart referred to in the column heading is a graphic depiction of an accounting system in which each significant step and control is identified. The numbers in the column indicate the step number in the flowchart that depicts the control cited. Obviously, only "yes" answers will be entered in this column.

Even if all the answers to the questionnaire are in the affirmative, you have no absolute assurance that an error will not be made or a misappropriation will never take place. Accounting literature points out that errors can result from misunderstandings of instructions, mistakes of judgment and personal carelessness, distraction or fatigue. Controls can be overridden by management or circumvented by collusion. Furthermore, controls that are effective today may become inadequate tomorrow as circumstances change. On the other hand, the internal controls questionnaire is unsurpassed as a tool for a rapid, substantially reliable evaluation of a company's control system. It helps identify weaknesses and points the way to alternative approaches.

APPENDIX: TOOLS FOR EFFECTIVE ACCOUNTING SYSTEMS AND INTERNAL CONTROLS

Exhibit 8.1

SAMPLE MONTHLY OPERATING STATEMENT FOR A MANUFACTURER

1. MONTHLY KEY INDICATOR REPORT

Month of _____

	Two Months Ago	Last Month	This Month
Cash on hand	$ _____	$ _____	$ _____
Receivables	_____	_____	_____
Inventories	_____	_____	_____
Payables	_____	_____	_____
Sales	_____	_____	_____
Sales order backlog	_____	_____	_____
Purchase orders outstanding	_____	_____	_____

Three-Month Moving Averages

	Last Month	This Month
Incoming order value	$ _____	$ _____
Order backlog value	$ _____	$ _____
Open purchase value	$ _____	$ _____

Key Ratios

	Last Month	This Month
Current ratio	_____	_____
Receivable turnover	_____	_____
Collection period	_____	_____
Inventory turnover	_____	_____
Days sales in inventory	_____	_____

2. BALANCE SHEET

_____ _____, 19_____

Assets

Current assets:

Cash $ _____

Accounts receivable _____

Inventory:

Parts and material $ _____

Work in process _____

Finished goods _____ _____

Prepaid expenses _____

Total current assets _____

Property and equipment:

Machinery and equipment _____

Office furniture and equipment _____

Leasehold improvements _____

Accumulated depreciation
and amortization (_____) _____

Other assets _____

Total assets $ _____

2. BALANCE SHEET, Continued

_____ _____, 19_____

Liabilities and Stockholders' Equity

Current liabilities:

Notes payable—
  First National Bank $ _____

Accounts payable—trade   _____

Accrued commissions   _____

Accrued interest   _____

Accrued payroll and payroll taxes   _____

Notes payable—stockholders   _____

Accrued taxes on income   _____

Other current liabilities   _____

Total current liabilities   _____

Long-term debt

Bonds payable $ _____

Notes payable—stockholders   _____   _____

Total liabilities   _____

Stockholders' equity   _____

Total liabilities and
  stockholders' equity $ _____

3. STATEMENT OF OPERATIONS FOR THE MONTH OF _____ AND THE _____ MONTHS ENDED _____, 19___

Current Month

	Plan		Actual	
	Amount	Percent	Amount	Percent
Sales	$ _____	100.0%	$ _____	100.0%
Cost of sales	_____	_____	_____	_____
Gross margin	_____	_____	_____	_____
Administrative	_____	_____	_____	_____
Marketing	_____	_____	_____	_____
Income from operations	_____	_____	_____	_____
Research and development	_____	_____	_____	_____
Interest	_____	_____	_____	_____
Other income (expense)	_____	_____	_____	_____
Income before provision for income taxes	_____	_____	_____	_____
Provision for income taxes	_____	_____	_____	_____
Net income	$ ======	====== %	$ ======	====== %

Year to Date

	Actual		Plan	
	Amount	Percent	Amount	Percent
Sales	$ _____	100.0%	$ _____	100.0%
Cost of sales	_____	_____	_____	_____
Gross margin	_____	_____	_____	_____
Administrative	_____	_____	_____	_____
Marketing	_____	_____	_____	_____
Income from operations	_____	_____	_____	_____
Research and development	_____	_____	_____	_____
Interest	_____	_____	_____	_____
Other income (expense)	_____	_____	_____	_____
Income before provision for income taxes	_____	_____	_____	_____
Provision for income taxes	_____	_____	_____	_____
Net income	$ ======	====== %	$ ======	====== %

4. SCHEDULE OF MANUFACTURING VARIANCES FOR THE MONTH OF _____
AND THE
_____MONTHS ENDED _____ _____, 19_____

Current Month Actual		Year to Date Actual
$ _____	Materials price variance	$ _____
_____	Overhead variance	_____
_____	Materials usage variance	_____
_____	Cost of sales adjustment	_____
_____	(Over) underapplied labor (from schedule of manufacturing costs)	_____
$ _____	Total variances	$ _____

5. SCHEDULE OF MANUFACTURING COSTS FOR THE MONTH OF _____ AND THE _____ MONTHS ENDED _____, 19___

	Current Month		Year to Date	
	Plan	Actual	Actual	Plan
Direct labor:				
Salaries and wages	$	$	$	$
Payroll taxes				
Insurance and benefits				
Subtotal direct labor				
Labor applied to inventory	( )	( )	( )	( )
(Over) underapplied labor	$	$	$	$
Manufacturing overhead:				
Indirect labor	$	$	$	$
Supplies and equipment rental				
Travel and entertainment				
Other operating costs				
Professional services				
Allocated occupancy expenses				
Depreciation and amortization				
Subtotal manufacturing overhead				
Manufacturing overhead applied	( )	( )	( )	( )
(Over) underapplied overhead	$	$	$	$

6. SCHEDULE OF RESEARCH AND DEVELOPMENT FOR THE MONTH
OF _____ AND THE _____ MONTHS ENDED _____, 19___

	Current Month		Year to Date	
	Plan	Actual	Actual	Plan
Project labor:				
Direct labor applied	$ _____	$ _____	$ _____	$ _____
Materials and parts	_____	_____	_____	_____
Outside engineering costs	_____	_____	_____	_____
Total project costs	_____	_____	_____	_____
Research and development overhead:				
Salaries and wages	_____	_____	_____	_____
Payroll taxes and benefits	_____	_____	_____	_____
Labor applied to manufacturing	(_____)	(_____)	(_____)	(_____)
Supplies	_____	_____	_____	_____
Rental equipment	_____	_____	_____	_____
Dues and subscriptions	_____	_____	_____	_____

231

6. SCHEDULE OF RESEARCH AND DEVELOPMENT FOR
THE MONTH OF _____ AND THE _____ MONTHS ENDED _____, 19 _____

| | Current Month | | | Year to Date | |
	Plan	Actual		Actual	Plan
Freight					
Equipment depreciation					
Travel					
Entertainment					
Telephone and communications					
Professional services					
Miscellaneous					
Allocated occupancy expenses					
Materials and parts					
Total	$	$		$	$

7. SCHEDULE OF MARKETING EXPENSE FOR _____ AND THE _____ MONTHS ENDED _____, 19___

	Current Month		Year to Date	
	Plan	Actual	Actual	Plan
Salaries and wages	$	$	$	$
Payroll taxes and benefits				
Casual labor				
Total salaries and benefits				
Supplies and equipment rent				
Travel and entertainment				
Commissions expense				
Professional services				
Advertising				
Trade shows				
Demonstration expense				
Bidding				
Other operating expenses				
Allocated occupancy expenses				
Total	$	$	$	$

8. SCHEDULE OF OCCUPANCY EXPENSE FOR THE MONTH OF _____ AND THE _____ MONTHS ENDED _____, 19____

	Current Month		Year to Date	
	Plan	Actual	Actual	Plan
Occupancy:				
Rent	$ _____	$ _____	$ _____	$ _____
Repairs and maintenance	_____	_____	_____	_____
Property taxes	_____	_____	_____	_____
Utilities	_____	_____	_____	_____
Miscellaneous	_____	_____	_____	_____
Subtotal	_____	_____	_____	_____
Allocation of occupancy expenses:				
Manufacturing	( )	( )	( )	( )
Research and development	( )	( )	( )	( )
Marketing	( )	( )	( )	( )
General and administrative	( )	( )	( )	( )
Total allocated expenses	( )	( )	( )	( )
(Over) underallocated occupancy expenses	$ _____	$ _____	$ _____	$ _____

9. SCHEDULE OF GENERAL AND ADMINISTRATIVE EXPENSES FOR
THE MONTH OF _____ AND THE _____ MONTHS ENDED _____, 19___

| | Current Month | | Year to Date | |
	Plan	Actual	Actual	Plan
Salaries and wages	$	$	$	$
Payroll taxes and benefits				
Total salaries and benefits				
Supplies				
Rental equipment				
Dues and subscriptions				
Postage				
Office equipment and depreciation				
Vehicle expense				
Travel and entertainment				

235

9. SCHEDULE OF GENERAL AND ADMINISTRATIVE EXPENSES FOR
THE MONTH OF _____ AND THE _____ MONTHS ENDED _____, 19__

	Current Month		Year to Date	
	Plan	Actual	Actual	Plan
Telephone and communications				
Insurance				
Professional services				
Taxes and licenses				
Continuing education				
Donations				
Amortization of leasehold improvements				
Miscellaneous				
Allocated occupancy expenses				
Total	$	$	$	$

10. SCHEDULE OF OTHER INCOME AND EXPENSE FOR THE _____ MONTHS ENDED _____, 19____ AND THE MONTH OF _____

	Current Month		Year to Date	
	Plan	Actual	Actual	Plan
Income:				
Interest income	$	$	$	$
Other income				
Subtotal				
Expense:				
Interest expense	( )	( )	( )	( )
Subtotal	( )	( )	( )	( )
Net total	$	$	$	$

11. SALES AND COST OF SALES

Thousands of Dollars

——— Sales
· · · · · · · · · Standard cost of sales
- - - - - - - Total cost of sales

| 105 |
| 100 |
| 95 |
| 90 |
| 85 |
| 80 |
| 75 |
| 70 |
| 65 |
| 60 |
| 55 |
| 50 |
| 45 |
| 40 |
| 35 |
| 30 |
| 25 |
| 20 |
| 15 |
| 10 |
| 5 |
| 0 |

APR MAY JUN JUL AUG SEP OCT NOV DEC JAN FEB MAR APR MAY JUN JUL AUG SEP

12. SHIPMENTS MONTH OF _____

Thousands of Dollars

——— Target

.... Actual

80
75
70
65
60
55
50
45
40
35
30
25
20
15
10
5

0 1 2 3 4 5 6 7 8 9 10 11 12 13 14 15 16 17 18 19 20 21 22 23 24 25 26 27 28 29 30 31

Day

Exhibit 8.2

INTERNAL CONTROL QUESTIONNAIRE[a] FOR CASH DISBURSEMENTS
(PURCHASES AND PAYMENTS CYCLE)

Control Objective

1. Control should be established over goods and services received as a basis for:
   a. Determining and recording the liability for goods and services received but not entered as accounts payable
   b. Where required, posting the items to detailed inventory records

---

Questionnaire	Flowchart Ref.	Yes	No

Initial recording of receipt of goods and services
   a. Are the following checked by suitable methods (for example by counting or weighing and inspecting goods received) and the results recorded at the time of their receipt for subsequent checking with the related invoices:
   (i) Nature, quantity, and condition of goods received (including property, plant and equipment, and major supplies such as fuel and stationery)?
   (ii) Major services received (to the extent practicable)?
   b. Are the receiving records (a) controlled in such a way that it can subsequently be established whether all the related transactions have been accounted for (for example, by sequentially prenumbering receiving reports or by entering receipts in a register), in respect of:
   (i) Goods [a(i)]?
   (ii) Major services [a(ii)]?
Liability for unprocessed invoices
   c. Are there adequate records of goods and services received which have not been matched with the related suppliers' invoices, in respect of:
   (i) Goods [a(i)]?
   (ii) Major services [a(ii)]?
   d. Where sequentially prenumbered forms are used (b) are all numbers accounted for as part of the control procedure over unmatched receipts (c) in respect of:
   (i) Goods [a(i)]?
   (ii) Major services [a(ii)]?
   e. Are unmatched records of goods and services received (c) reviewed on a regular basis, such as monthly, to determine the reasons for any such receipts that have not been matched within a reasonable period of time, in respect of:
   (i) Goods [a(i)]?

(ii) Major services [a(ii)]?
f. Are the results of the procedures in (e) reviewed and
approved by a responsible official?

Control Objective

2. Invoices and related documentation should be properly
checked and approved as being valid before being entered
as accounts payable.

Questionnaire	Flowchart Ref.	Yes	No

Detailed checking of documentation
  a. Are invoices for goods received checked as to:
    (i) Quantities and conditions of goods received (to re-
        ceiving records)?
    (ii) Nature and quantities of goods ordered (to pur-
        chase orders)?
    (iii) Prices and other terms (to purchase orders or sup-
        pliers' price lists)?
  b. Are invoices for services received compared with the
     underlying documentation (such as records of receipts
     [1.a.(ii)] completion reports, leases, records of meter
     readings) or if such documentation is not available, ap-
     proved by a responsible official?
  c. Are the following functions performed by separate indi-
     viduals:
    (i) Preparation of purchase orders?
    (ii) Preparation of receiving records?
    (iii) Checking of purchase invoices (2.a. and 2.b.)?
  d. Are credit (or debit) memoranda checked to confirm
     that:
    (i) They agree with the original record of the goods re-
        turned or claims made?
    (ii) Where applicable, the prices agree with original in-
        voice?
  e. Are the extensions and additions of invoices and credit
     (or debit) memoranda checked to an adequate extent?
  f. Do the invoices and credit (or debit) memoranda bear
     adequate evidence that the checking (2.a., 2.b., 2.c. to
     2.e.) has been carried out?
Approval of documentation
  g. Are invoices and credit (or debit) memoranda subject to
     final written approval by a responsible official prior to
     entry as accounts payable?
  h. Are adjustments to suppliers' accounts properly docu-
     mented?
  i. Are the adjustments and related documentation (2.h)
     reviewed and approved by a responsible official prior
     to entry in the accounts payable records?

Control Objective

3. Payments in respect of wages and salaries should be:
   a. Made only to company employees at authorized rates of pay
   b. Where required, in accordance with records of work performance
   c. Accurately calculated

Questionnaire	Flowchart Ref.	Yes	No

Standing payroll data
   a. Are the following authorized in writing:
      (i) Employees added to payrolls?
      (ii) Employees removed from payrolls?
      (iii) Rates of pay and changes in rates of pay?
      (iv) Payroll deductions other than the compulsory deductions (specify below)?
   b. Do persons other than those who prepare the payrolls provide the authorizations required in 3.a.?
   c. Are there adequate controls designed to ensure that the payroll reflects all authorized standing data (3.a.) and only such authorized data?

Transaction payroll data
   d. If employees are paid on the basis of time worked:
      (i) Is the payroll based on adequate time records?
      (ii) Where applicable, are the time records checked to supporting records of time spent (for example, time charges to jobs)? [3.d.(i)]
      (iii) Are the time records [3.d.(i)] approved?
      (iv) Do the time records [3.d.(i)] indicate that overtime has been properly authorized?
   e. If employees are paid on the basis of output, are the payments based on output records that are reconciled with production records that are under accounting control?
   f. If salaried or other employees not included in 3.d. or 3.e. are paid for overtime, is the payroll based on time records that indicate that overtime has been properly authorized?
   g. If employees receive commissions on sales, are the commissions based on sales records that are reconciled with sales (less, where applicable, returns) recorded in the books?

Payroll preparation
   h. Is there a check on the calculation of gross pay (for example, by agreeing in total with predetermined control totals or with cost records, or by sufficient checking of individual amounts), in respect of:
      (i) Employees paid for time worked (3.d.)?
      (ii) Employees paid for output (3.e.)?
      (iii) Employees paid for overtime (3.f.)?
      (iv) Employees paid commissions (3.g.)?

i. Are the calculations and additions of payrolls and payroll summaries checked to an adequate extent?
j. Do payrolls bear adequate evidence that the procedures in 3.h. and 3.i. have been completed?
k. Are payrolls subject to the final written approval of a responsible official before they are paid?
Payments to employees
  l. If employees are paid in cash:
    (i) Is cash withdrawn only for the net amount of the payroll?
    (ii) Do persons other than those who prepare the payroll physically control cash until it is distributed to employees?
    (iii) Are unclaimed wages promptly recorded and controlled by persons other than those who prepare the payroll?

Control Objective

4. Payroll deductions should be correctly accounted for and paid to the third parties to whom they are due.

Questionnaire	Flowchart Ref.	Yes	No
Initial control over deductions			
a. Are all payroll deductions recorded in separate control accounts?			
Checking of amounts to be paid to third parties			
b. Are payments of payroll deductions to third parties agreed to the related payrolls?			

Control Objective

5. Reimbursements of imprest and similar funds (such as postage and other franking meters, payroll deduction stamps) should be made only for valid transactions.

Questionnaire	Flowchart Ref.	Yes	No
Overall control of funds			
a. Are imprest and similar funds:			
(i) Maintained at a reasonable balance in relation to the level of expenditure?			
Expenditures from funds			
b. Are all disbursements from imprest and similar funds:			
(i) Supported by adequate documentation?			
(ii) Approved where appropriate?			
c. In the case of cash funds, are there reasonable limits on:			
(i) The size of individual disbursements?			
(ii) The extent to which personal checks of employees are cashed?			

(iii) Loans and advances such as for wages made from such funds?

Requests for reimbursement of funds

  d. Are all reimbursements made on an imprest basis?
  e. Are requests for reimbursement accompanied by details of expenditures and supporting vouchers?
  f. Are the reimbursements approved by an official who is not the custodian of the funds?

Control Objective

6. Disbursements from bank accounts should be made only in respect of valid transactions

Questionnaire	Flowchart Ref.	Yes	No

Preparation of checks and bank transfers

  a. Are checks and bank transfers prepared by persons other than those who initiate or approve any documents that give rise to disbursements for:
     (i) Payments of accounts payable?
     (ii) Payrolls and payroll deductions (control objectives 3 and 4)?
     (iii) Reimbursements of imprest and similar funds (control objective 5)?
  b. Are checks and bank transfers prepared only on the basis of evidence that the validity of the transactions has been confirmed in accordance with the company's procedures, in respect of:
     (i) Payments of accounts payable?
     (ii) Payrolls and payroll deductions (control objectives 3 and 4)?
     (iii) Reimbursements of imprest and similar funds (control objective 5)?
  c. Are checks and bank transfers for transactions that, because of their nature, do not pass through the normal approval procedures as referred to in 6.b. (such as purchase of investments, payment of dividends, repayment of debt), initiated only on the basis of proper documentation of the validity of the transactions?
  d. Is the documentation in 6.c. reviewed and approved in writing by a responsible official before checks and bank transfers are initiated?

Signing of checks

  e. Are checks signed by officials other than those who approve transactions for payment in respect of:
     (i) Payment of accounts payable?
     (ii) Payrolls and payroll deductions (control objectives 3 and 4)?
     (iii) Reimbursement of imprest and similar funds (control objective 5)?
     (iv) Other payments (6.c.)?

f. At the time of signing checks and bank transfers, does each signatory examine:
  (i) Original supporting documents (for example, invoices, payrolls, or imprest cash records) that have been checked and approved in accordance with the company's procedures (control objectives 2, 3, 4, and 5 and Question (6.c.)?
  (ii) Substitute documents (such as remittance advices or check requisitions) that provide adequate evidence of the validity of the related transactions?
g. Are the supporting documents effectively cancelled by, or under the control of, the signatories to prevent subsequent reuse?
h. If a mechanical check signer is in use, is there adequate control over the custody and use of the signer and the signature plates?

Control of checks and bank transfers after signing
  i. After signing, are checks and bank transfers forwarded directly to the payees (or to the bank with the bank transfer lists) without being returned to the originators or others who are in a position to introduce documents into the cash disbursements system?

Control Objective

7. General ledger entries arising from the payments cycle should be accurately determined.

Questionnaire	Flowchart Ref.	Yes	No

Classification of expenditures
  a. Is the coding of the following transactions for posting to general ledger accounts checked to an appropriate extent:
    (i) Invoices and other supporting documentation related to the payment of accounts payable?
    (ii) Payrolls?
    (iii) Reimbursements of imprest and similar funds?
    (iv) Disbursements from bank accounts not covered in (i) to (iii) above?
    (v) Depreciation of property, plant, and equipment?

9

Computer Systems Selection and Implementation

Once your accounting system has developed to the point where the procedural cycles are more or less continuous operations or your present data processing equipment is nearing the end of its useful life, you should begin to think about the possibility of investing in, replacing, or upgrading your computer system. As your business continues to grow, it is not unlikely that your present system will begin to show strain. Even before that happens, you may find that you cannot get timely information to help manage important operational matters such as inventory control, product line profitability or data needed to improve customer service.

Technological advances and attractive prices mean that the point of considering a computer or changing equipment happens earlier in a company's life cycle than ever before.

Competition, the need for quick access to accurate business information, and reductions in the cost of hardware and software have stimulated many emerging businesses to invest in computerized systems. As a result, businessmen who may not have the technical expertise to undertake feasibility studies or computer hardware evaluations are being asked to make decisions regarding the purchase and selection of computers. Mastering the basic terminology is simply not enough to enable them to decide wisely. Take for example, these common problems:

☐ Choosing an unnecessarily expensive and complex computer system

☐ Using a computer system for data that would be better processed by improved manual or semi-mechanized methods

☐ Choosing a computer that cannot be easily expanded to accommodate additional work

☐ Delegating systems development to staff who lack the proper technical skills or business understanding

☐ Choosing a computer with poor vendor support or inappropriate processing techniques.

To help the emerging business manager avoid these pitfalls, this chapter discusses six important areas—the value of a computer to your business, the computer environment, how to select the right computer, the costs, installation process, and procedures and controls of computer systems. By following the general guidelines given here, a businessman will be better equipped to assess computer needs, make informed decisions about appropriate equipment and help ensure continued functioning of the computer with adequate controls.

THE VALUE OF A COMPUTER TO YOUR BUSINESS

People first think of installing small business computers because they feel instinctively that cost savings and efficiency improvements might be achieved. They see that existing manual systems are strained or that current computer equipment is nearing the end of its useful life. Or, particular management problems—such as inadequate information for accounts receivable, inventory control or the need for improved customer service—may indicate that a new approach to information processing is needed.

Features Most Adaptable to Computerization

The features of a company's business that are usually computerized rely on the special characteristics of the computer, such as:

☐ The ability to carry out, accurately and quickly, simple tasks such as price calculations or wage calculations

☐ The capacity to store a large amount of data and use it easily for analysis and processing

☐ The ability to transfer common data among different systems (e.g., sales order information may be fed directly through a production planning and stock system to a sales accounting system and general ledger)

☐ The potential for relieving staff of routine tasks.

Although these accounting and production control operations are the ones that first come to mind, other specialized repetitive jobs equally suited to a small computer include general accounting, mailing lists, personnel records, vehicle scheduling and even word processing.

Benefits

Computer systems can yield considerable benefits:

☐ In order processing, quicker deliveries and more accurate order statistics

☐ In accounts receivable, faster routine billing and collections

☐ In inventory, reduced inventory investment and an improved inventory availability

☐ In purchasing, better cash management and an improved purchasing history

☐ In payroll, faster calculations and improved analysis of costs

☐ In general ledger accounting, more timely management reports

☐ In production planning, better use of labor production facilities.

Evaluating Your Computer Needs

Initially, you will have two questions to answer in connection with automation: First, Do I need it? and second, If so, how much, and what kind? These questions are not easy to answer; they require study and, unless you have a good knowledge of computerized accounting, a certain amount of expert assistance. If you act hastily, you risk committing a potentially costly blunder.

Preliminary Survey. Before beginning a detailed investigation of your computer needs, you have to establish the objectives you want to achieve. The reasons for considering computerization and the possible benefits should be set down in writing, taking into account overall business objectives, identifying high priority areas and establishing cost parameters.

One of the major advantages of computers with integrated software is combining separate clerical tasks and reducing duplication of information. For instance, once sales invoices are recorded in an invoicing application, the data can be reused for sales accounting and sales analysis without reinputting the information. So, during the preliminary survey, you should consider all applications related to priority areas; otherwise, systems can quickly outgrow the equipment as the opportunities for linking with other areas are understood. The preliminary review will identify:

☐ The reasons for considering computerization
☐ The overall objectives and the expected benefits
☐ The application areas to be examined
☐ The cost justification for the system.

Feasibility Study. If the preliminary survey is positive, your next step will be to carry out a more detailed feasibility study; the main objectives here are to determine if computerization will work, will be useful and is economically worth doing. Your feasibility study should include:

☐ An analysis of present systems highlighting strengths and weaknesses

☐ A detailed written outline of how the proposed systems will work so that company managers and personnel can understand and agree to the implications of the system

☐ An analysis of current and projected data volumes

☐ A proposed implementation timetable

☐ Estimates of the costs and benefits of the new systems.

No decision to replace an existing procedure with a computer system should be made without considering whether the same benefits would be more easily or inexpensively obtained in other ways. For example, it may be that redesigning forms and clerical procedures, improving filing systems and the layout of offices and workflows would be better than computerization.

You also run the risk that without a good understanding of the different types of computer and processing facilities, the system features developed and the related costs may be inappropriate for your organization. The natural tendency is to avoid the problem by calling in one or more computer suppliers. Although this seems a good way of obtaining free advice, computer salesmen often recommend an approach that demonstrates the best features of their own equipment but that is not necessarily the most suitable or cost-effective for your company. Ideally, therefore, you should not seek the advice of computer salesmen until you have a good understanding of your requirements. If expert advice is required, you should consider going to independent consultants, who have no affiliation to software or hardware manufacturers or suppliers.

THE COMPUTER ENVIRONMENT

The development of small business computers was led by a generation of computer manufacturers whose original work was in the scientific and educational fields. These firms developed a range of inexpensive processors geared to users working via multiple terminals. These processors were simple to operate and did not require special environmental conditions. With continued development, smaller, more compact processors became available with built-in terminal screens, memory and storage devices. These smaller processors, called microcomputers, entered the business arena with the introduction of accounting and office simplification software.

In general, there are three types of small business computer environments:

1. *Microcomputer.* Single terminal, diskette or hard disk storage, screen and letter quality dot matrix printer. Can be used as a terminal to a large computer system.
2. *Multi-Workstation Systems.* Two or more terminals connected via a network concept with multi-screens, printers and storage devices sharing information. Both networked microcomputers and minicomputers with attached terminals can be considered multi-workstation systems.
3. *Service Bureaus.* Access to computing capabilities either through manually generated forms or remote terminals connected via telephone.

Microcomputer

In today's business environment, the microcomputer is suitable for a wide variety of tasks. A typical microcomputer for business use consists of:

☐ A microprocessor with .2 to 1.0 million characters of memory
☐ Dual exchangeable diskette drives giving immediate access to 1.0 to 1.5 million characters of information or a hard disk with 20 to 40 million characters of storage
☐ A dot matrix printer capable of producing letter quality or near letter quality reports
☐ A visual display screen and keyboard.

The equipment can be used as a terminal providing local processing capabilities or linked via a network to other microcomputers or through telephone lines to a larger central computer.

The limitation of a single microcomputer is that, at present, the volumes of work are effectively limited to the maximum number of transactions that can be entered through one keyboard. Growth beyond these volumes can be covered by networking additional microcomputers. If networking of multi-microcomputers is expected, it would be more sensible to start with a microprocessor with expansion capabilities to support, when needed, multiple keyboards, display screens, printers and additional hard disk storage. Entry level microcomputers with network expansion capabilities can be purchased for under $10,000.

Multi-Workstation System

The multi-workstation systems offered by various manufacturers offer on-line, real time systems that allow each transaction—for example, a customer order—to be processed as soon as it is received. The latest equipment is typically based on multiple microcomputers and thus the distinction between networked microcomputers and terminal connected minicomputers is disappearing. At the same time, the power and facilities of multi-workstation systems have increased and are now rivalling small minicomputer mainframe computers costing approximately $50,000.

Typical multi-workstation computer systems configurations include two or more workstations/microcomputers with .5 to 4 million characters of memory, multiple dot matrix printers, 40 to 100 million characters of disk storage and an optional high-speed printer operating at 100 to 300 lines per minute.

Larger networked configurations can support local and/or remote operations. Simultaneously a sales clerk can be entering orders, while an accounts clerk enters cash sales transactions, a third makes an inventory inquiry, and a fourth develops a budget using a spread sheet application. Each area might be connected locally via a Local Area Network (LAN) or remotely using a Wide Area Network (WAN), all sharing the same business information.

The attraction of multi-workstation/networked computer systems is that they bring the facilities of powerful computers into the business office. Instead of completing input forms, sending them to a remote location for processing and then receiving a report listing data errors many hours or days later, the user can control the computer by entering data through the workstation and having it checked immediately for errors. The processing then takes place on individual transactions and causes an immediate response. Systems can, therefore, be designed in which, for example, an order for goods entered by a sales clerk can cause packing dispatch instructions and billing to be printed immediately on remote printers in separate areas.

Service Bureaus

Some organizations with limited resources find computer service bureaus an attractive and inexpensive approach to computerization or to the introduction of benefits and costs of computers. The majority of service bureaus developed by offering basic processing services. For example, copies of invoices and cash receipts for a week were grouped into batches and taken to the service bureau for data preparation and sales ledger processing. The service bureau would then return a series of printed reports, including customer statements, an aged accounts receivable listing and a complete listing of the ledger. As the demand grew, service bureaus offered remote computing services accessed by telephone using remote terminals or workstations located at the customer's site. In order to respond to the challenge of the small business computer, most service bureaus now offer a variety of remote data capture and communications capabilities. These capabilities include:

☐ Terminals that allow users to undertake their own data preparation, transmit it periodically to the bureau and have the resulting reports printed on their terminal

☐ Terminals (linked by telephone lines to the bureau) that allow data to be entered and checked and processing to be carried out either before the data are transmitted or after transmission.

Many service bureaus claim they can offer businesses levels of operational convenience, performance and inquiry facilities similar to those of the small business computer described earlier. Whether this claim is valid depends on individual circumstances.

Because communication costs have not fallen as fast as processor costs, equipment costs alone tend to favor the installation of a small business computer. However, since a major cost in the total computer package relates to systems and program development, a service bureau might offer a special service based on software packages that are already proven in operation and that may not be available on a small business computer. It is not unusual for a company to use a service bureau for this type of application, even though it may install its own small computer for day-to-day processing requirements.

HOW TO SELECT THE RIGHT COMPUTER

Your initial investigations will have determined the system and general type of computer facility you require. You will have also made a choice between a service bureau and an in-house computer. Your next step is to invite your selected suppliers to present their proposals.

To avoid future misunderstandings and to provide a consistent basis for comparing proposals, you must give the suppliers a written statement of requirements. This should contain:

☐ A brief description of the company, the existing processing systems and the environment in which the system must operate

☐ A description of the main purpose and features of each system required

☐ An indication of the volume and content of each of the input documents and output reports and, where necessary, a description of the intermediate processing steps to clarify the logic of any complex requirements

☐ Current and projected data volumes

☐ An itemized statement of information on costs, time frames, maintenance, experience and staffing that must be included in the suppliers' proposal.

The initial selection of suppliers invited to propose can present problems. Many specialist firms have developed links with computer manufacturers so that they act as prime contractors, offering both equipment and programs. These firms are usually referred to as "systems houses."

The result of this proliferation of suppliers has been to dramatically increase the choices facing a potential purchaser. There is a risk that you will waste time obtaining quotations from suppliers with inappropriate equipment or that you will omit suppliers with extremely suitable equipment and services from your proposal list; so again, consider getting expert independent advice or consult with other business associates.

THE CHOICE OF SOFTWARE

Closely linked to the selection of an equipment supplier is the choice of a method for developing the applications software. There are essentially three choices:

☐ Your organization can employ systems analysts and programmers and establish an in-house systems development capability.

☐ The computer supplier or a systems house can be contracted to undertake the systems and programming or supply off-the-shelf applications software.

☐ The systems and programming implementation can be directed by management consultants retained separately from the equipment contract.

Few small organizations will want to recruit their own systems analyst and programmers, especially if the systems have to be developed quickly. For this reason, the trend is toward using outside specialists. There are benefits in dealing with only one contractor, but a major disadvantage is that the supplier of the best hardware is frequently not the organization with the skills and experience to understand your systems requirements or to design and implement a solution to your problem. In fact, many computer manufacturers do not offer systems development support and refer customers to systems houses.

Evaluating Proposals

You should give suppliers a reasonable time in which to submit their proposals. You then need to assess the proposals using a set of criteria that relate to:

☐ The adequacy of the proposed equipment to process the current and planned workload within defined time limits

☐ The adequacy of the proposed terminal response times

☐ The ability to expand components of the equipment to handle increased workloads

☐ The versatility, reliability and ease-of-use of those computer programs (systems software) supplied with the equipment to control its operation

☐ The bidders' understanding of the application system requirements and their approach to system design

☐ The flexibility, suitability and user history of any proposed engineering packages

☐ The reliability of the equipment and the quality of engineering maintenance

☐ The value of the total services offered, recognizing that the lowest price is not necessarily the best.

Selecting a Service Bureau

To select a service bureau, you should follow a path similar to that described above, asking several bureaus to quote against a definition of requirements. The criteria to use for selection are also similar, but you should consider in addition the convenience and quality of the day-to-day operational service provided. Provision of contingency facilities and the degree of experience in your industry are also important.

COSTS OF A COMPUTER SYSTEM

Hardware

A computer capable of providing on-line processing through two terminals can be purchased for under $20,000. This basic price will normally be the figure initially quoted by the salesman to secure customer interest. However, essential additional expenses—for purchasing or developing systems and their associated programs—will increase this cost.

In common with other electronic products, such as pocket calculators and digital watches, the cost of computer equipment continues to decrease steadily. Unfortunately, the costs of developing the systems and programs have not followed this trend, and in common with other skill-based resources, these costs will probably continue to increase. The cost of developing a customized series of accounting systems on a small business computer will rarely be less than $25,000 and is frequently greater than the price of the equipment itself. The key factor is the complexity of the system requirements and the resulting effort needed to embody the logic of the system into a set of computer programs. There is no fixed relationship between the computer and software costs.

Although the costs of developing systems and programs appear high, the ultimate success of any system is more dependent on the quality of the work than on the equipment itself. For this reason, you should not try to make large savings in this area, since correcting any errors and shortcomings in the original system can be expensive.

Standard Packages

In order to help overcome the high cost of systems development work, certain equipment suppliers and specialist firms have developed standard packages for the more common processing applications. The packages may be purchased or leased for considerably less than it would cost to develop a customized system. Usually, no single package completely suits a particular organization's requirements, and the company may want to revise procedures to fit the package or modify the package for special requirements—but this can be as costly as developing a unique system if the changes are more than merely cosmetic.

Hidden Costs

Apart from the costs for systems development and programming, there are other expenses to consider:

☐ *Specialist Staff.* Even if development is subcontracted to a software house, you should assign an operator/manager to coordinate with the software house and consultants and to provide a degree of professional in-house expertise.

☐ *Engineering Maintenance.* This has traditionally run about 10% annually of the capital hardware costs for normal operation and can rise sharply if maintenance is done outside regular office hours.

☐ *Software Maintenance.* Systems and program maintenance for minor changes and extensions will recur and can be expensive.

☐ *Installation and Room Preparation.* This is normally a minor cost but in certain situations you may need to purchase an air conditioner and storage cabinets and install a special electrical circuit to avoid voltage fluctuation.

INSTALLATION PROCESS

When you have concluded the lengthy discussions leading to the decision to install a computer system and to select a particular supplier, (see Figure 9.1) there is a natural tendency to relax. Nothing could be more dangerous. It is in the next few months that the success or failure of the project will be determined.

Having chosen your system and your contractors, you are ready to enter the installation phase of computerization. This is a difficult period not only in a technical but also in a human sense. Computer equipment interfaces with people, and in certain circumstances, people have trouble getting used to it. It is important, therefore, to

Figure 9.1

proceed cautiously; obstacles that arise in this period tend to be difficult to remove later.

Unless the development phase proceeds with senior management involvement and encouragement, it is all too easy for the installed system to be inadequate, implementation delayed and the user staff ill-prepared. Any barriers and prejudices created in these circumstances may be extremely difficult to remove. In most organizations, the development phase should be controlled by naming an overall manager and, when appropriate, obtaining professional assistance on a scheduled basis. The manager is responsible for approving a detailed development and implementation plan for the installation phase.

Installation Plan. The tasks in a typical installation plan are:

☐ Specification of user requirements in each of the areas to be computerized

☐ Agreement to and acceptance of the specification by the users
  —. Design of supporting clerical procedures
  —. Production of a system and program specifications
  —. Preparation of computer programs.

☐ Preparation of user instructions

☐ Site preparation and installation of facilities such as:
  —. Communications systems
  —. Air conditioning
  —. Electrical connections and cabling
  —. Fire prevention and safety equipment
  —. Security systems
  —. Computer room furniture

☐ Installation of computer equipment

☐ Equipment acceptance testing

☐ Training of user staff

☐ Preparation of computer operating instructions

☐ Systems testing and analysis of systems test results

☐ Creation of computer master files

☐ Pilot and parallel running of each system and checking of results by users

☐ Systems acceptance by users

☐ Post-implementation review.

Remember, with careful planning you can avoid costly mistakes.

One of the major challenges to face when you automate is setting up controls to curb errors in and to prevent fraudulent manipulation of your automated procedures.

A small business computer system requires more specific controls than does a large one. As previously discussed, like their counterparts in middle-size and large organizations, smaller systems often incorporate integrated applications with on-line—that is, directly linked to the computer—input, processing, and updating of data files. Yet typically, the atmosphere of a small operation is informal and frequently involves multi-functions performed by one person. There may be difficulty keeping unauthorized persons away from the computer. In addition, small operations seldom have much in-house technical capability, so they cannot rely to the same degree as better-staffed, larger operations can on ad hoc investigations to review their automated activities.

Protection

Some people think that computer technology is so sophisticated that it doesn't need to be protected. But computer frauds have been committed by people who are not technically sophisticated. The best protection does not necessarily result from installing a better lock. Good security comes from management policies and procedures that encourage employees to use the locks or controls. Controls, however, are of little use if they are not used or periodically re-examined. Unless the accuracy of the information stored in your computer is continually edited, you will never detect any breaches of security. Generally, there is a decrease in the number of manual control procedures in a computerized environment, with the result that data receive less manual scrutiny and review.

Security. The two underlying security issues are:

☐ Data Integrity—the extent of control over the accuracy of information

☐ Physical Security—the vulnerability of your business and operations information (including the computer itself) to destruction or loss.

A computer makes mistakes in about the same way a typewriter makes typographical errors—with the assistance of the operator. Though some errors result from hardware or software errors—"bugs"—most result from operator errors, especially when entering new data. You can significantly reduce the possibility of error if your software has "error-catching" controls. These controls call attention to potential errors, such as unusually small or large figures, invalid codes or account numbers, or duplicate entries. The best way to ensure data integrity is to train your users thoroughly.

The physical security of your system can be protected in a number of ways. You should first control access to the equipment and software by locking the room and locking any cabinets in which diskettes are stored. It is also important to ensure that the computer itself is protected from physical abuse or damage, vandalism, environmental damage, and unauthorized use. These concerns may be addressed in the initial installation by securing a separate room for the computer.

In addition to the physical protection of data through backups and physically separate storage, care should be taken that more than one person knows how to access data if needed. Otherwise, the absence of key operators or persons with primary responsibility over the data could mean inaccessible data. It is critical that no one person be the exclusive user or have control over significant functions of the computer.

Backup. The best way to ensure the constant functioning and reliability of your system is to provide resources to fall back on if something goes wrong. First, make "backup" copies of programs and data stored on disks periodically. The time this process takes is well worth the effort. Having backup diskettes protects you against the diskette failure of one disk. Some businesses, for example, keep the same data on three different diskettes that are rotated every week or so—one is kept for use on the computer, another stored in the office, and a third kept off site (perhaps in a safe deposit box). Storing printed copies of important information offers additional insurance against loss of data.

Second, when you are entering data into the computer, be sure to transfer it to a diskette at reasonable intervals. The reason is that data in the computer's temporary (random access) memory depends on a constant current of electricity to remain accessible. A surge or spike in your electrical current could obliterate the contents of the computer's memory which would eliminate data that has taken you hours to prepare. If you store data at intervals, a power surge or brownout will result in the loss of minutes rather than hours of work.

Third, make sure you have backup personnel available. In a business environment, an important issue is whether computerization is personal or institutional. There is a grave danger in having the driving force behind the computer reside in one person, and also in having the computer regarded as "Jack's" or "Mary's". The risk, of course, is that if the person leaves, use of the computer could be disrupted, or even be lost entirely.

Some attention must be given to the issue of information "gate-keepers" and backup personnel. The truism that "information is power" is highly relevant when a business computerizes. Care should be taken that no one individual moves into a position of total control over major parts of the information contained in the computerized system. At least two people should be sufficiently familiar with each major application so that one can take over for the other in the event of vacation, illness or injury, or personnel transfer. Failing to provide for backup personnel raises the specter of the business being paralyzed in major areas of its operations.

Controls

In larger computer environments, input is balanced before it is processed; edit checks are performed in the data entry process; and systems controls that perform logic and range-boundary tests are built in. In addition, these controls check for characters in numeric fields and vice versa; produce error warning and exemption lists; and reconcile output. In other words, errors are expected and anticipated, and systems controls are an integral part of the system.

Information in a computer, however, can be changed without leaving any trace. Not all computer software provides the kinds of sophisticated audit trails to control security and data integrity that are found in larger computer software. Therefore, you must anticipate errors. Controls are absolutely essential in three areas: software verification, parallel testing during installation, and written documentation. Beyond the mechanical or electrical sources of error, the computer program itself may contain "bugs" or inaccurate instructions that cause flaws in the way the computer handles information. For these reasons, several operational procedures are critically important to assure the accuracy of a computer system.

☐ When the computer is first installed, it is critical to test it side-by-side with previous manual or other systems. This parallel test should continue until you are satisfied that the new system handles requirements accurately and can be relied upon to replace the previous system

☐ When software is first received, a duplicate of the original should be made, and then the original should be stored in a secure place. The duplicate copy should be the one used in the computer

☐ Printout should always be immediately spot-checked, item by item, if the accuracy of information is critical

☐ Underlying all of these procedures is the need for documentation—thorough and detailed references on how the system is organized, step-by-step procedures for entering and retrieving data, and procedures to follow if the system does not work as it should. Documentation should cover operation of both software and hardware, and any changes made to the system. Inadequate documentation, or no documentation at all, makes troubleshooting problems difficult or impossible. It also makes system operation heavily dependent on the abilities and memories of current users. If those personnel leave, the system may collapse.

Maintenance

Once the computer is running successfully, you may become aware of limitations in its responsiveness or capabilities. Of course, if something does go wrong, you should have a good service contract to back you up. Nonetheless, you can reduce or even eliminate many causes of computer failure by taking a few simple precautions. Whether or not problems surface, you should evaluate periodically your computer's performance and adequacy. The computer itself (the CPU and main memory) is actually the least delicate component in your system. Its integrated circuits have no moving parts and are as rugged as those in a transistor radio. Heavy and prolonged vibration may cause parts to unseat from their sockets, but this is highly unlikely. Still, even the most reputable microcomputers are known to "crash" now and then. Printers and disk drives are mechanical and can cause problems, as can on/off switches, keyboards, sockets that are frequently unplugged, and other mechanisms that have moving parts.

Breakdowns are inevitable even with a computer that has been well maintained. Normal wear and tear takes its toll on a computer as it does on any other machine. Computers are sophisticated, complex machines, so virtually everyone will need help sometime.

What if your computer or a vital peripheral like a printer or monitor breaks down? How quickly can you expect your computer to be operating again? If it is down for more than a few days, can you acquire a substitute promptly? Obviously, it is important to have a contingency plan, so check with your computer dealer. Find out what provisions can be made if your computer needs service. Substitutes may be needed in an emergency. Do not rely on a dealer's oral promises.

Post-Implementation Review. Installing a computer is not the last chapter in the process of computerization; for most businesses, it is merely the preface. As a computer is put into use, you may become aware of limitations in the original requirements study, or of limitations in the responsiveness of capability of the computer you acquired. Whether or not these problems surface, it is good business practice to evaluate periodically the performance and adequacy of your computer.

Proper evaluation and review require ongoing management of the computer—it cannot simply be plugged in and left alone. Once a computer is installed, greater demand may surface among your users. There is a tendency for users to need additional terminals, and to want additional applications, once they have been exposed to the initial capabilities—a classic case of rising expectations. It is easier, of course, to anticipate this demand before the computer is acquired; but in most cases, the demand must be accommodated after the computer is installed. Realize that as more applications are added, you may need to upgrade your computer.

An upgrade in computer capabilities may be needed in the first few months of operation, or may not arise for two or three years. The following are some symptoms of a need to upgrade computer capacity:

☐ An insufficient number of available terminals for those requiring terminal access

☐ The need to install applications that are beyond the system's current capabilities

☐ The lack of storage space on diskette or hard disk systems

☐ The need to undertake several processing steps in handling large files because of the system's inability to process all of the information on one storage device.

It is important to assess upgrading needs in the same systematic way that original computer requirements are addressed. This systematic approach is needed so that an upgrade decision will include all current and anticipated needs, and will not just respond to a specific capacity or application problem. In fact, an upgrading decision represents a good opportunity to recover from mistakes in the original computer requirements definition and selection process.

Before undertaking upgrading as the means to increase capacity, consider other, more immediate alternatives:

☐ Better computer file management procedures to reduce the disk storage requirements

☐ Work scheduling improvements to better utilize the available equipment and user time

☐ Low-cost additions to the current installation, including terminals and some upgrades in peripherals, such as higher-speed printers or larger capacity disk drives.

Finally, equipment and software compatibility is an important consideration when upgrading a system. If practical, new equipment should be compatible with existing equipment, in order to preserve prior investments.

HOW CONSULTANTS CAN HELP

The introduction of a computer system into an organization should be smooth; the aim is to ensure that the entire procedure is completed without disruption of day-to-day activities or major problems. To achieve this objective, management must make these decisions:

- ☐ Agree that a computer system is necessary
- ☐ Select the applications that can benefit from being computer-based
- ☐ Select the most suitable processing philosophy (e.g., batch processing or on-line, in-house computer or service bureau)
- ☐ Select the computer supplier best able to provide and maintain equipment matched to the application requirements
- ☐ Arrange for the system design and programming to be carried out by those with technical understanding of the chosen computer, an appreciation of the business and the ability to deliver systems on time and within budget
- ☐ Allocate sufficient top management time to all stages of the project—with emphasis on participation during system design—to ensure preparedness and commitment when the systems go live.

Given the importance of these decisions, there are advantages to seeking expert advice if the company has no previous experience in this area. During the feasibility study, a consultant can help you answer these questions:

- ☐ Is a computer really needed?
- ☐ If so, what areas in the organization will benefit the most?

☐ What is the processing philosophy?
☐ What are the priorities and time frame for installation?
☐ How much will it cost?
☐ What benefits can be expected?

Then, once agreement has been reached on getting a computer, a consultant can help select the right vendor by:

☐ Preparing a statement of requirements and a formal request for proposal
☐ Reviewing proposals for both software and hardware
☐ Selecting a vendor
☐ Advising on contractual questions.

During implementation, a consultant's assistance can be at three levels:

1. At the lowest level, the role is purely advisory, alerting management to danger signals that indicate problems at a later date if proper action is not taken.

2. At an intermediate level, support can be extended to include the design of the computer systems and supporting clerical procedures. In this situation, a consultant prepares user specifications for agreement with management, designs report formats, supervises systems testing, arranges for file conversion and trains the staff.

3. At the highest level of involvement, the consultant provides a complete implementation service by selecting and monitoring the programming effort in addition to the tasks described above. Under this arrangement, the consultant takes project responsibility from systems design through staff training.

Drawing on related experience in similar technical and industry fields, consultants can apply a fresh and independent view to problems that individual companies may be facing for the first time. Consultants are also well equipped to approach questions on the introduction of computers from the businessman's viewpoint in order to ensure that computers are used in ways that will bring the greatest benefits. And consultants can help avoid the pitfalls that so many nontechnical managers face as they judge their computer needs.

APPENDIX: CONTROLS

The American Institute of Certified Public Accountants identifies two major types of controls relevant to all computer installations: integrity and application controls.

Integrity Controls

Generally, integrity controls are aimed at the prevention or detection of fraud, misdirection of computer resources and concentration of functions in a computer. This kind of control is inherent in the plan of organization and operation of the computer activity and in the procedures for documenting reviewing, testing, and approving systems or programs. Other integrity controls include those built into the equipment, those over access to equipment, and certain others concerned with data or procedures and affecting overall computer operations. The following discussion focuses on integrity controls that are especially relevant to the needs of small businesses.

☐ *Controls on Access* include:
- —. Restricted access to terminals through use of key locks, badge readers, and so on
- —. Lockup of terminals when not in use
- —. Safe storage and periodic change of locks and keys
- —. Password requirement for sign-on to a terminal
- —. Periodic change in passwords.

☐ *Controls Supporting User Dependence on the System* include adequate fallback procedures fully documented.

☐ *Controls on Computer Personnel* include:
- —. A formal organization structure within the computer department
- —. Thorough checking of new employee references
- —. Prohibition on computer use by programmers and analysts working in other areas of the organization
- —. Involvement of management, users and auditors in new systems design and in system maintenance activities

—. Continuous logging of computer processing

Application Controls

Application controls relate to specific tasks performed by computer. They are designed to provide reasonable assurance that the system is recording, processing, and reporting data completely and accurately. Application controls are often categorized as input controls, processing controls, or output controls. A checklist of items to consider in defining application controls for a small business computer system follows:

☐ *Input Controls*
- —. Requirement for approval of all source documents
- —. Procedures for unauthorized forms
- —. Batching and totaling source documents
- —. Continuous logging of batches entered
- —. Required initialing of source documents
- —. Design of programs to: (1) validate all input data extensively; (2) require error correction before proceeding; and (3) accumulate totals during processing
- —. Data entry instructions for all functions
- —. Instructions for abnormal termination of processing
- —. Review of audit trails and logs

☐ *Processing Controls*
- —. Periodic balance of file controls against manually calculated totals
- —. Verification of processing date in month-end and year-end processing programs
- —. Checklist of functions to be performed
- —. Procedures for timely handling of suspense items

☐ *Output Controls*
- —. Schedules for preparation of reports

—. Verification of report totals against manually calculated totals

—. Incorporation of appropriate printing control techniques in reports

—. Checklist for report distribution

—. Procedures to prevent reports from remaining in the system too long

—. Password requirement for access to inquiry screens.

Other Controls

In addition to integrity and application controls, there are other basic controls that you should not overlook when you install your automated system. Most of these are concerned with physical security—a broad category that includes protection of equipment, software, and records (the latter largely from premature destruction). Provisions for contingencies (maintaining service in adverse circumstances) also comprise a category of controls.

10

Employee Benefit Plans

Employers are constantly faced with decisions on establishing and maintaining employee benefit programs. According to a study by the U.S. Chamber of Commerce, the cost of providing employee benefit programs amounts to approximately 40% of payroll. Some of these programs are income replacement programs such as retirement, savings, medical, life insurance and disability plans. Others are vacation, holidays, sick pay, etc., as well as Social Security, worker's compensation and unemployment insurance.

But employee benefit plans, which include pension, profit-sharing and welfare plans as well, also allow the owner-manager to accumulate wealth on a tax favored basis as well as attract, retain and motivate employees. In this chapter, a variety of benefit programs will be examined.

BASICS OF A WELL-DESIGNED PROGRAM

A well-designed benefit program should provide a level of benefits high enough to attract and hold key employees. In addition to being competitive, the plans should be cost-effective and designed to achieve maximum tax savings. An example of such a program is a 401(k) plan, which allows employees to save for retirement with before-tax dollars.

Details of the plans should be communicated to employees in a clear and positive manner so that the value of the programs provided are fully understood and appreciated.

An employer must also consider whether the plans are affordable. It is often difficult to terminate a plan or reduce benefits once they have been established, so the plan chosen should be appropriate for the company.

In an era of rapidly rising medical costs, many employers are establishing cost-containment programs in their hospital, surgical and major medical plans by increasing deductibles and limiting coverage paid. To control costs, employers often establish profit-sharing plans as opposed to retirement plans, with fixed obligations that must be met whether or not the company made a profit.

A well-designed benefit program should include plans that are coordinated with one another and with government benefits—including Social Security, Medicare, unemployment insurance and worker's compensation insurance—to reduce costs and preclude overlapping. For example, where a company has a long-term disability (LTD) insurance policy as well as a retirement plan, no disability benefits are paid out under the retirement plan until benefits under the LTD plan expire. Similarly, the benefit under the disability program is reduced (or offset) by some or all of the Social Security payable on disability.

NEED FOR EXPERTS

Benefits planning is highly complex. To accommodate the needs of even a midsized organization with a single plan would be difficult enough without the numerous applicable government regulations covering taxation and security of benefits. To develop your benefit package or evaluate an existing one, you must work with at least one professional—a benefits consultant or an actuary—and often it is advisable to consult a lawyer as well. Passage of various tax laws including the 1986 Tax Reform Act require amendments to existing qualified retirement, profit sharing and savings plans and the issuance of government regulations. In addition, the 1986 tax act requires for the first time that many companies amend their welfare plans including their medical, dental and life insurance programs to meet new nondiscrimination tests.

This chapter is designed to give you the basic understanding you will need to evaluate their recommendations properly.

QUALIFIED VERSUS NONQUALIFIED RETIREMENT PLANS

Retirement plans are either qualified or nonqualified. The Employee Retirement Income Security Act of 1974 (ERISA) and subsequent tax law changes, together with regulations and rulings issued by the Internal Revenue Service, establish rules for retirement plans. They cover minimum employee participation, prohibited discrimination, vesting, plan terminations, and so forth. If a plan meets these requirements, it is deemed qualified and receives favorable tax treatment. Plans that do not meet these requirements are nonqualified. This would include, for example, plans that are designed to provide particular benefits to a limited number of top executives. Nonqualified plans do not enjoy the favorable tax treatment accorded qualified plans.

The major advantages of a qualified plan are:

☐ Employer contributions to a qualified plan are tax deductible. Thus, the federal government contributes a portion of the plan's cost.

☐ The investment income and capital appreciation of the plan's assets are not taxed until distribution to plan participants or their beneficiaries.

☐ Company contributions do not become taxable income to an employee until the employee receives benefit payments.

☐ Lump-sum distributions receive special tax treatment if the employee meets certain requirements. Beginning in 1987, with limited exemptions, the treatment takes the form of a five-year forward-averaging provision whereby a lump sum distribution received after age 59 1/2 is divided by five and taxed using the tax rate for a single individual with no exemptions. The result is then multiplied by five to get the total tax due, which may be lower than the tax on the aggregate distribution at the graduated rates.

Qualified plans also have some notable disadvantages. For example:

☐ Certain types of retirement plans require a current cash outlay in the form of an annual contribution. (This is an expense item, however, which decreases reported income.) Employees with short service may be encouraged to leave the company in order to cash in on vested benefits.

☐ Administrative expenses, including the cost of in-house paperwork and fees for lawyers, actuaries and accountants, can be significant. These fees can be paid out of the trust assets or directly by the company.

☐ A qualified plan cannot discriminate in favor of key employees, (e.g., shareholders, owners, or highly compensated individuals). The Employee Retirement Income Security Act of 1974 (ERISA) and numerous IRS regulations specifically address this point. For purposes of the nondiscrimination requirements, employees of corporations that are members of a controlled group of corporations are considered to be employed by a single corporation. Therefore, years of service with any of the corporations must be counted for participation and vesting purposes, and the limitations on benefits and contributions apply as though the employees were employed by a single employer.

☐ A qualified pension plan that is terminated within 10 years of inception without a valid reason may be denied qualified status retroactively to its inception. In that event, employer income deductions for plan contributions will be disallowed for all open tax years. In addition, the benefits of the 25 most highly paid employees may be scaled down if the plan's benefits are not fully funded.

Qualified plans must meet a number of government requirements as follows:

☐ *Coverage Requirements.* For plan years beginning after 1988, new percentage and classification tests would replace existing employee coverage tests. A plan that does not meet the new percentage test would still satisfy the coverage requirements if it meets either the new ratio test or the new average benefit test.

—. *Percentage Test.* To meet this test, a plan must benefit 70% of all employees who are not highly compensated.

—. *Ratio Test.* This test would be met if the percentage of nonhighly paid employees covered by the plan equals at least 70% of highly paid employees that are covered.

—. *Average Benefit Test.* This test would be met if the plan satisfies the existing fair cross-section test and the employer-provided benefits for nonhighly compensated employees are, on average, at least 70% of the average employer-provided benefits of highly compensated employees.

—. *Fifty-Employee Rule.* A qualified plan would have to benefit the lesser of 50 employees or 40% or more of all employees, not counting employees excludable under the coverage rules.

☐ *Includable Compensation.* Generally, for years beginning after 1988, a $200,000 limit would be imposed on the amount of a participant's annual compensation that could be taken into account under any qualified plan for qualification and deduction purposes.

☐ *Accelerated Vesting.* For plan years beginning after 1988, the three current statutory vesting schedules would be replaced with five-year cliff vesting (100% vesting on completion of five years of service) or an alternative seven-year graduated vesting schedule (20% after three years of service and 20% for each year thereafter).

☐ *Limits on Contributions and Benefits.* The Tax Reform Act of 1986 modifies the limits on contributions and benefits under qualified plans.

— *Early Retirement Adjustments.* The $90,000 limit on the annual benefit payable under a defined-benefit pension plan is not directly reduced, but the act requires an actuarial reduction where retirement benefits begin before the participant has attained Social Security retirement age (presently, age 65).

—. *Other Reductions.* The $90,000 defined-benefit plan dollar limit would be phased in over the first 10 years of plan participation, rather than over years of service with the employer. Moreover, a new 10-year period of participation is required for certain increases in a plan's benefit structure.

—. *Special Cost-of-Living Accounts.* Defined-benefit pension plans could permit participants (other than certain key employees) to contribute to special accounts to provide post-retirement cost-of-living increases in their pension benefits.

☐ *Integration Rules Modified.* For plan years beginning after 1988, the rules under which qualified plans integrate (coordinate) their provision with Social Security benefits would be modified.

☐ *Deduction Limits for Qualified Plans.* In determining deduction limits under profit-sharing and stock bonus plans, credit carryovers are to be eliminated. Pre-1987 credit carryovers, however, would be permitted. The deduction limitation for an employer maintaining both a defined-benefit plan and a money-purchase pension plan is the greater of:

—. 25% of covered compensation

—. the amount necessary to satisfy the minimum funding requirements for the defined-benefit plan.

☐ An excess contribution (that exceeds applicable deduction limits) results in an annual 10% tax until the excess is eliminated.

☐ *Present Value of Accrued Benefits.* To determine the present value of a participant's accrued benefit, a qualified plan must compute the first $25,000 using an interest rate no greater than the Pension Benefit Guaranty Corporation (PBGC) rate. If the present value exceeds $25,000 (based on the PGBC rate), however, the plan may use an interest rate no greater than 120% of the PBGC rate to compute the entire present value.

☐ *Participant Loans.* Employees are allowed to borrow up to the present value of their accrued benefit. The maximum loan is $50,000 and must be repaid within five years. The only exception to the five-year repayment rule would be for the purchase of your own principal residence.

☐ *Excise Tax on Large Benefits.* Generally, a 15% excise tax is imposed on payments to individuals whose annual benefits distributed from all retirement plans, including IRAs and 403(b) tax-sheltered annuities, exceed the greater of $150,000 or 125% of the defined-benefit dollar limit in effect for the year.

☐ *In-service Withdrawals.* The tax rules (basis recovery rules) for distributions from contributory plans provide for the pro rata recovery of amounts attributable to after-tax employee contributions.

UNIFORM DISTRIBUTION REQUIREMENTS

All tax-favored retirement plans (including profit-sharing and pension plans, 403(b) tax-sheltered annuities and IRAs) are subject to uniform distribution rules.

Commencement Date

Beginning in 1989, distributions would generally be required to begin in April 1 following the year an individual attains age 70 1/2. The minimum payout rules would generally require that distributions be made over the life expectancy of the participant or the joint lives of the participant and a designated beneficiary. A 50% nondeductible excise tax would be imposed for failure to satisfy the minimum payout rules.

Premature Distributions

A 10% penalty tax is imposed on a distribution before age 59 1/2 from any tax-favored retirement plan (other than a distribution on account of death or disability) to any participant. Exceptions include:

☐ Periodic or annuity payments for the life (or life expectancy) of the participant or the joint lives of the participant and a designated beneficiary, commencing with separation from service

☐ Distributions to participants who have attained age 55 and satisfied the plan's early retirement provisions

☐ Distributions used to pay deductible medical expenses

☐ Certain distributions prior to March 15, 1987

☐ Payments to an alternate payee under a qualified domestic relation order.

With the assistance of an expert benefits consultant, you can usually create a plan that meets the needs of the company and its employees and takes into account the numerous technical provisions.

QUALIFIED PLANS

Qualified plans generally fall into one of two categories: defined-benefit and defined-contribution.

Defined-Benefit Pension Plans

In a defined-benefit pension plan, the employer contributes the amount necessary to provide a specific benefit. The benefit is generally payable monthly and is stated as a sum of money or a percentage of average compensation times years of service.

A typical plan might call for lifetime payments beginning on retirement, of $1,000 a month or 50% of average salary. The benefit is usually a function of at least one, and sometimes all, of the following factors:

☐ *Age* at which benefits begin

☐ *Service* accumulated at termination of employment, often including service before adoption of the plan

☐ *Salary* earned during employment or during a shorter period, such as the five or 10 years before retirement.

The amount of the employer contribution is actuarially determined using these factors together with the expected investment return on plan assets, and the probabilities of termination of employment due to all causes, including death and disability.

There are six mathematical models, called actuarial cost methods, that may be used to determine annual pension costs. No matter which is used, the maximum annual retirement benefit that can result is the lesser of either $90,000 or 100% of the average annual compensation for whatever three consecutive years have the highest total. To qualify for this maximum, an employee must have at least 10 years of plan participation. This dollar limitation is scheduled to be adjusted upward each year beginning in 1988 in accordance with changes in the consumer price index.

Sometimes the employer's contribution will be defined in terms of a range extending from the minimum funding amount required by ERISA to the maximum contribution that will be tax deductible. If the employer contributes more than the minimum funding requirement, the excess amounts build up a credit that may be used in future years to offset that requirement. Not all actuarial cost methods provide this feature, so it is important to discuss the choice of method with your actuary.

Financial Accounting Standards Board (FASB) Statement No. 87, *Employer's Accounting for Pensions*, outlines accounting methods and prescribes a single actuarial method that must be used for valuing pension liability and periodic expense for accounting and reporting purposes. Employers may want to consider the actuarial method they have adopted for funding purposes and whether it is the same or differs from the method that must be used for accounting pur-

poses. The same method does not have to be used for both purposes.

A Tool for the Owner-Manager. It is possible for an owner-manager to allocate a large portion of defined-benefit pension plan contributions to owners and key employees under the following
conditions:

- ☐ The owner-manager has long service, is older than 45 (approximately) and is highly paid
- ☐ Other employees have short service, are young and are at the
  lower end of the pay scale.

Restrictions apply to level of contributions and benefits that are
payable to key employees, if a pension plan is deemed "top-heavy."
A defined-benefit pension plan is considered top-heavy if the present value of accrued benefits of key employees exceeds 60% of the
present value of accrued benefits of all plan participants. Key employees are those employees who at any time during the current or
preceding year were included in one of the following four categories:

- ☐ One percent owners earning more than $150,000
- ☐ Employees owning the 10 largest interests in the company
- ☐ Officers receiving compensation greater than 150% of the de-
  fined-contribution plan maximum annual addition for the year.
  (For 1987, and the following several years, this will be 150%
  of $30,000, or $45,000.)
- ☐ An owner of 5% of the employer.

Top-heavy plans are subject to special rules affecting vesting,
contributions, and benefits. Although the rules will generally increase costs for employers maintaining these plans, the benefits for
key employees will still be substantial in most situations. Top-heavy
plans will continue to provide immediate deductions for contributions, tax-free accumulations of trust earnings and favorable income
tax treatment for certain plan distributions.

Advantages and Disadvantages. A defined-benefit pension plan offers these advantages:

☐ The plan provides a definite benefit on which participants can rely

☐ There may be a degree of flexibility in funding

☐ The plan can provide a benefit formula that automatically takes into account salary increases

☐ Benefits, at least in part, are insured by the government through the Pension Benefit Guaranty Corporation

☐ Service before the effective date of the plan can be recognized.

The following are disadvantages:

☐ The plan usually requires a minimum annual contribution. It is for this reason that some employers choose profit-sharing plans

☐ Administrative costs may be higher than they are in other plans because of the actuarial calculations required

☐ The company assumes responsibility for the plan's investment performance. If the investment yield is less than anticipated, the company's contributions may have to increase to meet the promised benefits

☐ If the plan is terminated, the company may be liable to the government's Pension Benefit Guaranty Corporation for the difference between the present value of guaranteed benefits and the plan's assets, up to 30% of the company's net worth.

Defined Contribution Plans

The main advantage of a defined contribution program is that annual company contributions are predictable and controllable. If the program is such that the employer contribution is determined by a formula, then the annual expense for the plan is easily budgeted. If the plan provides for fully discretionary contributions, then the employer has total control over the cost of the plan. The main disadvantage of a defined contribution plan is that older employees may not have sufficient time remaining in their careers to accumulate account balances that will provide adequate retirement benefits.

The following pages discuss some of the various types of defined contribution plans.

Money Purchase Pension Plans

One type of defined contribution plan is a money-purchase pension plan. In this plan, the employer's contribution is fixed, but the benefits are not. The amount of contributions and investment accumulated in the plan determines the level of benefits available to participants.

For each employee there is an individual pension account to which the employer promises to contribute annually. The amount is almost always defined as a percentage of the participant's pay. The maximum contribution permitted is 25% of salary, up to $30,000, for any one participant. As with defined-benefit pension plans, this dollar limitation is adjusted for cost-of-living increases.

Top-heavy plan rules apply to defined-contribution plans. A defined-contribution plan is top-heavy if more than 60% of the account balances have been accumulated on behalf of key employees. Investment earnings, including realized and unrealized gains and losses, are also allocated to individual participant accounts. At retirement, the employee withdraws funds from his or her account to satisfy retirement needs.

A money-purchase pension plan favors the owner-manager under the following conditions:

☐ The owner-manager is young and has little or no service

☐ Other employees, regardless of their age and service, are at a level of pay lower than that of the owner-manager.

The following characteristics of a money-purchase pension plan are advantageous:

☐ The contribution can be easily determined

☐ Administration is simpler than it is for a defined benefit pension plan, and consequently administrative costs are lower

☐ There is no potential liability to the Pension Benefit Guaranty Corporation

☐ Contributions are allocated to individual accounts, which employees can easily understand.

The following characteristics are disadvantageous:

☐ There is no flexibility in funding

☐ The employee bears the investment risk

☐ There is no promised retirement income on which the employee can rely

☐ Service prior to establishment of the plan cannot be effectively recognized

☐ The company must maintain records of individual employee accounts.

Profit-Sharing Plans

Another type of defined contribution plan is a profit-sharing plan. Under a profit-sharing plan, the contribution is usually established in relation to some aspect of profitability, such as a percentage of pretax profit. Thus, in most profit-sharing plans, no contribution would be required in any year in which there were no profits. (In certain plans structured along profit-sharing lines, management does accept a contributory obligation not contingent on profits; see thrift plans in this chapter.) The rules for plan qualification call for a "substantial and recurring" contribution; *recurring* is usually construed by pension consultants as not less than once every three years, if there are profits.

A profit-sharing plan can be designed without *any* specified contribution formula; that is, the amount of the contribution, if any, is entirely at the discretion of management, subject, of course, to the above-mentioned regulatory requirement. Also, since enactment of the 1986 Tax Reform Act, employer contributions under a qualified profit-sharing plan do not have to be limited to or geared to profits.

The maximum annual company contribution is limited to 15% of the *aggregate* compensation of all the plan members. As with a defined-contribution pension plan, however, the maximum amount that may be allocated to any *individual's* account in any year is 25% of pay, up to $30,000. Again, the dollar amount will be adjusted annually on the basis of the consumer price index.

Under a profit-sharing plan, any amounts forfeited by employees who terminate before they are 100% vested may be reallocated to the individual accounts of the remaining participants or used to reduce future company contributions.

A profit-sharing plan is ideal for a business where the following conditions exist:

- ☐ The owner-manager is young
- ☐ The company desires flexibility in funding
- ☐ There is rapid turnover of employees. The correspondingly high level of forfeitures augments the interest of the remaining plan participants. (Forfeitures are, however, included with contributions to determine the maximum amount that may be allocated to any member's account.)

The advantages of money-purchase pension plans also apply in general to profit-sharing plans. A profit-sharing plan, however, has the major advantage of flexible annual contributions. The chief drawbacks of profit-sharing plans are:

- ☐ An owner-employee with long service cannot shelter as much income as under a defined-benefit pension plan, especially if the other employees are younger and have short service.
- ☐ There is no flexibility in funding when the contribution is specified in the plan (by formula, for example).
- ☐ There is no promised retirement income on which employees can rely.
- ☐ The employee bears the investment risk.
- ☐ Service prior to the establishment of the plan cannot be effectively recognized.

☐ The company must maintain records of individual employee accounts.

Employee Stock Ownership Plan (ESOP)

These plans are designated to invest primarily in employer securities and generally distribute these securities to terminating or retiring employees. The 1986 Tax Reform Act generally retains and adds to existing provisions favorable to ESOPs. The act provides an estate tax exclusion for 50% of the proceeds of certain sales of employer securities to ESOPs. The exclusion would apply to sales made after the date of enactment and before 1992. Dividends paid on ESOP stock that are used to repay the ESOP loan will be deductible.

For plan terminations before 1989, the act provides special rules encouraging the transfer of surplus assets from a terminated defined-benefit plan to an ESOP. The amount transferred will not be includable in the employer's income and will not be subject to the proposed 10% excise tax on asset reversions.

Upon reaching age 55 with 10 years of participation, a participant would have to be allowed to direct the investment of 25% of his or her account balance. This election would have to be offered every year from age 55 until the first plan year after age 60, when the participant would be permitted a one-time opportunity to diversify a full 50% of his or her account balance. A plan would meet this requirement either by distributing the portion of the account balance eligible for diversification or offering at least three investment options to the employee.

Unless a participant elects otherwise, a participant's account balance would generally have to be distributed within five years of separation from service, or upon repayment of the ESOP loan, if later. Currently, a plan is permitted to delay distribution until a participant reaches normal retirement age, even after separation from service.

Other Qualified Plans

Not all benefit plans fall neatly into one or another of the basic categories described in the preceding discussion. Certain plans feature characteristics of both defined-benefit and defined-contribution plans. Moreover, some plans have features that are distinct from any so far discussed. The following subsection deals with the more common of these variants.

Floor Plans. A floor plan is a money-purchase pension plan or profit-sharing plan with a promised, defined benefit. In recent years, these plans have been referred to as account-balance plans. At retirement, employees receive the greater of the desired benefit or the amount that can be provided by their individual account balances. The principal advantages of floor plans are:

- [ ] The contributions are allocated to individual accounts that employees can easily understand
- [ ] The plan can be designed to favor the owner-manager (within the constraints imposed by the new top-heavy rules)
- [ ] There is a promised minimum retirement income on which the employee can rely
- [ ] Service before the effective date of the plan can be recognized.

The following are the chief disadvantages of the plans:

- [ ] There is a potential liability to the Pension Benefit Guaranty Corporation
- [ ] Each annual contribution must be supported by an actuarial valuation
- [ ] Records of individual employee accounts must be maintained
- [ ] The employer assumes downside investment risks by being responsible for minimum benefits, or the floor.

Combination of Pension and Profit-Sharing Plans. Many organizations start out with pension plans and later add profit-sharing plans to increase retirement benefits and to provide incentives to younger employees. Conversely, many begin with a profit-sharing plan and later add a pension plan when fixed commitments can be safely undertaken. And there are companies that have both types of plans at the outset.

The maximum deductible contribution allowed when a company combines a money-purchase pension plan or a profit-sharing plan with a defined-benefit pension plan is 25% of the greater of the annual pay of plan participants or the minimum funding requirement for the defined-benefit plan. If, therefore, the minimum required contribution to the defined-benefit plan equals or exceeds 25% of pay, no additional contribution can be made to the profit-sharing plan or the money-purchase pension plan.

Under the current IRS position on comparability of benefits, a company in designing its plans may take into account the benefits an employee will receive at retirement from all company-sponsored qualified plans and Social Security. Thus, it may be advantageous to a company to include different groupings of employees in defined-benefit and defined-contribution plans to provide the highest level of benefits to highly paid employees at the least cost to the company. However, to meet the new minimum participation rule of the 1986 Tax Act, beginning after 1988, a plan would have to benefit the lesser of 50 employees or 40% or more of all employees, not counting employees excludable under the coverage rule. The new 50-employee or 40% rule will apply separately to each qualified plan.

Thrift Plans. Employee thrift or savings plans are retirement plans that call for employee and employer contributions. The plans are structured like defined-contribution plans. The employer's contribution is a function of the amount or rate of the employee's contribution—which is, of course, voluntary. For example, the employer might contribute 50 cents for every dollar from the employee. Thus, by limiting the amount of employee contribution by up to 6% of pay, management can limit its own contribution.

A thrift plan may be of the pension or the profit-sharing type. Besides providing employees with an incentive to save on a regular basis, thrift plans also offer them tax advantages. Neither company contributions nor fund earnings are taxable to the plan participants until distributed. Company contributions are tax deductible when made.

Cash or Deferred-Compensation 401(k) Plans. Employers may offer elective deferred-compensation arrangements to employees. Each eligible employee can decide whether to receive cash or to have the same amount contributed by the employer to a qualified profit-sharing or stock bonus plan. These plans, referred to as 401(k) plans, must meet stringent antidiscrimination rules. Company contributions are deductible and are not taxed to the employee until withdrawn from the plan.

Employers may offer the cash or deferred-compensation choice to employees in a number of ways. For example, many have amended existing thrift plans to allow employee contributions eligible for company matching contributions to be made with pretax dollars. Another way is to have all or part of an annual bonus contributed by the employer to the 401(k) plan.

Individual Retirement Accounts. Individual retirement accounts are available to individuals, including those who are active participants in company qualified plans. However, the Tax Reform Act of 1986 restricts the amount of IRA contributions that higher-paid employees can make to an IRA if he or she is a member of a qualified plan.

As in qualified plans, the income earned by IRA assets is not taxable until distributed. Substantial penalties are imposed, however, if withdrawals are made before age 59 1/2, except in the event of death or disability.

Keogh Plans. The Keogh, or HR-10, plan is a qualified pension plan that can be used to benefit individuals who are self-employed. Keogh plans receive the favorable tax treatment afforded qualified plans which benefit employees.

Most Keogh plans are defined-contribution plans. Defined-benefit plans are permitted and should be considered because they allow credit for service rendered prior to plan adoption, thus giving the potential for contributing more than $30,000 a year for the benefit of individuals with high earned income.

The following chart explains the differences between these two types of Keogh plans.

Defined-Contribution	Defined-Benefit
Profit-sharing plans—lesser of 15% of aggregate compensation or $30,000; Money-purchase plans—lesser of 25% of compensation or $30,000.	Actuarially determined—same as corporate defined-benefit plan limits.

The repeal of the Keogh rules existing before 1984 and addition of top-heavy plan restrictions effectively eliminated the differences in the rules for corporate and non-corporate plans. Only minor differences remain. As a result, there is now no incentive for professionals to incorporate their practices in order to obtain greater retirement benefits.

Simplified Employee Pension Plans. Simplified employee pension plans (SEPs) may be adapted by a corporation, a partnership or a sole proprietorship. SEPs combine many of the features of Keogh and IRA plans. They do not, however, offer the favorable tax treatment on distribution offered by qualified plans. Also, SEPs must cover all employees who have attained the age of 21 and have completed three years of service. Beginning in 1989, employees who participate in SEPs maintained by small employers (25 or fewer employees) can make up to $7,000 in elective deferrals if certain requirements are met.

Employees who participate in a simplified employee pension (SEP) maintained by a small employer (fewer than 25 employees) can make up to $7,000 in elective deferrals as long as 50% of the employees make deferrals. The deferral percentage for each highly compensated employee cannot exceed the average deferral percentage (ADP) for all other participants by more than 25%.

INCENTIVE STOCK OPTIONS

Repeal of tax-favored treatment for capital gains under the 1986 Tax Reform Act eliminates an important tax advantage currently available under Incentive Stock Options (ISOs). However, ISOs would continue to provide a deferral of tax attributable to the "bargain element" at the date of exercise. The act repealed the requirement that ISOs must be exercised in the order granted. This requirement currently makes ISOs unavailable to companies that have experienced a decline in stock prices. The act also modifies the $100,000 limit that currently applies to the value of ISOs granted to any employee in one year. As revised, the limit would apply to the value of ISOs that became exercisable in one year.

RETIREMENT FUNDING ARRANGEMENTS

The more common funding arrangements used for retirement plans and related administrative cost considerations are highlighted in the following subsections.

Individual Insurance Policies

Many retirement plans with 25 or fewer participants are funded with individual whole-life insurance policies and an auxiliary fund. The fund holds pension plan assets required over and above the cash values of the individual insurance policies. The company purchases whole-life insurance on the participants' lives at a guaranteed annual cost. These policies are owned by the retirement plan, and the company is allowed a deduction for the premiums paid. Often the insurance company agrees to assume most of the administrative burden connected with the plans at little or no charge.

The chief drawbacks of this kind of funding are high commissions and the low yields realized under individual insurance policies. In most cases, group life insurance outside the retirement program will give more benefits for the same contributions. In addition, group programs offer the participants major tax advantages over individual policies. (See Individual versus Group Life Insurance in this chapter.)

Group Insurance Contracts

Retirement plans that use contemporary group insurance contracts have a choice of two general types of contracts: the Deposit Administration (DA) contract, or the Immediate Participation Guarantee (IPG) contract. Funds are not allocated to individual participants under these contracts.

Under a DA contract, the insurer guarantees the rate of interest credited to the pension fund for a specified number of years. At the end of the specified period, the insurer may revise the interest guarantees on the basis of investment performance and actual expenses during the period. If the company refuses to accept the revised guarantees, it can opt out of the plan, but at a price—specifically, a penalty imposed for contract termination.

The IPG contract works much like an equity account in that the interest credited represents the actual investment result achieved by the insurance company. Actual expenses incurred are charged against the fund. Thus, there is no need for periodic revision of the rates based on experience. This type of contract is usually designed for plans with an annual contribution in excess of $50,000. Like DA accounts, IPG contracts have clauses designed to deter termination of the contract.

Banks and Savings and Loan Institutions

Banks and savings and loan institutions have many investment arrangements available. For small pension funds, banks usually recommend that a plan invest assets in one or more pooled funds, such as an equity fund, a fixed-income fund short-term fund or a balanced equity and fixed-income fund.

Banks and savings and loan associations provide limited administrative services. They will often allocate contributions to individual accounts under a defined contribution pension or profit-sharing plan, but they do not provide actuarial services. You will probably need consultants to assist you in this and other administrative aspects.

WELFARE BENEFIT PLANS

For most companies welfare plans generally consist of accident and health plans, life insurance and disability insurance programs. Some companies also provide dependent care assistance, group legal service plans and educational assistance programs. The types of programs and the level of coverage provided can vary significantly depending on a company's needs and workforce.

The benefit packages offered by various insurers in the health and welfare area differ widely in coverage and in cost. It is essential, therefore, to shop around before you adopt a particular plan.

GROUP BENEFITS

The owner-manager should be aware that the Tax Reform Act of 1986 establishes new eligibility and benefit nondiscrimination tests for health plans and group-term insurance plans. These provisions would generally not take effect until January 1, 1988. The application of the new rules would be further delayed if regulations are not issued by three months preceding that date.

Except in very special cases, failure to use at least one employee benefit plan is incompatible with good business practice. There is no shortcut to benefits planning; you must work out the optimal arrangement for yourself and your employees in the light of your objectives, the annual cost, flexibility in funding, administrative costs and taxation. A qualified benefits consultant is indispensible to this process.

The following are some basic checklist questions the owner-manager should follow in evaluating who should administer the welfare program:

☐ *How Flexible Are the Benefits Packages?* Will you be locked into one kind of plan or policy? Or will you be able to pick and choose—and change if you want to? What options are available? The answers to these questions will tell you whether you can adopt, or switch to, cost containment measures like second opinions or elective surgery, certification requirements for hospital admissions (which eliminates hospital stays for treatment available on an out-patient basis), raising the deductible each employee must pay and reducing coverage to less than 100% of costs.

☐ *What Market Size Does the Insurance Company Specialize In?* Some insurance companies concentrate on large groups, and peg their premium rates accordingly. Others specialize in small companies. You might be able to realize significant savings by signing with, or switching to, an insurer that is appropriate for your company.

☐ *What "Pool" Will the Insurance Company Put You In?* Unless your company is large enough to be experience rated, which means premiums are based on your own claims history, your funds will go into some type of pool. A pool might include the entire community of small businesses or an industry group. Your rates will be based on this pool's history so it's important to shop for the right pool. For example, if you're in a service industry where employees—younger and more highly paid than the general workforce—don't tend to use as many medical services, you might look for an insurer that will place you in a service industry pool.

☐ *At What Point Will the Insurer Experience Rate You? When Will It Offer You Funding Alternatives?* If you expect future personnel increases, you might want to pick an insurer for the long term— one that will start giving you options when the company is fairly small—even if the insurer or these options cost a little more at present.

☐ *How Are Rates Developed and on What Basis Do They Change?* Rates may be based, for example, on the experience rating of your company or pool. You will want to know how, and how often, this experience rating is reviewed. In some states, Blue Cross-Blue Shield rates for pooled small businesses are regulated; the state insurance commissioner has to approve changes, and the commissioner can veto all or part of an increase.

☐ *How Fast Have Rates Been Going Up?* A company with lower premiums might be hiking them faster than more expensive insurers. Particularly where small differences are involved, it might be wiser to pick the company that will charge a little more right now. For example, say one insurer asks $2,500 a year per employee, but has hiked its rates an average of 10% a year over the past five years. If this trend continues, you'll be paying about $4,027 five years from now, depending on how the hikes are spread out and calculated. Another insurer may charge $2,000 per employee, but has raised rates an average of 20% a year. In this case, your rate in five years could be in the $4,759 range. As the premium amounts get larger, so do the differences.

TYPES OF WELFARE PLANS

Accident and Health Insurance

The major forms of accident and health insurance include hospital insurance, surgical and medical insurance, major medical, dental and disability income coverage.

Premiums paid by an employer for accident and health benefit plans are generally tax deductible as ordinary and necessary business expenses. Amounts received by employees under employer-financed accident and health plans are generally excluded from their gross income as are premiums paid by an employer for such coverage. Thus, amounts received as reimbursement for medical care are not taxable. However, payments received under a disability income plan, which are made by the employer, are included in the employee's taxable income and subject to federal income tax and FICA taxes. For this reason, some programs are designed so that the employee pays the premiums for disability coverage. In such a case, payments made under the plan are not subject to income or FICA tax.

Self-employed persons, who are not now permitted deductions for medical benefits, will be allowed to deduct 25% of health insurance premiums through 1989.

Uninsured Medical Reimbursement Plans

Uninsured medical plans are subject to the same limitations on excludability that are applicable to insured plans and also must comply with special stringent nondiscrimination rules. Where amounts paid to highly compensated employees fail to satisfy these nondiscrimination rules, they are treated as excess reimbursements and are taxable to those individuals. Highly compensated employees are defined as the five highest-paid officers, shareholders of more than 10% of the company and the highest-paid 25% of all employees.

To avoid this taxation of benefits, many companies establish insured excess medical plans to cover key individuals. However, these arrangements will now have to be reviewed under the 1986 Tax Reform Act's new standards of nondiscrimination coverage for medical plans.

HEALTH AND WELFARE FUNDING ARRANGEMENTS

For some companies, there are health insurance options other than the traditional group insurance policy. The two major options are self-funding and alternative insurance. Both are touted as cash-flow protectors, but they may be unavailable or inadvisable for many small companies.

How the Options Work

Alternative funding comes under titles like "minimum premium" and "split fund." To understand how it works, you have to look first at regular health insurance. Normally, you have a cash reserve at the insurance company that collects little or no interest. With alternative funding, you hold onto the reserves yourself and can invest them in a more profitable way, resulting in higher interest. The insurance company will probably charge you a "lost-interest fee," but you can still come out ahead. The higher interest your money earns, less any fee, is your cash-flow savings.

Self-Insurance

Self-insurance means the employer accepts all of the risk of claims costs, setting aside reserves according to actuarial assumptions (calculations of what claims it can expect) or otherwise meeting liabilities. It may still pay to have an insurance company administer the program.

Who Can Use It. Alternative funding is available to any company large enough to be experience-rated. Insurance company policies vary. Although alternative funding is available for companies with as few as 25 employees, a more typical cutoff is about 100.

Self-insurers are generally larger. The predictability of regularly scheduled premiums may be more important to smaller companies than the possibility of savings. Self-insurance has a risky downside. Obligations may turn out to be more than you expect. You might also need more staff, depending on how you choose to administer your program. Also, you'll have to consult with professionals to sort through a number of legal and technical questions to set up a plan.

Individual versus Group Life Insurance

The premiums for group insurance are lower than those for individual policies. Also, individual insurance policies do not permit, except indirectly, coordination with other benefits, including those provided by the employer and those associated with the death and disability features of Social Security.

A major advantage of group insurance over individual life is that the first $50,000 of coverage is not taxable to the employee under group insurance, but the premiums are deductible by the employer. At death, the beneficiary has no reportable income. Further, through assignment, it is possible for the death benefits to be kept out of the insured's estate.

Nevertheless, individual insurances can be appropriate, especially where large amounts are needed for only a few individuals. Some of these applications are:

For life insurance policies purchased by employers after June 20, 1986, the act disallows an employer's deduction for interest on policy loans in excess of $50,000 from policies on the lives of officers, employees or owners of the business.

Buy-Sell Agreements. These agreements are used in partnerships or closely held companies. They provide that on the death or disability of one of the owners (or partners), the remaining owners (or partners) will automatically buy out that owner's interest in the business. In these arrangements, individual disability insurance can be as important as individual life insurance.

Insuring Key People. Corporations whose success is contingent on certain key individuals purchase insurance to protect the company or carry it through a transition period on one such individual's death or disability.

Ensuring Liquidity for Estate Tax Purposes. Individual life insurance can guarantee total or partial coverage for estate taxes on large estates.

CAFETERIA PLANS

A cafeteria or flexible compensation plan allows each eligible employee to select from a variety of nontaxable benefits and cash, without being taxed because of "constructive receipt." Under the doctrine of "constructive receipt," if an employee can choose between cash and nontaxable benefits, the employee is generally taxed even if the nontaxable benefit is chosen. Cafeteria plans that meet the requirements of the tax laws are an exception to this doctrine and, thus, nontaxable benefits are protected against taxation. A cafeteria plan may offer a choice among some or all of the following:

Nontaxable Benefits

☐ Health care benefits, including many benefits allowed by the Internal Revenue Code but not covered under a group contract

☐ Group term life of up to $50,000 insurance

☐ Deferred compensation under a cash or deferred arrangement as defined in IRC Section 401(k) (other forms of deferred compensation may not be offered)

☐ Dependent care assistance

☐ Group legal services.

Taxable Benefits

☐ Direct cash payments
☐ Group term life insurance in excess of $50,000

Cafeteria Plan Requirements

Section 125 of the Internal Revenue Code includes stipulations to determine whether a flexible compensation plan that includes taxable and nontaxable benefits should be taxed or not. If the requirements of IRC Section 125 are met, no tax is imposed on the nontaxable benefit the employee selects. If these requirements are not met, an employee will be taxed to the extent that a taxable benefit could have replaced the chosen benefit. Generally, the requirements include:

☐ *Participation.* Only employees and former employees may participate. Benefits may also be provided for beneficiaries of participants. The plan must be available to a nondiscriminatory classification of employees beginning in 1989. Special new nondiscrimination rules will apply.

☐ *No Deferred Compensation.* Only profit-sharing or stock bonus plans that include a cash or deferred arrangement governed by IRC Section 401(k) are allowed as part of a cafeteria plan.

Types of Flexible Compensation Plans

Flexible compensation plans generally fall into five basic categories. For purposes of this discussion they will be described as the modular plan, the core plan, the benefits bank, the unlimited choice plan and the mini-flex plan.

The Modular Plan

This version consists of several "modules" or packages of benefits. All of the modules have the same type of benefits but they offer a varying mix of coverage.

For example, a modular plan might offer employees a choice of one of the following:

1. Life insurance—1 times salary. Health insurance with a $100 deductible and coinsurance of 80% above the deductible, plus a $1,000 out-of-pocket stop-loss feature.
2. Life insurance—2 times salary. Health insurance with a $500 deductible, coinsurance of 80% above the deductible, a $2,000 out-of-pocket stop-loss feature and dental care.
3. Life insurance—3 times salary. Health insurance with a $1,000 deductible and no coinsurance, plus vision and dental care.

The modular plan has the advantage of being relatively easy to administer, although pricing the various benefits may be difficult. Another possible problem is adverse selection, which occurs when benefits are chosen primarily by those who would use them frequently with a corresponding rise in average claims. This tends to drive up the cost of the benefit. In a modular plan, this may be remedied by linking certain benefits to each module to spread the risks.

The Core Plan

All employees receive a basic or "core" benefit package. In addition, each employee is credited with a certain number of benefit dollars that can be used to enrich the core benefits or purchase additional benefits. Each employee is given credits; these might be the same for all employees or might be a percentage of compensation. Individuals must allocate their benefit dollars prior to participation. Any unused benefits are forfeited.

The following is an example of a core plan. When the plan was adopted, the company reduced its previous benefits to a core and added some options.

ABC Company Previous Benefits Package

☐ Life insurance—4 times salary

☐ Health insurance with no deductible and no coinsurance

☐ Short-term disability pay—up to 12 months

☐ Vacation—3 weeks

☐ Holidays—12

☐ Profit-sharing plan with 401(k) feature.

Core Benefits

☐ Life insurance—1 times salary

☐ Health insurance with $500 deductible and 80% coinsurance

☐ Short term disability—6 months

☐ Vacation—2 weeks

☐ Holidays—10

☐ Profit-sharing plan with 401(k) feature.

Options

☐ Additional life insurance

☐ Lower deductible on health insurance

☐ Longer disability pay period

☐ More vacation

☐ More holidays

☐ Vision care

☐ Dental care

☐ Dependent care assistance.

This type of core program requires careful analysis to establish proper pricing and subsequent monitoring to ensure continued pricing accuracy. It may also be necessary to link certain benefits to avoid adverse selection and poor employee choices.

The Benefits Bank

The benefits bank is a variation on the core plan that has significant additional advantages in implementation and administration.

The savings achieved by reducing previous benefits to a core package is put into a benefits bank for allocation to participants. Each participant receives a dollar credit that may be used for a variety of nontaxable benefits.

The benefits bank type of core program allows flexibility without many of the pricing and administrative difficulties associated with other programs. Many companies could use their present claims administration in connection with benefits bank payments. For example, an employee would have the following benefits under a core plan:

- ☐ Life insurance—2 times salary
- ☐ Health insurance—$500 deductible or 80% coinsurance
- ☐ Dental
- ☐ Short-term disability
- ☐ Long-term disability—50% of salary.

The following options could be purchased with money in the benefit bank account.

- ☐ Life insurance—1 or 2 times salary
- ☐ Health insurance—reimbursement for premium, coinsurance, the deductible and other eligible unreimbursed expenses
- ☐ Long-term disability—66 2/3% of salary
- ☐ Vision care
- ☐ Dependent care assistance.

In addition, a properly designed program may result in significant cost containment in future years. In the year of adoption, a company will merely shift to the benefits bank all or part of the amounts saved by reducing the core benefit package. In later years, however, cost containment may be achieved by limiting benefit bank increases to the cost of living index or increases in national average wages. Over a period of years this cost containment could be substantial, and yet employees would retain the same basic health protection with added flexibility to purchase meaningful benefits.

Unlimited Choice Plans

Each employee is given a fixed dollar amount of credits. The amount might be the same for all employees or might be a percentage of compensation. The credits are to be used to purchase one or more benefits. There is no core of benefits.

For example, employees might be offered the following benefit choices:

☐ Life insurance
—. 1 times salary
—. 2 times salary
—. 3 times salary
☐ Health insurance
—. $100 deductible, 80% coinsurance, $250 stop-loss
—. $250 deductible, 80% coinsurance, $500 stop-loss
—. $500 deductible, 80% coinsurance, $1,000 stop-loss
—. $1,000 deductible, 80% coinsurance, $2,000 stop-loss
☐ Short-term disability pay
—. 1 year maximum
—. 6 month maximum
☐ Long-term disability benefits
—. Vision care
—. Dental care
—. Dependent care.

An unlimited choice plan will be complicated to administer. Also, there might be problems if employees use poor judgment in making their choices. For example, an employee might not choose any health care coverage at all and then encounter a very expensive medical emergency that could conceivably throw him into personal bankruptcy. Adverse selection may also present a problem. However, it is possible to link certain benefits to minimize adverse selection and poor employee choices.

The Mini-flex Plan

This plan uses salary reduction to pay the employee's share of contributory benefits. Employees make these contributions with pretax dollars rather than after-tax-dollars.

For example, suppose an employee is paying $75 per month for health insurance and $15 a month for group life insurance premiums. Under the mini-flex plan, this employee's salary would be reduced by $90 per month and all of the premiums would be paid by the employer. The employee's take-home pay would actually increase as a result of reduced income tax withholding.

This plan is easy to administer but it does not offer the employee a choice of benefits.

Sources of Flexible Compensation Funding

A flexible compensation plan can be funded through employer contributions and employee contributions.

Employer contributions may be generated from:

☐ Savings achieved by reducing the present benefit program
☐ Additional payroll costs.

Employee contributions may come from:

☐ Payroll deductions (after-tax dollars)
☐ Salary reduction (pretax dollars).

Reducing Present Benefits

One source of employer contributions to a flexible compensation plan is the savings achieved by reducing the present benefit program to basic core coverage. For instance, if the employer presently provides health insurance with a $100 deductible and 80% coinsurance, this program could be reduced to provide a $1,000 deductible with 100% coinsurance. Similarly, life insurance policies now covering several times salary could be scaled back to one times salary coverage.

The savings from these reductions can be used to provide additional benefit choices such as dental care, vision care and dependent care assistance. Employees could also choose to be covered by the original benefit program instead of the new benefits. Thus, flexibility can be offered at little additional cost by redesigning the existing benefit structure.

Salary Reduction

This is another source of contributions to a flexible compensation plan. Salary reduction is particularly relevant to flexible compensation plans because it enables employees to pay for certain benefits with pretax dollars instead of after-tax dollars. If an employee chooses salary reduction, the employer makes a contribution for one or more nontaxable benefits in an amount corresponding to the salary reduction. The contribution is treated for tax purposes as an employer contribution and is not subject to federal income tax if spent on a nontaxable benefit. The employee is taxed only on his or her reduced salary.

The following example illustrates the use of a salary reduction agreement in a cafeteria plan:

In addition to its basic benefits package, ABC Company provides each employee with credits worth $2,000 that can be used for medical reimbursement, group legal services, dependent care assistance and cash or deferrals under a 401(k) plan. In order to make these benefits more available to employees, ABC Company also offers a salary reduction agreement in which employees can reduce their salaries up to an additional $2,000 each. These amounts can then be used in addition to the original employer contributions to pay for extra benefits. As a result, each employee can spend up to $4,000 on cafeteria plan benefits.

Consider an employee with a salary of $25,000 who agrees to a salary reduction by $2,000 to pay for nontaxable benefits, such as dependent care and legal expenses, that would otherwise have to be paid for with after-tax dollars.

An employee in the 15% tax bracket who elected to reduce his or her salary by $2,000 would save $300 in taxes. The savings to an employee in the 28% bracket would be $560.

The Internal Revenue Service has stated that an employee must make an advance decision on how to allocate funds. Any money remaining in an employee account at the end of the plan year is forfeited.

OTHER ISSUES

Social Security Taxes and Benefits

Social Security (FICA) tax is not imposed on nontaxable benefits under a cafeteria plan (except cash or deferred arrangements under IRC Section 401(k)). Therefore, both employers and employees save on FICA taxes. This saving may be accompanied by reduction in Social Security benefits, but in most instances these benefits will be only slightly reduced.

The Potential for Cost Containment

The continued growth in medical care expenditures is of increasing concern to both the government and employers, and many innovative approaches to reducing the rate of increase are under consideration. The enactment of hospital reimbursement controls under Medicare (in TEFRA and the Social Security Amendments of 1983) are only the beginning of federal efforts to slow the growth of health care spending. Similarly, many employers have joined local health care coalitions in an attempt to reduce the amounts they spend on employee health insurance.

Cafeteria plans are one way of reducing the rate of increases in medical care expenditures. For example, the benefit bank approach generally reduces health benefits to catastrophic coverage and shifts the saving to a benefits bank. Employees can spend their allocated share of benefit credits on medical reimbursement or other nontaxable and taxable benefits. The future cost of catastrophic coverage is likely to be far less than continued comprehensive basic health coverage for all employees. And while the general cost of health coverage may continue to escalate at a rapid pace, the benefits bank increases can be controlled.

Employee benefit trade magazines and financial journals have provided hard evidence that cafeteria plans can save companies significant amounts of money and can reduce costs related to a medical plan.

This approach not only offers direct savings in health benefit costs, but also gives employees a financial stake in the cost of health care. It is hoped that this employee involvement will result in downward pressure on health care costs in general to the extent that demand for medical services is reduced.

Employer costs can also be reduced by using salary reduction to pay for a portion of employer-provided benefits. If offered in a benefits bank program—where the employer is funding part of the benefits bank and offering new benefits that may have previously been paid for with after-tax dollars—this approach is generally well received by employees.

* * *

Now that the features of several types of employee benefit plans have been examined, we believe it is important for the owner-employer to evaluate the specifics of the company's benefit program. Sweeping changes to our federal income tax system are significantly affecting the employee benefits area. Every company should make a detailed review of existing programs to determine what changes need to be made and the most appropriate method.

11

Tax Strategies

Sweeping changes in the tax laws during the 1980s are having a dramatic effect on businesses. What were once straightforward tax-planning decisions now require serious deliberation to choose business structure, accounting methods, financing arrangements and the structure of day-to-day transactions. Chapter 5 discussed the various forms of doing business; this chapter will describe various tax strategies associated with starting a new business and continuing its operations.

INCEPTION OF BUSINESS

Start-Up Considerations

There are several elections and decisions that must be made either before your business begins or during the initial year of operations. Which options are appropriate will depend on the structure of the business. These options should be taken into consideration in choosing the structure of your business operations.

Tax Year-End. Selection of a tax year is an important planning opportunity that could provide initial tax savings or income deferral for most regular corporations. However, the Tax Reform Act of 1986 (TRA '86) virtually eliminated this planning opportunity for most partnerships, S corporations and personal service corporations by requiring them to adopt the tax year of their principal partners or shareholders (usually a calendar year). These entities can only use a fiscal year-end if they can show that it constitutes the natural year-end for their particular business. This became even more difficult to demonstrate under TRA '86. Regular corporations may adopt any year-end they choose.

In selecting a tax year several factors, such as natural business year, year-end of principal shareholder/employees, timing of various elections, etc., should be taken into consideration. The tax year-end selected ordinarily also should be used in keeping books and records for your business operations to eliminate complicated adjustments between book and tax information.

Accounting Methods. The term "accounting method" refers to the rules for computing taxable income and, more specifically, the timing of the recognition of specific items of income and deductions. There are two overall methods of accounting that may be used in keeping books and records and computing taxable income—the cash method and the accrual method. In addition, there are several special methods that will affect the tax treatment of certain items of income and expense.

Cash versus Accrual. TRA '86 imposed strict limitations on the use of the cash method of accounting. In general, corporations and partnerships with corporate partners (other than S corporations and personal service corporations) must use the accrual method of accounting unless average gross receipts of the business over a three-year period do not exceed $5 million annually.

S corporations, sole proprietorships, certain personal service corporations and partnerships with no corporate partners may use the cash method of accounting. However, if your business is involved in the production, purchase and sale of merchandise, and thus maintains inventories for ultimate sale to the customer, you must use the accrual method.

Under the cash method of accounting, income is reported when actually or constructively received and expenses are deducted when paid. For businesses using the accrual method, income is included and deductions are allowable in the year when all events have occurred that either fix the right to receive the income or establish the liability, and the amount can be determined with reasonable accuracy.

The election to use a particular accounting method is ordinarily made by using that method on the business entity's first tax return. It is usually necessary to obtain permission from the Internal Revenue Service (IRS), and possibly one or more states, to change established accounting methods—either the overall method or the treatment of specific items. Normally, requests are made within the first 180 days of the taxable year for which the change is to be effective.

Planning Idea

Businesses that provide services will generally find it beneficial to use the cash method of accounting. This will allow income to be deferred until actually received. Even though expenses may not be deducted until paid, service businesses typically have fewer expenses than manufacturing, retailing and other ventures, so the benefit from income deferral should outweigh the negative aspects. Caution: The business must be eligible to use the cash method of accounting.

Other Methods. There are several other accounting methods that apply to specific income and expense items, including:

☐ Depreciation methods
☐ Inventory methods
☐ Long-term contract methods
☐ Installment sale method
☐ Elections to expense or capitalize certain items (e.g., research and development costs, circulation expenditures, intangible

drilling costs)

☐ Amortization of organization costs and start-up expenditures.

Several of these methods are discussed later in this chapter or in other chapters of this book.

Start-Up Elections

Start-Up Expenditures. Start-up expenditures include amounts paid to investigate the acquisition of a business, create a business or in anticipation of future business activity. These costs must be capitalized and may be amortized over a period of not less than 60 months, beginning with the month in which the active trade or business begins. The election to amortize these costs should be made in a statement attached to the return for the tax year in which the amortization period begins.

Organizational Expenditures. Organizational expenditures include costs incurred in creating the entity, such as legal fees, accounting fees and incorporation fees. These amounts must be capitalized, and may also be amortized over a period of not less than 60 months. A statement electing to amortize these costs should be made with the tax return for the taxable year in which business begins.

Syndication costs and costs associated with issuing stock of a corporation, or interests in partnership, must be capitalized and may *not* be amortized.

Research and Development Costs. You may either expense research and development (R&D) costs or capitalize and amortize these costs over a period of not less than 60 months. The treatment may vary from project to project. For purposes of this election, research and development costs include those incurred in experimentation or in the laboratory.

The election to capitalize and amortize these costs is made in a statement attached to the return for the first taxable year to which the election is applicable. The election to expense these costs is made by deducting them on the return for the taxable year in which the business first incurs the expenses. You may also be eligible for the R&D credit, which will be discussed later in this chapter.

First-year Expensing of Assets. In general, costs associated with acquiring an asset must be capitalized and depreciated over the life of the asset. There are numerous rules that prescribe the life and methods to be used in computing depreciation. In general, you may use either an accelerated depreciation method or the straight-line method. In addition, certain taxpayers may be eligible to expense up to $10,000 annually of the costs associated with acquiring depreciable personal property during the year. The $10,000 amount phases out dollar-for-dollar for expenditures in excess of $250,000 per year.

Intangible Drilling Costs. Costs incurred drilling oil and gas wells and preparing the wells for production must generally be capitalized and recovered through depletion or depreciation. However, you can elect to deduct rather than capitalize these costs. The election is made by deducting these costs on the return for the first year in which they are paid or incurred. Failure to deduct these expenses in a timely fashion will result in automatic capitalization of these costs.

Construction Period Interest and Taxes. In general, construction period interest and taxes must be capitalized and added to the basis of the property being constructed. Construction period interest includes interest directly or indirectly attributable to construction.

Planning Idea   Prior to filing the first income tax return of the entity, make sure all possible elections have been considered and, if necessary, included with the tax return.

Summary. There are many decisions that must be made either before your business begins or prior to filing its first tax return. Each of these decisions deserves careful consideration, because faulty judgments or failures to make elections may result in unintended or adverse tax consequences for you and your company.

DEBT VERSUS EQUITY

Chapter 4 discusses in detail the types of financing available to a business, including the advantages and disadvantages of using debt versus equity. Although the initial ratio of indebtedness to capital investment depends on the owner-manager's objectives and the existing market, as a business owner you should also consider the impact of this decision on your personal financial situation.

When much of the capital of the business is provided by owner-managers, it is generally advantageous to obtain the capital in the form of debt. The owner-manager is taxed only on the interest, which is deductible by the company. Generally, no further tax consequences result when the business repays the debt.

If the capital of a business is structured as equity, any repayment by the company probably would be taxed to the owner-manager as a dividend, unless it is treated as a return of capital. Regardless of the tax consequences to the owner-manager, the corporation is not entitled to a deduction for repayment of equity capital.

Although the use of debt may be more beneficial from an income tax standpoint, using too much debt may create a thin-capitalization problem and prompt the IRS to reclassify debt as equity. There are no set rules to determine whether a business is thinly capitalized, but some of the factors to consider are:

- [ ] Lack of a written obligation to pay a specified amount on demand or on a specified date
- [ ] Failure to provide a fixed interest rate
- [ ] A high ratio of debt-to-equity
- [ ] The percentage of debt held by each shareholder is the same as his percentage of stock ownership
- [ ] Debt is convertible into stock of the corporation.

There are numerous factors to be considered in the debt versus equity decision. Careful planning in the initial stages of business will help avoid the adverse tax consequences associated with reclassification of debt as equity. As noted above, these include potential taxability to the shareholder on repayment, and interest payments that are not allowed as deductions to the corporation. See Chapter 5 for additional issues to be considered in the debt versus equity question when considering different forms of doing business.

OPERATIONAL ISSUES

Owner Compensation

Once a business is doing well and has adequate cash flow, the owner-manager will have to consider whether to invest revenue in business expansion or withdraw it for personal use. If the funds are withdrawn, payments generally should be made as salaries rather than as dividends. In most cases, the tax consequences to an owner-manager will be the same whether the payments are salaries or dividends, but dividends are not deductible by the company. (In a partnership, the return of capital generally will neither be taxable to the partner nor deductible by the partnership.) Once a decision has been made to withdraw excess funds as salaries, the amount and timing of the payments must be considered.

Reasonable Compensation. In determining the amount of compensation, keep in mind that the IRS can challenge the amount as excessive or unreasonable. If salaries are considered unreasonable, no deduction will be allowed for the excess portion, and the excess could be treated as a dividend to the owner-manager. There are numerous factors that might support a substantial salary; for example, if little or no salary was paid during the start-up years or if the owner-manager has made a major contribution to the success of the company.

The IRS has considered the following factors to determine whether compensation is unreasonable:

☐ Extent of involvement in the business

☐ Importance of the owner-manager's contribution to the success of the company

☐ Salary levels of similar individuals in comparable companies

☐ History of dividend payments.

There are several factors that should be considered to determine a reasonable salary. These include the relationship between wages and retirement benefits, other forms of compensation, accumulated earnings problems (discussed later in this chapter), demands of other executives, as well as the effect on reduced earnings and profits and how they will affect the company's ability to obtain financing.

Business and Owner-Manager Tax Rates. There are many tax implications connected with owner-manager compensation and withdrawal of excess funds from a business. These issues should be considered not only in choosing the form of business but also in future years when the corporation is doing well.

The adverse tax consequences of certain cash distributions and the issue of unreasonable compensation for an owner-manager are not present where a business operates as a sole proprietorship. These issues are mitigated where S corporation status is elected. However, there are numerous other factors, discussed in Chapter 5, that may discourage one from using a sole proprietorship, or may preclude or prevent an S corporation election.

Salary received by an owner-manager is taxed as ordinary income. The business should be entitled to a deduction for the entire amount unless a portion is considered unreasonable. The major planning opportunity here involves the tax rates of the employer and employee to reduce combined taxes for the current year.

As a result of TRA '86, the maximum tax rate for corporations exceeds that for individuals. Thus, the use of an S corporation or partnership should generally be more beneficial unless earnings are low enough that compensation deductions would reduce a corporation's taxable income to the point where its effective tax rate would be lower than the individual's. This would reduce the double tax associated with regular corporations. The tax brackets of both the owners and the entity are critical to making this analysis.

If a business plans to distribute all or most of its income currently, the S corporation or partnership form are preferable to a regular corporation. The income will be taxed only once, at the shareholder or partner level. The double tax on corporate income and the problems of unreasonable compensation can be avoided. The advantages and disadvantages of corporations, partnerships and S corporations are discussed in greater detail in Chapter 5.

Timing. Timing the payment of business earnings to owner-managers is an important planning opportunity available to defer taxes. If the business uses the accrual method, bonuses and other compensation may be accrued at year-end but not paid until the beginning of the following year for owner-managers who own 50% or less of the business. The compensation will generally be deductible when accrued and taxable to the recipient when received, assuming the individual uses the cash method of accounting. Income tax may be deferred if the business and employee use the same taxable year.

There are, however, certain hazards associated with these year-end accruals, including *constructive receipt* and the requirement that the timing of a deduction match the income inclusion of payments to certain owner-managers.

Constructive Receipt. If an officer or other employee has unrestricted authority to decide when a payment is made, the IRS may contend that it was "constructively" received, that is, received in fact though not in form, and thus, should be taxed in the current year. This risk can be minimized if the board of directors decides that bonuses will be paid in the following January or February, and will be determined by a formula based on the current year's financial results. This action must be taken early in the year; otherwise, the IRS may contend that bonuses to owner-managers are really disguised dividends. The IRS is especially likely to take this position if the decision comes after it is apparent that profits will be better than expected.

Payments to Shareholders or Partners. An accrual-method business that accrues expenses for payments to cash-method *related parties* is not permitted to deduct those expenses until payment is actually made. A regular corporation and an individual who owns more than 50% of the value of the corporate stock, directly or indirectly, are considered related parties. In a partnership, any person who owns any capital interest or profits interest is considered a related party. In an S corporation, any person who owns any stock of the corporation is a related party. These rules may also apply to payments between certain related entities.

In the case of an individual owning 50% or less of the stock of the corporation, accrued bonuses or wages payable at year-end may be deducted by an accrual method business, if payment is made within 2 1/2 months after year-end. If payment is not made within the 2 1/2 month period, a deduction will be permitted only when the expense is paid.

The purpose of these provisions is to match the inclusion and deduction of various items and prevent abuses associated with tax deferral under prior law. These rules apply not only to compensation but also to other payments between related parties.

Fringe Benefits

Fringe benefits are in-kind compensation made available to owners and their employees in addition to base salary. Generally, fringe benefits are taxable, but special rules provide for exclusion of certain fringe benefits from gross income.

In structuring owner and employee compensation, your company should be aware of the tax consequences of the fringe benefits it offers. In general, an employee must include in income the amount, if any, by which the fair market value of the taxable portion of the fringe benefit exceeds the sum of the amount the employee pays for such benefit. Under these rules, virtually all fringe benefits will be taxable to employees unless they fall under a specific exception.

There are four general categories of benefits that employees don't have to include in income:

☐ No-additional-cost services
☐ Qualified employee discounts
☐ Working condition fringes
☐ *De minimis* fringes.

No-Additional-Cost Services. An employee may use certain services provided by the employer without any additional income if:

☐ The same service is offered to customers

☐ The employee provides substantial services in the same line of business, and

☐ The employer does not incur substantial additional costs in providing the service to the employee.

Qualified Employee Discounts. An employee may also receive certain discounts on property or services that the employer offers to customers in the ordinary course of business, excluding real property and personal property commonly held for investment. For merchandise, the discount exclusion is limited to the employer's gross profit percentage for that line of business for the previous year. For services, the discount exclusion is limited to 20% of the regular selling price. As with the no-additional-cost service fringe benefit, the discount must be for property or services offered for sale to customers in the ordinary course of the line of business in which the recipient-employee performs substantial services.

Working Condition Fringe Benefits. The value of a working condition fringe benefit may also be excluded from an employee's gross income. Working condition fringe benefits include any property or service provided by an employer that, if paid for by the employee, would give rise to a trade or business expense deduction. The personal use of any benefit will not qualify for exclusion. In addition, the benefit must be related to the employee's duties in the employer's business. Working condition fringe benefits include items such as employer-provided transportation, consumer goods furnished to employees for product tests and demonstrator autos furnished to dealer salespersons. Specific rules for employee use of a company auto are discussed in greater detail in the next section.

De Minimis Fringe Benefits. A *de minimis* fringe benefit includes any property or service provided infrequently to employees where the value of the benefit is so small as to make accounting for it administratively impractical. Some common benefits include typing of personal letters by company secretaries, personal use of a company copy machine, holiday gifts of low value and company picnics.

Benefits not qualifying for exclusion would include season tickets to sporting events, memberships in country or athletic clubs and regular use of an employer-provided auto for commuting.

Vacation Pay. Employers often establish vacation pay plans for their employees. In general, vacation pay is subject to deferred compensation provisions that preclude a current deduction for accrued compensation paid more than 2 1/2 months after the end of the year. However, there is an election available to employers that allows them to deduct accrued vacation pay currently if it is expected to be paid during the taxable year or within 8 1/2 months after the close of the taxable year. The election must be made in a statement attached to the tax return for the first year in which a vacation pay plan is maintained.

Planning Idea

> In order to ensure deductibility of accrued vacation pay, the vacation pay plan should include language that requires employees to take their vacation within 8 1/2 months after the close of the taxable year.

Medical Expense Reimbursement. In addition to the fringe benefits listed above, there are a few other fringe benefits that may be provided tax-free to employees. One such benefit commonly offered by companies is a medical expense reimbursement plan.

The company may provide for reimbursement of medical expenses incurred by an employee and his family, including those expenses not covered by the company's medical insurance plan, such as visits to the dentist, glasses and the deductibles under an insurance policy. There are three ways to fund this type of plan:

☐ *Purchase of Additional Insurance.* Currently, medical insurance may be provided on a discriminatory basis; that is, it can cover any number of employees. However, it should be noted that because of recent tax legislation these benefits are taxable to highly compensated employees beginning in 1988 or 1989 if provided under a discriminatory arrangement. Under current law, the premiums are deductible by the company and the benefits (including premiums paid by the company) are tax-free to the employee. "Administrative services only" plans, in which premiums equal losses incurred plus a fee for processing claims, generally will not qualify as insurance for this purpose. However, employers will be able to deduct claim amounts and administrative costs when paid or incurred.

☐ *Adoption of a Nondiscriminatory Self-Insurance Plan.* The plan must provide reimbursement by the company of the medical expenses on a nondiscriminatory basis. In testing for discrimination, those employees under age 25 and those who do not have at least three years of service can be disregarded. (Union members may be excluded if collective bargaining covers medical benefits.) The payments are deductible by the company and tax-free to recipients.

☐ *Adoption of a Discriminatory Self-Insured Medical Reimbursement Plan.* The plan can cover one or more officers. Although the payments may be deductible by the company, they are taxable to the recipient.

Summary. Numerous fringe benefits can be provided to employees. In determining compensation and fringe benefit arrangements, care should be taken to ensure that, to the extent possible, all benefits provided will be deductible by the company and that such benefits will not be taxable to the employee.

Travel, Meal, and Entertainment Expenses

There are few expense items that give rise to more disputes with the IRS than amounts claimed for travel, meals and entertainment. The usual controversy is over whether a particular item of expense is deductible and, if so, the actual amount of the item incurred. An understanding of the rules governing these deductions should help minimize challenges by the IRS, or at least arm you for the battle.

20% Disallowance. TRA '86 imposed a significant limitation on deductions for business meals (including those while away on travel) and entertainment. In general, deductions for these expenses will be limited to 80% of the amount otherwise allowable. Travel expenses (except meals) generally are not subject to the 20% disallowance rule. However, there are additional limitations on travel-related deductions, as noted below.

Travel Expenses. Travel expenses are the reasonable costs incurred by a self-employed individual or an employee while traveling away from home. Travel expenses incurred for personal activities are, of course, not deductible.

An employer may claim a deduction for travel expenses only if he has actually paid for, or is obligated to pay for, the expense. In addition, the recordkeeping requirements discussed below must be met. If an employee is not fully reimbursed for the travel expenses he has incurred, the unreimbursed portion will generally be deductible by the employee on his personal tax return as an itemized deduction (subject to a 2% adjusted gross income floor), provided the recordkeeping requirements have been met. The most common type of travel expenses include:

- [ ] Air, rail and bus fares
- [ ] Operation and maintenance of an automobile while away from home
- [ ] Taxi fares or other transportation costs to and from airports, hotels, etc.
- [ ] Meals and lodging while away from home (see additional limitations below)
- [ ] Cleaning and laundry expenses
- [ ] Telephone charges
- [ ] Tips incidental to a legitimate travel expense.

Ordinary and Necessary. "Reasonable," in a travel expense context, means "ordinary and necessary." An expense is ordinary if it is the type normally incurred in the company's line of business; it need not be recurring. An expense is generally considered necessary if it is helpful in the production of income.

Travel expenses deemed lavish or extravagant will be disallowed. What is lavish or extravagant is a question of judgment. An expense will not be considered lavish or extravagant merely because it exceeds a specified dollar amount or because it was incurred traveling first class, staying at a first-class hotel or dining at a first-class restaurant.

Away from Home. Travel expenses must be incurred while away from home. Generally, the metropolitan area where the principal or regular place of business or employment is located is considered home, regardless of the location of the individual's family residence. If an employee has no principal place of business, his home is the place where he maintains his family residence.

Away from home, for tax purposes, means away for a period longer than the normal workday, if the time away is long enough to require rest.

Business Purpose. Travel expenses must be incurred for business rather than for personal activities to be deductible; sightseeing expenses on a business trip would not be deductible. Expenses incurred by a spouse or friend on a business trip are deductible only if the presence of these parties on the trip serves some substantial business purpose.

TRA '86 imposed new limitations on the type of travel expenses that may be deducted. Under these rules, costs associated with investment seminars (unrelated to the taxpayer's trade or business) and certain educational and charitable travel will not be deductible.

Planning Idea	A portion of costs incurred on a family vacation may be deductible with proper planning. Where appropriate, a business aspect may be incorporated into a vacation. A greater benefit will result if business is the predominant purpose for the travel. In addition, expenses attributable to a spouse may be deductible if the spouse's attendance has a substantial business purpose.

Entertainment Expenses. Entertainment expenses generally include the cost of recreation or amusement incurred in connection with the active conduct of a business, such as entertaining guests at nightclubs, restaurants, sporting events, theaters or country clubs. Other entertainment activities could include providing food and drink, a hotel room or use of an automobile or private plane to a business customer or his family. In order for entertainment expenses to be deductible, they must be either directly related to or associated with business.

Direct Relation to Business. An entertainment expense must meet all of the following conditions to be considered directly related to the active conduct of a business:

- [ ] At the time of the expense, there was more than a general expectation of deriving income or some other specific benefit at some time in the future
- [ ] A business discussion was maintained with the person being entertained during the period (discussed later) when the entertainment was taking place
- [ ] The primary purpose of the combined business and entertainment meeting was to transact business
- [ ] The expense must be applicable to the individual and person or persons with whom trade or business is conducted.

The IRS presumes that entertainment expenses incurred in a clear business setting are directly related to the business. Generally, the following situations are considered to be clear business settings:

- [ ] Entertainment at a hospitality room at a convention
- [ ] Entertainment of civic or business leaders at public events to obtain publicity
- [ ] Entertainment when no meaningful social or personal relationship exists between the person being entertained and the person entertaining.

If the entertainment does not take place in a clear business setting, you should document that a substantial business discussion occurred during the entertainment. If the entertainment occurs at a place where there is little or no possibility of conducting a business discussion, the expenditure will generally not be considered to have met the directly related test.

Associated with a Business. Even if an expense is not directly related to the business, it will still be deductible if it is associated with it. To be associated with the business, the entertainment must have directly preceded or followed a bona fide business discussion. What constitutes a bona fide business discussion depends on facts and circumstances. The facts should indicate that the parties actively conducted a discussion, meeting, negotiation or some other type of business transaction.

Generally, a business discussion will be considered to directly precede or follow entertainment if the discussion and entertainment took place on the same day. If the entertainment and business discussion do not occur on the same day, then a determination will be made based on the facts, including the place, date and duration of the business discussions and whether the business associate or the person entertained is away from home, and if so, when he arrived and departed.

Other Criteria. As with travel expenses, only those entertainment activities that are deemed ordinary and necessary, that are not lavish or extravagant, and for which proper records are maintained are deductible.

Entertainment Facilities Owned by the Taxpayer. Any property that a taxpayer owns, rents, or uses primarily for entertainment, amusement, or recreation will be classified as an entertainment facility. The costs of operating and maintaining such a facility are not deductible. However, the costs associated with business activities held within the facilities should be deductible provided that the facility is used primarily in furthering a trade or business and the expense is directly related to business. Entertainment facilities include items such as yachts, hunting and ski lodges, vacation homes and swimming pools.

A facility is deemed to have been used primarily in the furtherance of a trade or business if, based on the number of days of actual
use, the facility is used more than 50% of the time for business
purposes. Even if the 50% threshold is met, a deduction is allowed
only for costs directly related to business. If the 50% threshold is
not met (e.g., a club is used 45% of the time for business), no
expenses may be deducted — not even the 45% directly related to
business.

Country Club Dues. Country clubs and business luncheon clubs
are often ideal places to entertain customers, suppliers, bankers and
others potentially beneficial to the business. You can deduct dues
and fees charged by country clubs if more than 50% of the use of
the club is for business purposes — that is, directly related to and
primarily in furtherance of the business. The proportion of business
use is determined by comparing the number of days (not dollars)
used for business purposes with total days used. Under outstanding
regulations, luncheon club dues are not required to meet the 50%
threshold test, but only the tests of whether they are directly related
to or associated with business.

Limitations. Ticket costs in excess of the face value of a ticket are
not deductible. If the rental cost of private luxury boxes at sporting
events exceeds the cost of regular box seat tickets, the deduction
for the excess will be phased out and completely eliminated for
taxable years beginning in 1989.

As mentioned previously, entertainment expenses, including expenses associated with entertainment facilities, are subject to the
20% disallowance rule. If an employer reimburses an employee for
entertainment expenses, the 80% limitation will apply to the employer. If the entertainment is treated as compensation to the recipient, the disallowance rule does not apply and the entire amount
would be deductible by the employer. The employee would report
the compensation as income and would deduct the entertainment
expense subject to the 80% limitation and the substantiation rules.
Employer-paid recreational expenses, such as holiday parties, are
excepted from any limitation.

Business Meals. You can deduct the cost of business meals if the expenditure is ordinary and necessary to the conduct of your trade or business and either the "directly related to" or "associated with" test is met. These tests are nearly identical to those discussed above for entertainment expenses. In addition, the expense must be substantiated with adequate documentation and may not be lavish or extravagant.

Limitations. The 20% disallowance rule will apply to those expenses otherwise qualifying for deduction. In addition to the typical business meal involving you and your business associates, the limitation will apply to meals taken while traveling away from home on business and meals furnished on employer premises.

If a business meal is treated as compensation to an employee, the cost is fully deductible by the company. If an employer reimburses an employee for the cost of a business meal, the employer is subject to the 80% limitation. The cost of meals provided as part of certain banquet meetings will not be deductible after 1988. (These amounts can be deducted in full during 1987 and 1988.)

Recordkeeping. In order to claim deductions for travel, entertainment and business meals, the substantiation requirements must be met. There are two permissible methods for substantiating these expenses—"adequate records" or "sufficient corroborative evidence."

Adequate Records. Under the adequate records method, you must use account books, diaries, logs, statements of expense or similar records supported by documentary evidence such as receipts, paid bills, etc. The records should be made at or near the time of the expenditure and any business meal or entertainment expense over $25 should be supported by documentary evidence. Such evidence is required for travel expenses regardless of amount. Records should include the amount, time, place, business purpose and business relationship, where applicable.

Sufficient Corroborative Evidence. If you do not maintain adequate records, the substantiation requirement may be met by using sufficient corroborative evidence. The evidence can be your own written or oral statements containing sufficient detailed information to support the deduction. However, remember that written evidence created at or near the time of the expenditure generally will have the highest credibility. Estimates of expenses will no longer be sufficient; the so-called *Cohan* rule can no longer be used to substantiate meal and entertainment expenses.

These recordkeeping requirements apply to nearly all types of expenses incurred in connection with travel, entertainment and business meals, including business meals and travel away from home. There are a few situations where substantiation is not required, such as certain meals for employees provided on the employer's business premises, expenses treated as compensation and expenses relating to recreational activities for employees.

Planning Ideas

There are several items that should be considered in developing the business meal and entertainment policies of a company. With proper planning, a company can ensure the greatest benefit from these expenditures.

☐ Require employees to maintain records of all business expenses with meal costs separately stated

☐ Determine whether the business or employees will be subject to the 80% limitation and set policies accordingly

☐ Structure meal allowance policies to qualify as *de minimis* fringe benefits, if possible

☐ Establish written policies as to necessity, frequency and business purpose of business/client and employer/employee business meals and entertainment.

Automobiles and Other Listed Property

The Tax Reform Act of 1984 (TRA '84) imposed special limitations on depreciation and other deductions associated with "listed property" that is used for both business and personal purposes. Listed property includes assets such as automobiles, property used for entertainment or recreation and computer equipment. The law also imposed strict recordkeeping requirements to substantiate deductions associated with the use of listed property.

In general, the limitations on depreciation and other deductions are based on the proportion of business and personal use of the property. The depreciation deduction for automobiles is subject to even further limitation.

Automobiles. In the case of a self-employed individual or an employee who owns his own auto, expenditures will be deductible only when they relate to the business use of the auto. Unreimbursed costs incurred by an employee will be allowed as a miscellaneous itemized deduction only when all such deductions exceed 2% of adjusted gross income. Costs attributable to personal use, including commuting to and from work, are not deductible.

To determine deductible expenses, an individual may use either his actual expenses or the optional mileage method, whereby the amount of the expense is based on business mileage. If one car is used for both business and personal purposes, actual costs must be allocated between the business and nonbusiness portions based on mileage. As discussed below, it is essential to maintain mileage records to support these deductions.

Where the company provides an auto to either owner or employee, associated costs are deductible in full by the employer, provided that the employee or owner is taxed on the value of any personal use. The recordkeeping requirements must also be met. Deductible automobile expenses include the cost of fuel, oil, repairs, maintenance, insurance, licenses, washing, automobile club memberships and depreciation.

Depreciation. Whether the auto is owned by an employee or the company, there are limitations on both the annual depreciation deduction and the method used to compute depreciation.

If the business use of the auto is 50% or less, the straight-line method must be used to compute depreciation and first-year expensing is not allowed. If business use exceeds 50%, accelerated depreciation (ACRS) and additional first-year expensing are available to the taxpayer. However, if business use declines to 50% or less in future years, the accelerated portion of the depreciation will be restored ("recaptured") in the year use declines.

In general, personal use will constitute "business use" for purposes of the 50% test if the fair market value of the personal use of the auto is included in the employee's compensation. However, personal use by a more-than-5% owner-manager, the value of which is included in compensation, will not constitute business use. Whether or not the employee is a 5% owner, the employer may still depreciate 100% of the cost of the auto but the method—accelerated versus straight-line—may differ.

Dollar Limitations. Regardless of the method used to compute depreciation, the deduction will be limited to $2,560 for the first year, $4,100 for the second year, $2,450 for the third year and $1,475 for each succeeding year. These amounts are adjusted for inflation after 1988. The dollar limitation for the first year also applies if additional first-year expensing is elected.

Leased Automobiles. In general, the lessee of an automobile may deduct all costs associated with the business use of the auto, including lease payments. However, the benefit of these deductions is limited in a manner comparable to the restrictions that would apply if the auto had been purchased. The lessee is required to include in gross income an amount based on the fair market value of the auto and the business use. The amount included in income is determined using IRS tables.

Employee Compensation. If an employee uses an employer-provided auto for personal use, the fair market value of this use, less any amount paid by the employee to the employer, must be included in the employee's compensation. The employer's deduction is limited to actual costs associated with the automobile. Since the employer has deducted the costs as automobile expenses, no additional deduction may be taken for the compensation associated with personal use by an employee. There are several methods that may be used to determine the value of the personal use including special rules that apply where the auto is used only for commuting. An employer also can treat 100% of the value of the auto use as compensation, in which case the employee would be entitled to deductions for any business use of the automobile.

Other Listed Property. The limitations on deductions relating to "other listed property," such as computer equipment, are similar to those for automobiles. Business use must exceed 50% in order for the owner to take accelerated depreciation and/or additional first-year expensing. However, depreciation on this property is not subject to annual dollar limitations. The regular limitation for additional first-year expensing will apply if this provision is elected. (The limitation for additional first-year expensing is equal to the lesser of $10,000 or taxable income. The $10,000 amount is reduced dollar-for-dollar to the extent that the cost of eligible assets placed in service during the year exceeds $200,000.)

Leased property. If other listed property is used more than 50% for business purposes, the lessee is not required to include an amount in gross income (as discussed above under Leased Automobiles). However, if business use is 50% or less, a one-time amount must be included in income based on a formula and IRS tables.

Planning Idea

Prior to acquiring a company auto or other listed property, you should analyze the tax consequences of both a lease and purchase. Depending on the circumstances, it may be more beneficial for owner-managers to use their own automobiles. All possibilities and factors should be considered, including the tax brackets of both the business and owner-managers.

Substantiation and Recordkeeping. All deductions claimed for listed property must be substantiated either by adequate records or sufficient corroborative evidence. These terms are defined above under the recordkeeping requirements for travel, entertainment and business meals. Because the most credible evidence is an adequate record maintained at or near the time of the expenditure, it is advisable to maintain a diary or log where feasible. Supporting records should contain the amount of acquisition and maintenance costs for the property, the business use and total use, and the time and place.

There are several exceptions and short-cuts to these requirements that may apply, depending on the actual use of the property. In addition, if the employer treats all of the employee's use of an auto as personal use, the employer is exempted from the recordkeeping requirements and the employee must keep records in order to deduct any expenses for business use of the auto.

Planning Idea   Develop logs or expense reports that can be used to capture all of the information required to substantiate deductions. Establish company policy on the use of these logs or reports.

Summary. The rules for listed property are very detailed. To obtain the greatest benefit from using listed property in a business, these rules should be reviewed periodically and in connection with acquisition of any listed property.

Research and Development Activities

Many businesses are involved in research and development (R&D) activities. The expenses incurred for these activities may provide substantial tax savings through both deductions and credits. You can either deduct or elect to capitalize and amortize research and experimental expenditures as discussed earlier in this chapter. Most of these expenditures may also be used to compute the Credit for Increasing Research Activities, or the R&D credit.

Deductible Expenditures. To deduct (or capitalize and amortize)

R&D expenses, the costs must be incurred in connection with your trade or business and must represent research and development costs in the experimental or laboratory sense. Expenditures incurred for contract research may also qualify. In general, deductible costs include those incident to the development or improvement of a pilot model, plant process, product, formula, invention or other similar property. Costs associated with marketing, routine inspections and improvements, ordinary testing and trial production runs don't qualify as R&D expenses. However, these costs should be deductible as ordinary and necessary business expenses.

Development of Computer Software. Costs associated with developing computer software or modifying previously developed software generally will not qualify as R&D expenses. However, programming costs paid for new or significantly improved computer software may qualify if the operational feasibility of such software is seriously in doubt.

Expenditures Qualifying for the Credit. If the costs incurred are considered R&D expenses, they will generally qualify for the R&D credit. However, under TRA '86 it will be more difficult for these expenses to qualify for the credit. The expenditures must be technological in nature, useful in developing a new or improved business component and associated with experimentation for a functional purpose.

The credit applies only when there is an increase in research activities. This is determined by comparing current-year expenses to a base period amount. The credit will equal 20% of the excess. In-house research expenses (e.g., wages and amounts paid for supplies) and 65% of certain contract research expenses qualifies for the credit. There is also a similar 20% credit available to those taxpayers who make payments to qualified organizations for basic research.

Computer Software. The test to determine whether research costs for developing computer software qualify for the R&D credit differs from the test for determining whether these costs qualify as R&D expenses. In general, research costs incurred developing computer software for internal use will not qualify for the R&D credit unless the software is used in connection with certain research activities. If the research expenses qualify for the credit, the costs incurred for developing computer software to be used conducting this research should qualify for the credit.

Computer Software Royalty Income. Many companies are engaged in the business of developing and licensing computer software. Whether the related expenses are R&D expenses and the treatment of the royalties received under a licensing arrangement may be tax planning issues.

As discussed later in this chapter, certain closely held companies that receive substantial passive income may be subject to the personal holding company (PHC) tax. Prior to the TRA '86, many companies ran into PHC problems as a result of these software royalties. The TRA '86 added a provision that allows companies to exclude software royalties from PHC income if certain requirements are met. Thus, the use of a corporate entity to develop and license software should be more feasible.

TAX ACCOUNTING MATTERS

Inventories

Many small companies are engaged in businesses that require them to maintain inventories. As discussed earlier in this chapter, these companies must use the accrual method of accounting. In addition, they must select a method for valuing their inventory. Several factors must be considered to determine the best inventory method for a particular business, including the type of product being sold and the direction of the overall economy.

Undervaluation. Many small businesses undervalue inventories in an attempt to minimize taxable income. This may be accomplished by creating liberal reserves for obsolescence or excess quantities. In addition to being an improper accounting method, intentional understatement of inventories can constitute fraud and company officers could be subject to civil and criminal penalties. There are several other disadvantages to undervaluing inventories including:

☐ The undervalued portion may not be insured under the company's property and liability insurance policy

☐ Banks probably will not lend against the undervalued inventory

☐ The company's balance sheet may understate the real financial strength of the business

☐ Product pricing, ordering lead times and warehouse requirements are all difficult to determine without reliable inventory data

☐ Full value for the inventory may be difficult to obtain if the entire business is sold

☐ Possible shrinkage through theft or error could go undetected with undervalued inventory.

While the undervaluation of inventories may have adverse consequences, there are significant tax planning opportunities available where a permissible method is used to value inventories.

The Last-In, First-Out Method. An effective method for minimizing taxable income during a period of rising costs is to value inventory using the last-in, first-out (LIFO) method. Under this method, inventory is valued on the basis of the oldest costs and current costs are expensed as part of cost of sales. Consequently, in times of rising prices, the current, more expensive products are included in cost of sales, while the older, less expensive ones are included in inventory for valuation purposes.

There are two overall LIFO inventory methods—the dollar-value method and the unit method. Under the dollar-value method, LIFO inventory is grouped into pools of *substantially similar* items and a separate LIFO inventory value is computed for each pool, based on the total dollar value of the pool. Under the unit method, a separate LIFO inventory pool is established for *each type* of inventory item and a separate LIFO inventory value is calculated for each pool, based on the quantity of items on hand in the pool. Since most companies' inventories consist of numerous types of items, the dollar-value method is used more often because it simplifies calculations.

Unlike other changes in inventory methods, a change to the LIFO method does not require prior approval by the IRS. The LIFO method may be elected when a business files its income tax return. If it is used for tax purposes, it must also be used for financial reporting purposes. Thus, the decision to use LIFO must actually be made prior to issuance of the financial statements, if this occurs before the return is filed. Once the LIFO method is elected, a change of methods must be approved by the IRS.

There are both advantages and disadvantages to using the LIFO method:

Advantages

☐ In times of rising prices, taxable income is lower and, therefore, federal and state income taxes are deferred. (Before adopting LIFO, you should consider the likelihood of inventory prices falling below base-year prices at some point in the future.)

☐ Income tax payments, quarterly or total, are reduced.

☐ Lower income taxes will increase cash flow and, therefore, reduce borrowings.

Disadvantages

☐ Lower financial statement earnings and inventory values may adversely affect items such as loan agreements or pension and profit sharing plans that are based on earnings formulas. Existing agreements may have to be modified if LIFO is elected. (If financial statements are provided to banks, supplemental disclosures may reflect earnings and net worth on a FIFO, or current-cost basis.)

☐ A sale, merger or public offering could be adversely affected by the lower earnings.

☐ LIFO inventory must be valued at cost for tax purposes. In the year in which LIFO is elected, inventory writedowns in beginning inventory must be included in income ratably over a three-year period.

☐ Non-LIFO companies in the same industry will show higher financial earnings.

☐ LIFO inventory calculations are more complicated.

☐ Ending inventory balances less than beginning inventory can trigger ordinary income.

Over a period of years, the difference between current inventory prices and the LIFO price can be quite substantial. The difference in these prices, multiplied by the company's income tax rate, equals the LIFO tax savings. Furthermore, the higher current year inventory prices can be shown in footnotes to the company's financial statements. As a result, inventories can be managed more effectively and the inventory can serve as loan collateral and will be eligible for insurance.

The First-In, First-Out Method. Under the first-in, first-out (FIFO) method of inventory valuation, the cost of units purchased most recently is used to determine inventory value and the cost of older units is used to compute cost of goods sold. In times of falling prices, FIFO will be beneficial for the same reason that LIFO is best when prices are rising. In recent years, some high technology industries, such as manufacturers of computers and telecommunications equipment, have found it advantageous to use FIFO.

Inventories of Wholesalers, Retailers and Manufacturers. In addition to the various methods for valuing inventories, there are rules that set forth costs that must be included in inventory. A manufacturer must capitalize both direct and indirect production costs as inventory costs. In the case of a wholesaler or retailer, all costs incurred acquiring goods must be capitalized as inventory costs. Starting in 1987, wholesalers and retailers must capitalize the following additional costs:

☐ costs incident to purchasing inventory (e.g., wages of employees responsible for purchasing)

☐ repackaging, assembly and other costs incurred in processing goods

☐ offsite costs of storing goods (e.g., rent or depreciation, insurance premiums and taxes attributable to the warehouse and wages of warehouse personnel)

☐ the portion of general and administrative costs allocable to these functions.

Change in Inventory Method. Prior approval from the IRS is required to change your inventory method. Permission must be obtained even if the present inventory method is incorrect. Any income resulting from a voluntary change in accounting method can be spread over a number of years. The maximum spread period for most inventory changes is three years.

Capital Gains and Gain Deferral

Before TRA '86, the sale of assets used in a trade or business (other than assets such as inventory or accounts receivable), generally meant favorable tax consequences for the seller. Gains from the sale of property held for more than six months were taxed at preferential long-term capital gain rates, although in many cases the law required all or a portion of the gain to be characterized as ordinary income if the asset had been depreciated prior to sale, or if losses on similar property had been taken during the five preceding tax years. If an asset was sold at a loss, it was generally deductible as an ordinary loss. This treatment was preferable because of the limitations imposed on capital loss deductions.

TRA '86 eliminated preferential treatment of capital gains, which are now taxed as ordinary income. In addition, the law generally retains the limitations imposed on the deductibility of capital losses. For individuals, capital losses that exceed capital gains may offset dollar-for-dollar only $3,000 of ordinary income. In the case of a corporation, capital losses may only be used to offset capital gains.

As a result of these changes, many planning opportunities and tax-saving strategies have disappeared. However, there are still several planning opportunities that relate to the timing of tax consequences rather than reduction of the amount of tax.

One factor to consider in timing any taxable disposition of depreciable personal property is that no ACRS (depreciation) is allowed in the year of disposition. Depending on the situation, it may be preferable to take a depreciation deduction in the current year and report a higher gain in a subsequent year than to report a smaller gain in the current year without any depreciation. If investment credit (ITC) recapture is still an issue, it may be beneficial to defer the sale to reduce or eliminate potential ITC recapture. Other methods for deferring gain are discussed below.

Installment Sales. If you are planning to sell property at a gain, you may consider financing the sale and receiving payments in installments. This technique may be used to postpone recognition of the gain and payment of related taxes until installment payments are received.

TRA '86, however, reduced the benefit of installment sales (where the selling price exceeds $150,000) by inputing deemed payments. Based on a ratio of total indebtedness to total assets, a portion of the amount owed on an installment obligation will be treated as received each year. Gain recognition is based on the deemed payments rather than on actual payments.

There are several factors to consider in determining whether to finance the sale. These include the credit standing of the buyer, the impact of the original issue discount and imputed interest provisions and your income tax bracket for the year(s) in which gain will be recognized. In addition, any gain attributable to depreciation recapture must be recognized in the year of sale, even if no payments are received in that year. Gain may be recognized due to either the deemed payment rule or depreciation recapture in years when little or no cash is received. You should make sure that adequate cash will be available to pay any tax due.

Like-Kind Exchanges. Another method of gain deferral involves a like-kind exchange. In general, real estate and certain other business or investment property (other than stock) can be exchanged for property of a like-kind without current tax on the gain. However, if cash or other property (referred to as "boot") is received in the exchange, any gain, based on the fair market value of the cash and/or other property received, must be recognized.

A like-kind exchange should be considered if a gain would be realized on the disposition of the asset and you plan to replace the asset with similar property. Even if the owner of the replacement property is not willing to make a trade, it may be possible to arrange a multiple party transaction to achieve tax deferral.

Generally, any like-kind property must be identified and the exchange completed not more than 180 days after the transfer of the original property.

There may be situations in which a like-kind exchange is not the best strategy. If you have expiring net operating or capital loss carryovers, it may be preferable to recognize the gain in the current year. Another consideration is that an outright sale at a gain, followed by the purchase of a similar asset, will generally give rise to considerably larger depreciation deductions. This is because the tax basis of property received in a like-kind exchange is the same as that of the property surrendered, increased by any recognized gain from the receipt of boot.

Because long-term capital gains no longer receive preferential treatment under TRA '86, transactions with no recognition, such as like-kind exchanges, have taken on increased tax planning significance. In determining whether to use a like-kind exchange, your overall tax situation must be considered.

Involuntary Conversions. You may be able to defer gain recognition if your property is destroyed (by casualty, theft, seizure, condemnation, etc.) and compulsorily or involuntarily converted into similar property or money. The replacement property must be similar or related in service or use, and if money is received, all of it must be used to acquire the necessary replacement property within two years after the close of the first taxable year in which any part of the gain upon conversion is realized. Gain must be recognized if the money received exceeds the cost of the replacement property. A loss through condemnation must always be recognized.

Passive Losses

For quite some time, certain kinds of investments have been used to shelter both earned income and portfolio income (e.g., dividends, interest, royalties, etc.). However, the tax savings associated with these investments diminish considerably as a result of TRA '86. The new law imposes strict limitations on the deductibility of losses and utilization of credits generated by certain "passive activities."

The passive activities to which this provision applies generally involve the conduct of a trade or business in which the investor does not materially participate on a regular, continuous and substantial basis. All limited partnerships and rental activities are considered passive activities. A separate set of rules govern the deductibility of losses from rental real estate.

Limitations. Under the new rules, passive activity losses generally can be offset only against passive activity income, and credits from passive activities are allowed only for the amount of actual tax liability arising from passive activity income. Losses and credits disallowed in one taxable year may be carried forward indefinitely. Any unused losses or credits may be utilized in full to offset future year's passive income, or upon a complete taxable disposition of the property constituting the passive activity. The passive loss limitation generally applies to individuals, estates, trusts, partnerships, S corporations and personal service corporations.

Regular corporations that are closely held (five or fewer shareholders own 50% or more of the stock) are subject to slightly different limitations. Passive losses may also be used to offset active trade or business income but not portfolio income.

S corporation shareholders who do not materially participate in the corporation's activities must treat their share of income or loss as passive. Thus, operating income from a profitable S corporation may currently offset the passive losses of a passive shareholder.

The passive loss limitation is effective for tax years beginning after 1986 with a four-year phase-in period.

Rental Real Estate. Individuals who actively participate in rental real estate activities (e.g., management of rental property) are allowed to deduct up to $25,000 annually of losses attributable to rental real estate if they exceed income from passive activities. The $25,000 allowance will be gradually reduced if the individual's adjusted gross income (AGI) exceeds $100,000 and completely eliminated if AGI exceeds $150,000.

Summary. As a result of these provisions, many investments will no longer be effective to provide shelter against income tax liabilities. You may want to consider using a regular corporation to invest in passive activities since the passive loss provisions do not apply unless the corporation is closely held. However, there may be disadvantages to using a corporation as discussed in Chapter 5.

Premature Accruals/Prepayment of Expenses

In an attempt to reduce taxable income in a particular year, taxpayers have devised various methods to accelerate deductions at year-end by either prepaying expenses or establishing a liability for an expenditure. Because such transactions may have allowed deductions before the expenses were incurred, new laws were enacted to attack these arrangements.

Premature Accruals. Under the accrual method of accounting, an expense is deductible when all events have occurred that establish the fact of the liability and the amount can be determined with reasonable accuracy. In addition, "economic performance" must take place before a deduction can be claimed. The economic performance requirement is designed to ensure that the time value of money is taken into account.

Economic performance normally occurs when property or services are provided, when property is used or when one provides property or renders services to satisfy a liability. For example, if a company signs a five-year management contract, management fees will be deductible only as the services are performed. Items of a recurring nature (e.g., year-end accrual of wages) generally will not be subject to the economic performance requirement if economic performance occurs within 8 1/2 months after year-end.

Workers' compensation and tort liabilities are subject to a special set of rules. Economic performance for these items does not occur until payment is made. The recurring item exception described above does not apply to these items.

Prepayment of Expenses. Before TRA '86, certain tax shelters, whether on the cash or accrual method of accounting, were not permitted to deduct prepaid expenses until economic performance occurred and the expenses were paid or incurred. The term "tax shelter" includes not only ventures that have a principal purpose of minimizing tax, but also enterprises (other than corporations that are not S corporations) for which sales of interests must be registered with federal or state agencies and enterprises where more than 35% of the losses are allocable to investors with limited liability. All these tax shelters must use the accrual method of accounting for their expenses.

Seller-Financed Transactions/Original Issue Discount

In the past, some taxpayers have attempted to obtain tax benefits by providing for little or no interest in structuring seller-financed transactions. The seller would benefit by converting ordinary interest income into long-term capital gain while the purchaser is still able to deduct the amount from ordinary income through depreciation. In addition, in a situation where the note provided for the payment of interest, a cash method seller could defer the inclusion of interest income while an accrual method purchaser was able to accrue a deduction for interest under the same sales contract.

In response to these abuses, there are now rules that recharacterize part of the purchase price as interest if the contract does not provide for adequate interest. If interest must be imputed, the original issue discount (OID) rules require the seller and buyer to recognize interest under the accrual method of accounting and, thus, properly match the inclusion and deduction of interest. After TRA '86, recharacterizing interest income as capital gain no longer results in any significant tax savings. However, the imputed interest rules still apply.

Original Issue Discount. The original issue discount rules will apply to most obligations issued for nontraded property. Under these rules, the interest income received by the seller will generally be matched with the interest deduction of the borrower. This is accomplished by comparing the stated interest rate with a test rate provided by the IRS. If sufficient interest is not unconditionally payable annually on a compounded basis, interest will be imputed at a specified rate. (The rates are determined monthly based on the average yields on federal obligations and will vary depending on the term of the obligation.)

For certain debt instruments where the stated principal does not exceed $2.8 million (adjusted for inflation after 1989), taxpayers may be eligible to use a 9% safe-harbor rate. If the interest rate is at least 9% compounded semi-annually, no interest will be imputed. This safe-harbor will not be very useful if the market interest rate is substantially below 9%.

Interest income must generally be recognized by the seller and interest expense deducted by the buyer on an economic accrual basis regardless of their methods of accounting. However, if the principal amount of the debt instrument does not exceed $2 million (adjusted for inflation after 1989) and the seller uses the cash method of accounting, both the seller and buyer may use the cash method to report interest if both parties do so and all of the requirements are met.

Certain transactions, such as the sale of a principal residence, sales of personal use property and sales involving total payments of $250,000 or less, are exempt from the OID provisions. However, these transactions may be subject to a different set of rules governing deferred payment transactions. Under these rules, interest will be imputed as under the OID provisions. However, interest income and expense will be reported under the accounting methods employed by the parties to the transaction.

Below-Market-Interest-Rate Loans. Prior to TRA '84, interest-free loans and loans with below-market interest rates were used to shift income among related parties. Under the new provisions, these loans are recharacterized as arm's-length transactions by first imputing a payment from the lender to the borrower to fund the correct amount of interest which is followed by a deemed payment of adequate interest by the borrower.

These rules apply in several situations, including gift loans, loans between a shareholder and corporation and loans between an employer and employee.

In a gift-loan situation (i.e., loans between friends and relatives), there will be a deemed gift of the imputed interest from the lender to the borrower, followed by a payment of interest from the borrower to the lender. In addition to the income tax consequences to both parties because of the interest payments, there may also be gift tax consequences to the lender on the deemed transfer of funds used in making the interest payments. In a shareholder/corporation situation, the imputed payment will be considered either a dividend or contribution to capital.

There will be income tax consequences for both parties as a result of the deemed interest payment. If the loan is from an employer to an employee, the deemed payment will be compensation and each party would have offsetting income and expense amounts, for interest and compensation, over the term of the loan.

The timing of the gift and income tax consequences associated with the transaction will vary depending on whether the loan is a term loan or a demand loan. In addition, the rate used to determine the imputed interest must generally be adjusted to correspond to the period for which the interest is being imputed.

There are several exceptions to the imputed interest provisions. For example, there are generally no income or gift tax consequences if the amount of a gift loan between an individual borrower and lender does not exceed $10,000. A similar exception applies to corporate/shareholder and employer/employee loans. Loans made in connection to property transactions are subject to the OID rules discussed above.

MISCELLANEOUS CONSIDERATIONS

Income Shifting

In the past, various methods have been used to shift investment income to family members in lower tax brackets to reduce the over-all tax burden on family income. For example, bonds or securities could be transferred to an elderly parent to support the parent. The income generated by these investments would be taxed at the parent's presumably lower tax rate. Upon the parent's death, the investments could be returned to the original owner, possibly without estate-tax consequences for the parent's estate.

TRA '86 included provisions that limit some of the benefits of shifting income to children under 14. However, there are still tax-saving opportunities in shifting income to other family members. The transfer of income-generating assets may be either temporary or permanent. If the transfer is permanent, there may be significant estate-tax savings in addition to income tax savings. With careful planning, gift tax consequences can also be minimized (see Chapter 12).

The income tax savings associated with these transfers can be significant. For example, assume an individual owns investment property that generates taxable interest income of $10,000 per year. The following table illustrates the interest remaining after taxes if the property is transferred to other family members.

| | AFTER-TAX INCOME | |
Recipient	1987	1988 and thereafter
Married individual in top bracket	$ 6,150	$ 6,700
Dependent child under 14[1]	$ 6,480	$ 6,955
Dependent child 14 or over[1]	$ 8,647	$ 8,575
Parents, if both are over 65	$10,000	$10,000
Nongrantor Trust[2]	$ 7,695	$ 7,878

[1]This assumes no other taxable income and no itemized deductions.
[2]This may be affected by distributions and certain other rules.

Shifting Income to Dependent Children

Children Under 14. As illustrated in the table above, TRA '86 limits the tax benefits associated with shifting income to children under 14. Under these provisions, unearned income, such as interest and dividends, will generally be taxed at the greater of the parents' top marginal rate or the child's own marginal rate for earnings in excess of $1,000. These rules apply regardless of the source of unearned income.

Clifford Trusts. Prior to TRA '86, Clifford trusts were often used to shift income to children. The trusts were set up as reversionary trusts with a term of more than ten years. This allowed trust distributions for the life of the trust to be taxed at the beneficiary's marginal rate. Under the new rules, these trusts are treated as grantor trusts where income earned on the property is taxable to the grantor. Although certain existing Clifford trusts will continue to qualify for beneficial treatment, Clifford trusts will no longer be effective in reducing taxes by shifting income to dependent children.

Shifting Income to Other Family Members

Irrevocable Trusts. One method of shifting income involves the use of an irrevocable trust. Assets are transferred to the trust, and income generated from the assets may either be distributed and taxed to the beneficiary or retained and taxed at the trust level. The assets may not revert back to grantors or their spouses.

In establishing the trust, the tax brackets of the grantor, beneficiaries and trust should be considered. Since income generated by the trust would be considered unearned income, there would be little, if any, benefit from an income tax standpoint if trust income is distributed to a beneficiary who is under the age of 14.

Gifts. Income may also be shifted by transferring cash or property through an outright gift. This is discussed in more detail in Chapter 12.

Interest-Free Loans. In general, you can loan money to another family member without charging interest if the amount of the loan to any one person does not exceed $10,000. Interest earned on the borrowed funds, if any, would be taxed to the borrower. As discussed later in this chapter, these loans must be structured carefully in order to avoid imputed interest income.

Hiring Family Members. You may be able to reduce the overall taxes that you, your family and your business pay if you hire family members in your business and pay them wages. Hiring retired parents or student children who have little or no taxable income provides the greatest tax savings. Wages paid to children under 14 will not be taxed at the parents' tax rates since compensation is considered earned income. In order for the employer to deduct these wages, the family member must actually perform services and the compensation must be reasonable and in line with what nonfamily employees would earn for similar work.

There may be adverse tax consequences associated with hiring certain family members. For example, children who are under the age of 19 or are full-time students for at least five months during the year may be claimed as dependents regardless of their earnings. However, the dependency exemption will be lost if the child contributes more than half of his own support or, in the case of a child over 19 (and not a full-time student), if he or she earns more than the amount of the personal exemption. Social Security benefits for older family members may be reduced if earnings exceed a specified level. Another factor to consider is that both the employer and employee will generally be required to make Social Security contributions. In addition, deductions by an accrual-method taxpayer may be deferred until the compensation is included in a related taxpayer's income. All of these factors should be taken into consideration in hiring family members and determining the amount of compensation.

State Tax Considerations

The reduction in recent years in effective federal tax rates, together with the reduction in federal revenue-sharing with the states, have brought about a significant increase in state and local business taxes. In fact, many businesses are currently paying more tax dollars to state and local taxing authorities than they are to the federal government. Therefore, it is prudent for a business to focus on planning opportunities to counter the impact of the ever-increasing state and local tax burden.

Careful planning prior to implementing a business decision may provide alternative means to accomplish the desired business purpose and still minimize the state and local tax burden. There are several tax strategies to reduce state and local taxes that, if properly applied, can produce significant state tax savings.

Location of Business Activities. A major consideration in forming a new business should be the effect of state taxes. Many smaller businesses will want to incorporate and conduct their activities based on the location of the owners. However, in other situations, the company may be larger or have an opportunity to conduct business in more than one state. In these situations, state and local tax planning opportunities should be considered. Each state has its own rules for taxing businesses where operations are conducted both in and outside the state. Some states also impose taxes on companies that have incorporated in the state even though no business is conducted within the state.

State tax planning in these situations involves the distinctions between methods of allocating and apportioning business activity in different states. Being taxable in more than one state does not mean the payment of more tax. In fact, it could reduce the overall state tax payable.

If the business is conducted in more than one state, most state laws provide for the division of business activity through a mathematical formula. The factors involved are property, payroll and sales or receipts. The ratio of the total of the factors within each state with the right to impose a tax to the total of the factors everywhere may be less than 100%. In that instance not all income is taxed at the state level. Another advantage can be to apportion income to states with lower tax rates and reduce the overall effective state tax rate. In any case, the ability to apportion business activity between various states can create state tax savings.

For example, a company that has 100% of its income subject to tax by New York state will have an effective state tax rate of 10%. If the company can make itself subject to tax in a state with a 4% income tax and divide its income 50% to New York and 50% to the other state, its overall effective state tax rate can be reduced to 7%.

To be held taxable in any state, the enterprise must have some "minimum contact" with the state attempting to impose the tax.

Generally, if a company's only business activity or contact within a state consists of "mere solicitation" of orders for tangible personal property by the company's employees or representatives, and the orders are sent outside the state to be filled and the goods delivered from outside the state, the state is prohibited from imposing its income tax. This prohibition from tax by the state is important in avoiding state tax or attempting to be taxed in order to acquire the right to apportion business activity. Also, the prohibition applies only to state *income* taxes, therefore, the mere solicitation of activities within a state may give cause for imposing other state taxes such as sales/use or gross receipts tax. Each state is free to make its own determination of what constitutes mere solicitation. Various state court decisions have indicated that there is some need for additional activity to go beyond mere solicitation and subject a business to state income taxes.

The decisions have not produced a clear definition, however, and, depending on the state, may produce different results in identical cases. Business entities whose activities are other than sales of tangible personal property, such as service companies, may find that they are liable for state income taxation with only a limited presence in the state.

As noted above, mere solicitation in a state may subject a company to a gross receipts tax, franchise tax or net worth taxes. Even a company with no income would still have a taxable liability. Obviously, before initiating extensive business activities in a particular state, the state taxing schemes should be reviewed.

Another concern for companies with orders for products from states outside its normal business area is sales and use tax. Shipping goods into a state may not subject the company to corporate income/ franchise taxes, but it may create a sufficient contact to require collection of sales and use taxes. A sales and use tax generally is imposed on the consumer of the product, but if the seller fails to properly collect and remit the tax the seller is liable for the tax. Because the rules establishing responsibility to collect sales tax are broader than the minimum contacts necessary to impose corporate income taxes, the taxpayer must not assume that an absence of corporate taxation in a state means there is no responsibility to collect sales and use tax in that state.

In many cases, special-purpose entities, such as holding companies, finance companies, sales or service companies and real estate companies, can be useful in state tax planning—both in limiting exposure to tax in particular jurisdictions and in minimizing the tax burden through appropriate shifting of income or business activities. Several states may require that affiliated entities be included in a combined or consolidated state income tax return and, in many cases, combination or consolidation will in fact be beneficial to the taxpayer.

Accumulated Earnings Tax

Successful companies often accumulate substantial earnings over the years. In many cases, there is no desire to distribute the earnings to the owners. Higher salaries may not be justifiable and dividends, which would be taxable to the shareholders, would not be deductible by the corporation. Furthermore, retained earnings can often be invested at attractive yields, and by retaining these earnings in the company, the second level of tax (on owners) can be deferred.

But if a corporation accumulates earnings beyond its reasonable needs, the IRS may assess the accumulated earnings tax. The tax is imposed at a rate of 27.5% on the first $100,000 of the amount deemed excessive (accumulated taxable income) and 38.5% on the remainder. Normally, the IRS will consider only liquid assets to determine the excess amount. To impose the tax, the IRS must demonstrate that the amount in question was accumulated solely to avoid income taxes.

The taxpayer can rebut this contention by showing that the company has sound reasons for retaining earnings. Acceptable reasons include:

☐ The existence of significant debt or other liabilities
☐ Plans for expansion, documented by sketches, architectural designs and board minutes
☐ Current or threatened litigation

☐ A requirement to redeem shares of a deceased shareholder.

It is essential that the company continually evaluate its earnings situation. If a quantitative analysis suggests the possibility of an accumulated earnings tax penalty, there are several steps that may be taken to help avoid an assessment:

☐ Electing S corporation status

☐ Planning business transactions during the year to get the best possible results under the IRS formulas used to test for accumulated taxable income

☐ Planning, documenting and implementing programs requiring use of funds

☐ Reducing taxable income through various tax-deferral techniques, such as installment sales or changes in inventory accounting methods

☐ Increasing compensation to shareholder-officers (taking into consideration the unreasonable compensation issue)

☐ Amending retirement plans to provide increased benefits

☐ Raising dividends

☐ Becoming a member of a consolidated group.

The accumulated earnings tax does not apply to S corporations, partnerships or individuals.

Personal Holding Company Tax

Closely held corporations that receive a sizable amount of passive investment income, such as dividends, interest and rent, may be taxed on that income if they are deemed personal holding companies. This tax is in addition to the normal income tax. To be classified a personal holding company (PHC), at least 50% of the value of a company's stock must be owned directly or indirectly by not more than five shareholders at any time during the last half of the taxable year. In addition, a substantial portion of the company's income must be from passive sources.

There is an objective test to determine whether this requirement is met. If both the ownership and income tests are met, the company will be subject to the PHC tax, which is 28% (38.5% in the case of 1987 tax years only) of undistributed PHC income. If the company is operating at a loss, undistributed PHC income may be negative and thus, the PHC tax would be zero. If it appears that the company will be subject to the PHC tax, it can pay out dividends to help reduce or eliminate the liability.

If a company is in danger of being treated as a personal holding company, the following alternatives should be considered:

☐ Enhance operating rather than passive income

☐ Manage and evaluate transactions with related companies; consider filing consolidated returns

☐ Reassess the distribution of stock ownership

☐ Select investments to avoid or postpone taxable investment income

☐ Review dividend policy prior to year end

☐ Elect S corporation status.

Collapsible Corporations

Among the most complex of Internal Revenue Code provisions is Section 341, which attempts to deny capital gain treatment if an enterprise is sold before it has realized a substantial portion of the income from the business activity for which it was originally organized.

For example, assume a corporation is organized to construct a building and, upon completion, the shareholders sell their shares to another owner or operator of the facility. Under the collapsible corporation provisions, the gain on the sale would be treated as ordinary income based on the theory that such gain is attributable to construction profit rather than capital appreciation.

As a result of TRA '86, these provisions are less detrimental since capital gains are now taxed as ordinary income. However, taxpayers' capital losses may be limited if they don't have capital gain from other sources to offset such losses. The collapsible corporation pro-

visions may become more meaningful at some point in the future
if preferential treatment of capital gains is restored.

Collapsible Partnerships

Provisions relating to sale of partnership interests or dissolution
of partnerships are designed to deny capital gains tax treatment. If
a partner sells his interest in the partnership, ordinary income taxes
must be paid on any gain that represents appreciation in property
owned by the partnership that would have produced ordinary income had that property been sold by the partnership. Therefore, if
a partnership owns "substantially appreciated inventory" or has
"unrealized receivables," all or part of the gain on the sale of an
interest by a partner will be treated as ordinary income. As with
the collapsible corporation provisions, these rules are less detrimental now that capital gains are taxed as ordinary income.

Transactions Between Related Parties

Many provisions of the Internal Revenue Code apply to transactions between related parties. The definition of the term "related"
differs among the various rules that apply a related party test. Most
of these provisions use the concept of constructive ownership to
determine whether the parties are related. Under this concept, an
individual, corporation or other entity may be treated as constructively owning stock that it does not actually own if there is a close
relationship among the actual owners.

For example, assume that Jones owns 100% of Ace Corporation
and that Best Corporation is owned 51% by his daughter and 49%
by her husband. Under the constructive ownership provisions, Jones
is deemed to own the shares actually owned by his daughter and
therefore, would be in control of both corporations—control being
defined as 50% ownership of the value of voting power. If Jones
were to sell all or part of his shares in Ace to Best, the gain would
generally be treated as a dividend taxable at ordinary rates. Jones
would thus be in the distressing tax position of having received a
dividend from a corporation in which he actually owns no shares.

Because of the potential for adverse tax consequences, any contemplated transaction between related parties should be reviewed to determine the relationship of the parties in the transaction and the effect of the constructive-ownership provisions.

Reallocation of Income and Expense. The IRS has the power to reallocate items of income and of deduction between related parties. The theory is that these parties must deal with one another as they would if unrelated; stated another way, all transactions must be at "arm's length." (Unfortunately, this theory has not been easy to implement, and the body of law covering it is copious and growing.)

The arm's-length standard applies to sales of goods, services, rentals and licensing agreements. It can apply to leases between affiliates; for example, if a lessor is deemed to be charging insufficient rental to an affiliated lessee, additional income may be imputed to the lessor. This could have adverse results if the additional income to the lessor is taxed at a higher rate than the tax benefit of the corresponding rent deduction to the lessee.

This power of reallocation is often applied to dealings between domestic entities and their foreign affiliates. In many foreign countries, tax rates are substantially lower than those in the United States. If a U.S. manufacturer organizes a subsidiary in a low-tax country to act as a local distributor of the company's product, there is nothing to stop the manufacturer from setting the selling price to the affiliate at a level that would minimize the profit to the U.S. company and maximize the income of the affiliate. In these circumstances, the IRS has the power to step in and reapportion the total income so that a larger part is attributed to the U.S. company. The IRS has the same power over domestic entities.

Sale of Depreciable Property. When a taxpayer sells real estate or depreciable fixed assets, the depreciation recapture rules require that all or a portion of the gain attributable to depreciation be treated as ordinary income. The remaining gain generally qualifies for capital gain treatment.

However, if depreciable property is sold to a related party, the entire gain will be treated as ordinary income. Among the categories of related parties subject to this provision are an individual and his 80%-or-more-owned corporation, or two corporations 80%-owned by the same individual. The rationale for this treatment is that the purchaser would otherwise be able to take ordinary income deductions on the purchase prices in the form of future depreciation, whereas the seller would have a capital gain on the same property. Again, due to the treatment of capital gains as ordinary income under the TRA '86, this provision is no longer as detrimental.

If property is sold to a related party at a loss, the loss will generally not be allowed. For purposes of this provision, related parties include members of a family, an individual and his 51%-or-more-owned corporation, and two corporations that are members of the same controlled group.

Sale of Stock. If a taxpayer is conducting a business through two or more corporations that he controls (e.g., one corporation to own land and buildings and another to operate the business housed in the buildings), he cannot sell all or part of the stock of one corporation to the other and be eligible for capital gain treatment as he would be if the shares had been sold to an unrelated purchaser. The transaction would be treated as a taxable dividend distribution in the amount of the selling price from the purchasing corporation to the shareholder. Thus, if Jones, the owner of all of the shares of both Ace Corporation and Best Corporation, were to sell part of his Ace shares, which cost him $10,000, to Best for $30,000, Jones, instead of having a $20,000 capital gain, would most likely be taxed on the receipt of a $30,000 dividend from Best.

12

Estate Tax Planning

The primary objective of estate planning is to make sure that your will and other documents accomplish what you want them to accomplish. Other objectives are:

☐ To minimize estate and income taxes
☐ To provide funds to pay debts and estate taxes
☐ To arrange for capable management of assets.

DESIGNATING YOUR ASSETS

Estate planning begins with an understanding of the assets that make up your estate. The following lists of the major categories of personal assets are designed to help you prepare an inventory. Personal property includes:

☐ Interest in a business (sole proprietorship, partnership interest, or stock)
☐ Life insurance policies
☐ Stocks and bonds held for investment
☐ Tax shelter investments (usually limited partnership interests)

☐ Deferred compensation

☐ Bank accounts

☐ Automobiles

☐ Jewelry

☐ Art objects and collectibles

☐ Household furnishings.

Deferred compensation may include:

1. Unpaid salary or bonus as of date of death. A carefully planned company death benefit may be excluded from your taxable estate provided you had no access to or control over it during your lifetime.
2. Payments received under a qualified pension and profit-sharing plan, a Keogh plan and an IRA.

Real property includes:

☐ Home (principal residence)

☐ Vacation home

☐ Investment real estate

Where an asset is insured, make sure that the insurance policy agrees with the ownership. Otherwise, the assets may be included in the estate of the insured if he predeceases the owner.

Jointly Held Property

The joint ownership of property by spouses is widely prevalent but is not necessarily advantageous from an estate or an income tax planning standpoint. Normally, property transferred as part of an estate is valued at fair market value at the time of death or six months later rather than at cost. When the surviving spouse later sells the asset, the fair market value at which he or she received the property from the estate is the basis on which gain or loss on the sale is reckoned. To the extent this value exceeds the original cost, the taxable gain will be lower. With jointly held property, however, only one-half is included in the estate of the decedent. Accordingly, only one-half receives a step-up in basis. (Property held jointly is treated as owned one-half by each spouse regardless of how much each contributed to the purchase price.) Therefore, the taxable gain on sale will be greater than it would have been if the property were originally owned entirely by the deceased.

ESTATE AND GIFT TAXATION

The rules governing the taxation of gifts and estates are highly developed. The recommendations in this discussion are premised on a knowledge of a few rules that can be briefly summarized. They focus primarily on federal estate and gift taxation.

Valuation

Transfers by gift or by bequest are taxable; gifts, to the giver; bequests, to the estate. In general, the value of an item for gift-tax purposes is the market value at the time the gift is made; the value for estate-tax purposes is the value at time of death or, under certain circumstances, six months from date of death. With gifts of life insurance policies, the equivalent of market value is replacement value—that is, replacement cost—at the time of transfer. This also applies to transfers of policies by bequest, which, strictly speaking, can take place only when the insured is not the decedent.

Deductions and Exemptions

Most transfers of property between spouses are allowed a 100 percent marital deduction. Gifts to anyone are generally subject to an exclusion for each recipient, and there is an additional one-time exemption (in the form of a credit) based on the aggregate of the estate and total lifetime gifts.

The Marital Deduction. Virtually everything you leave your spouse, whether outright or in the form of a legal life estate or trust, will be free of federal estate taxes. There is one catch; your spouse's estate will be subject to estate tax on his or her death. Furthermore, unless the spouse remarries, there will be no marital deduction available to that estate. This means that if the largest part of your spouse's estate came from your bequest—and that estate did not diminish appreciably in his or her hands—the tax on your spouse's estate might well be larger than the tax was on yours, even if your estate, including distributions to your other beneficiaries, was considerably larger. Community property is eligible for the marital deduction as well as a qualified terminable interest life estate (see "Testamentary Trusts" in this chapter).

The unlimited marital deduction affects tax years beginning in 1982. It applies to a provision in a will, whenever executed, which leaves your estate to your spouse. It does not, however, apply to a formula provision (phrased in terms of a "maximum marital deduction") in a will drafted before September 12, 1981. The only exception applies when the law of the testator's state treats the inclusion of the formula clause as a provision, *ipso facto*, for the unlimited marital deduction. If you have not taken the necessary steps to qualify for the new deduction, your marital deduction will follow the pre-1982 formula—that is, $250,000 or one-half of adjusted gross estate, whichever is greater. If it were not for this rule, pre-1982 wills that mention the marital deduction, especially those designed to take full advantage of that deduction, could, now that the term denotes the new unlimited deduction, cause the survivor to inherit more of the decedent's estate than intended.

Because of the loss of the new deduction, failure to change a will made before September 12, 1981 could operate to trigger liability for an estate tax where no tax would be due under the new marital deduction.

The Nonmarital Gift Exclusion. You can give up to $10,000 each year tax free to any person, with no limit on the number of recipients. If you give with your spouse's consent, that amount may be doubled. This exclusion also applies to trusts if the beneficiary receives a "present interest" (see "The Gift Tax" in this chapter) in the trust. Thus, if you have four adult children and four grandchildren, you and your spouse could give them a total of $160,000 annually on a tax-free basis.

The Unified Credit for Estate and Gift Taxes. In addition to these annual exclusions, you are entitled to a credit against amounts in excess of these exclusions. In 1987 and thereafter, the exemption equivalent of this credit is $600,000 or, with the consent of your spouse, $1,200,000. On your death, the basis for assessing the estate tax will be the combination of the fair market value of the property you bequeath and the value of the taxable gifts you made since 1976—a combination termed the "transfer tax base." To the tax calculated on this base is applied and unified credit for estate and gift taxes.

This is how the credit works. Assume that A gives away after 1976 $600,000 over and above the marital exclusion, and dies in 1987, leaving an estate of $1,400,000. His estate's transfer tax base is $2,000,000; that is, the $600,000 in gifts added to the gross estate. The tax computed on this base is $780,800, but this amount is reduced by the unified credit equivalent of $600,000, or $192,800, to produce a net estate tax of $588,000. Had the tax been computed on the gross estate alone, it would have been $512,800—$75,200 less than the actual tax.

Generally, the sooner you use the unified credit exemption the better, because the present value of the exemption is greater than the future value.

STRATEGIES FOR GIVING AND BEQUEATHING

To determine the optimal planning approach for disposing of your possessions, you will probably have to weigh a host of considerations: external, such as rules and economic trends, and internal, such as your age, means, and needs. In the following discussion we focus on some of the more important principles involved, illustrating with representative situations.

Utilizing the Marital Deduction

Because your spouse's estate will be subject to taxation without—

unless he or she remarries—benefit of the marital deduction, it is advisable to withhold from your bequest to your spouse an amount equal to the unified credit exemption. This amount, at least, will be removed from all possibility of subsequent taxation as part of his or her estate. You can use the unified credit exemption currently by gift or, ultimately, by bequest.

The marital bequests can be made either directly or through a trust under which your spouse would receive the income and, under certain conditions, the principal as well. The following example illustrates how foregoing the full permissible marital deduction can reduce the total tax on the combined value of both estates.

Assume that D dies in 1987, leaving an estate of $2 million entirely to his wife, who has no property of her own. On D's death, Mrs. D receives the $2 million free of estate taxes, due to the marital deduction. If Mrs. D never remarries and her estate is $2 million at her death, the estate tax will be $588,000, leaving $1,412,000 for their heirs, their two children. If, on the other hand, D left $600,000 directly to the children or in the form of a nonmarital trust, with income payable to Mrs. D during her life and with the children as remainder beneficiaries, the $1,400,000 estate remaining to the widow would be liable on her death for a tax of $320,000. The $1,080,000 remaining in the widow's estate after taxes, added to the first $600,000, would give the children a total of $1,680,000—$268,000 more than they would have received under the first option.

Another way to reduce taxes is to equalize the total holdings of husband and wife. Thus, in the preceding example, if D left his wife $1 million the total estate taxes for husband and wife would be $306,000—$14,000 less than the $320,000 ultimately assessed on the $1,400,000 received by the wife in the bequest of the entire estate. On the other hand, half of the estate tax, $153,000, is paid on D's death, with the balance payable when the wife dies. The use of $153,000 might be worth more than the $14,000 saved. Nevertheless, the equal-estate arrangement is definitely advantageous when the spouses die simultaneously or the surviving spouse dies very shortly after the first spouse.

The Common Disaster Threat. If you and your spouse die as the result of the same occurrence, such as an airplane crash or a fire, it may not be possible to establish which of you succumbed first. The laws of many states provide that where there is any doubt about order of death, each spouse is deemed to survive with respect to his or her own property. If this presumption is sustained, the marital deduction will be lost and if the spouse has no other assets, her $600,000 exemption equivalent will be wasted. To counter this presumption, it should be stipulated in your will that in the event of doubt the husband is deemed to have died first. The testamentary provision is standard in form and is known as the common disaster clause. Many wills with this clause also establish a formula for equalizing the two estates in the event of a common disaster.

If the wife dies after the husband, but not more than six months later, she would derive little benefit from the estate. To simplify administration and, in some cases, to save taxes as well, a couple should consider providing in their will for nullification of all or part of the bequest to the wife if she dies within the six-month period—not later, or the amount of the marital deduction will be taxed as part of the husband's estate. Of course, you and your spouse should consider this contingent cancellation provision when you draft your wills, to make sure that all of your beneficiaries are provided for according to your wishes.

Tax Reasons for Giving

If your net worth is greater than your needs, you should consider making gifts to your family or other beneficiaries during your lifetime. By this expedient, you can materially reduce taxes on your estate at the price of accelerating transfers to those who will ultimately receive the transfers. This can be accomplished, within limits, by taking advantage of the $10,000 annual exclusion and the marital deduction. (The reduction in the taxable value of your estate that you achieve by making a gift must be reckoned as the value of the property given *plus* any future appreciation realized on the property and/or income earned on it between the time you gave it and the time of your death.)

If everything, or nearly everything, is in your name, it is a good idea to utilize your spouse's lifetime credit as well as your own. If he or she predeceases you and you have been taking the exemption only for yourself, his or her exemption will be lost for lack of any-thing to which to apply the credit equivalent of that exemption. Because of inflation, the tax benefit of using up the gift-tax credit while you are alive may be greater than letting the credit shelter your estate from taxation after your death. On the other hand, ap-preciated property given by you during your lifetime will, when sold, generate taxable income to the recipient, because he or she must assume your cost basis, increased only to the extent of any gift tax you paid, which is attributable to appreciation up to the date of the gift in excess of your basis. If the property is transferred after your death, the recipient's basis will be its value at the time of death—presumably far higher than the cost basis. Of course, jointly held property received by your spouse is, as discussed earlier, a special case.

Vehicles for Bequests and Gifts

Bequests and gifts need not be outright; both may be accom-plished by use of trusts.

Testamentary Trusts. If there is any doubt that your spouse can properly manage the property left to him or her, or that the property remaining at the time of his or her death will go to parties on which you both agreed, you should use the trust vehicle.

The General-Power-to-Appoint Trust. With this kind of trust, the surviving spouse receives the income from the property during his or her lifetime but has no power over the trust assets except to dispose of them as he or she pleases either during lifetime or under the terms of his or her will. If the spouse fails to exercise this right—that is, to provide for disposition—the property will go to parties that you have designated in your will. The property used in funding this kind of trust must be either income producing or convertible to income producing at the behest of the survivor. For example, two types of assets that are not considered income producing are stock in a closely held corporation that is not paying a dividend and various types of tax shelters.

The Qualified-Terminable-Income Trust (Qtip). Under this arrangement, your spouse will also receive the income currently, and on his or her death the parties you have designated will receive the property. The same requirements that the property be income producing or convertible to income producing that apply to the general-power-to-appoint trust apply here as well. The main advantage of this trust is that your spouse cannot change your ultimate beneficiaries. (In some states, this type of trust does not qualify for the state marital deduction.)

The Estate Trust. Here, the income need not be paid currently to the surviving spouse, but when he or she dies, any undistributed income, together with the remaining corpus, is distributed to his or her estate. The main advantage of this trust is that it can be funded with non-income producing property, whereas the main disadvantage is that the property passes under the surviving spouse's will.

In all three of the preceding trusts, the property qualifying for the marital deduction in the estate of the first spouse to die will be included in the surviving spouse's taxable estate.

Trusts for Gifts. Trusts are also extensively used in gift giving. As long as the trust, or the beneficiary of the trust, is in a lower income tax bracket than you are, you will save taxes on the trust income. Of course, transfers to a trust are taxable gifts and, to the extent they exceed the allowable deduction, use up the lifetime credit.

Insurance

If you have life insurance policies, whether ordinary, group term, or any other type, provision for transferring ownership of the policies and disposition of the proceeds on the death of the insured should be a major factor in your estate-tax planning. The general rule is that the proceeds of an insurance policy are included in the taxable estate of the insured if the insured owned the policy within three years of death. It is immaterial who took out the policy , paid the premium, or is the beneficiary, provided that it is not you or your estate. These proceeds are not taxable income to the beneficiary, so if you keep them out of your estate, they will escape taxation entirely.

The most obvious way to exclude the proceeds from your estate is to give the policy away during your lifetime, making the recipient the beneficiary of the policy as well as its owner. Except where a policy has a high cash surrender value, the tax cost of the gift is generally modest. For example, term insurance policies, even those with double-indemnity provisions or accidental death benefits, do not usually have much value during the life of the insured. (Company group term insurance has virtually no value.) If you give the policy directly (and through certain types of trust arrangements) the gift-tax exemption will apply not only to the value of the policy but also to payments of premiums you make after giving it. Finally, gifts of insurance policies normally involve no significant management or administrative problems until the death of the insured.

Requirements for Divestiture. In giving an insurance policy, you must divest yourself of it completely and irrevocably. If you retain any control over the policy, the tax benefits of the transfer will almost certainly be denied. The following rights or powers over the policy are criteria or, in legalese, "incidents" of ownership:

☐ The right to change the beneficiary

☐ The right to cancel or surrender the policy and receive its cash value, if any

☐ The right to assign or sell the policy or revoke an assignment

☐ The right to pledge the policy for a loan

☐ The right to borrow against the cash surrender value of the policy. If the borrowing takes place before the transfer and the payments of interest or principal are carried on after the transfer, there will be no incident of ownership, because the insured will derive no further economic benefits from the policy.

In construing ownership, the courts look beyond the forms of law to facts and circumstances. Thus, you may be considered to have retained control over the policy if you are the controlling shareholder in a corporation that formally owns the policy. On the other hand, a policy given pursuant to a divorce, and maintained by you solely for the benefit of your ex-spouse and that of the children will not be included in your estate. (The theory is that you do not have effective control over the insurance because the divorce decree gave your ex-spouse a vested interest in the policy.)

When Donee-Beneficiary Predeceases Donor-Insured. If your spouse owns insurance on your life, his or her will should specifically bequeath ownership of the policy to an individual—other than yourself—or to a trust for such individual's benefit.

If the owner-beneficiary predeceases the insured, the value of the policy—which is not the face amount of the policy—at the date of death will be included in the owner's estate. (The value of an insurance policy before the death of the insured will generally consist of the interpolated terminal reserve value—slightly more than cash surrender value—plus any unearned premiums.)

The Irrevocable Life Insurance Trust. The safest way to divest yourself of an insurance policy is to assign ownership of the policy to an irrevocable life insurance trust for the beneficiary, thus avoiding all incidents of ownership, including—but not limited to—acting as trustee.

The irrevocable life insurance trust may be the appropriate vehicle for gifts of insurance, not only for your spouse but also for other members of your family. With this kind of trust, you can achieve maximum flexibility by conferring discretionary powers on the trustee. For example, your trustee can be authorized to provide for the needs of the beneficiaries as they arise, by invading the corpus of the trust. The trustee can be empowered to use trust funds to lend money to your estate or buy assets from it to provide it with funds to pay taxes. To obtain the benefits of this arrangement, however, you must live at least three years after the assignment.

The Gift Tax. An insurance policy, even if it has no cash value, is valued for gift-tax purposes at replacement value as of the time the gift is made. Although (as pointed out earlier) this value is usually no more than a fraction of the proceeds, with certain policies—notably, whole life—it can be significant. One way to reduce the gift tax on a policy is to borrow against its cash surrender value before assigning the policy; the loan will reduce the policy's net value. Another way is to split the policy into several parts and transfer one part at a time. Finally, you might be able to retain the cash surrender value of the policy and assign only the amount at risk, that is, the face amount less the cash surrender value.

In one set of circumstances, there is a hidden gift-tax trap to watch for. If your spouse receives a policy on your life as a gift and names his or her children as beneficiaries, the full proceeds of that policy on your death may be treated as a taxable gift from him or her to them. The standard way to prevent this from happening is to assign the policy to the children who are the beneficiaries.

Gifts to Trusts. An outright gift of an insurance policy is, like the gift of almost any marketable item, treated as a transfer of a present interest and, therefore, is eligible for the $10,000 annual gift-tax exclusion. Payment of premiums by the donor after the transfer is treated in the same way if the beneficiary owns the policy. If, however, you place an insurance policy in a trust, the transfer will usually be deemed a gift of a future interest, and the value of the policy as well as subsequent payments of premiums will not qualify for the exclusion. (With certain types of trust, this can be prevented, as is explained later.) In either case, you can pay the premiums directly to the insurance company without risk of having an incident of ownership.

If you wish to put an insurance policy into a trust for the benefit of a minor—the usual practice, rather than to give full possession during minority—you can ensure that the gift will be one of a present interest and therefore eligible for the gift-tax exclusion. The key is to stipulate that the beneficiary is to receive full ownership of the policy including proceeds, if any, plus an accumulated earnings at the age of 21. (In addition, it is advisable to give the trustee the power to dispose of the policy.) Another approach that should have the same result is to give the beneficiary the annual right to withdraw from the trust $5,000 or 5% of the value of the policy, whichever is greater.

Caveat. The estate-planning aspects of insurance are tricky, thanks to the variety and complexity of insurance policies and the vehicles for holding and transferring them. If you have given, or intend to give, insurance on your life, you should consider utilizing the services of a lawyer of an estate planner. That your death within three years of donating a policy would throw the proceeds into your estate argues for early action.

Sale of Remainder Interest in Property

"Ownership" of Property. A property owner has two separate and distinct interests in property: a present interest and a future interest. A life estate is a present interest in property with its owner—the life tenant—retaining general control over the property, as well as its use, enjoyment and income during his or her lifetime. A remainder interest is a future interest in property which enables the owner—the remanderman—to obtain possession and full title to the property only after the life tenant has died.

Remainder Interest Sale. For a fraction of its overall value, a property owner can make a lifetime sale of a remainder interest in his or her property to a family member. The purchase price would be the actuarial value of the remainder interest as determined by Treasury Regulations.

The following are the Treasury Regulations' percentage costs of a remainder interest in property:

Seller's Age	Percentage Cost of Remainder
40	8.429%
50	15.257
60	25.509
70	39.478
80	56.341

Tax Considerations. Although there are uncertaintes in this area of law, it appears that the sale of a remainder interest for its actuarial share of the property's fair market value should remove the entire property from the life tenant's gross estate. Thus, an estate tax of up to 50% could be avoided both on the present value of the property and on any future appreciation. Any sales proceeds that were not used by the life tenant would, of course, be included in his or her gross estate.

The life tenant's income tax basis is apportioned between the retained life interest and the remainder interest sold. Thus, a gain on the sale of the remainder interest may result. The current tax cost could be diminished by selling the remainder interest on an installment basis.

Although the remainderman receives the entire property for a fraction of its value, his or her adjusted basis is only the amount actually paid. Assuming the remainderman sells the property shortly after the life tenant's death, an income tax of up to 28% (at today's rates) would result. This tax cost, however, is much less than an estate tax of up to 50%.

Estate Freezing

If your corporation is closely held as well as a substantial part of your estate—both likely conditions—you should consider freezing the size of that asset in your estate and diverting future appreciation to your beneficiaries. It is much easier to do this at a reasonable tax cost now than it is to dispose of future accumulated wealth.

Recapitalization. The most common way to freeze the value of a closely held corporation is to recapitalize it so that you and your beneficiaries will hold a particular mix of voting and nonvoting common or preferred stock. If your beneficiaries are already shareholders, an exchange of their holdings may be necessary to achieve this end. If you are the sole shareholder, then you must make the beneficiaries shareholders, making sure their participation follows the pattern of holdings you want. If you are a joint equity holder with outsiders who are not to be beneficiaries, your exchange program will probably have to involve them. In any case, you should be able to accomplish the recapitalization without incurring any tax. The following examples illustrate several estate-freezing arrangements based on varying goals.

EXAMPLE 1. A business man, the sole shareholder of a corporation, wishes to turn over this business, while living, to his two sons, who are active in the corporation. At the same time, he wishes to provide for his wife, who wants to be independent of the children. The first objective he accomplishes as follows: he capitalizes the company and exchanges all of his common stock for a package of new common and preferred, with the par value of the nonvoting preferred comprising about 80% of the company's net worth. He then gives the common stock to his sons. (If the value of the common stock is less than $1,200,000, the father can use his credit and that of his wife to avoid all federal tax on the gift.) The effect of these moves is to freeze the value of the father's interest in the company so that all future appreciation will accrue to the common stock owned by the sons. For the second objective—providing for his wife—the dividend-paying preferred stock is ideally suited. If the dividend is fixed and cumulative, it is not at the discretion of the children.

If the second son were not active in the business but the father wanted to protect that son's interests, the father could create two classes of common stock (in addition to the preferred)—Class A common with full voting rights, and Class B with highly restricted voting rights—giving Class A to the active and Class B to the other son. Alternatively, the father could make the common stock non-voting, or he could put the gift to the second son in a trust of which the first son is trustee with the right to vote the stock.

If the father wished the active son to realize the entire future appreciation, he could give that son all the common stock and allow the second son only the preferred. Under this arrangement, the second son would be buffered against a decline in the value of the business under the first son's management.

If the father wished to retain control of the business, he could give the preferred stock full voting rights. Because there would be more preferred shares than common shares, he would retain voting control of the corporation. To ensure that the sons would have complete voting control over the corporation on his death, he would make them trustees of the marital trust.

A variation on this planning technique could occur if S corporation status was either in place or contemplated. While a split of the company's ownership between more than one class of stock is not allowed, it is possible to create voting and non-voting common stock. In this context, it may be desirable to create two marital trusts, one of which can be phrased to include language making it a "qualified subchapter S trust" that is specifically allowed to hold S corporation stock, while the other trust would only have to conform to the requirements satisfying a marital estate tax deduction. (See the appendix to this chapter for a comparison of the requirements of a Qtip trust with a qualified subchapter S trust funded by a will.)

EXAMPLE 2. A businessman, A, is sole shareholder in a corporation with a fair market value of $3,000,000. None of A's children are active or interested in the enterprise, but several key employees would like to acquire significant equity holdings, although their combined capital is only $100,000. Our entrepreneur wants to protect his children's interests and to accommodate the employees.

He capitalizes his holdings into $2,500,000 of preferred stock and $500,000 of common and sells 20 percent of the common to the key employees. (He could have gone as high as 40 percent, if he were willing to let the corporation make a loan of $100,000 to them to buy an additional 20 percent interest. The loan could be repaid in future years with the aftertax proceeds of their bonuses.) The preferred stock he uses in an active program of gifts to his wife and children. He also enters into a buy-sell arrangement with the corporation whereby, on his death, all of his remaining stock and his family's stock will be redeemed. As a precaution against the possibility that the corporation will not have enough liquid assets to satisfy the claim, the redemption will be carried out in installments spread over a number of years. (When a closely held business comprises more than 35 percent of the adjusted gross value of an estate, the estate is not compelled to pay federal inheritance taxes on the value of that business for four years and has an additional 10 years to complete payment.)

EXAMPLE 3. Two entrepreneurs, each owning 50% of a company, are concerned about continuity of control for both families when one entrepreneur dies. They recapitalize, creating a package of non-voting preferred and voting common. On the death of one, the company could redeem or the survivor could buy the nonvoting stock owned by the estate of the deceased. The equal division of the voting interests would continue.

Tainted Stock. One obstacle to estate freezing is that the preferred stock issued in a recapitalization will be "tainted"; that is, if the stock is sold during the lifetime of the recipient, the full proceeds of the sale will be taxed as ordinary income. If tainted stock is given to charity, the charitable deduction is limited to the taxpayer's cost basis. Although the taint is purged at death, it may limit the taxpayer's flexibility during his or her lifetime; the stock is less valuable for a gift program, for example. The common stock retained, however, need not be tainted and, if not, can be used for gift tax purposes.

Valuation Problems. A difficult problem to contend with when you recapitalize your company is what value to assign to the corporation and the securities to be issued. For example, in setting the dividend on preferred stock, you have to weigh the desirability of a low-dividend obligation against the fact that if the dividend rate is too low by current business standards, the IRS may value your preferred stock at far below par and assign the difference to the common stock. The higher value of the common stock would hardly be advantageous for gift-tax purposes. (If the preferred is noncumulative and the dividends are in arrears, any gap between par and true value will be greater than it would otherwise be.)

The IRS has taken the position that the fair market value of stock must be determined in accordance with the facts in each case. It is unrealistic to assume that the IRS will accept a valuation at par with a dividend of only 6%, when preferred stocks of quality listed corporations are yielding 10% or more. In a case involving a charitable gift of 6% noncumulative, nonvoting preferred stock, the Tax Court applied substantial discounts in valuing the stock for purposes of determining the amount of the charitable deduction.

In general, whenever a closely held company is recapitalized or reorganized and certain parties receive more than they gave up, the possibility exists that the difference will be taxed either as a gift from those who received less than they contributed or as compensation to those who received more. Thus, as in Example 2, if the key employees are deemed to have acquired the common stock in a bargain purchase, they may have received compensation to the extent of the bargain portion.

The valuation problem is the major reason why many proposed recapitalization plans are never completed. The taxpayer may be reluctant to load the corporation with a heavy dividend requirement, with its resulting drain on working capital. With adroit tax planning, however, the problem can be minimized, if not eliminated.

Redemptions. After your spouse's death, it may be desirable for your company to repurchase some of the preferred stock from his or her estate. This must be planned carefully. The amount redeemed generally cannot exceed death taxes plus funeral and administrative expenses. Any additional amount may be taxed to the estate as a dividend.

Selling the Business. If you decide to sell your business rather than to keep it in the family, you will probably be faced with a tax on the appreciation in its value over your cost basis. One way to avoid the tax is to have a publicly owned company acquire your business via a tax-free exchange of stock. The disadvantage of this expedient is that it results in your family's losing control over a substantial portion of its net worth; that is, the family holdings would now consist of a minority interest in a company controlled by others.

The Personal Holding Company. Another approach would be to have the corporation sell its assets and retain and reinvest the proceeds, thereby perpetuating itself as a family personal holding company. The corporation would probably realize only a small capital gain, and it is possible that it would realize none. From an estate-planning point of view, this arrangement can be very advantageous. The courts have been generous in allowing substantial discounts in valuing the stock of a personal holding company held by an estate. Discounts ranging from 20% to as high as 55% have been approved. Even the IRS has been willing to concede a substantial discount, and many cases have been settled at the appellate level with discounts of 25% or more. (For a discussion of personal holding companies, see Chapter 6.)

CONCLUSION

By now you should realize that the preparation and execution of an estate plan requires expert advice. Although what is appropriate for one taxpayer may be inappropriate for another, the main objective of all tax planning is to fulfill the testator's wishes at a minimum tax cost, satisfy liquidity needs, and provide for capable management. With proper planning, which includes gift giving during your lifetime, you should be able to reduce the value of the estate while preserving a degree of control, minimize or avoid a present gift tax on the transfer, and pass on more "value" than meets the eye to your family.

APPENDIX: COMPARISON OF THE REQUIREMENTS OF A QTIP TRUST WITH A QUALIFIED SUBCHAPTER S TRUST FUNDED BY A WILL

	Requirement of: Qtip Trust / S Trust	
1. The income beneficiary must be entitled to all the income from the property, payable annually or at more frequent intervals.	Yes	Yes
2. The trust must have only one current income beneficiary. IRS Code Sec. 1361(d)(3)(A)(i), and 2056(b)(7)(B)(ii)(I).	Yes	Yes
3. Only the current income beneficiary may receive any part of the corpus during his or her lifetime. IRS Code Sec. 1361(d)(3)(A)(ii), and 2056(b)(7)(B)(ii)(II).	Yes	Yes
4. The current income beneficiary must be a U.S. citizen or resident. IRS Code Sec. 1361(d)(3)(B).	No	Yes
5. An irrevocable election must be made.	Yes	Yes

13

Selling to the United States Government

The U.S. government is the world's largest buyer of goods and services. In this chapter, we explain how the government buys and what it expects of sellers.

BEFORE THE AWARD (PREAWARD)

Identifying the Customer

The first step is to determine which agencies need the goods or services you have to offer. You can generally rely on the Small Business Administration (SBA) field offices serving your area to pinpoint government agencies that are potential customers. A request for information from the SBA must be accompanied by enough data about your facilities and products to enable it to form an accurate idea of your capabilities. Better yet, contact the local SBA personally and discuss your capabilities.

Another excellent source of information is the *Commerce Business Daily*, which is published Monday through Friday (except on federal legal holidays) and sometimes on Saturday by the U.S. Department of Commerce in cooperation with government purchasing agencies. In this publication you will find a daily list of U.S. government procurement solicitations, subcontracting leads, contract awards, sales of surplus property and foreign business opportunities. The publication is on file at SBA and Department of Commerce field offices and is available by subscription via first-class mail from: Superintendent of Documents, *Commerce Business Daily*, Government Printing Office, Washington, D.C., 20402.

If you are near a military base or a Defense Supply Agency station, find the bid room, where current requirements are posted for public inspection. If you want to develop a new product, do not overlook participation in the Small Business Innovative Research (SBIR) program, which is heavily supported by the Department of Defense (DOD), National Aeronautics and Space Administration (NASA) and the Department of Energy (DOE).

Above all, do not overlook the numerous opportunities for subcontracting. The local office of the Defense Contract Administration Services (DCAS) will have a small-business representative who can help identify government prime contractors that you should contact. The office is listed in the telephone directory under Department of Defense.

Getting Listed with Government Agencies

After learning which agencies or prime contractors buy the products or services you can supply, you should ask the purchasing representatives of these agencies or firms to send you the necessary forms to have your company placed on their lists of potential suppliers, usually termed "bidder lists." These lists are made up of companies—manufacturers, wholesalers, construction, contractors, consultants and others—that have registered with the purchasing offices as suppliers of an item or service, and have provided printed information on their operations to demonstrate their qualifications as a vendor.

In addition, if you are applying for a listing with a military agency, attach a note on any defense items your company has supplied in the past. Each product or service listed should be carefully described. If possible, the government specifications that product or service meets or could meet should be listed.

After contacting a government agency, you will probably receive a Standard Form 129 (Solicitation Mailing List Application) that must be completed. Many bid lists are being computerized, particularly in the Department of Defense. As a result, you may receive both a Standard Form 129 and a specially developed form identifying the products or product lines that the agency purchases.

You should enclose a letter with the completed form requesting notification of the lists you are to be included on and notification of contract awards (referred to as placement lists).

Even before receiving assurance of placement on supplier lists, you should explore opportunities to sell to agencies that do not have your name and to which you have never applied. The *Commerce Business Daily* and comparable commercial publications are helpful here.

SOLICITATION CONTENT

Every government solicitation document, whether it is an invitation for bids under the sealed bidding procedure or a request for proposals under negotiated procurement, contains the following information:

Requirements for a Responsive and Sound Bid or Proposal

The requirements are usually presented in a work statement or specification. These also include delivery schedules, data to be furnished by both parties and other important requirements.

The specification can be used by the applicant as the basis for his or her estimates. In a negotiated purchase, agencies usually require proof of financial stability as well as capacity to fulfill the contract requirements. You may be asked to furnish your company's financial statements along with your proposal. Even if this information is not requested with your proposal, it may be requested at a later date.

Terms and Conditions

These cover the following points, among others:

☐ Funding and payment

☐ Performance monitoring

☐ Inspection and acceptance of finished products

☐ Subcontractors

☐ Use of government property

☐ Disputes

☐ Changes in the contract

☐ Termination (with or without prejudice to the contractor).

Several of these provisions are discussed in this chapter's section on submitting the proposal and implementing the contract.

Procedural Instructions

Information essential to preparing bids or proposals includes opening and closing dates, authorization for alternative bids and instructions to the contractor on the format of a proposal and criteria for evaluating proposals.

Policy Provisions

Most solicitations contain provisions reflecting the government's socioeconomic and financial policies. You may be asked to certify or attest to compliance with these policies not only when you submit a bid or proposal but also at intervals during the life of the contract.

These policies can be classified as either business or public. Business policies deal with matters such as contingent fee payments, use of current cost or pricing data and independent price determination. Public policies cover matters such as fostering small business, improving employment, wages and working conditions, equal employment opportunity, encouraging domestic purchasing (such as the Buy American Act) and promoting a cleaner environment.

Nondiscrimination in employment, wages and working conditions are the subjects of two major policy provisions.

Equality of Employment Opportunity

This policy became law as a result of a series of presidential executive orders. Most contracts contain an equal opportunity clause forbidding discrimination against any job applicant or employee because of race, color, religion, sex, age or national origin. Both contractors and subcontractors may be required to file compliance reports in connection with this provision.

Adherence to Local Standards for Wages and Working Conditions

Under the Davis-Bacon Act of 1931, contractors and subcontractors working on public construction projects, including buildings, cannot pay lower wages than those prevailing in the municipality or other local jurisdiction in which the project is located. The Secretary of Labor has the power to determine what the prevailing wage is, and that determination if final and conclusive. The Services Contract Act of 1965 extended this concept to "service employees" and included fringe benefits in the wage computation.

To fill some of the gaps in these laws, the Walsh-Healey Public Contracts Act requires contractors furnishing goods in excess of $10,000 to conform to "prevailing minimum wages," again as determined by the Secretary of Labor. Generally, the wages meant are the national minimums for similar work in the industry or similar industries. In some cases the Secretary has set higher minimums. In addition, the law forbids the contractor from using child or convict labor and requires compliance with occupational safety and health regulations.

TYPES OF PROCUREMENT

Federal purchasing offices buy supplies and services through sealed bids, competitive negotiation, sole-source negotiation and by set-asides for small business or labor surplus areas, using sealed bids or competitive negotiation. The sealed bid procedure is the most formal and the least flexible, but the authorities are careful to preserve the element of competition wherever possible in all awards.

By law, contracting officers must promote full and open competition in government procurement, except for certain exclusions such as set-asides, or whenever a specific authority prevents full and open competition. Even under the exclusions and specific authority, the maximum competition possible must be promoted. Methods of procurement will be discussed later in this chapter.

Sealed Bids

In a sealed bid, a purchasing office sends invitations for bids (IFB) to prospective bidders taken from the bidders list. The purchasing agency, however, may want a greater number of bidders than it can get from its own files. In that case, the agency may advertise for bidders.

An IFB will include or tell you how to get a copy of the specifications for the item, which describe in detail quality and other requirements. It will also include instructions for the preparation of bids, and will state conditions of purchase, delivery and payment.

The contact is awarded to the bidder whose bid is considered the most advantageous to the government in terms of price, delivery and other factors, provided the bidder is considered competent to carry out the contract. A purchasing officer may reject all bids received if prices seem unreasonable or it appears there has been collusion or bad faith on the part of the bidders. Estimated costs and anticipated profit are not revealed. These purchases are exempt from PL 87-0653 (Truth in Negotiation) and cost accounting standards.

Prerequisites. The sealed bid procurement process must meet certain prerequisites:

☐ Adequate competition for the procurement
☐ Adequate specifications describing the government requirement
☐ Time enough to carry out formal advertising
☐ A price basis for determining which organization will be awarded the contract.

Competition is ordinarily considered adequate if there are at least two organizations able and willing to handle the contract. To establish this fact, agencies can undertake a certain amount of investigation.

Don't assume that sealed bidding always takes more time than negotiated procurement. With sensitive procurements, however, the last prerequisite cited above can be more easily expedited. When considerations other than price are critical to the awarding of a contract, these factors cannot always be specified in the invitation.

There usually aren't precise and accurate requirements for research and development projects so conventional bidding on these projects is rare.

Processing of Bids. Sealed-bid procurement is a highly proceduralized and formal process. All bids must arrive sealed and be opened publicly in a designated place at an appointed time, as set forth in the bid invitation. This procedure is designed so no one can unfairly benefit from any of the bids.

At the public opening, the bids are abstracted—that is, the price offered by each bidder is publicly posted and revealed to all interested parties. After bid opening, all bidders must remain in the competition while the government evaluates received bids and determines the winning bidder. This rule is known as the firm-bid rule. Exceptions to the rule may be made where a mistake has been discovered.

Constraints on Communication. Normally, during the formal sealed-bid process you will not be permitted to communicate with an offering agency except on a formal, written basis. Whether you have submitted a bid when you make your inquiry is immaterial. This policy aims to prevent any party from extracting more information than any other. Government agencies sometimes hold prebid conferences at which questions may be asked to facilitate equal and simultaneous disclosure of information to all parties.

After all bids have been submitted, do not expect officials to tell you the names and number of firms solicited, or to disclose the terms and conditions received from individual bidders, proprietary data included in bids or anything that may prompt any party to raise a claim of prejudice or preference.

Evaluating Bids. Bids are evaluated using four criteria: responsiveness, price, nonprice factors and bidder responsibility.

Responsiveness. Responsiveness means adherence to the precise terms set forth in the solicitation document, such as specifications, quantities to be delivered, schedules and other stipulations, whether these terms are required by regulations or developed for this particular purchase. You will be excluded from further consideration if your bid is determined to be nonresponsive.

Price. The price determined is the true or effective price as opposed to the quoted price. A number of factors account for the distinction. For example, as a matter of principle, any discounts offered by the bidder reduce the effective price. The terms on which discounts are available, however, must be advantageous to the government. Thus, if you offer a discount for early payment, the maximum payment delay for which the discount is available must exceed the buyer's standard payment delay as stipulated in the IFB.

Other adjustments that will be made to determine the effective price are for such factors as transportation, government inspection, use of government property and any other elements set forth in the IFB. Any adjustments in your bid price must be in accordance with the requirements specified in the invitation. Thus, you will have the opportunity to consider these factors when developing your bid.

Nonprice Factors. Factors not related to price that may enter into the evaluation of bids include delivery schedules and the availability to the government of proprietary data. The IFB will identify these factors and indicate the weight they will be given in the evaluation process. In addition, certain priorities may apply if the low bids of two or more competitors are equal and the bids are otherwise equal in all respects. Under these conditions, the award decision may be governed by the small-business or the labor surplus area set-aside programs, according to the Federal Acquisition Regulations (FAR 6.203).

Bidder Responsibility. Under government policy, a contractor who cannot be classified by the contracting officer as a responsible contractor cannot be awarded a government contract. There are several bases the contracting officer must use to evaluate the responsibility of potential sources. Two of the most important are the contractor's capacity to perform the work, including ability to comply with the government's specified delivery schedule and ability to finance the work costs until government payment is received. These two elements are known as *capacity* and *credit*.

Acceptance, Rejection, and Award. Ordinarily, the contract is awarded during the acceptance period specified in the IFB. If this is impossible, the contracting officer will obtain an extension from each bidder. The award is made by furnishing to the successful bidder a properly executed award document or a notice of award in a format determined by the procuring agency.

A government agency may terminate bidding at any stage without awarding the contract. This means bidders have wasted time and money invested in preparing bids. There are many reasons for cancelling a sealed-bid procurement. The most common are:

☐ Indications of collusion among the bidders
☐ Ambiguities or defects in the specification
☐ No further need for the supplies or service

If this should happen, you will be notified and told why the action was taken. The government assumes no liability for your bidding costs.

Mistakes in Bids. As in any formal offer, the consequences of mistakes in bids can range from trivial to catastrophic.

Disposition Before Award. Contract officers have two ways to handle a mistake in a bid: they can allow a correction or a withdrawal of the bid. In practice, the officer may be reluctant to let you withdraw if it seems possible to correct the error.

In general, the officer will allow correction if *both* of the following conditions are met:

- ☐ The change would not alter the relative standing of the bidders
- ☐ The error—usually clerical—cannot be traced to a document or the original bid.

Do not assume, however, that any error you claim will be uncritically accepted. The officer may decide that there was no error and that you are merely looking for a chance to get in a last-minute change or to back out of the bidding. In that case, you may not be allowed to make the change or to withdraw.

Disposition After Award. If you have accepted the contract on the basis of a bid that contains an error, you will have more difficulty getting an adjustment than you would have had adjusting the bid before acceptance. But if you can show that the error was obvious—either because it created a conflict with other features of the bid or because it produced an estimate clearly out of proportion to the whole procurement—you can have the contract rescinded. Otherwise, your contract will stand, unless the change favors the government.

Types of Contracts. There are two types of contracts used in sealed bid procurement: the firm fixed-price contract (FFP) and the fixed-price contract with escalation (FPE). In an FFP, the contractor assumes 100% of the monetary risk of performance; with an FPE, the government accepts some of the risk, according to Federal Acquisition Regulations (FAR 14.1040).

Procurement by Negotiation

Negotiated procurement is generally used only when sealed bids are not feasible. As the term *negotiated* implies, this method normally involves a discussion between the government agency and the potential supplier. Virtually all facets of the proposed relationship may be covered. In addition to price, performance, and quality requirements, the contractor's management structure and the availability to the contractor of government facilities may be discussed.

Negotiated purchases are usually competitive. In certain circumstances, however, the government recognizes that sole-source or noncompetitive procurement is essential. The most common reason for a noncompetitive negotiated procurement is that one organization or individual is believed to be far better able than others to supply the needed goods or services within the required time.

Even here, however, there is an element of competition. If as a result of the discussions it appears that the agency's confidence is misplaced, another contractor will be solicited.

In contrast to sealed bidding, communications don't have to be confined to formalized written inquiries. The very nature of the procedure precludes this kind of restriction. Nevertheless, the same restrictions apply to sensitive information (see the section on constraints on communication in this chapter).

The negotiation process seeks to reach a mutually satisfactory agreement between you and the government on all contract matters. Negotiations can be handled through letters or telephone discussions or through more formal face-to-face discussions.

The government's stated objective is to pay a fair and reasonable price for the product or service it is buying. You must therefore be prepared to support your costs and profit. This includes ensuring that all factual items can be supported and that estimates are based on sound, logical bases.

Before a negotiation, you may wish to read Chapter 8 of the *Armed Services Pricing Manual*, which discusses negotiation requirements and various negotiation techniques used by the government. The manual may be purchased from the Superintendent of Documents, Attention: Mail List Section, U.S. Government Printing Office, Washington, D.C. 20402, at a nominal price.

Competition in Contracting Act of 1984. This law requires full and open competition in all federal procurement. (All previous laws on federal procurement had indicated that "advertised procurement" was the preferred method.)

The current law is not applicable to:

☐ Contracts under small-purchase procedures

☐ Contracts under the SBA 8(a) program (minority awards)

☐ Contracts using other procedures expressly authorized by statute

☐ Modifications under the terms of an existing contract

☐ Orders placed under requirements contracts or definite-quantity contracts

☐ Orders placed under indefinite-quantity contracts awarded in conformance with the full and open competition standards.

The exception for contracts covered by statutory procedures is for those using other than full and open competition. The situations where expressly authorized procedures are applicable are:

☐ Only one responsible source

☐ Unusual and compelling urgency

☐ Industrial mobilization or experimental, developmental or research work

☐ International agreement

☐ Authorized or required by statute

☐ National security

☐ Public interest.

To use the exceptions, there must be a written justification or determination and findings. Contracts awarded under these exceptions are usually negotiated based on cost estimates or are based on catalog or market prices of commercial items or services sold to the public in substantial quantities.

The Truth in Negotiation Act. This statute requires that where there is reasonable expectation that a negotiated procurement will exceed $100,000, the contractor must submit cost or pricing data in support of this proposal. The requirement, which is subject to certain exceptions, applies not only to new procurement actions but also to any negotiated contract modification that exceeds $100,000, even though the original procurement action may have been formally advertised and therefore exempt from the requirement. The regulation also allows the contracting officer to apply this requirement where an original procurement or modification is less than $100,000.

The law stipulates that submitted cost or pricing data must be current, complete and accurate at the time of the negotiation agreement and that the contractor must so certify to the contracting officer. In addition, the contractor is held responsible for obtaining the same information from any subcontractors who are awarded subcontracts in excess of $100,000.

To implement these provisions, the standard negotiated contract provides for an audit of performance records. If the cost and pricing data previously submitted and certified are overstated at the time of submission and certification, the government has the right to reduce the agreed-on price by the amount of the overstatement.

Finally, the statute requires the contracting officer to negotiate with all contractors "in the competitive range"—that is, those that have passed preliminary scrutiny.

SUBMITTING THE PROPOSAL

Every RFP or IFB includes the following vital parts:

Work Statement. This describes the service or product desired. Be sure you understand what it says. Some requirements may refer only to a Military Specification (MIL-SPEC) number. The MIL-SPEC may require packaging in wood crates, while you normally use pasteboard boxes. Failure to review the cited specifications could result in increased costs or the inability to be responsive.

General Clauses. These are often called "boiler plates." Normally, you will find a list of all possible clauses referenced to the Federal Acquisitions Regulations (FAR) or to an FAR supplement. The contemplated clauses are marked with an X. Be sure you know what each clause says. Some marked clauses may not apply to you or may be clauses you do not want to accept. It may be possible to get them changed or removed in negotiation.

Special Clauses. These are nonstandard but apply to your special circumstances. They may be negotiable.

"Reps and Certs." These are representations and certifications that you must take care to answer correctly because they will become part of the contract. If you answer them incorrectly, you may be judged unresponsive or the contract may be cancelled.

Funding and Payments. This provision tells you how the government will provide money for the contract and how you will be paid. It includes progress payments in fixed-price contracts.

Performance and Monitoring. This provision reveals whether you are required to report progress on the contract. If so, it could have an impact on cost.

Inspection and Acceptance. This provision tells you how the government will perform inspection and acceptance, which is required before you can get paid.

Subcontracts. This provision tells you whether the government must approve subcontracts and when.

Proposal Requirements. This provision covers what kind of proposal is expected. Sealed-bid proposals usually are accomplished by inserting the bid price on the award portion of Standard Form 33. Negotiated procurement can range from inserting a price on the Standard Form 33 to completing a Standard Form 1411 or 1412 with all of the required backup explained in FAR 15.804-6.

The proposal is your sales pitch. More elaborate proposal requirements will require a *Technical Proposal*, which describes your approach to satisfying the government requirement, and a *Management Proposal*, telling how you are or will be organized to perform the task. These two volumes will be submitted separately from the *Cost Proposal*, which states your price. This price includes costs you estimate for completing the task plus your proposed profit.

THE NEGOTIATING PROCESS

Negotiations may be carried out in writing or orally. The contracting officer will point out apparent ambiguities, uncertainties or deficiencies in your proposal and will give you a reasonable opportunity to clarify, correct or otherwise strengthen it. The office may conclude the negotiation process by asking the contractors for a best and final offer and advising them of a cutoff date.

Criteria for Choice. Selection is based on the contracting officer's judgment on which contractor or proposal offers the greatest advantage to the government, "price and other factors considered." This means that a higher-priced offer may be selected over lower-priced offers if other factors, especially technical superiority, are found to outweigh the price factor.

Debriefings. If your proposal is turned down and you wish to know why, the offering agency will grant you an explanatory or debriefing conference. At this session, you can learn in general terms the factors that weighed against you. If you plan to do business with the government on a regular basis, you should take advantage of this opportunity to improve your bargaining skills.

Protests. If you believe the government's evaluation of your bid or proposal has not been properly carried out, or if there is a defect in the procurement process, you have the right to protest. Protests can be registered before or after the award. You can file your protest with the contracting officer or you can protest directly to the Comptroller General. The authorities are obliged to give a written protest full consideration and to reply specifically to each point raised. On the other hand, there is little use in protesting unless you have put together a convincing case supported by facts.

Contract Types. In FAR Part 16, the following contracts are cited for use by federal agencies in negotiated purchasing:

☐ Firm-fixed-price (FFP)
☐ Fixed-price with escalation (FPE)

☐ Fixed-price incentive (FPI)

☐ Fixed-price redeterminable prospective (FPRP)

☐ Fixed-price redeterminable retroactive (FPRR)

☐ Cost reimbursement (CR)

☐ Cost sharing (CS)

☐ Cost plus incentive fee (CPIF)

☐ Cost plus a fixed fee (CPFF)

☐ Time and materials (T&M)

☐ Labor hour (LH)

☐ Letter (LC)

☐ Indefinite delivery (IDC)

These contracts range from the stringent fixed-price type, in which price is predetermined when the contract is awarded, to the cost type, in which the procurement price is determined in an audit of performance costs undertaken after completion of the work. Between these extremes is a spectrum of pricing arrangements varying in flexibility. One of the most common is the fixed-price incentive, in which the contractor and the government agree to share cost overruns and underruns on a predetermined formula. Contracts based on costs incurred plus a percentage of costs are illegal in government contracts.

IMPLEMENTING THE CONTRACT

When you accept a contract you begin a relationship with the government agency that will last the life of the contract. Implementation of contract terms will involve administrative procedures of varying complexity. Some of these are discussed below.

Administrative Considerations

Four of the terms and conditions of the contract (some of which are listed in the section on submitting the proposal) merit a closer look. These are funding and payment, inspection and acceptance, changes in the contract and termination.

Funding and Payment. In a fixed-price contract, you will be paid either at the completion of the work or, in the most common arrangement, in a series of partial payments based on partial delivery and acceptance. Under a cost-reimbursement contract, you will receive the funds on presentation of an invoice and verification of the cost incurred during contract performance.

Inspection and Acceptance. Basically, the inspection and acceptance clause gives the contracting officer the right to inspect your production process at reasonable intervals during the life of the contract. The clause also entitles the officer to inspect your finished product before accepting it and to refuse acceptance for cause. If your product can be judged against specifications, the purchaser may be satisfied with simple proof of conformity. In that case, you should set up an efficient quality-control system. If the contracting officer is satisfied that you have such a system, you may be subjected to little or no surveillance.

Ordinarily, once the government accepts your product it has no recourse, at least for that particular run or batch, unless it can prove fraud or demonstrate that the defects defy ordinary inspection techniques. Some contracts, however, require the contractor to grant the purchaser an extended warranty, valid after acceptance.

Changes in the Contract. All government contracts contain a clause giving the purchaser broad authority to make changes affecting the contracted work. If you incur additional costs because of these changes, you have the right to request additional compensation—even with a fixed-price contract. You must submit a written request for the adjustment within 30 days after receiving written notice of the intended change.

Sometimes, contract provisions are altered informally at the contractor's or the government agency's request. There is always the possibility that later, when you request compensation for expenses resulting from the change, the official who made the commitment has been replaced or has lost all record of it, or the person who directed the change may not have had the authority to do so. Only the contracting officer can alter the contract terms or conditions, and the change must be in writing.

Termination. Your contract with a government agency will contain a provision for termination at the convenience of the government or by default. Termination at the government's convenience is usually because of a change in its needs or a cutoff of essential funds. In any case, you are entitled to compensation, but you should be prepared for some delay and considerable red tape.

When you are terminated for default, you are held responsible. The government will contend that you either failed to make a delivery of acceptable quality on schedule or were not making adequate progress toward fulfilling the contract.

In the latter case, you must be given notice of the government's intention to terminate and an opportunity to show why this action should not be taken. Normally a default relieves the government of the obligation to pay you anything, even amounts to cover costs previously incurred. Furthermore, the government may recover from you any excess costs incurred to obtain the needed goods or services elsewhere.

Delays. Delays in meeting delivery schedules are a major cause of termination by default. Often a government agency will accept a late delivery, prompting the contractor to believe that lateness will be ignored. Unfortunately, acceptance of your late delivery does not necessarily constitute a waiver of the government's right to declare you in default. Therefore, if your ability to meet delivery schedules is impeded and you are not at fault, it is very important that you request an immediate adjustment in the schedules, including, if necessary, an extension of the life of the contract. Once the machinery for termination has been set in motion, you may be able to save yourself from being sued by proving you were not to blame, but you may have a difficult time reversing the termination decision.

ACCOUNTING AND PRICING

Since the cost proposal is so important to winning a government contract and assuring that the experience is financially rewarding, accounting and pricing should be addressed. Unlike most commercial cost accounting, for government contracts it is a *total cost absorption technique*. That means that if a cost is to apply to the government contract, it must be specifically identified in the contract or grouped and then apportioned to the contract on a basis that includes all of the contractor's similar activity.

A work-in-process technique must be developed that will capture all such costs in the time frame in which they are incurred. Conceptually, this work-in-process isn't closed until the contract is completed. Many contractors accomplish this by using memorandum records that can be reconciled to the general ledger. This is acceptable to the government and preserves the established management accounting system.

Selected Cost Elements

The handling of certain cost elements illustrates why the memorandum records are often an effective method.

General and Administrative Expenses. Government contract costing requires that general and administrative expenses be pooled and allocated to all activities of a contractor. The most common method is to allocate expenses as a percentage of total costs incurred. This allocation may be made monthly at a budgeted or estimated annual rate, but at the end of the year it must be adjusted to the actual annual rate. Allocating these costs on the actual monthly rate is not acceptable. Generally accepted accounting principles would normally treat general and administrative expenses as period costs. In government accounting, all work-in-process costs incurred in a year will bear the general and administrative rate of that year, regardless of when they are recognized as cost of sales.

Independent Research and Development Costs. These costs must be treated like jobs in government contracts, in that they will be included in the allocation base of applicable indirect expenses. Total indirect research and development costs plus applicable indirect expenses are allocated to government contracts like general and administrative expenses. Some contractors include this element with their general and administrative expense.

Depreciation. Under Cost Accounting Standards (CAS), the method for determining depreciation is unlike the way any firm would compute depreciation for financial accounting or tax purposes. There are rigid rules for determining costs to be depreciated, determining the life of the asset and selecting the method used. Asset cost is the actual cost less estimated residual value. Life of an asset is the documented actual period similar assets were used. The method can be any recognized method acceptable by the IRS, whether used in financial statements or not. Companies exempt from CAS (such as small businesses) must use the same depreciation used for financial reporting, provided the method is acceptable for federal income tax purposes.

Overhead or Indirect Expenses. These costs include all amounts that are not direct costs or general and administrative expenses. They are grouped into homogeneous pools and then allocated so a fair share of the annual cost is given to all work in the base. Like general and administrative expenses, a budgeted rate can be used monthly, but it must be adjusted at year-end to actual costs.

Facility Capital Cost of Money. This is an imputed cost designed to compensate the contractor for use of capital assets based on net book value. It is rarely included in the books of accounts and is applied to individual jobs, similar to the application of overhead expenses.

Proposals. You will be expected to determine the price of the work called for in the proposed contract using accounting data. A Standard Form 1411 is used to transmit the cost proposal, but is in no way complete even if item prices are shown on the form. A summary of the cost elements and the rationale for the estimated value of each element must be attached. You will be expected to use historical accounting data to back up your estimate.

For example, you may show that the average cost of one hour of an engineer's time costs $20.00 as of your last payroll. You anticipate that by the time the engineer performs this job, the average rate will be 5% higher. You would, therefore, price the engineer at $21.00 per hour. Other costs, such as materials or equipment rentals, may be based on written quotations or catalog prices. These same techniques will be applied and shown for all cost elements. In some cases, you may have no data and will have to make a raw estimate. You state this in the backup. Remember that, whatever basis is used for cost projections, you will need to certify that all of the data is current, accurate and complete.

Cost Allowability. Allowable costs for a government contract are defined by the government. FAR Par 31 contains 51 specific cost areas that identify each cost as allowable, partly allowable (limits) or unallowable. Those costs that are unallowable or exceed certain limits must be excluded from proposals and actual cost presentations. This means that even if a cost is properly included in financial statements and properly deducted for tax purposes it may not be properly used to price or cost government contracts.

Cost Accounting Standards. FAR Part 30 covers Cost Accounting Standards (CAS), which were originally the subject of Public Law 91-379, and applied only to military contracts. Now, however, CAS applies to all federal government procurements. Small business is exempt from the provisions of CAS, but since many of the standards have been included in the Cost Principles (FAR Part 31), no one is totally exempt. The standards incorporated into the cost principles are not onerous, but may not coincide with some practices of a typical commercial cost-accounting system.

POSTAWARD ADMINISTRATION

After you have been awarded a contract, you may be selected for a postaward conference. This will likely happen if it is your first contract or there are complex technical or financial matters. At this conference, you learn how and when you should contact the administrative contracting officer and auditor, how you get paid, how inspections will work, your responsibilities under special clauses, etc. If you have any questions, no matter how trivial, this is the time to ask them.

If your contract contains the cost reimbursable clause or progress payment provisions, you will want to negotiate provisional billing rates for overhead, general and administrative expenses and facility capital cost of money. To do this, prepare a proposal showing your budget for these items each year and send it to the auditor and contracting officer. You may receive a letter accepting your "provisional billing rates" or the rates may be audited, followed by negotiation of acceptable billing rates. Usually, these rates are slightly lower than you think they should be because it is the government's objective not to overpay. These rates will be used to reimburse your actual costs on a regular basis. For cost reimbursable contracts, these rates are adjusted after your fiscal year-end. You will be paid or owe the difference between actual rates and provisional rates (FAR 42.704).

Businesses with large government contracts (not just large businesses) may be subject to formal reviews in:

- ☐ Quality assurance
- ☐ Estimating system
- ☐ Insurance and pension
- ☐ Employee compensation.

The findings of these reviews may be used to disallow costs or may serve as a basis for relying on the contractor's systems.

Expect the government to pay you in 30 days or less. If it takes longer, you may be entitled to interest on the billing. Progress payments are generally much faster. But if you make any billing errors, the bill will probably be returned and the payment period will start over.

To bill for reimbursement of cost, you will use Standard Forms 1034 and 1035 (Public Voucher for Purchases and Services Other Than Personnel). Usually, any fixed fee included in the contract can be billed at the fixed-fee rate times the costs being billed. A small percentage of the fee billed will be withheld until a reserve is built up to assure proper close-out of the contract. Once the fixed amount of the fee is billed, you can't bill further fees, even if you continue to bill cost. Conversely, if the contract is completed before the estimated cost is used up, you can bill for any fixed fee not already billed.

Fixed price contracts are billed to the government at the price indicated in the contract as the items are delivered. If you take progress payments, the government will deduct an amount to liquidate the payments made as progress payments. Normally, the liquidation rate will be the same as the progress payment rate. On long-term contracts (over two years), a lower liquidation rate can be negotiated so that the liquidation on price will not include the actual profit indicated.

SUMMARY

Dealing with the government can be financially rewarding, but it can also be frustrating. Government contractors frequently overlook the favorable aspects of government contracts, while concentrating on undesirable aspects.

Some of the more troublesome areas of doing business with the government are: (i) the extent of detailed oversight by auditors and inspectors; (ii) funding instability in the annual appropriation process; (iii) overemphasis on competition; (iv) the exposure caused by required certifications and (v) the need to comply with a host of specific regulations, socioeconomic objectives and statutes applicable only to government contracts.

On the positive side, government contracting (i) is financially rewarding; (ii) provides the opportunity to develop advanced technologies partially or entirely at government expense that can be applied to the commercial marketplace; (iii) provides financing not available in most commercial work, since monthly progress payments or partial billings are authorized; (iv) provides a balanced business base that can help absorb fixed overhead costs, and (v) provides the opportunity to display corporate patriotism.

One might conclude that the rewards outweigh the burdens. However, as in any complex venture, one needs to know the ground rules of the game if success is to be assured.

14

Going Public

The expression "going public" describes the process of offering for sale to the general public securities—generally common or preferred stock or bonds—of a privately owned company.

Usually a company begins to think about going public when the funding required to meet business growth has exceeded the company's debt capacity.

In an Initial Public Offering (IPO), a company may sell its unissued securities to raise additional capital, so the company receives all of the proceeds—called a primary offering. Alternatively, securities that belonged to the owners of the company may be sold, whereby the owners receive the proceeds—called a secondary distribution. Sometimes the offering may be a combination, for the benefit of shareholders and the company.

The President of the United States in a recent report to Congress on the state of small business noted that small companies with total assets under $500,000 issued more than 68% of all IPOs. The typical issue from this group had a median value of $2 million, or four times the companies' preoffering asset value.

Although small corporations did not participate in the public equity market for many years, these statistics indicate that many are now active. The President's report stated a major contributor to this activity is the effort by the Securities and Exchange Commission (SEC) to reduce issuing costs and registration and reporting burdens on small companies. The SEC began simplifying the registration process by adopting Form S-18, which applies to offerings of less than $7,500,000, reduced disclosure requirements. It was intended to reduce costs and accelerate the registration process. Regulation D continued the trend that started with the adoption of Form S-18 by establishing exemptions from registration for offerings up to $500,000 over a twelve-month period as well as larger offerings described in this chapter. By these actions, the SEC has made access to equity markets easier for smaller companies.

Owners of growth-oriented closely held companies who read this may begin to have visions of their company's name appearing in the New York Stock Exchange listings. Equity capital from the public is very attractive. After all, the purchasers of a company's common stock are paid no interest on their investment. The corporate officers do not guarantee its repayment, marketability, or value; and, as far as the corporation is concerned, the investment is permanent.

An investor is motivated to purchase a new stock issue only if it appears to be a better investment than a low or no-risk alternative, such as an insured certificate of deposit or Treasury Bill. A stock's value will increase only if, over time, the public places a higher value on the security than at the initial offering. Although the market value of a company's stock is affected by many factors, performance is the major factor. Since the company's performance may be dependent on its access to capital for expansion, equipment needs, acquisitions, major sales or distribution, investors want all or a major portion of an offering's proceeds to be available. An IPO is much less attractive when a substantial amount of the proceeds go to the present owners. Consequently, IPOs are almost always primary offerings or offerings where only a small number of shares held by owners are included.

In this chapter, only federal government regulations are discussed. Anyone considering issuing securities should be sure to comply with appropriate state and federal securities laws. We intend to provide you with the benefit of our experience by reviewing the process of going public, informing you of the pros and cons and removing some of the mystique that surrounds this major event in a company's life.

THE DECISION

The decision to go public requires in-depth analysis. Although going public offers many attractive advantages, it also has many disadvantages to be weighed carefully. Once you make the decision, it's time-consuming and costly to retreat to nonpublic status. Some of the principal advantages and disadvantages that must be considered before making the decision are summarized here.

ADVANTAGES

Access to Long-Term Capital

A privately owned company may have limited sources of capital. For the most part, a company expands by reinvesting its undistributed earnings and by looking to its owners, banks, or institutional lenders for additional capital funds. Without more capital, the company's earning capacity may be restricted, the ability of the owners to provide capital may be limited and borrowing must be repaid with interest. Sale of the company's stock, however, provides permanent non-interest-bearing capital. Furthermore, once the company and its securities are known to the investing public, future stock offerings may be easier to sell, assuming no adverse change in its affairs.

Subsequent Capital Needs

When securities are offered for sale to the public, they must first be registered with the SEC. Once the company has gone through the SEC's registration process, succeeding issues ordinarily take less to process. Registered companies may, under certain circumstances, also qualify to use simplified registration forms when offering additional securities.

Expansion Through Business Combinations

When a company's securities have an established market, it's easier to negotiate mergers or acquisitions using the company's own securities. When a privately owned company wants to acquire another business, it's difficult to trade stock for the acquired entity since it's impossible to measure clearly the market value of the stock. With publicly held shares, however, the value of those shares is easier to determine, since the daily market stock quotations show the value that the investing public places on the shares. All other things being equal, the owners of a private company are often more interested in merging with a public company than with another private company because the shareholders may prefer to exchange their holdings for a readily marketable security.

Owner Diversification and Liquidity

If all or most of your wealth is invested in your business, going public offers a chance to sell part of those holdings for cash and diversify your investments. Most owners would like to limit the number of shares sold to raise enough cash yet retain control of the business.

Estate-Tax Planning

In the event of your death, your shares in the company you own must be valued to determine the taxable value of your estate. If substantial estate taxes are due, your executors could be forced to sell the company to raise the cash needed to pay estate taxes. When a company's shares are widely owned by the public and the stock is actively traded on an exchange or in the over-the-counter market, the value and marketability of the securities for estate-tax purposes can be more clearly established—and the estate's liquidity increased.

Marketability of Investments

You want to dispose of a part of your holdings during your lifetime to be in a more liquid position. This is, of course, easier if there are established markets for your company's securities. It's also easier for you or any other shareholder to borrow money with collateral consisting of securities that have an established market than with securities having no market.

Employee Benefit Plans and Incentives

When a company is publicly owned, it's possible to establish stock compensation arrangements that will serve to attract and keep key personnel. Stock option plans, for example, may be more attractive to officers and other key personnel than generous salary arrangements, since these plans provide the employee with a sense of ownership and the opportunity to share in any stock price appreciation as well as tax advantages.

Public Awareness of Business

Every shareholder is a potential customer. The company often benefits when its shares are owned by the public, especially if the company sells a consumer product or service. The more widespread the distribution of shares, the greater the public's awareness of the company's products or services.

DISADVANTAGES

Lack of Operating Confidentiality

The registration statement and subsequent reports to shareholders require disclosure of many facets of your company's business, operations and finances that may never before have been known outside the company. Some particularly sensitive areas of disclosure are the remuneration of officers and directors; the security holdings of officers, directors and major shareholders ("insiders"); details regarding stock option plans and deferred compensation plans; and extensive financial information, including sales, costs of sales, gross profits, net income, borrowings, and sales to major customers.

Pressure on Short-Term Performance

Prior to going public, you can operate your business independently—taking whatever risks you wish, secure in the knowledge that it's only your money (or the bank's) at stake. Once the company becomes publicly owned, you acquire as many partners as you have shareholders and are accountable to them.

In a closely held company, management has the flexibility to focus attention on long-term goals, even if earnings in the near term suffer. In a public company, the investor's return depends on the company's performance, as well as the overall market's performance. Shareholders expect steady growth in areas such as sales, profits, market share and product innovation. Management must balance short-term strategies to achieve growth with long-term goals. For example, management may believe that a substantial advertising and marketing campaign will result in a profitable product line within a year or two. In the interim, however, the cost of the campaign will depress earnings. Management must weigh the potential long-term benefits against shareholder reaction, the effect on the market value of the stock and the risk that the long-term sales goal may not be achieved. Finally, business flexibility may be limited, such as in sale of the company and election of officers, which may require the vote of the shareholders. In addition, the ability to act quickly is inhibited because management must wait on voting to take place.

Restrictions on Management

After the public offering, the officers, directors, and principal holders of the company's equity securities and their relatives will probably become subject to insider trading provisions under SEC regulations. Because they have access to information before the public does, they must exercise caution in trading in the company's equity securities and discussing the company's affairs. For example, gains they realize in closed transactions (purchase and sale or sale and purchase) within a six-month period may be recoverable by the company if gains are from insider information.

Initial Cost of Offering

The process of going public is expensive and time-consuming. Preparation of the registration document is a complicated process that occupies the time of many people within the organization and several outside experts. Ordinarily, the documents must pass critical review by two different lawyers, the company's and the underwriter's. The financial statements must be audited by an independent public accountant. In addition, the printing bill alone is often quite substantial.

Possible Loss of Management Control

If more than 50% of the company's shares are sold to the public, the original owners could lose control of the company. This is especially likely if most of the shares sold to the public are in the hands of a few individuals who could challenge management, and possibly obtain control of the company by voting themselves on the board of directors at the annual stockholders' meeting. If, however, the shares held by the public are widely distributed, management could exercise control, even though it owns less than 50% of the shares.

Accounting and Tax Practices

Owner-managers are typically more concerned with tax savings than with earnings per share and their accounting practices may be designed solely for the purpose of minimizing taxes on income. Their financial statements may not have been audited or even prepared in accordance with generally accepted accounting principles (GAAP). If this applies to you, be prepared to put your "accounting house" in order before going public. Conforming financial statements to prescribed rules and GAAP is a condition of filing with the SEC, and the cost and other implications of the changes you might have to make to meet the SEC standards could be significant.

Ongoing Costs

After going public, companies become subject to the SEC's periodic reporting requirements which vary with the number of share-holders and major company changes. The reports are designed to keep the information in the registration statement up-to-date—requiring maintenance of adequate financial staff and professional assistance, and adding significantly to the company's cost of doing business.

Demand for Dividends

As the owner of a private company, you may have declared dividends depending on your needs or sections of the Internal Revenue Code dealing with unreasonable compensation or accumulations of earnings (*see chapter 11 of this book*). As a public company you may have to adopt a regular dividend policy if shareholders demand it. Generally, investors in companies that have "gone public" do not expect a dividend during the first several years of public life. They expect earnings to be reinvested to ensure long-term viability.

WHO SHOULD GO PUBLIC

Many companies may have capital needs that could be satisfied by going public. Individual, institutional, regional or industry-specific investors also have needs. After evaluating what it offers to the investing public and the demands of investors, management may decide that traditional debt financing or owner capital infusion can satisfy their capital needs.

Here are some questions you should ask to determine whether your company is a public offering candidate:

☐ Has the company demonstrated a sustained or increasing growth rate high enough to attract investors? Generally, a company that outpaces the industry average in growth will have a better chance of attracting prospective investors than one with marginal or inconsistent growth. Many companies that have successfully gone public have shown market support for their product or service that would sustain a 25-50% annual growth rate for a five-year period. This growth potential should be even larger if institutional investors are expected to buy shares in the company.

☐ Has the company reached the point where prospects for maintaining a strong sales and earnings growth trend in the future are reasonably good? Underwriters usually consider a company as an IPO candidate when they have at least $10 million in sales and profitability of approximately $1 million or more. The exception: the early stage company that has mitigated the investment risk.

☐ Are the company's products or services highly visible and of interest to the investing public? The established company can satisfy these requirements with historical data while the early stage company must use projections. Usually, the early stage company qualifies as an IPO candidate based on the uniqueness of its product or service. In addition, it should have reached the stage in its development where the risks usually associated with a venture capital investment—product development, manufacturing capability, market acceptance and market size—have been reduced.

☐ Does management believe it can meet the disclosure and financial reporting requirements and other associated demands that will be made by the newly acquired "business partners" and the regulatory authorities? In an established company as well as an early stage company, the quality of the management team is a key factor. Since registration requirements and analyst meetings require detailed analysis and descriptions from executive management, they must have credibility to the investing public; the organization must have depth and quality in leadership and skill. Financial reporting requirements for both the SEC and shareholders must be provided on a timely basis. To meet these requirements, a system of management controls and financial reporting is necessary to maintain credibility and investor confidence after the IPO.

If you can answer these questions or have put together a plan to improve the company's ability to qualify as an IPO candidate then the remaining portion of this chapter provides information necessary to understand the process and consequences of going public.

HOW TO GO PUBLIC

The Securities Act of 1933 requires that a registration statement, such as Form S-1 or S-18, be filed with the SEC before an offering to sell securities is made public. It also prohibits the actual sale of securities unless the required registration statement has become effective.

The registration statement has two parts. Part I is the prospectus, which must be provided to anyone who has been made an offer to purchase the securities or ultimately buys them. Part II contains supplemental data and is available to the public at the offices of the SEC or by mail.

An offering of more than $7.5 million must be registered using Form S-1, and offerings of up to that amount can be filed using Form S-18. There are several exemptions from registration requirements. For example, regulation A is for certain public offerings not exceeding $1.5 million, used infrequently because underwriters' opportunities are reduced due to the limited amount of capital that can be raised. Regulation D rules 504, 505, and 506 are for offerings that do not exceed $500,000, $5 million and unlimited respectively.

A registration using Form S-1 includes business information in both narrative and financial format.

Registration Statement: Part I

Part I of the registration statement, also known as the prospectus, contains basic information including:

- [ ] Company business and properties
- [ ] Degree of risk associated with the company's business
- [ ] Use of proceeds
- [ ] Underwriter's compensation
- [ ] Significant legal proceedings
- [ ] Extent of the company's competition
- [ ] Securities being offered
- [ ] Names of directors and officers and their remuneration

☐ Options outstanding to purchase securities

☐ Company's financial history, as follows:

—. Detailed financial statements that include a balance sheet for each of the last two fiscal year-ends and other statements for each of the last three years that have been audited by an independent public accountant and, depending on the timing, interim unaudited financial data

—. Selected financial data, for five fiscal years and possible interim periods, including such items as revenues, net income, earnings per share and long-term debt

—. Management's description of the company's financial condition in terms of liquidity and capital resources, and its explanation of any factors that have significantly affected or may affect the company's operating results.

The prospectus generally serves two purposes. The first is as a selling document to prospective buyers of the securities. The second is as a basis of legal protection for the issuing company and its officers. It ensures that a prospective purchaser has been provided with relevant information about the company so he or she can make an informed judgment with respect to his or her investment.

The dual functions that the prospectus serves may, however, be in conflict with each other. Management naturally wishes to tell the prospective investors about the company's past achievements and to predict successful operations. At the same time, to guard against possible litigation from purchasers of the securities who may claim they were misled, management must make sure that it adequately discloses the risks.

Registration Statement: Part II

Part II of the registration statement contains supplemental data, which is not required to be provided to each prospective investor, including such items as:

☐ Listings of the registrant's subsidiaries

☐ Certain data on recent sales of unregistered securities

☐ Listings of financial statements and copies of certain documents filed as exhibits

☐ Descriptions of marketing arrangements

☐ Details of the expenses of the offering

☐ Supplemental financial statement schedules supporting certain financial data.

Form S-18 reduces disclosure requirements and has resulted in a more timely and less expensive registration process for many companies. While many requirements of Form S-18 are the same as for Form S-1, the major differences to consider are:

☐ *Financial Statements.* S-18 requires that two fiscal years are audited and prepared in accordance with GAAP, while S-1 requires three fiscal years audited and presented in accordance with more detailed SEC regulations.

☐ *Narrative Disclosures.* S-18 requires less detailed description of business, operations and performance than S-1 does.

☐ *Filing.* S-18 allows for regional filing in one of the nine regional offices of the SEC, while all S-1 filings are made with the SEC's Division of Corporate Finance in Washington, D.C.

The appropriate form to file depends generally on the size of offering and interpretation by legal counsel specialized in securities.

WHO CAN HELP

Once you've decided to go forward with a public offering, the next task is to assemble the registration team. It consists of management, your legal counsel, the underwriter, the underwriter's legal counsel, your independent accountants, a financial printer and, in some cases, a financial public relations firm. In addition to the help provided by the team, the SEC can also assist through the Division of Corporate Finance Office of Small Business Policy. The personnel of the SEC's regional offices can respond to any questions on federal securities laws. In addition, SEC rules and regulations are available through the U.S. Government Printing Office.

The Underwriter

The principal role of the underwriter is to sell securities to the public. The underwriter also plays a significant role in advising you on the financing opportunities, structuring the transaction and determining the proper timing of the offering. The choice of underwriter is important because the investment bankers who perform these services vary widely in quality, cost and range of services. Most companies will have established a relationship with an investment banker or had preliminary discussions prior to selection. It's usually a good idea to make contact with an underwriter a year or two before the offering. Here are some of the factors to be considered in selecting the underwriter.

Reputation. The underwriter should have a good reputation in the investment community and among others who have used its services. The firm should be particularly well known in the company's target market—institutional investors, for example.

Experience. The underwriter should have experience and success with underwritings similar to yours in number of shares and dollar amount. The underwriter should also have experience analyzing and understanding your industry, since it must communicate the IPO opportunity and support the after-market through investor analysis.

Market-Making Capabilities. The underwriter should be able to attract a large number of investors and to generate enough interest in the stock to maintain a good market after the initial offering. Furthermore, the underwriter's distribution network should support the nationwide or regional image of your company and the appeal of its stock.

Ability to Provide Other Investment Banking Services After the Offering. The underwriter should be prepared to assist in locating additional sources of public or private capital and general financial counseling.

Fees To Be Charged. The underwriter's commissions and expenses for performing the brokering functions should be competitive.

The best way to gather information on the underwriter's capabilities is to ask the officers of other companies who have used its services. Your accountant and lawyer—both have frequent contact with underwriters on a regular basis—should also be reliable sources of recommendations. Ultimately, management must interview several underwriting firms and ask for proposals from each. References of other offerings the firm has underwritten should be obtained and contacted.

The underwriter's commitment to your stock is crucial, considering the time, effort, and money invested in the public offering process. You should fully comprehend different types of underwriting available before you choose an underwriter.

Types of Underwriting. When the underwriter is selected, a letter of intent should be signed that outlines the proposed terms of the offering and acknowledges the underwriter's intention to execute an underwriting agreement before the conclusion of the registration process. The letter of intent is not a binding agreement to underwrite the offering, but rather a preliminary understanding of the terms of the offering. It outlines the underwriter's compensation, any reimbursement for expenses and defines the type of underwriting. The following types of underwriting may be entered into:

☐ *Best Efforts.* The underwriter agrees to use its best efforts to sell as many shares as possible and is not obligated to purchase any unsold securities. This means you incur the time and cost to prepare to go public with no guarantee the shares will be sold. Even if the company's shares are not sold, outside members of the team are still compensated on an hourly basis, except for the underwriters. In addition to their commission for a successful offering of generally up to 10% of the amount raised, underwriters normally require a nonrefundable fee on their engagement to cover initial expenses. Should the deal fail to close, you remain responsible for a substantial bill for professional services in addition to the nonrefundable fee.

☐ *Best Efforts, All or None.* The offering is cancelled if the underwriter is unable to sell the entire issue. Should the deal fail to close, you are responsible for the cost of professional services in addition to the nonrefundable fee.

☐ *Firm Commitment.* The underwriter agrees to buy all of the stock being offered for sale and thereby assumes the risk for any unsold securities. You are responsible for the cost of professional services, but the offering proceeds are guaranteed when the underwriting becomes effective.

The Underwriting Agreement. Regardless of the type of underwriting, the actual underwriting agreement generally is not signed until the registration statement becomes effective. It's important to understand that even though your company may incur considerable expense in anticipation of an offering, there is no advance assurance that the offering will actually take place. A reputable underwriter, however, will generally not turn away without a valid reason.

Normally, the underwriting agreement is a document of 10-15 pages that covers various matters including:

☐ The type of offering

☐ Agreement by the company to sell and the underwriter to purchase a certain number of shares at a designated price

☐ Warranties by the company on the completeness and accuracy of the information included in the registration statement

☐ Indemnification of the underwriter against liabilities arising under federal securities laws

☐ Conditions or events that must occur before the underwriter is obligated to pay for the securities, normally including receipt of an acceptable "comfort letter" from the company's independent accountants and a representation letter from the company's counsel stating that the company has met all legal requirements to complete the offering

☐ Time and location of the closing.

Many of the factors that should be considered in selecting the underwriter—such as reputation, experience, service and fees—are for the most part equally applicable to the selection of the other team members.

Counsel for the Company

The competence of company legal counsel and its familiarity with SEC rules and regulations and the registration process are critical to timely and effective coordination. Counsel's principal role is to advise the company on compliance with provisions of the securities acts and with the various state and federal laws the company and the offering will be subject to. Counsel also oversees the progress of the various members of the registration team, ensures the timeliness and completeness of the process, and coordinates the resolution of any questions arising from the SEC review and the filing of the necessary amendments. Should any conferences with the SEC be necessary, counsel would be expected to attend them with the company's representative.

Counsel for the Underwriter

Counsel for the underwriter is selected by the underwriter and is generally responsible for drafting the underwriting agreement and reviewing the registration statement and any related agreements and contracts that are filed as exhibits. Counsel's principal objective is to ensure the registration statement is complete and not misleading.

The Independent Accountant

The independent accountant's principal responsibilities in preparing a registration statement are:

☐ Examining and expressing an opinion on the various financial statements that must be included in the document

☐ Reading, in depth, the text portion of the registration statement in order to identify any inconsistencies that may require changes or corrections to the text or the financial statements

☐ Issuing a letter (called a "comfort letter") to the underwriters, covering, in general, the financial statements' compliance, in both form and content, with applicable SEC regulations and describing any adverse changes in the company's financial position since the last audited balance sheet.

The Financial Printer

The financial printer is responsible for having the prospectus printed and ready for distribution. A printer that is convenient—since most printing will be done overnight—aware of SEC regulations and sensitive to the accuracy and speed required in a public offering is a necessary and important member of the team.

THE PROCESS

Once you've selected the underwriter and the other members of the registration team, you can start the public offering process. It generally commences with an organizational conference attended by the members of the registration team, including:

☐ The chief executive and financial officers of the company
☐ Counsel for the company
☐ A representative of the underwriters
☐ Counsel for the underwriters
☐ The independent accountant
☐ The financial printer.

Matters usually discussed at the organizational meeting include the nature of the offering, the appropriate SEC registration form and the anticipated filing date. A detailed registration timetable for each member of the team, which indicates the date each step is to be completed, is also developed (see appendix to this chapter for a public offering outline you could use for planning purposes).

At this first meeting it's important to assess your ability to make the transition. The systems and controls that support your financial statements must be reliable and in place. This is important because at the time of the offering the underwriters or the SEC may require accurate interim or stub information in addition to annual financial statements to proceed with the offering.

This is also your last opportunity to estimate what the process will cost, and what portion of the company will be sold. The underwriter's discount or commission can range from 5 to 15% of the total funds raised. The amount you agree to will depend on the total offering amount, the market rate for current offerings and the underwriter's effort to sell the stock. Also, depending on the total discount amount, certain expenses may be reimbursed and warrants (subscription rights to buy stocks) provided. While the underwriter's discount is not a cost until you close, all other services must be paid even if the offering does not close. Legal fees, depending on the extent of disorder (housekeeping) and state security filings (called Blue Sky) could range from $50,000 to $150,000. Accountants' fees, depending on the audit requirements and scope of the underwriter's comfort letter, could fall in the same range. Printing costs, based on length of the documents, color and picture use, and revisions could reach $100,000. If the offering is successful you will also be faced with SEC, NASD, Blue Sky and registrar and transfer agent fees.

Based on a survey of IPOs, total expenses for underwriters, attorneys, accountants and printers ranged from less than 10% to over 35% of the gross offering.

The entire process generally requires several months and in capsule form consists of the following:

- ☐ The initial registration statement
- ☐ Filing and SEC review
- ☐ The amended registration statement
- ☐ The preliminary ("red herring") prospectus
- ☐ Financial analyst meetings (road shows)
- ☐ The due diligence meeting

☐ The price amendment and the underwriting agreement

☐ Closing

Once a preliminary understanding with the underwriters has been reached, a "quiet period" begins when the company is subject to SEC guidelines regarding publication of information outside of the prospectus. The opportunity to enhance awareness of the company, its name, products and geographic markets will be limited, since any publicity that creates a favorable attitude towards the securities could be considered illegal. However, continuation of established, normal advertisements and financial information is acceptable. The timetable should include strategies for enhancing company visibility, as market awareness and acceptance of the offering could reduce an underwriter's sales efforts and, as a result, lower offering costs.

The Initial Registration Statement

The form and content of the registration statement are prescribed by the SEC. The type of information included in the statement will vary to a certain extent depending on the particular registration form called for in the filing.

Generally, the responsibility for the preparation of the nonfinancial portions of the registration statement falls upon counsel for the company. Preparation of the financial portions usually rests with the company's financial management in consultation with outside accountants.

Filing and SEC Review

Registration statements filed by first-time issuers are subjected to review by SEC staff specialists—generally consisting of a lawyer, accountant and financial analyst. The group may also consult with other staff experts depending on industry specializations. The staff reviews the documents filed to determine full and fair disclosure, particularly whether the document contains any misstatements of fact or omissions of material facts. The SEC review, however, cannot assure accuracy or completeness of the data.

The review of financial data is performed by a staff accountant who reads the entire prospectus and remainder of the registration statement to become familiar with the company and its business. The staff accountant may also refer to published annual and interim reports and newspaper articles for information regarding the company and its industry. The accountant's review is primarily directed at the financial statements and other financial data and the independent accountant's report. The purpose is to determine whether the data comply with SEC requirements and the applicable pronouncements of the American Institute of Certified Public Accountants and the Financial Accounting Standards Board, as well as with the various SEC staff interpretations and policies dealing with accounting and auditing issues.

Although the securities laws contemplate a review of registration statements filed with the SEC, they do not specify the review procedures to be followed by the SEC in processing these documents. The "informal" procedures followed have been developed by the SEC to make comments available to registrants and to permit necessary revisions of a registration statement without formal proceedings. The informal-comment technique has proved to be an effective method of communicating and resolving questions and defects before permitting a registration statement to become effective.

After the review, the SEC generally issues a letter that sets forth questions, deficiencies and suggested revisions found in its review. The letter, referred to as a letter of comment, is generally mailed to the company's counsel.

To save time in the registration process, company counsel generally maintains close contact with SEC staff while the registration statement is being reviewed. Counsel often arranges to receive staff comments by telephone to expedite preparing the required amendment and/or response. Sometimes, a formal letter of comment is not even issued. Telephone contact is often used in connection with review of a registration statement amendment that has been prepared in response to comments raised by the SEC on a previous filing. This method to communicate SEC comments is generally used by registrants and their underwriters as a time-saving measure.

For a carefully prepared document, staff comments are usually relatively few in number and minor in character. Whatever the nature of the comments, each must be addressed and resolved before the registration statement can become effective. If the comments are well-founded and significant, the registration statement must be approximately amended. Although differences of opinion sometimes exist as to the propriety of a particular comment or request, comments and suggestions made by the SEC often prove to be constructive and appropriate and, in the effort to save filing time, are usually complied with rather than challenged.

The Amended Registration Statement

After necessary revisions have been identified, preparation of a revised statement begins. Amendments to the initial registration statement may also be necessary as a result of significant business developments occurring subsequent to the original filing date—for example, a material change in the business or financial condition of the company. If the change is materially adverse, the underwriter could stop the offering since it could render the stock unsalable. On the positive side, a major pending lawsuit could be settled favorably and disclosure would remove any uncertainty about the company and its future. Generally, the changes that go into the revised registration statement require reprinting the statement.

The Preliminary ("Red Herring") Prospectus

Even before the amended registration is filed, a preliminary prospectus is sent to brokers and prospective purchasers. Circulation of the preliminary prospectus is important to forming the underwriting syndicate of various brokerage companies that the underwriter assembles to distribute the stock. SEC rules require that this prospectus substantially conform to the requirements of the Securities Act and that the cover page bear, in red ink (hence the term "red herring") the caption "Preliminary Prospectus." The following statement must be printed on the cover in type as large as that generally used in the body of the prospectus:

A registration statement relating to these securities has been filed with the Securities and Exchange Commission but has not yet become effective. Information contained herein is subject to completion or amendment. These securities may not be sold nor may offers to buy be accepted prior to the time the registration statement becomes effective. This prospectus shall not constitute an offer to sell or the solicitation of an offer to buy, nor shall there be any sale of these securities in any State in which such offer, solicitation or sale would be unlawful prior to registration or qualification under the securities laws of any such State.

The SEC rules also stipulate that the preliminary prospectus may omit the offering price, underwriting discounts or commissions, discounts or commissions to dealers, amount of proceeds, or other matters dependent on the offering price.

Financial Analyst Meetings (Road Shows)

Timing plays as important a part as any other factor in determining the final price of the shares. Almost any company that went public during the late 1960's and mid-1980's (great bull markets) would have done so at a higher offering price than in the mid-1970's (the worst bear market since the 1940's). In addition to cyclical market factors, particular industries go through "hot" and "cold" periods. Unlike the private sale of stock, where negotiations can be in the form of face-to-face meetings, stock sold through the public market is basically priced by market psychology.

For potential investors to learn about the company, the underwriter will arrange for financial analyst and brokers' meetings—usually called road shows. These meetings are usually handled by the president and key management (such as the chief financial officer). The credibility you project through your presentation and ability to respond to potential inestors' and brokers' questions will be a major influence in the success of your offering.

The Due Diligence Meeting

After the registration statement is filed, but before it becomes effective, the principal underwriter holds a due diligence meeting.

The reason can be found in a provision of the SEC rules stating that, except for the company and its principals, no person will be held civilly liable in connection with untrue statements or material omissions in SEC filings if he or she can prove that

> he had, after reasonable investigation, reasonable ground to believe and did believe, at the time such part of the registration statement became effective, that the statements therein were true and that there was no omission to state a material fact required to be stated therein or necessary to make the statements therein not misleading.

The meeting is attended by the principal underwriter and often by members of the underwriting group, as well as the company's principal officers, counsel for the company, counsel for the underwriter and the independent accountant. The usual procedure is for the underwriters to question the company representatives on the company and its business; products; competitive position; recent developments in finance, marketing, operations and other areas and future prospects.

The Price Amendment and Underwriting Agreement

When a registration statement has been filed, the registrant and the underwriter have generally agreed on the securities—both in number of shares and dollar amount—to be sold. In almost all cases, however, the issuer and the underwriter have not yet determined the final price to offer the securities to the public, the exact amount of underwriter's discount or commission and the net proceeds to the registrant. The negotiation and final determination of these amounts depend on a number of factors, as discussed earlier, including past and present performance of the company and conditions in the securities markets and the prices of securities of companies in similar industries at the time the registration statement becomes effective.

The agreed-on price should reflect a discount amount based on anticipated after-market share value of the company. An offering at the high end of a range may not provide adequate investor return, resulting in a weak or depressed after-market. While pricing at the low end may result in a run-up immediately following the offering; after a period of trading the stock should settle at the anticipated after-market share value. The price per share and number of shares will also have an impact on the after-market.

Market perceptions of the risk inherent in a stock are sometimes related to the per-share value. A company with a market value of $5 per-share value may be perceived to be speculative, while a $10 stock may not. An IPO of $15 may be considered overpriced. In addition to the price, the number of shares offered should be sufficient to ensure broad distribution and liquidity.

Upon completion of negotiations with the underwriter—usually about the time the registration statement is ready to become effective—the agreement is signed by authorized representatives of the company and the underwriter. At this time, the final amendment to the registration statement is prepared, including as applicable, the agreed-on offering price, underwriter's discount or commission, and the net proceeds to the company. This amendment is called the price amendment. If the staff of the SEC's Division of Corporation Finance has no important reservations with respect to the registration statement, the registrant and underwriter will customarily request that the offering be declared effective immediately—referred to as requesting "acceleration." If acceleration is granted, the underwriter may proceed with the sale of securities to the public.

Closing

The closing date—generally specified in the underwriting agreement—is usually 10 days to two weeks after the effective date of the registration statement. At the closing, the company delivers the registered securities to the underwriter and receives payment for the issue. Various legal documents are also exchanged as well as an updated comfort letter prepared by the independent accountant.

AFTER YOU GO PUBLIC

Once you have gone public it takes considerable effort to maintain your company's market position. The excitement of an IPO must be maintained or trading will decline and liquidity for the owner through a future secondary offering, as well as other IPO benefits, will not be realized. Effective distribution and support of the stock and continuing security analyst interest is necessary after you go public. A strategy for after-market support can be determined with the assistance of a financial public relations firm. It usually includes choosing an individual within the company to handle shareholder relations.

The SEC will require the company to file certain periodic reports to keep the investing public informed. This requirement will continue as long as certain investor and asset tests are met.

Reporting Requirements After Going Public

No discussion of going public would be complete without consideration to the obligations of the now-public company to provide information to its shareholders.

Legal counsel should be consulted about when a company is obligated to file a particular report with the SEC or the type of report to be filed. The following is an overview of the general filing requirements and common reports.

Form	Description
10K	Annual report to the SEC. It discloses, in detail, information about the company's activities, financial condition and results of operations. It also contains the company's annual financial statements.
10-Q	Quarterly report required for each of the first three quarters of the fiscal year. It includes condensed financial data and information on significant events.
8-K	Report filed in the case of a change in control, bankruptcy or a change in independent accountants.

| Proxy or informa-
tion statements | Data furnished to shareholders so they can
decide how to assign their proxies (votes). |

In addition, public companies must provide annual reports to shareholders with financial information similar to that included in Form 10-K.

To meet the various reporting requirements imposed on them, public companies must maintain an adequate financial staff, supported by legal counsel and knowledgeable independent accountants.

EXEMPT OFFERINGS

The importance of small businesses to the U.S. economy and their ability to gain access to equity markets is a major concern of the Congress and the SEC. Congress enacted the Small Business Investment Incentive Act in 1980 to expand exemption of certain public offerings or private placements from registration with the SEC.

In 1982, Regulation D was adopted by the SEC to coordinate limited offering exemptions and streamline the existing requirements, which reduce the cost of compliance applicable to private offerings and sales of securities. So if you are in need of limited capital, you can still sell stock in your company under an exempt offering and avoid the cost of a public offering.

While Regulation D simplifies the process, the company is not exempted from the antifraud provisions of the securities laws. You must still provide the prospective investor with adequate information to make an informed decision. In addition, while the offering may be exempt from federal registration, it may be subject to state requirements. Regulation D permits the following offerings:

- ☐ Sale of securities totalling up to $500,000 over a twelve-month period.
- ☐ Sale of securities totalling up to $5,000,000 over a twelve-month period. Investors must meet the SEC's definition of "accredited investor," except for up to 35 of them which the SEC

allows to be nonaccredited. An accredited investor, in general, is an individual or institution that is knowledgeable and has adequate net worth to make such investments.

☐ Sale of an unlimited amount of securities if all the investors, except for the up to 35, are accredited. The nonaccredited investors must meet the definition of a "sophisticated" investor. In general, a sophisticated investor is one who is capable of evaluating the merit of the investment venture.

Why Use an Exempt Offering?

There are advantages as well as disadvantages to raising money through an exempt offering.

Advantages

Business strategy. Investors in exempt offerings are generally long-term oriented. In addition, you will probably know them as individuals. This could mean less pressure on management to obtain short-term results at the expense of long-term growth.

Time. With fewer requirements and no SEC review, an exempt offering can be completed more rapidly than a registration statement.

Disclosure. Continuous reporting requirements are necessary only for certain issuers. The limited number of investors also limits disclosure of information that you may prefer to keep confidential.

Cost. Because the compliance regulations are reduced, so are the related professional fees. Also, the exempt offering documents can be produced on the company's word processor, allowing you to avoid substantial printing costs.

Disadvantages

Offering limitation. Exempt offerings limit the amount of capital that can be raised and could restrain the company's growth potential.

Price. Generally your company's market valuation will be higher using an IPO. Investors in exempt offerings will demand a substantially larger share of ownership to offset the lack of liquidity and the risk that the company may never go public.

Investors. Investors in an exempt offering will want eventually to liquidate their holdings at a profit. Investor exit can be realized by participating in a public offering, a sale of the company or by having the company buy the shares back.

Liquidity. The shares of an exempt offering cannot be freely traded. They are therefore less desirable for use as loan collateral, since value based on a market price per share is not readily available.

Selling a portion of your company to raise needed capital is a major decision. An exempt offering may be the appropriate decision for the company that has limited capital needs and is not ready to go public.

PUBLIC OFFERING OUTLINE

Date	Action	Responsibility
	Discuss outline	(1)
	Interview SEC counsel	(1)
	Select SEC counsel	(1)
	Select board members	(1)
	Review corporate name	(1)(4)
	Interview financial public relations firm	(1)
	Prepare financial information for three years	(1)

Implement recommendations for changes to accounting and management information system	(1)(2)
Interview underwriters	(1)
Develop business plan	(1)(2)
Establish management organization	(1)
Interview financial printer	(1)
Confirm board members	(1)
Select financial public relations firm	(1)
Begin examining financial statements	(2)
Implement business plan	(1)
Release notification of going public to press	(1)(6)
Select underwriter	(1)
Select financial printer	(1)
Hold public offering organization meeting	(1)(2)(3)(4)
Develop investor relations plan	(1)
Start registration statement	(1)(2)(4)
Draft annual report to stockholders	(1)(2)(4)(5)(6)
Review draft of registration statement	(1)(2)(3)(4)(5)
Review draft of annual report to stockholders	(1)(2)(4)(6)

Final approval of regis-tration statement (without numbers)	(1)(2)(3)(4)(5)
Final approval of annual report to stockholders (without amounts)	(1)(2)(3)(6)
Complete examination of financial state-ments and release for inclusion in registra-tion statement and annual report to stockholders	(1)(2)
Review and approve registration statement	(1)(2)(3)(4)(5)
File with SEC	(1)(4)
Distribute prospectus	(3)
Receive comments from SEC	(1)(4)
File amendments to cover SEC comments	(1)(2)(3)(4)(5)
Hold due-diligence meeting	(1)(2)(3)(4)
Registration effective	(1)(3)
Complete settlement	(1)(3)

---

[1]Management
[2]Independent accountant
[3]Underwriter
[4]SEC counsel
[5]Financial printer
[6]Financial public relations firm

15

Measuring Business Performance

A business does not have to be troubled for a performance measurement to be meaningful. An analogous situation would be a person's periodic physical examination—you do not have to be ill to reap some peace of mind or to determine that changes may be in order to improve your health. All businesses can use evaluations as they grow.

When trade creditors, lenders or potential or existing shareholders request financial information, an evaluation of the business is being performed. A creditor's evaluation may be concerned with current health and short-term viability—the business's ability to pay for goods or pay its debt obligations. A shareholder's focus may be both short- and long-term—what is the value of a share now and what kind of return can be expected on the investment?

A performance evaluation can identify areas that need improvement. The process can spotlight a department that may seem to be performing adequately but not be performing at the same level of prior periods or the competition, in light of the resources (salaries and other costs) used by the department. You may also find out that a function thought to be performing poorly, says sales, is really performing well in light of problems in another area, production say. You may then decide to focus more attention on production problems.

In this chapter we discuss various approaches for a self-evaluation of your business and highlight some possible solutions to problems identified. We also present some "Red Flags" that third parties may focus on, and a diagnostic questionnaire that can be used to identify weaknesses, or to supplement findings of the objective evaluation. We also include a list of over 80 ideas to increase revenues and operating efficiency and decrease expenses.

METHODS OF EVALUATION

When you walk out onto the shop floor and observe all of the equipment running and your work force busy fulfilling the day's production and shipping goals, you are making an evaluation. You may speak to the foreman, ask a few questions and make a few suggestions, and then proceed to the sales department and make further evaluations. This is the typical "hands-on" daily assessment that many entrepreneurs use. It is one method of evaluation.

However, there are other matters to consider: How are you doing versus your business plan? What return are you getting on dollars invested in the business? How do you match up against the competition? Are there ways to improve performance? Answers to these questions may not come from your hands-on assessment. They may require other evaluation and measurement approaches. It is not necessary to have elaborate systems or extraordinary amounts of time. Many of the best performance evaluation tools are flash reports, daily or weekly, that provide a hands-on assessment of operational or financial performance.

More formal performance measurements may be accomplished· with objective or subjective evaluations. An objective evaluation is based on quantifiable measures; sales and net income for a period are examples. A subjective evaluation is qualitative and therefore judgmental; it is concerned with how the business is being managed. To evaluate the effectiveness of a one-time marketing program may be essentially a subjective exercise. The exercise becomes somewhat more objective if continuing programs are matched against prior results or against a plan developed using a history of results.

The objective and subjective approaches can be differentiated in terms of ends and means. Objective measures of performance focus on the accomplishment or the end result. Subjective measures focus on the process or means by which the end result is achieved. By incorporating both objective and subjective measures of performance into the evaluation process, you will be able to benefit from the advantages of each.

Objective Measures of Performance

For many entrepreneurs, the most appropriate objective measure of performance is the personal financial benefits derived from owning a business. These benefits include not only salary and direct fringe benefits, such as medical and life insurance and perhaps a retirement plan, but also indirect benefits, such as travel and entertainment, use of an automobile, a country club membership and other items of value the owner can extract from the business.

These benefits, however, are not a measure of the viability of your business. That viability is determined with a broad spectrum of criteria, which in turn may be best expressed by ratios, a useful tool in summarizing data in a form that can be more easily understood and provide a basis for monitoring and comparison.

Indiscriminate use of a multitude of ratios as a means of measuring performance can be confusing. Ratios by themselves are difficult to interpret. How, for example, should you react when profitability for the period is up but your average return (net income) per dollar invested in the business is down? Is the average-return decrease a sign of poor performance?

There are two questions that must be answered. First, which ratios are meaningful for your business? Second, what should the ratios you calculate be measured against?

We suggest that your identification of meaningful ratios begin with the appropriate analytical focus, or performance area. Among the most frequently asked questions about a business are: What are your sales? How profitable are you? How much cash do you generate? What is your return on investment or equity?

Table 15.1 presents each of these questions as an "analytical focus" and summarizes the advantages and disadvantages of each as indicators of performance or trends.

For analytical purposes, we believe that return on equity (ROE) is generally the best measure of performance. When using this measure, you should increase net income by the excess of your salary and benefits, less the income tax benefits derived, over what you would otherwise expect to be earning as an employee elsewhere. This measure is appropriate because each investor has alternatives for his or her investable funds, ranging from a relatively risk-free investment in government debt obligations to the comparatively risky investment of the business itself. (However, if the amount of equity is relatively low and the working capital is provided from a highly leveraged debt position, return on investment may be substituted.) A business must earn over time a rate of return greater than what the owner could have earned by investing in a relatively safe debt obligation. Otherwise, existing shareholders would be better served by liquidating their investment in the business and simply buying a Treasury bill.

An advantage of using ROE as the primary focus is that it can be explained, with mathematical precision, by performance with regard to profitability, asset turnover and financial leverage. The formula is:

$$\text{ROE} = \frac{\text{net income}}{\text{shareholders' equity}}$$

$$= \frac{\text{net income}}{\text{revenues}} \times \frac{\text{revenues}}{\text{assets}} \times \frac{\text{assets}}{\text{shareholders' equity}}$$

Shareholders' equity and assets are average balances for the period. Each of the three components of ROE can in turn be viewed as:

$$\frac{\text{net income}}{\text{revenues}} = \text{measure of profitability}$$

$$\frac{\text{revenues}}{\text{assets}} = \text{asset turnover}$$

$$\frac{\text{assets}}{\text{shareholders' equity}} = \text{financial leverage}$$

Table 15.1

**ALTERNATIVE ANALYTICAL FOCUSES:
SUMMARY OF ADVANTAGES AND DISADVANTAGES**

Analytical Focus	Advantage	Disadvantages
Revenue or sales	Easy to calculate	Ignores the cost of revenues
	Measurable for short periods of time (even daily)	Ignores amount of assets needed to generate revenues
Net income	Reflects expenses that accompany generation of revenues	Greatly affected by non-cash charges such as depreciation and amortization
	Relatively easy to understand and calculate	Ignores amount of assets needed to generate revenues
Cash flow [a]	Theoretically measures cash-generating capability of the entity	Ignores amount of assets needed to generate revenues
Return on investment [b]	Measures net results of operations in comparison with assets utilized	Does not differentiate between effects of equity and debt financing
Return on equity [c]	Measures efficiency with which shareholders' investment is utilized	Sometimes of limited meaning where shareholder investment is minimal
	Easily related to the factors of profitability, asset turnover and financial leverage	

[a] Cash flow is frequently calculated by adding back noncash charges such as depreciation and amortization to net income.

[b] There are many variations in the calculation of ROI. A frequently used one is: net income plus interest expense, depreciation and amortization divided by stockholders' equity plus long-term debt.

[c] ROE is frequently calculated by dividing net income (for the period) by average stockholders' equity (during the period).

Profitability is the amount of profits generated compared with sales for the period. Asset turnover measures how efficiently assets such as receivables, inventory and plant and equipment are being used in generating sales. Financial leverage measures the value of assets being financed by shareholders' money rather than by money provided by creditors. These three ratios may be thought of as second-level performance indicators.

Entrepreneurs, Inc. had assets and shareholders' equity of $2,700,000 and $1,250,000, respectively, at the end of 1985. The following example displays a calculated ROE for 1986 and 1987:

	1986	1987
Revenues	$3,100,000	$3,500,000
Net income	$260,000	$294,000
Assets	$3,200,000	$4,200,000
Shareholders' equity	$1,510,000	$1,950,000

Calculated ROE:
  Net income ÷
Average
    Shareholders'
equity
	18.8%	17.0%

What caused the decrease in ROE? To answer this question, let's review the second-level performance indicators.

	DOLLARS IN 000s	
	1986	1987

Profitability:
net income
revenues
	$260
	$3,100 =
	    8.4%
		$294
		$3,500 =
		    8.4%

Asset turnover: revenues assets (ave.)	$3,100 $2,950 = 1.05	$3,500 $3,700 = .95

Financial leverage:	$2,950		$3,700	
assets (ave.)				
Shareholders'	$1,380 = 2.14		$1,730 = 2.14	
equity (ave.)				

We can see that the profitability and financial-leverage ratios are unchanged year-to-year. The focus is now narrowed to the decreased asset-turnover ratio. The analysis can go on to a third-level performance indicator.

Third-level performance indicators are included as Exhibit 15.1 in the Appendix to this chapter. Thus, for the above example, not only can return on equity be measured by profitability, asset turnover and leverage, but the asset turnover problem can be further evaluated by receivables turnover, inventory turnover and fixed-asset turnover. This presentation creates an analytical framework through which one can understand the components (or causes) of changes in any one ratio. Understanding the components of the changes then highlights areas for taking action to improve results.

By themselves, ratios have limited value. In the above example, without a year-to-year comparison, there was no basis upon which to determine that 1987 may have been a "down" year. In addition to comparisons to prior years, ROE should be interpreted in conjunction with such data as the return projected for future years, the return generated by similar businesses and yields on alternative investments.

Developing a Base of Comparative Information. There are numerous sources of information that can be used to help evaluate performance. The most readily available, and hence probably most frequently used, is historical data. We will use the hypothetical results of Company XYZ Inc. (Table 15.2) as an aid in presenting a discussion of comparative information.

Historical Comparisons. Knowing that company XYZ Inc.'s return on equity for the past six years was 6%, 8%, 10%, 11%, 11.5%, and 12% adds meaning to an evaluation. This historical information demonstrates that performance has been improving steadily.

Historical data, however, has some limitations. It may not even be available, as in a start-up situation. Even if it is available, over-reliance on comparisons with historical data may lead to mediocre performance. Management may strive only to improve on the poor results of prior periods. Further, changes in accounting principles used during periods being compared must be adjusted for. Changes in conditions must also be considered—for instance: a new product line, a new geographic territory or more debt financing and interest costs. You must adjust for changes or break out segment data to develop meaningful comparisons.

Comparisons with Plan or Budget Data. Another basis for comparison is the plan or budget for the entity. Thus, if the ROE for the year is 12%, this figure takes on added meaning when compared with a budgeted return of 14%. The value of comparing the actual ROE to budget depends, of course, on the quality of the budget. To some, the budget is little more than an extrapolation of past performance. In such cases, using the budget as a comparative source has the same limitation as using historical performance—the comparison may not get to the root of mediocre performance.

Similarly, if planned or budgeted data is based on unrealistically formulated objectives, the value of the comparison is weakened if the ROE is set too high; for example, comparison with the year's results may show a less favorable performance than the facts warrant. Assuming performance standards in the budgeting process have been set objectively, however, comparison of actual results with budgeted results can be worthwhile.

Industry Comparison. Comparisons with historical and budgeted data can be supplemented by comparisons with industry data. Data on performance of companies in a given industry may be available from three important sources:

☐ Trade and industry groups

☐ Government, primarily federal, especially the Department of Commerce

☐ Private compilers of data for public use, such as Robert Morris Associates, Standard & Poor's and Dun & Bradstreet

An enhancement of the comparison with industry groups is a comparison with specific companies in the industry group. Because industry data covers both good and poor performers, overall industrial comparisons seldom provide the kind of insights that can be applied in improving performance. On the other hand, the equivalent data on a company that is similar in size and scope of operations to your own may be very useful. The identification of these similar companies and subsequent comparative analysis can be quite worthwhile.

Unfortunately, developing an appropriate peer group and gaining access to information on the peers is difficult, because many may be privately held companies for which performance information is not available. You may want to inquire whether your lender, your accountant or other professionals can provide you with industry data.

When you make industry comparisons, be sure that the data is accurate, timely and essentially comparable. Comparing a gasoline retailer to a gasoline wholesaler is of little value to the wholesaler looking to evaluate the performance of the business. The impact of minor differences—for example, in accounting for inventory costs—can be factored into any analysis.

Tabular Analysis of ROE. Table 15.2 depicts what an analysis of Company XYZ's ROE might look like using four comparative bases: historic (own data), peer group, industry and yields on long-term government bonds. The table shows that XYZ's ROE performance, although improving in absolute terms over the last five years, has been mediocre relative to the performances of its peer group, especially Companies A and B. Company B has been a consistently high-ranking performer, although its performance has not shown the dramatic progress of Company A, which over the last five years has progressed from the worst performer to the best performer in the peer group. The strong showing of these two companies has raised the peer-group performance average over XYZ's performance, even though Companies C and D have not performed well.

Although XYZ's improvement in ROE in the latest year was notable, it was still less than that achieved by the peer group and the industry as a whole. The performance of all companies, except A and B, and of the industry as a whole was poor in the last year in comparison with the yield on the less risky government bonds.

Table 15.2
COMPARATIVE ANALYSIS OF RETURN ON EQUITY

Company	1987 Projected %	1987 Actual %	Rank	1986 Actual %	Rank	1985 Actual %	Rank	1984 Actual %	Rank	1983 Actual %	Rank
A	NA	14.9	1	13.5	2	12.0	3	10.4	3	7.9	5
B	NA	14.8	2	14.2	1	14.1	1	14.2	2	14.4	2
XYZ	14.0	12.0	3	11.5	3	11.0	4	10.0	4	8.0	4
C	NA	11.9	4	11.2	4	13.2	2	14.3	1	14.6	1
D	NA	8.2	5	8.0	5	8.1	5	7.9	5	8.1	3
Peer group average	12.4	11.7		11.7		11.4		10.6			
Industry average	11.9	11.3		11.6		11.2		10.5			
Long-term government bond yield	12.1	11.2		8.9		7.9		7.4			

The table demonstrates the power of comparative analysis. Suddenly XYZ's performance, which without comparative analysis had seemed to be good because of the consistent progress in increasing ROE, on a relative basis is poor. To begin to understand why XYZ is not performing as well as Companies A or B would require comparative analysis of other factors in the ratio hierarchy or analytical framework.

Timing the Objective Evaluation. Using an analytical framework such as ROE and a full comparative analysis requires information on peer company and industry performance. Information on your company's performance should be available on a timely basis but, unfortunately, the other information will often be available only on an annual basis. If the peer group is composed of public companies, limited quarterly data may be available. Companies operating in regulated industries may publish data monthly and in some cases even weekly or daily.

Typically, a full comparative analysis can be done only once a year. This is probably just as well, given the limited resources you may have for this kind of activity. By itself, the ROE analytical focus and framework does not require data from outside the company. Therefore, it should be calculated more often than the comparative analysis is undertaken. As with any data-gathering project, you should assign responsibility and prepare a timetable for development of the analysis.

Because of the objective nature of these measures, the calculations can easily be performed by you or one of your employees. The real challenge is analyzing the results to identify how performance improvements can be made and the causes of the performance. Determining why something has occurred may take additional time, but therein lies the larger payoff of identifying opportunities for improving performance. Delaying an evaluation of performance exposes your business to the risk of poor performance continuing undetected. Remember that mere summaries of data without such analysis, interpretation and corrective action are almost certainly a waste of time.

In the meantime, do not forget the values of the hands-on evaluations previously mentioned. Using a monthly key indicator report (described in Chapter 8) to summarize performance will reduce this risk. Also, a daily or weekly flash report should be considered— these report on a key element or two that you identify as vital to the business.

If you manufacture a readily measurable product, units of production per day may be key. If high volume revenues are required, dollars of orders booked per day or sales per salesperson per day or week may be the key. If you are in a service-oriented business, persons available per day may be a key indicator. Similar to the more formal approaches, these indicators only have value when interpretation and corrective action follow closely behind the identification of problems.

Subjective Measures of Performance

You are probably involved to some extent in subjective evaluation every working day. As discussed earlier, when you walk out to the shop floor to see how production is running, you are engaging in an evaluation. But such evaluations are seldom systematically performed; rather, they occur "ad hoc," squeezed between other activities or in response to a crisis. To be effective, subjective evaluation must be systematic and planned to cover every activity. This is not to say that periodic systematic evaluation should replace ad hoc evaluation; rather, it should supplement it. Through ad hoc evaluation, you can pick up obvious performance deficiencies and act quickly to correct them.

The Management Process. The activities of any manager can be classified into five major categories:

Planning   Comparing alternative objectives, selecting the optimal ones and determining the methodology and schedule for achieving them.

Organizing   Establishing a formal structure that defines the duties of people working together to accomplish planned objectives.

Staffing   Providing and developing capable and experienced personnel in sufficient numbers to meet organizational needs.

Directing   The leadership and effective management of people by guiding and monitoring their efforts.

Controlling   Reviewing activities and correcting deviations from planned results.

Functions of a Business. Almost every business is involved in the following functions:

Marketing   Determining what product will be sold, where, at what price and with what promotions.

Purchasing   Purchasing or obtaining the goods that will be sold or used in production.

Production   Conversion of purchased material into finished goods.

Sales   Following through on the marketing analysis and moving product through a distribution network.

Distribution   Transporting finished goods.

The primary functions above need to be coupled with effective support functions such as accounting, finance, legal, personnel and EDP data processing/information systems.

When the management processes and functions are combined, we have a summary of all management activities. This summary can be depicted as a matrix, shown in Figure 15.1.

The matrix can be read either across rows or down columns. Reading across the first row, we see that to perform the function of marketing properly one needs to be involved in all five of the management processes: planning, organizing, staffing, directing and controlling. Reading down the first column shows that planning should be done in connection with each of the business functions of marketing, purchasing, production, sales and distribution. Keep in mind that the number of boxes is not necessarily indicative of the number of managers or even employees, for in smaller companies one person may handle several of these activities.

By providing an overview of all management activities, the matrix identifies those that must be subjectively evaluated to see how each is being performed and how performance might be improved. This evaluation, as pointed out earlier, lacks the mathematical precision inherent in the objective evaluation process.

Conducting the Subjective Evaluation. Using the matrix in Figure 15.1 as a guide, you should develop a schedule for reviewing each activity on a cycle of no more six months. Ideally, the focus of the analysis should alternate between functions—that is, first marketing, then purchasing, then production—and processes—that is, first planning in all five functions, then organizing in all five functions, and so on.

For each activity, there must be a comparison between how the activity is performed and how it should be performed. But how do you derive a standard for how an activity should be performed? Primarily from your experience and past observations of how your company performed the activity or how some other company performs it. Your standard might also be influenced by the ideas of qualified authorities expressed in business periodicals, books and lectures.

Summarizing Subjective Assessments

You may find it useful to quantify assessments made in your subjective evaluation. This can be accomplished using the matrix previously introduced, and a functional evaluation chart as follows:

1. Does not perform.
2. Attempts to perform but lacks experience.
3. Performs at reasonable level.
4. Consistently performs very well.
5. Outstanding performance.

Functions	Processes				
	Planning	Organization	Staffing	Directing	Controlling
Marketing					
Purchasing					
Production					
Sales					
Distribution					

Figure 15.1 Matrix of Business Functions and Management Processes

Applying the quantified functional evaluations will lead to a quantified matrix. Figure 15.2 provides an example of how the matrix may look.

The quantified matrix allows for a consise top-level summary of the company's strengths and weaknesses. In management, the company performs extremely well in Planning while performing poorly in Controlling. Purchasing is the top performer, while Distribution is poorest. In Management, training of all key managers may be necessary; for instance, a program on controlling deviations from planned results may be introduced. Further, specific functions that need overall management improvements are highlighted; for instance, the Distribution function.

These procedures merely highlight performance matters. The solutions will be developed only after taking action on the data gathered.

The Diagnostic Questionnaire. The diagnostic questionnaire in the Appendix to this chapter (Exhibit 15.2) highlights some of the many questions to ask as part of your analysis.

In making a subjective evaluation, you can, of course, use second opinions. For example, the accountant's review of controls or the consultant's evaluation of a firm's planning process can provide useful input into the evaluation process. Naturally, you must be sure of the qualifications of anyone you consult.

RED FLAGS

When third parties review your business, they are making both objective and subjective evaluations. Some "Red Flags" that third parties use to identify potential problems should be of use to you also. We have summarized below the probable interests of a lender, when probing for problem areas, with respect to business and management policies and procedures:

1. *Highly leveraged, thinly capitalized*
   - Healthy profits are needed to finance future operations.
   - The company is vulnerable to changes in business and economic cycles.
2. *One-person management*

- Viability of the company depends on one person—the entrepreneur.
- The entrepreneur has little or no financial expertise.
- Despite substantial growth, management has not changed.
- In periods of rapid growth, there is no program for training middle management.

Functions	Planning	Organization	Staffing	Direction	Controlling	Total
Marketing	5	3	3	2	1	14
Purchasing	5	3	4	4	1	17
Production	4	4	3	3	2	16
Sales	3	4	4	2	2	15
Distribution	3	1	2	2	1	9
Total	20	15	16	13	7	
Average	4.0	3.0	3.2	2.6	1.4	

Figure 15.2 Quantified Performance Matrix of Business Functions and Management Proc

3. *Poor management communications*

- Financial advisers (e.g., bankers and auditors) are not kept up-to-date on the company's plans.
- Accountants are not consulted on finance decisions.
- Communication between the company's bankers, accountants and lawyers is discouraged.

4. *Few management tools*

- Management does not issue regular reports.
- Systems and procedures are outdated and ineffective.
- Sales and order backlogs are not analyzed.
- Marketing plans are based on intuition rather than research.

5. *Insufficient financial controls*

- Control procedures are lax and often unmonitored.
- Management does not consider controls important and will override them.

6. *Late financial statements*

- Annual reports are not available until several months after year-end.
- Monthly or quarterly reports are not issued.
- Decisions are based on outdated or incomplete financial data.

7. *Variations in accountant's reports*

- Quality of the figures in the financial statements is uncertain.
- Auditor gives a "going-concern qualification."

8. *Sales growth with no bottom-line increase*

- Emphasis is on sales volume, not profitability.
- Only a small percentage of earnings makes it to the bottom line.

9. *Lack of inventory records*

- Company does not have perpetual inventory records.

- Management relies on inventory estimates until year-end physical inventory is performed.
- Inadequate cost systems result in improper capitalization of certain costs.

The above items include both objective and subjective assessments. If you recognize any of these "Red Flags" it is time to take some action—either immediate corrections or developing a framework for further analysis.

PERFORMANCE IMPROVEMENT

Performance improvement is often identical to profit improvement, which can be brought about in one or more of the following ways:

☐ Increasing the volume of profitable business
☐ Decreasing the expenses associated with generating business
☐ Using assets more efficiently.

The Appendix to this chapter contains an "idea list" (Exhibit 15.3) of potential opportunities in each of these three areas. The idea list does not present absolute techniques but should serve as an alert or memory jogger for profit-improvement opportunities. You must always take into account all aspects of your business and your competition. For instance, requiring your customers to cover the cost of shipping on goods returned for credit is a possible cost-cutting technique; however, if your competition has no such policy, this can cost you a future order. The risk of customer losses must be considered.

The Procedure

Merely identifying opportunities for improving performance is not enough. Action must be taken to implement the findings. A logical procedure for accomplishing this would involve the following steps:

☐ Determining alternative means of operating in the area under analysis

☐ Evaluating the impact of operating by alternative means

☐ Selecting the appropriate alternative

☐ Blueprinting the implementation of selected alternatives

☐ Determining priority of alternatives selected for implementation

☐ Assigning responsibility and timetable for implementation

☐ Monitoring implementation

☐ Monitoring results periodically after implementation, reevaluating as necessary.

Performance improvement need not be a formal or cumbersome process. Some opportunities for improvement will be obvious. On the other hand, some possibilities, because of their scope and implications, cannot be properly weighed without a written analysis. For example, deciding whether to purchase a machine that will replace five laborers requires projection of expenses with and without the purchase. Factors in the decision include projected sales volume, machine capacity, product profitability, machine reliability, financing costs, peripheral equipment needs, projected wage scales, payroll taxes, tax benefits and utility costs.

SUMMARY

This chapter has cited detailed techniques for measuring performance, identifying opportunities for improvements and making improvements. The real key to improving performance lies not with these techniques, however, but rather with you. Improvement can occur only if you want it to and if you are openminded about the changes that may be necessary.

APPENDIX: TOOLS FOR MEASURING AND IMPROVING BUSINESS PERFORMANCE

Exhibit 15.1
Ratio Performance Indicators (Third Level)

Performance Indicator	Formula for Ratio
Return on equity	$\dfrac{\text{net income}}{\text{shareholders' equity}}$
Profitability	$\dfrac{\text{net income}}{\text{revenues}}$
Gross margin	$\dfrac{\text{revenue less cost of goods sold}}{\text{sales}}$
Production-purchasing efficiency	$\dfrac{\text{cost of goods sold}}{\text{revenues}}$
Selling efficiency	$\dfrac{\text{selling expense}}{\text{revenues}}$
Administrative efficiency	$\dfrac{\text{general and administrative expenses}}{\text{revenues}}$
Effective tax rate	$\dfrac{\text{income taxes}}{\text{pretax profit}}$
Asset turnover	$\dfrac{\text{revenues}}{\text{assets}}$
Receivables turnover	$\dfrac{\text{revenues}}{\text{average receivables}}$
Inventory turnover	$\dfrac{\text{cost of goods sold}}{\text{average inventory}}$
Fixed-asset turnover	$\dfrac{\text{revenues}}{\text{average fixed assets}}$
Leverage	$\dfrac{\text{assets}}{\text{shareholders' equity}}$ or $\dfrac{\text{total debt}}{\text{shareholders' equity}}$
Current ratio	$\dfrac{\text{current assets}}{\text{current liabilities}}$
Quick ratio	$\dfrac{\text{cash and receivables}}{\text{current liabilities}}$

Exhibit 15.2
Diagnostic Questionnaire for Performance Evaluation

Management Processes

(Applicable to the entire business, including all business functions)

Planning:

Is there a long-range plan that sets out objectives and a course of action
for each of the business functions?
Is there a long-range financial forecast?
Is there a detailed budget against which actual performance is compared
and significant variances analyzed?
Do all personnel understand who reports to whom?
How is morale and the general work environment?
Is there a backup for key personnel?

Staffing:

What is being done to identify and attract personnel in keeping with pro-
jected needs?
How are potential employees and existing employees evaluated?
Has a benefits package been designed that will facilitate hiring and reten-
tion of personnel?
What means of improving motivation of personnel have been identified?
Have training programs been developed?
Are there career plans for key personnel?

Directing:

Is there a clear description of each employee's responsibilities and duties?
Does each employee know his or her objectives?
Is there periodic feedback on progress against objectives and means for
improving performance where it is deficient?

Controlling:

Have you put in place a system for timely reporting of activity in such
major functions as:
  Marketing?
  Purchasing?
  Production?
  Distribution?
Is there a system for timely reporting of financial results with comparison
to budgeted results?
Has a cost system for identifying product costs been developed?

Are results of operations promptly analyzed and appropriate corrective action identified?

Is corrective action promptly implemented?

Business Functions

Marketing:

Have marketing objectives and strategies been clearly defined?

Has the market been identified and analyzed—where it is, who the customer is, who the noncustomer is, and why; decrease or increase in market size, anticipated changes and their impact?

Is there a long-term sales forecast by broad product category or dollar volume for use in planning production facilities, manpower or long-range procurement?

Is a product-by-product review of profitability, continuance, composition and obsolescence conducted to answer such questions as:

    Do a few products account for a large percentage of sales?

    Should low-volume items be trimmed?

    Is any product line threatened by social or technological changes?

Are sales and profitability results regularly analyzed and compared with budget by product line, customer, market, territory, salesperson, outside agent and distribution channels?

Are short-term sales forecasts prepared for successive periods showing type of product, number of untis, unit sales and price?

Are short-term sales forecasts supplied to production management for developing manufacturing plans and to financial management for developing a profit plan?

Have active programs in market research, new markets and new product development been established?

Is there a formal mechanism for new-product review and approval? Are marketing responsibilities clearly assigned?

Is compensation of salespersons structured to promote sales of high gross-margin items?

Is there periodic performance evaluation of brokers, distributors and manufacturers?

Is there periodic review of advertising effectiveness?

Do you regularly prepare reports on bids submitted versus invitations to bid, sales commitments received versus bids submitted and analysis of reasons for lost bids?

Are periodic returns and claims reports listed by customer?

Have you established periodic reports on variations from established prices and significant terms listed by customer, product or salesperson?

Has budget control of advertising effectiveness been implemented?

Has an expense budget been prepared, with estimated cost for each sales segment (product, customer type, territory and so on) and expense classification?

Do you bill back unusual customer-caused costs, such as excessive handling and special packaging?

Are customer invoices and credit memoranda being issued promptly?

Purchasing

Have purchase authorizations on frequently used articles been reduced through a systematic stocking program?

Are purchase authorizations for frequently used articles under a stocking program based on lead time plus safety-stock considerations, or is periodic planning being used?

Do purchase authorizations designate the date materials are required?

Do purchase authorizations for specialized components or equipment include technical and performance specifications?

Have statements of purchasing policies been issued covering:

Corporate relationships, particularly buying responsibilities?

Competitive buying, source selection and bidding?

Maintenance of multiple buying sources to protect continuity of supply?

Rules on commitments and contracts?

Reciprocity?

Conflict of interest?

Is the purchasing function centralized so that locations do not compete with one another, thereby maximizing purchasing power?

Is full use being made of nationwide buying contracts and blanket purchase commitments as a means of maximizing purchasing power?

Have purchasing personnel been supplied with summaries of commodity buying and supplier buying volumes to facilitate negotiations with suppliers?

Does the purchasing agent participate in decisions on standardization, value analysis and lease-versus-buy options to purchase equipment under lease?

Is there a plan to ensure that materials are delivered within the time specified on purchase commitments?

Are there up-to-date procedures to foster use of accurate weights and weighing routines (that is, periodic testing of scales or use of statistical sampling techniques)?

Is there a policy on acceptance or nonacceptance of overshipments or undershipments?

Is the purchasing agent informed quickly when shipments are received or when they are overdue, as well as of the quantity and quality of each?

Are payments deferred until due date?

Is purchasing tied in closely with inventory analysis and control?

Are perpetual inventory records maintained on all important items?

Have there been significant book-to-physical-inventory adjustments? If so, why?

Has the rate of back-order change been analyzed?

Have there been interruptions in production schedules due to lack of materials? If so, why?

Is the customer-service measurement system functioning properly?

Have machine setup costs increased significantly? If so, why?

Are product delivery schedules being met?

Are work-in-process increases disproportionate to sales?

Are scrap costs rising faster than they should?

Production:

Has short-term production and inventory forecasting been developed?

Has plant productivity improved?

Is labor utilization continually reassessed to determine how it can be improved?

Are seasonal peaks and lows in plant operations minimized to the fullest degree possible?

Do supply sources offer the optimal combination of reliability and competitive price?

Do you minimize production costs through efficiencies in material, handling, materials management, plant layout, shop scheduling, maintenance programs, quality control, control over labor usage, product design and research and development programs?

Is overtime authorized before it is actually incurred?

Do records indicate whether production schedules are met and the reasons for any deviations?

Does the system ensure periodic identification, review and disposal of slow-moving or obsolete stock?

Is the cost accounting system using the same basic data and/or records as the production system?

Is there in effect a standard cost system, developed by element or expense for each significant operation, each important cost center and each product?

Does the cost system identify and facilitate control over direct (variable) product costs?

Are you utilizing production management that includes organization charts, job descriptions and clear-cut assignments of responsibility?

Are production and production changes initiated only on written request?

Does preparation of time cards, time sheets and attendance records distinguish between direct and indirect costs and facilitate control over those costs?

Is production management furnished with "bills of material" or route sheets listing parts and quality of each required to produce one unit of a particular product or subassembly?

Do production management route sheets specify what must be produced, how, where and in what sequence?

Are labor assignments based on route documents specifying operations to be performed, time allowed, sequence of operations, machines to be used and alternative routings when feasible?

Is preventive maintenance utilized to curb machine downtime?

Is there an up-to-date system of inventory control?

Distribution:

Are distribution costs including demurrage reviewed?

Do you determine means of distribution by evaluating items such as:
   Truck?
   Common carrier?
   Contract carrier?
   Rail?

Are opportunities to back-haul identified?

Do you monitor the condition of goods on delivery?

Support—Finance:

Have you identified opportunities to increase earnings from surplus cash by maintaining minimum bank balances in demand accounts?

Have you identified opportunities to improve collection of receivables through:
   Generating bills more promptly?
   Designing appropriate incentives for customer prompt payment?
   Reducing mail and processing time through utilization of a lockbox?

Are opportunities to reduce inventories through proper purchasing and production procedures identified (see "Purchasing" in this questionnaire)?

Do you identify and dispose of assets not needed for operations?

Have all asset acquisitions been evaluated on the merits of leasing versus buying?

Is insurance coverage reviewed to keep programs in line with needs and changing conditions?

Has a plan been developed for enhancing your relationships with financial institutions to reduce your interest rates on borrowing?

Support—EDP

Have the costs and capabilities of service bureaus versus a company-operated facility been evaluated?

Have systems development plans of various departments been ranked for priority of implementation?

Are EDP systems and procedures documented?

Have adequate security measures been implemented for protection from loss due to errors, fraud, embezzlement, sabotage, malicious mischief and accidental destruction?

Exhibit 15.3
Techniques for Improving Efficiency

The following is a list of ideas for increasing revenues, decreasing expenses, and operating more efficiently.

Techniques	Cut Purchase Costs	Cut Freight Costs	Maximize Working Capital	Cut Scrap	Reduce Downtime	Cut Labor Costs	Cut Administrative Overhead	Increase Revenues
							Objectives	
Reduce variety of articles in stock	X		X				X	
Standardize preferred items	X				X		X	
Define roles of purchasing personnel at different levels of large organization	X		X				X	
Evaluate vendor quality, delivery and cost performances	X		X		X			
Provide enough time to shop the market	X							
Centralize negotiations for major items, including freight	X	X						
Use traveling requisitions							X	
Give purchasing personnel a free hand in vendor selection, based on operating specifications	X				X			
Issue complete purchase orders for significant transactions	X							
Reduce rush procurement	X	X			X		X	
Prescribe preferred routing for incoming bulk items		X			X			
Seek competitive bids for significant transactions	X							

458

Establish floor below which bids will not be obtained					X
Subject all buying contracts to periodic review	X				
Develop approved vendor list for highly technical purchases	X			X	
Combine related items on purchase orders	X				X
Conduct make-or-buy studies					X
Use purchase order copy as receiving report	X	X			
Test-weight bulk commodities					X
Authorize telephone releases for minor items bought on contract					X
Eliminate useless copies made by receiving clerks	X	X			
Stagger incoming loads to eliminate demurrage and shipping overtime				X	
Speed up invoice processing to avoid discount losses	X				
Set up plant delivery system				X	
Signal vendor overshipments to buyers for bargaining purposes					
Negotiate terms with suppliers affecting packaging, pallets and so on					X
Reduce distance between receiving and storage facilities					X
Set up inspection schedule for incoming goods to curb acceptance of damaged items	X		X		

Action item	1	2	3	4	5	6	7
Step up billing to vendors of rework	X						
Bill freight to vendors on rejected shipments		X					
Pass minor invoice discrepancies	X						X
Control slow-moving inventories and initiate time for disposal actions	X	X				X	X
Establish reorder points and economic ordering or production quantities	X	X			X		X
Plan use of inventory space					X		
Maintain current locator files in storerooms							
Establish technologically significant materials codes	X				X	X	X
Shift burden of carrying inventory to suppliers	X				X		X
Introduce self-help storeroom bins for inexpensive items							X
Install storeroom facilities to cut metals on site	X						
Determine optimum buying sizes for metals	X	X					
Recharge flashlight batteries instead of buying new ones	X						
Clean gloves instead of buying new ones	X						
Use rebuilding services for valves, instruments, and so on	X						
Use nonoriginal equipment sources for spares	X						
Circumscribe addition of new articles to stock	X	X					X

- Correlate forecasting data for marketing and production
- Control off-sheet discounts
- Control application of freight terms to customers
- Consider freight factor in setting selling prices
- Develop standard routing guides for outgoing shipments
- Signal premium freight for investigation
- Establish prompt control over freight claims
- Negotiate favorable terms with freight audit agency
- Highlight unprofitable territories, products, customers, warehouses
- Act as self-insurer on rental cars
- Negotiate hotel rates on guaranteed basis
- Use compacts rather than big cars
- Use coach class on planes
- Stratify salespersons' calls on basis of customer needs
- Capture order information near source
- Use self-checking capabilities of computers
- Check new customer credit *before* shipment
- Train order-input clerks to reduce need for editing
- Signal costly piecemeal order releases by customers

Invoice special warehousing or packaging services

Invoice cancellation charges where practical

Report physical percentage-of-contract completion versus dollar percentage

Reduce delays before production order reaches floor

Avoid emergency inventory transfers from plant to plant

Eliminate duplications on operating and accounting records

Take inventory cycle counts at low of stocks

Consider adapatability of current stocks when planning engineering changes

Substitute second shift for overtime

Avoid split labor assignments of high-rate persons to lower-rate jobs

Monitor machine running speeds to avoid breakdowns

Stabilize labor force by level loading

Plan maintenance jobs

Reduce fire insurance premiums by complying with inspection reports

Invest excess cash

Monitor unemployment insurance claims where experience rating is a factor

Negotiate interruptible rates with utilities where practical

INDEX

A
Moment's
Liberty

———

The Shorter Diary
Virginia Woolf

ABRIDGED AND EDITED BY
ANNE OLIVIER BELL

INTRODUCTION BY
QUENTIN BELL

A Harvest Book
Harcourt Brace & Company
SAN DIEGO NEW YORK LONDON

Library of Congress Cataloging-in-Publication Data
Woolf, Virginia, 1882–1941.
A moment's liberty: the shorter diary/Virginia Woolf; edited by Anne
Olivier Bell; introduction by Quentin Bell.
p.   cm.
ISBN 0-15-161894-1
ISBN 0-15-661912-1 (pbk.)
1. Woolf, Virginia, 1882–1941 — Diaries.   2. Novelists, English — 20th
century — Diaries.   I. Bell, Anne Olivier.   II. Title.
PR6045.072Z466   1990
828'.91203 — dc20   90-33428
[B]

Printed in the United States of America
F H I G

Contents

Introduction

THIS is an abridged version of the diaries which Virginia Woolf wrote in the years between 1915 and 1941. Those diaries were published in full between 1977 and 1984 in five profusely annotated and carefully indexed volumes, and were furnished with an introduction by me. The purpose of that introduction was to preface a hitherto unpublished text, one which could hardly fail to interest scholars or enthusiasts for whom, indeed, the learned apparatus of those volumes was supplied. This present work is aimed at a more general public, which may well include many who are unfamiliar with the other writings of the diarist. In fine, my earlier task was to introduce the diaries; my present one, to introduce Virginia Woolf the writer.

Such an essay is appropriate inasmuch as the diary is on the whole a very simple and straightforward, though hastily written, record, and for this reason a good starting-point for anyone who has had the very sensible idea of adventuring into this fertile province of literature. The novice will very likely have heard ill of the writer I am trying to present. She was, we are frequently told, snobbish, elitist, and malicious. The reader will be able to form his or her own opinion of this. Here I would only point out that some other diarists, as for instance Pepys and Boswell, also had their faults of character but that, to put it mildly, their occasional lapses from perfection do not make them less readable. But there are other charges, more serious in the eyes of a prospective reader, which should be examined. It must be allowed that in Virginia Woolf's novels there are passages which baffle the common reader. In her critical writings she is always lucid; but in the fictions her disregard of what I should call narrative, her interest in the obscure emotions and the workings of the human mind, and her indifference to the more humdrum facts of everyday life, result in obscurities which can confound us. *The Waves* is not an easy read, and most of the earlier fictions present difficulties which are sometimes formidable. The diary, on the other hand, is almost always plain sailing. Virginia Woolf sets herself, at the end of her working morning or between tea and dinner, to record the pains and delights of her days. No prose could be less 'studied', and if anything is at all unclear it is because the diarist is in a hurry to dash down her experiences. Writing about herself and her life she does not disdain the commonplace. Whereas the characters – if they can be called characters – in *The Waves* scarcely seem to have such a thing as an income, Virginia Woolf, as a diarist, does not refrain from making notes on the price of eggs.

In that earlier introduction to which I have alluded, I committed myself to the kind of value judgment which I usually avoid, and declared that the diaries rank with the greatest of her novels, that they are a masterpiece. But the question may now arise: do they still look like a masterpiece now that they have been boiled down to a fifth of their original size? I think they do. Indeed I would suggest that in some respects the deletions of the editor have enhanced the merits of the original text.

The story which unfolds in these pages may be divided into three parts. Firstly, the years of recovery (1915–22) – recovery, that is, from the terrifying mental breakdowns of Virginia Woolf's early married life and, with the restoration of her health, the beginnings of her reputation as a writer, the publication of her first and second novels, and of a few strikingly original short stories which indicated the direction that she was to take. Secondly, the years of ascent (1922–31), in which, writing what are now her most celebrated novels, she formed and developed her own style, each book, beginning with *Jacob's Room* and culminating in *The Waves*, bringing new problems, new triumphs, and new fame. Thirdly, the final phase (1931–41), the phase of wealth, celebrity and distress. This coincides with a deterioration in her world and in the world at large, which was drifting with fearful speed towards barbarism and war, a catastrophe for which her grand remedy was feminism. Those years saw her long and painful struggle to write *The Years*, and the final triumph, as we can now see it, of *Between the Acts*, a novel which was published posthumously and which might have been altered if she could have been saved from the fear of insanity and from suicide.

In each period we see the writer sustaining old friendships and starting new ones. From the first Virginia was a central figure, with her sister Vanessa Bell, in what is called Bloomsbury, and her Bloomsbury friendships were formed long before these diaries were begun. The Great War had done something to disperse and to change the group, but familiar figures like Maynard Keynes, Desmond MacCarthy, Lytton Strachey, E. M. Forster and Roger Fry provide material for some valuable portraits; and to these may be added more recently introduced younger fellow-writers, Katherine Mansfield and T. S. Eliot. We do get an occasional glimpse of the corridors or waiting rooms of power: the afternoon when Virginia's cousin Herbert Fisher, then a cabinet minister, invited himself to tea and told her that the war had been won; or the memorable visit to the Woolfs' Sussex house of Sidney and Beatrice Webb, planning a socialist future for Britain. Such encounters did bring her momentarily close to the world of military and political action, although in neither case was she left with much admiration for the chief actors.

In the second period, as she enters her forties, we find the author rising and adventuring into the world of rank and fashion, if we may thus describe Lady Colefax and Lady Cunard, and that much more important connection (for it was sentimental) with Knole and the Sackvilles. At the other end of the social spectrum we may notice – indeed we cannot possibly escape – the long tragi-comic saga of Nelly Boxall, the Woolfs' living-in servant who, it seemed, could neither live with Virginia nor without her, so was continually giving notice and continually withdrawing it, exasperating her mistress who however was sufficiently attached to her to be culpably weak in dealing with her moods.

It was a token of her success that Virginia was now invited to meet the leaders of her profession. T. S. Eliot had for long been a friend, but now she encountered celebrated older writers such as Arnold Bennett, H. G. Wells, Shaw, Yeats, Max Beerbohm and George Moore; and to this phase of her career we owe a memorable portrait of Thomas Hardy. Also, for her curiosity was catholic, a description of the total eclipse of the sun in 1926.

In the last phase there were still new friends to be made, notably Dame Ethel Smyth, one of the most remarkable as well as one of the most tiresome of her admirers. She also enjoyed the company of younger poets and writers – William Plomer, Christopher Isherwood, Stephen Spender and others. But the 1930s was a time of mourning: Lytton Strachey was the first to die, and after him Dora Carrington, Roger Fry, Ottoline Morrell, Ka Arnold-Forster and other, younger, people: Francis Birrell, Stephen Tomlin, and her nephew, Julian Bell.

To these lists of persons, which I hope will give the reader a notion of the kind of society to be met with in these pages, one should add a multitude of other things: birds and weather, landscape and London streets, the pleasures of walking, of conversation, of listening to music; the peculiarities of university life, the insufficiencies of ceremonies; the list is endless and would soon become pointless; but it is perhaps worth observing that Virginia is one of the few women to give us a first-hand description of a military operation: she witnessed and described one of the most crucial engagements of the Battle of Britain – even if she was unaware of its significance.

It has been said that Bloomsbury was an exclusive society which repulsed all would-be visitors with icy scorn and had no use for outsiders. To some extent this was true of Virginia's sister, but it is not true of the other members of that group, especially Virginia. There were, to be sure, some relationships which she found irksome, as for instance that with her mother-in-law Mrs Woolf, but her no doubt tedious conversations with unwelcome guests, however exasperating when experienced, became, when confided to her diary, a theme of great comic value. From the point of view of Leonard or of her doctor, such encounters could be dangerous: they might give rise to headaches and make of her a solitary invalid, with nothing to record but her own state of mind (not that such observations were without interest), or worse still might bring the diary to a halt. But whenever she has the strength to write and give expression to her curiosity, sympathy, malice or sense of humour, she becomes immensely readable. Inevitably, in a manuscript which was written in haste by a writer who normally arrived at her meaning by a series of successive drafts, there must be some superfluities which she would have struck out. Here in the abridged version an attempt is made to give added momentum and clarity by means of tactful deletion. One hopes that the intelligent reader will see the material advantages of this operation. But of course in avoiding one difficulty one may fall into another: the pleasure of reading these pages may lead him to complain that the book is too short.

QUENTIN BELL, *1989*

Editorial Note

WHEN Virginia Woolf died in 1941, she left a series of diaries, thirty volumes in all, written between 1915 and her death. From these her husband Leonard extracted those passages primarily concerned with her own preoccupations as a writer, and published them in 1954 under the title *A Writer's Diary*. After his death in 1969 his wife's copyrights were inherited by her sister Vanessa Bell's surviving children, and it fell to them to decide on any further publication of her remaining manuscripts, including her letters and diaries. The decision was taken that both these should be published in full. Accordingly the *Letters*, edited by Nigel Nicolson and Joanne Trautmann, appeared in six volumes between 1975 and 1980, and the *Diaries*, edited by me, in five volumes from 1977 to 1984, both series being extensively and scrupulously annotated and indexed. In the nature of things, this formidable array of volumes is somewhat intimidating to the general reader, who may have neither time, money, nor inclination to expend on such a scale. So now the Hogarth Press – the publishing business started on a hand-press in the Woolfs' Richmond dining room almost three-quarters of a century ago – is publishing a single-volume selection of Virginia Woolf's letters under the title *Congenial Spirits*, and this volume, *A Moment's Liberty*, an abridged version of her diary.

In reducing the original five volumes to one I have had to jettison some four-fifths of their contents. My purpose has been to preserve the overall character of the original, to follow the autobiographical thread, and to present a comprehensible and readable distillation of the 2,000 or so pages of Virginia's manuscript diaries. To do so I have omitted a host of figures altogether and rationed the appearances of others; I have (reluctantly) omitted the diaries Virginia kept on her travels – which may well deserve separate publication; I have deliberately reduced the space allowed to Virginia's reflections on the conception, progress and reception of her work, for these are given full scope in *A Writer's Diary*; and for the rest, I have cut and condensed wherever I could do so without impairing the quality, language, and sense of the original text. I have also, with heroic self-abnegation, omitted all my informative footnotes. (For the deprived, they are always to be found in the five-volume complete edition.) Instead, I have provided introductory summaries to each year to give a background to the subjects engaging Virginia's interest; and I have included in the Index brief details of the people she mentions.

As this shortened diary is designed to be easily read and enjoyed, I have amended Virginia Woolf's wayward punctuation, have spelled out the many abbreviations she employed in her rapid rush to set down her thoughts and impressions, and have occasionally inserted (in square brackets) a name or a word or two to help the reader.

Virginia Woolf's diaries have since 1979 been housed in the admirable Henry W. and Albert A. Berg Collection of English and American Literature in the New York Public Library (Astor, Lenox, and Tilden Foundations), together with a great number of her other manuscripts.

It remains for me to thank my step-sister Chloe Green and my daughter-in-law Imogen Bell for particularly valuable and expert help in time of need.

ANNE OLIVIER BELL

1915

Adeline Virginia (b.1882) was the third of the four children of the second marriage of Leslie Stephen – Victorian man of letters and editor of the Dictionary of National Biography *– and his wife Julia, widow of Herbert Duckworth. The family, with the children of both parents' earlier marriages, lived in a large house at Hyde Park Gate, Kensington, with a staff of servants headed by the cook Sophie, removing each summer for several months to St Ives in Cornwall. Julia Stephen died in 1895, and (Sir) Leslie in 1904; that autumn, led by Vanessa, the eldest, the younger Stephens set up house at 46 Gordon Square, Bloomsbury, an unfashionable district where they felt able to loosen the shackles of Kensington convention. When Thoby Stephen left Trinity College, Cambridge – where his brother Adrian was to follow him – he brought his friends to Gordon Square, and his sisters were able first to be present at and soon to participate in the sort of free-ranging discussions on all manner of subjects which these intelligent and high-spirited young men had enjoyed at the University, and which were denied to most nicely-brought-up young ladies of that period. Among these visitors several were to become lifelong friends – Lytton Strachey, Saxon Sydney-Turner, Desmond MacCarthy. Two – Clive Bell and Leonard Woolf – were to become the husbands of Vanessa and Virginia Stephen.*

In 1906 Thoby Stephen died of typhoid fever contracted on a family expedition to Greece, and shortly afterwards Vanessa married his friend Clive Bell; Virginia and Adrian, leaving 46 Gordon Square to the Bells, moved a short distance to Fitzroy Square and subsequently, in 1911, to Brunswick Square, where they shared their household with the economist Maynard Keynes, Duncan Grant the painter and, home on leave after seven years as a colonial administrator in Ceylon, Leonard Woolf. The following year, in August, Virginia and Leonard were married. Virginia's nervous instability had long been an anxiety to her family; now Leonard was to bear it in aggravated form: she fell into depressions, refused to eat, and, in 1913, attempted suicide. Under his devoted care she gradually recovered, living for the most part in the country house she had leased before her marriage, Asheham in Sussex; and, after the outbreak of war in 1914, she was fit enough to return to London – or rather, its outskirts. In October she and Leonard took lodgings at 17 The Green, Richmond-on-Thames, with a Belgian landlady, Mrs Le Grys, and set about looking for a home of their own.

The Stephen sisters had resolved in their nursery that Vanessa would be a painter and Virginia a writer, and neither of them ever wavered from their chosen destinies.

From 1904 Virginia had published reviews and articles, mainly in The Times Literary Supplement; *her first novel,* The Voyage Out, *had been accepted by her half-brother the publisher Gerald Duckworth in 1913, although its appearance was delayed until March 1915 owing to her breakdown, and she was at work on her second,* Night and Day. *Leonard Woolf, who resigned from the Colonial Service in order to marry Virginia, had published two novels,* The Village in the Jungle *in 1913 and* The Wise Virgins *in 1914. But although Virginia had inherited a modest private income, this was insufficient to support two – particularly in view of the heavy medical and nursing expenses she had incurred, and Leonard turned to journalism as a source of income, becoming more and more concerned with political matters.*

Virginia Woolf wrote her diary at 17 The Green, Richmond, each day between 1 January and 2 February 1915; ten days later there are three further pages, and then no more.

1915

17 The Green, Richmond

Friday 1 January
We were kept awake last night by New Year Bells. At first I thought they were ringing for a victory.

Saturday 2 January
This is the kind of day which if it were possible to choose an altogether average sample of our life, I should select. We breakfast; I interview Mrs Le Grys. She complains of the huge Belgian appetites, & their preference for food fried in butter. If they eat thus in their exile, how must they eat at home, she wonders? After this, L. and I both settle down to our scribbling. We lunch; and read the papers, agree that there is no news. I read *Guy Mannering* upstairs for twenty minutes; and then we take Max for a walk. Halfway up to the Bridge, we found ourselves cut off by the river, which rose visibly, with a little ebb and flow, like the pulse of a heart. One of the queer things about the suburbs is that the vilest little red villas are always let, and that not one of them has an open window, or an uncurtained window. One house had curtains of yellow silk, striped with lace insertion. The rooms inside must be in semi-darkness; and I suppose rank with the smell of meat and human beings. I believe that being curtained is a mark of respectability – Sophie used to insist upon it. And then I did my marketing. Saturday night is the great buying night; and some counters are besieged by three rows of women. I always choose the empty shops, where I suppose one pays a halfpenny a pound more. And then we had tea, and honey and cream; and now L. is typewriting his article; and we shall read all the evening and go to bed.

Sunday 3 January
It is strange how old traditions, so long buried as one thinks, suddenly crop up again. At Hyde Park Gate we used to set apart Sunday morning for cleaning the table silver. Here I find myself keeping Sunday morning for odd jobs – typewriting it was today – and tidying the room – and doing

3

accounts which are very complicated this week. I have three little bags of coppers, which each owe the other something. We went to a concert at the Queen's Hall, in the afternoon. Considering that my ears have been pure of music for some weeks, I think patriotism is a base emotion. By this I mean that they played a National Anthem and a hymn, and all I could feel was the entire absence of emotion in myself and everyone else. If the British spoke openly about WCs, and copulation, then they might be stirred by universal emotions. As it is, an appeal to feel together is hopelessly muddled by intervening greatcoats and fur coats. I begin to loathe my kind, principally from looking at their faces in the tube. Really, raw red beef and silver herrings give me more pleasure to look upon. But then I was kept standing forty minutes at Charing Cross Station, and so got home late, and missed Duncan [Grant] who came here. Moreover, London on a Sunday night now, with all its electric globes half muffled in blue paint, is the most dismal of places. There are long mud coloured streets, and just enough daylight and insufficient electric light to see the naked sky, which is inexpressibly cold and flat.

Monday 4 January
Philip [Woolf] came after luncheon, having four days leave. He is sick to death of soldiering – told us tales of military stupidity which pass belief. The Colonel says "I like well dressed young men – gentlemen" and gets rid of recruits who sink below this level. In addition to this, the demand for cavalry at the front is exhausted, so that probably they will stay at Colchester for ever. Another dark, rainy day. An aeroplane passed overhead.

Tuesday 5 January
We worked as usual: as usual it rained. After lunch we took the air in the Old Deer Park, and marked by a line of straw how high the river had been; and how a great tree had fallen across the towing path, crushing the railing beneath it. Three bodies were seen yesterday swiftly coursing downstream at Teddington. Does the weather prompt suicide? *The Times* has a queer article upon a railway smash, in which it says that the war has taught us a proper sense of proportion with respect to human life. I have always thought we priced it absurdly high; but I never thought *The Times* would say so. L. went off to Hampstead to give the first of his lectures to the Women's Guild. He did not seem nervous: he is speaking at this moment. The Belgians downstairs are playing cards with some friends, and talk – talk – talk – while their country is destroyed. After all, they have nothing else to do.

4

Wednesday 6 January

L. went off at 10 a.m. to give his second lecture at Hampstead. The first was a great success, as I knew it would be. He finds the women much more intelligent than the men; in some ways too intelligent, and apt on that account, not to see the real point. No one except a very modest person would treat these working women as he does. Clive [Bell], or indeed any other clever young man, would give himself airs; and however much he admired them pretend that he didn't.

I wrote all the morning, with infinite pleasure, which is queer, because I know all the time that there is no reason to be pleased with what I write, and that in six weeks or even days, I shall hate it. Then I went to London, and asked at Gray's Inn about Chambers. They had a set vacant; and I at once envisaged all sorts of charms, and let myself into them with a thrill of excitement. But they would be perfect for one, and impossible for two. Next I saw a flat in Bedford Row, which promised divinely, but on asking at the agents, was told they had just been instructed to let it furnished only – And now, of course, I am convinced that there is no flat in London to equal it! I could wander about the dusky streets in Holborn and Bloomsbury for hours. The things one sees – and guesses at – the tumult and riot and busyness of it all –

Now I have to decide whether I shall go up again, to a party at Gordon Square. On the one hand, I shirk the dressing and the journey; on the other I know that with the first chink of light in the hall and chatter of voices I should become intoxicated, and determine that life held nothing comparable to a party. I should see beautiful people, and get a sensation of being on the highest crest of the biggest wave – right in the centre and swim of things. On the third and final hand, the evening's reading by the fire here – and smoking and talking to L. in what stands for slippers and dressing gown – are heavenly too. And as he won't urge me to go, I know very well that I shan't. Besides, there is vanity: I have no clothes to go in.

Thursday 7 January

No – we didn't go to the Gordon Square party. Leonard got back too late, and it rained; and really, we didn't want to go. I started off after lunch today, first to go to the Foundling Hospital and ask whether they would let us have Brunswick Square – or half the house; then to the Omega [Workshops] to buy Janet [Case] a shawl, and then to tea with Janet. Brunswick Square is already practically let to a retired Ceylon Civil Servant, called Spence, who may however be willing to let the two upper floors, which would suit us very well. I became, of course, possessed with a passion to have Brunswick Square. When I got out, it was raining. I walked to the Omega however and bought my stuff from a foolish young woman in a

Post Impressionist tunic. I went to Hampstead, and was allowed up to Janet. She is in bed, and will have to stay in bed for weeks. Still, she is trained to be brave, and so unselfish by nature that other people really interest her. We talked about Leonard, and life in London and Hardy's poems which she can't re-read – too melancholy and sordid – and the subjects not interesting enough. I don't agree. It grew late; and she suggested that I should dine there and go with L. to the Peace Debate at the Women's Guild. I couldn't face dinner, so I retreated to the Public Library. On the way I walked through one of the worst downpours I have ever been in. My shoes squeaked so with wet as I walked up the Library that I was ashamed. Then I dined at a cabman's eating house – the only dining place, and very good. Coarse, but clean and sober. At eight I met L. at 28 Church Row. The rooms are old white panelled rooms; one was full of working women. It was a comfort to see how they roar with laughter, like schoolgirls. It was very good. The women impressive as usual – because they seem to feel, and to have such a sense of responsibility.

Friday 8 January
I went to Chancellors [Richmond Estate Agents], to ask whether there was any news of Hogarth [House]. At first the man said no. When I told him that we might take a house in London, he at once confessed that he had twice seen the present tenant, and that she does not like the house. Is this invented, and, if not, is there some good reason why she does not like it? It seems likely that we shall have to choose between Brunswick and Hogarth -- unless both fail us.

Sunday 10 January
I was sitting typewriting this morning when there came a tap at the door; and someone whom I thought at first was Adrian, appeared; it was Walter Lamb however, fresh from the King. Whenever he has seen the King he comes to tell us. He insisted that we should go for a walk with him in Richmond Park. What did we talk about? We forgot about the King, and Walter told us a long inexpressibly dreary story about the inefficiency of the French soldiers. Whatever Walter says, has the same flat, smooth, grey surface; and his voice alone would dull the fieriest poesy in the world. His life now lies among respectable, semi-smart, rich people, whom he half-despises, so that his accounts are always a little condescending. The one passion of his life is for eighteenth century building. He is perfectly suited by Kew, and the Royal Academy, and the Royal family. He refused to lunch with us, saying that he had lived on pheasants all the week, and rhubarb was forbidden him, on account of his acidity.

I heard last night that old Spence won't let any part of Brunswick Square.

6

Monday 11 January

Leonard was in his bath this morning, and I was lying in bed, when I heard a commotion next door, and then someone rushed downstairs crying in a strange, unnatural voice "Fire! Fire!" As it was obvious that the house was not on fire, to any large extent, I put on my waterproof and slippers before I looked out of the window. I then smelt paper burning. I then went into the passage, and found smoke pouring from the open door of the next room. There was clearly time to escape, so I withdrew; and heard Lizzy return with the lodger; and heard her begin "I only put a bit of paper to draw the fire –" Later, I heard that the paper had caught; the draperies on the mantelpiece had caught; the screen had caught; the woodwork had caught. As every room in the house is lined with dry old wood, loosely papered over, ten minutes, I think, would have put the fire beyond water jugs – The wonder is how we have escaped so far, considering Lizzy. Yesterday she smashed two very nice bits of china for us.

We went up to London this afternoon: L. to see the editor of the *New Statesman* about an article on Diplomacy, I to go over a flat in Mecklenburgh Square. I went on to Day's Library and L. to the London Library. He has to write an article of 1200 words by Wednesday noon.

Tuesday 12 January

Cecil [Woolf] came to luncheon, in mufti, I observed. In fact they are both entirely sick of the army, and see no chance of going to the front. Nevertheless, Cecil thinks of being a permanent soldier, because the life is better than a Barrister's life. On the other hand, he and Philip may go to the colonies. The odd thing about the Woolf family, to me, is the extreme laxness of it. In my family, the discussions and agitations that went on about the slightest change in one's way of life were endless; but with the Woolfs it doesn't much seem to matter whether they turn farmer, run away with another man's wife, or marry a Polish Jew tailor's daughter. Perhaps the Woolfs haven't a family tradition. It gives a sense of freedom anyhow. From all this, obviously I have nothing to say.

Wednesday 13 January

L. went off to the *New Statesman* office this morning with his article. I lunched here, and then went to Day's, to get more books. The West End of London fills me with aversion; I look into motor cars and see the fat grandees inside, like portly jewels in satin cases. The afternoons now have an elongated pallid look, as if it were neither winter nor spring. I came back to tea. L. arrived – having seen Gordon Square and Maynard [Keynes] (who says German finance is crumbling) and Saxon [Sydney-Turner], who is recovering from influenza.

Thursday 14 January

We were woken this morning (I see this is going to become a stock phrase like 'Once upon a Time' in a faery story) by a thumping throbbing sound as if a motor omnibus were on the roof, endeavouring to start. Experience told now, however, that Lizzy had merely made a huge kitchen fire, when there was no water in the pipes. When L. turned on the tap, steam issued, as if it were Siegfried's dragon at Covent Garden, and then came floating bits of pipe, and the water was rust red. We wrote all the morning. After lunch we set off to Kingston in order to buy some charming cups, which are to be had there for a penny each. If Lizzy doesn't go, and continues to behave as though each day were her last, we must give her something cheap to break her rage against. We came home on top of a bus. Leonard is going up to hear the Fabians discourse; I think I shall indulge in a picture palace.

Friday 15 January

I went to my picture palace; and L. to his Fabians; and he thought, on the whole, that his mind and spirit and body would have profited more by the pictures than by the Webbs, and the doctors, who were talking about their etiquette. There were two or three superb pictures; but as usual, the drama is very boring. I wish one liked what everyone likes. The Hall was crowded, roars of laughter, applause &c.

We walked to Hogarth this afternoon, to see if the noise of schoolchildren is really a drawback. Well – I wonder what we shall do. I'd give a lot to turn over thirty pages or so, and find written down what happens to us. We are dining early, and going to a Hall – an unheard of dissipation – though there was a time when I went out to operas, evenings, concerts &c, at least three times a week. And I know we shall both feel, when its over, 'really a good read would have been better.'

Saturday 16 January

I think the Hall (Coliseum) last night *was* worth while – in spite of drawbacks. What I like in Halls are 'turns' – comic singers, or men imitating Prima Donnas, or Jugglers. I don't like one act plays. It takes me a whole act to get into a play, and so one act plays are mostly sheer boredom. Therefore I was disappointed to have three one act plays. However, there was a man who sang like a Prima Donna; and a patriotic Revue. We left, just as an Eastern jar, coloured grey and violet, shot up in the middle of the stage.

We wrote this morning. I took Max along the River, but we were a good deal impeded, by a bone he stole, by my suspenders coming down, by a dogfight in which his ear was torn and bled horribly. I thought how happy

I was, without any of the excitements which, once, seemed to me to constitute happiness. L. and I argued for some time about this. Also about the worthlessness of all human works except as a means of keeping the workers happy. My writing now delights me solely because I love writing and don't, honestly, care a hang what anyone says.

Monday 18 January
This afternoon we went over the houses in Mecklenburgh Square; which has led to a long discussion about our future, and a fresh computation of income. The future is dark, which is on the whole, the best thing a future can be, I think.

Tuesday 19 January
We walked in Richmond Park this afternoon; the trees all black, and the sky heavy over London; but there is enough colour to make it even lovelier today than on bright days, I think. The deer exactly matched the bracken. But L. was melancholy. When I analyse his mood, I attribute much of it to sheer lack of self confidence in his power of writing; as if he mightn't be a writer, after all; and being a practical man, his melancholy sinks far deeper than the half assumed melancholy of self conscious people like Lytton, and Sir Leslie and myself. There's no arguing with him.

Wednesday 20 January
Having finished a chapter, I went off buying small fragments of things part of the morning – For one thing, I saw a mass of pinkish stuff in the fishmongers, and bought it – Cods' Roe. Maynard Keynes came to dinner. We gave him oysters. He is like quicksilver on a sloping board – a little inhuman, but very kindly, as inhuman people are. We gossiped at full speed. Then we talked about the war. We aren't fighting now, he says, but only waiting for the spring. Meantime we lavish money, on a scale which makes the French, who are fearfully out at elbow, gape with admiration. We are bound to win – and in great style too, having at the last moment applied all our brains and all our wealth to the problem.

Friday 22 January
When L. pulled the curtains this morning, practically no light came in; there was a kind of greyish confusion outside – soft swirling incessant snow. This has gone on all day almost, sometimes changing to rain. The Green itself is very lovely; and lights up the room with its pure white glare. But the streets become brown directly. Of course, in this House of Trouble, the pipes burst; or got choked; or the roof split asunder. Anyhow in the middle of the morning I heard a steady rush of water in the wainscot; and

9

Mrs Le Grys, Lizzy and various people have been clambering about the roof ever since. The water still drips through the ceiling into a row of slop pails. We are going to hear the Fabians at Essex Hall.

Saturday 23 January

The Fabians were well worth hearing; still more worth seeing. The interest was watching Mrs [Beatrice] Webb, seated like an industrious spider at the table; spinning her webs (a pun!) incessantly. The hall was full of earnest drab women, and of broad nosed, sallow, shock headed young men, in brown tweed suits. They all looked unhealthy and singular and impotent. It was all very dull and sensible, and the idea that these frail webspinners can affect the destiny of nations seems to me fantastic. But it was well worth going, – and I have now declared myself a Fabian. Oliver and Ray [Strachey] dined with us. Oliver as usual, very prompt, impatient and rather testy. Ray solid and capable and soothing. We discussed the war.

Monday 25 January

My birthday – and let me count up all the things I had. L. had sworn he would give me nothing, and like a good wife, I believed him. But he crept into my bed, with a little parcel, which was a beautiful green purse. And he brought up breakfast, with a paper which announced a naval victory (we have sunk a German battleship) and a square brown parcel, with *The Abbot* in it – a lovely first edition. So I had a very merry and pleasing morning – which indeed was only surpassed by the afternoon. I was then taken up to town, free of charge, and given a treat, first at a Picture Palace, and then at Buszards [Tea Rooms]. I don't think I've had a birthday treat for ten years; and it felt like one too – being a fine frosty day, everything brisk and cheerful, as it should be, but never is. We exactly caught a non-stop train, and I have been very happy reading father on Pope, which is very witty and bright, without a single dead sentence in it. In fact I don't know when I have enjoyed a birthday so much – not since I was a child anyhow. Sitting at tea we decided three things; in the first place to take Hogarth, if we can get it; in the second, to buy a printing press; in the third to buy a bull dog, probably called John. I am very much excited at the idea of all three – particularly the press. I was also given a packet of sweets to bring home.

Wednesday 27 January

Mrs Woolf and Clara came to dinner. Mrs Woolf has the mind of a child. She is amused by everything, and yet understands nothing – says whatever comes into her head – prattles incessantly, now good humoured, now ill humoured. She told us how she used to go to bed with a basket of socks by her side, so as to start darning first thing in the morning.

Thursday 28 January
Leonard off again to lunch with the Webbs. I decided to go to London, for the sake of hearing the Strand roar, which I think one does want, after a day or two of Richmond. Somehow, one can't take Richmond seriously. One had always come here for an outing, I suppose; and that is part of its charm, but one wants serious life sometimes. A new servant has come today. Lizzy left, carrying a brown paper parcel and whistling loudly – I wonder where she has gone?

Saturday 30 January
L. went to Chancellors this morning about Hogarth. They will let us know on Monday for certain.

Sunday 31 January
O dear! We quarrelled almost all the morning! and it was a lovely morning, and now gone to Hades for ever, branded with the marks of our ill humour. Which began it? Which carried it on? God knows. This I will say: I explode; and L. smoulders. However, quite suddenly we made it up (but the morning was wasted), and we walked after lunch in the Park, and came home by way of Hogarth, and tried to say that we shan't be much disappointed if we don't get it. After tea I started reading *The Wise Virgins*, and I read it straight on till bedtime, when I finished it. My opinion is that its a remarkable book; very bad in parts; first rate in others. A writer's book, I think, because only a writer perhaps can see why the good parts are so very good, and why the very bad parts aren't very bad. I was made very happy by reading this; I like the poetic side of L. and it gets a little smothered in Blue-books, and organisations.

Monday 1 February
We went up to London – L.. to the London Library, I to Day's. I walked with him across the Green Park. In St James Street there was a terrific explosion; people came running out of Clubs; stopped still and gazed about them. But there was no Zeppelin or aeroplane – only, I suppose, a very large tyre burst. But it is really an instinct with me, and most people, I suppose, to turn any sudden noise, or dark object in the sky, into an explosion, or a German aeroplane. And it always seems utterly impossible that one should be hurt.

We have just been rung up by Chancellors, who wish us to see the owner of Hogarth tomorrow. In fact it seems quite likely at this moment that we shall get Hogarth. I wish it were tomorrow. I am certain it is the best house to take.

Tuesday 2 February
Well, it is tomorrow; and we are certainly nearer to Hogarth than we were. We have done little else and thought of little else all day.

There are no entries in VW's diary for the next ten days

Saturday 13 February
There was a great downpour this morning. I am sure however many years I keep this diary, I shall never find a winter to beat this. It seems to have lost all self control. We wrote; and after luncheon L. went to the Library, and I went to a concert at the Queen's Hall. I got by luck a very good place, for the Hall was nearly full – and it was a divine concert. But one of the things I decided as I listened (its difficult not to think of other things) was that all descriptions of music are quite worthless, and rather unpleasant; they are apt to be hysterical, and to say things that people will be ashamed of having said afterwards. They played Haydn, Mozart no. 8, Brandenburg Concerto, and the Unfinished. I daresay the playing wasn't very good, but the stream of melody was divine. It struck me what an odd thing it was – this little box of pure beauty set down in the middle of London streets, and people – all looking so ordinary, crowding to hear, as if they weren't ordinary after all, or had an ambition for something better. I was annoyed by a young man and woman next to me who took advantage of the music to press each other's hands. And other people eat chocolates, and crumbled the silver paper into balls.

Sunday 14 February
Rain again today. I cleaned silver, which is an easy and profitable thing to do. It so soon shines again. Philip came, and he and L. went for a walk. He lunched with us and stayed talking till 3.30, wanting to talk about himself perhaps and had to go back to Colchester, where the only tolerable thing is the oysters.

Monday 15 February
We both went up to London this afternoon; L. to the Library, and I to ramble about the West End, picking up clothes. I am really in rags. It is very amusing. With age too one's less afraid of the superb shop women. These great shops are like fairies' palaces now. I swept about in Debenham's and Marshall's and so on, buying, as I thought, with great discretion. The shop women are often very charming, in spite of their serpentine coils of black hair. Then I had tea, and rambled down to Charing Cross in the dark,

making up phrases and incidents to write about. Which is, I expect, the way one gets killed. I bought a ten and elevenpenny blue dress, in which I sit at this moment.

1917

Virginia Woolf's record of daily life at The Green, Richmond, early in 1915 was brought to an end by the onset of a very severe mental breakdown. Soon after she became ill - mad, she called it - Leonard took possession of Hogarth House in Paradise Road, Richmond, and it was here and at her rented country house, Asheham in Sussex, that Virginia slowly recovered under the care of professional nurses, the last of whom left towards the end of the year, when she was able to resume a comparatively normal, if cautious, life. In February 1916 her household was augmented by two living-in servants, Nelly Boxall the cook and her impetuous friend Lottie Hope, who were to serve and to exasperate Virginia for many years to come. As Leonard became more and more involved in political activities, Virginia resumed her connection with The Times Literary Supplement, *and from 1916 onwards she contributed a regular stream of book reviews to this and other periodicals. Early in 1917 the Woolfs realised their intention (recorded by Virginia on her birthday in 1915) to buy a printing press, and that summer they issued their first hand-printed publication,* Two Stories. Written and Printed by Virginia and L. S. Woolf, *and then began to set* Prelude, *the long short story by Katherine Mansfield, whom they had met some time earlier. Thenceforth the preoccupations and satisfactions of the 'Hogarth Press' were an ever-present factor in their lives.*

Richmond is some distance from central London, but nevertheless the Woolfs maintained an active social life. Friends readily came out to meals, to walk with them in the neighbouring parks or to stay overnight; they themselves frequently went up by train to meetings, concerts, libraries, parties and so forth in London. Their circle included those drawn in through Leonard's political interests - in particular the doughty Margaret Llewelyn Davies, the General Secretary of the Women's Co-operative Guild; ramifications of family on both sides; and old friends such as Desmond MacCarthy and Roger Fry who were joined by a younger generation - Cambridge graduates like 'Ka' Cox, Karin Costelloe (who had married Adrian Stephen in 1914), Alix Sargant-Florence and, from the Slade School of Fine Art, Saxon Sydney-Turner's Egeria, Barbara Hiles, and Lytton Strachey's devotee, Dora Carrington.

Inevitably the war was a continuing background to their lives; four of Leonard's brothers joined the army; one was killed; and he himself was called up in May 1916 but, concerned rather for Virginia's than his own welfare, he obtained from their doctors certificates of unfitness for military service (he suffered from an uncontrollable nervous tremor of the hands). Many of their circle had conscientious objections to the war, including Virginia's brother Adrian and her brother-in-law Clive Bell – who was nominally doing farm work on the estate of the Liberal MP Philip Morrell and his aristocratic wife Lady Ottoline at Garsington, near Oxford, which they had made a refuge for artists, intellectuals, and Conscientious Objectors. Clive and Vanessa, whose sons Julian and Quentin were born in 1908 and 1910, had some time since effected an amicable detachment, though both retained rooms in their former home in Gordon Square, the lease of which had been taken over by Maynard Keynes. Clive was engaged in a long affair with Mary Hutchinson; and Vanessa had fallen in life-long love with the painter Duncan Grant (both incidentally cousins of Lytton Strachey); and it was to enable him and his friend David (Bunny) Garnett to obtain agricultural work (upon which their exemption from military service depended) that Vanessa had moved her household to Charleston, an isolated farmhouse which Leonard had found about four miles from Asheham, which was to remain her, Duncan and Clive's country home until their deaths some half a century later.

_1917_

Monday 8 October
This attempt at a diary is begun on the impulse given by the discovery in
a wooden box in my cupboard of an old volume, kept in 1915, and still able
to make us laugh at Walter Lamb. This therefore will follow that plan –
written after tea, written indiscreetly, and by the way L. has promised to
add his page when he has something to say. We planned today to get him
an autumn outfit in clothes, and to stock me with paper and pens. This is
the happiest day that exists for me. It rained steadily of course. London
seems unchanged. We walked through Gough Square; Dr Johnson's house
a fine, very well kept place, not so shabby as I expected. A little square,
folded in behind Chancery Lane, and given over to printing presses. This
is the best part of London to look at – not I now think to live in.

Tuesday 9 October
We had a horrid shock. L. came in so unreasonably cheerful that I guessed
a disaster. He has been called up. It was piteous to see him shivering,
physically shivering, so that we lit his gas fire, and only by degrees became
more or less where we were in spirits; and still, if one could wake to find
it untrue, it would be a mercy.
   We took a proof of the first page of K[atherine] M[ansfield]'s story, _The
Prelude_. It looks very nice, set solid in the new type. We had a short walk
by the river. As it is a fine, fairly still evening, perhaps I shall have a raid
to describe tomorrow. I forget how many people rang us up this morning,
Alix [Sargant-Florence] for one, who wants to start her work apparently;
and we have a liver and bacon Clumber [spaniel] in view, the property of
a man taken for the army.

Wednesday 10 October
No air raid; no further disturbance by our country's needs. We walked
down the river, through the park, and back to an early tea. At this moment,
L. is bringing the 17 Club into existence. I am sitting over the fire, and we

have the prospect of K. Mansfield to dinner, when many delicate things fall to be discussed. We notice how backward the leaves are in falling and yellowing here compared with Asheham. It might still be August, save for the acorns scattered on the path – suggesting to us the mysterious dispensation which causes them to perish, or we should be a forest of oaks.

Thursday 11 October
The dinner last night went off; the delicate things were discussed. We could both wish that one's first impression of K.M. was not that she stinks like a – well civet cat that had taken to street walking. In truth, I'm a little shocked by her commonness at first sight; lines so hard and cheap. However, when this diminishes, she is so intelligent and inscrutable that she repays friendship. We discussed Henry James, and K.M. was illuminating I thought. Today poor L. had to go the round of doctors and committees. His certifications are repeated. He weighs only 9 stone 6 pounds.

Sunday 14 October
We were rung up and asked to dine with the Bells in Soho, and this, I regret to say, led to much argument: the night was wet, and L. didn't want – old arguments in short were brought out, with an edge to them. So we went dolefully enough, and found the place, behind the Palace [Theatre], dined with Roger [Fry], Nina Hamnett, Saxon and Barbara [Hiles] and a party such as might figure in a Wells novel; I enjoyed it though, and L. was a model of self-control. Clive's remarks tended to prove that he is at the centre of everything, but not so aggressive as usual.

Then on Saturday – what happened? Saturday was entirely given over to the military. We are safe again, and, so they say, for ever. Our appearance smoothed every obstacle. I waited in a great square, surrounded by barrack buildings, and was reminded of a Cambridge college – soldiers crossing, coming out of staircases, and going into others; but no gravel and no grass. A disagreeable impression of control and senseless determination. A great boarhound, emblem of military dignity I suppose, strolled across by himself. L. was a good deal insulted: the doctors referred to him as 'the chap with senile tremor', through a curtain. Mercifully the impression slowly vanished as we went about Richmond. Herbert [Woolf] came to tea, bringing the dog, Tinker, a stout, active, bold brute, brown and white, with large luminous eyes. We have taken him for a walk, but directly he is loosed, he leaps walls, dashes into open doors, and behaves like a spirit in quest of something not to be found. We doubt rather if we can cope with him.

We are to have Alix and Lilian [Harris] to dinner.

Monday 15 October
Alix and Lilian were much as usual last night. Alix has the same air of level headed desperation, solid, capacious, but as low in tone as a coal cellar. However we found her very anxious to take on our work; and comes to learn tomorrow.

Tuesday 16 October
We started printing in earnest after lunch, and Alix came punctually; was instructed, and left on her high stool while we took the air with Tinker, who jumped from a parapet into a boat covered with tarpaulin, crashed through, and out again, unhurt though surprised. We came back, and Alix solemnly and slowly explained that she was bored, and also worried by her two hours composing, and wished to give it up. A sort of morbid scrutiny of values and of motives, joined with crass laziness, leads her to this decision; and I expect it will lead her to many more. She has a good brain, but not enough vitality to keep it working.

Wednesday 17 October
I went up to the show of pictures at Heal's this afternoon. Ottoline [Morrell] was not at her ease; closely buttoned up in black velvet, hat like a parasol, satin collar, pearly, tinted eyelids, and red gold hair. Needless to say one saw nothing of the pictures. Aldous Huxley was there – infinitely long and lean, with one opaque white eye. We had tea with Roger. I was very much conscious of strain – Ott languid, and taking refuge in her great ladyhood, which is always depressing. I walked with her in the downpour to Oxford Street, she buying me crimson carnations, without cordiality.

Friday 19 October
The sweetness of Ka [Cox]'s nature, so we thought, is triumphing over the bureaucracy which threatened to straitwaistcoat all her charm. Not but what office life isn't a pool past which one has to lead her. She spent the night, was down with her leather case in hand to catch an early train. I had a letter from Nessa about servants, and so went up to Mrs Hunt's [Domestic Agency] this afternoon. Not a parlourmaid to be had. With some skilful manipulation of trains, I reached the Æolian Hall, paid my shilling and heard a very long and very lovely Schubert octet. Coming out, I saw a grey, shockheaded woman without a hat – Alix; and we had tea at Spikings. She has a kind of independence and lack of concern for appearances which I admire. But as we walked up and down Dover Street she seemed on the verge of rolling up the usual veil of laughter and gossip and revealing her sepulchral despair – poor woman. "Where are you going now Alix?" "I really don't know." "Well, that sounds dismal! Don't you look forward to

say eleven tomorrow morning?" "I merely wish it didn't exist that's all!"
So I left her, hatless, aimless, unattached, wandering in Piccadilly.

Saturday 20 October
Happily, or she might say unhappily, for Alix she didn't presumably wander
in Piccadilly all night, or the great bomb which ploughed up the pavement
opposite Swan & Edgar's might have dug her grave. It turns out that a
Zeppelin came over, hovered unseen for an hour or two and left.

Sunday 21 October
Lytton [Strachey] came to luncheon, and Goldie [Goldsworthy Lowes Dick-
inson] to dinner – so we must have talked for six or seven hours. We walked
down the river and through the Park, Lytton in good spirits, having finished
a book of 100,000 words [*Eminent Victorians*], though now pretending that it
can't be published. He means to leave London and live 'for ever' in the country.
It seems a good thing that one's friends should try experiments. Poor old
Goldie is evidently beyond that stage. This war seems to possess him, to leave
little over. In fact he looked very shrunk and worn; infinitely good, charming,
devoted, every ounce of vitality rightly applied – no time for experiments, not
enough curiosity perhaps, though extreme kindliness and sympathy, which
in the case of young men, becomes amorous.

Monday 22 October
The moon grows full, and the evening trains are packed with people leaving
London. We saw the hole in Piccadilly this afternoon. Traffic has been
stopped, and the public slowly tramps past the place. Swan & Edgar has every
window covered with sacking or planks; you see shop women looking out
from behind: 'business goes on as usual' so they say. Our London Library
stands whole, however, and we found our books, and came home in the tube,
standing the whole way to Hammersmith, and have just come in.

Tuesday 23 October
Another lapse in this book, I must confess; but if I do it against my humour
I shall begin to loathe it; so the one chance of life it has is to submit to
lapses uncomplainingly. I remember though that we walked, printed, and
Margaret [Llewelyn Davies] came to tea. How pale these elderly women
get! The rough pale skin of toads, unfortunately: Margaret in particular
easily loses the flash of her beauty. This time we were whelmed in the
Co-op revolution; I get an occasional swinge of the tail which reminds me
of the extremely insignificant position I have in this important world. I get
a little depressed, a little anxious to find fault – a question of not being in
the right atmosphere. L. I suppose feels the same about Gordon Square.

Thursday 25 October
Saxon and Barbara dined with us; Saxon as usual when with her – gentle and giving off a sound as of a boiling, but not over boiling, kettle; speechless of course. As she has only simple direct things to say, I.. and I were a little sleepy; but we have arranged that she is to take up printing. I am going to Asheham on Monday with Saxon.

Sunday 28 October
Still no raids, presumably the haze at evening keeps them off, though it is still and the moon perfectly clear. The numbers who have gone out of London this week must feel a little foolish.

Friday 2 November
L. is giving a lecture at Birkenhead at this precise moment, and will then I suppose travel all night across England before reaching me. I feel as if I'd moved about a great deal; kept moving to keep myself warm. I mean Asheham and Charleston were rather in the nature of distractions, so as not to think how strange and solitary I was. Not solitary in the literal sense of course. Yesterday at Charleston it rained all day, so I sat in; writing in the morning; sitting in the Studio after luncheon. Duncan painted a table, and Nessa copied a Giotto. I unpacked all my bits of gossip. They are very large in effect, these painters; very little self-conscious; they have smooth broad spaces in their minds where I am all prickles and promontories. Nevertheless to my thinking few people have a more vigorous grasp or a more direct pounce than Nessa. Two little boys with very active minds keep her in exercise. I like the feeling that she gives of a whole nature in use. In working order I mean; living practically, not an amateur, as Duncan and Bunny [Garnett] both to some extent are of course. I suppose this is the effect of children and of responsibility, but I always remember it in her. A love of the actual fact, is strong in her.

But I was glad to come home, and feel my real life coming back again -- I mean life here with L. One's personality seems to echo out across space, when he's not there to enclose all one's vibrations. This is not very intelligibly written; but the feeling itself is a strange one – as if marriage were a completing of the instrument, and the sound of one alone penetrates as if it were a violin robbed of its orchestra or piano. A dull wet night, so I shall sleep.

Saturday 3 November
I woke 5 minutes before 7, and lay listening, but heard nothing, and was about, at 8 o'clock, to flatten out all my expectations when I heard L. at the door and there he was! With the softness of a mouse he had let himself in and breakfasted. We talked for as long as we could; divine contentment at being once more harmonious.

Tuesday 6 November

The melancholy fact is that Tinker, at the present moment, 5.30, is lost. He was let out in the garden and presumably escaped. We took the bus to Kingston; visited for the last time let us hope in our lives, the Recruiting Office, and after waiting in the familiar room with the two wooden benches, the towel hanging up and the khaki coat, L. was summoned, and given his paper which states that he is 'permanently and totally disabled.' We suppose this might fetch £500 if sold. However we were rather dashed by the loss of the spaniel whom we had come to like.

Saturday 10 November

Another melancholy fact is that I've let all these days pass – two of them because I was out late, the third, Friday, because I was too gloomy; and we were both too argumentative, to make writing possible. However to deal with the dissipations first. Nessa was up, and I had a Bloomsbury afternoon. I went to the Omega where Roger was convoying three chattering Frenchwomen round the show, and giving the impression as usual that French manners and language have a peculiar relish for him. The pictures glimmered through the dusk; and I was chiefly impressed by the Gertlers; Vanessa, too, very good; Duncan, I thought, a little pretty or tending to be. Nessa came and we left, I buying an apricot coloured coat on my way. I had tea in Gordon Square, which always puzzles me under the new arrangement, there being no sitting room. This was the prelude to a party on Thursday, to which I went, through the wet and the dirt, a very long expedition for two hours of life, though I enjoyed it. The usual sensation of being in a familiar but stimulating atmosphere, in which all the people one's in the habit of thinking of, were there in the body. A great many mop headed young women in amber and emerald sitting on the floor. I spent most of my time with Oliver [Strachey], and as the clock struck 10 I got up and went – an example of virtue if ever there was one. And now we see how the gloom came about. L. was testy, dispiriting, and tepid. We slept. I woke to a sense of failure and hard treatment. This persisted, one wave breaking after another, all day long. We walked on the river bank in a cold wind, under a grey sky. Both agreed that life seen without illusion is a ghastly affair. Illusions wouldn't come back. However they returned about 8.30, in front of the fire, and were going merrily till bedtime, when some antics ended the day.

Monday 12 November

Today we've been to London, as usually happens on Monday. We went to the Omega, and in came Roger, which embarrassed me a little, partly because of his own pictures, and also because I don't like talking of art in front of him. He was in process of painting a table though, and disappeared. Then we went to Gordon Square, and who should open the door but Clive? He asked us in, and there was Mary Hutchinson in one of the big armchairs, a piteous half moon of a woman, to my thinking. She seems so crushed and submissive always.

Tuesday 13 November
We began our printing off this afternoon, and we printed 300 copies of the first page [of *Prelude*], but we should be glad of another press, though the results are very good for the most part. L. is making up a lecture he's giving at Hammersmith; I'm to preside over the Women's [Co-operative] Guild.

Wednesday 14 November
L. gave his lecture; I presided over my guild. It always puzzles me to know why the women come, unless they like sitting in a room not their own, gas and light free, other women on other chairs. They don't pay much attention apparently.

Thursday 15 November
We printed off another page, very successfully, which took till tea time, and then we went round in the semi-darkness to the little printer [owner of The Prompt Press] who will come round any moment now to see the room for the press.

Monday 19 November
The little printer came round at the end of the last page, and stayed perhaps one hour. We have advanced £10, and for that bought the cutting press, and stipulated that the printing press shall be here by January 14. On Friday we went to a concert, walking out when the English piece came on. Tea at Spikings, with some of the upper classes; who looked like pet dogs threatened with a cold bath. They were talking of the scarcity of motor cars. I bought a pair of stockings and then home. The stockings were in preparation for Garsington. We came back from that adventure two hours ago. It's difficult to give the whole impression, save that it wasn't much unlike my imagination. People strewn about in a sealingwax coloured room: Aldous Huxley toying with great round disks of ivory and marble – the draughts of Garsington; [Dorothy] Brett in trousers; Philip [Morrell] tremendously encased in the best leather; Ottoline, as usual, velvet and pearls; two pug dogs. Lytton semi-recumbent in a vast chair. Too many nick nacks for real beauty, too many scents, and silks, and a warm air which was a little heavy. Droves of people moved about from room to room all Sunday. After tea I had perhaps an hour over a log fire with Ottoline. On

the whole I liked [her] better than her friends have prepared one for liking her. Her vitality seemed to me a credit to her, and in private talk her vapours give way to some quite clear bursts of shrewdness. The horror of the Garsington situation is great of course; but to the outsider the obvious view is that Ottoline and Philip and Garsington House provide a good deal, which isn't accepted very graciously. In such conditions I think Ott deserves some credit for keeping her ship in full sail, as she certainly does. We were made immensely comfortable; a good deal of food; the talk had frequent bare patches, but then this particular carpet had been used fairly often. By talking severely to Philip, L. made him come up to Parliament today. He is a weak amiable long suffering man, who seems generally to be making the best of things, and seeing the best of people whom by nature he dislikes.

Thursday 22 November
On Wednesday Barbara came to make a start, and the machine thereupon completely struck work, and as our stock of K's ran out, she could only set four lines. This she did however, quickly and without fault, so that she promises well. She bicycled from Wimbledon, her small crop head, bright cheeks, brilliant waistcoat give her a likeness to some vivacious bird; but I don't know that I think this very emphatic appearance particularly interesting.

I dined with Roger and met Clive. We sat at the low square table covered with a bandanna, and eat out of dishes each holding a different bean or lettuce; delicious food for a change. We drank wine, and finished with soft white cheese, eaten with sugar. Then, taking a splendid flight above personalities, we discussed literature and aesthetics. Roger asked me if I founded my writing upon texture or upon structure; I connected structure with plot, and therefore said 'texture'. Then we discussed the meaning of structure and texture in painting and in writing. Then we discussed Shakespeare, and Roger said Giotto excited him just as much. This went on till I made myself go precisely at 10. And we discussed also Chinese poetry; Clive said the whole thing was too distant to be comprehensible. Roger compared the poetry with the painting. I liked it all very much (the talk I mean); the atmosphere puts ideas into one's head, and one can speak them straight out and be understood – indeed disagreed with. Old Roger takes a gloomy view, not of our life, but of the world's future.

Monday 26 November
Today I went into London with my manuscript; and Leonard – which entry was broken off somehow – but my recollection is that L. found Desmond [MacCarthy] at the London Library; together they look up the word f—— in the slang dictionary, and were saddened and surprised to

see how the thumb marks of members were thick on the page. My afternoon was by comparison chaste; though I'm hardly proud of the fact that I completely lost my way in seeking Printing House Square. A kind man in uniform took me to *The Times* at last.

Monday 3 December

On Saturday L. gave a lecture at Hampstead. But we had to race off in the Tube to Leicester Square to dine with Barbara, Saxon and a young woman; then on to *Figaro* at the Old Vic. It's perfectly lovely; breaking from one beauty into another, and so romantic as well as witty – the perfection of music, and vindication of opera.

On Sunday we heard of Cecil |Woolf|'s death, and Philip's wounds.

Wednesday 5 December

Our apprentice weighs rather heavily upon us. For one thing her presence is rather in the way of our complete comfort. It may be her youth; something highly polished so as to reflect without depth about her – On the other hand, she's nice, considerate; one can be open with her. The real drawback is her work. Today has been spent by L. in the futile misery of trying to print from one of her pages which won't lock up. As the other page had to be entirely taken down and re-set, her work amounts to *nil*; less than nil, considering L.'s time wasted. A bitter cold day too.

Thursday 6 December

Nothing was further from our minds than air raids; a bitter night, no moon up till eleven. At 5 however I was wakened by L. to a most instant sense of guns: as if one's faculties jumped up fully dressed. We took clothes, quilts, a watch and a torch, the guns sounding nearer as we went down stairs to sit with the servants wrapped in quilts in the kitchen passage. Slowly the sounds got more distant, and finally ceased; we unwrapped ourselves and went back to bed. In ten minutes there could be no question of staying there; guns apparently at Kew. Up we jumped, more hastily this time. Servants apparently calm and even jocose. Guns at one point so loud that the whistle of the shell going up followed the explosion. Then silence. Cocoa was brewed for us, and off we went again. Having trained one's ears to listen one can't get them not to for a time; and as it was after 6, carts were rolling out of stables, motor cars throbbing, and the prolonged ghostly whistlings which meant, I suppose, Belgian work people recalled to the munitions factory. At last in the distance I heard bugles; L. was by this time asleep, but the dutiful boy scouts came down our road and wakened him carefully.

Today we have printed, and discussed the raid, which, according to the

Star I bought was the work of twenty-five Gothas, attacking in five squadrons and two were brought down. A perfectly still and fine winter's day, so about 5.30 tomorrow morning perhaps –

Friday 7 December
But there was no raid; and as the moon wanes, no doubt we are free for a month. Happily no apprentice today, which gives a sense of holiday. Nessa was up about a governess, so I ended my afternoon in one of the great soft chairs at Gordon Square. I sat alone for twenty minutes, reading a book on Children and Sex. When Nessa came we had tea and it was discovered that Clive and Mary were in the house; the same party as usual. As usual to my liking; so much alive, so full of information of the latest kind; real interest in every sort of art; and in people too. I rather expect L. to disagree with all this. I judge by the amount of animation of brain produced in myself. Not that Mary Hutchinson opens her lips, but she has an air of mute sympathy. Nessa had to go round to Roger's, and I walked with her, buying sausages and cheese for a supper party on the way. Roger is becoming one of the successes of the day as a painter of perfectly literal and very unpleasant portraits.

Sunday 9 December
Lytton came to tea. I was alone, for L. went to Margaret. I enjoyed it very much. He is one of the most supple of our friends; I don't mean passionate or masterful or original, but the person whose mind seems softest to impressions, least starched by any formality or impediment. There is his great gift of expression of course, never (to me) at its best in writing; but making him in some respects the most sympathetic and understanding friend to talk to. Moreover, he has become, or now shows it more fully, curiously gentle, sweet tempered, considerate; and if one adds his peculiar flavour of mind, his wit and infinite intelligence, he is a figure not to be replaced by any other combination. Intimacy seems to me possible with him as with scarcely any one; for, besides tastes in common, I like and think I understand his feelings – even in their more capricious developments; for example in the matter of Carrington. He spoke of her, by the way, with a candour not flattering, though not at all malicious. "That woman will dog me" – he remarked. "She won't let me write, I daresay." "Ottoline was saying you would end by marrying her." "God! the mere notion is enough – One thing I know – I'll never marry anyone –" "But if she's in love with you?" "Well, then she must take her chance." "I believe I'm sometimes jealous –" "Of her? that's inconceivable –" "You like me better, don't you?" He said he did; we laughed. He brought us his Gordon. Next day he was to take the book to Chatto & Windus.

Tuesday 11 December

The infliction of our apprentice. I own that I sounded the very depths of boredom with Barbara. She gives out facts precisely as she received them – minute facts about governesses and houses. And no doubt of her own adequacy crosses her mind; all so nice, honest, sensible, how can there be a flaw; And the time passed; she missed her train; waited on for another – waited until 6.10 – and my evening fretted away without sensation, save of one standing under the drip of a water spout.

Wednesday 12 December

This morning ruined by the tears and plaints of Lottie [Hope], who thinks her work too hard, and finally demanded higher wages, which she could easily get, and so could Nell [Boxall]. I lost my temper, and told her to get them then. Up came Nelly in a conciliatory mood regretting Lottie's outburst, though pointing out the hardships of our printing-room, so untidy – work endless; had meant to ask a rise in February – everyone's wages raised. We were very amicable; but Lottie's taunts seemed to me unpleasant – At last she went.

Thursday 13 December

By careful arrangement I limited the reconciliation scene with Lottie to fifteen minutes at eleven sharp. She sobbed; repented; took back everything she'd said; all a fabrication about overwork, and the more people we had and the more mess we made the better she liked it. She kissed me and went off, like a chastened child, leaving me with a mixture of pity and (I suppose) self complacency. The poor have no chance; no manners or self control to protect themselves with; poverty degrades, as Gissing said.

Monday 17 December

Monday, as I think I've noted before, is our marketing day – but I'm forgetting Molly MacCarthy and Walter Lamb last night –

I forget who it was that came in at this moment; and I have excuse for forgetting, since it is now *Thursday 3 January 1918*, and we're just back from Asheham. I remember though that the last days were full of people. Walter and Molly as I began to relate. And then, I can remember that we had Ka; who contemplates resignation; and then, the night after, Bob [R. C. Trevelyan]; with his pockets bulging with Georgian poetry, his talk all of books and prices asked for printing, and number of copies sold, in the midst of which Nelly burst in to say that the Take Cover had sounded. So we had our dinner party in the cellar; Bob talking at such a rate that it was necessary to listen at the window for the guns, loud enough though they were. After that – the very next night – we went to the 17 Club dinner; a great deal of eating by some two hundred people at long tables. Next day we went to Asheham, and the journey was the worst in our record – five hours; spent mostly outside Clapham Junction; fog, bitter cold; every move stopping short in a minute or two. Motored out, I remember, and found the roads under snow; but very pleasant coming into the drawing room, save that we were without milk. One of the coldest and finest of Christmases. Rather to our relief, we spent it alone. There was the usual visit from Maynard and Clive. But what I like most about Asheham is that I read books there; so divine it is, coming in from a walk to have tea by the fire and then read and read – say *Othello* – say anything. It doesn't seem to matter what. And then the trees, spare and leafless; the brown of the plough, and yesterday, downs mountainous through a mist. Solitary sportsmen beat up duck and snipe on the marshes. Windows were almost always frozen in the morning, and each blade rough with frost. Partridges would come and sit in the field, lifeless little lumps they looked, half stiff with cold perhaps.

Clive, by the way, enlivened Christmas by a small book of verse – the prose fantastically foppish, the verse very pretty and light, to my mind (by which I mean not altogether to L.'s mind).

So we come to an end of the year, and any attempt to sum it up is beyond me, or even to cast a final glance at the evening paper, with news from Russia, which has just come in and drawn L. to remark: "A very interesting state of things –" "And what's going to happen?" "No human being can foretell that."

The End

1918

Although little reference to it is made in her diary, concurrently with all her other activities, social, domestic and journalistic, Virginia was writing her second novel, Night and Day, *which she reported 'finished' in November this year, although it was six months before she submitted it to her half-brother the publisher Gerald Duckworth. The most notable extension of her customary round was her now frequent resort to the 1917 Club in Soho, a meeting place for socialists and intellectuals which Leonard had helped to bring into existence. On her expeditions to London she found it convenient to drop in there in the afternoon, after perhaps delivering her copy for Bruce Richmond, the editor of* The Times Literary Supplement *(1918 and 1919 were her most prolific years as a journalist), or getting books from the London Library, in the expectation of finding tea, congenial company and gossip.*

Leonard meanwhile was becoming increasingly involved in the Labour movement, writing, researching and lecturing; in September he was appointed editor of the International Review. *Virginia's own contribution to the betterment of society was to preside over the local branch of Margaret Llewelyn Davies's Women's Co-operative Guild, which met at Hogarth House and for which she found speakers, often from among her own friends.*

The possibilities inherent in their embryo Hogarth Press continued to attract both Leonard and Virginia, in spite of their amateurishness as printers; moreover it attracted writers too. While still working on Katherine Mansfield's Prelude, *they were approached with a request that they might print James Joyce's* Ulysses, *refused by commercial printers fearful of prosecution under obscenity laws. Virginia was both repelled and impressed by the manuscript, and Leonard would have liked to undertake it, but of course the task was far beyond their capacities. In November T. S. Eliot came to dine at Hogarth House, the beginning of a long and respected friendship; his seven* Poems *became the fourth publication of the Hogarth Press, and was followed four years later by* The Waste Land, *both set up and printed by the Woolfs themselves.*

The war growled on in the background, but finally came to its end, after surges and relapses of hope; Virginia notes the privations and alarms it caused; but though travel was precarious and difficult, she and Leonard managed to make several country visits to friends including the Morrells at Garsington, to Lytton Strachey, now installed at Tidmarsh in Berkshire attended by his devoted Carrington, to Roger Fry near Guildford, and to their own Asheham; and it was while they were here that on

Christmas Day Vanessa gave birth at Charleston to Angelica, her daughter by Duncan Grant, and Julian and Quentin, her two little Bell sons, were brought over to stay with their Aunt Virginia.

_1918_

Friday 4 January

There's no reason after all why one should expect special events for the first page of a new book; still one does: and so I may count three facts of different importance: our first use of the 17 Club; talk of peace; and the breaking of my tortoiseshell spectacles. This talk of peace (after all the most important of the three) comes to the surface with a kind of tremor of hope once in three months; then subsides; then swells again. What it now amounts to, one doesn't even like to guess; at any rate, one can't help feeling something moving. The 1917 Club is a success, on the basis of one tea. We met Alix, already an habitué by the fire; together with a knot of very youthful revolutionaries, one officer, and two sallow democratic officials. The rooms are light, bear traces of Omega, and are less formal than usual. Before this, I did my usual round; L. passing his afternoon in committees.

Saturday 5 January

We went to Hampton Court. We walked across Bushy Park, and along a raised bank beneath trees to the river. It was cold, but still. Then we took a tram to Kingston and had tea at Atkinsons, where one may have no more than a single bun. Everything is skimped now. Most of the butcher's shops are shut; the only open shop was besieged. You can't buy chocolates, or toffee; flowers cost so much that I have to pick leaves instead. We have cards for most foods. The only abundant shop windows are the drapers. Other shops parade tins, or cardboard boxes, doubtless empty. (This is an attempt at the concise, historic style.) I suppose there must be some undisturbed pockets of luxury somewhere still; but the general table is pretty bare. Papers, however, flourish, and by spending sixpence we are supplied with enough to light a week's fires.

Sunday 6 January

Alix and Fredegond [Shove] for supper. The talk, after flaunting round Clive, Barbara, Garsington &c, settled upon conscience, social duties, and Tolstoy. Gerald [Shove] read Tolstoy the other day, and determined to give up tobacco, but now argues that Tolstoy's commands were for men of looser life than he, so that he may smoke cigarettes. He thinks seriously of starting a nursery garden after the war, and threatens to give up their capital. "What's the use of that?" L. demanded. "That's the worst of all things to do. We don't want people to live on thirty shillings a week." "Psychologically it may be necessary if one is to abolish capitalism" I remarked. "I don't agree" said Alix. "Besides who would he give his capital to?" "In the ideal state everyone would have £300 a year" L. went on. "Please tell me some reason that I can remember to take back to Gerald" Fredegond pleaded. I forget now what the reason was. "He's got an awful conscience" she continued. "He ate a large Christmas dinner, and then he and his brother sent out for preserved fruit and when they had finished them they were miserable. 'We've behaved like pigs!' they cried. They were both miserable." L. gave us a great many reasons why we should keep what we have, and do good work for nothing. I still feel, however, that my fire is too large for one person. I'm one of those who are hampered by the psychological hindrance of owning capital.

Tuesday 8 January

To the printer's today, and find him calmly asserting that he can't really send the Press on the 14th. Can't find anyone to move it. This is cool as he took our ten pounds on the understanding we should have the press without fail.

Wednesday 9 January

The 17 Club is something of a lure; certainly promises better conditions for tea than a shop. So, having gone for my spectacles, I went to Gerrard Street. Found Fredegond and Faith [Henderson] there, also a large semi-circle of Cambridge youths, and one or two others. I was amused at the repetition of certain old scenes from my own past – the obvious excitement, and sense of being the latest and best (though not outwardly the most lovely) of God's works, of having things to say for the first time in history; there was all this; and the young men so wonderful in the eyes of the young women, and young women so desirable in the eyes of the young men, though this was not perceptible to me sitting elderly upon my sofa. However, then I was summoned to have my tea at the far end of the room; and Lytton came in. We tried still to overhear young Cambridge, and Lytton finally decamped, on my daring him, to that party.

I then had some private talk with Faith. According to her Nick [Bagenal, her brother] is getting a great deal of pain from the Saxon Barbara Nick combination. His claims are disregarded; Barbara prefers Saxon; and seems to be ashamed of the unintellectuality of Nick. She won't take him to see her Bloomsbury friends. Bloomsbury, I think, will have one more corpse to its credit; for poor Barbara's attainments aren't such as to give her a very secure footing there; and to my thinking a marriage with Nick offers more solid value than a cold blooded and only semi-real attachment with Saxon.

Friday 11 January
Another sedentary day, which must however be entered for the sake of recording that the Lords have passed the Suffrage Bill. I don't feel much more important – perhaps slightly so. Its like a knighthood; might be useful to impress people one despises.

Saturday 12 January
The hope of peace all broken up again; policies once more running in every direction, as far as one can tell.

Monday 14 January
We had Saxon to dinner on Saturday. He was at his lowest ebb. Even his gestures are weariful. He has been nowhere, seen no one. Played chess with Leonard, was beaten which didn't add to his spirits, and left burdened with the mysteries of this unintelligible world.

On Sunday, Clive came to tea; he hadn't long settled in when the Shoves arrived; and we spent an hour or two in gossip. After Clive went, Fredegond and Gerald stayed to dinner, and were more at their ease. Fredegond has a great turn for mimicry. She mimicked Karin [Stephen] bursting into tears one night from a sense that Maynard &c didn't want to see her. In fact the dominion that 'Bloomsbury' exercises over the sane and the insane alike seems to be sufficient to turn the brains of the most robust. Happily, I'm 'Bloomsbury' myself, and thus immune; but I'm not altogether ignorant of what they mean. And its a hypnotism very difficult to shake off, because there's some foundation for it. Oddly, though, Maynard seems to be the chief fount of the magic spirit. Talk about capital with Gerald; he says he means to part with his, but I guess that he always has some scruple to play with as an intellectual exercise.

Friday 18 January
Another skip, partly due to my writing a long letter to Nessa, which drained up some of the things I should have said here. But I like this better than

letter writing. On Thursday and Friday we worked away at printing. Unvarying cold and gloom, which turns now to rain, now to snow. This is the Hell of the year. We seem to mark time in the mud.

Monday 21 January

[On Sunday] Lytton came to tea; stayed to dinner, and about 10 o'clock we both had that feeling of parched lips and used up vivacity which comes from hours of talk. But Lytton was most easy and agreeable. Among other things he gave us an amazing account of the British Sex Society which meets at Hampstead. They were surprisingly frank; and fifty people of both sexes and various ages discussed without shame such questions as the deformity of Dean Swift's penis; whether cats use the w.c.; self abuse; incest – incest between parent and child when they are both unconscious of it, was their main theme, derived from Freud. I think of becoming a member. Lytton at different points exclaimed *Penis*: his contribution to the openness of the debate. We also discussed the future of the world; how we should like professions to exist no longer; Keats, old age, politics, Bloomsbury hypnotism – a great many subjects.

Wednesday 23 January

I see I've forgotten yesterday; but it was uneventful. L. went up to a meeting, Barbara was left in control of the Press, and I took a walk by myself. I went along the river to Marble Hill. I must retract what I said about the Hell of the year. We have glimpses of Heaven. I sat by the river watching a boat launched, and half expected to see buds on the willows. River very high, swift and yellow, testifying to the floods higher up. They say its been raining heavily; I daresay it has, but such is the civilisation of life in London that what with fires, electric light, underground railways and umbrellas, how can one take notice of the weather. We dined early and had the Guild. As usual, L. and I were the only people to speak; as usual it was only when talk drifted near food that one of the women broke silence. She wanted a bread shop. Oddly phlegmatic these women for the most part; with a passive sort of pleasure in sitting there and watching like so many pale grey sea anemones stuck to their rocks. Still, the children, the housework – excuses enough if one troubled to look.

Today we printed; and I made two little excursions into Richmond. The bakers' windows now provide almost nothing but little plates of dull biscuits; sections of plain cake; and little buns without any plums. If you see a plum, it is invariably a decoy plum; there are no others. This transformation scene has been stealing on imperceptibly; last year were we still allowed iced cakes? Its unthinkable!

Friday 25 January
My Birthday. L. slid a fine cow's horn knife into my hand this morning. Nelly has knitted me a pair of red socks which tie round the ankle, and thus just suit my state in the morning. Barbara came, and together we 'dissed' four pages, and L. printed off the second four at the printers – altogether a fine day's work. At this rate Katherine's story will be done in five weeks.

Saturday 26 January
Today we went to Kew. Snowdrops, dwarf cyclamen, some miniature rhododendrons out; also the points of some squills or crocuses coming through the grass and dead leaves.

Monday 28 January
I went to have my tooth finished, winding up for tea at the Club, which becomes as Goldie said "quite a family party". You come in to find half a dozen pairs of legs radiating from chairs towards the fire. You hear, or I heard, 'its a case of revolution or evolution' and then, if you've heard enough, you seek the *Manchester Guardian*, and hide yourself for precisely ten seconds. Fredegond, with apologies, breaks through the barrier. "But they're so fearfully dull, and I must talk something that isn't politics". That something, so far as I remember, was Ottoline, Alix, poetry, love. Home I went, and there was a raid of course. From 8 to 1.15 we roamed about, between coal hole, kitchen, bedroom and drawing room. I don't know how much is fear, how much boredom; but the result is uncomfortable, most of all, I believe, because one must talk bold and jocular small talk for four hours with the servants to ward off hysteria. Next morning ——

Tuesday 29 January
– the after effects of the raid were swept aside by Barbara. "Virginia, I shan't come on Friday because I'm going to be married." "You're going to marry – ?" "Yes, Nick [Bagenal]." "And Saxon?" "Saxon doesn't mind. Nothing's to be changed. We're all agreed."

These are the terms. I don't myself think that she wishes to be married; but has convinced herself that she should. She showed no wish to be congratulated or in any way fussed over. She stayed and printed as usual.

Wednesday 30 January
Up to a concert and tea with Ottoline. She is perched in the smallest bedroom of a Bloomsbury hotel, moulting, depressed, untidy, overdressed. Not much talk of interest to me, though friendly and not so overpowering in certain directions as usual.

Friday 1 February
A day of fog in patches. Last night the worst fog they say for thirty years, and old gents who escaped the raid walked in numbers over the edge of platforms and were crushed. A cook stepped into the Thames; people walked by rapping our railings to keep the road.

Tuesday 5 February
Karin came to give her lecture. She arrived at tea time. I can't help being reminded by her of one of our lost dogs – Tinker most of all. She fairly races round a room, snuffs the corners of the chairs and tables, wags her tail as hard as she can, and snatches at any scrap of talk as if she were sharp set; and she eats a great deal of food too, like a dog. This extreme energy may be connected with deafness. She has become a Bolshevik. Socialism is nibbling at our friends in a curious way. She and Adrian have scruples about the size of their income, and wish to earn money. She gave her paper on League of Nations well, though speaking too quick. She stayed the night. But I see that Adrian must find her energy, her not fastidious or critical but generous and warm blooded mind, her honesty and stability, a great standby –

Saturday 2 March
What is the use of finishing a sentence left unfinished a month ago? Here we are; evening; I came back from Asheham, or rather Charleston, an hour ago. After Karin went that Wednesday, rather a monotonous time began for me. Influenza began on the Friday; I was kept in bed eight days; on the next Tuesday we went to Asheham. For nine of our ten days we saw no one; but the days melted into each other like snowballs roasting in the sun. On Thursday Nessa came for the night, and I went back with her to Charleston for Friday night, L. taking the servants up to town. On Saturday morning Nessa, Duncan and I sat in the studio and gossiped. Part of the time we discussed art. They say there's no one worth considering as a painter in England today – no one like Katherine Mansfield or Forster even with whom its worth discussing one's business. In France this is reversed. Nessa showed me Saxon's letters. He has been very unhappy, and made out his moments of exaltation and depression with his usual minuteness. I left at 1.15, walking in a high wind with two parcels slung across my shoulders, to Glynde; through the park. Back here for tea.

Tuesday 5 March
The Guild meets tonight for Nick [Bagenal] to address it.

Wednesday 6 March

Again one has to wonder why the women come – what inducement there is in such a passive employment as sitting silent, half asleep, in a chair for an hour. Nick was in the right style for them too; simple, detailed, casual, much at his ease. He spoke for an hour. His matter of fact way of speaking and common sense also struck me. He seemed in good spirits; proud of Barbara, and telling me how after the war they'd like to live in the country and make good furniture after designs by Carrington.

We now have a mania for gambling over Demon patience. I lost four shillings over this in a week.

Friday 8 March

Going up in the lift at Holborn the other day I stood next a boy of fourteen or so, whose head only was visible among the crowd. I noticed that it was an extremely interesting, sensitive, clever, observant head; rather sharp, but independent looking. One couldn't tell from his cap whether he was well off or not. I came to the conclusion that he was the son of an officer with whom he stood. When we got into the street I looked at once at his legs. His trousers had holes in them. From that one could judge what a wretched affair his life will be.

Saturday 9 March

We went to a meeting called a 'Suffrage Rally' in Kingsway this afternoon. The hall was fairly well filled; the audience almost wholly women, as the speakers were too. The pure essence of either sex is a little disheartening. Moreover, whether its a meeting of men or of women, one can't help wondering why they do it. I get one satisfactory thrill from the sense of multitude; then become disillusioned, finally bored and unable to listen to a word. In truth this meeting seemed to beat the waves in vain. The vote being won, only great eloquence could celebrate the triumph. None were eloquent.

We had tea at the 17 Club. One room was crowded, and silent; at the end of the other Aldous Huxley and a young woman in grey velvet held what should have been a private conversation.

Monday 11 March

I spent seven shillings on books this afternoon; a fact to be recorded, since its the only mention of buying books this year, or last, perhaps. As a matter of fact I've accumulated twelve shillings as *Times* money; add five shillings for a birthday present, and I have seventeen shillings – an unparalleled sum. First, however, I beat the town for chocolate or sweets. In the whole of the stores, not one ounce of choc to be had; but some simple square drops, such as one used to buy in a bag for a penny. Half a crown will now buy a pound of them. Half a crown in the old days would have bought a coal-scuttle full. Then I went on the top of a bus, for the day was of the quality of June, only fresher, and sadder too, to Nutt's shop to get a Leopardi; then to Mudie's where I bought Mill on Liberty; then to the Charing Cross Road where I bought *The Happy Hypocrite* by Max Beerbohm; and *Exiles of the Snow*, by Lancelot Hogben. In this way I laid out seven shillings.

Poor Hogben's book is precisely the dreary imitative stuff one might have expected; or even worse than one might have expected – what Lytton would call 'illiterate'; under the influence of Swinburne, incredibly ungifted, and weakly rebellious.

Tuesday 12 March
I may say that I'm 'rejected by *The Times*'. Its the second week of my rejection; and it has the result of making me write my novel [*Night and Day*] at an astonishing rate. If I continue dismissed, I shall finish within a month or two. It becomes very absorbing.

Thursday 14 March
My dismissal is revoked. A large book on Pepys arrived, which I spent the evening reading, and now another on Swinburne awaits me at the Railway station. I'm divided whether one likes to have books, or to write fiction without interruption.

Monday 18 March
On Saturday the chatter began. Lytton and Carrington came to tea – she apple red and firm in the cheeks, bright green and yellow in the body, and immensely firm and large all over. The talk has run off my mind, so that I don't suppose there was anything said of great importance. Carrington going out of the room for a second, Lytton explained that he would like to stay with us without her, could it be managed. He asked me to review his book. I agreed without thinking. On second thoughts I don't much want to write under surveillance, or to ask for the book of a friend. On Sunday the burden of visitors was oppressive. Gerald [Duckworth] and Saxon lunch; Saxon tea; Barbara, Nick, Middleton Murry dinner. Gerald's likeness to a pampered overfed pug dog has much increased. The feebleness of his hold on life save through the stomach must be fearful. His commercial view of every possible subject depressed me, especially when I thought of my novel destined to be pawed and snored over by him. Saxon at his least urbane and most insignificant. He was beaten at chess, and went, as if not wishing to meet Nick and Barbara. Nick was the only cheerful one of us.

Poor Murry snarled and scowled with the misery of his lot. He works all day, and writes when he comes home. Worst of all, Katherine has been very ill with haemorrhage from the lungs, out in France, and has to be brought home, which is difficult, in order to see how bad she is. But I thought him very much more of a person and a brain than I had thought him before. I had a good deal of talk about books with him, such as one couldn't have with Nick – though he's read Jane Austen, and can keep his end up by natural good sense and taste. Barbara was almost blotted out; scarcely spoke, I think. They went first; Murry stayed on, for a time, discussing French writers and Thomas Hardy. He will never write another novel, he says. Poetry is a short cut and "life seems to me now very precarious."

Friday 5 April
Off we went to Asheham on Thursday [21 March], in such a burst of summer heat that people in the Tube pulled blinds down. The daffodils were out and the guns could be heard from the downs. Even to me, who have no immediate stake, and repudiate the importance of what is being done, there was an odd pallor in those particular days of sunshine. Our visitors broke in upon the moods which weave so thick a texture into life alone at Asheham. First Lytton. Then we waited, with eyes upon the avenue, for the appearance of Barbara. She never came though, and upon Sunday I had a letter telling the almost incredible story of her repeated attempts to get into a train; how for three days she went to Victoria; never got in, and finally spent Easter alone in her studio, expecting, so we are told, to find herself in some nine months short of a fortnight, the mother of a child. Lytton was with us one day less than a week. We had short, and to me, very intimate talks; intimate in the sense that he will understand from the sight of the tail what the whole body of the thought is in one's mind. These thoughts were for the most part about books; but books include a good deal of life. I suspect that he is now inclined to question whether Eminent Victorians, four in number, and requiring four years for their production, are quite enough to show for his age and pretensions. I suppose the contrast (and to me there is a contrast) between his achievements and L.'s achievements made itself felt to him. Then he was sick one morning. His ebb of health is very low; and certainly health does make one careful, perhaps a little peevish, spiritually. Then James [Strachey] and Noel [Olivier] came. Our patience wore rather thin. Visitors do tend to chafe one, though impeccable as friends. L. and I discussed this. He says that with people in the house his hours of positive pleasure are reduced to one; he has I forget how many hours of negative pleasure; and a respectable margin of the acutely unpleasant. Are we growing old? But this time food

difficulties certainly increased one's discomfort. One day we came back from a long walk to find the third of a loaf of bread on the table. No more to be had in the house. This was due to bad management on Nelly's part, but then at Asheham it's very easy to manage badly and needs considerable thought, cycling and carrying, to manage even tolerably. The relief of being back in comparative plenty and anyhow next door to shops is quite recognisable. We came up on Friday.

Saturday 6 April

This morning I had a letter from Barbara telling me that Nick was danger-ously wounded on the 30th; they have operated. The last news said he was well through the operation. If he recovers, perhaps he won't be sent out again – but who knows? At least she has had the blow soon. But the state of waiting for telegrams and letters, and this baby in prospect, must be as fair a combination of torture as human beings can invent for each other. Rain all day till this moment when it has turned brilliant. Plum blossom in the garden, and flowers very healthy looking.

Sunday 7 April

We are just back from tea with Barbara and Saxon in the Studio. Nick is already moved to another hospital and has written himself, so at least he must be in no immediate danger. The couple in the interior were almost too perfect an illustration of the post impressionist spirit for my taste. Even the black and white cat seemed decorated by the Omega. Whitewash in which the hairs of the brush remain, a striped pole, Burnet for the covers, china dogs for the mantelpiece, check cottons wherever you looked, and to the censorious eye one or two uncertainties of taste or reversions to an earlier stage, as for example a bead necklace hanging on a nail. I don't think Saxon had anything to say; he reminded me of a hen who has laid an egg – but only one. We did not like Hampstead. The vulgarity of Richmond is always a relief afterwards.

Monday 8 April

There is an awkward moment between coming back from London and dinner which is the salvation of this book. For some reason one can't settle to read, and yet writing seems the proper channel for the unsettled irritable condition one is generally in. Perhaps this condition is intensified by tea at the 17 Club, particularly if one happens to meet Roger in the Charing Cross Road, in his wideawake hat with four or five yellow French books under his arm. He is the centre of a whirlwind to me. Under this influence I was blown straight into a book shop, persuaded to lay out three shillings and seven pence on a French novel, made to fix a day for coming to Durbins, invited to a play and fairly overwhelmed – made to bristle all over with ideas, questions, possibilities which couldn't develop in the Charing Cross Road. Of course he was in a hurry to keep an appointment, and to produce one or two plays somewhere – ill too, so he said, but somewhat relieved in his mind by reading Fabre, who makes him see that after all our war, hideous though it is – but here we parted.

Wednesday 10 April
A very wet dark day. Printed. I set one page in one hour and fifteen minutes – my record. At this rate, the book might be done in a month. I had a letter from Miss Harriet Weaver yesterday asking whether we would consider printing Joyce's new novel [*Ulysses*], which no other printer will do, owing presumably to its sentiments. They must be very warm, considering the success he had with his last. She is to come here, though we can hardly tackle a book. I like this dipping into the great bran pie.

Saturday 13 April
A cold dismal day, and very bad news in the newspapers. Stout red-faced elderly men are visibly perturbed. And Ireland has Conscription. If one didn't feel that politics are an elaborate game got up to keep a pack of men trained for that sport in condition, one might be dismal; one sometimes is dismal; sometimes I try to worry out what some of the phrases we're ruled by mean. I doubt whether most people even do that. Liberty, for instance.
   Last night Desmond rang us up. I'm afraid our friends' motives won't stand scrutiny. His book comes out on Monday; he, though forgetting everything, yet remembers a vague joking promise of mine, uttered at least a year ago, to review it in *The Times*. He is sending me a copy. I'm now debating how to deal with these damned authors –

Thursday 18 April
Harriet Weaver appeared. Here our predictions were entirely at fault. I did my best to make her reveal herself, in spite of her appearance, all that the Editress of *The Egoist* ought to be, but she remained inalterably modest, judicious, and decorous. Her neat mauve suit fitted both soul and body; her grey gloves laid straight by her plate symbolised domestic rectitude; her table manners were those of a well bred hen. We could get no talk to go. Possibly the poor woman was impeded by her sense that what she had in the brown paper parcel was quite out of keeping with her own contents. But then how did she ever come in contact with Joyce and the rest? Why does their filth seek exit from her mouth? Heaven knows. She is incompetent from the business point of view and was uncertain what arrangements to make. We both looked at the MS which seems to be an attempt to push

the bounds of expression further on, but still all in the same direction. And so she went.

Then I went to [Roger Fry's house near] Guildford. I don't see how to put three or four hours of Roger's conversation into the rest of this page; it was about all manner of things: on growing old; on loneliness; on religion; on morality; on Nessa; on Duncan; on French literature; on education; on Jews; on marriage; and on the *Lysistrata*. We woke next morning to find the hills covered in snow, and came up in a bitter wind and rain to the Omega; so to Gordon Square; where first the new Delacroix and then the Cézanne were produced. There are six apples in the Cézanne picture. What can six apples not be? I began to wonder. There's their relationship to each other, and their colour, and their solidity. To Roger and Nessa, moreover, it was a far more intricate question than this. It was a question of pure paint or mixed; if pure which colour; emerald or viridian; and then the laying on of the paint; and the time he'd spent, and how he'd altered it, and why, and when he'd painted it – We carried it into the next room, and Lord! how it showed up the pictures there, as if you put a real stone among sham ones.

All day it rained, and L. was out to tea. I went to the Guild, which pleased me by its good sense, and the evidence that it does somehow stand for something real to these women. In spite of their solemn passivity they have a deeply hidden and inarticulate desire for something beyond the daily life; I believe they relish all the pomp of officers and elections because in some way it symbolises this other thing. They wish me to get them a speaker on Sex Education, Mrs Hiscoke telling us that she had had to get a friend to explain the period to her own daughter, and she still feels shy if the daughter is in the room when sexual subjects are discussed. She's twenty-three years old.

Today I got Desmond's book, sent, I'm sorry to say, by request of the author.

Sunday 21 April
The weather goes on with its wind and rain and occasional snow. I went to a concert at the Palladium this afternoon; but on the whole I regretted it. A man called Julian Clifford played Mozart as if it were a Dream Waltz, slowly and sentimentally with a kind of lugubrious stickiness. I must now write to Desmond, who has been telephoning, I fear, with thoughts of that review.

Friday 26 April
There are five or six days missed out – I don't remember why, but partly at least because there wasn't much to say. On Wednesday Lottie spilt half

a case of type on the floor, so that I had to spend four hours in sorting every compartment – about the most trying work there is.

Wednesday 1 May

On Saturday we went to Hampton Court, the first visit for a long time. We had a tremendous talk about the Equator. In the middle of a demonstration with two pebbles, Jack Radcliffe passed (or so I thought). This diverted my attention. A serious reprimand had to be administered. It was discovered that I took the Equator to be a circular mark, coloured dull red, upon the end of a football. The ignorance and inattention combined displayed in this remark seemed so crass that for about twenty minutes we couldn't speak. However, I was forgiven, and told about the tropics of Cancer and Capricorn. The question originally was about the time of moon and sun rise and setting in different months.

On Sunday Desmond came after dinner. He has the hard sea-worthy look of an old salt, cased in stiff black, with a few gold scrolls about him. But within this shell he is as tender and vague as ever, and very tired after his day's work [at the Admiralty] which results, he is alarmed to find and so are we, in practical action upon his evidence. He yawned, and couldn't stir himself up, though L.'s yawns were partly the cause of this. Late at night he took to reading Joyce's MS aloud, and in particular to imitating his modern imitation of a cat's miau, but L. went to bed, and though capable of spending a night in this manner, I had compunction, and decoyed Desmond upstairs, collecting books as we went. Next morning, having observed that breakfast at 8.30 would possibly be early enough, he stayed talking about books till 10, and rambled off quite out of tune for his office.

Friday 3 May

By Bus and tube to Hampstead, and to tea with Margaret [Llewelyn Davies]. Janet [Case] was there in those decorous draperies with which people compromise between art and fashion in Hampstead. Lilian [Harris] semi-recumbent upon a green pillow, Margaret immensely fat and broad; all black. I felt this to be the heart of the woman's republic. L. came in, and we had a long semi-political argument arising out of Milk combines, about government.

Monday 6 May

I went to London on my usual round; the one I like best. In my beatific state I forgot the principal thing I'd gone for: a typewriter ribbon; but never mind; that will be another day's treat. Mudie's [Library] I don't altogether like because I'm kept waiting, but I love Holborn, and the Charing Cross Road, and I rather like turning into the 17 Club, and finding or expecting to find someone I want to talk to. I don't like buying hats though. Presently Leonard came, with Adrian. Adrian looks immensely long, and his little bow tie somehow gives him a frivolous rather than distinguished air, as if a butterfly had settled on him by mistake. He has some job in an office. We gossiped. Blood is a very strong tie; so much can be taken for granted, after the first shyness. We went on to the London Library, and so home.

Tuesday 28 May

To take up the pen directly upon coming back from Asheham shows I hope that this book is now a natural growth of mine – a rather dishevelled, rambling plant, running a yard of green stalk for every flower. But first let me recall Janet, Desmond, Katherine Mansfield and Lilian; there were others – yes, there was Harry Stephen and Clive. Each left me with a page full of comments, but useless now partly I think from my habit of telling these incidents over to people, and the telling leaves a groove in my mind which gives a hardness to the memory, stereotypes it, makes it a little dull. Katherine was marmoreal, as usual, just married to Murry, and liking to pretend it a matter of convenience. She looks ghastly ill. As usual we came to an oddly complete understanding. My theory is that I get down to what is true rock in her, through the numerous vapours and pores which sicken or bewilder most of our friends. It's her love of writing I think. But she is off to Cornwall.

At Asheham we had Roger, a picnic, and I spent a night at Charleston. That is by way of company. But the important thing was the weather. We had the best display of flowers yet seen – wall flowers in profusion, columbines, phlox, and as we went huge scarlet poppies with purple stains in them. The peonies even about to burst. Last night at Charleston I lay with my window open listening to a nightingale, which beginning in the distance came very near the garden. Fishes splashed in the pond. May in England is all they say – so teeming, amorous, and creative. I talked a good deal with Nessa – much about servants and other possibilities. Roger and I croaked a kind of frogs' chorus together – how we loved and admired and were only snubbed for our pains – Nessa sitting almost silent, stitching a dress by lamplight.

Thursday 6 June

These gaps are accounted for by the weather. Its not weather for drawing up to the fire and settling in. Carrington came to tea with me [and] stayed over two hours; and I think that by itself is a sign of youth. She is odd from her mixture of impulse and self consciousness; so eager to please, conciliatory, restless, and active. I suppose the tug of Lytton's influence deranges her spiritual balance a good deal. She has still an immense admiration for him and us. She looks at a picture as an artist looks at it; she has taken over the Strachey valuation of people and art; but she is such a bustling eager creature, so red and solid, and at the same time inquisitive, that one can't help liking her. She posted me up in all the gossip. Lytton complains that the critics haven't attacked his judgments. They have copied each other and complimented him without much fineness. Still his book goes into another edition. I haven't yet read it through.

Friday 7 June
L. was told the other day that the raids are carried out by women. Women's bodies were found in the wrecked aeroplanes. They are smaller and lighter, and thus leave more room for bombs. Perhaps it is sentimental, but the thought seems to me to add a particular touch of horror.

Monday 17 June
Another gap of ten days. Ray [Strachey] for the night. Ray lectured the Women's Co-operative Guild. How strange it is to see one's friends taking their fixed shape! She has the look of conscious morality which is born of perpetual testifying to the right. She has grown heavier, more dogmatic. She speaks in all the counties of England. She has lost such feminine charm as she had; she seems mature. But she is made of solid stuff; and this comes through and pleased me, and L. likes her better than the cropheads. Ray tends to think us a set of gifted but good for nothing wastrels.

Murry and the Sangers came here to supper last Sunday. Murry was pale as death, with gleaming eyes, and a crouching way at table that seemed to proclaim extreme hunger or despair. Charlie has his wintry brightness still; but after dinner such a duet of despair was croaked by Murry and Dora as warmed the cockles of Dora's heart. 'At Christmas' said Murry, 'I was near suicide; but I worried out a formula which serves to keep me going. Its the conception of indifferentism. I have hope no longer. I live in two layers of conscience' (but I forget what these were). Dora egged him on, and sounded his praises. But to us he seemed less nice, perhaps more anxious for effect, this time than before.

Monday 24 June
[Mark] Gertler and Kot [S. S. Koteliansky] dined with us. Gertler is a plump white young man, got up for the occasion very sprucely in sponge-bag trousers. The word he would wish one to use of him is evidently 'powerful'. There is something condensed in all Jews. His mind certainly has a powerful spring to it. He is also evidently an immense egoist. He means by sheer will power to conquer art. I felt about him, as about some women, that unnatural repressions have forced him into unnatural assertions. He

examined our furniture and pictures. He likes shiny lodging house things best, he said. He has never felt akin to anyone. He thinks himself very much cleverer than most painters. Kot sat indulgently silent.

We had a visit from Margaret; which opened with a tremendous broadside of co-operative shop: lamentations, aspirations and too sanguine expectations; all exaggerated, so I felt, in comparison with their real value. Margaret stayed till the last train. She is a fine specimen of the public woman; a type, after all, no less marked than the literary type, though not yet so fully observed and recorded. Their eccentricities keep me amused, when to tell the truth, I've ceased to follow their plots and denunciations. They have the habit of considering themselves driven to death, overwhelmed with work, without a possibility of rest; and never once since I've known her has Margaret owned to any state of health save that of being very tired. But these peculiarities are not more than jokes to me; and the directness and superb vigour of her character always overcome me with admiration.

Before tea this afternoon I finished setting up the last words of Katherine's story – 68 pages.

Thursday 27 June
Mrs Woolf and Herbert dined with us on Tuesday. She has, I think, the qualities of a person who has never altogether grown up, in spite of nine children and all her cares. She gossips and enjoys herself, and somehow deals with life very freely and easily and with the liveliest childlike interest in it all, mixed with the most absurd conventions. She chattered away. "But Rasselas says the truth – a very fine truth" she observed. "Happiness is never perfect – I've never found perfect happiness – always something missing, Virginia." Herbert cordial, distant, and detached as usual.

Monday 1 July
We've talked a great deal since I wrote last. First there was the party at the Club on Friday. All sorts of people one half knew from the papers – men with shaggy hair and great eyebrows – women cadaverous or flamboyant – [Ramsay] Macdonald, Huysmans, Mrs Despard, [J. H.] Thomas and so on. We dined with Adrian and Karin, a good dinner; at 9 we went on to Ray's party – a dull affair, neither respectable nor bohemian. On Saturday I went to tea with Janet – but my hand shakes so with carrying parcels that I can't write.

Friday 5 July
Today L. printed off the last of *Prelude*, only the title page and dedication still to do.

Tuesday 9 July
I can't fill up the lost days, though it is safe to attribute much space in them to printing. The title page was finally done on Sunday. Now I'm in the fury of folding and stapling, so as to have all ready for glueing and sending out tomorrow and Thursday. By rights these processes should be dull; but its always possible to devise some little skill or economy, and the pleasure of profiting by them keeps one content.

Wednesday 10 July
We have sent off our first copies this evening, after spending the afternoon in glueing and covering. They surprised us when done by their professional look. I must read the book through after dinner, partly to find possible faults, but also to make up my mind how much I like it as literature.

Adrian and Karin dined here last night, and he spoke to the Guild on Peace – very composed, clear, well spoken. He has traces of the judicial mind and manner. The women would all have peace tomorrow, on any terms, and abuse our government for leading us on after a plan of their own. When asked to join a Peace Meeting in Hyde Park on Sunday, Mrs Langton, as spokeswoman, intimated that on no account could they violate the Sabbath. What a terrible grip Christianity still has – she became rigid and bigoted at once, as if God himself had her in his grasp. That I believe is still the chief enemy – the fear of God. But I was tactful enough to keep this view dark.

Friday 12 July
Great storms have been beating over England the last three days, God being, as usual, spiteful in his concessions, and now threatening to ruin the harvest. I owe God a grudge for his effect upon the Guild.

I suppose a great many tongues are now busy with Katherine Mansfield. I myself find a kind of beauty about the story; a little vapourish I admit, and freely watered with some of her cheap realities; but it has the living power, the detached existence of a work of art. I shall be curious to get other opinions.

Tuesday 16 July
Monday was as usual a day for London and tea at the Club. I was so foolish as to fritter three shillings – one and sixpence on the blue penholder with which I write, and when I don't write, suck; one and sixpence on paper, at a grossly extravagant shop in Pall Mall. I justified these extravagances by the fact that you can get into the National Gallery for nothing. I spent an hour wandering there. But I see why I like pictures; its as things that stir me to describe them. I don't want to read stories or emotions or anything

into them. But the atmosphere of picture galleries, always gloomy, is worse than ever now, when the glory of war has to be taught by a life-size portrait of Lord Kitchener, and almost life-size battle scenes.

Wednesday 17 July
We glued fifty copies of *Prelude*. So far our present supply is ample. It seems doubtful whether we shall sell more than a hundred. Clive writes a tolerant but not enthusiastic letter about it.

Thursday 18 July
All the copies that we glued yesterday have gone white in the back. We don't know the cause. [Bruce] Richmond rang up to offer me Rupert [Brooke]'s Life [by Edward Marsh] for next week. I told him that I should like to explain Rupert to the public. He agreed that there was much misunderstanding. "He was a very jolly sort of fellow" he said. I'm trying to get letters out of James [Strachey].

Tuesday 23 July
On Saturday we went to Tidmarsh [Berkshire]. From the point of view of country there is nothing that we at least can say for it; though the house and garden are nice enough. Lytton and Carrington were alone. No servant was visible and most of the waiting seemed to be done by Carrington. She is silent, a little subdued, makes one conscious of her admiring and solicitous youth. If one were concerned for her, one might be anxious about her position – so dependent on Lytton and having so openly burnt the conventional boats. She is to run her risk and take her chances evidently. Lytton was fresh from the Duchess of Marlborough and [Lord] d'Abernon, who is taking his play in hand. Whatever there is in the way of London society is, I suppose, now open to him. He is making his investigations not with a view to a permanent settlement; rather to round off his view of human nature. He declared he knows more different sorts of people than any of us; but we disputed this. A great deal of talk about Rupert. The book is a disgraceful sloppy sentimental rhapsody, leaving Rupert rather tarnished. Lytton very amusing, charming, benignant, and like a father to Carrington. She kisses him and waits on him and gets good advice and some sort of protection. He came up with us on Monday.

Saturday 27 July
On Wednesday I had one of my field days. To London, first to meet James at the Club. He was to tell me about Rupert for my article. His first words however were "Have you heard of Ka's engagement to Arnold-Forster?" This annoyed me considerably. I am glad that she should marry, though

she bade fair to be a marked spinster, but marriage with Will Arnold-Forster will be merely a decorous and sympathetic alliance, making her more of a servant of the state than ever. Then, as James had a medical examination, we couldn't say much about Rupert, save that he was jealous, moody, ill-balanced, all of which I knew, but can hardly say in writing. Fredegond appeared next; having spread my rumour about Ka, which may not be true, and I hope it isn't, I went up to Gordon Square; Nessa in and out of the room all the time; and of course Clive and Mary appeared; and then everything goes over the same little rapids. We all dined at the Mont Blanc. Clive has never forgiven me – for what? His personal remarks always seem to be founded on some reserve of grievance, which he has decided not to state openly. But he paid for my dinner, and we wound up good temperedly. The rain pelted down and I rushed for my train.

By rights of importance I should remark that today L. was asked to stand for Parliament. I haven't yet turned my mind that way. A natural disposition to think Parliament ridiculous routs serious thought. But perhaps it isn't so ridiculous as speeches make one suppose.

Monday 29 July

I'm paralysed by the task of describing a week end at Garsington. I suppose we spoke some million words between us; listened to a great many more, chiefly from the mouth of Mrs [Mary Agnes] Hamilton, who strains at her collar like a spaniel dog, and has indeed the large hazel staring eyes of one of them. There was Gertler, Brett, Ottoline, three children and Philip. Happily the weather was fine, the food good, and we flowed about happily enough, and without serious boredom. In fact, for some reason I was rather well content. My bed was like layer upon layer of the most springy turf; and then the garden is almost melodramatically perfect, with its grey oblong pool, and pink farm buildings, its soft whitish grey stone and enormous smooth dense green yew hedges. Down these paths we wandered; once or twice with Ott; once with Mrs Hamilton. She hasn't a penny of her own; and has the anxious hard working brain of a professional, earning her living all the time. I'm not sure though that she didn't compare very well with Ott. Some time after tea we three meandered off 'to the woods'. But we never got there of course. Halfway up a hill in the sun, she stopped, leant on her parasol, looked vaguely across the landscape, and began a discourse upon love. "Isn't it sad that no one *really* falls in love nowadays? Its the rarest, rarest thing – I mean they don't see each other ideally. They don't feel that every word is something too wonderful just because the other has spoken it." Here, chiefly in order to get us home, I said that love meant a great many different things; and that to confine it to romantic love was absurd. I also maintained that one could love groups of people, and landscapes. Unluckily this remark led Ott to lean on her parasol once more, and look longingly at a wheatfield. "Yes. I love that – just for itself – the curve of that wheatfield seems to me as divine as any human being. I love literature too –" "I love quite absurd things – the Independent Labour Party for instance," said Mrs Hamilton. At last we got moving again, and we asked the poor old ninny why, with this passion for literature, she didn't write. "Ah, but I've no time – never any time. Besides, I have such wretched health – But the pleasure of creation, Virginia, must transcend all others." I said it certainly did. We trailed back through the village, where all the peasants were lounging in the road, with their pipes and their dogs and their babies. The most affable and, I'm afraid, obsequious greetings were exchanged; the dazzling appearance of Ott and her pearls seeming to strike the agricultural labourer neither as wrong nor ridiculous, but as part of the aristocratic show that he's paid for. No one laughed. They seemed all very anxious to please. "Very nice people, aren't they?" she said when we came in; and I daresay nothing for the next three hundred years will make them otherwise.

I was taken to Gertler's studio and shown his solid 'unrelenting' teapot (to use Brett's word). He is a resolute young man; and if good pictures can be made by willing them to be good, he may do wonders. No base motive could have its way with him; and for this reason I haven't great faith in him. Its too moral and intellectual an affair; or perhaps the natural gift is not abundant enough to cover his conscience and will power. He says straight out what he thinks; his art an agony often, as he told me. But at last he understands that he wishes to paint form in the brightest colours. Form obsesses him. I advised him, for art's sake, to keep sane; to grasp, and not exaggerate. But he can think pianola music equal to hand-made, since it shows the form, and the touch and the expression are nothing.

Asheham House

Wednesday 31 July
Arrived at Asheham. I sit as if in the open air – the drawing room providing only a shell of shade in the intense heat. The air dances over the field. The garden is overgrown, and the flowers crushed out.

We spent yesterday doing jobs in London. I saw a dead horse on the pavement – a literal case of what politicians call dying in harness, and rather pathetic to me – to die in Oxford Street one hot afternoon, and to have been only a van horse; and by the time I passed back again he was removed.

Saturday 3 August
There's nothing but rustic news to record, since as we expected the Murrys have put us off. Katherine writes that she's ill. I can't help guessing that she may be rather hopelessly ill. The weather hasn't held good. Yesterday was as wet a day as England often produces. We went mushrooming in the evening, and got a handkerchief full. So one of our great excitements has begun again. Perhaps we're rather pleased to be alone after all.

Monday 12 August
(I believe this is near about the anniversary of our wedding day, six years ago).

Friday 16 August
My visit to Charleston and L.'s to York are both partly responsible for this skip. My visit to Charleston was spent mostly in sitting in the drawing room and talking to Nessa while she made herself a small brown coat. Duncan wandered in and out; sometimes digging a vegetable bed, sometimes painting a watercolour of bedroom china, pinned to a door. In the evening there was the lumpish Bunny, inclined to be surly; and Nessa inclined to take him up sharply. What did we discuss? There was Ka's engagement, concerning which Duncan had a good deal to say; one of his statements being that Arnold-Forster is forty-five, and always has been. When Nessa and I were alone, I suppose we discussed the two parrokeets and money, which is not any longer such a distant, speculative sort of commodity as it used to be – at least to her. We discussed the children too; the sort of talk that runs on when one knows all the facts, but wishes to ascertain how they've changed position; Gertler's notions of painting; Duncan's fame; Bunny's socialism. Bunny thus defines his position: all capitalists are wrong; therefore for him to live upon Vanessa is good, inasmuch as she enjoys money that she has no right to, and could not possibly spend her interest better than by maintaining him. This evolved from a sentimental declaration by him that he ought to spend his life in giving honey to his friends for nothing. His brain must be a tangle of sentiments and half-realised socialism. I bicycled back on Wednesday and found L. and we were very happy, until it came to the fat bacon – when, alas –!

Monday 19 August
It is possible that we may have solved the problem of having visitors – not to see them. At this moment Adrian and Karin are in the house, as an occasional sound from the drawing room proves. But we only meet at meals; so that it is possible to think of things to say in the intervals.

Carrington came for the weekend. She is the easiest of visitors as she never stops doing things – pumping, scything, or walking. After trudging out here, she trudged to Charleston, and only came in at eleven last night, just as we were shutting the windows. Poor lugubrious Bunny escorted her, protesting that a ten mile walk was nothing compared to the joy of having some one to talk to. She trudged off again this morning to pack Lytton's box or buy him a hair brush in London – a sturdy figure, dressed in a print dress, made after the pattern of one in a John picture; a thick mop of golden red hair, and a fat decided clever face, with staring bright blue eyes.

Saturday 24 August
I confess that I shirk the task which has accumulated for seven days of describing our visitors. They are with us for another week; so I need not try to hit them this very moment. I hesitate a little to write evil of my guests, nor do I think evil – exactly. I refer, in rather crablike fashion, to something coarse, material, insensitive about Karin. She has no concealed vices. Would she be more interesting if she had? She is not stupid; or dull; or trivial; on the contrary she is bright, capable and stirring: stirring Adrian to read books upon economics, and even stirring him to learn shorthand which according to her is useful in a literary career. She intends him to have a career. Outwardly we are all good friends, talkative and in agreement, and not relying on gossip merely to despatch dinner with. We talk about the Labour Party, and politics, and anarchy, and government. And in her way she's a nice honest creature, not so sure of herself when it comes to taste; and knowing it too – though taste has led her, alas, to embroider a pair of shoes which Adrian obediently wears.

Friday 30 August
Here we are almost at the end of August, and finishing off Adrian and Karin's visit. They go to Charleston tomorrow. There is an element of criticism in our relationship, based partly on Karin's manners, appetite and appearance. Her appetite is frankly a schoolboy's. "What beef!" she exclaimed today. "Don't you feel elated at the sight of good meat?" Meals add a sort of romance to her life such as I in my way get, shall we say, from the post or the newspapers. L. on the other hand is irritated, and being irritated by superficial disagreeables finds deeper causes for them than I altogether agree with. Our usual method is to begin "Why did Adrian marry her?" Then I say "I can quite understand it – she has energy" and so on. Then L. says "I'd a thousand times rather have married Ka – in fact I'd rather have married any one in the whole world. I couldn't sit in the same room with her." Still, I do see why Adrian married her. First and foremost she makes him like other people. He has always, I believe, a kind of

suspicion that whereas other people are professionals, he remains an amateur. She provides him with household, children, bills, daily life, so that to all appearances he is just like other people. I believe he needs constant reassurance on this point; and takes delight in her substantiality. He is very proud of her vitality. I suppose it provides him with a good deal of the stuff of life, which he does not provide for himself.

Yesterday I bicycled to Charleston, lunched, and came home in the evening. It was the first autumn day, warm, softly blue, and blurred with haze. Duncan spent the night before with us. He stumbled along until, by means which he only knows the secret of, he had us all laughing until the tears came. His chief effort was a description of Lady Strachey reading aloud. Then we discussed the bursting of people's bladders, the National Gallery, incest, perhaps, and other gossip. All sitting in the drawing room, until it grew too dark to see. We have lamps almost at dinner; but not quite.

Sunday 8 September
At anyrate today I am the wife of an Editor. Leonard got a letter to tell him that he is to get his first number [of the *International Review*] out in January. The idea is very amusing and stimulating too. I like playing with imaginary offices, and sheets of notepaper, and little boys with buttons, and myself walking up the steps to take a cup of tea, and surveying the Strand from the window. Then long galley proofs; distinguished foreign visitors; telegrams from distant capitals; general importance and glory; yes, a very nice prospect even on its picturesque side, which I admit is the one most perceptible to me.

Ka, another letter says, is to be married at 11 tomorrow. I can't help reading into her letter a sort of protest as to the merits of Will, and her love for him. Yet even so, I think of her as a rounder warmer more complete person than she was single. I suppose I had got into the habit of seeing her faithful solitary lonely till the end of time; I like happiness too well to be very fastidious about the husband.

Yesterday poor Bunny came for the night, bringing eight combs of honey, for which he charges half-a-crown each. How we were robbed at Brighton! Three shillings for a mixture of milk and saccharine. Poor old Bunny! He is as if caked with earth, stiff as a clod; you can almost see the docks and nettles sprouting from his mind; his sentences creak with rust. He can only lay hands on the simplest words. However by dint of kindly treatment we softened him. We wanted to know about mushrooms; and upon all funguses he is an authority. Then he could tell us about the agricultural labourers' Union, which is being half secretly organised even among our Freds and Wills. He has a humanity which is not at all theoretical.

He talks to the German prisoners, who are social democrats, only fought because they would be shot for refusing, and consider the whole war a device of the aristocracy. Bunny looks forward to a democratic future. I sacrificed half my morning and sat with him hemming handkerchiefs.

Tuesday 10 September
I spent the first five minutes with this book before me trying to fish two drowned flies out of my ink pot on the tip of my pen; but I begin to see that this is one of those undertakings which are quite impossible – absolutely impossible. Not Darwin or Plato could do it with the tip of my pen. At Asheham I naturally bethink me of Darwin and Plato; but in this I am not singular. My intellectual snobbishness was chastened this morning by hearing from Janet that she reads *Don Quixote* and *Paradise Lost* and her sister Lucretius in the evenings. Janet holds the characteristic view that *Don Quixote* is more humorous than Shakespeare. The coarseness of Shakespeare I can see would distress her; she would deal with it intellectually. All her generation use their brains too scrupulously upon books, seeking meaning rather than letting themselves run on for pleasure, which is more or less my way, and thus naturally richest and best.

Wednesday 18 September
I have let the first freshness of the Webbs fade from my mirror. I wonder how I can recapture the curious discomfort of soul which Mrs Webb produces each time I see her again? In the intervals one forgets; in a second it comes over one again. There's something absolutely unadorned and impersonal about her. She makes one feel insignificant, and a little out of key. She represses warmth or personality. She has no welcome for one's individuality. She divines a little what one's natural proclivities are, and she irradiates them with her bright electric torch.
It was a pouring wet day, on Saturday; not a day for geniality. Webb however has some coat to shake; she is bare as a bone. We sat down to tea, without George Young. They eat quickly and efficiently and leave me with hunks of cake on my hands. After tea we were soon disposing of our topics, and I began to feel nervous, lest our cupboards should be bare. Then George Young appeared, having like all Youngs, rejoiced in his battle with distance and wet. Liked the walk, he said. While he changed, Mrs Webb rapidly gave me her reasons for saying that she had never met a great man, or woman either. At most, she said, they possessed remarkable single qualities, but looked at as a whole there was no greatness in them. Shakespeare she did not appreciate, because a sister, who was a foolish woman, always quoted him wrong to her as a child. Goethe might conceivably have been a great man. Then, this having been dealt with, down came

L. and George Young, and they all pounced together upon some spot of interest floating far out beyond my ken. I think it was to do with the General Election and the views of the private soldiers.

After dinner Mrs Webb plunged from brisk argument to unconcealed snoring. Then Sidney had his turn. I thought he spoke a little quick to conceal the snores, but you have only to ask him a question and he can go on informing you till you can hold no more. He sketched his idea of a Supernational Authority. The work of Government will be enormously increased in the future. I asked whether I should ever have a finger in the pie? "O yes; you will have some small office no doubt. My wife and I always say that a Railway Guard is the most enviable of men. He has authority, and he is responsible to a government. That should be the state of each one of us." And then we discussed L.'s plans of a state so contrived that each person has to do some work. Here there was a long argument upon the growing distance between men of different social grades and professions. I asked (in reporting conversations one's own sayings stand out like lighthouses) one of my most fruitful questions; viz: how easy is it for a man to change his social grade? This brought down a whole shower-bath of information, but let us say that the Webbs' shower-baths are made of soda water. They never sink one, or satiate. Webb told us how many scholarships were won in London in a given year, and also reported upon the educational system of East Sussex, which bad though it is, is slightly better than that of West Sussex. "I myself" he said "came too early to profit by secondary education. My parents were lower middle class shopkeepers, possessed, like so many of their kind, with a blind determination to educate their sons somehow, but without the ghost of a notion how to set about it. They hit on the plan of sending me and my brother abroad to France and Germany; and so we learnt French and German at least. I can still read them, though I seldom do." Our talk must have dealt fully with education, for I remember that Mrs Webb woke with a start and delivered herself of a statement upon the German 'wrong turning', and put Young right on some point about the division of character and intellect. He was simple enough to separate them and to prefer what he was quite unable to define. She thrust him through and through with her rapier, but he persisted.

Next day, which was said to begin for the Webbs at 5.30, when they begin tea-drinking in their bedroom, I had to withdraw in order to do battle with a very obstinate review. My ideas were struck stiff by the tap of Mrs Webb's foot, up and down the terrace, and the sound of her rather high, rather mocking voice, discoursing to L. while she waited either for Webb to come or the rain to stop. They walked on the downs, till lunch. I must now skip a great deal of conversation and let us suppose that Sidney and Beatrice and I are sitting on the roadside overlooking Telscombe, smoking cigarettes, in bright sunshine. The downs were at their best; and set Mrs Webb off upon landscape beauty, and recollections of India, which she turns to when lying awake at night, relishing the recollection more than the reality. Sidney, one perceives, has no organ of sight whatever, and pretends to none. Mrs Webb has a compartment devoted to nature. So briskly narrating their travels and impressions, which were without respect for British rule, we set off home. I saw them from behind, a shabby, homely, dowdy couple, marching with the uncertain step of strength just beginning to fail, she clutching his arm, and looking much older than he, in her angularity. Their clothes looked ill dusted, and their eyes peering in front of them. My few private words came, as I knew they would come, when Mrs Webb detached us two together, passing Southease Church. She asked me about my novel, and I supplied her with a carefully arranged plot. I wished, so at least I said, to discover what aims drive people on, and whether these are illusory or not. She promptly shot forth: "Two aims have governed my life; one is the passion for investigation by scientific means; the other the passion for producing a certain good state of society by those investigations." Somehow she proceeded to warn me against the dissipation of energy in emotional friendship. One should have only one great personal relationship in one's life, she said; or at most two – marriage and parenthood. Marriage was necessary as a waste pipe for emotion, as security in old age when personal attractiveness fails, and as a help to work. We were entangled at the gates of the level crossing when she remarked, "Yes, I daresay an old family servant would do as well." In old age people become of little account, she said; one speculates chiefly upon the possibility, or the impossibility of a future life. This grey view depressed me more and more; partly I suppose from the egotistical sense of my own nothingness in her field of vision. And then we wound up with a light political gossip and chapter of reminiscences, in which Mr and Mrs Webb did their parts equally. And so to bed; and to my horror, in came Mrs Webb early next morning to say Goodbye, and perched in all her long impersonality on the edge of my bed, looking past my stockings drawers and po. This has taken so long to write that we are now arrived at

Monday 23 September
and so many things have accumulated, that I can hardly proceed to that masterly summing up of the Webbs which I intended. I had meant to point out the good qualities which come from such well kept brisk intellectual habits; how open minded they showed themselves; how completely and consistently <u>sensible</u>. That, I think, deserves a line under it. Good sense seems to me their invariable characteristic. Sidney is the warmer and more human of the two, and one could even commit the impropriety of liking

him personally, which one can hardly do in the case of Mrs Webb. How stoically with his perpetual little smile, he remarked that they are now sixty, and therefore may expect a stroke within the next five years; but if he could arrange things with the divine messenger, he would compound somehow to die precisely at the same moment with 'my wife'.

I went over to Charleston last Tuesday and was shown his shells by Quentin; sat with Nessa and laid bare my sorrows, which she can more than match; and then Clive and Mary arrived in a motor car for tea – so many were their parcels and bags; and indeed Mary produced chocolates, cakes and sweets in abundance. I'm ashamed to say that that is my chief impression. She was, as usual, mute as a trout – I say trout because of her spotted dress, and also because, though silent, she has the swift composure of a fish. I walked home shoving my bicycle, too badly punctured to ride.

Then on Saturday we went to Lewes by train and bought a two-handled saw, and fish, and envelopes, and then met Gertler at the station and came out here. Whether our exclamations on parting from our guests are good evidence, I don't know, but on this occasion we both cried "Good God, what an egoist!" We have been talking about Gertler to Gertler for some thirty hours; it is like putting a microscope to your eye. One molehill is wonderfully clear; the surrounding world ceases to exist. But he is a forcible young man, as hard as a cricket ball; and as tightly rounded and stuffed in at the edges. We discussed – well, it always came back to be Gertler. He hoards an insatiable vanity. However, as I say, he has power and intelligence, and will, one sees, paint good interesting pictures, though some rupture of the brain would have to take place before he could be a painter.

HOGARTH HOUSE, RICHMOND

Saturday 12 October
The first week in London is always one of the richest; and the rich weeks always tend to pass unrecorded. I have my anniversary to celebrate also; this diary is one year old, and looking back I see how exactly one repeats one's doings. For example this week we went to buy an overcoat for L.; last year we bought boots. Again there was the question of a party; again what I may euphemistically call an 'argument'. Nessa was in London too; and I dined with her and Clive, only there was Duncan too, and we dined at Gordon Square. But Lord Grey's meeting has no counterpart last year; nor could I possibly have written then, as I can now write that tomorrow morning's paper may bring news of an armistice. Possibly the fighting will be over this time next week. Whatever we have done this week has had this extraordinary background of hope; a tremendously enlarged version of

the feeling I remember as a child as Christmas approached. The Northcliffe papers do all they can to insist upon the indispensability and delight of war. Grey's meeting was impressive as meetings go, which is not saying very much of course. He said nothing but what one has read and agreed with about a League of Nations, but he said it simply, and for a 'great statesman' to have sense and human feeling and no bombast does produce an odd sense of wonder and humility in me, as if human nature were worth something after all. There was an enormous audience, and as we left people were passing about the rumour that the Kaiser had abdicated.

I went on to my dinner at Gordon Square; thence to the Coliseum with Nessa, where we had to sit out an infinite length of Miss Clarice Mayne, after which we saw our [Diaghilev] ballet – Sche – (I can't achieve either the spelling or the speaking of it) which isn't one of the best, and when I saw it I remembered it better done at Covent Garden. Maynard who has the generosity and something of the manner now of an oriental prince, had hired a brougham for Nessa – an infinitely small, slow, antiquated carriage drawn by a very liverystables looking quadruped. Roger, Duncan, Maynard, Nessa and I all crammed in and padded along slowly across London to Chelsea. Somehow we passed Ottoline, brilliantly painted, as garish as a strumpet, displayed in the midst of omnibuses under an arc lamp; and she reappeared in the Sitwell's drawing room. I had made acquaintance with the two Sitwell brothers the day before and had been invited to the party. That very morning a review by me of Edith Sitwell's poems had appeared in *The Times*. Edith Sitwell is a very tall young woman, wearing a permanently startled expression, and curiously finished off with a high green silk head-dress, concealing her hair, so that it is not known whether she has any. Otherwise, I was familiar with everyone, I think. My complete mastery of evening parties is shown by the indifference with which I am deserted, and the composure with which I decide upon my next choice. I was a good deal impressed by this; and how calmly too, I looked at my watch, and saw it was time to leave, and went out alone, and drove to Sloane Square, not excited, not depressed, but contemplative and introspective.

Tuesday 15 October
I did not think I should so soon have to describe a meeting with a cabinet minister – though I admit that we seem to be drifting into a circle where the great officials are sometimes to be found. This is the doing of the *International Review*, mainly; but Herbert Fisher's visit was very obviously due to old family affection. I was sitting down alone to tea on Sunday, L. being gone to Sutton to speak about our colonies and the servants out, when the bell rang. On opening the door, there were Olive and M. Heseltine and Herbert Fisher. The Heseltines went off, and Herbert came in, as they

had arranged beforehand. Was I nervous or proud? I don't think I felt a moment's agitation. For one thing he has lost his lean intellectual look; his hollow cheeks are filled; his eyes with that pale frosty look which blue eyes get in age; his whole bearing very quiet, simple, and when not speaking, rather saddened and subdued. Anyhow we talked without stopping and without difficulty.

"We've won the war today" he said at once. "The Germans have made up their minds they can't fight a retreat. The General Staff has faced the fact, and they've had what I think the considerable courage to admit it. There is now a good prospect of a complete defeat of the German army." Foch says "I have not yet had my battle". Despite the extreme vindictiveness of our press and the French press, Herbert believed that we are going to baulk Foch of his battle, partly because the Germans will accept any terms to avoid it. "Lloyd George has told me again and again that he means to be generous to the Germans. We want a strong Germany, he says." The Kaiser will probably go. "O I was a great admirer of the Germans in the beginning. I was educated there, and I've many friends there, but I've lost my belief in them. The proportion of brutes is greater with them than with us. They've been taught to be brutal. But it hasn't paid. No one can face another war. Why in ten years they could blot out London by their aeroplanes. But the proportion of men who have never been hurt, or even seen anything horrible is very large; thousands and thousands of soldiers all wanted the war conditions of life to go on 'without these bloody shells.' There'll be trouble when they come back. They'll find their old lives too dull. I'm going to educate them, its true; but that won't begin yet – not in my time. Very likely I shall go back to Oxford to teach."

So we talked on. I tried to think it extraordinary but I found it difficult – extraordinary, I mean, to be in touch with one who was in the very centre of the very centre, sitting in a little room at Downing Street where, as he said, the wireless messages are racing through from all over the world, a million miles a minute; where you have constantly to settle off-hand questions of enormous difficulty and importance – where the fate of armies does more or less hang upon what two or three elderly gentlemen decide. Importance seems to give people an appearance of simplicity; they are very courteous; but somehow no longer spontaneous people; the taint of the family butler is on them. But this was more visible when L. came in. Alone with me Herbert was very friendly and quiet; and gave himself no airs of dignity.

Friday 18 October
It is quite obvious of course that for some reason perhaps not creditable to me I think Herbert Fisher worth many more words than Ka say, or Saxon,

both of whom have dined here since. My theory is that for some reason the human mind is always seeking what it conceives to be the centre of things – I don't know what I call it; but I distinctly visualise it as a possession rather more in Herbert Fisher's hands than in other people's. I write hurriedly, giving no account of our suspension over what one of the papers calls 'the precipice of peace'. The truth is that nothing much more definite is yet known about peace.

Thursday 24 October
We are just in from Kingston – today being a holiday, and there heard the paper boys shouting out about the President [Wilson]'s message, which we bought and devoured. The main points are that he is keeping negotiations going; he discriminates too, between the German people and the Kaiser; he will consider an armistice with the one but only complete surrender with the other. Anyhow, the question is now laid before England and France.

Saturday 26 October
We had a day in London yesterday – somehow the charm of those days is not quite what it was. Am I getting blasé – is the 17 Club less enthralling? We went to the Omega show, met Roger there, were invited to tea at his studio, discussed the change in Duncan's style, representation, reality, and so on again. We dined at a very hot place in Soho. On again to the Club, where Leonard made his speech about Austria Hungary. As usual I find him not only very clear but with the right degree of passion to be interesting.

Monday 28 October
As I write this, the post brings a letter from [T. S.] Eliot asking to come and see us. To my great surprise a voice upon the telephone developed into the voice of Lady Mary Murray; asking us to lunch yesterday. We changed lunch to tea and went off to More's Gardens, a block of flats on the Embankment. A tea party is the least natural of situations, and produces the utmost amount of discomfort I think. Still it was the respectability that weighed me down. There are certain dun coloured misty days in autumn which remind me of the Murrays' atmosphere. The cleanliness of Gilbert was remarkable; a great nurse must rub him smooth with pumice stone every morning; he is so discreet, so sensitive, so low in tone and immaculate in taste that you hardly understand how he has the boldness to beget children. Maliciously enough, I felt that his simplicity was maintained in the face of years of worship and adulation, and that the proper thing to say is 'How wonderfully simple dear Gilbert Murray is!' But his niceness was unmeasured. The Toynbees came in. I had a long rigmarole with Arnold about his office and his learning and so forth; I think I frighten him; or

perhaps I'm not used to the Oxford manner. Its suavity and politeness are strange to me.

Wednesday 30 October
Just in from a walk in the Park on this incredibly lovely autumn day. We talked of peace: how the sausage balloons will be hauled down, and gold coins dribble in; and how people will soon forget all about the war, and the fruits of our victory will grow as dusty as ornaments under glass cases in lodging-house drawing-rooms. How often will the good people of Richmond rejoice to think that liberty has been won for the good people of Potsdam? I can believe though that we shall be more arrogant about our own virtues. *The Times* still talks of the possibility of another season, in order to carry the war into Germany, and there imprint a respect for liberty in the German peasants. I think the distance of the average person from feelings of this sort is the only safeguard and assurance that we shall settle down again neither better nor worse.

Sunday 3 November
On Saturday, we had one of our Hampstead afternoons, L. going to Margaret, I to Janet. I've done the same thing so often. I've found her in that green distempered room, with the ugly pictures. Tea is prepared. I am pressed to eat more of everything. Questioned about butter and coal. And then Janet talked to me about literature, and I fell into a passing gloom. She says that a great many novels are written, and it seems fairly evident that none are 'immortal'. I suppose I referred this to my own novels. But I fancy that what depressed me was not only the personal question, but the smell of musty morality; the effect of talking to some one who seems to want all literature to go into the pulpit; who makes it all infinitely worthy and safe and respectable. I was also depressed at the implied criticism of *The Voyage Out*, and the hint that I had better turn to something other than fiction. Its the curse of a writer's life to want praise so much, and be so cast down by blame, or indifference. The only sensible course is to remember that writing is after all what one does best; that any other work would seem to me a waste of life; that on the whole I get infinite pleasure from it; that I make one hundred pounds a year; and that some people like what I write.

Saturday 9 November
We began to set up *Kew Gardens* this week – Thursday was the first day of it I think. On Wednesday I went up to Hampstead; found the tall ugly villa looking over the valley where the Murrys live. Katherine was up, but husky and feeble, crawling about the room like an old woman. How far she is ill, one can't say. She impresses one a little unfavourably at first – then more

favourably. I think she has a kind of childlikeness somewhere which has been much disfigured, but still exists. Illness, she said, breaks down one's privacy so that one can't write –

Monday 11 November
Twenty-five minutes ago the guns went off, announcing peace. A siren hooted on the river. They are hooting still. A few people ran to look out of windows. The rooks wheeled round, and wore for a moment the symbolic look of creatures performing some ceremony, partly of thanksgiving, partly of valediction over the grave. A very cloudy still day, the smoke toppling over heavily towards the east; and that too wearing for a moment a look of something floating, waving, drooping. So far neither bells nor flags, but the wailing of sirens and intermittent guns.

Friday 15 November
Peace is rapidly dissolving into the light of common day. You can go to London without meeting more than two drunk soldiers; only an occasional crowd blocks the street. But mentally the change is marked too. Instead of feeling that the whole people, willing or not, were concentrated on a single point, one feels now that the whole bunch has burst asunder and flown off with the utmost vigour in different directions. We are once more a nation of individuals. Some people care for football; others for racing; others for dancing; others for – oh well, they're all running about very gaily getting out of their uniforms and taking up their private affairs again. The streets are crowded with people quite at their ease; and the shops blazoning unshaded lights. Yet its depressing too. We have stretched our minds to consider something universal at any rate; we contract them at once to the squabbles of Lloyd George, and a General Election. The papers are unreadable.

The first effect of peace on our circle is to set Desmond loose, and to bring Gerald Shove up to London saying that he must find a way of making £500 a year. Before long the crowd of out of work intellectuals looking for places will be considerable. Desmond is doing what he knows how to do supremely well – going later and later to the office every day and taking longer for lunch, and sometimes not going back again. This he proposes to continue for a fortnight; then to fold up his blue and gold coat for ever – unless by cutting off the brass buttons he can make it do for an ordinary coat. His spirits are very high.

I was interrupted somewhere on this page by the arrival of Mr Eliot. Mr Eliot is well expressed by his name – a polished, cultivated, elaborate young American, talking so slow, that each word seems to have special finish allotted it. But beneath the surface, it is fairly evident that he is very intellectual, intolerant, with strong views of his own, and a poetic creed. I'm sorry to say that this sets up Ezra Pound and Wyndham Lewis as great poets, or in the current phrase 'very interesting' writers. He admires Mr Joyce immensely. He produced three or four poems for us to look at – the fruit of two years, since he works all day in a Bank, and in his reasonable way thinks regular work good for people of nervous constitutions. I became more or less conscious of a very intricate and highly organised framework of poetic belief; owing to his caution, and his excessive care in the use of language we did not discover much about it.

Saturday 30 November
I see I've been rather slack, and I can't remember now exactly what's made me slack. Certainly not the General Election. Saxon dined here, talking of death without enthusiasm. He knew for certain that he would die on a certain day last summer and then – didn't. One night we went to the Russian dancers [at the Coliseum]; and it was incongruous enough to see what they offered the tolerant good tempered public who had been bellowing like bulls over the efforts of a man to nail a carpet down. They were tolerant, but, as I fancied, a little bit contemptuous of all this posing and springing against a flat blue wall. What a queer fate it is – always to be the spectator of the public, never part of it. This is part of the reason why I go weekly to see Katherine Mansfield up at Hampstead, for there at any rate we make a public of two.

Saturday 7 December
On Thursday I lunched with Roger in order to hear the following story. Mrs McColl to Mr Cox of the London Library: "Have you *The Voyage Out* by Virginia Woolf?" "Virginia Woolf? Let me see; she was a Miss Stephen, daughter of Sir Leslie. Her sister is Mrs Clive Bell I think. Ah, strange to see what's become of those two girls. Brought up in such a nice home, too. But then, they were never *baptised*."

Roger and I get on very well now; more genuine and free than we were, under the shadow of Gordon Square. At last, inevitably late, I go on to the 17 Club. Alix I found intoning pompously downstairs, with a perverted likeness to a colonel of the upper classes holding forth upon the iniquity of Bolshevism. Her theme is the iniquity of colonels; the method seems much the same; even the voice.

Monday 16 December
Back from a week-end with Roger. Lips, therefore, rather sore with talk, though his range is so wide, and we both have such a number of things to say that I, certainly, was neither bored nor satiated. It was polling day in

Guildford, as in other parts of the world, and Roger very gloomy about the future of the world. All Sunday, in spite of rain and fog he painted till the sky was black, having been grey through the time of daylight. I feel little hope about his pictures, but had to counterfeit an opinion as to the effect produced on the solidity of a bowl by a morning's work on it. He said that he grudged every hour of daylight spent not painting. We visited the National Gallery together this morning; I thought a Rembrandt 'very fine' which to him was mere melodrama. A little El Greco conveyed little till he illumined it; showed how it held more real colour than any other picture there. Then Ingres was repulsive to me; and to him one of the most marvellous of designs. I always feel, too, that to like the wrong thing, or fail in sufficiently liking the right, jars on him, like false notes, or sentimentality in writing.

Tuesday 17 December

I go to Asheham on Friday. Nessa has asked us to have the children for a fortnight when the new baby is born. This is now imminent, and she fixes the 28th for the exact day. We shall have one week entirely alone, at Asheham, the greatest and most unmixed pleasure this world affords; enhanced very much in my mind by the absence of servants. I am going to read through my novel and determine what to do with it.

We have printed off the text of *Kew Gardens*.

1919

As the war receded there were renewed contacts with circles which to a large extent Virginia had outgrown. Since the death of Sir Leslie Stephen in 1904 and his children's removal to Bloomsbury and to a very different outlook on society, Virginia, far more than Vanessa, harboured a certain loyalty to, as well as a writer's curiosity about, old friends and family connections from the 'respectable' Kensington world in which she had been brought up. Members of the aristocracy – Thynnes, Cecils – whom she had got to know through her intimate friendship with Violet Dickinson, a county neighbour of the Duckworth family, break surface from time to time in her diary. The death of 'Aunt Anny' – Thackeray's daughter, whose sister was Leslie Stephen's first wife, and whom Virginia had portrayed in Night and Day – is recorded; she died, aged eighty-one, at Freshwater in the Isle of Wight, the home ground of an earlier generation of eminent Victorians – Tennyson, G. F. Watts and his momentary bride Ellen Terry, and Virginia's own great-aunt Julia Margaret Cameron, the pioneer photographer – about whom she later wrote Freshwater, her only play. But in general she was more concerned with the future than the past, and with her developing relationships with new friends like Katherine Mansfield and T. S. Eliot. In May the Hogarth Press published Eliot's Poems, her own Kew Gardens, and a long poem by J. Middleton Murry (Katherine's husband), who had recently been appointed editor of the Athenaeum, to which journal Virginia was to make frequent contributions during this year and next, as well as producing almost weekly reviews for the TLS. In October her second novel, Night and Day, was published by her half-brother Gerald Duckworth.

But the most serious upheaval in the Woolfs' affairs this year was caused by their receiving in March six months' notice to vacate Asheham, which Virginia had rented since 1911. Reluctant to leave the neighbourhood she had grown to love, and where her sister now also had her foothold, Virginia impulsively bought a small house for £300 in the county town of Lewes; but dispirited by Leonard's tepid reaction to her enterprise, they subsequently secured Monks House at Rodmell, across the Ouse valley from Asheham, into which they moved their belongings in September and which was to remain their country home for the rest of both their lives.

1919

Monday 20 January
The fortnight in bed was the result of having a tooth out, and being tired enough to get a headache – a long dreary affair, that receded and advanced much like a mist on a January day. One hour's writing daily is my allowance for the next few weeks; and having hoarded it this morning, I may spend part of it now, since I am much behindhand with the month of January. I note however that this diary writing does not count as writing, since I have just reread my year's diary and am much struck by the rapid haphazard gallop at which it swings along, sometimes indeed jerking almost intolerably over the cobbles. Still if it were not written rather faster than the fastest typewriting, if I stopped and took thought, it would never be written at all; and the advantage of the method is that it sweeps up accidentally several stray matters which I should exclude if I hesitated, but which are the diamonds of the dustheap. If Virginia Woolf at the age of fifty, when she sits down to build her memoirs out of these books is unable to make a phrase as it should be made, I can only condole with her and remind her of the existence of the fireplace, where she has my leave to burn these pages to so many black films with red eyes in them. But how I envy her the task I am preparing for her! There is none I should like better. Already my thirty-seventh birthday next Saturday is robbed of some of its terrors by the thought. Partly for the benefit of this elderly lady, I intend to spend the evenings of this week of captivity making out an account of my friendships and their present condition, with some account of my friends' characters; and to add an estimate of their work, and a forecast of their future works.

Wednesday 22 January
Two days more were spent in bed, and today counts as my first of complete health.

How many friends have I got? There's Lytton, Desmond, Saxon; they belong to the Cambridge stage of life; very intellectual, cut free from Hyde

Park Gate; connected with Thoby; but I can't put them in order, for there are too many. Ka and Rupert and Duncan, for example, all come rather later; they belong to Fitzroy days; the Oliviers and all that set are stamped as the time of Brunswick Square; Clive I put a little aside; later still there are the cropheads, Alix, Carrington, Barbara, Nick, Bunny. I must insert too the set that runs parallel but does not mix, distinguished by their social and political character, headed perhaps by Margaret and including people like Goldie, Mrs Hamilton, and intermittent figures such as the Webbs. I have not placed Ottoline or Roger, and again there are Katherine and Murry and outlying figures such as Ray and Oliver. Gertler I must omit (and Mary Hutch too) for reasons which if my account gets written I might give; and Eliot I liked on the strength of one visit and shall probably see more of, owing to his poems which we began today to set up.

This is a very partial account, but I shall never place half of them accurately unless I start straight away. Lytton and Desmond and Saxon then. Well, I cherish a considerable friendship for each of them; the worst of it is how seldom we meet. With Lytton and Desmond till last month tethered to a stool in the Admiralty, months pass without a sight of them. The season of letter writing is over for all of us, I think; or perhaps we need different correspondents. Brilliant letters we wrote each other once, partly for the sake of being brilliant, and we were getting to know each other then, and there was a thrill about it (I speak of my own feelings.) But when we do meet, there is nothing to complain of. Lytton again is famous these last six months, but as that was a matter of course since his first six months there is not much surprise or change in it. Nothing is easier or more intimate than a talk with Lytton. If he is less witty, he is more humane. I like Carrington though. She has increased his benignity. O yes, if he were to walk in at this moment we should talk about books and feelings and life and the rest of it as freely as we ever did, and with the sense, on both sides I think, of having hoarded for this precise moment a great deal peculiarly fit for the other.

Friday 24 January
To resume. There are three words knocking about in my brain to use of Stracheys, – a prosaic race, lacking magnanimity, shorn of atmosphere. Roger's version is that all, except Lady Strachey, lack generosity. But then one must combine with this a great variety of mental gifts, and gifts of character – honesty, loyalty, intelligence of a spiritual order. One might almost attribute what I mean in Lytton's case at least to lack of physical warmth, lack of creative power, a failure of vitality warning him not to be spendthrift but to eke out his gifts parsimoniously, and tacitly assume his right to a superior share of comfort and opulence. In matters of emotion

this has a slightly stingy appearance. Mentally of course it produces that metallic and conventionally brilliant style which prevents his writing from reaching, to my judgment, the first rate. It lacks originality, and substance; it is brilliant, superbly brilliant journalism, a supremely skilful rendering of the old tune. But when I think of a Strachey, I think of someone infinitely cautious, elusive and unadventurous. To the common stock of our set they have added phrases, standards, and witticisms, but never any new departure; never an Omega, a Post-Impressionist movement, nor even a country cottage, a Brunswick Square or a printing press. We Stephens, yes, and even Clive, with all his faults, had the initiative, and the vitality to conceive and carry our wishes into effect because we wished too strongly to be chilled by ridicule or checked by difficulty. Even in the matter of taking Tidmarsh Lytton had to be propelled from behind, and his way of life insofar as it is unconventional, is so by the desire and determination of Carrington.

Thursday 30 January
Such is the cold today that I doubt I can go on with my disquisition. I must note for future use, the superb possibilities of Freshwater, for a comedy. Old Cameron dressed in a blue dressing gown and not going beyond his garden for twelve years, suddenly borrows his son's coat, and walks down to the sea. Then they decide to proceed to Ceylon, taking their coffins with them, and the last sight of Aunt Julia is on board ship, presenting porters with large photographs of Sir Henry Taylor and the Madonna in default of small change.

Tuesday 4 February
Let me try to account for the fact that Lytton has 'dominated' (why, even the word is his) a generation at Cambridge, and make it square with my disparaging remarks. How did he do it, how is he so distinct and unmistakable if he lacks originality and the rest? Is there any reputable escape from this impasse in saying that he is a great deal better than his books? or am I too chary of praise for those books? Am I jealous? Do I compare the six editions of *Eminent Victorians* with the one of *The Voyage Out*? Perhaps there's a hint of jealousy; but, if I underrate, I think the main cause is that while I admire, enjoy up to a point and up to a point agree, I'm not interested in what he writes.

Desmond has *not* rung up. That is quite a good preface to the description of his character. The difficulty which faces one in writing of Desmond is that one is almost forced to describe an Irishman: how he misses trains, seems born without a rudder to drift wherever the current is strongest; how he keeps hoping and planning, and shuffles along, paying his way by talking so enchantingly that editors forgive, and shopmen give him credit and at least one distinguished peer leaves him a thousand in his will.

Saturday 15 February
What a disgraceful lapse! Eleven days unrecorded. Still I think if I were a painter I should only need a brush dipped in dun colour to give the tone of those eleven days. I should draw it evenly across the entire canvas. Yesterday, Friday, I had one of my occasional galas. Dressed in my best I went to Sickert's pictures, which I here pronounce the pleasantest, solidest most painter-like show in England. And there I met Clive and Mary; Clive in his fur coat, Mary in the more subdued style of the New English [Art Club]. Later, Clive, Mary and I strolled chattering like a perch of parrokeets, to Verreys. Mary had a dutiful visit to pay her husband in hospital. So we sat and talked in an inner room – a pleasant, dissipated place, parquet floor, curved bar, little tables, green and gold flourishes, dilapidated George the IVth style, and empty at this hour, save for some dubious ladies. Our intercourse was very gay, vibrant, like that of stringed instruments. Duncan passed through – a strange shaggy interlude, but always and inevitably harmonious. He blinked as if newly exposed to the light, crumbled his brioche, and gulped down his coffee, stammering out his half articulated but immensely expressive words. Somehow, too soon, he hoisted himself into an astonishing long straight black coat, like a non-conformist minister's, hitched down his red waistcoat, and started off in a vague determined way to Victoria Station. And then we sat on, Clive and I, talking of writing, of my writing chiefly, which he praises sufficiently to give his strictures a good deal of force. Mary came in and interrupted, or rather influenced the current of our discourse, for she hardly spoke, and then we turned out into Regent Street where the lamps were lit, and the shop opposite had all its windows full of bright clothes against a green stage scene, and so strolling in the spring twilight and laughing still we made our way through Soho, and I left them, in a street with many jewellers' windows.

Tuesday 18 February
Here I sit waiting for Alix, who can't be coming to disburden herself of confidences as I supposed; and thus my mind returns by way of her fickleness to my friends. Where was I? Desmond, and how I find him sympathetic compared with Stracheys. It is true; I'm not sure he hasn't the nicest nature of any of us. I don't think that he possesses any faults as a friend, save that his friendship is so often sunk under a cloud of vagueness and effectively prevents us from meeting. Perhaps such indolence implies a slackness of fibre in his affections too – but I scarcely feel that. It arises rather from the consciousness which I find imaginative and attractive that

things don't altogether *matter*. Somehow he is fundamentally sceptical. Yet who is more tolerant, more appreciative, more understanding of human nature? It goes without saying that he is not an heroic character. He finds pleasure too pleasant, cushions too soft, dallying too seductive, and then, as I sometimes feel now, he has ceased to be ambitious. His 'great work' (it may be philosophy or biography now, and is certainly to be begun, after a series of long walks, this very spring) only appears, I believe, in that hour between tea and dinner, when so many things appear not merely possible but achieved. Yet it is true that he has the floating elements of something brilliant, beautiful – some book of stories, reflections, studies, scattered about in him, for they show themselves indisputably in his talk. I can see myself going through his desk one of these days, shaking out unfinished pages from between sheets of blotting paper and deposits of old bills, and making up a small book of table talk, which shall appear as a proof to the younger generation that Desmond was the most gifted of us all. But why did he never do anything? they will ask.

At any rate in his own intermittent way Desmond is faithful. So much one may affirm of Saxon too, who comes next on my list. But Saxon's fidelity is almost that of the senile old collie, or broken down ass – the pensioner who can draw upon a memory of the past for a seat at one's table in perpetuity. He has little to give at the moment, life has not been generous to him. His possessions are old friendships, old memories – things we've talked of ages ago. Unlike the rest of us he has had no renewal of life in marriage; his hopes in that direction have been crushed. Therefore he comes disconsolately, asking rather than giving; asking at this moment that I shall accept Barbara at his hand – return her to him enriched with the glow of my approval. However, poor Saxon's life is now in the uncomfortable and unbecoming season which is so painfully well reproduced out of doors. Sleet, and mud and chill, and nothing growing. He has summed up his own position accurately as that of one who finds himself lonely if alone, and bored if in company. But faithful – there is something worth having in Saxon's fidelity; something that makes his most meagre visitation not altogether fruitless. One is aware, even after two hours of tepid and almost entire silence, that he is strictly true, genuine, unalloyed.

At any rate I rest on the thought of Saxon with some relief after hovering for the past two months in a state of uncertainty over the thought of Katherine [Mansfield] Murry. It is at this moment extremely doubtful whether I have the right to class her among my friends. Quite possibly I shall never see her again. Upstairs I have letters in which she speaks of finding the thought of me a joy, dwelling upon my writing with excitement; I have letters making appointments, pressing for visits, adding postscripts of thanks and affection to visits already paid. But the last is dated December, and it is now February. The question interests, amuses, and also slightly, no very decidedly pains me. The truth is, I suppose, that one of the conditions unexpressed but understood of our friendship has been precisely that it was almost entirely founded on quicksands. We have been intimate, intense perhaps rather than open; but to me at anyrate our intercourse has been always interesting and mingled with quite enough of the agreeable personal element to make one fond – if that is the word – as well as curious. I was at pains to go up to Hampstead every week since mid October or November, I suppose. And then what happened? I go away for Christmas, and we send small bright presents. I add to mine one if not two long and affectionate letters; I propose to come as soon as I get back. My time in bed prevented this. But meanwhile, for no reason given or to be guessed at with any certainty, she falls silent; I get no thanks, no answers, no enquiries.

Friday 21 February
But all this is made to appear rather fine drawn and exaggerated by the simple fact that I have a letter this morning from Katherine herself asking me to tea on Monday and explaining how some new treatment gives her fever for two days and makes it impossible for her to see people.

Tuesday 25 February
The truth is I shirk the gigantic task of giving an account of Sunday's teaparty, at which I met Sir Henry Newbolt and Lady, Lady Cromer, the Bruce Richmonds, and a scattering of gallant bald cavalry officers, and mounds of South Kensington dowager respectability who must be nameless. But the amiability of South Kensington is disarming. A kind of modesty veils what is so prominent and disagreeable in the intellectuals. They have an air of saying "I am no one – no one at all. My only function is to be agreeable. Another cup of tea? Do for goodness sake take this arm chair – and let me fetch you a slice of bread and butter –" That's my impression of the moment; though for some reason it doesn't encourage one to say anything more interesting than Thank you and please don't trouble, and other phrases of the kind. Of no. 23 Cromwell Houses, fronting the stuffed beasts [the Natural History Museum], and quite capable of staring them out of countenance, I will only say that it is furnished on the great South Kensington principle of being on the safe side and doing the thing handsomely. Good Mrs Samuel Bruce went to the Autotype Company and ordered the entire Dutch school to be sent round framed in fumed oak. And so they were; and just covered the staircase walls, leaving an inch or two's margin in between. The drawing room – no, I can't write it all out; memory preserves only the shoulders of a horse on a gilt easel, and three large

seascapes, like slabs of thick bread and butter. The company was decorous and fur bearing as usual; and the music like the voice of spirits in another world enticing the hopelessly damned. But how nice they are too!

Very well: but now we come to another of the ornate and decorated tribe; try as she will she can never lay aside her coronet; I mean poor dear old Ottoline. We dined at Gatti's together last night. She has the slim swaying figure of a Lombardy poplar – the ridges and hollows of the cheeks are the only sign of her years (forty-seven I make them); and a feeble mincing step on the street, like that of a cockatoo with bad claws. She has an indomitable spirit – plucking life out with those same gouty claws as if she were young and had illusions by the score. As we sat at dinner Ott picked up scraps of talk from the other diners, and admired their profiles. And so round to Gordon Square where we found Clive at the top of the house, where I used to stand and write, in the largest arm chair ever seen, by the finest fire, with a screen across the door to keep the draught out, as affable as a cockatoo and as brightly coloured as a macaw. I left them together and lost my train.

Wednesday 5 March
Just back from four days at Asheham, and one at Charleston; I sit waiting for Leonard to come in, with a brain still running along the railway lines, which unfits it for reading. But oh, dear, what a lot I've got to read! The entire works of Mr James Joyce, Wyndham Lewis, Ezra Pound, so as to compare them with the entire works of Dickens and Mrs Gaskell; besides that George Eliot; and finally Hardy. And I've just done Aunt Anny [Lady Ritchie], on a really liberal scale. Yes, since I wrote last she has died, a week ago today to be precise, at Freshwater, and was buried up at Hampstead yesterday. I suppose my feeling for her is half moonshine; or rather half reflected from other feelings. Father cared for her; she goes down the last, almost, of that old 19th Century Hyde Park Gate world. Unlike most old ladies she showed very little anxiety to see one; felt, I sometimes think, a little painfully at the sight of us, as if we'd gone far off, and recalled unhappiness, which she never liked to dwell on. Also, unlike most old Aunts she had the wits to feel how sharply we differed on current questions; and this, perhaps, gave her a sense, hardly existing with her usual circle, of age, obsoleteness, extinction. For myself, though, she need have had no anxieties on this head, since I admired her sincerely; but still the generations certainly look very different ways.

Asheham was, I suppose, a qualified success only. Starting out to fetch milk on one of these days we met Gunn [the bailiff] and heard our fate. We're to go in September. He wants Asheham to live in with his old mother. Oh dear Oh dear! Each time I walked up the drive I thought how nothing was ever so perfect. If it weren't for the devil of starting something new in me, I should be in despair. On the whole we incline to aim at Itford farm house – a house that could be made very attractive, with its view and its sun. We have grown out of gentlemen's houses.

Charleston is by no means a gentleman's house. I bicycled round there in a flood of rain, and found the baby asleep in its cot, and Nessa and Duncan sitting over the fire, with bottles and bibs and basins all round them. Duncan went to make my bed. Their staff at this moment consists simply of Jenny, the sharp Jewish looking cook; and she having collapsed, spent the afternoon in bed. By extreme method and unselfishness and routine on Nessa's and Duncan's parts chiefly, the dinner is cooked, and innumerable refills of hotwater bottles and baths supplied. One has the feeling of living on the brink of a move. In one of the little islands of comparative order Duncan set up his canvas, and Bunny wrote a novel in a set of copy books. Nessa scarcely leaves the baby's room, or if she appears for a moment outside, she has instantly to go off and talk to Dan, Jenny's young man and the future support of Charleston, or to wash napkins, or bottles, or prepare meals. Then Quentin had just been suspected of measles – The atmosphere seems full of catastrophes which upset no one; the atmosphere is good humoured, lively, as it tends to be after three months of domestic disaster. In these circumstances, I daresay I had no more than thirty minutes consecutive talk with Nessa. But I broke off in full tide, and had to trudge through the mud to Glynde – such mud that when I went into the land àgent, the sleek little clerk looked from my head to my boots in expostulation – as if such a figure couldn't possibly require a house with seven bedrooms and a bathroom. Unhappily there seems little chance of finding one. I've said nothing of my niece, who must be called so formally, since they've cancelled Susanna Paula, and can think of nothing else. She is a wistful, patient, contemplative little creature, examining the fire very meditatively, with a resigned expression, and very large blue eyes.

Wednesday 12 March

Clive gave me dinner at the Café Royal, which did not much interest me as a show, rather to his disappointment. However towards the end of dinner a woman of doubtful character dining alone with a man threw her glass on the floor, made a great rattle of knives and plates, upset the mustard pot and marched out like an indignant turkey cock. Was this moment, with the eyes of the diners upon her, what repaid her? Was it for this that she protested? Anyhow she left her man very crestfallen, trying to appear nonchalant; and I daresay that was what she wanted. I couldn't help thinking of the dreary scene in the flat next morning – the tears, the recriminations, the reconciliation – and next Sunday they'll dine, I suppose, at another restaurant.

This morning we had notice to quit [Asheham] from Hoper [the owner], and the further blow that he will not let us have the Itford Farm.

Wednesday 19 March
Life piles up so fast that I have no time to write out the equally fast rising mound of reflections, which I always mark down as they rise to be inserted here. I meant to write about the Barnetts, and the peculiar repulsiveness of those who dabble their fingers self approvingly in the stuff of others' souls. The Barnetts were at any rate plunged to the elbow; red-handed if ever philanthropists were. Is it chiefly intellectual snobbery that makes me dislike them? – is it snobbery to feel outraged when she says 'Then I came close to the Great Gates' – or reflects that God = good, devil = evil. Has this coarseness of grain any necessary connection with labour for one's kind? And then the smug vigour of their self-satisfaction! Never a question as to the right of what they do – always a kind of insensate forging ahead until, naturally, their undertakings are all of colossal size and portentous prosperity. Perhaps the root of it all lies in the adulation of the uneducated, and the easy mastery of the will over the poor. And more and more I come to loathe any dominion of one over another; any leadership, any imposition of the will. But I can only scratch the surface of what I feel about these two stout volumes [*Rev. Canon S. A. Barnett: His Life, Work and Friends* by his wife, Henrietta Barnett, 1918].

On Monday after many failures I met Murry at the Club and we had our talk about the *Athenaeum*. Success has already begun to do for Murry what I always said it would do. He is more freshly coloured, even in the cheeks, than when we last met. Why, he chuckled like a schoolboy; his eyes shone; his silences were occupied with pleasant thoughts, I think; not that he would admit that to edit the *Athenaeum* was much more preferable to a place in a government office. He talked so much about his plans, and with such zest that we sat there from 4.45 to 6.30, or past, and I had to rush. We went over all his names, and tried to think of others, but agreed that once our intimate friends were gone through the field was mown of its poppies. Katherine will do four novels every week – pray to God she don't do mine! I feel the acid in her once more – since she doesn't take the trouble to write a card to fix an engagement; but I shall try to go up there tomorrow and judge the situation with my own eyes.

Today we finished printing Eliot's poems – our best work so far by a long way, owing to the quality of the ink.

Saturday 22 March
The inscrutable woman remains inscrutable I'm glad to say; no apologies, or sense of apologies due. At once she flung down her pen and plunged, as if we'd been parted for ten minutes, into the question of Dorothy Richardson; and so on with the greatest freedom and animation on both sides until I had to catch my train. But something – something dark and catastrophic possibly to do with Murry – has taken place since we met. So much she hinted; but said she wished now to forget it – But this was a momentary revelation as I left. Otherwise, as I say, we chattered about the *Athenaeum* mostly, and I was much complimented to hear how much they wish for my writing. And again, as usual, I find with Katherine what I don't find with the other clever women a sense of ease and interest, which is, I suppose, due to her caring so genuinely if so differently from the way I care, about our precious art. Though Katherine is now in the very heart of the professional world – four books on her table to review – she is, and will always be I fancy, not the least of a hack.

Thursday 27 March
Our dinner last night at the Isola Bella was rather a brilliant affair in the Bohemian style, with a great deal of wine, and talk of books and pictures, and a general air of freedom and content. At the end of dinner the Padrone (Clive chattered Italian with the greatest gusto) brought a large sketch book, in which Nessa and Duncan and Roger all drew pictures, and we were rewarded by a bottle of Marsala. We talked by the way a great amount of *Athenaeum* gossip, all secretly delighted with our own importance; Clive and Roger to do art criticism, the most brilliant list of contributors on record.

Wednesday 2 April
Yesterday I took *Night and Day* up to Gerald [Duckworth], and had a little half domestic half professional interview with him in his office. I don't like the Club man's view of literature. For one thing it breeds in me a violent desire to boast: I boasted of Nessa and Clive and Leonard; and how much money they made. Then we undid the parcel, and he liked the title, but found that Miss Maud Annesley has a book called *Nights and Days* – which may make difficulties. But he was certain he would wish to publish it; and we were altogether cordial. I had tea at Gordon Square; then dinner at the Isola Bella; talk with Clive and Duncan; Clive insisting that Eliot dislikes me, and further trying to convince us that Nessa, Roger, himself, Lytton and I are the most hated people in London; superficial, haughty, and giving ourselves airs – that, I think, is the verdict against the ladies. I admit I hate not to be liked.

Thursday 10 April

A great skip, how accounted for I scarcely know. I have to read one book a day – such is the life of a hack. The Eliots, Walter and Marjorie [Strachey] dined here on Sunday; I amused myself by seeing how sharp, narrow, and much of a stick Eliot has come to be, since he took to disliking me. His wife a washed out, elderly and worn looking little woman, who was relieved to find Walter Lamb with his stories about the King provided for her; and indeed Walter seemed to both the ideal of manhood. Gumbo held forth in her most vivacious and commanding style.

Saturday 12 April

These ten minutes are stolen from *Moll Flanders*, which I failed to finish yesterday in accordance with my time sheet, yielding to a desire to stop reading and go up to London. But I saw London, in particular the view of white city churches and palaces from Hungerford Bridge through the eyes of Defoe. I saw the old women selling matches through his eyes; and the draggled girl skirting round the pavement of St James's Square seemed to me out of *Roxana* or *Moll Flanders*. Yes, a great writer surely to be thus imposing himself upon me after two hundred years. A great writer – and Forster has never read his books! I was beckoned by Forster from the [London] Library as I approached. We shook hands very cordially; and yet I always feel him shrinking sensitively from me, as a woman, a clever woman, an up-to-date woman. Feeling this I commanded him to read Defoe, and left him, and went and got some more Defoe, having bought one volume on the way.

Herbert Fisher astounded us by asking himself to lunch tomorrow, and we have been to Kew, and seen the Magnolia trees in blossom.

Thursday 17 April

We saw the magnolia tree in blossom next day with the Minister for Education himself. He is a strange mixture of ascetic and worldling. The lean secluded man now finds himself dazzled by office, and with all his learning and culture swept away by men of vitality and affairs. Such a tribute as he paid to Winston [Churchill] might have been paid by some dazzled moth to a lamp. He seems to see nothing clearly, or else some notion of responsibility forbids him to say what he thinks. He hums and haws when asked a plain question. His whole aspect is that of a worn and half obliterated scholar made spruce by tailors and doing his best to adopt the quiet distinguished manner of those who govern. In private he is a kindly, even affectionate gentleman, simple by nature, though tarnished with a supercilious superficial manner which leads him to dally urbanely and in a way which belittles them with art and letters and everything but politics. We took him to Kew, and chatted of Oxford and Walter Pater, and how Chesterton is a genius, and George Moore another, by way of relief from politics. And he approved of nature too, and likened the Thames beneath a shower to a picture in the Louvre. He stood still on the bank for some minutes, taking in the impression, not as a person who is accustomed to looking at things looks, but rather as a man who collects objects for the good of his soul. So it was too with the buds of the magnolia at Kew.

I could fill this page with gossip about people's articles in the *Athenaeum*, since I had tea with Katherine yesterday and Murry sat there mud-coloured and mute, livening only when we talked his shop. He has the jealous partiality of a parent for his offspring already. Heinemann has rejected Katherine's stories; and she was oddly hurt that Roger had not invited her to his party. Her hard composure is much on the surface.

Thursday 24 April

On Easter Monday we went up to visit the Murrys and see Hampstead Heath. Our verdict was that the crowd at close quarters is detestable; it smells; it sticks; it has neither vitality nor colour. How slow they walk! How passively and brutishly they lie on the grass! How little of pleasure or pain is in them! But they looked well dressed and well fed; and at a distance among the canary coloured swings and roundabouts they had the look of a picture. Very little noise they made; the large aeroplane that came flying so steadily overhead made more noise than the whole crowd of us. Why do I say 'us'? I never for a moment felt myself one of 'them'. Yet the sight had its charm: I liked the bladders, and the little penny sticks, and the sight of two slow elaborate dancers performing to a barrel organ in a space the size of a hearthrug. Katherine and Murry and Murry's brother met us at their door. We thought she would have enjoyed herself, from the likeness of her prose to the scene; on the contrary, she was disgusted. We had rather a stiff tea.

Last night the Coles [G.D.H. and Margaret] dined here, and gave me my first view of them. Sharp, positive, hard minds; in tense taut bodies; in Cole's case the mouth seems fixed in a kind of snarl at the world. A positive domineering young man he seemed; and she, with less force, equally sure of herself. A good laugh would do them both good; yet how laugh with those tight stretched drums for cheeks, and those curled sneering lips? I don't accuse either of them of a desire to be savage or destructive; I write from the outsider's unsympathetic point of view. But Leonard, though he works at their works, is still humane and deliberate. Its the perpetual strife that strings them up in this way, I think; no speculative or contemplative imaginative power seems to be left them. This I write from the recollection of them which came to me on waking. 'I don't like the Coles' I said to myself, before I had time to set my faculties to work upon this judgment.

Tomorrow we go down to Asheham for ten days; alone; leaving the servants to clean here, and intending to find a house for £35 if we can, for that is our solution at present.

Monday 5 May

The day mother died twenty something years ago. The smell of wreaths in the hall is always in the first flowers still; without remembering the day I was thinking of her, as I often do – as good a memorial as one could wish. Ah but how happy we've been at Asheham! It was a most melodious time. Everything went so freely;   but I can't analyse all the sources of my joy.

Wednesday 7 May

To recapitulate the events of Asheham is no longer in my power, or perhaps, since they were mainly of a spiritual nature requiring some subtlety to relate, I'm too lazy to try. Happiness – what I wonder constitutes happiness? I daresay the most important element is work, and that rarely fails either of us now.

A letter from Gerald to say he has read *Night and Day* with 'the greatest interest' and will be delighted to publish it. I suppose, as I go to the trouble of copying his words verbatim, that I was a good deal pleased by them. The first impression of an outsider, especially one who proposes to back his opinion with money, means something; though I can't think of stout smooth Gerald smoking a cigar over my pages without a smile.

I got over to Charleston and had a night and morning alone with Vanessa – so far as she can ever be alone. Living is fairly bare at the moment. They have all the necessaries; but not an ornament. My life, by comparison, seems padded at every turn. But they all looked as vigorous as possible. As usual, a good deal of domestic talk; sleep in the ground floor room at night, where this time last year about I heard the nightingales, and the fishes splashing in the pond, white roses tapped at the window; that night when I was told that [baby] Angelica was in evidence. Nothing but wind and rain this time, and no coal in the house.

Monday 12 May

We are in the thick of our publishing season: Murry, Eliot, and myself are in the hands of the public this morning. I read a bound copy of *Kew Gardens* through, having put off the evil task until it was complete. The result is vague. It seems to me slight and short.

On Friday I had tea with Katherine and Murry, with whom I now adopt a manner of motherly badinage; which is less fatiguing than the intellectual pose.

Friday 16 May

This week we've had Ottoline, and Lytton, and I've been to see Violet Dickinson. Let me attempt Ottoline, since her hat and veil on the sofa beside me recall her. She struck her unmistakable note on entering the room; rayed with green and blue, like the Cornish sea, and magnificently upright and held together; her blue blood giving her the carriage of assurance and self-respect which is rare among the intellectuals. Certain layers of powder showed upon the steeps of her face – but when you reflect that she's close on fifty – and has cropped her hair like a boy! Of course we talked personalities; and she was kindly, and well wishing, though considerably bewildered, and bewailing as usual her disasters in friendship, and inclined to blame everyone but herself. L.'s verdict was that she was 'very nice'; the first time he has ever said that. Perhaps she was on her good behaviour – but if so, she was capable of wrapping herself in her great Spanish cloak, and sallying out into the street without her hat; she's altogether such a fancy dress character that a hat more or less seems immaterial. We put her into her train with young officers who looked up startled; and despatched her to Waterloo.

Next day there was Lytton. I need not repeat the stock observations upon his mellow good humour. It is more to the point to chronicle a renewed sense of affection, which has never been seriously in abeyance. We scrutinised the condition of his soul, with his help, very closely. Ottoline had professed some alarm. We came to the conclusion that it would be absurd not to have this butterfly's season among the great.

I broke from Lytton with regret, and paid my visit to Violet; but she would have been hurt had I shirked it, to judge at least by her pleasure at seeing me. Its odd how people of fifty remain exactly fifty. She hasn't changed a hair for twenty years, which must be the length of our friendship. We take things up precisely as we left them; a year's gap makes no difference. When I come onto the verge of the respectable classes I'm always much struck by their unexpectedness: Violet is as much of a democrat as I am; as little of an Imperialist; she blames England; she has no hate of Germany; she sends clothes to Russia; and yet she lives in Manchester Street, and consorts chiefly with people like the Horners and the Thynnes. Beatrice Thynne has inherited a quarter of a million; two large properties, and one of the finest libraries in England; she has no idea what to make of them; visits them in a distracted way to see which she'd like to live in; can't make up her mind to settle in either, and finally spends most of her time in Gray's Inn, looked after by a charwoman.

Sunday 18 May
Our seductive sweetness appears still to be drawing bees from all quarters. As we left lunch there was a great rapping on the door, and the hall immediately filled with strangers, who eventually became Roger, Pamela [his daughter], and a strange silent foreign woman whom from her grey hair I took to be Margery Fry. We pitched on the grass, under a shower of apple blossom; and there sat until tea; and then Logan [Pearsall Smith] came; and we only fell silent at half past six or even later; nor was there a moment of repose, neither for tongue nor brain. [Logan] is a very well brushed, bright eyed, rosy cheeked man, seemingly entirely satisfied with life, which he appears to have mastered: visiting each of its flowers, like a bee. These flowers he keeps stored in his waistcoat pocket: lines from Jeremy Taylor, Carlyle, Lamb, &c. An epicurean, I suppose; a little frosty, I conjecture; though kindly and humane of course, rather than human.

Sunday 25 May
The day recalls the fact that we lunched with the Webbs this time last week. The Webbs were very quotable. Mrs Webb's brilliant idea of municipal bricks for children, inscribed with the names of organisations so that in putting them together they would learn their civic duties was almost too much in character to be suitable. Even Sidney had his mild joke at her.

Lytton came to tea on Friday and half maliciously assured me that my industry amazed him. My industry and my competence, for he thinks me the best reviewer alive, and the inventor of a new prose style, and the creator of a new version of the sentence. He asserted that he was disgusted by his own stereotyped ways: his two semi-colons; his method of understatement; and his extreme definiteness. Without agreeing, I conveyed my sense of his dangers, and urged him to write plays – stories - anything to break the mould of the early Victorians. After a volume on Victoria in the same manner, he is going to attempt it. But the money – he must make money – he can't write reviews.

Monday 9 June
A week at Asheham has intervened. An odd thing happened to me at Asheham, where I count upon becoming clearer and more concentrated. The very opposite of this took place. I dozed and drowsed and seemed to feel the sun in my brain sending all my thoughts to seek repose in the shadow. I write there at an open window looking onto the field; and the field was gilt with buttercups; the sheep were tempting in their indolence; in short, I used to find the morning gone and only a few lines written. The loveliness of Asheham once again brimmed the cup and overflowed. Wild ideas seized us of building a house. To give up every foothold in that region

seemed unthinkable. With the notion of building a house running strongly in my mind I went to Charleston for a night and was there disabused of such fantasies very completely. Nessa and I quarrelled as nearly as we ever do quarrel now over the get up of *Kew Gardens*, both type and woodcuts; and she firmly refused to illustrate any more stories of mine under those conditions, and went so far as to doubt the value of the Hogarth Press altogether. An ordinary printer would do better in her opinion. This both stung and chilled me. Anyhow I left in a rather crumpled condition, and paused in Lewes in no cheerful mood, with three hours, moreover, to spend there. To pass the time, more than anything, I asked Mrs Wycherley [Estate Agent] about houses; and she bethought her of one newly on the market, small, old, actually in Lewes, and perhaps a little humble for one used to lodge at Asheham. Off I went up Pipes Passage, under the clock, and saw rising at the top of the sloping path a singular shaped roof, rising into a point, and spreading out in a circular petticoat all round it. An elderly and humble cottage woman, the owner, showed me over. How far my satisfaction with the general oddity and character of the whole place were the result of finding something that would do, that one could conceive living in, that was cheap (freehold £300) I don't know; but as I inspected the rooms I became conscious of a rising desire to settle here; to have done with looking about; to take this place, and make it one's permanent lodging. In short I took it there and then, being egged on by Wycherley's hesitation, and hints of a purchaser who had already asked for the refusal. The end of the story, which I must curtail, is that we have bought the Round House, and are now secure of a lodging on earth so long as we need sleep or sit anywhere.

Tuesday 10 June
I must use up the fifteen minutes before dinner in going on again, in order to make up the great gap. We are just in from the Club and from tea with James. His news is that Maynard in disgust at the peace terms has resigned; kicked the dust of office off him, and is now an academic figure at Cambridge. But I must really sing my own praises, since I left off at the point when we came back from Asheham to find the hall table stacked, littered, with orders for *Kew Gardens*. They strewed the sofa, and we opened them intermittently through dinner, and quarrelled, I'm sorry to say, because we were both excited, and opposite tides of excitement coursed in us, and they were blown to waves by the critical blast of Charleston. All these orders – 150 about, from shops and private people – come from a review in *The Times Literary Supplement* in which as much praise was allowed me as I like to claim. And ten days ago I was stoically facing complete failure! The pleasure of success was considerably damaged, first by our quarrel, and second, by the necessity

of getting some 90 copies ready, cutting covers, printing tables, glueing backs, and finally despatching, which used up all spare time and some not spare till this moment.

Saturday 14 June

Yesterday I had a Hampstead field day; first the Murrys, then Adrian and Karin, and finally dinner – it was 8.30 by the time I got it – with Ray and Dorothy Bussy. A very severe review of Murry, a severe review of Eliot, appeared in the *TLS* on Thursday. I don't see why they choose to come down so hard upon Murry; and I wish they hadn't. I attribute the extreme depression of him and Katherine at least partly to this. And I felt gorged and florid with my comparative success. Poor Murry pretended not to mihd, but much like a small boy sticking it out that caning doesn't hurt. A poem is a very sensitive part to be beaten. But Katherine looks so ill and haggard that I suppose health may make a great part of her depression. She is going to San Remo for a year in September. Murry means to live alone in the country. I don't see how, all this being so, they can look forward to their future. Anyhow I went off rather sombre, leaving them to their spare lonely meal, nothing seeming to grow or flourish round them; leafless trees.

Wednesday 18 June

I went off, as I now remember, to call on Adrian, as I was early for Ray; and found that strange couple just decided to become medical students. After five years' training they will, being aged thirty-five and forty-one or so, set up together in practice as psycho-analysts. Here is another chance; visions of success and a busy crowded, interesting life beguile him. Halfway through, I suppose, something will make it all impossible; and then, having forgotten his law, he will take up what – farming or editing a newspaper, or keeping bees perhaps. I don't see that it matters at all, so long as they always have some carrot dangling in front of them.

Yesterday, Tuesday, I was treated to ices at Gunter's by Clive. It was all the same as before. Little tables; long rather dark shop; numbers of gilt chairs; discreet buffet; elderly waitresses in black; and couples scattered all about silently, or almost silently, absorbing ices and sugared cakes. We strolled out of the solemn cave and sauntered through the purest 18th Century London to the Green Park where we sat on hard green chairs, and watched people passing down the little slope towards the Palace. This being, I suppose, the sixth week without rain the grass is already haycoloured and slippery. We gossiped, speculated, and reminisced. Very easy, agreeable talk to my mind, and then what an age I've known him! How much we've been through side by side – these infrequent meetings are little islands upon which one stands surveying the flood racing away in the past; looking out over the future, safely and with very little anxiety just at present. He talks of going to Paris in the autumn, to see what's on; and he's given up his book, and finds that articles of 2,000 words exactly suit him. He thinks of subjects in his bath. He makes money. He spends it on ices and dinners at the Café Royal. He dines out every night, enjoys every moment, and feels his senses quicker and stronger as time goes on. We agreed in finding life very delightful, though very different for each of us.

Monday 23 June
If I hadn't had since midday to settle myself, I should still be twanging and twittering with Garsington. But parties don't fluster me as they used. I don't much care now about the great question of hair; I am resigned to my station among the badly dressed, though the speeding up of my blue dress, and doubts as to its beauty scarcely seem to confirm that statement. However this may be, I enjoyed Garsington saying to myself 'The worst moment will be when I come into the drawing room in my blue dress before dinner.' I planned thus to get dressed quick and come in before Ott which is not difficult as Ott never gets dressed quick. Mercifully I need not face Garsington squarely and draw its picture. I observed that the sealing wax red drawing room is a good deal smaller this visit than last, and last visit than first. That's what happens to people too. The population was floating and changing. Goldie and I were permanent; Aldous Huxley came for one night. I shall leave out several names if I try to count them. I think Goldie was the principal element in the week end, that is to say that he took upon him the brunt of Sunday morning, and meal times; three hours sitting on a hard seat with Ott and me, Philip sometimes, Gertler occasionally, and Aldous off and on was a trial; but for us all it was well surmounted. I did not guess the time once. When Philip suggested a visit to the pigs I was ready but not over-ready. Ott needled away at her embroidery, losing her needle once, and crouching on all fours behind the seat, while Goldie and I went on talking. This seemed to me to typify her modest position; so long as people talk she doesn't much want to interfere, and she listens, especially if people's characters are discussed. Yet it struck me as strange –

Thursday 3 July
What struck me as strange? Perhaps I meant to finish by trying to define the sense of purposelessness which now and then besets me – Suppose we do settle exactly what Roger's character is, and what degree of spite to allow Clive – well this is too far gone for recapturing, though there was a queer enough sequel a day or two later at Asheham. We went there on the Thursday following, and came back yesterday. I can't give much space to Philip's letter though; [it] was all about my lack of heart and his terror of

me; to which I have rejoined 'if I'm Bloomsbury, you're Mayfair'; to his
bewilderment, as I hope. But this is moonshine. The solid fact is that we
own, besides the Round House, Monks House at Rodmell, with three
quarters of an acre of land.

We own Monks House (this is almost the first time I've written a name
which I hope to write many thousands of times before I've done with it)
for ever. It happened thus. As we walked up the steep road from [Lewes]
station last Thursday on our way to inspect the Round House, we both
read out a placard stuck on the auctioneers' wall. 'Lot 1. Monks House,
Rodmell. An old fashioned house standing in three quarters of an acre of
land to be sold with possession.' "That would have suited us exactly" L. said
as we passed, and I, loyal to the Round House, murmured something about
the drawbacks of Rodmell, but suggested anyhow a visit to the place; and
so we went on. I think a slight shade of anti-climax had succeeded my
rather excessive optimism; at any rate, the Round House no longer seemed
so radiant and unattainable when we examined it as owners. I thought L.
a little disappointed. The bedrooms were very small. The garden not a
country garden. Anyhow it seemed well to plan a visit to Rodmell on the
following day. I bicycled over against a strong cold wind. This time I flatter
myself that I kept my optimism in check. 'These rooms are small', I said
to myself; 'The kitchen is distinctly bad. There's an oil stove, and no grate.
Nor is there hot water, nor a bath, and as for the earth closet I was never
shown it.' These prudent objections kept excitement at bay; yet even they
were forced to yield place to a profound pleasure at the size and shape and
fertility and wildness of the garden. There seemed an infinity of fruitbearing
trees; unexpected flowers sprouted among cabbages. There were well kept
rows of peas, artichokes, potatoes; and I could fancy a very pleasant walk
in the orchard under the apple trees, with the grey extinguisher of the
church steeple pointing my boundary. On the other hand there is little view
– There is little ceremony or precision at Monks House. It is an unpretending
house, long and low, a house of many doors, on one side fronting the street
of Rodmell, and wood-boarded on that side, though the street of Rodmell
is at our end little more than a cart track running out on to the flat of the
water meadows. There are, if memory serves me, no less than three large
outhouses of different kinds, and a stable; and a hen house – Our fruit and
vegetables are said to flourish under the care of a single old man who for
forty years has spent his spare time in tending these trees for the late Mr
Jacob Verrall. All this made a happy kind of jumble in my brain, together
with the store of old fashioned chairs and tables, glass and furniture with
which every inch of room space is crowded. I came back and told my story
as quietly as I could, and next day L. and I went together and made a
thorough inspection. He was pleased beyond his expectation. The truth is

he has the making of a fanatical lover of that garden. In short, we decided walking home to buy if we could, and sell Round House, as we conjecture we can. Eight hundred we made our limit, which, according to Wycherley, gave us a good chance of possession.

The sale was on Tuesday. I don't suppose many spaces of five minutes in the course of my life have been so close packed with sensation. The room at the White Hart was crowded. I looked at every face for signs of opulence, and was cheered to discover none. But then, I thought, getting L. into line, does *he* look as if he had £800 in his pocket? Bidding began. Someone offered £300. "Not an offer," said the auctioneer, who was immediately opposed to us as a smiling courteous antagonist, "a beginning." The next bid was £400. Then they rose by fifties. Wycherley standing by us, silent and unmoved, added his advance. Six hundred was reached too quick for me. The auctioneer egged us on. I daresay there were six voices speaking, though after £600, four of them dropped out, and left only a Mr Tattersall competing with Mr Wycherley. We were allowed to bid in twenties; then tens; then fives; and still short of £700. Seven hundred reached, there was a pause; the auctioneer raised his hammer, very slowly; held it up a considerable time; urged and exhorted all the while it slowly sank towards the table. "Now Mr Tattersall, another bid from you – ten pounds? five pounds? no more? for the last time then –" *dump*! and down it came on the table, to our thanksgiving – I purple in the cheeks, and L. trembling like a reed – "sold to Mr Wycherley." We stayed no longer. Out we went into the High Street, and very nearly quarrelled over the address of Roger's house.

Thursday 8 July
We went on however, L. to Asheham, and I to Charleston, where there was Maynard, and a good deal of brisk talk. He is disillusioned he says. No more does he believe, that is, in the stability of the things he likes. Eton is doomed; the governing classes, perhaps Cambridge too. These conclusions were forced on him by the dismal and degrading spectacle of the Peace Congress, where men played shamelessly, not for Europe, or even England, but for their own return to Parliament at the next election. He resigned, and is now a don at Cambridge, daily rejecting profitable offers made him by houses of business, willing, according to Duncan, to pay £4,000 a year for his attendance for a short time daily. We all came up to London early next day. We had an afternoon's gaiety at the Ballet, and then went back to Gordon Square, everything a little glittering and unreal, as usual after the country and in Nessa's presence.

Friday, the 4th, I went to tea with Katherine, since I begin to feel my visits numbered, how seriously I don't know, but once she gets abroad, what's to bring her back? Murry, poor man, pale and sad as usual, for she is again only just out of bed.

Thursday 10 July
Last night I dined at the Savoy Grill Room with Clive. It is long since I had taken part in the great ceremony of dinner with others believing in it, assisting at it, and dressing for it. Fish and meat and melon and ices have come to their own again. Clive parted with a good deal of paper money. He pointed out to me Picasso and Mme Picasso making off for the ballet. We drove back to Gordon Square and talked about the problems of literature. I wonder if I talk nonsense about writing to Clive? On the whole I believe that he has an odd gift for making one talk sense. He's so eager that one should talk sense; his enthusiasm is the engaging thing about him – deducting the tribute of his enthusiasm for me. Moreover, whatever one may think of his taste in life, however one may feel him a little battered and dusty in the pursuit of pleasure, still there's his honesty; his vivacity; his determination not to be bored, and not to bore. In his own way he is somehow a figure.

Saturday 12 July
In public affairs, I see I've forgotten to say that peace was signed; perhaps that ceremony was accomplished while we were at Asheham. I've forgotten the account I was going to write out of the gradual disappearance of things from shop windows; and the gradual, but still only partial reappearance of things. Sugar cakes, currant buns, and mounds of sweets. The effect of the war would be worth describing, and one of these days at Monks House – but why do I let myself imagine spaces of leisure at Monks House? I know I shall have books that must be read there too. But this dressing up of the future is one of the chief sources of our happiness, I believe. There's still a good deal of the immediate past asserting its claim on me. I met Morgan Forster on the platform at Waterloo yesterday; a man physically resembling a blue butterfly – I mean by that to describe his transparency and lightness. I like Forster very much, though I find him whimsical and vagulous to an extent that frightens me with my own clumsiness and definiteness. Then I bought my bag of coffee, and so up to Katherine, with whom I spent my hour very happily. Indeed, I like her more and more; and think we have reached some kind of durable foundation.

Saturday 19 July
One ought to say something about Peace Day, I suppose, though whether its worth taking a new nib for that purpose I don't know. In ten minutes or so the Richmond procession begins. I fear there will be few people to

applaud the town councillors dressed up to look dignified and march through the streets. Rain held off till some half hour ago. The servants had a triumphant morning. They stood on Vauxhall Bridge and saw everything. Generals and soldiers and tanks and nurses and bands took two hours in passing. It was they said the most splendid sight of their lives. But I don't know – it seems to me a servants' festival; something got up to pacify and placate 'the people' – and now the rain's spoiling it. There's something calculated and politic and insincere about these peace rejoicings. Moreover they are carried out with no beauty, and not much spontaneity. Yesterday in London the usual sticky stodgy conglomerations of people, sleepy and torpid as a cluster of drenched bees, were crawling over Trafalgar Square, and rocking about the pavements in the neighbourhood. The one pleasant sight I saw was due rather to the little breath of wind than to decorative skill; some long tongue-shaped streamers attached to the top of the Nelson column licked the air, furled and unfurled, like the gigantic tongues of dragons, with a slow, rather serpentine beauty. (And now, in the rain, under a grey brown sky, the bells of Richmond are ringing – but church bells only recall weddings and Christian services.) I can't deny that I feel a little mean at writing so lugubriously; since we're all supposed to keep up the belief that we're glad and enjoying ourselves. So on a birthday, when for some reason things have gone wrong, it was a point of honour in the nursery to pretend. Years later one could confess what a horrid fraud it seemed; and if, years later, these docile herds will own up that they too saw through it, and will have no more of it – well – should I be more cheerful?

Sunday 20 July
Perhaps I will finish the account of the peace celebrations. What herd animals we are after all! – even the most disillusioned. At any rate, after sitting through the procession and the peace bells unmoved, I began after dinner to feel that if something was going on, perhaps one had better be in it. I routed up poor L. and, seeing that the rain was stopped, we went out just before ten. Explosions had for some time promised fireworks. The doors of the public house at the corner were open, and the room crowded; couples waltzing; songs being shouted, waveringly, as if one must be drunk to sing. A troop of little boys with lanterns were parading the Green, beating sticks. Not many shops went to the expense of electric light. A woman of the upper classes was supported dead drunk between two men partially drunk. We followed a moderate stream flowing up the Hill. Illuminations were almost extinct half way up, but we kept on till we reached the terrace. And then we did see something – not much indeed, for the damp had deadened the chemicals. Red and green and yellow and blue

balls rose slowly into the air, burst, flowered into an oval of light, which dropped in minute grains and expired. Rising over the Thames, among trees, these rockets were beautiful; the light on the faces of the crowd was strange; yet of course there was grey mist muffling everything, and taking the blaze off the fire. It was a melancholy thing to see the incurable soldiers lying in bed at the Star and Garter with their backs to us, smoking cigarettes, and waiting for the noise to be over. We were children to be amused. So at eleven we went home. Today the rain has left us in no doubt that any remaining festivities are to be completely quenched.

Thursday 24 July

Last night we had Forster and the Bussys. Morgan is easily drowned even by the vivacity of the Bussys. He is an unworldly, transparent character, whimsical and detached, caring very little I should think what people say, and with a clear idea of what he wishes. I don't think he wishes to shine in intellectual society; certainly not in fashionable. He is fantastic and very sensitive; an attractive character to me. He resembles a vaguely rambling butterfly; since there is no intensity or rapidity about him. To dominate the talk would be odious to him. He subsided in a chair; or strolled about the room, turning over the pages of a book. Even when the Bussys had gone, we made little direct headway. He will come to Asheham if we pay his fare. He has only £26 in the bank. I liked this simple way of explaining things.

MONKS HOUSE, RODMELL.

Sunday 7 September

I suppose this is the first day upon which I could easily sit down and write in my long suffering and by this time I hope tolerant diary. The move was accomplished in one day, thanks chiefly to the organisation of L. who tied all the books in lots. Two waggon loads, one leaving about ten, another at six did the job, and we managed to roost about the house somehow or other that night. Much remains to be done inside the house, though the main arrangements are now made. But for some days one's mind is distracted by perpetually dwelling upon the changes round one; it works with an effort. This is wearing off slightly, though I write this as if I were raising seven stone on my pen instead of the usual number of ounces. However from all the difficulties, advantages and disadvantages of the place, I think the upshot is wholly favourable. One gains much in the way of variety here; there are more walks, and endless interests in the garden, though nothing of the flawless beauty of Asheham.

Thursday 12 September
Duncan and Nessa have just been over unexpectedly to tea. Other people's incursions always leave me tremulous. They break in upon a mood of depression, deep according to L.; to me of the consistency of September mist. Why is it, I wonder? Partly that for ten days I don't think I've had a letter; then I expect something unpleasant from Macmillans [USA]. Here I make my forecast. 'We have read *Night and Day* with the deepest interest, but hardly think it would appeal to our public over here.' Though I foretell this, and see that written down it is negligible as criticism, yet I want to have that unpleasant moment over. And the publication of *Night and Day* may perhaps send an occasional tremor through me for all my boasting. If that is pronounced a failure, I don't see why I should continue writing novels. These are the usual writer's melancholies.

Saturday 13 September
Well, Macmillan's letter came this morning, and is neither so good nor so bad as it might have been. They read with great interest, think *Night and Day* a fine work, but not likely to appeal to a wide public in America, and too long to be, at this season, worth reprinting. But they propose to take 500 or 1000 sheets from Gerald; the same number of *The Voyage Out*, and understand that I will offer them my next book. On the whole, I'm rather pleased than otherwise. I shall accept, I suppose, since there's scarcely time to try elsewhere. But I don't think Macmillan had much to do with my depression. Do I envy Nessa her overflowing household? Perhaps at moments; everything flourishing and humane there; perhaps I can't help a contrast which never occurs when I'm in full flood of work. I made these comparisons yesterday, when I lunched there and spent the afternoon and rode home. I had meant to say something about these queer spiritual states. They interest me, even when I'm the subject. And I always remember the saying that at one's lowest ebb one is nearest a true vision. I think perhaps nine out of ten people never get a day in the year of such happiness as I have almost constantly; now I'm having a turn of their lot.

Sunday 14 September
Well, I don't think my turn of their lot is a very serious matter. We went for our first Sunday walk today. In order to counteract the tremendous draw of the garden we have arranged two walks a week, on Sundays and Wednesdays. Today we went on the downs towards Kingston. We saw the sea at Brighton and the sea at Eastbourne to right and left of us. I must try a little Plato now – to prove that concentration is as easy here as elsewhere.

Sunday 21 September
By paying five shillings I have become a member of the Lewes public library. It is an amusing place – full of old ghosts; books half way to decomposition. A general brownness covers them. They are as much alike outwardly as charity schoolchildren. Most have shed their boards years ago, and been recovered in brown paper.

Sunday 28 September
Cut off as we are from all human intercourse I cannot be sure even of the date. It is said that the entire railways of England are on strike; the miners, and perhaps the transport workers, are with them. This happened yesterday morning, or rather late the night before; and though we got our papers through late in the evening, we are without posts. The signalman gave us some information yesterday, and believes himself to be striking against a reduction of fourteen shillings a week in his wages. His strike pay comes to sixteen shillings a week. How with prices what they are the strike can be kept up more than a day or two is difficult to see. He expects a settlement tomorrow; but like all the rest, he knows far less about the reasons and machinations than we do – L. at any rate. At present, what with Sunday and the quiet one imagines on the lines, a queer deep silence seems to lie upon us. We post letters knowing they won't get further than Lewes. There is talk of a motor car service. The Government make a show of courageous determination. We are on war rations, and told to be brave and good. Not since coaching days has the village of Rodmell been so isolated as it is at the present moment. Yet a state of siege has a certain smugness and self-sufficiency about it. No one can interrupt. If it lasts another day or two the food difficulty will begin. Then there's the question of getting back on Thursday.

Yesterday we went over to Asheham, plundered the hollow of its mushrooms, and then got in at the drawing room window. I don't know whether its one's accommodating temper that painted the place a little shut in and dismal, with the vast hollow behind and the straight view between trees in front. I thought it lacking in variety, this time, and colour – but I expect this is one of the devices of the imagination. Anyhow Monks improves, after the fashion of a mongrel who wins your heart. We have been planting tiny grains of seed in the front bed, in the pious or religious belief that they will resurrect next spring as Clarkia, Calceolaria, Campanula, Larkspur and Scabious. I shan't recognise them if they do; we are planting at a venture, inspired by seedsman's language: how they stand high and bear bright blue petals.

Tuesday 30 September

This is opened to record the Strike bulletin. Nothing has happened. All railways are silent. I went into Lewes yesterday and found a kind of modified Sunday prevailing. There were numbers of motors with luggage and the pampered rich. Rumour – shop keepers, that is to say – predicts a long strike. Who's in the right, they don't say: 'anyhow its bad for us'. In our private world the discomfort is mostly what we imagine for the future. We can make no plans anyhow. The papers are just in, shrunk to single sheets, and untrustworthy in their extreme – *Daily Mail* and *Herald*; trustful in the middle perhaps, *Daily News*. So far nothing but persistent hostility on both sides; no overtures.

Wednesday 1 October

The strike remains, so far as we can judge, the same. On the other hand, rumours of the strike change from hour to hour. A post came this morning. The postman is reported to say that all trains are running as usual. The signalman appears. Situation unchanged; much depressed. Then Dedman [gardener] comes to pick apples. A notice is in the post office, he says, that trains are as usual. Nelly goes to Lewes. Comes back 'frightened' so she says. A few trains only, into which you get at your own risk. We went down to the signalman with books and offers of help. His wife met us; he being at Newhaven. A fiery, impulsive, vigorous woman about to bear her fifth child. She was urging him to give in. Public opinion was against them, she said. Then she explained that they had only saved six shillings. With their strike pay this can't long keep off hunger. Then she couldn't see the rights of it. "They're like children who've had their sweet and don't want to give up their penny" she said, often enough to show that she'd used the argument often to him. They must give it up sooner or later, so why not now.

HOGARTH HOUSE, RICHMOND

Tuesday 7 October

Home yesterday. The 'docile herds' whom I describe on Peace Day are not so deluded after all. They have held the country up for eleven days, I think. We did a little to support them too, and kept one man on strike who would have gone back without our pound. Still, what's to be read in the papers is hardly fit for my private page.

I began reading the first volume of my diary; and see that its second anniversary is now reached. I don't think the first volume makes such good reading as the last; a proof that all writing, even this unpremeditated scribbling, has its form, which one learns. Is it worth going on with? The trouble is, that if one goes on a year or so more, one will feel bound on that account to continue. I wonder why I do it. Partly, I think, from my old sense of the race of time: 'Time's winged chariot hurrying near' – Does it stay it?

Saturday 11 October
For the first time I went up to London yesterday in the first place to buy gloves; in the second to have tea at Nessa's flat. Lytton we ran into at the Club on coming back – composed, agreeable, permanently shone upon, and completely sure of himself – ah, but infinitely charming into the bargain. Success, I believe, produces a kind of modesty. It frees you from bothering about yourself. He was flattering to me, as usual; but then I'm *not* a success. Did I not hear from Macmillan today that Messrs Duckworth's charges are prohibitive? So my chance of appearing in America is gone. But I'm showered under with review books.

Tuesday 21 October
This is Trafalgar day, and yesterday is memorable for the appearance of *Night and Day*. My six copies reached me in the morning, and five were despatched, so that I figure the beaks of five friends already embedded. Am I nervous? Oddly little; more excited and pleased than nervous. In the first place, there it is, out and done with; then I read a bit and liked it; then I have a kind of confidence, that the people whose judgment I value will probably think well of it, which is much reinforced by the knowledge that even if they don't, I shall pick up and start another story of my own.

Thursday 23 October
The first fruits of *Night and Day* must be entered: 'No doubt the work of the highest genius' Clive Bell. Well, he might not have liked it; he was critical of *The Voyage Out*. I own I'm pleased; yet not convinced that it is as he says. The people whose judgment I respect won't be so enthusiastic as he is, but they'll come out decidedly on that side, I think. Moreover, in a way which I can't defend to L., I do respect Clive's judgment. It's erratic, but always springs from a direct feeling. I think I feel most doubtful about Morgan; after getting his report I shall be quite at ease. Three or four people count, and the rest, save as a senseless clapping of hands or hissing, are nowhere.

Thursday 30 October
If I could treat myself professionally as a subject for analysis I could make an interesting story of the past few days, of my vicissitudes about *Night and*

Day. After Clive's letter came Nessa's -- unstinted praise; on top of that Lytton's: enthusiastic praise; a grand triumph; a classic; and so on; Violet's sentence of eulogy followed; and then, yesterday morning, this line from Morgan: 'I like it less than *The Voyage Out*.' Though he spoke also of great admiration, and had read in haste and proposed re-reading, this rubbed out all the pleasure of the rest. Yes; but to continue. About 3 in the afternoon I felt happier and easier on account of his blame than on account of the others' praise - as if one were in the human atmosphere again, after a blissful roll among elastic clouds and cushiony downs. Yet I suppose I value Morgan's opinion as much as anybody's. Then there's a column in *The Times* this morning; high praise; and intelligent too. I hope this week will see me through the reviews, I should like intelligent letters to follow; but I want to be writing little stories; I feel a load off my mind all the same.

Saturday 1 November
Never have I been so pressed with reviewing. I think I might slack off if *Night and Day* succeeds. Happily the book begins to recede from the front of my mind.

Thursday 6 November
Sydney [Waterlow] and Morgan dined with us last night. The doubt about Morgan and *Night and Day* is removed; I understand why he likes it less than *The Voyage Out* and, in understanding, see that it is not a criticism to discourage. Perhaps intelligent criticism never is. All the same, I shirk writing it out, because I write so much criticism. We talked very easily, the proof being that we (I anyhow) did not mind silences. Morgan has the artist's mind; he says the simple things that clever people don't say; I find him the best of critics for that reason. Suddenly out comes the obvious thing that one has overlooked.

Saturday 15 November
I have never been so neglectful of this work of mine; but there have been substantial difficulties. We were with Lytton last Sunday; on Monday I was at the dentist, and back just in time for Molly Hamilton; Tuesday I wrote letters; Wednesday, at a concert, with Violet Dickinson immediately after; Thursday Molly MacCarthy, for tea and after tea; Friday to Margaret and Lilian, and so here I am, sitting after Saturday tea, a large warm meal, full of currants and sugar and hot tea cake, after a long cold walk.

If I shut my eyes and thought of Tidmarsh, what should I see? Carrington a little absorbed with household duties; secreting canvas in the attic; Saxon mute and sealed till Sunday night, when he flowered for a time and talked of Greek; Lytton - a more complex situation. Good and simple and tender

-- a little low in tone; a little invalidish. If I'd married him, I caught myself thinking, I should have found him querulous. He would have laid too many ties on one, and repined a little if one had broken free. He was in his usual health (as they say); but the sense of living so much for health, and assembling so many comforts round him with that object is a little depressing. But what I feel for Lytton is as true as ever it was. We sit alone over the fire and rattle on, so quick, so agile in our jumps and circumventions. On his table were the latest editions of Voltaire. His books were as primly ranged and carefully tended as an old maid's china. I was in the vein to feel highly 'creative', as indeed he said he thought me. But he declared himself entirely without that power. He can invent nothing he says; take away his authorities, and he comes to a full stop. Perhaps this is true of all Stracheys.

Molly Hamilton still strains at her leash like the spaniel of my legend. It is a rough eager mind, bold and straightforward, but O dear – when it comes to writing! Her courage impresses me – the sense she gives of a machine working at high pressure all day long – the machine of the professional working woman. A tailor made coat costing £16 is essential she said to exact respect in an office.

I think Violet Dickinson must be skipped. So we skip to Molly who took her tea in the kitchen, and lastly we approach the heights of Hampstead – the immaculate and moral heights of Hampstead. Had I the energy left I would write out that scene of revelation and explanation with Margaret, since in thirty minutes we traversed more ground than in the past three years. Tentatively she began it – how Janet and she felt that perhaps – they might be wrong, but still in their view – in short my article on Charlotte Brontë was so much more to their liking than my novels. Something in my feeling for human beings – some narrowness – some lack of emotion – here I blazed up and let fly. So you go on preaching humanity, was the gist of what I said, when you've withdrawn, and preserve only the conventional idea of it. But its you that are narrow, she retaliated. On the contrary, I'm the most sympathetic, the most human, the most universal of people. But the idea of herself as a forcible intense woman, excluding the greater half of the human heart staggered her. She took the blow well. It was as if one had suddenly drawn some curtain. She must think it over, and write to me she said.

Friday 28 November
This gap can easily be accounted for by recalling the old saying (if it is one) that when things happen, people don't write. Too many things have happened. Within this last fortnight the *International Review* has come to an end; both servants are going; two publishers have offered to publish *Night and Day* and *The Voyage Out* in America; Angelica has stayed with us –

together with a greater number than usual of dinners, letters, telephone calls, books to review, reviews of my book, invitations to parties and so forth. It was the dinner parties that led Nelly to give notice last Monday. She did it in a way which makes me think she would be glad now to change her mind. She would this moment if I asked her. But on the whole I'm not going to ask her. Let alone the recurring worry of these scenes we both incline to try a new system of dailies, which never ceases to attract us. We mean to make the attempt now. No one could be nicer than Nelly, for long stretches. But the fault is more in the system of keeping two young women chained in a kitchen to laze and work and suck their life from two in the drawing room than in her character or mine.

Katherine Mansfield wrote a review which irritated me – I thought I saw spite in it. A decorous elderly dullard she describes me; Jane Austen up to date. Leonard supposes that she let her wish for my failure have its way with her pen. But what I perceive in all this is that praise hardly warms; blame stings far more keenly; and both are somehow at arms length. Yet it's on the cards, I suppose, that *Night and Day* is a marked success.

I'm reading Ethel Smyth [*Impressions that Remained*, 1919]. I wish it were better – (odd that I wrote that genuinely meaning it). What a subject! But of course, not knowing how to write she's muffed it. The interest remains, because she has ridden straight at her recollections, never swerving and getting through honestly, capably. Honesty is her quality; and the fact that she made a great rush at life; friendships with women interest me.

Friday 5 December

This last week L. has been having a little temperature in the evening, due to malaria, and that due to a visit to Oxford; a place of death and decay. I'm almost alarmed to see how entirely my weight rests on his prop. And almost alarmed to see how intensely I'm specialised. My mind turned by anxiety, or other cause, from its scrutiny of blank paper, is like a lost child – wandering the house, sitting on the bottom step to cry.

Saturday 6 December

On Tuesday I lunched with the [Lord Robert] Cecils. Perhaps this is my first appearance as a small Lioness. The Bibescos wished to meet me; Lord Cranborne has a great admiration for me. Lord Robert was congenial as usual, long, loose, friendly and humorous, in spite of the crucifix on his watch chain. Lord Cranborne much of a Cecil in appearance, modest and gentle, with a long sallow face, no chin, and shiny blue coat and trousers. I stayed talking with Nelly [Cecil] when the rest were gone – about adders, about servants, George Eliot, and *Night and Day*.

Sunday 28 December
Probably the last entry this year, and not likely to be the most articulate. Twenty-two days gap to be accounted for chiefly by illness: first L.'s which dribbled on; then much in the same way I was attacked – eight days in bed, down today on the sofa, and away to Monks House tomorrow. It was influenza – what they call a low type, but prolonged, and sponging on the head as it always does. Not much to say therefore, even if I could say it. But I've read two vast volumes of the Life of [Samuel] Butler and am racing through Greville Memoirs – both superbly fit for illness. Oh yes, I've enjoyed reading the past year's diary, and shall keep it up. I'm amused to find how its grown a person, with almost a face of its own.

L.'s book not yet out; but we have six copies in advance. Servants determined to stay for ever and ever. No news of the sale of *Night and Day*, but private opinion highly pleasing to me. *International Review* amalgamated with *Contemporary [Review]*, and L. to keep his office and his virgins. We think we now deserve some good luck. Yet I daresay we're the happiest couple in England.

1920

As she entered her thirty-ninth year the tentative form for a new novel began to take shape in Virginia's imagination; it developed into Jacob's Room, *which was to occupy her for the next two years or so. This novel was an important development, her discovery of a style suited to her mind and imagination. Meanwhile in the Hogarth Press, the Woolfs continued with their modest endeavours – a story by E. M. Forster, biblical stories by Logan Pearsall Smith, and Gorky's* Reminiscences of Tolstoi, *the first of a series of short Russian works brought to them by the Ukrainian exile Koteliansky, which led Leonard, and later Virginia, to study Russian in order to collaborate with him over the translations. Towards the end of the year the business of the Press occupied so much of the Woolfs' time they once again determined to enlist a helper; and in October Ralph Partridge, ex-officer, Oxford graduate, protégé of Lytton Strachey and the ardent wooer of Carrington, started part-time work at Hogarth House.*

Towards the end of 1919 Vanessa and her children had returned to London so that the boys might go to school; and Gordon Square, where they now occupied two floors at the top of Adrian and Karin Stephen's house, no. 50, again became a magnet for Virginia. She, beginning to 'feel a little famous', half enjoyed and half deplored the social demands increasingly made upon her, both as hostess and guest, from which she and Leonard escaped from time to time to Rodmell, removing there, as became their fixed custom, for eight to ten weeks in summer, and inviting their friends for weekend visits. This year saw the inauguration by Desmond's wife Molly MacCarthy of the 'Memoir Club' in which the members – all intimate friends – would meet for dinner and then read aloud their frank reminiscences – a seed-bed for biographical revelations which survived until the 1950s.

At the end of April Katherine Mansfield, who for her health's sake had spent the winter by the Mediterranean, returned to her Hampstead home, and once again Virginia – in spite of the hurt of Katherine's caustic review of Night and Day *in the* Athenaeum *– was drawn by a shared passion for their 'precious art' into renewing her affectionate relationship with this enigmatic, and now seriously ill, fellow writer. In August she went up to London from Rodmell to say goodbye to her for the last time; Katherine returned to the Riviera in September, and Virginia never saw her again.*

_1920_

Monks House, Rodmell

Wednesday 7 January
This is our last evening. We sit over the fire waiting for post – the cream of the day, I think. Yet every part of the day here has its merits. The house is empty by half-past eleven; empty now at five o'clock; we tend our fire, cook coffee, read, I find, luxuriously, peacefully, at length. Every day or nearly I've walked towards a different point and come back with a string of matchings and marvels. Five minutes from the house one is out in the open, a great pull over Asheham; and, as I say, every direction bears fruit. Once we went over the cornfield and up onto the down. The long down grass pale, and as we pushed through it, up got a hawk at our feet, seeming to trail near the ground, as if weighted down – attached to something. It let the burden fall, and rose high as we came up. We found the wings of a partridge attached to a bleeding stump, for the hawk had almost done his meal. We saw him go back to find it. Further down the hill-side a great white owl 'wavy in the dusk', flew behind the hedge as we came past. Village girls were returning, and calling out to friends in doors. So we cross the field and churchyard, find our coke burnt through to red, toast the bread – and the evening comes.

L. has spent most of his time pruning the apple trees, and tying plums to the wall. To do this he wears two jackets, two pairs of gloves; even so the cold bites through. These last days have been like frozen water, ruffled by the wind into atoms of ice against the cheek; then, in the shelter, forming round you in a still pool.

Hogarth House, Richmond

Saturday 10 January
So the New Year is broached: ten days of it already spent. The 1917 Club has the merit of gathering my particular set to a bunch about 4.30 on a week day. There, returning on Thursday, I found Clive (I heard him from

the stairs), Morgan, Fredegond and dim background figures just worth a nod turning out to be Oliviers – varieties of Oliviers. Now Clive showed as gaslight beside Morgan's normal day – his day not sunny or tempestuous but a day of pure light, capable of showing up the rouge and powder, the dust and wrinkles, the cracks and contortions of my poor parrokeet. He makes me feel the footlights myself. The blend of the two was not agreeable; or rather not comfortable.

Wednesday 14 January
Leonard's book [*Empire and Commerce in Africa*] is out today. To judge by his calm, you would not think it. Great gales in the way of weather; a French ship sunk in the Bay of Biscay; a Cornish steamer too wrecked off Swanage; and on our windows such a battering at night that we woke twice. Violent gusts leaping out of the heart of complete calm – a suggestion of animal savagery; or human frenzy. But what with glass and brick we humans do pretty well.

Saturday 17 January
Now Desmond for the night; I'm writing dully, wishing, though I love Desmond, for a solitary night. He has been made successor to Eagle [J. C. Squire] on the *Statesman*.

Tuesday 20 January
Years ago as a child I made up a wise saw to the effect that if one didn't expect a party to be nice it was and t'other way round. So Desmond's visit was easy, refreshing, and passed without hitch. We had a fine store of talk to keep us going. The story of his voyage – the squall at sea; arrival at Cape Town; Mrs Paley's surprise – his wire 'Desmond sailed' arriving 'Desmond failed' – (as indeed he might probably have done) – all this in the lovely soft voice. Then much talk of the *New Statesman* – projects without number. Secretly, I think, he was much excited and pleased. Five hundred assured, two hundred and fifty of it dependent on a weekly article, signed Affable Hawk (this is a dead secret). Off we went after tea to Roger's, all across Europe to the Brecknock Arms [Camden Town]. As we both depend upon holding to a button naturally we did not arrive easily. The house very high and narrow, with many large rooms, and a bright lining of pictures. Roger to my eyes slightly shrunken, aged? Can one use that word of him? And I don't know how much I colour him from my own depression – for I guessed he didn't much care for *Night and Day*. He showed freakish by side of Desmond's benevolence.

Wednesday 21 January
It would be easy to take up the line that Roger's praise is not worth having, since it is balanced by what appears an irrational prejudice. If the prejudice is on your side, well and good. I sometimes fancy that the only healthy condition is that of doing successful work. Roger's work never meeting with the right sort of appreciation, he suffers perpetually from an obscure irritation. The main form it takes is irritation against England; I fancy I can trace it elsewhere also. He is testy without much occasion, and too easily reverts to grievance, how art critics hate him, how its only in France that they care for his pictures – If I'm sincere, however, I see that I'm led to infer all this from what I note in my own disposition under a cloud. For one thing, I find it difficult to write. I held my pen this morning for two hours and scarcely made a mark. The marks I did make were mere marks, not rushing into life and heat as they do on good days. Perhaps Roger was the first cloud; Desmond may have contributed a little; and then how many silly things I did yesterday.

Saturday 24 January
Oh dear, this talk of novels is all turned sour and brackish by a visit to Mrs Clifford. She must have supplied herself with false teeth since I saw her – twenty years ago; and her hair frizzed out is surely browned by art; but she remains otherwise the same – large codfish eyes and the whole figure of the nineties – black velvet, morbid, intense, jolly, vulgar – a hack to her tips, with a dash of the stage – 'dear', 'my dear boy'; "Did you know Leonard, that I was only married for three years, and then my husband died and left me with two babies and not a penny – so I had to work – oh yes, I worked, and sold the furniture often, but I never borrowed." However the pathetic is not her line. But if I could reproduce her talk of money, royalties, editions, and reviews, I should think myself a novelist; and the picture might serve me for a warning. Having years ago made a success, she's been pulling the wires to engineer another ever since, and has grown callous in the process. Her poor old lips pout for a pat of butter; but margarine will do. She keeps her private and very rancid supply on some of the little tables that those distressing rooms are lumbered with: she has a review of herself in the *Bookman* and a portrait, and a paper of quotations about *Miss Fingal*. Moreover, I had a feeling that in these circles people do each other good turns; and when she proposed to make my fortune in America, I'm afraid a review in *The Times* was supposed to be the equivalent. Brave, I suppose, with vitality and pluck – but oh, what an atmosphere of rancid cabbage and old clothes stewing in their old water! We went away laden with two of the cheap flaring books – "Are you going to take my mangy works! To tell the truth I'm in debt –" Yes, but was that why we

were asked to tea? Not altogether, I suppose, but partly; subconsciously. And now, you see, all colour is taken from my boasting, a second edition of *The Voyage Out* needed; and another of *Night and Day* shortly. Oh dear there must be an end of this! Never write for publishers again anyhow.

Monday 26 January

The day after my birthday; in fact I'm thirty-eight. Well, I've no doubt I'm a great deal happier than I was at twenty-eight; and happier today than I was yesterday having this afternoon arrived at some idea of a new form for a new novel. Suppose one thing should open out of another – and yet keep form and speed, and enclose everything, everything? For I figure that the approach will be entirely different this time: no scaffolding; scarcely a brick to be seen; all crepuscular, but the heart, the passion, humour, everything as bright as fire in the mist. The theme is a blank to me. Anyhow, there's no doubt the way lies somewhere in that direction; I must still grope and experiment but this afternoon I had a gleam of light.

Yesterday being my birthday and a clear bright day into the bargain showing many green and yellow flushes on the trees, I went to South Kensington and heard Mozart and Beethoven.

Saturday 31 January

At present the battle in our circles is between James and Desmond. James wishes to 'stab humbug dead'. Desmond and I wish, on the contrary, to revive it like a phoenix from its ashes.

Wednesday 4 February

The mornings from 12 to 1 I spend reading *The Voyage Out*. I've not read it since July 1913. And if you ask me what I think I must reply that I don't know – such a harlequinade as it is – such an assortment of patches – here simple and severe – here frivolous and shallow – here like God's truth – here strong and free flowing as I could wish. The failures are ghastly enough to make my cheeks burn – and then a turn of the sentence, a direct look ahead of me, makes them burn in a different way. On the whole I like the young woman's mind considerably – and my word, what a gift for pen and ink! I can do little to amend.

Friday 13 February

Again many lapses and the same excuses. For some time now life has been considerably ruffled by people. Age or fame or the return of peace – I don't know which – but anyhow I grow wearied of 'going out to tea'; and yet can't resist it. To leave a door shut that might be open is in my eyes some form of blasphemy. That may be; meanwhile I neither write my diary nor read my Greek. There was a lunch party at the Café Royal on the day of Duncan's private view to record: twelve guests; everything handsomely done; I stimulated and fuddled with wine; a queer assortment of the usual and the unusual. I fancy Duncan would rather have done without fuss, and he slunk off after lunch, leaving us to visit the show. Meanwhile I say nothing and have nothing to say of Duncan's pictures. They spun in my head like the white wine I'd drunk; so lovely, so delicious, so easy to adore. However I only caught glimpses here and there as well dressed people moved across them. Next day I bought one of Duncan's pictures.

I must skip over forgotten days and alight at Ottoline's last night. Yet I don't know that I can describe an evening party – Philip and I sitting together watched the door open and people come in. There were more of the shady smart sort than of old; or so they looked to me since I did not know them. There were Eliots and Huxleys and Forster and – all the rest. My single diversion was a dialogue with W. J. Turner, an inarticulate, infinitely modest man, with nice vague eyes, seeming to wish to tell the truth; yet too shy to be ready with it. At a party now I feel a little famous – the chances are people like Turner whose names I know, also know my name. I must have one coloured figure though in my black and white; I must spare a phrase for the sealing-wax green of Ottoline's dress. This bright silk stood out over a genuine crinoline. She did control the room on account of it. Yet I dreamt all night of her disillusioned with a weak pouting face, revealing her inner discontent. Indeed I can't help thinking her unhappy!

Sunday 15 February
But the Webbs! I find the hour of 1.30 on a cold blowy day, precisely fitting to them. As we walk down Grosvenor Road the old papers blow and the middle classes parade in their Sunday clothes. The houses have a red raw look. Factory chimneys face the windows across the river. There is no sun or warmth. Then there's the mutton and the cabbage and apple tart – all adequate but joyless. Bad cigarettes. A little whisky. The drawing room now a glacial white with water colours hung accurately apart. Mrs Webb displaying shark like teeth. Webb daubed red, and clumsily thick in person. No longer am I frightened; only dreary and dismal, and rasped all over by the sense of so hideous a prospect. Mrs Webb told me it was wrong to prevent L. from going into Parliament; we want men of subtle intellect and – But what is 'right' and who are 'we'? Frostily friendly she said goodbye. One deals with the situation more easily, but the horror of it increases with familiarity. Shall we become like that too? I stamp up and down the platform to warm myself; steep my hands in hot water, crouch over the fire, but still I'm irritated and exacerbated.

Wednesday 3 March

So then at the end of that week we went to Rodmell, and are back again two days ago. But I've numbers of old clothes in my dirty clothes basket – scenes, I mean, tumbled pell mell into my receptacle of a mind, and not extracted till form and colour are almost lost. I suppose 'going out to tea' continued; oh, there was a dinner at Gordon Square, when Mary, becoming almost peevish in her bedroom refused to part with hairpins: I made a note of that scene. Desmond was there: Desmond warm, affectionate, the oldest friend, so I sometimes feel; perhaps the best.

Then there was Roger's speech at the Club and my first effort – five minutes consecutive speaking – all very brilliant, and opening the vista of that form of excitement not before glimpsed at. Dined with Nessa and Duncan in Soho. Saw the woman drop her glove. A happy evening. Then off to Monks – and here I should write large and bright about the SPRING. It has come. It has been with us over a fortnight. Daffodils all out; garden set with thick golden crocuses; snowdrops almost over; pear trees budding; birds in song; days like June with a touch of the sun – not merely a painted sky but a warm one. Now we've been to Kew. Almond trees out.

Saturday 6 March

Tuesday and Wednesday here in Richmond printing. Then on Thursday, dine with the MacCarthys, and the first Memoir Club evening. A highly interesting occasion. Seven people read – and Lord knows what I didn't read into their reading. Sydney [Waterlow], to whom the occasion was one of some importance, signified as much by reading us a dream – in reality a parable – altogether a queer, self-conscious, self analytic performance, interesting to me. Clive purely objective; Nessa starting matter of fact; then overcome by the emotional depths to be traversed; and unable to read aloud what she had written. Duncan fantastic and tongue – not tied – tongue enchanted. Molly literary about tendencies and William Morris, carefully composed at first, and even formal; suddenly saying "Oh this is absurd – I can't go on" shuffling all her sheets. "These meagre Welsh, these hard-headed Scots – I detest them – I wanted to be the daughter of a French marquise by a misalliance with –" That was the tone of it. Roger well composed; story of a coachman who stole geraniums and went to prison. Good: but too objective. I doubt that anyone will *say* the interesting things but they can't prevent their coming out. Before this by the way, I saw Nessa's new home, no. 50 [Gordon Square] and looked in upon Adrian and Karin doing biology in their dining room.

Tuesday 9 March

In spite of some tremors, I think I shall go on with this diary for the present. I sometimes think that I have worked through the layer of style which suited it – suited the comfortable bright hour after tea. Never mind: I fancy old Virginia, putting on her spectacles to read of March 1920 will decidedly wish me to continue. Greetings! my dear ghost. Several good books can be written still; and here's the bricks for a fine one.

To return to the present owner of the name: on Sunday I went up to Campden Hill to hear the Schubert Quintet – to see George Booth's house – to take notes for my story – to rub shoulders with respectability – all these reasons took me there, and were cheaply gratified at seven-and-sixpence. Whether people see their own rooms with the devastating clearness that I see them, thus admitted once for one hour, I doubt. Chill superficial seemliness; but thin as a March glaze of ice on a pool. A sort of mercantile smugness. Horsehair and mahogany is the truth of it; and the white panels, Vermeer reproductions, Omega table and variegated curtains rather a snobbish disguise. The least interesting of rooms: the compromise; though of course, that's interesting too. I took against the family system. Old Mrs Booth enthroned on a sort of commode in widow's dress; flanked by devoted daughters; with grandchildren somehow symbolical cherubs. Such neat dull little boys and girls. There we all sat in our furs and white gloves.

Monday at the Club, which I see I've ceased to describe.

Thursday 18 March

If this diary were the diary of the soul I could write at length of the second meeting of the Memoir Club. Leonard was objective and triumphant; I subjective and most unpleasantly discomfited. I don't know when I've felt so chastened and out of humour with myself – a partner I generally respect and admire. 'Oh but why did I read this egotistic sentimental trash!' That was my cry, and the result of my sharp sense of the silence succeeding my chapter. It started with loud laughter; this was soon quenched; and then I couldn't help figuring a kind of uncomfortable boredom on the part of the males; to whose genial cheerful sense my revelations were at once mawkish and distasteful. What possessed me to lay bare my soul! I saw Nessa yesterday, and she guessed at none of this – which indeed Leonard firmly assured me was a miasma on my part due to late nights &c.

Saturday 10 April

We sped to Rodmell, which accounts for another formidable break. By the way, Morgan keeps a diary, and in his diary Morgan writes conversation – word for word, when the humour takes him. I don't know that the humour takes me to describe our Easter at Monks House. To describe Monks House would be to trench upon literature, which I can't do here; since we only slept by snatches last night, and at 4 am turned a mouse out of L.'s bed. Mice crept and rattled all night through. Then the wind got up. Hasp of the window broken. Poor L. out of bed for the fifth time to wedge it with a toothbrush. So I say nothing about our projects at Monks, though the view across the meadows to Caburn is before me now; and the hyacinths blooming, and the orchard walk. Then being alone there – breakfast in the sun – posts – no servants – how nice it all is!

I'm planning to begin *Jacob's Room* next week with luck. (That's the first time I've written that.)

Thursday 15 April

Rain has come – what I mind much more is the black sky: so ugly. Yesterday I think I was unhappy all day long. What book can I settle to read? I want something that won't colour my morning's mood – something a little severe. My notion is to write this [book] in chapters straight off; not beginning one unless I can count on so many days clear for finishing it.

Saturday 17 April

To the Bach Festival [at Central Hall, Westminster] last night; as I settled into my seat, a voice said Virginia! It was Walter Lamb. The egg shaped man – the billiard ball man – sat by me, and told me a great deal about Bach. Bach was very beautiful, though the human element in the choir always distracts me. *They* aren't beautiful; all in greens, greys, pinks, blacks, fresh from the suburbs and high tea. The hall seemed to suit them better than the music.

Tuesday 20 April

Saw the birth of Ka's son in *The Times* this morning, and feel slightly envious all day in consequence. To the Bach choir last night; but one of our failures. I'd made out on waking such a perfect day; and one by one my events missed fire. Such a good morning's writing I'd planned, and wasted the cream of my brain on the telephone. Then the weather; great bouncing gusts all set about with rain soaking one; buses crowded; left typewriting paper in the bus; a long time waiting at the Club – Then Bach unaccompanied isn't easy – though at last I was swept up to the heights by a song. Anna Magdalena's song. I walked a few steps beyond Herbert Fisher coming out; followed him across the empty lamplit purlieus of Westminster, saw him step so distinguished, yet to my eye so empty, into Palace Yard, and so to take part in ruling the Empire. His head bent – legs a little wavering – small feet – I tried to put myself inside him, but could only suppose he thought in an exalted way which to me would be all bunkum. Indeed, I feel this more and more. I've had my dive into their heads and come out again, I think.

Saturday 24 April
Morgan came for a night. Very easy going. I wish I could write his talk down. "I must now write a postcard. Yes, I must really catch the first post if possible. I'll take it myself – is there time still? I'll tell you what it is. The seat is being painted. The boy is so stupid he'll paint it after its been rained upon. Then it will be ruined." "Nonsense" said L. "It won't hurt it." "But are you sure?" "Positive." "Oh then I'll let it alone – if you're quite sure. My mother is having the seat painted green. She wouldn't let me do it, and the boy is dreadfully stupid. I found him putting on the paint without having scraped the old paint off first." &c . . .
    This is very like Morgan; so too his reliance on Leonard. "Where d'you get your boots? Are Waterman pens the best?"

Wednesday 5 May
We have had a Thursday to Tuesday at Rodmell; which accounts, as I say, making my apology to this book, in which so few pages seem to have been written. As we sat down to dinner on Saturday, Desmond rapped at the door. Desmond (this is L.'s saying not mine, and I quote it to avoid speaking grudgingly myself) produces a sense of frowst in the room. It rained; he lay back, smoking cigarettes, eating sweets and opening novels which he never read. Being an editor has drugged the remnants of ambition in him, and he is now content. Content is disillusioning to behold: what is there to be content about? It seems, with Desmond now, always afternoon.

Saturday 8 May
Yesterday I had tea with Saxon at the Club; and, remembering old lonely evenings of my own, when the married couple seemed so secure and lamplit, asked him back to dinner. I wonder though whether his loneliness ever frightens him as mine used to frighten me. I daresay office work is a great preservative.

Tuesday 11 May
It is worth mentioning, for future reference, that the creative power which bubbles so pleasantly on beginning a new book quiets down after a time, and one goes on more steadily. Doubts creep in. Then one becomes resigned. Determination not to give in, and the sense of an impending shape keep one at it more than anything. I'm a little anxious. How am I to bring off this conception?
    L. is up in London seeing his constituents. Eight gentlemen are waiting

on him to learn his views. Though it was summer till 3.30, it is now brushed with blackness, and I must shut the window and put on my jersey. Nessa comes back on Friday. Clive and Mary are in Paris.

Tuesday 18 May

Gordon Square begins again and like a snake renews its skin outworn – that's the nearest I can come to a quotation. [No. 50] Gordon Square different – like a looking glass version of 46. You are let in, by a strange servant, go up bare steps, hear children crying at various stages, go up and up – till you reach what is, in the real Gordon Square, servants' bedrooms. Nessa is right at the top. Well we talked till I left at 8; interrupted though by Lytton, Angelica, and Julian. Lytton said that James and Alix are to be married in three weeks. But though satisfactory, I find no excitement in this. They know each other too well to stir one's imagination thinking of their future, as one does with most engagements. Then, talk talk; and as we were despatching the superficial and reaching the easy-intimate, I had to tear off, in the rain, to Wigmore Hall. Sat between Oliver and Saxon; and these musical people don't listen as I do, but critically, superciliously, without programmes.

Thursday 20 May

Up yesterday with peonies to Nessa. Then I went on with L. to dine with the Coles in Chelsea. The Coles are Webbs in embryo – with differences of course. I'm used to being at ease with clever young men, and to find myself stumped, caught out, leg before the wicket at every turn is not pleasant. Never was there such a quick, hard, determined young man as Cole; covering his Labour sympathies, which are I suppose intellectual, with the sarcasm and sneers of Oxford. Then there's a bust of [William] Morris on the side board, too much to eat, Morris curtains, all the works of all the classics, and Cole and Mrs hopping on the surface like a couple of Cockney sparrows. The whole effect as of electric light full in the eyes – unbecoming at my age. One can see Mrs Cole rapidly becoming the cleverish elderly fox terrier type of intellectual woman – as it is not a shade or valley in her mind. Cole, grinning like a gutterpipe demon took us to the door – so spry, alert, virile, and ominous.

I have written to Katherine. No answer.

Monday 24 May

A real bank holiday – blazing weather, sound of buses unceasing – crowds like queues in the streets – and we spent it properly going to Hurlingham to see polo, of which I must make this rapid note. You get the impression that the turf is india-rubber – so lightly do the horses spring – touching it and up again – Captain Lockit galloping down with his stick like a Persian rider with a lance. A large white ball is then thrown in the midst. The horses twirl and dart; almost like long lean cats their scamper after the ball; only as they come past you hear a roar in the nostrils. But the bounce and agility of them all knotted together pawing the ball with their feet indescribable; passing in a second from full gallop to delicate trot as the ball is dribbled almost between their feet. This is the game of the officers of England. Each had eight ponies, and one lasted in this frenzy of freshness only seven minutes. Anyhow it was well worth seeing.

Summer has set in two days ago. Yesterday for the first time we lunched out of doors.

Wednesday 26 May

L. has been adopted as the Labour candidate of the seven Universities; may even be writing his letter of acceptance upstairs now. We are having the kitchen re-built at a cost of £80 at Monks House. And the night Morgan and Nessa dined here we saw a fire. Three minutes of excitement – great flames shooting up behind the playground; then a glow as of red yellow gauze, with sparks rising and falling; then a lovely sight when the hose shot into the air, wrapping itself in light and soaring like a rocket. A pouring crackling noise all the time, and now and then wood crashing.

This morning Katherine writes a stiff and formal note thanking me for my kind postcard, and saying she will be delighted to see me, though 'grown *very* dull'. What does this mean – *she* hurt with *me*? Anyhow I go on Friday to find out, unless stopped as is always possible.

Monday 31 May

Back from Monks an hour ago, after the first week-end – the most perfect, I was going to say, but how can I tell what week-ends we mayn't spend there? The first pure joy of the garden I mean.

I had my interview with Katherine Mansfield on Friday. A steady discomposing formality and coldness at first. Enquiries about house and so on. No pleasure or excitement at seeing me. It struck me that she is of the cat kind: alien, composed, always solitary and observant. And then we talked about solitude, and I found her expressing my feelings, as I never heard them expressed. Whereupon we fell into step, and as usual, talked as easily as though eight months were minutes – till Murry came in. We chatted as usual. Aldous was our butt. But Murry going at length, Katherine and I once more got upon literature. A queer effect she produces of someone apart, entirely self-centred; altogether concentrated upon her 'art'; almost fierce to me about it, I pretending I couldn't write. "What else is there to do? We have got to do it." Then asked me to write stories for the *Athenaeum*.

"But I don't know that I can write stories" I said, honestly enough, thinking that in her view, after her review of me, anyhow, those were her secret sentiments. Whereupon she turned on me, and said no one else could write stories except me – *Kew Gardens* the right 'gesture', a turning point. "Well but *Night and Day?*" I said, though I hadn't meant to speak of it. "An amazing achievement" she said. "Why, we've not had such a thing since I don't know when –" "But I thought you didn't like it?" Then she said she could pass an examination in it. Would I come and talk about it – lunch – so I'm going to lunch; but what does her reviewing mean then? Anyhow, once more as keenly as ever I feel a common certain understanding between us.

Saturday 5 June
I've gone back into winter clothes; its bitter windy; and the sun sparks and glints instead of burning. It burnt on Derby Day though – the day I lunched with Katherine and had two hours of priceless talk – priceless in the sense that to no one else can I talk in the same disembodied way about writing; without altering my thought more than I alter it in writing here. (I except L. from this.) We talked about books, writing of course: my own. Then I said "You've changed. Got through something"; indeed there's a sort of self command about her as if having mastered something subterfuges were no longer so necessary. She told me of her terrific experiences last winter – experience of loneliness chiefly; alone in a stone house [at Ospedaletti] with caverns beneath it into which the sea rushed; how she lay on bed alone all day with a pistol by her; and men banged at the door. Murry sent a balance sheet of his accounts; came at Christmas with plum pudding and curd cheese; "Now I'm here, its all right". Then she went to him for assurance; didn't get it; and will never look for that particular quality again. I see what she means, vaguely. She is nervous about her book coming out; fearing lest she hasn't done enough. Anyhow, I enjoyed myself; and this fragmentary intermittent intercourse of mine seems more fundamental than many better established ones.

Tuesday 8 June
One of my field days yesterday – National Gallery – there met Clive – ices at Gunters – dine with Nessa. My drive to Waterloo on top of a bus [was] very vivid. A bright night; with a fresh breeze. An old beggar woman, blind, sat against a stone wall in Kingsway holding a brown mongrel in her arms and sang aloud. There was a recklessness about her; much in the spirit of London. Defiant – almost gay, clasping her dog as if for warmth. How many Junes has she sat there, in the heart of London? How she came to be there, what scenes she can go through, I can't imagine. O damn it all, I say, why can't I know all that too? Perhaps it was the song at night that seemed

strange; she was singing shrilly, but for her own amusement, not begging. Then the fire engines came by – shrill too; with their helmets pale yellow in the moonlight. Sometimes everything gets into the same mood; how to define this one I don't know – It was gay, and yet terrible and fearfully vivid. Nowadays I'm often overcome by London; even think of the dead who have walked in the city. Perhaps one might visit the churches. The view of the grey white spires from Hungerford Bridge brings it to me; and yet I can't say what 'it' is.

Thursday 17 June

Today is Cup Day at Ascot; which I think marks the highest tide of the finest society's greatest season – all superlatives that mean little to me – save as I catch the hum of wheels in Piccadilly on a fine afternoon, and passing carriages look in and see powdered faces like jewels in glass cases. One must be young to feel the stir of it. Yet the fine weather gives us too our sudden acceleration: dinner parties; Memoir Club; invitations; coming one on top of another.

I lunched at Gordon Square for Roger's show: got stuffed in the head with wine and talk and sat there not very comfortably. A toast to Roger missed fire somewhat – so, I fear do the pictures, which fill three rooms garishly, as with coloured sheets of tin, not one being yet bought. Lytton and I stood in a window, and he told me how he lived for ambition; he wants influence not fame; not Maynard's influence, but the influence of some old gentleman on whose 80th birthday people present addresses – he wants to deal little words that poison vast monsters of falsehood. This I declared to be unattainable. But I believe it to be what he wishes. Tea at Gunters; dinner at Nessa's; and so home, a little bruised about the lips, thirsty for a great draught of solitude, which was not given me; since we dined next with the Murrys, next with Roger, and last night had the Memoir Club here, of which I'm too sleepy to give any notice.

Wednesday 23 June

Poor Roger has only sold three or four sketches. There the innumerable pictures hang, like ugly girls at a dance, and no one bids a penny piece. According to Nessa, he can talk of nothing else, and they're at their wits ends to say the right things – since what is to be said, save that bad pictures don't sell?

Tuesday 29 June

Back from Rodmell, which was disappointing, as if held to our lips the cup of pleasure was dashed from them. One day was consumed by Saxon and Barbara. Poor Barbara has the fixed lines of premature maturity. Such a grind and a drudge her life is as fills me with pity – For she seemed to have no choice. First Nick, then the child – and all her lines laid down for her for life, by the hand of fate, for she can't leap them. Our generation is daily scourged by the bloody war. Even I scribble reviews instead of novels because of the thick skulls at Westminster and Berlin. Saxon was airy and sprightly. The kitchen a success I think, but then I'm not a cook.

Tuesday 6 July
Too much to write as usual, but we work like navvies at binding Morgan [*The Story of the Siren*], and have no time for frivolity. Festivities get wedged in where convenient. It looks as though Morgan might boom, though I don't, as a critic, see altogether what the reason is.

Tuesday 13 July
Oh the servants! Oh reviewing! Nelly has vacillated between tears and laughter, life and death for the past ten days; can't feel an ache anywhere without sending for me or L. to assure her that aches are not certainly fatal. Then she cries. Never, never, never will she get over it, she says. The doctor comes. Innumerable pills and draughts consumed. Sweats, sleepless nights, recur. And nothing the matter save what one of us would call an upset inside and take a pill for. This drives us to accept invitations, since if anyone comes here, the atmosphere lowers. But where have we been? Indeed I see myself cutting covers incessantly.

Now for Oh reviewing! – Three weeks I think have passed without a word added to *Jacob*. How is one to bring it through at this rate. Yet its all my fault – why should I do *The Cherry Orchard* and Tolstoy for Desmond, why take up the Plumage Bill for Ray? But after this week I do no more.

MONKS HOUSE, RODMELL

Monday 2 August
Bank Holiday. I'm in the middle of baking a cake, and fly to this page for refuge, to fill in moments of baking and putting in my bread. Our season ended unexpectedly; the blind falling with the light still in the sky. If I were not ashamed of my egotism, I could give a literal meaning to my metaphor – seeing that I had to leave Nessa's great party at 11 in order to be home, not to disturb L., and be ready for packing and going next morning. Poor L., utterly driven for a month at last confessed to feeling tired, and was indeed on the verge of destruction. As a hobby, the Hogarth Press is clearly too lively and lusty to be carried on in this private way any longer. Moreover, the business part of it can't be shared, owing to my incompetence.

The future, therefore, needs consideration. This being so, we fled a week earlier than intended. On Monday I went up, to say good bye to Katherine Mansfield, was inveigled into a night at 46 [Gordon Square] and could write many pages on my reflections on sleeping in London again. The ease and rapidity of life in London a good deal impressed me – everything near at hand, to be compassed between lunch and tea, without setting out and making a job of it. Katherine asked me to review her book; I cried off on the ground that to review spoils the reading. They are coming to Eastbourne, so my farewell is deferred.

Thursday 5 August
I write *Jacob* every morning now, feeling each day's work like a fence I have to ride at, my heart in my mouth till its over, and I've cleared, or knocked the bar out. (Another image, unthinking it was one.)

Tuesday 10 August
I have spent the whole afternoon yellow washing the earth closet. I can now reckon up my labours: dining room distempered and cleaned; bannisters painted blue; stairs white; and now the earth closet. Coming home on Sunday, a hot still day, Leonard initiated a scheme for the future of the Press. We are going to offer [Ralph] Partridge a share in it, baiting this perhaps minute titbit with the plumper morsel of secretaryship to L. About the middle of dinner L. developed this further: why not buy a complete printing outfit? Why not? Run a shop too, perhaps. Ramifications spring unceasingly from this centre. Its a pleasant thing, come autumn, to make plans. Nelly still mysteriously diseased, and that being so we implore her to stay away –

Friday 20 August
Mrs Dedman cajoled us there by calling it a Sussex funeral, and promised that the bearers would wear smock frocks. But only six were to be found in the village; so the plan was given up; Mr Stacey was lowered to his grave by black farm labourers, two of whom managed to tumble into the grave as they lowered him. Smock frocks exist however, as she proved by showing us grandfather's, and a fine piece of stitchery it is, with a pattern appropriate to Rodmell, distinct from all other villages. The entire male population of Kingston village came out of church after the coffin; brown faces, white hairs, showing on top of coal black coats. The clergy acted with such portentous gloom that even now I daresay they scarcely feel comfortable. The day was cold; a thunder shower purple in the sky. As usual the service seemed chill, awkward, unmanageable; everyone subduing their natural feelings, and seeming to play a part because the others did.

The coffin was a pale grey, wreaths attached by strings. Whether the Catholic form is warmer, I know not. I saw one man shredding a few grains of dust at the right moment. But the ceremonial spirit is entirely absent. We never catch fire. Then the awkwardness of old Sunday coats and hats. I feel Sunday clinging to my clothes like the smell of camphor.

Wednesday 25 August

For the third time this summer, I went to London on Monday, paid five shillings for a plate of ham, and said goodbye to Katherine. I had my euphemism at parting; about coming again before she goes; but it is useless to extend these farewell visits, and after all, visits can't do away with the fact that she goes for two years, is ill, and heaven knows when we shall meet again. These partings make one pinch oneself as if to make sure of feeling. Do I feel this as much as I ought? Am I heartless? And then, after noting my own callousness, of a sudden comes the blankness of not having her to talk to. So on my side the feeling is genuine. She wants to live in an Italian town and have tea with the doctor. But we propose to write to each other – She will send me her diary. Shall we? Will she? If I were left to myself I should; being the simpler, the more direct of the two. Strange how little we know our friends.

So I missed my train; and what I wanted most in the world was to catch it and travel back with L.

Tuesday 31 August

The last day of August – and what a day! November in the city without the lights. Then the schoolchildren singing, and as I write Lottie chatter-chattering – so I'm out of mood. Detestable grey sky – life has too few days to waste them thus. I must walk my temper off upon the downs. But first I've Partridge and Carrington to deal with. Another step has been taken in life: we have a partner and a secretary at a cost of £100. Rash, I suppose; but then what's the point of life if one's not rash? Anyhow we step out boldly, and if the Press is to live, it had better run a risk or two. The young man, aged twenty-six, just left Oxford, is a superb body – shoulders like tough oak; health tingling beneath his skin. Merry shrewd eyes. He has been religious; is now socialistic; literature I don't suppose counts for much: he's written an essay on Milton, which Carrington was not struck by. Carrington is ardent, robust, scatterbrained, appreciative, a very humble disciple, but with enough character to prevent insipidity. A little ashamed of Partridge, I thought her. But what shoulders! what thickness of bone! Well, how will it turn out? What shall we print?

Wednesday 8 September

Lytton, Mary, Clive, came here yesterday, discussed immortality; and I find my bid for it is as letter writer. What about poor *Jacob* then? and hadn't I better drive my pen through sheets that pay of a morning, in the intervals of writing letters? Oh vanity, vanity! how it grows on me – how I swear to crush it out – Learn French is the only thing I can think of. Then I didn't like Mary; she saying sharp things and then hard, and I unable to say out loud 'Well then, why come and sit on my lawn?' Why does she? L. at tea put me right: Mary Hutchinson is one of the few people I dislike, I said. No: he replied: one of the many you dislike and like alternately.

Wednesday 15 September

Nelly by the way has now had, I suppose, every organ in her body examined, and is pronounced healthy with the exception of her teeth. So that shot of mine seems the true one.

Lytton has been with us from Friday to Tuesday. We walked all the way to Kingston, talking, back over the flats, talking. Save for shadows that cross and leave him ruffled, he is now uniformly amiable. At night we had the first two or three chapters of [*Queen*] *Victoria* – Disgraceful to say I was twice overcome with sleep, owing to our wood fire; but the liveliness of it is such as to make one forget whether its good or not. I don't know what qualities it has. I suspect it depends too much upon amusing quotations, and is too much afraid of dulness to say anything out of the way. Not at all a meditative or profound book; on the other hand, a remarkably composed and homogeneous book. A miracle in the matter of condensation and composition I suspect. But we are to read it when done. Blessed with fine weather, I could look from my window, through the vine leaves, and see Lytton sitting in the deck chair reading. He wore a white felt hat, and the usual grey clothes; was long and tapering as usual; looking so mild and ironical, his beard just cut short. As usual, I got my various impressions: of suavity, a gentle but inflexible honesty; lightning speed; something peevish and exacting; something incessantly living, suffering, reflecting moods. Still he can withdraw in that supercilious way that used to gall me; still show himself superior to me, contemptuous of me – of my morality that is, not of my mind. Well, I can walk and talk with him by the hour.

Sunday 19 September

Eliot is separated only by the floor from me. The odd thing about Eliot is that his eyes are lively and youthful when the cast of his face and the shape of his sentences is formal and even heavy. Rather like a sculptured face – no upper lip; formidable, powerful, pale. Then those hazel eyes seeming to escape from the rest of him. We talked – America, Ottoline, aristocracy, printing, Squire, Murry, critics. "And I behaved like a priggish pompous little ass" was one of his comments upon his own manner at Garsington. He is decidedly of the generation beneath us – I daresay superior – younger, though.

Monday 20 September

To go on with Eliot, as if one were making out a scientific observation – he left last night directly after dinner. He improved as the day went on; laughed more openly; became nicer. I kept myself from being submerged, though feeling the waters rise once or twice. I mean by this that he completely neglected my claims to be a writer, and had I been meek, I suppose I should have gone under – felt him and his views dominant and subversive. He is a consistent specimen of his type, which is opposed to ours. Unfortunately the living writers he admires are Wyndham Lewis and Pound – Joyce too, but there's more to be said on this head. He told me he was more interested in people than in anything. He can't read Wordsworth when Wordsworth deals with nature. His turn is for caricature. He wants to write a verse play in which the four characters of Sweeney act the parts. Now he wants to describe externals. Joyce gives internals. His novel *Ulysses* presents the life of man in sixteen incidents, all taking place (I think) in one day. This, so far as he has seen it, is extremely brilliant, he says. Perhaps we shall try to publish it. Joyce himself is an insignificant man, wearing very thick eyeglasses, a little like Shaw to look at, dull, self-centred, and perfectly self assured. There is much to be said about Eliot from different aspects; his mind is not yet blunted or blurred. He wishes to write precise English; but catches himself out in slips; and if anyone asked him whether he meant what he said, he would have to say no, very often. Now in all this L. showed up much better than I did; but I didn't much mind.

Sunday 26 September

But I think I minded more than I let on; for somehow *Jacob* has come to a stop, in the middle of that party too, which I enjoyed so much. Eliot coming on the heel of a long stretch of writing fiction (two months without a break) made me listless; cast shade upon me; and the mind when engaged upon fiction wants all its boldness and self-confidence. He said nothing – but I reflected how what I'm doing is probably better done by Mr Joyce. Then I began to wonder what it is that I am doing: to suspect, as is usual in such cases, that I have not thought my plan out plainly enough – so to dwindle, niggle, hesitate – which means that one's lost.

Went to Charleston for the night; and had a vivid sight of Maynard by lamplight – like a gorged seal, double chin, ledge of red lip, little eyes, sensual, brutal, unimaginative: one of those visions that come from a chance attitude, lost so soon as he turned his head. I suppose though it illustrates something I feel about him.

Eliot has sent me his poems, and hopes to maintain contact during the winter.

Friday 1 October
Here we are at the last day; the boxes with apples standing open – Yes, undoubtedly the best summer so far, in spite of execrable weather, no bath, one servant, and an earth closet down a winding glade. To that verdict we both set our hands. Even the schoolchildren's voices, if one thinks of them as swifts and martins skirling round the eaves, exhilarate instead of annoying. We now give them apples, rejecting their pence, and requiring in return that they shall respect the orchard. They had already stripped several trees. Nelly, by the way, returns. I must try to say nothing sharp, though inclined to. After all, without education, -- there are excuses.

One of the charms of Rodmell is the human life: everyone does the same thing at the same hour. Everyone is in his, or their garden; lamps are lit, but people like the last daylight. What I mean is that we are a community.

HOGARTH HOUSE, RICHMOND

Monday 18 October
This is a long break, and perhaps I should not fill it now if it were not that I am in from the Club, and can't settle to anything. Yet we have been back seventeen days, have seen a number of people, and harboured more thoughts than there are words in my mind. Who have we seen? The usual people, Nessa and Duncan, Clive, Mary, Stracheys, Stephens, Ka, Arnold-Forsters, – Kot, too, who came to bring us Tchekhov, and was so excited over it and other projects as to twang like a fiddle, instead of solemnly resounding as usual like a full barrel of beer. We are well launched upon the work of the Press. Partridge – Ralph I should call him -- is putting his ox's shoulder to the wheel, and intends to do 'hurricane' business. We are bringing out *Three Stories* by L.; my book [*Monday or Tuesday*]; (printed for an experiment by McDermott): and have in view Tchekhov, Eliot, Roger, possibly Lytton's essays.

Monday 25 October
(first day of winter time). Why is life so tragic; so like a little strip of pavement over an abyss? I look down; I feel giddy; I wonder how I am ever to walk to the end. But why do I feel this? Now that I say it I don't feel it. The fire burns; we are going to hear *The Beggar's Opera*. Only it lies

about me; I can't keep my eyes shut. It's a feeling of impotence: of cutting no ice. Here I sit at Richmond, and like a lantern stood in the middle of a field my light goes up in darkness. Melancholy diminishes as I write. Why then don't I write it down oftener? Well, one's vanity forbids. I want to appear a success even to myself. Yet I don't get to the bottom of it. Its having no children, living away from friends, failing to write well, spending too much on food, growing old – I think too much of the whys and wherefores; too much of myself. I don't like time to flap round me. Well then, work. Yes, but I so soon tire of work – can't read more than a little, an hour's writing is enough for me. Out here no one comes in to waste time pleasantly. If they do, I'm cross. The labour of going to London is too great. Nessa's children grow up, and I can't have them in to tea, or go to the Zoo. Pocket money doesn't allow of much. Yet I'm persuaded that these are trivial things: its life itself, I think sometimes, for us in our generation so tragic – no newspaper placard without its shriek of agony from some one. Unhappiness is everywhere: just beyond the door; or stupidity which is worse. Still I don't pluck the nettle out of me. To write *Jacob's Room* again will revive my fibres, I feel. And with it all how happy I am – if it weren't for my feeling that it is a strip of pavement over an abyss.

Wednesday 10 November
Nessa's room at Gordon Square is becoming what the drawing room at 46 was five or six years ago. I go there and find that astonishing brightness in the heart of darkness. Julian coming in with his French lesson; Angelica hung with beads, riding on Roger's foot; Clive claret coloured and yellow like a canary; Duncan vague in the background, sitting astride a chair, looking with blurred eyes rather dimly. Altogether I sometimes feel that not to have a refuge here would be a bad thing – I don't know. Ralph hints at a plan of sharing a London house with us – which tempts me, on some days.

Sunday 13 November
L. now translating Tchekhov, and I must set to on my share, I suppose. Ralph comes twice a week or so, an indomitable, perhaps rather domineering, young man; loves dancing; in the pink of health; a healthy brain.

Tuesday 23 November
We see too many people for me to describe them, had I the time. I have lived the past two weeks methodically, printing till dark, allowing myself a day off, arranging things rather successfully; so my strip of pavement (I bag that phrase for *Jacob*) widens.

Sunday 5 December
The Memoir Club was fearfully brilliant – I mean I was; and Leonard so much more impressive with so much less pains; and Morgan very professional; and Mary never laughed once at my jokes. Well, I shall laugh loud at hers next Wednesday to make up. Eliot and Goldie dined here t'other night – a successful party. A cold in the head made me desperate like wine – nothing seemed to matter. I laughed in the grim marble face and got a twinkle back. What a big white face he has beside Goldie's mobile brown monkey one! A mouth twisted and shut; not a single line free and easy; all caught, pressed, inhibited; but great driving power somewhere – and my word what concentration of the eye when he argues! We discussed criticism, and I find he thinks himself a poet. A little human laughter comes very welcome to him, as I guess, and I think he would willingly break up his formal ways. My guess is that he wishes to detach himself from sets, and welcomes us as an escape. Then – what? Gerald Duckworth engaged – does that count as news? dinner at the Toynbees, but I can't go into that. What do I want to go into? How hard we work – that's what impresses me this winter: every compartment stuffed tight, chiefly owing to the press. Whether we can keep it up, I don't know. Then both so popular, so well known, so much respected – and Leonard forty, and I nearing it, so there's not much to boast of. In my heart, too, I prefer the nondescript anonymous days of youth. I like youthful minds; and the sense that no one's yet anybody.

Sunday 12 December
Nearing the end of the year. Everything muffled in snow and crisp with frost, streets knobbed and slippery; hands grimy as cold for some reason always makes them. Here we sit over the fire, expecting Roger – whose book is out; as everyone's book is out – Katherine's, Murry's, Eliot's. None have I read so far.

Scenes now come to mind. Gordon Square at tea time – All those branches twisting themselves so fluently, like the Laocoon; so I saw them from Ralph's upper room. Then there's Lytton coming round to tea. At once we plunge, even on the cold pavement, into literature. So we pace to Nessa's door. And Ralph? Well, I wouldn't marry Ralph – A despot. True. But what's to happen to Carrington? She can't live indefinitely with me – Perhaps with him? Door opens, in I go; up I go; children there; sit over the stove; Nessa draws pictures for Angelica. And home again.

Molly Hamilton next. I'm enlarging my sphere, not very widely, but I take pains to accept what's offered. When accepted, I feel that I must make the most. It's not for nothing that I go out to tea. So there we sit, scratching on the match box. "I'm assistant editor to the *Review of Reviews* – at a salary of £570!" she cried. And so her mother can live in London; and she's launched; poor Molly can do all this by chaining herself to the desk. There the desk was and books laid out as you see them in shops. Did the match burst into flame? Yes, I think so, about happiness, and human beings. I forget my first view of Molly, going down the Strand the night of the Cenotaph; such a lurid scene, like one in Hell. A soundless street; no traffic; but people marching. Clear, cold, and windless. A bright light in the Strand; women crying Remember the Glorious Dead, and holding out chrysanthemums. Always the sound of feet on the pavement. Faces bright and lurid – poor Molly's worn enough by that illumination. I touched her arm; whereupon she jumped, like some one woken. A ghastly procession of people in their sleep.

Sunday 19 December
I ought to say how happy I am, since one of these pages said how unhappy I was. I can't see any reason in it. My only guess is that it has something to do with working steadily; writing things out of my head; and never having a compartment empty. I can't help suspecting that both Mr and Mrs Woolf slowly increase in fame; that helps to fill compartments. My book seems to me rather good. L.'s book seems to him (so I interpret) rather good. I am entreated to write for the *TLS*.

So we reach the end of the year; which is for us cheerful, I think. For one thing we want to get to Rodmell; to see what has happened to the garden. I shall like a soft grey walk. Then the post. Then reading. Then sitting in the chimney corner. We take the servants and ensure comfort, for by contriving it, we're now on the best of terms with them. Left to myself I should invite people down – then probably regret it. But this is dawdling and rambling – never mind – this poor book must take what it can get and be thankful. (I use my new blotter, just given me by L., for the first time.)

1921

During the first half of 1921, besides working on Jacob's Room, *Virginia was as usual making frequent contributions to journals, although one of her favoured outlets, the* Athenaeum, *was now ceasing its independent existence owing to the decision of its editor, Middleton Murry, to join his ailing wife Katherine Mansfield abroad. In February Virginia attended his farewell dinner in Gordon Square.*

In 1920 Leonard had been selected as the Labour Party candidate for the Combined Universities' parliamentary seat, and though in general he pursued the attendant fatigues of this calling without Virginia's physical support, in March this year she accompanied him to Manchester when he addressed his potential constituents in the University there. And soon afterwards they took the train to spend Easter in her beloved Cornwall.

By early June Virginia's energetic social, literary and printing activities had brought her to a state of collapse, which necessitated a period of rest and quiet. After a further two months' summer break at Monks House, she returned to Richmond early in October, and finished Jacob's Room *a month later, though a further eight months were to elapse before she considered it fit to show to Leonard.*

This autumn, after summer holidays spent at Charleston, Vanessa with her children and Duncan had decamped to St Tropez where Roger Fry also was staying, thus removing one segment of Virginia's intimate circle; but there were other friends to see, walks to take in Richmond Park, more reviewing for the TLS, *and the ever-present demands of the Hogarth Press which, with the advent of their new assistant Ralph Partridge and of a new printing machine, increased rather than diminished. The Woolfs found themselves ineluctably becoming professional publishers, although most of the necessary operations – type-setting, stitching, binding, and still some of the actual printing – were carried out by themselves in the living rooms of their home. Virginia's own* Monday or Tuesday, *published early in April, was a characteristic product of this period. And their second collaboration with Koteliansky,* The Note Books and Reminiscences of Anton Tchekhov *by Maxim Gorky, also published in April, attracted a wider renown and brought further manuscripts to the Hogarth Press. However the problems attendant on such success – in particular the need for a working assistant – became a perennial source of strain. The regular presence of Ralph Partridge (who this year succeeded in persuading Carrington to marry him) in their house and at mealtimes grew more and more trying to the Woolfs; and though Virginia admired his vitality and enjoyed his confidences, they became less and less convinced of its benefits.*

1921

Hogarth House, Richmond

Tuesday 25 January

Here have I waited twenty-five days before beginning the new year; and the twenty-five is, not unfortunately my twenty-fifth, but my thirty-ninth birthday; and we've had tea, and calculated the costs of printing Tchekhov; now L. is folding the sheets of his book, and Ralph has gone. I'm at a crisis in *Jacob*: want to finish in 20,000 words, written straight off in a frenzy. And I must pull myself together to bring it off. Lytton has asked to dedicate *Victoria* to me, which pleases me, and I stipulate, from vanity, for my name in full.

Monday 31 January

Just back from Tidmarsh, from the Club, from Harrison's [dentist], from losing two books on a bus. Lytton keeps his books amazingly tidy, like books on the stage. L. much depressed on Sunday morning and working out how many hours remained, before breakfast. Indeed, Saturday night was hard going. Lytton lapsed into gentle indifference, tired, depressed perhaps. Carrington I think grows older, and her doings are of the sort that age. Next day was better. Carrington and Ralph tactfully made out lists of summer flowers in the dining room. "You ought to have dedicated *Victoria* to Carrington" I said. "Oh dear no – we're not on those terms at all." "Ottoline will be enraged" I said. Yes, he thought she might be. The manuscript was there, and once I began reading it, I couldn't stop myself. Talk of going to Italy at Easter with the party but – One of the 'buts' is the Press. I sometimes think that L. and I are settling in too soundly. And now, am I to learn Russian with him and Kot? If he can read it and solace his age with it I shall be furious. But I'm broiling as I write and can't settle to anything, and detest going away, and vow never to do it, but to work, work, work –

Saturday 5 February
Jealousy or ambition has won the day, and I've just had my first Russian lesson and mortgaged my time to the extent of doing three lessons weekly. L. is mumbling Russian as I write. Have I done a great deal of work in pursuance of my vow? Books begin to drop in, and so long as I can do them every other week I rather like the relief from *Jacob*; I am beginning the last lap; and it is a sprint towards the end, difficult to keep up.

Wednesday 16 February
Russian is snatching all the time spared for this book. I can only keep up with L. by running as hard as I can. Everyone prophesies an early end. But I feel myself attached to an express train. With Kot and Leonard dragging me, I must be pulled through somehow.

   We have dined twice at the Cock [Tavern]. Pale, marmoreal Eliot was there last week, like a chapped office boy on a high stool with a cold in his head, until he warms a little, which he did. We walked back along the Strand. "The critics say I am learned and cold" he said. "The truth is I am neither." As he said this, I think coldness at least must be a sore point with him. Then there was Murry's farewell dinner at 46 [Gordon Square]. I sat next Murry. He posed, I thought; looked anguished and martyred. Then, at the end, I asked after Katherine. Poor man! he poured himself out. We sat on after the others had gone. Apparently she is worse – dying? God knows. She is desperately depressed, thinks her book bad, can't write. Murry asked me to write to her. She feels herself out of things, left alone, forgotten. As he spoke with great feeling, and seemed to be very miserable, I liked him, felt with him, and think there can be no doubt that his love for Katherine anyhow is sincere.

Friday 18 February
I have been long meaning to write a historical disquisition on the return of peace; for old Virginia will be ashamed to think what a chatterbox she was, always talking about people, never about politics. Moreover, she will say, the times you lived through were so extraordinary. They must have appeared so, even to quiet women living in the suburbs. But indeed nothing happens at one moment rather than another. The history books will make it much more definite than it is. The most significant sign of peace this year is the sales; just over; the shops have been flooded with cheap clothes. Pre-war prices, so they say. Food has fallen a penny here, a penny there, but our books scarcely show a change. Servant girls aged twenty get £45 wages. And *The Times* pays me three guineas instead of two for a column. But I think you'll find all this written more accurately in other books, my dear Virginia: for instance in Mrs Gosse's diary and Mrs Webb's. I think it

true to say that during the past two months we have perceptibly moved towards cheapness – *just* perceptibly. It is just perceptible too that there are very few wounded soldiers abroad in blue, though stiff legs, single legs, sticks shod with rubber, and empty sleeves are common enough. Also at Waterloo I sometimes see dreadful looking spiders propelling themselves along the platform - men all body, legs trimmed off close to the body. There are few soldiers about.

To change the subject, Rose Macaulay dined here last week – something like a lean sheep dog in appearance – harum scarum – humble – too much of a professional, yet just on the intellectual side of the border. Might be religious though: mystical perhaps. Not at all dominating or impressive; I daresay she observes more than one thinks for. Clear pale mystical eyes. A kind of faded moon of beauty: oh and badly dressed.

Monday 21 February
We dined with Roger the other night; and found Sydney [Waterlow]. After dinner we turned over sketches in the studio – not the pleasantest occupation for a cold night. Still old Roger has a quality of imagination which attracts me - loose and warm and genuine, in contrast to the costive judicial Sydney, who was catching us out all the time. Sydney looks melancholy; is touched with grey. This gives him an air of distinction. Then we had Quentin and Julian for Sunday, packed Julian home with a temperature, and I put him to bed. Quentin ran in to see Angelica. I liked to think of all this set going in the younger generation.

Tuesday 1 March
We came back from Rodmell yesterday; and Rodmell was all gold and sunshine. The one dismal element was provided by the human race. We went to tea at the Rectory. My book [*Monday or Tuesday*] is back from the printer, who has added the final eyesore – a brown back. There it is in masses, and I can't read it, for fear of howlers, printer's as well as writer's.

Morgan goes to India, and I think for ever. He will become a mystic, sit by the roadside, and forget Europe, which I think he half despises. In thirty years time he may turn up again, give us an amused look, and return to the East, having written a little unintelligible poetry. He has no roots here. And the news made me melancholy. I like him, and like having him about. But we shan't see him again. He sails on Friday.

Sunday 6 March
But perhaps I colour my view of Morgan from my painter's box. At any rate, Bob [Trevelyan] at the Cock the other night made it all seem very reasonable and desirable – "a trip to India just the thing for him – a relief

after his ... well, his mother is trying sometimes – very fond of him of course; devoted to him and he ..." This in the usual Bob style, hinting little defects and mysteries with one corner of his mouth, praising with the other.

Nessa approves of *Monday or Tuesday* – mercifully; and thus somewhat redeems it in my eyes. But now I wonder a little what the reviewers will make of it – this time next month. The general line will be that I am becoming too much in love with the sound of my own voice; not much in what I write; indecently affected; a disagreeable woman. The truth is, I expect, that I shan't get very much attention anywhere.

Sunday 13 March

Eliot dines here tonight, alone, since his wife is in a nursing home, not much to our regret. But what about Eliot? Will he become 'Tom'? What happens with friendships undertaken at the age of forty? Do they flourish and live long? I suppose a good mind endures, and one is drawn to it, owing to having a good mind myself. Not that Tom admires my writing, damn him.

Nessa has influenza; slightly; and I'm glad to see how solicitous dear old Duncan is, waiting on her, and taking thought for her, better I think than Clive ever did.

Friday 18 March

Just back from two days at Manchester. I fancied myself writing this account, and how good it would be; what lots of things I had to say; and now the pen brings blankness. Well I was kept awake by business men talking in slow steady almost continuous voices in the room above till 1.30; and we were up early, breakfasted and caught a train, and so home, travelling all through the great rocky moors of Derbyshire – places so solitary they might be eighteenth century England; great sweeps of country all sunny and gloomy with bare rocks against the sky; and then behold a row of east end slum houses, with a strip of pavement and two factory chimneys set down in the midst. The houses are all stone, bleak, soot stained, different from our cottages; not cottages at all, but streets. Suddenly, in the palm of a wide valley you come on a complete town – gasworks, factories, and little streams made to run over stone steps and turn engines I suppose. "Yes" I said to Mrs Unwin, "Derbyshire is a very fine country." We were standing in a pit at the University, below us a row of chairs, on which sat Professors Unwin, Findlay, Goldman (a financier) and Weiss. Leonard then got up and made his speech, a very vigorous one. We sat round on hard benches, with ink pots, or the holes for them, in front of us.

All Manchester streets are the same, and all strung with tramlines. You hear bells striking all the time. Then there are no tea shops, but great cafés; and no little shops, but all big drapers. Then there's Queen Victoria, like a large tea cosy, and Wellington, sleek as a mastiff with paw extended; none of this was quite English, or at least London. The people were lower middle class, no sprinkling of upper class. But my observation of the university type was more profound. Mr and Mrs Weiss gave a dinner in the refectory before L.'s second speech; and there they all were – professors and wives, elderly people, depressed looking, with the manner of dons, but not the extreme confident eccentricity of first rate brains. But how supercilious I thought myself, and ultimately how much pure merit seemed in them. The women were dowdy; oh yes, but they too had fought for the right. Professor Unwin told me he had been arrested three times for attending seditious meetings during the war. Mrs Weiss said her husband had resigned because the University refused to accept a Conscientious Objector, upon which they thought the better of it. And yet there is no surface brilliancy; not a scrap of romance. It is a little familiar professional society, trying to keep up the standards, which (perhaps wrongly) I suppose must be hard work in Manchester, or am I merely snobbish in thinking it harder to say clever things and write clever books in Manchester than in Cambridge? Old Mrs Herford and Professor Findlay sat patiently looking at the tablecloth with nothing to say, like two old horses who have been working in the fields all day together. L., in the large room after dinner, was emphatically first rate. "Are you a politician?" they asked me. "Do you do much organising work?" I said I listened. Why was I there then? Oh for the fun of spending ten pounds in Manchester and seeing the Zoo. So we went to the Zoo; and I daresay I could write something interesting about that – a pale stone desert given over to charwomen and decorators; a few bears; a mandrill, and a fox or two – all in the desolation of depression.

Tuesday 22 March
Here we are on the verge of going to Cornwall. This time tomorrow we shall be stepping onto the platform at Penzance, sniffing the air, looking for our trap, and then – Good God! – driving off across the moors to Zennor – Why am I so incredibly and incurably romantic about Cornwall? One's past, I suppose; I see children running in the garden. A spring day. Life so new. People so enchanting. The sound of the sea at night. And now I go back 'bringing my sheaves' – well, Leonard, and almost forty years of life, all built on that, permeated by that: how much so I could never explain.

ZENNOR, CORNWALL

Wednesday 30 March
This is the last evening, and L. is packing, and I'm not in the mood for
writing, but feel superstitiously that I should like to read something actually
written in Cornwall. By looking over my left shoulder I see gorse yellow
against the Atlantic blue. And we've been lying on the Gurnard's Head, on
beds of samphire among grey rocks with buttons of yellow lichen on them.
You look down onto the semi-transparent water -- the waves all scrambled
into white round the rocks -- gulls swaying on bits of seaweed -- rocks now
dry now drenched with white waterfalls pouring down crevices. We took
a rabbit path round the cliff, and I find myself a little shakier than I used
to be. Still however maintaining without force to my conscience that this
is the loveliest place in the world.

HOGARTH HOUSE, RICHMOND

Friday 8 April
Ten minutes to eleven a.m. And I ought to be writing *Jacob's Room*; I can't,
and instead I shall write down the reason why I can't -- this diary being a
kindly blank faced old confidante. Well, you see, I'm a failure as a writer;
my book [*Monday or Tuesday*] out (prematurely) and nipped, a damp
firework. A short notice [in the *TLS*] scrambled through, put in an obscure
place, rather scrappy, complimentary enough, but quite unintelligent.
I mean by that that they don't see that I'm after something interesting.
So that makes me suspect that I'm not. Oh and Lytton's book is out
and takes up three columns: praise, I suppose. My temper sank and sank
till for half an hour I was as depressed as I ever am. To rub this in
we had a festival party at 41 [Gordon Square]: to congratulate Lytton;
which was all as it should be; but then he never mentioned my book;
and for the first time I have not his praise to count on. What depresses
me is the thought that I have ceased to interest people -- at the very
moment when, by the help of the Press, I thought I was becoming more
myself.
    Roger is staying with us. I think he has the nicest nature among us -- so
open, sincere, and entirely without meanness; always generous, I think,
and somehow hearty? He throws out a tremendous laugh. We went to the
Bedford Music Hall last night, and saw Miss Marie Lloyd, a mass of
corruption -- long front teeth -- a crapulous way of saying 'desire', and yet
a born artist -- scarcely able to walk, waddling, aged, unblushing. A roar of
laughter went up when she talked of her marriage. She is beaten nightly

by her husband. I felt that the audience was much closer to drink and beating and prison than any of us. The coal strike is on.

Sunday 10 April

I must note the symptoms of the disease, so as to know it next time. The first day one's miserable: the second happy. There was an Affable Hawk on me in the *New Statesman* which at any rate made me feel important (and its that that one wants).

Tuesday 12 April

I must hurriedly note more symptoms of the disease, so that I can turn back here and medicine myself next time. Well; I'd worn through the acute stage, and come to the philosophic semi-depressed, indifferent, when L. dropped into my ear the astonishing news that Lytton thinks 'The String Quartet' 'marvellous'. This did for a moment flood every nerve with pleasure, so much so that I forgot to buy my coffee and walked over Hungerford Bridge twanging and vibrating. I'm not nearly as pleased as I was depressed; and yet in a state of security. What I had feared was that I was dismissed as negligible.

Friday 15 April

Lytton rang up this morning, and I asked him about his book. "Are you smothered in laurels?" "Well, rather depressed," he said, and so he sounded. "I'm in the middle; and then I shall write to you about it." "And I'm writing to you about yours" he answered. He's sold, so they say, 5,000 copies this week, and another edition is printing. I have sold just 300. Well, but that doesn't prove my immortality, as I insinuate. One ought to write more of this occasion, since I suppose in twenty years' time the publication of *Queen Victoria* will be thought an important matter; but these things aren't important to us.

A queer sort of stillness seems already settling down on us, as of Sunday. This is the foreboding of the General Strike. L. has just come in with a paper which says that nothing has been done to patch up the strike. Therefore at 10 tonight, unless something happens meanwhile, all trains, trams, buses, mines, and perhaps electric light works come to an end. The servants have been to the Co-ops and brought back a week's groceries. We have a bundle of candles. Our most serious lack is coal, as Nelly forgot to order any. Still, Heaven knows why, I don't believe the strike will happen.

Sunday 17 April

And I was perfectly right. The strike didn't happen. The Triple Alliance had split: the railwaymen and transport workers refusing to go on with it, and leaving the miners by themselves. Presumably the miners will have to give in, and I shall get my hot bath, and bake home made bread again; yet it seems a pity somehow, – if they're to be forced back and the mine owners triumphant. I think this is my genuine feeling, though not very profound. It is fairly obvious that working people are well enough satisfied to prefer going on working.

Monday 18 April
Just back from lunching with a Cabinet Minister. I mean, of course, Herbert Fisher. We think he asked us in order to apologise for – everything. He said he had neither the physical force nor the combativeness to carry things through. He said he hated Parliament. A political life is dull, and wastes all one's time he said; one is always listening to dull speeches, frittering time away. He leaves home at 10, gets back at 11 p.m. and then has a bundle of papers to go through. And then he was careful to explain that the public is ridiculously in the dark about everything. Only the Cabinet knows the true spring and source of things he said. That is the only solace of the work. A flood tide of business flows incessantly from all quarters of the world through Downing Street; and there are a few miserable men trying desperately to deal with it. They have to make tremendous decisions with insufficient evidence on the spur of the moment. Then he pulled himself up, and said, solemnly, that he is going to Geneva to initiate peace – disarmament. "You are the great authority upon that, I understand", he said to Leonard. Anyhow I confess it seemed to me, sitting opposite to Leonard in that brown ugly room with its autotypes of Dutch pictures, that Leonard was an authority and Herbert a thin-shredded thread paper of a man.

Friday 29 April
Every afternoon for a week I've been up to the Æolian Hall; taken my seat right at the back; put my bag on the floor and listened to Beethoven quartets. Do I dare say listened? Well, but if one gets a lot of pleasure, really divine pleasure, and knows the tunes, and only occasionally thinks of other things – surely I may say listened. We are just back from the 5th. We had tea with Lytton, Carrington and Ralph.

Tuesday 3 May
Hamilton Fyfe in the *Daily Mail* says that Leonard's story will rank with the great stories of the world. Am I jealous? Only momentarily. But the odd thing is that I immediately think myself a failure. I feel fine drawn, misty, attenuated, inhuman, bloodless and niggling out trifles that don't move people. A full stop in *Jacob*, owing partly to depression. But I must pull together and finish it off. I can't read it as it is.

Sunday 15 May

Whit Sunday – dull, wet, and cold; so that on the whole we don't blame the coal strike for keeping us here over the fire instead of Monks House. By this time I think Carrington will have made up her mind one way or t'other. She must have had an odious Sunday. But still she *must* make up her mind. So I told Ralph on Friday, broaching that topic after all these months of silence. He did it himself, rather, by telling me of his gloom of the night before: his loneliness. He was very shrewd and bitter about Carrington. "She thinks herself one of the little friends of all the world" he said. Then he said she was selfish, untruthful, and quite indifferent to his suffering. So people in love always turn and rend the loved, with considerable insight too. He was speaking the truth largely. But I expect he was biassed; and also I expect – and indeed told him – that he is a bit of an ogre and tyrant. He wants more control than I should care to give – control I mean of the body and mind and time and thoughts of his loved. There's his danger and her risk; so I don't much envy her making up her mind this wet Whit Sunday.

Monday 23 May

So Carrington did make up her mind to become Partridge · no, that is precisely what she is determined not to do; and signs herself aggressively Carrington for ever. If people ever took advice I should feel a little responsible for making up Ralph's mind. I mean I am not sure that this marriage is not more risky than most. Certainly she is not in love; and he has the obdurate Anglo-Indian in him. But still, if she couldn't face the prospect of a week-end breach, or of a journey alone to Italy, she had no alternative. So they were married on Saturday.

We have been to Rodmell, and as usual I come home depressed – for no reason. Merely moods. Have other people as many as I have? That I shall never know. And sometimes I suppose that even if I came to the end of my incessant search into what people are and feel I should know nothing still.

Thursday 26 May

I sat in Gordon Square yesterday for an hour and a half talking to Maynard. Sometimes I wish I put down what people say instead of describing them. The difficulty is that they say so little. Maynard said he liked praise; and always wanted to boast. He said that many men marry in order to have a wife to boast to. But, I said, its odd that one boasts considering that no one is ever taken in by it. Its odd too that you, of all people, should want praise. You and Lytton are passed beyond boasting – which is the supreme triumph. There you sit and say nothing. I love praise, he said. I want it for the things

I'm doubtful about. He was going to some official dinner. He gets £120 for an article –

Thursday 2 June
The day after Derby Day, the very height of the season, I suppose; anyhow of leaf and flower. People turn up regularly though with little planning on our part. Madge Vaughan on Friday; Kot on Saturday; Roger; Fredegond. Will these names recover anything in ten years' time of the last week of May 1921? Madge asked to come; so we had her. She is curiously changed. She has become ordinary. Yet she has her gaiety and her vitality which protect one from the worst boredom. But not Leonard or Roger. They were out of hand with misery. And this was the woman I adored! I see myself now standing in the night nursery at Hyde Park Gate, washing my hands, and saying to myself 'At this moment she is actually under this roof.'

Sunday 5 June
Murry has written against our Tchekhov in the *Nation*. As for Kot, yesterday he couldn't keep his seat for fury. He verged on the voice and language of the public house. Is Murry 'a damned swindler'? Suppose we admired Murry's writing, would he change his tune? In my theory he's all parched for praise – run mad for lack of it. Yet it goes against my psychology to think people scoundrels. I don't know – at this moment I incline to think him a damned swindler – only a swindler so plausible that he'll become Professor of English Literature in the University of Oxford.

Tuesday 7 June
Eliot, by the way, saw no truth in Murry's article. "He is extremely clever" he said. "But you don't mean that in a good sense", I said. "Oh no; not at all." And Eliot astounded me by praising *Monday or Tuesday*. This really delighted me. It pleases me to think I could discuss my writing openly with him. *Ulysses* he says is prodigious.

MONKS HOUSE, RODMELL

Monday 8 August
What a gap! How it would have astounded me to be told when I wrote the last word here, on June 7th, that within a week I should be in bed, and not entirely out of it till the 6th of August – two whole months rubbed out. These, this morning, the first words I have written – to call writing – for sixty days; and those days spent in wearisome headache, jumping pulse, aching back, frets, fidgets, lying awake, sleeping draughts, sedatives, digi-

talis, going for a little walk, and plunging back into bed again – all the horrors of the dark cupboard of illness once more displayed for my diversion. Let me make a vow that this shall never, never, happen again; and *then* confess that there are some compensations. To be tired and authorised to lie in bed is pleasant; then, scribbling 365 days of the year as I do, merely to receive without agitation of my right hand in giving out is salutary. I feel that I can take stock of things in a leisurely way. Then the dark underworld has its fascinations as well as its terrors. Later, I had my visitors, one every day; so that I saw more people than normally even. Roger, Lytton, Nessa, Duncan, Dorothy Bussy, Pippa [Strachey], Carrington, James and Alix – all these came; and were as detached portraits – cut out, emphatic, seen thus separately compared with the usual way of seeing them in crowds. Lytton, I note, is more than ever affectionate. One must be, I think, if one is famous. One must say to one's old friends 'All my celebrity is nothing – nothing – compared with this.' And that was what he did say too.

Tuesday 9 August
Nessa &c have had a splendid summer of dissipation. I don't envy it; I don't want it; I want nothing but quiet and an active brain. Yet I have a worm of uncertainty moving at the foundations of this pleasant life: cultivated voices and a cultivated dog barking wake us on Sunday mornings. The truth is, Rodmell is a colony for Georgian poets, and though I am all for letting live, and not reading their works, it is hard and indeed intolerable that I should have to let them live next door to me.

Wednesday 10 August
But how is one to arrive at the truth? I have changed the *Daily News* for the *Morning Post*. The proportions of the world at once become utterly different. The *Morning Post* has the largest letters and the double column devoted to the murder of Mrs Lindsay; Anglo-Indians, Anglo-Scots, and retired old men and patriotic ladies write letter after letter to deplore the state of the country; applaud the *Morning Post*, the only faithful standard bearer left. They lament the downfall of England, which is flourishing as usual in the *Daily News*. But the *Daily News* has become a vivacious scrapbag. News is cut up into agreeable scraps, and written in words of one syllable. I may well ask, what is truth?

Thursday 11 August
A fortnight already gone. It goes too quick – too quick. If only one could sip slowly and relish every grain of every hour! For, to speak the truth, I've thought of making my will for the first time during these past weeks.

Sometimes it seems to me that I shall never write out all the books I have in my head, because of the strain. The devilish thing about writing is that it calls upon every nerve to hold itself taut. That is exactly what I cannot do – Now if it were painting or scribbling or making patchwork quilts or mud pies, it wouldn't matter.

Thursday 18 August
Nothing to record; only an intolerable fit of the fidgets to write away. Here I am chained to my rock: forced to do nothing; doomed to let every worry, spite, irritation and obsession scratch and claw and come again. This is to say that I may not walk, and must not work. Whatever book I read bubbles up in my mind as part of an article I want to write. No one in the whole of Sussex is so miserable as I am; or so conscious of an infinite capacity of enjoyment hoarded in me, could I use it. I hear poor L. driving the lawn mower up and down, for a wife like I am should have a label to her cage. She bites! Still if one is Prometheus, if the rock is hard and the gadflies pungent, gratitude, affection, none of the nobler feelings have sway. And so this August is wasted. Only the thought of people suffering more than I do at all consoles; and that is an aberration of egotism, I suppose. Seldom penetrated by love for mankind as I am, I sometimes feel sorry for the poor who don't read Shakespeare, and indeed have felt some generous democratic humbug at the Old Vic, when they played *Othello* and all the poor men and women and children had him then for themselves. Such splendour, and such poverty. I am writing down the fidgets, so no matter if I write nonsense.

Saturday 10 September
I recovered, and we took to seeing houses – without the least success, except that the rides to and from were successful. Much more important (to me) than anything else, was my recovery of the pen; and thus the hidden stream was given exit, and I felt reborn. I started an article upon the obscure, and should have finished it today had not Lytton come. However I gained by the exchange. We talked and talked; and always dislodged some new nugget, the deeper we went. He is going to write a play, "I am going to meet my Waterloo" – that is to say he is going to have a shot at the creative. If that fails, he dooms himself to history for ever – perhaps a history of English literature. Writing is an agony, we both agreed.

Monday 12 September
It is true that we are alone again, but I cannot take up my pen, partly, I think, from superstition. I said goodbye to James and Alix [Strachey] at 9 this morning; therefore the whole day is contaminated. James remains precisely where he was – the only human being, Alix says, fit for the

contemplative life, which is the highest. To look on comprehendingly is, she says, better than to create. But James claims no such eminence. He is the least ambitious of men – low, muted, gentle, modest – selfish of course, but not blind-selfish, not at all possessive, masculine, or dominating. I caught Alix in profile and saw her old, masterly, advanced; always in the same coat and skirt, which indeed renews itself as if it were her natural covering.

Lytton, by the way, talked about s——y; and agreed that the b.'s are all namby pambies and sentimentalists. He is himself, he said. To be a b. one must be unvirile, unpossessive, very nice indeed, but tending to be sentimental. And then their tastes become so degraded.

Wednesday 14 September
There was a very great storm three nights ago. I had to light my candle for support. Next morning our plum tree was down, and a great tree snapped some feet from the ground in the churchyard. The cottagers have been busy snatching up the twigs; the larger branches belonging, perhaps, to the Rector. More rain fell that night than in the three previous months, yet L. is not satisfied. Our garden is a perfect variegated chintz: asters, plumasters, zinnias, geums, nasturtiums and so on: all bright, cut from coloured paper, stiff, upstanding as flowers should be. I have been planting wallflowers for next June.

Thursday 15 September
It is the loveliest of evenings – still; the smoke going up straight in the quarry; the white horse and strawberry coloured horse feeding close together; the women coming out of their cottages for no reason, and standing looking; the cock pecking in the midst of his hens in the meadow; starlings in the two trees; Asheham fields shorn to the colour of white corduroy; Leonard storing apples above my head. Will this recall anything? I am so anxious to keep every scrap, you see.

A letter from Morgan this morning. He seems as critical of the East as of Bloomsbury, and sits dressed in a turban watching his Prince dance, quite unimpressed. He is not impressed by *Queen Victoria* either. Flimsy, he says, compared with Macaulay, which was perhaps what I meant.

I heard from Roger the other day, all in a hubblebubble about Murry's sneering pinpricking article. He is so angry that he can talk of nothing else. We must go on doing what we like in the desert Roger says, and let Murry climb the heights, as he certainly will.

The birds are moving about like nets full of fish; they turn sideways and vanish; sideways again, and become full of black spots.

Monday 19 September
Miss Green [Leonard's secretary] has been for the week-end, and a more comfortable guest does not exist. One need not bother about her; yet, at meal times, she proves brisk and fresh. Her father was a professor, or teacher, of geology at Oxford. Her mother, a Unitarian, and a liberal, with a great admiration for Gladstone. When Minna was nine her father died. She has lived all over England; and is fearfully independent – marches about, protected by her extreme plainness, unmolested, and unnoticed; yet has a strong will of her own; and observes, and won't be put upon. She is one of the regiment of the wage earning women's republic. Now she is off to spend a fortnight in Germany – a country which she thinks very beautiful. I said there were too many signposts and plaster statues. She would have none of it.

Wednesday 28 September
Eliot's visit passed off successfully, and yet I am disappointed to find that I am no longer afraid of him –

HOGARTH HOUSE, RICHMOND

Wednesday 2 November
This was the very last thing I wrote at Rodmell – so I suppose. I ought to run over the five weeks or so left out; and really cannot; for I have seen so many people; and so much has happened; though we are where we are. A printing machine is waiting at Richmond Station, and will be delivered at 8 a.m. tomorrow. Ralph is putting his back to the wheel, a very solid obdurate back. Some of our luncheons have been stormy, or rather silent, with sudden raps of opposition from the third party. But we have got along so far. In two days' time – during the week-end at any rate – I hope to finish *Jacob*. And one of these days I must read it. We go to Rodmell on Friday. I see I can think of nothing worth saying.

Tuesday 15 November
Really, really – this is disgraceful – fifteen days of November spent and my diary none the wiser. But when nothing is written one may safely suppose that I have been stitching books; or we have had tea at 4 and I have taken my walk afterwards; or I have had to read something for next day's writing, or I have been out late. We went to Rodmell, and the gale blew at us all day; off arctic fields; so we spent our time attending to the fire. The day before this I wrote the last words of *Jacob* – on Friday November 4th to be precise, having begun it on April 16th, 1920; allowing for six months

interval due to *Monday or Tuesday* and illness, this makes about a year. I have not yet looked at it.

We dined with Clive on Friday. Aldous and Mary and Maynard there. All the time I felt Mary solicitous, even affectionate; and sure enough, as I left she took my hand, said "I don't like this plan of quarrelling" and asked me to come and see her.

Poor Lilian – poor Margaret. They sit beside the corpse of the Women's Guild; the blinds are drawn; they are sad and white, brave, tearless, but infinitely mournful. When one leaves a life work at sixty, one dies. One ought to work – never to take one's eyes from one's work; and then if death should interrupt, well, it is merely that one must get up and leave one's stitching – one won't have wasted a thought on death. Margaret says in her work one gets superannuated. One must give it up. A very cruel work then; and she is left without husband or child.

Wednesday 16 November

It is pouring; but we say Thank God it is warmer. It has been freezing for a week. We go to bed under red blankets, quilts, fur coats. But now, as I say, it is raining. I take in the *Westminster Gazette*. For some politics are beginning to interest me, as I suppose they interest City men – like a football match. One might become a virulent Socialist – or a Conservative? It is a game. I mean by that that I don't think of ends (nor does any one else) but of means. I get no letters nowadays, so I read my paper. Did I describe the advent of the Press? Nelly panic struck, thinking it would come through the kitchen floor. How do you invent these fears? I asked her. But never have we been so peaceful domestically for so long.

Friday 25 November

L.'s forty-first birthday. My apology for not writing is quite truthfully, the Hogarth Press. Roger's woodcuts, 150 copies, have been gulped down in two days. I have just finished stitching the last copies – all but six. Last week-end we spent at Tidmarsh. I remember so little; for with old, worn, creased, shabby, intimate friends, it runs so easily; no rapids, or waterfalls; room for everything; and no damned brilliance. And it was all very warm and the details – such as cups and plates – were exquisite. Carrington and Ralph have a gigantic four poster bed.

Saturday 3 December

I dined with the Sangers last night, and enjoyed society. I wore my new black dress, and looked, I daresay, rather nice. That's a feeling I very seldom have; and I rather intend to enjoy it oftener. I like clothes, if I can design them. So Bertie Russell was attentive, and we struck out like swimmers who knew their waters. Bertie is a fervid egoist – which helps matters. And then, what a pleasure – this mind on springs. "If you had my brain you would find the world a very thin, colourless place" he said. "But my colours are so foolish" I replied. "You want them for your writing" he said. "God does mathematics. That's my feeling. It is the most exalted form of art." "Art?" I said. "Well there's style in mathematics as there is in writing" he said. "I get the keenest aesthetic pleasure from reading well written mathematics. My brain is not what it was. I'm past my best – and therefore, of course, I am now celebrated. In Japan they treated me like Charlie Chaplin – disgusting. I shall write no more mathematics. Perhaps I shall write philosophy. The brain becomes rigid at fifty – and I shall be fifty in a month or two. I have to make money." "Surely money is settled upon Russells by the country?" I said. "I gave mine away years ago, to help promising young men who wanted to write poetry. From twenty-eight to thirty-eight I lived in a cellar and worked. Then my passions got hold of me. Now I have come to terms with myself. I am no longer surprised at what happens. I don't expect any more emotional experiences. I don't think any longer that something is going to happen when I meet a new person." I said I disagreed with much of this. Yet perhaps I did not expect very much to happen from talking to Bertie. I felt that he had talked to so many people. Thus I did not ask him to come here – I enjoyed it though a good deal; and got home and drank cocoa in the kitchen.

Sunday 11 December
Both the servants have German measles, and for three days we have been servants instead of masters.

Sunday 18 December
Here it is practically the end of the year, and more pages left blank than seems to me altogether wholesome. But my diary dwindles, perversely enough, when the stuff for it is most abundant. There was Roger here for tea and dinner yesterday; the day before I had to go plundering the shops for presents after tea; Thursday, I had to put in semicolons to my Henry James article and then rush to catch a train to Hampstead to dine with Brett and Gertler. Tomorrow we dine with Adrian. Roger's visit went off specially well. I mean we are grown rather intimate, and sit talking at our ease – practically of everything. I see in this one of the good effects of middle age. Roger grudges every minute now that he doesn't paint. So we reflected upon these strange, on the whole merciful, dispensations, by which Roger always sees masterpieces ahead of him and I see great novels – We have our atmosphere of illusion, without which life would be so much duller than it is.

Our luck seems, at last, to be in again. With luck we may have £400 instead of £250; and we might buy a motor car; and we might buy the meadow; and we might run up another lodge, and we might take in a new strip of garden. And so on and so on.

Monday 19 December
I will add a postscript on the nature of reviewing. "Mrs Woolf? I want to ask you one or two questions about your Henry James article –" First (only about the right name of one of the stories). "And now you use the word 'lewd'. Of course, I don't wish you to change it, but surely that is rather a strong expression to apply to anything by Henry James? I haven't read the story lately of course – but still my impression is –" "Well, I thought that when I read it; one has to go by one's impressions at the time." "But you know the usual meaning of the word? It is – ah – *dirty* – Now poor dear old Henry James – At anyrate, think it over, and ring me up in 20 minutes." So I thought it over and came to the required conclusion in twelve minutes and a half.

But what is one to do about it? He [Bruce Richmond] made it sufficiently clear not only that he wouldn't stand 'lewd', but that he didn't much like anything else. I feel that this becomes more often the case, and I wonder whether to break off, or to pander, or to go on writing against the current. Anyhow, for the present I shall let it be.

To add to Leonard's trophies, the Webbs have asked him to edit a book; the League of Nations Union offer to reprint *International Government*; and *The Village in the Jungle* is sold among other rare first editions at six shillings. All very good.

1922

Virginia started the year with influenza, the sequelae of which lasted into the summer and involved consultations with doctors and specialists. But despite her uncertain health, she enjoyed a lively social life. Friends came to see her at Richmond; she and Leonard were able to spend Easter and Whitsun at Monks House, and to visit Lytton Strachey and his co habitees at Tidmarsh; and in July she went once again to Garsington at the invitation of Lady Ottoline Morrell. At the beginning of August the Woolfs removed to Sussex; and here too they were beset with visitors, including Lytton Strachey, T. S. Eliot, and E. M. Forster, back from India. Vanessa and her household were again in residence at Charleston, a few miles off.

Vexed by the editorial timidity of the TLS, Virginia determined at the start of the year to give up reviewing – she wrote but five all told this year – and concentrated on revising Jacob's Room, *which Leonard read in July and pronounced her best work. It was published (though not printed) by the Hogarth Press – its largest undertaking so far – in October (thereafter all Virginia's books were published by the Press), and had a mixed reception. But already in the summer she had begun a story she referred to as* Mrs Dalloway, *and this gradually expanded into a full-length novel, given poignancy by the accidental death in October of an important figure from her youth, Kitty Maxse, who was to some extent the model for Mrs Dalloway.*

In July Leonard accepted a post writing on political matters for the weekly Nation & Athenaeum; *and in November his electioneering activities were concluded by the General Election, in which he came bottom of his poll, although the Labour Party as a whole made considerable gains. But concurrently with his political interests, the Woolfs were increasingly concerned with the question of their Hogarth Press. This year it issued nine titles; and the problem of coping with the work involved became acute: Leonard in particular found Ralph Partridge more and more irritating and less and less dependable; Ralph, for his part, encouraged by Lytton Strachey, foresaw an influential and expanding future for himself in the management of the Press. There were endless discussions; alternative solutions proposed; well-to-do aspiring partners investigated; established publishers' enticing offers considered . . . In the end a solution presented itself as if in answer to Virginia's prayer: an intelligent young woman longing to dedicate herself to printing. Ralph was to go; Marjorie Thomson would replace him; and Leonard and Virginia would keep control of their own creation.*

On 14 December, dining with Clive Bell, Virginia made a new acquaintance: Mrs Harold Nicolson, who preferred to be known by her maiden name, Vita Sackville-West.

1922

HOGARTH HOUSE, RICHMOND

Tuesday 3 January
Home last night, after ten or eleven days at Monks House – days when the wind blew from every quarter at the top of its voice, and great spurts of rain came with it, and hail spat in our fire, and the lawn was strewn with little branches, and there were fiery sunsets over the downs. In the morning I wrote with steady stoicism my posthumous article upon Hardy. No more reviewing for me, now that [Bruce] Richmond re-writes my sentences to suit the mealy mouths of Belgravia; it is odd how stiffly one sets pen to paper when one is uncertain of editorial approval. That is the true reason why I give up; joined with the economic reason that I make as much by other means. Leonard planted, pruned, sprayed, though the cold and the wet and the wildness made his behaviour a heroism to be admired, not comprehended. Tonight my reading begins.

Sunday 22 January
'Tonight my reading begins' did I say? And two nights later I was shivering over the fire and had to tumble into bed with the influenza. Happily, it has been a mitigated lapse – not complete like the summer's. Nessa just back from France, alighting for a fortnight, and then off again to Paris. But what am I to say about her? All very gay in French boots, hat, and check shirt; with that queer antique simplicity of surface which I compare to the marble cheeks of a Greek statue.

Saturday 4 February
Another fortnight spent in bed. Indeed, almost as I put down my pen I was seized with a second attack, lay in bed like a piece of timber, and am still in bed, sitting up, looking at the fire, and my temperature a shade above normal. I think this second attack was more wearisome than the first, and I have seen very few people. Nessa came again. How painful these meetings are! Let me try to analyse. Perhaps it is that we both feel that we can exist independently of the other. The door shuts between us, and life flows on

again and completely removes the trace. That is an absurd exaggeration. The truth is she was a little depressed, ostensibly because no one had mentioned painting to her in the course of three weeks. "I have seen all the cleverest people," she said "and not one mentioned painting. I hung two of our latest paintings in Maynard's room, and he never noticed them." "Surely Clive?" I said. "Oh Clive knows nothing whatever about it" she replied. All this tends to make her turn to Paris as her dwelling place. But then there are the children, Julian at school, Quentin coming home nightly. And then there is Duncan. "And after all there is nothing binding in our relationship", she said. "Its quite different from yours." And so this ruffled me. I set out to prove that being childless I was less normal than she. She took offence (the words are too strong). Told me I shouldn't enjoy café life in Paris. Told me I liked my own fireside and books and my friends' visits; implied that I was settled and unadventurous. Implied that I spent a great deal upon comfort. As we had only two hours together, and she left for Paris next morning, and perhaps I shan't see her till May, I felt a sort of discontent, as the door closed behind her. Indeed, we are at the moment a little tremulous again. What to do about Ralph? – about the Press? Ralph works in the basement, and leaves the machine dirty. Yesterday he slipped off leaving L. to go down and clean up. Upon this crystallised all our grumblings of the past – They are to the effect that he is lazy, undependable, now industrious, now slack, all corroded by Lytton – the old story, which one has heard so often from the victims of the old serpent. Should we part company? I suspect the work is not possible for an educated and vigorous young man.

Tuesday 14 February
[On] Monday [Dr] Fergusson came in and pronounced that my eccentric pulse had passed the limits of reason and was in fact insane. So I was laid in bed again, and set up my state in the drawing room, where I now write sitting up in bed, alongside the fire, so that perhaps I shall be up and creeping this time next week. Katherine Mansfield bursts upon the world in glory next week [*The Garden Party*]; I have to hold over *Jacob's Room* until October, and I somehow fear that by that time it will appear to me sterile acrobatics. Nevertheless, such is life, that I am very tolerably amused; see a good many people. And Adrian is so happy and genial that I am really pleased. An unambitious man, with good brains, money, wife and children is, I daresay, the most fortunate of us all. "Oh well" he said talking of his medical career, "it's something to do. It's easier now to go on than to stop" he said. Like the whole family, he has this distinguished, cool, point of view, which always makes him good company, and admits him to any society – if he wished for any society, which needless to say, he doesn't.

Wednesday 15 February

I thought to myself, as Lytton was talking, Now I will remember this and write it down in my diary tomorrow. And as I thought that, everything melted to mist. People don't say things, except in biographies. True, Lytton was smooth and mild and melancholy beyond his wont; but with intimates, when talk is interesting, one sentence melts into another; heads and tails merge; there is never a complete beast. But he was back again in his old pre-*Eminent Victorians* despondency, partly, I guessed, because the publishers are chilly about his essays; partly because he can't think of a plot for a play.

Friday 17 February

I meant to write about death, only life came breaking in as usual. I like, I see, to question people about death. I have taken it into my head that I shan't live till seventy. Suppose, I said to myself the other day, this pain over my heart suddenly wrung me out like a dish cloth and left me dead? – I was feeling sleepy, indifferent, and calm; and so thought it didn't much matter, except for L. Then, some bird or light I daresay, or waking wider, set me off wishing to live – wishing chiefly to walk along the river and look at things.

Saturday 18 February

Three dozen eggs at present prices work out at 10/6. Three dozen = 36. Four eggs for breakfast work out at twenty-eight a week. This leaves eight over for cooking. I have an egg now every night for dinner. I make these calculations not with a view to an essay upon national economy, though that comes in. My weekly books – these are in my mind. For according to the papers, the cost of living is now I don't know how much lower than last year; whereas my books remain about the same. You can't question Nelly much without rubbing a sore. She threatens at once to send up a cheap meal "And Mr Woolf won't like that." There! Not a very grievous itch; and quelled by the sight of the new Byron letters just come from Mudies. But after six weeks influenza my mind throws up no matutinal fountains. A little air, seeing the buses go by, lounging by the river, will, please God, send the sparks flying again.

Monday 6 March

The cat lets this mouse run a few steps once more. I have walked for ten minutes only, according to the directions of Dr Sainsbury, who after examining me for an hour said – many things; among them that we can't go abroad. But I am back again, after two months this very day, sitting in my chair after tea, writing; and I wrote *Jacob* this morning, and though my temperature is not normal, my habits are: and that is all I care for.

Sunday 12 March
This book dwindles. Yet many portraits are owed to it – I have seen people – and people. Eliot, Clive, Violet, – if no one else. Of these Eliot amuses me most – grown supple as an eel; yes, grown positively familiar and jocular and friendly, though retaining I hope some shreds of authority. I mustn't lick all the paint off my Gods. He is starting a magazine; to which twenty people are to contribute; and Leonard and I are among them! So what does it matter if Katherine Mansfield soars in the newspapers, and runs up sales skyhigh? Ah, I have found a fine way of putting her in her place. The more she is praised, the more I am convinced she is bad. What, then, did we discuss? He has written a poem of forty pages, which we are to print in the autumn. This is his best work, he says. He is pleased with it; takes heart, I think, from the thought of that safe in his desk. Clive, via Mary, says he uses violet powder to make him look cadaverous. I am seeing Clive rather frequently. He comes on Wednesdays; jolly, and rosy, and squab: a man of the world; and enough of my old friend, and enough of my old lover, to make the afternoons hum. But, oh dear me, after nine weeks claustration, I want to vault the wall, and pick a few flowers. The ethical code of Bloomsbury allows poaching; and I'm amused to see how a change of relationship, a middle-aged relationship, offers new experiences.

Then I hit Morgan on the wing. He had come to London that very day, and so came here, and was, we thought, depressed to the verge of inanition. To come back to Weybridge, to come back to an ugly house a mile from the station, an old, fussy, exacting mother, to come back having lost your Rajah, without a novel, and with no power to write one – this is dismal, I expect, at the age of forty-three. The middle age of b——s is not to be contemplated without horror. But he was charming, transparent; and told us as much as we could get out. A year's absence fills one too full for many drops to issue upon turning the bottle upside down. He told us about the sparrows that fly about the Palace – No one troubles about them. "I used to shout at them sometimes. The squirrels sat on the piano. I used to row on the lake which was nice. The Indians were too heavy to row. There were black hills. A very nice climate, but dull. There were sparrows only. In other parts the birds were so lovely – I thought of you Virginia (which pleased me). It is a very nice life; but one wants other people to talk to. It is much nicer than this. I felt no enthusiasm at seeing my native cliffs again." That was obvious. Off he went, carrying a very heavy metal plate, to dine with Aunt Rosalie at Putney.

Friday 24 March
Still invalided, I sit and receive visitors almost daily; and say nothing about them here. People are neglected, and accumulate, up and up and up. Clive

is the most persistent; we talked from 4.30 to 10.15 the other day. It is clear that I am to rub up his wits; and in return I get my manners polished. I hear of supper parties; elicit facts about drink and talk and goings on. He enjoys *every*thing – There is no truth about life, he says, except what we feel. It is good if you enjoy it, and so forth. Obviously we reach no heights of reason. Nor do we become completely intimate. A little colour is added to taste. We have our embrace; our frill of sentiment. Impossible, as Nessa says, to talk without it. But I perceive, chiefly through his letters, that once a fortnight is the pitch of our relationship.

Thursday 30 March
It is snowing now, large loose watery flakes; they fall straight; there is no wind. Muddy water is in the evening sky, and we began summer time last Sunday, so the evening sky is prolonged.

Thursday 27 April
Just back – not from the Club, but from Rodmell, and fingers are so cold I can't close them on my pen. It is blackening for another downpour. This is the worst spring on record. Twenty-seven days of bitter wind, blinding rain, gusts, snowstorms, storms every day. So Rodmell was mitigated joy.

Sunday 11 June
Disgraceful! disgraceful! disgraceful! From the 27th day of April to this, not a word has been recorded. And I only write now to excuse myself from copying out a page or two of *Jacob*. The depression of a return from Rodmell is always acute. Perhaps this continued temperature may be some sort of cause for my ups and downs. Yet the ten days at Rodmell passed smoothly. One lives in the brain there – I slip easily from writing to reading with spaces between of walking – walking through the long grass in the meadows, or up the downs. And so of course, coming back from Rodmell – blank – reason for blank forgotten as well as blank's contents.

Friday 23 June
I think I've been working too hard; talking too much; to open this book. Working at copying *Jacob* after tea. As for the talk, it has been all about love and lies with Ralph. We have had a mad bull in the house – a normal Englishman in love; and deceived. His stupidity, blindness, callousness, struck me more powerfully than the magic virtues of passion. I began by believing his story – that Carrington had lied in matters of such importance that their relations were now forever damaged. But he concealed some essentials; how he had treated her, so as to foster lies. His passions are like those in books. And he thinks this fine. "But I am like that." "You're a

maniac" I said. Indeed I shouted it in the train coming back from Roger's lecture. "I should have left you if you had treated me like that." He does not answer. It was the stupidity of virility that impressed me.

We have seen a great many people. Roger's lectures provide a rendezvous. Eliot dined last Sunday and read his poem. He sang it and chanted it and rhythmed it. It has great beauty and force of phrase; symmetry; and tensity. What connects it together, I'm not so sure. But he read till he had to rush, and discussion thus was curtailed. One was left, however, with some strong emotion. *The Waste Land*, it is called; and Mary Hutch, who has heard it more quietly, interprets it to be Tom's autobiography – a melancholy one. Yes, Mary kissed me on the stairs. That was after the Memoir Club. Lytton and Morgan read; and our standard is such that little is left for me to hint and guess at. They say what they mean, very brilliantly; and leave the dark as it was before. Morgan, who is now out and about again, very calm, serene, like a kettle boiling by some private fire, spent the night here, and we sat round the table and discussed his book. *Jacob* is being typed by Miss Green, and crosses the Atlantic on July 14th. Then will begin my season of doubts and ups and downs.

Monday 17 July
Back from Garsington, and too unsettled to write – but then this does not count as writing. It is to me like scratching; or, if it goes well, like having a bath – which of course, I did not get at Garsington. I don't know that any incident burnt through the long windy cold day. I liked old [Augustine] Birrell's stories. He is a very well matured vintage: the barrel round and tight and mellow; and the wine within bright and sweet, and not lacking tang either. Ottoline has her little green book room with the gilt pillars stuffed with pretty yellow books. There I sat, crouching over the fire, and we talked, rather on our guard – a little toothless perhaps. Much disillusioned she said she was, but now indifferent to disillusionment. So we had the case of Aldous Huxley – a pretty poor one. There is Murry pleading and whining to be taken in, with a view to Oxford honours, so Birrell shrewdly said. Still we were low in tone – had she not had an operation on her bladder two days before? But energy ran like whips through her.

Leonard has been offered [H. N.] Brailsford's post [leader-writer and foreign affairs specialist] on the *Nation*; and has taken it.

I am finishing *Jacob's Room*. Grizzel [a dog] now belongs to us. We dine in the drawing room – the dining room being given over to print and Ralph (he annoys us both considerably). My temperature goes on, as usual, and Dr Hamill thinks that my right lung is suspicious. Fergusson says no. And perhaps I shall have to see Sainsbury to settle it.

Wednesday 19 July
Today Ralph has a story that Maynard and Lytton are to buy the *English Review* from Austin Harrison, set him up as drudge, pay their contributors £10.10 a thousand words, and beat all rivals. If Ralph wants it, then I think Lytton may agree; not otherwise. At Garsington they were getting up a subscription to give Tom £300, and so free him from journalism. These two bits of gossip seem to belong together.

Saturday 22 July
My conscience drives me again to write. Clive came to tea yesterday, and offered me only the faded and fly-blown remnants of his mind. He had been up late. So had I – at the pictures. For my own part, all my strings are jangled by a night out. Dissipation would rot my writing (such as it is, I put in, modestly). The question yesterday was about Lytton and the *English Review*. Would it be good or bad for his writing? Ralph says that he is very depressed; blocked by the play he can't write – and never will be able to write, say I; and if he lubricated himself with journalism, he might reel off some history or biography, and so pass by the play unmoved; and this is his line, and a good one too, I say. If Lytton takes it, Ralph is to be business manager, and leave us. Well? We are polite, but we don't sigh. Ralph is in mischief again. Poor young man! For really he was never meant for intellectual whirlpools. No; he was meant for punts in backwaters, gramophones, ices, flirtations, a pretty wife, large family, and interests in the City. We have bad luck with our prentices. Next time we must stipulate for eunuchs.

Hamill sticks to it that my right lung is wrong. Fergusson finds nothing. Pneumonia germs have been discovered. And my case is to be laid before Sainsbury on the 9th – all rather a bore.

Wednesday 26 July
On Sunday L. read through *Jacob's Room*. He thinks it my best work. He calls it a work of genius; he thinks it unlike any other novel; he says that the people are ghosts; he says it is very strange; he found it very interesting, and beautiful, and without lapse (save perhaps the party) and quite intelligible. I cannot write this as formally as it deserves, for I was anxious and excited. But I am on the whole pleased. Neither of us knows what the public will think. There's no doubt in my mind that I have found out how to begin (at forty) to say something in my own voice; and that interests me so that I feel I can go ahead without praise.

Friday 28 July

The affairs of the Partridges have engrossed us for two hours again. Partridge's conduct is that of the village Don Juan. Again, he behaves like a bull in a garden. He is a male bully, as L. says. I am reminded of the tantrums of Adrian and Clive. There is something maniacal in masculine vanity.

MONKS HOUSE, RODMELL

Thursday 3 August

Twice a year I make good resolutions – in August and October. My good resolution for August is to work methodically, yet with the grain not against it. Often, my wisdom teaches me, good resolutions wither because forced. And modern science teaches us to respect pleasure, or that is my reading.

We ended our season last Monday at the Commercio [Restaurant], with Clive and Roger. Roger came in with his hair flying and his coat flying carrying canvases – his mouth open, his eyes searching round – and we had our usual talk. Clive had his bits of gossip. To Gordon Square afterwards; Nessa had the mumps downstairs. Duncan drifted in, soft haired, vague, gentle as usual. Roger undid his canvases, and leant two portraits of Logan [Pearsall Smith] against the sofa. "Yes, I think that is the best portrait I have done so far" he said. He is fifty-five I suppose; and still thinks he is about to begin to paint as he should – a merciful dispensation – a carrot to lure him across the desert. But it is no desert to Roger. Every faculty is used and burnished, and some fairly on the way to be worn out. He suffers, consults doctors, aches and shivers, but eternally goes on. The perfect man, as I told him, and as indeed I believe him to be. He is off to spend the summer painting with Derain. It is his obsession now – to paint, paint, paint. Nothing else is worth doing.

Yesterday I walked to the top of Asheham hill, and found colonies of mushrooms on the way. The house now looks a little rigid and fixed, the country shut in, and severe compared with this. But the garden here is a lovely patch – open and airy with views of the hills.

Wednesday 16 August

I should be reading *Ulysses*, and fabricating my case for and against. I have read 200 pages so far – not a third; and have been amused, stimulated, charmed, interested by the first two or three chapters – and then puzzled, bored, irritated, and disillusioned as by a queasy undergraduate scratching his pimples. And Tom, great Tom, thinks this on a par with *War and Peace*! An illiterate, underbred book it seems to me: the book of a self taught working man, and we all know how distressing they are, how egotistic, insistent, raw, striking, and ultimately nauseating. When one can have the cooked flesh, why have the raw? But I think if you are anaemic, as Tom is, there is a glory in blood. Being fairly normal myself I am soon ready for the classics again. I may revise this later. I do not compromise my critical sagacity. I plant a stick in the ground to mark page 200. For my own part I am laboriously dredging my mind for *Mrs Dalloway* and bringing up light buckets.

I see I have said nothing about our day in London – Dr Sainsbury, Dr Fergusson, and the semi-legal discussion over my body, which ended in a bottle of quinine pills, and a box of lozenges, and a brush to varnish my throat with. Influenza and pneumonia germs, perhaps, says Sainsbury, very softly, wisely, and with extreme deliberation. "Equanimity – practise equanimity Mrs Woolf" he said, as I left; an unnecessary interview from my point of view; but we were forced into it by one step after another on the part of the bacteriologists. I take my temperature no more till October 1st.

Meanwhile there is the question of Ralph. This – it is the old question of his lumpiness, grumpiness, slovenliness, and stupidity versus his niceness, strength, fundamental amiability and connections.

Tuesday 22 August

I should like very much to account for my depression. Sydney Waterlow spent the week-end here; and reproduced in his heavy lifeless voice exactly the phrases in which Murry dismisses my writing. I cannot write *Mrs Dalloway*. Indeed it is fatal to have visitors, even like Clive for one day, in the middle of a story. I had just got up steam. All that agony now has to begin again. And Sydney is always a feather bed on a hot night – ponderous, meritorious, stuffy. No one ever suffered so acutely from atmosphere as I do; and my leaves drooped one by one; though heaven knows my root is firm enough. Ah, but how divinely happy we were until 12.30 on Thursday when Clive boarded the enchanted island with news from the world. Never have I been so happy in my life. The day was like a perfect piece of cabinet making – beautifully fitted with beautiful compartments. The odd thing is that neither of us wishes for visitors. Of course they threaten us from all sides – no: leave me, leave me, is all I say: to work my brain.

Saturday 26 August

Today is fine, and yesterday we went to Charleston by the Bus, for the first time. After all, one must respect civilisation. Charleston is as usual. One hears Clive shouting in the garden before one arrives. Nessa emerges from a great variegated quilt of asters and artichokes; not very cordial; a little absent minded. Clive bursts out of his shirt; sits square in his chair and bubbles. Then Duncan drifts in, also vague, absent minded, and incredibly wrapped round with yellow waistcoats, spotted ties, and old blue stained painting jackets. His trousers have to be hitched up constantly. He rumples his hair. However, I can't help thinking that we grow in cordiality, instead of drifting out of sight. And why not stand on one's own legs, and defy them, even in the matter of hats and chaircovers? Surely at the age of forty . . .

I dislike *Ulysses* more and more – that is think it more and more unimportant; and don't even trouble conscientiously to make out its meanings. Thank God, I need not write about it.

Sunday 3 September
Perhaps the greatest revolution in my life is the change of nibs – no longer can I write with my old blunt tree stump – people complained. But then the usual difficulties begin – what is to take its place? I should be reading the last immortal chapter of *Ulysses*; but I'm hot with Badminton in the orchard, and we dine in thirty-five minutes. I'm fretful with people. Every day will now be occupied till Tuesday week.

Wednesday 6 September
Visitors leave one in tatters; yet with a relish for words. Phrases roll on my tongue – which, really one can't produce for the delectation of my mother-in-law and Flora: who are now on their way back to Lewes; Carrington and Partridge being on their way to Chiddingly; the Sangers being on their way up Asheham Hill; and Lytton beginning to consider being on his way here.

We had our premeditated interview last night, with Ralph lying on the bed up here. Did his face show any change as Leonard went on – very forcible, measured, and impersonal. "Things have been unsatisfactory in my opinion" and so on. Ralph put up no more defence than a flock of sheep, which is disarming. Carrington is going to sit out his infidelities; which she does with her lips shut. She is going to paint. But she will never be a young woman again.

We had a great chatter party on Monday – Maynard, Nessa, Duncan, the Sangers. But how could I repeat the talk? Maynard is going to build a house: Nessa and Duncan are going to draw an income for ten years from it. It is to be a hotel, perfectly appointed, in a field off Beanstalk Lane – eight suites of rooms, with eight bathrooms, kitchens, waterclosets, surrounding a courtyard; in short a Peacock novel in stone; soon filled with characters. No doubt we have re-arranged life almost completely. Our parents were mere triflers at the game – Maynard, besides being our greatest living economist, has a dancer for a mistress, and is now preparing to stage a Mozart ballet; interviews the Coliseum Manager; is an expert on contracts. Then Duncan is going to dance with Lydia [Lopokova]. And Roger – but I need not go through the list; for my point is the same – we have all mastered the art of life, and very fascinating it is.

I finished *Ulysses*, and think it a misfire. Genius it has I think; but of the inferior water. It is underbred, not only in the obvious sense, but in the literary sense. A first rate writer, I mean, respects writing too much to be tricky; startling; doing stunts. I'm reminded all the time of some callow board school boy, full of wits and powers, but so self-conscious and egotistical that he loses his head, becomes extravagant, mannered, uproarious, ill at ease, makes kindly people feel sorry for him, and stern ones merely annoyed; and one hopes he'll grow out of it; but as Joyce is forty this scarcely seems likely. I have not read it carefully; and only once; and it is very obscure; so no doubt I have scamped the virtue of it more than is fair. I feel that myriads of tiny bullets pepper one and spatter one; but one does not get one deadly wound straight in the face – as from Tolstoy, for instance; but it is entirely absurd to compare him with Tolstoy.

Thursday 7 September
Having written this, L. put into my hands a very intelligent review of *Ulysses*, in the American *Nation*; which, for the first time, analyses the meaning; and certainly makes it very much more impressive than I judged. Still I think there is virtue and some lasting truth in first impressions; so I don't cancel mine.

Tuesday 12 September
Lytton drove off an hour ago; and I have been sitting here, unable to read or collect myself – such is the wreckage dealt by four days of conversation. I told Lytton I should try to write down his talk – which sprang from a conversation about Boswell. But said Lytton, I never do talk. One night he gave us a complete account of the prison system, based on reports which he has been reading – thoroughly, with mastery, and a kind of political ability which impresses me. He would have been an admirable ruler of an Indian province. However, as usual, there was one main theme to which we returned – Ralph and Carrington. Both weigh upon poor old Lytton who feels himself in the position of a father, is slightly in love, yet sees, with his usual candour, all the faults and drawbacks.

Tuesday 26 September
A great many things have happened, unrecorded. This has been the most sociable summer we've ever had. Sometimes I feel as if, instead of sleeping

through the months in a dark room, I'd been up in the light all night. Clive and Mary came: Mary in grey silk stockings; was very affable; sat on the floor. Morgan came on Friday; Tom on Saturday. My talk with Tom deserves writing down, but won't get it for the light is fading; and one cannot write talk down either, as was agreed at Charleston the other day. There was a good deal of talk about *Ulysses*. Tom said the book would be a landmark, because it destroyed the whole of the 19th Century. It left Joyce himself with nothing to write another book on. He thought that Joyce did completely what he meant to do. But he did not think that he gave a new insight into human nature – said nothing new like Tolstoy. (Light now fails – 7.10 after a bad rainy day.)

Wednesday 27 September
While Tom and I talked in the drawing room, Morgan wrote an article up here; or flitted through; humble, deprecating, chubby like a child; but very observant. Tom's head is all breadth and bone compared with Morgan's. He still remains something of the schoolmaster, but I am not sure that he does not paint his lips. After Joyce, however, we came to ticklish matters – the Eliot fund; the upshot of it was that Tom won't leave the Bank under £500, and must have securities – not pledges. So next morning, when Ott's letter and circular arrived, aiming at £300, I had to wire to her to stop.

For the rest the week-end was chilly and stormy. We had one blow on the hills. Tom left before dinner. Then we snuggled in, and Morgan became very familiar; anecdotic; simple; gossiping about friends and humming his little tunes. I was impressed by his complete modesty (founded perhaps on considerable self assurance). Compliments scarcely touch him. There is something too simple about him – for a writer perhaps – mystic, silly, but with a child's insight; oh yes, and something manly and definite too.

Wednesday 4 October
Our last whole day. From the weather point of view, the summer has been altogether disappointing. It has promised and then withheld. We have not had seven consecutive good days. Spiritually speaking, we have made some progress in Rodmell society. I was struck by the bloodlessness of philistines the other day at the Rectory. They seem far less alive than we intellectuals, so pale, so watery, so mild. I am a little uppish, though, and self assertive, because [Donald] Brace wrote to me yesterday 'We think *Jacob's Room* an extraordinarily distinguished and beautiful work, and we delight in publishing it' – or words to that effect. As this is my first testimony from an impartial person I am pleased.

HOGARTH HOUSE, RICHMOND

Saturday 8 October
Back again, over the fire at Hogarth House. But the day has been spoilt for me – so strangely – by Kitty Maxse's death; and now I think of her lying in her grave at Gunby. I read it in the paper. I hadn't seen her since, I guess 1908. I could not have kept up with her; she never tried to see me. Yet, yet – these old friends dying without any notice on our part always – it begins to happen so often – saddens me: makes me feel guilty. I wish I'd met her in the street. My mind has gone back all day to her; in the queer way it does.

Saturday 14 October
Kitty fell, very mysteriously, over some bannisters. How did it happen? Some one presumably knows, and in time I shall hear. "It seems rather melancholy that it should come to an end like this" Nessa said; but she was putting Angelica to bed, and we could not dig in our past. I have seen Nessa, Maynard, Lydia [Lopokova], Desmond, Saxon, Lytton, Frankie Birrell and Margery Fry, all within this week; and had two letters, from Lytton and Carrington, about *Jacob's Room*; and here we are on the verge of publication. My sensations? – they remain calm. I want to be through the splash and swimming in calm water again. I want to be writing unobserved. *Mrs Dalloway* has branched into a book; and I adumbrate here a study of insanity and suicide: the world seen by the sane and the insane side by side – something like that; and to be more close to the fact than *Jacob*; but I think *Jacob* was a necessary step, for me, in working free.

Sunday 29 October
There was the *Times* review on Thursday – long, a little tepid, I think; saying that one can't make characters in this way; flattering enough. Of course, I had a letter from Morgan in the opposite sense – the letter I've liked best of all. We have sold 650, I think; and have ordered a second edition. My sensations? – as usual, mixed. I shall never write a book that is an entire success. This time the reviews are against me, and the private people enthusiastic. Either I am a great writer or a nincompoop. But I want to be quit of all this. I don't want to be totting up compliments, and comparing reviews. I want to think out *Mrs Dalloway*.
　　Our position becomes more and more complicated. Clearly we cannot go on publishing seriously with Ralph attached to us like a drone. At anyrate the labour and worry of getting out a long book makes me decided not to do it again on the present system. We have to go to Tidmarsh next week to explain the position. Carrington says that Lytton is most anxious

for some arrangement, and the uncertainty is trying Ralph's nerves. Yet this nervous man makes no attempt to do the most ordinary things for us. L. has to tie parcels every morning. Ralph catches no earlier or later trains. Thursday morning he spent at the tailor's.

The election is beginning to roar in the newspapers. L. has a chance of getting in. We have bitten off a large piece of life – but why not?

Tuesday 7 November
We had a stormy week-end at Tidmarsh, and I'm afraid I have concluded that Ralph must go. His jealousy, and irrationality, combined with his fixed determination to make a permanent hobby out of what's a profession to us, make the position less and less possible. Yet, I am sorry, and like him, and the association. On the other hand what fun to spring off and make a good job of it! Suppose one could get a young man or woman of wits who would work violently and rashly.

Monday 13 November
Reviews are now favourable and utterly contradictory, as usual. I am quite able to write away without bother from self-consciousness, now; which shows that my splash is over. And now I have a multitude of pleasant jobs on hand, and am really very busy, and very happy, and only want to say Time, stand still here; which is not a thing that many women in Richmond would say I think. I walked in the Park, bought two wild duck and six snipe, all fresh and bleeding, just shot at Beaconsfield by two poachers I suspect. I paid eight and sixpence, thus introducing a good deal of stir in Hogarth House kitchen.

Monday 27 November
I need not say that my wild duck stank like old sea weed and had to be buried. But I cannot dally over this incident, which in tamer days might have provided some fun, because I have such a congeries of affairs to relate. There is the Press to be chronicled. At the Club we overheard one of those usual shabby, loose, cropheaded, small faced bright eyed young women [say] that she was tired of teaching and meant to become a printer. When she went into the writing room, I followed her, plucked her out, and revealed us to her as proprietors of the Hogarth Press. Yesterday she and 'a friend' came to tea. This friend we called mistakenly Jones; he being [C. E. M.] Joad, of the 1917 Club; a philosopher; a sturdy short man, with very bright round eyes, hair touched with grey, cocksure, reposing much weight upon the sterling quality of his intellect, and thus dispensing with the graces and amenities, as usual with sterling young men. He tipped one of my chairs on two legs, and ate a large tea, keeping close watch over Marjorie's interests at every point. For it

was evident that she was ready to bind herself hand and foot to us, and make fantastic promises. Still, she has been thoroughly educated, must earn her living, and has written, Joad says, a first rate novel. Well its not quite written, she said; being of course far more modest and less self confident than Cyril. "We are going to be married in February" she said. "And I mean to go on working after I'm married." I should say she is twenty-five or six; quick, impulsive, but with a steel thread in her from earning and learning, which is an invaluable property, and one that gives an edge to the rest. In short she might take us on and make a life work of it. Joad, who detests my books, may be an obstacle; since he may try to impose his literary views upon us; but I don't know. Moreover, we both liked him, and her too (but she was less self assertive, passed the cake, praised the dog, and sensitively appraised the situation with antennae quivering, woman like). We all kept our heads very creditably, insisted upon strict business dealings, and are to meet again on Sunday week. But where then does Ralph come in? He looks a little glum, and says very little.

Sunday 3 December

But these are historic days. The Hogarth Press is in travail. Heinemanns made us a most flattering offer – to the effect that we should give our brains and blood, and they would see to sales and ledgers. But we sniff patronage. If they gain, we lose. We have decided for freedom and a fight with great private glee. This brought on an argument with Ralph last Friday; he brought forth a plan obviously concocted at Tidmarsh, by which we are to become a company, Lytton, L. and I for partners, with Ralph remaining as he is. Lytton is said to hint a possibility that we should have all his work. At first tempting, this plan becomes to us less and less feasible. At this moment we incline to Miss [Marjorie] Thomson and freedom. Why, after all, should we conciliate Ralph? And is it not better to end this perpetual strain of friendship's burden – hurting Lytton's feelings that is, by failing to consider how fast poor Ralph's heart beats after a conversation with us? But there is a serious reason, and not mere restlessness, in our need for re-organisation. We are both giving all our spare time, and still there is far more work than we can do. At this rate, we have work for not three people but four or five or six.

This autumn has been perhaps the busiest of my dilatory life. People and books – I sing that to the tune of Women and Wine, which comes in *The Beggar's Opera*. I dined with Mary on Friday, met Clive and Aldous; Aldous very long, rather puffy, fat faced, white, with very thick hair, and canary coloured socks, is the raconteur; the young man of letters who sees life. We all said we despised reviewers and told little stories to our own advantage.

Friday 15 December

I have fifteen minutes before my solitary dinner, L. dining with Sangers, after a terrific Hogarth Press discussion ending in the final parting with Ralph. I am too muzzy headed to make out anything. This is partly the result of dining to meet the lovely gifted aristocratic Sackville-West last night at Clive's. Not much to my severer taste – florid, moustached, parakeet coloured, with all the supple ease of the aristocracy, but not the wit of the artist. She writes fifteen pages a day – has finished another book – publishes with Heinemanns – knows everyone. But could I ever know her? I am to dine there on Tuesday. The aristocratic manner is something like an actress's – no false shyness or modesty – makes me feel virgin, shy, and schoolgirlish. Yet after dinner I rapped out opinions. She is a grenadier; hard; handsome; manly; inclined to double chin. Dear old Desmond moped like a tipsy owl in his corner, affectionate and glad to talk to me, I think. He said something about the French admiring *Jacob*, and wishing to translate it.

As for Ralph – that question certainly can't be settled before L. comes in. Why did he make me, and L., so furious by saying, in his sulky schoolboy voice, that if this crisis hadn't happened, he would have had a nice surprise to offer us at Easter? – something of Lytton's presumably. I think the kernel of our discontent lies in that sentence. So far as I can see, Ralph's disappearance would leave us more freedom, but give us more work. We should have to make further arrangements. But the basis would be sound, which is the great thing. If we keep Ralph, there will be constant disease. I think by our own merits now we attract all the young.

1923

Virginia began the year in a mood of depression – dispelled for a moment by a grand and enjoyable fancy-dress party in Gordon Square – which persisted until the spring; it was caused in part by her continuing ill-health, and aggravated by financial anxieties. Leonard had been receiving a regular income from the Nation & Athenaeum; *the control of the paper now changed hands, Maynard Keynes becoming Chairman of the new board, and Leonard's future was uncertain. The burden of maintaining two houses, two servants, the Hogarth Press and its adherents, all weighed on Virginia, and she forced herself to take on more paid journalism and postpone work on the two books now occupying her thoughts – a collection of essays which became* The Common Reader, *and the development of her* Mrs Dalloway *stories into a full-length novel (which for a time she called* The Hours*). The constant presence in her house of Ralph Partridge – who did not leave until March – and the new assistant Marjorie Thomson, added to her discomfort. And the news of Katherine Mansfield's death in January intensified her feelings of uneasy dejection.*

The previous year Virginia had been involved in an abortive scheme to enable T. S. Eliot to leave his employment in a bank so that he might devote his energies to writing; now she saw an opportunity to further this aim by getting him appointed literary editor of the Nation *under its new management; but instead Leonard was offered the post; and the Woolfs set off at the end of March for a four-week holiday in Spain – their first foreign journey since their honeymoon – in a much happier frame of mind. They travelled via Paris and Madrid to the extreme south, where they stayed with Gerald Brenan – a friend of the Partridges – for a week.*

Back in Richmond, Virginia again responded to the allurements of social life; Vanessa was in Gordon Square; the indefatigable hostess Lady Sibyl Colefax began to invite Virginia to her luncheon parties; she attended the first performance of the Sitwells' Façade; *she spent a weekend at Garsington; and the inconvenience and limitations of living in the suburbs became an increasing source of discontent. But it was some months before she could get Leonard to concede that her health no longer warranted this exile, and agree to her looking for a house for them in Bloomsbury.*

In September the Woolfs interrupted their summer stay at Monks House and made their way to Studland in Dorset where Maynard Keynes had rented a house with his future wife, the Russian ballerina Lydia Lopokova. Here their fellow guests were two young men, Raymond Mortimer, a rising literary critic, and George (Dadie) Rylands, who the following year was to join the Hogarth Press for a while, and who became a great favourite with Virginia.

At Monks House and again in Richmond in the autumn, Virginia worked steadily at both her books, and at articles – the first version of her 'Mr Bennett and Mrs Brown' appeared in New York in November and was reprinted in the Nation & Athenaeum *in December. The Woolfs were at Monks House for ten days at Christmas; they spent a night at Charleston, and bored Vanessa with talk of the* Nation.

1923

HOGARTH HOUSE, RICHMOND

Tuesday 2 January
If I were a dissembler I should date this the last day of 1922. So it is to all intents. We came back from Rodmell yesterday, and I am in one of my moods, as the nurses used to call it, today. And what is it and why? A desire for children, I suppose; for Nessa's life; for the sense of flowers breaking all round me involuntarily. Here's Angelica – here's Quentin and Julian. They make my life seem a little bare sometimes; and then my inveterate romanticism suggests an image of forging ahead, alone, through the night; of suffering inwardly, stoically; of blazing my way through to the end – and so forth. The truth is that the sails flap about me for a day or two on coming back. And it is all temporary: yes let me be quite clear about that. Years and years ago, after the Lytton affair, I said to myself, walking up the hill at Bayreuth, never pretend that the things you haven't got are not worth having; good advice I think. And then I went on to say to myself that one must like things for themselves; or rather, rid them of their bearing upon one's personal life. One must venture on to the things that exist independently of oneself. Now this is very hard for young women to do. Yet I got satisfaction from it. And now, married to L., I never *have* to make the effort. Perhaps I have been too happy for my soul's good? And does some of my discontent come from feeling that? I could not stay at 46 [Gordon Square] last night, because L. on the telephone expressed displeasure. Late again. Very foolish. Your heart bad – and so my self reliance being sapped, I had no courage to venture against his will. Then I react. Of course its a difficult question. For undoubtedly I get headache or the jump in my heart; and then this spoils his pleasure, and if one lives with a person, has one the right – So it goes on.
　　Middle Age then. Let that be the text of my discourse. I'm afraid we're becoming elderly. We are busy and attach importance to hours. I have my correspondence to finish, says L. today. I don't laugh. But we must not let our hobbies and pleasures become objects of fetish worship. L., I think, suffers from his extreme clarity. He sees things so clear that he can't swim,

156

float and speculate. And now we have such a train attached to us that we have to go on. Nessa, though, who might so easily plead ties and circumstances, rides much more freely than we do. She will spend Easter travelling with the children, for instance. We have to make money – that is true. We have to have a house; two houses; two servants; a press; a Thomson; a Ralph. Yet most of this is for my sake; and am I honest in wishing it otherwise? I will leave it here, unfinished, a note of interrogation – signifying some mood that recurs, but is not often expressed.

Sunday 7 January
Let the scene open on the doorstep of number 50 Gordon Square. We went up last night, carrying our bags, and a Ceylonese sword. There was Mary Hutchinson in lemon coloured trousers with green ribbons. And so we sat down to dinner; off cold chicken. In came Roger and Adrian and Karin; and very slowly we coloured our faces and made ready for number 46. The drawing room was full, miscellaneous, and oriental for the most part. Suppose one's normal pulse to be 70: in five minutes it was 120; and the blood, not the sticky whitish fluid of daytime, but brilliant and prickling like champagne. This was my state, and most people's. We collided, when we met; went pop, used Christian names, flattered, praised, and thought (or I did) of Shakespeare. At any rate, I thought of him when the singing was doing – Shakespeare I thought would have liked us all tonight. Gumbo distorted nursery rhymes; Lydia [Lopokova] danced; there were charades; Sickert acted Hamlet. We were all easy and gifted and friendly and like good children rewarded by having the capacity for enjoying ourselves thus. I daresay no one said anything very brilliant. I sat by Sickert, and liked him, talking in his very workmanlike, but not at all society manner, of painting, and Whistler; of an operation he saw at Dieppe. There is something indescribably congenial to me in this easy artists' talk; the values the same as my own and therefore right; no impediments; life charming, good and interesting; no effort; art brooding calmly over it all; and none of this attachment to mundane things, which I find in Chelsea.

As parties do, this one began to dwindle, until a few persistent talkers were left by themselves. Lytton and I sat side by side on the sofa. "And what do you think of the Tidmarsh Press?" [he said]. And this was his crafty way of telling me that Ralph means to set up on his own, after the Hogarth model, after Easter. Lytton was anxious to sound me. Should we think it poaching? I said I should say sharp things, but there was quite enough work for two. But Lytton was not altogether urbane. He is possessive. His baby shall have his toy, and he shan't share it with anyone else this time. Well – so be it. Love is the devil. No character can stand against it. But this passed in our trivial champagne-pricking way. And so, at 3 I suppose, back to no. 50. And so we breakfasted together this morning, with the church bells ringing, and all the houses full of Stracheys, Grants, Stephens and Bells and Partridges – a wet grey morning, in the heart of London, where I am so seldom at that hour.

Tuesday 16 January

Katherine has been dead a week, and how far am I obeying her 'do not quite forget Katherine' which I read in one of her old letters? It is strange to trace the progress of one's feelings. Nelly said in her sensational way at breakfast on Friday "Mrs Murry's dead! It says so in the paper!" At that one feels – what? A shock of relief? – a rival the less? Then confusion at feeling so little – then, gradually, blankness and disappointment; then a depression which I could not rouse myself from all that day. When I began to write, it seemed to me there was no point in writing. Katherine won't read it. Katherine's my rival no longer. Then, as usual with me, visual impressions kept coming and coming before me – always of Katherine putting on a white wreath, and leaving us, called away; made dignified; chosen. And she was only thirty-three. And I could see her before me so exactly, and the room at Portland Villas. I go up. She gets up, very slowly, from her writing table. A glass of milk and a medicine bottle stood there. Everything was very tidy, bright, and somehow like a doll's house. She (it was summer) half lay on the sofa by the window. She had her look of a Japanese doll, with the fringe combed quite straight across her forehead. Sometimes we looked very steadfastly at each other, as though we had reached some durable relationship through the eyes. Hers were beautiful eyes – rather doglike, brown, very wide apart, with a steady slow rather faithful and sad expression. Her nose was sharp, and a little vulgar. Her lips thin and hard. She looked very ill – very drawn, and moved languidly, drawing herself across the room, like some suffering animal. I suppose I have written down some of the things we said. And then she was inscrutable. Did she care for me? Sometimes she would say so – would kiss me – would look at me as if (is this sentiment?) her eyes would like always to be faithful. She would promise never never to forget. That was what we said at the end of our last talk. She said she would send me her diary to read, and would write always. For our friendship was a real thing, we said. It would always go on whatever happened. What happened was, I suppose, faultfindings and perhaps gossip. The surroundings – Murry and so on – and the small lies and treacheries, the perpetual playing and teasing, cut away much of the substance of friendship. Yet I certainly expected that we should meet again next summer, and start fresh. And I was jealous of her writing – the only writing I have ever been jealous of. For two days I felt that I had grown middle aged, and lost some spur to write. That feeling is going. I no longer keep seeing her with her wreath. I don't pity her so much. Yet I have the feeling that I shall think of her at intervals all through life. Probably we had something in common which I shall never find in anyone else. I think I never gave her credit for all her physical suffering and the effect it must have had in embittering her.

I have been in bed, 101, again.

Sunday 28 January
A certain melancholy has been brooding over me this fortnight. I date it from Katherine's death. The feeling so often comes to me now – Yes, go on writing of course but into emptiness. I'm cock – a lonely cock whose crowing nothing breaks – of my walk. However then I had my fever, and violent cold, was in and out of bed for a week. In casting accounts, never forget to begin with the state of the body.

We have now had Thomson twice – Marjorie I should and do call her, and she comes tomorrow full time. She has a little too much powder and scent for my taste, and drawls. In short she is not upper class. But she has honest intent eyes, and takes it seriously, which, as she is quite without training, is as well. My only fear is lest she should prove a flibbertigibbet. Her quickness of movement, keenness, and dependability are so far a great gain on Ralph. There he sits thick as an oak and as angular. We have heard no more of the Tidmarsh Press.

Much talk of the *Nation*, which, as I should have recorded, is sold to Maynard and a group, and our future once more quite uncertain.

Wednesday 7 February
Nessa's wedding day. Reflections suppressed. I must describe Cambridge. We walked from the station, cold, starry, dismal; then familiar; King's College Chapel; hasty wash and dress, and dine with [J. T.] Sheppard. He was in evening dress. A good deal of raw time had to be manufactured. I had romanced so much about Cambridge that to find myself sitting there was an anti-climax. Then off in the motor to the ADC [Theatre]. I think I was genuinely excited, rather than moved, by *Oedipus Rex*. The plot is so well tied; the story's race so fast. Then the young men's faces, pink and plump under their wigs, moved me. And so to bed; with King's bell saying very pompously all through the night the hour. We were happy and busy all Sunday, first Sheppard, then Pernel [Strachey]; sitting on the Backs, strolling up to Newnham, then lunching with the Shoves. So to the [G. E.] Moores. Then to Maynard's: I must say the pleasantest sitting room I have ever been in, owing to the colours and paintings, curtains and decorations of Bell and Grant. Here we dined well. The party began after a few brilliancies on my part about religion: emotional capital which I did not

know how to invest, I said. And Maynard kept the old ball smartly rolling. Indeed we were rather talk-dazed. And as people arrived, I suppose one's eyes tire; one's brain stales.

The depression which I mentioned comes partly from the uncertainty about the *Nation*. Leonard thinks himself a failure. And what use is there in denying a depression which is irrational? Can't I always think myself one too? And our depression comes too from the time of year, wet and wan, and from Thomson's drawling voice, and Ralph's stubbornness. I think Thomson and Ralph daily for lunch and tea, and the need for bright talk, depress also; and I shall be glad when the 15th March arrives.

Saturday 10 February

The omens are, I think, more favourable. Then we have £40 from income tax return – I seem to see a feather floating favourably from that region where the Gods abide. So I said as we walked in the cemetery this afternoon. It is now our plan (a day old) to walk from 2 to 3; print from 3 to 5; delay our tea; and so make headway. Ralph sticks on, defiant, argumentative, and gives one the lowest opinion of the manly virtues.

Monday 19 February

How it would interest me if this diary were ever to become a real diary: but then I should have to speak of the soul, and did I not banish the soul when I began? What happens is, as usual, that I'm going to write about the soul, and life breaks in. Talking of diaries sets me thinking of old Kate [Stephen], in the dining room of 4 Rosary Gardens; and how she opened the cabinet and there in a row on a shelf were her diaries from January 1, 1877; all the same to a t. And I made her read an entry; one of many thousand days, like pebbles on a beach: morning, evening, afternoon, without accent. Oh how strangely unaccented she is, sitting there all of a piece, with the mute sagacity of elephant or grey mare! Orderly solidity marked every atom there. The vases stood on mats: each was supplied with a tuft of mimosa and maidenhair. The Christmas cards – six – were ranged on the mantelpiece. Red tiles newly dusted. Green walls. Objects that came from India. And said Kate I intend to live to 1944 when I shall be eighty-four. And on her last day she will say to the charwoman who attends her, Bring me the diaries which you will find in the cabinet; and now, put them on the fire. I scarcely tried to disturb what had the sculptured classic appearance of alabaster fruit beneath glass.

In scribbling this, I am led away from my soul, which interests me nevertheless. For it is the soul I fancy that comments on visitors and reports their comments, and sometimes sets up such a to-do in the central departments of my machinery that the whole globe of me dwindles to a button head. I think this dwindling is often the result of talking to second rate people. They make the world pinchbeck.

We had a surprise visit from the Nicolsons. She [Vita] is a pronounced Sapphist, and may, thinks Ethel Sands, have an eye on me, old though I am. Snob as I am, I trace her passions five hundred years back, and they become romantic to me, like old yellow wine. Harold is simple downright bluff; wears short black coat and check trousers; wishes to be a writer, but is not I'm told and can believe, adapted by nature. Soul, you see, is framing all these judgments, and saying, this is not to my liking, this is second rate, this vulgar; this nice, sincere, and so on. My soul diminished, alas, as the evening wore on.

And we are still in suspense. Maynard is on the war path. And also I am trying to pull wires, to seat Tom at the *Nation* as literary editor. Yes, I am grown up. I give advice. I am a little bored indeed, and could wish that poor dear Tom had more spunk in him, less need to let drop by drop of his agonised perplexities fall ever so finely through pure cambric. One waits; sympathises; but it is dreary work.

Tuesday 6 March
Undoubtedly this has been a very unpleasant quarter. I date our misery from January 3rd. The main grievance has been this *Nation* affair, which hangs over us, lifting, then lowering, as it is at the present moment – low and black over our heads. On April 7th our income ceases; Maynard has made us no definite offer – but that I think is assured so far as L. goes. But that is only £120 p.a. and we shall have to scrape up the rest rather dismally, doing journalism, I suppose. But it is not the money trouble that worries us: but something psychological. The gloom is more on L.'s side than on mine. Mine is a gloom like a mist that comes and goes. I dip into different circles – and come home either exalted or depressed. Then the social question rises between L. and me. Are we becoming 'respectable'? Shall we dine with the [Bruce] Richmonds? L. says no. I regret it. Yes, somehow I regret it seriously, this shutting of the door upon suburban studies. I love the chatter and excitement of other people's houses. I want to make life fuller and fuller. Never mind, I say; once I get my claws into my writing and I'm safe. Eliot slightly disillusions me too; he is peevish, plaintive, egotistical; what it amounts to is that poverty is unbecoming.

Saturday 17 March
We now read plays at 46 [Gordon Square]. 46 is become a centre. For how long we don't know, as Maynard's marriage approaches. 46 has been very pleasant to me this winter. Two nights ago the Nicolsons dined there. Exposed to electric light eggs show dark patches. I mean we judged them

both incurably stupid. He is bluff, but oh so obvious; she, Duncan thought, took the cue from him, and had nothing free to say. There was Lytton, supple and subtle as an old leather glove, to emphasise their stiffness. It was a rocky steep evening.

And then? Ralph is gone, casually, without good bye. I have seen Osbert Sitwell, Sebastian Sprott and Mr [Raymond] Mortimer. As Nessa says, we are becoming fashionable.

Friday 23 March
L. has just come in with an offer from Maynard of the literary editorship of the *Nation*. Well, that's unexpected. Here have I been toiling these three weeks to make Eliot take it; finally he shied; and this is the result. No doubt there are drawbacks, but it means safety for the moment, indeed luxury. And to me it opens interesting vistas – but here I am with the typhoid germs and can't write.

*   *   *

Friday 11 May
The long break deserves a line, since I shall scarcely commemorate it otherwise. Have I not, with infinite labour, written for the first number of the *Nation* 'To Spain'? Am I not sitting waiting for L. to 'come back from the office' like other wives? It annoys me to be like other wives. Ah there he is! No: damn it; only Nelly gone out. As I say, I cannot go into the journey, Spain, Paris, et cetera. I stayed in Paris by way of facing life. I meant to use this diary to pull myself up from a fortnight's debauch of journalism, *Nation*'s affairs, and so on. So far we don't feel the *Nation* blood of our blood. It may turn that way. We work very hard at it. It has temptations and attractions. I like having the pick of new books. People crowd and press for work. It is mildly amusing to say, now don't worry, I'm not going to give you any. I have been so often in their position. But these delights are not very profound.

Sunday 13 May
Karin was here yesterday. Adrian is altogether broken up by psycho-analysis. His soul rent in pieces with a view to reconstruction. The doctor says he is a tragedy: and this tragedy consists in the fact that he can't enjoy life with zest. I am probably responsible. I should have paired with him instead of hanging on to the elders. Karin says we shall see a great change in three months. For my part, I doubt if family life has all the power of evil attributed to it, or psycho-analysis of good.

Morgan told me that when he and Mortimer discussed novelists the other day they agreed that Lawrence and I were the only two whose future interested them. They think of my next book, which I think of calling *The Hours*, with excitement. This does encourage me.

Monday 4 June

But I cannot describe Garsington. Thirty-seven people to tea; a bunch of young men no bigger than asparagus; walking to and fro, round and round; compliments, attentions, and then this slippery mud – which is what interests me at the moment. A loathing overcomes me of human beings – their insincerity; their vanity – A wearisome and rather defiling talk with Ott last night is the foundation of this complaint – and then the blend in one's own mind of suavity and sweetness with contempt and bitterness. Her egotism is so great. Yet on Saturday night I liked her. Lord David [Cecil] is a pretty boy. Puffin [Anthony] Asquith an ugly one – wizened, unimpressive, sharp, like a street boy. [Edward] Sackville-West reminded me of a peevish shop girl. They have all the same clipped quick speech and politeness, and total insignificance. What puts me on edge is that I'm writing like this here, and spoke so differently to Ott. I'm over peevish in private, partly in order to assert myself. I am a great deal interested suddenly in my book. I want to bring in the despicableness of people like Ott; I want to give the slipperiness of the soul. I have been too tolerant often.

And then there was Mrs Asquith. I was impressed. She is stone white; with the brown veiled eyes of an aged falcon; and in them more depth and scrutiny than I expected; a character, with her friendliness, and ease, and decision. Oh if we could have had Shelley's poems, and not Shelley the man! she said. Shelley was quite intolerable, she pronounced; she is a rigid frigid puritan; and in spite of spending thousands on dress. She rides life, if you like; and has picked up a thing or two, which I should like to plunder and never shall.

Wednesday 13 June

Nessa is back and the London season of course in full swing. So I judged yesterday in the Æolian Hall, listening, in a dazed way, to Edith Sitwell vociferating through the megaphone. There was Lady Colefax in her hat with the green ribbons. Did I say that I lunched with her last week? That was Derby Day and it rained, and all the light was brown and cold, and she went on talking talking, in consecutive sentences like the shavings that come from planes, artificial, but unbroken. It was not a successful party, Clive and Lytton and me.

I should be describing Edith Sitwell's poems [*Façade*], but I kept saying to myself 'I don't really understand . . . I don't really admire.' The only view, presentable view that I framed, was to the effect that she was monotonous. She has one tune only on her merry go round. And she makes her verse keep step accurately to the Hornpipe. This seems to be wrong.

Tuesday 19 June
I took up this book with a kind of idea that I might say something about my writing – which was prompted by glancing at what Katherine Mansfield said about *her* writing in *The Dove's Nest*. But I only glanced. She said a good deal about feeling things deeply; also about being pure, which I won't criticise, though of course I very well could. But now what do I feel about *my* writing? – this book, that is, *The Hours*, if that's its name? One must write from deep feeling, said Dostoevsky. And do I? Or do I fabricate with words, loving them as I do? No I think not. In this book I have almost too many ideas. I want to give life and death, sanity and insanity; I want to criticise the social system, and to show it at work, at its most intense – But here I may be posing. Am I writing *The Hours* from deep emotion? Of course the mad part tries me so much, making my mind squint so badly that I can hardly face spending the next weeks at it.

One thing I do feel pretty certain about and here confide it to my diary – we must leave Richmond and set up in London. The arguments are so well known to me that I can't bother to write them down. Leonard remains to be converted, and my God, the move – the horror – the servants. Still this is life – never to be sitting down for longer than one feels inclined.

Thursday 28 June
This may be life; but I doubt that I shall ever convert L. and now sit down baffled and depressed to face a life spent, mute and mitigated, in the suburbs, just as I had it in mind that I could at last go full speed ahead. For the capacities in me will never, after forty, accumulate again. And I mind missing life far more than he does, for it isn't life to him in the sense that it is life to me. But half the horror is that L. instead of being, as I gathered, sympathetic, has the old rigid obstacle – my health. And I can't sacrifice his peace of mind, yet the obstacle is surely now a dead hand, which one should no longer let dominate our short years of life – oh to dwindle them out here, with all these gaps, and abbreviations! Always to catch trains, always to waste time, to sit here and wait for Leonard to come in, to spend hours standing at the box of type with Marjorie, to wonder what its all for – when, alternatively, I might go and hear a tune, or have a look at a picture, or find out something at the British Museum, or go adventuring among human beings. Sometimes I should merely walk down Cheapside. But now I'm tied, imprisoned, inhibited. All I can do is to pretend I'm writing something very important, or reading with a view to a book I shall never write. This is the pith of my complaint. For ever to be suburban. L. I don't

think minds any of this as much as I do. But then, Lord! what I owe to him! What he gives me! Still, I say, surely we could get more from life than we do – isn't he too much of a Puritan, of a disciplinarian, doesn't he through birth and training accept a drastic discipline with too Spartan a self control? There is, I suppose, a very different element in us; my social side, his intellectual side. This social side is very genuine in me. Nor do I think it reprehensible. It is a piece of jewellery I inherit from my mother – a joy in laughter, something that is stimulated by contact with my friends. Moreover, for my work now, I want freer intercourse, wider intercourse – and now, at forty-one, having done a little work, I get my wages partly in invitations. I might know people. In Richmond this is impossible. Either we have arduous parties at long intervals, or I make my frenzied dashes up to London, and leave, guiltily, as the clock strikes 11.

Saturday 8 July
It is now the hottest day of the year, and I don't want to grumble; having seen many people – Anyhow, if a move is to be made, it can't be till the autumn, or new year. Anyhow, I am content at present, or moderately so. I can't help thinking myself about as successful journalistically as any woman of my day. But that is not saying much. I wish I could write *The Hours* as freely and vigorously as I scribble *Freshwater, a Comedy*. Its a strange thing how arduous I find my novels; and yet *Freshwater* is only spirited fun; and *The Hours* has some serious merit. By the way, on re-reading this book I resolved to write rather more carefully, and to record conversations verbatim. It is difficult to write carefully, as I am always having at this book by way of killing time, filling time, or writing out the fidgets. As for recording conversations, nothing is harder.

Sunday 22 July
A great many conversations to record: dined with [Raymond] Mortimer and Scofield Thayer the other night and went on with them to Mary's. Mortimer is Oxford; he is all angle and polish. Wears a swallow tail white waistcoat; wants brilliancy not intimacy, is half a dandy. Scofield Thayer was a cautious hardheaded American, edited the *Dial*. Like Mortimer he buys modern pictures. But the talk was too formal and too conventional to bear writing out; or I can't do it. A good account of flying from Thayer: "The pilot said he wouldn't start. The company had sold three seats instead of two. But I had taken my passage ten days before. I wouldn't budge. Some luggage was left. One man took his dachs. But we felt overweighted. Then we got above a storm. One leant over and saw the lightning dashing up at one's face. It was terrible. I looked at my feet. One man kept going to the side and being sick. The other kept saying It is bad It is bad. And

we all knew we were overweighted. Suddenly the engines stopped. We pitched up and down. We expected the whole thing to crash. The dog sat quite calm. Then after ten minutes the engine began again. Towns looked like the handle of that salt cellar. Never again, no. And the pilot said he'd been guiding with one hand and fumbling with the other and suddenly touched the right spring by chance, and the engine started. But we might just as well have dashed to the ground."

Friday 28 July

These days before going, as we do on Wednesday, are too dissipated for serious reading writing living or thinking. This half year has kept me on the hop. I like that; agitating though it is. I've taken my fences, as I say, and got some good gallops for my trouble. Never settle, is my principle in life; and I try to put it in practice, but in talk more than in action I daresay. My theory is that at forty one either increases the pace or slows down. Needless to say which I desire. But, to be just, my activity is also mental. I'm working variously and with intention. And I'm going to work hard, hard, hard, in every sense at Rodmell. Also I shall explore – take a motor bus ride along the downs one day – see Steyning and Arundel and so on.

MONKS HOUSE, RODMELL

Monday 6 August

I have ruined my morning's work by making bread and buns, which require constant voyages to the kitchen. We went over to Charleston yesterday. Although thinking quite well of ourselves, we were not well received by the painters. There they sat like assiduous children at a task in a bedroom – Roger, Nessa, and Duncan; Roger on chair in foreground; Nessa on sofa, Duncan on bed. In front of them was one jar of flowers, and one arrangement of still life. Roger was picking out his blue flower very brightly. For some reason, the talk was not entirely congenial. Clive was sitting in the drawing room window reading Dryden. Hollyhocks, decapitated, swam in a bowl; there was a loaf for tea, and a long slab of cake. Roger, I can't help thinking, has become a little querulous with years. His grievances torment him; he talks of them too much. After tea, Angelica had her dolls' tea party in the window, and beat Clive, and when he cried, ran of her own accord and picked him a flower – which was a sensible womanly act. She is sensitive – minds being laughed at (as I do). "Don't laugh at me" she said, petulantly, to Roger.

Saturday 29 August

I've been battling for ever so long with *The Hours*, which is proving one of my most tantalising and refractory of books. Parts are so bad, parts so good. I'm much interested; can't stop making it up yet – yet. What is the matter with it?

Clive has an egg – a turkey's egg – for a head now – quite bald; never a hair will grow any more. Mary was shrinking, childlike, not attending when I read my play, but very anxious to say the right thing. Chocolates she brought; she wore tight grey Alpaca, with large buttons, and she powdered and re-powdered in the drawing room. Going to the dogs was discussed.

Thursday 30 August

My goodness, the wind! Last night we looked at the meadow trees, flinging about, and such a weight of leaves that every brandish seems the end. I read such a white dimity rice puddingy chapter of Mrs Gaskell at midnight in the gale, *Wives and Daughters* – I think it must be better than *Old Wives' Tale* all the same.

Wednesday 5 September

Our week end was Francis Birrell and Raymond Mortimer. Frankie spills out the whole contents of his head like a nice little boy; never stops talking. Mortimer is a curious half breed. An Oxford young man, inclined to smartness, dress and culture. His soul is uneasy in Cambridge company. He flatters. He is not very simple, candid or talkative, like chatterbox Frankie who is as open as daylight. "My father is a solicitor – lives at Exmouth, and has really been a bachelor since the death of my mother. She died when I was quite small. No I don't mind being an only child at all. I am quite happy. If I had two thousand a year, I should never write. I should buy pictures and travel." We discussed writing novels on Asheham Hill. But he can't write novels himself. Doesn't see why he should; has no originality. Likes pictures perhaps best, because there's Picasso in painting and no one to match him in writing. At the same time we were talking about Clive Bell who had been to luncheon, talking a great deal. "He seems to me a perfectly happy and developed man, and he enjoys life too." Then Vanessa: "She has such a lovely voice, and then she's very lovely to look at. Her personality too is very impressive," he said. In short "You can't imagine what it has been to me getting to know Bloomsbury. They're different human beings from any I thought possible."

I began for the fifth but last time, I swear, what is now to be called *The Common Reader*; and did the first page quite moderately well this morning.

Tuesday 11 September

Here we are back from 'The Knoll', Studland. It was reckoned that we could have got to France in less time. I wanted to observe Lydia as a type for Rezia; and did observe one or two facts. It was very hot at Lulworth, and we sat with the sun in our eyes on a verandah having tea. Suddenly she got cross, frowned, complained of the heat, seemed about to cry, precisely like a child of six. She was concerned to know what Leonard meant by coupling her with me among the 'sillies'. "It means that you can both be beaten," Maynard said. Maynard is grown very gross and stout, especially when he wraps his leopard-spotted dressing-gown tight round his knees and stands in front of the fire. He has a queer swollen eel-like look, not very pleasant. But his eyes are remarkable, and as I truly said when he gave me some pages of his new book to read, the process of mind there displayed is as far ahead of me as Shakespeare's. True, I don't respect it so much. The poet Rylands was there and Mortimer. Dadie's hair (he became Dadie at 10 a.m. Monday at Poole Station) is precisely the colour and consistency of the husk of straw. Add to this a blue cornflower coloured tweed suit, his apple red face, and blue eyes and you have – well, merely a cornflower to me, but to Raymond the most intoxicatingly beautiful young man that it is possible to imagine. We motored to Lulworth on Sunday, or rather to Warbarrow, which we climbed and walked five miles over the down. My shoes interfered with my pleasure rather. But I thought of the year 1830, and how most of England then looked as this coast looked, bays with their sweep untenanted, only coast guards and grey cottages, and rowing boats making off to little ships. And then I caught a view or two which I've no doubt will keep for some years and then be used. The clear water was very moving to me, with the pale stones showing under it like jelly fish. Lulworth of course was all skittles. Then we stopped, Maynard liking I think to be showman, at Bindon Abbey, having just before seen the old Manor house where Tess [of the D'Urbervilles] slept, or lived. At Bindon Lydia lay in her pink jacket with the white fur in a Bishop's tomb – a kind of shaped tank sunk in the earth on the way up to the Calvary. She lay quite still, acting death, her muscular dancer's legs in white silk stockings lying with the soles of the feet touching, and Maynard and I standing by. What did she think about? About Maynard, and her death, and what would happen before? Heaven knows. We sat on the mound of the Calvary, and Maynard talked about palaeolithic man. To return: – Dadie has an ingratiating manner of pawing ladies old enough to be his mother. He threw out an idea that he might join the Press. The printing mania has come upon him. He asked lightly, for he is not emphatic and very happy I should think, with all his interests and successes, and no inhibitions and good health, and money in prospect, and an editor to print his poems, and a year more at Cambridge, and a possible fellowship and so forth – he asked lightly whether he might lodge with us in the holidays, and pay his way by working the press. So you see how the future branches and extends: I mean there are ways down the forest; roads leading to right and left hitherto unseen.

Tuesday 18 September
Leonard's day in London, and before I walk off to meet him I may as well write here. We have had visitors – Lytton and the Partridges, unexpectedly; then Nessa and Duncan; then Morgan for the week-end. There are times when I want no one, times when I relish the commonest animated slug. I am worn smooth with talk at the moment. Yet how good, kind, tender, and clever we all are! Not much talk of interest with Lytton. He pounced on our books. Oh books, books! he cried. Fame has made him confident, taken from him I suppose some charm, turned it to strength of some kind. Very well. We all grow old; grow stocky; lose our pliancy and impressionability. Even Morgan seems to me to be based on some hidden rock. Talking of Proust and Lawrence he said he'd prefer to be Lawrence; but much rather would be himself. He is aloof, serene, a snob, he says, reading masterpieces only. We had a long gossip about servants. But it grows cold and dark; I shall walk off to meet L.

HOGARTH HOUSE, RICHMOND

Monday 15 October
This last entry seems long ago. And I meant to record for psychological purposes that strange night when I went to meet Leonard and did not meet him. What an intensity of feeling was pressed into those hours! It was a wet windy night; and as I walked back across the field I said Now I am meeting it; now the old devil has once more got his spine through the waves. And such was the strength of my feeling that I became physically rigid. And there was something noble in feeling like this; tragic, not at all petty. Then cold white lights went over the fields; and went out; and I stood under the great trees waiting for the lights of the bus. And that went by; and I felt lonelier. But I could control all this, until, suddenly, after the last likely train had come in I felt it was intolerable to sit about, and must do the final thing, which was to go to London. Off I rode, without much time, against such a wind; and again I had a satisfaction in being matched with powerful things, like wind and dark. I battled, had to walk; got on; drove ahead; dropped the torch; picked it up, and so on again without any lights. Saw men and women walking together; thought, you're safe and

happy and I'm an outcast; took my ticket; had three minutes to spare, and then, turning the corner of the station stairs, saw Leonard, coming along, walking very quick, in his mackintosh. He was rather cold and angry (as perhaps was natural). And then, not to show my feelings, I went outside and did something to my bicycle. Also I went back to the ticket office, and said to the humane man there, "It's all right. My husband caught the last train. Give me back my fare", which he did. And I got the money more to set myself right with Leonard than because I wanted it. All the way back we talked about a row at the office; and all the time I was feeling My God, that's over. I'm out of that. Its over. Really, it was a physical feeling, of lightness and relief and safety. And yet there was too something terrible behind it – the fact of this pain, I suppose; which continued for several days. I think I should feel it again if I went over that road at night. But I have not got it all in, by any means.

My first activity has been to see houses. So far I have seen the outsides of two. And the problem is a difficult one. Its my wish to live in London, no one else's. How far can this wish bear the weight of the removal, the expense, the less pleasant surroundings, and so on? Here we are tight wedged in printing and editing. And we have Dadie in prospect. This young man with hair like the husk of corn, says he wishes to devote his life to the Hogarth Press, and is writing to that effect to Leonard. This will begin in June. He shall be a partner, and take over the work; and we shall supervise, and by degrees it will become more and more important, and we shall be the benefactors of our age; and have a shop, and enjoy the society of the young, and rummage and splash in the great bran pie, and so never, never stop working with brains or fingers or toes till our limbs fly asunder and the heart sprays off into dust. Such is my fancy picture.

Saturday 3 November
And now I've found a house: 35 Woburn Square. Yes, shall I write that address often? Certainly I hope to. For me it would be worth £500 a year in pleasure. Think of the music I could hear, the people I could see, easily, unthinkingly? And then comes before me the prospect of walking through the city streets; starting off early and walking say to Wapping. Why this so obsesses my mind I don't know. But I have wasted my time drawing a plan of 35 on the opposite page. Nothing runs away with time like these house dreams. I must read Sophocles. After twenty years I now know how to read Greek quick (with a crib in one hand) and with pleasure. This is for the eternal book. And my mind whips off to rents – how much can we ask for this house? I'm heartless about poor old Hogarth, where for nine years we have been so secure.

Friday 16 November

No we didn't take 35 Woburn Square, and the colour has gone out of it, and I don't want to write about it at the moment. I'm back from lunch [with] Lady Colefax and in rather a fritter, too much so to read Euripides. Indeed, I've been talking to Hugh Walpole – not an impressive man – a man who protests too much; an uneasy, prosperous, vain man, who harbours some grudge against clever intellectuals and yet respects them, would like to be one. He has the look of a kindly solicitor or banker; red cheeks; very small bright eyes; a genial, but not profound or cordial manner. An uninteresting mind, and really not able to cast a shadow even upon me. I did not feel knocked over, dashed to pieces, or anything very vividly, except that he was slightly in awe of me. As for Lady Colefax, there she sits painted and emphatic at the head of her table, broad cheeked, a little coarse, kindly, glass-eyed, affectionate to me almost, capable, apparently disinterested – I mean if she likes to listen to clever talk and buy it with a lunch of four courses and good wine, I see no harm in it. Its a taste, not a vice. Off we streamed at 3.

So to the Tate with Lytton. Lytton and I don't need much preliminary. "Here's my book – *Queen Victoria* – in French. I daresay it reads better in French." He has almost bought a house near Hungerford, in the downs. There are no drains and no water. Still I advised the leap, as I always advise leaps. And then there was [Boris] Anrep, and his tinted [Blake mosaic] floor, all raying out in greens and browns, like the waves of a sea; not a good metaphor, for it is really very compact, strong, and contained. Droves of schoolchildren kept sweeping over it. He explained it to me, smelling rather too much of whisky.

Monday 3 December

Back from Rodmell; unable to settle in; therefore I write diary. An odd psychological fact – that I can write when I'm too jangled to read. Moreover, I want to leave as few pages blank as possible; and the end of the year is only some three weeks off. Oh there's Adrian's catastrophe to record – now two weeks old. Nessa rang me up in the middle of dinner with Tom here. "Adrian and Karin are going to separate." You could have knocked me down with a feather. The devoted and inseparable couple! They'd been unhappy for years. They hadn't quarrelled. Nessa says, and Clive says, that Karin did it. She felt all I used to feel: the snub; the check; the rebuke; the fastidiousness; the lethargy. Poor old Adrian; undoubtedly the *DNB* crushed his life out before he was born. It gave me a twist of the head too. I shouldn't have been so clever, but I should have been more stable, without that contribution to the history of England.

Wednesday 19 December
I don't know if this is my last chance of writing. I am so stifled with work of all sorts, society of all sorts, and plans of all sorts, that I can't pour a pure stream from my tap. I must briefly touch on Dadie; house problem not settled; Maynard threatening to cut down reviews; Leonard at this moment threatening to resign; publishing, writing, doing Hardy and Montaigne and the Greeks and the Elizabethans and *The Hours*; accepted in America, neglected by all prize givers, very happy, very much on the go – that's my state, at the moment of writing, 6.14 p.m. on Wednesday aforesaid.

1924

On returning to Richmond from Monks House at the New Year, Virginia lost no time in pressing on with her plan to move into London, and by 9 January she had found her house -- 52 Tavistock Square, Bloomsbury, on which, after the usual agitations, the Woolfs secured a ten-year lease from the Bedford Estate. In spite of Leonard's reservations, the problem of the servants, and all the practical dispositions to be made, Virginia's determination carried them forward, and the move took place on 13 March. In the meantime she still found time for some social distractions, including meeting Arnold Bennett and enjoying another encounter with the philosopher Bertrand Russell, who had been her sister-in-law Karin Stephen's tutor at Cambridge. At a farewell dinner given by the Nation to the poet Edmund Blunden, Virginia talked to Katherine Mansfield's widower Middleton Murry, and confirmed her low opinion of his character.

Installed in their new home on the top two floors of 52 Tavistock Square, Virginia felt herself at the hub of her world: Vanessa round the corner in Gordon Square; friends at hand to come or to go to; concerts, theatres, films within easy reach; and in the basement the busy life of the Hogarth Press, with Marjorie Thomson at work, Dadie Rylands coming as potential manager, and manuscripts pouring in. They published fourteen books this year, including small paper-bound works by Eliot, Roger Fry, E. M. Forster, Robert Graves and Virginia herself; and the first volumes of the Collected Papers of Sigmund Freud, Leonard having secured the English rights to the publications of the International Psycho-Analytical Library. Notwithstanding the increased bustle of her life, Virginia managed to write a great deal of journalism, largely unsigned contributions to the Nation; and in October, she records that she had finished Mrs Dalloway, which she had worked at steadily since moving house.

The Woolfs were at Monks House for Easter; in May they stayed with Lytton Strachey and attendant Partridges at Tidmarsh, and later in the year at Lytton's new home, Ham Spray House in Wiltshire; they went to Cambridge, where Virginia read a paper, 'Character in Fiction', to the Society of Heretics; in July they were at Garsington.

Although after first meeting Harold Nicolson and his wife Vita Sackville-West at Clive Bell's and on one or two further occasions Virginia had decided that they were both incurably stupid, the acquaintance was fostered by Vita, who in July this year invited Virginia to lunch with her father Lord Sackville at Knole, his vast baronial *mansion in Kent, and then to her own home, Long Barn, nearby. Virginia's imagination was stirred by the visit and her hostess, who was to become her most beloved woman friend. Vita came for a night to Monks House in September, overaweing Nelly by her rank, and making Virginia very conscious of the shabby imperfections of her own and Vanessa's cherished homes. But the initial benefit of this relationship was to the Hogarth Press, who published Vita's* Seducers in Ecuador *(dedicated to Virginia), and were to become her main publishers for many years to come.*

By the end of the year Dadie Rylands had decided that the life of a printer and publisher was not for him, and proposed a Cambridge friend, Angus Davidson, to succeed him, which he did on 10 December; he spent Christmas with the Woolfs at Monks House.

1924

HOGARTH HOUSE, RICHMOND

Thursday 3 January
This year is almost certainly bound to be the most eventful in the whole
of our (recorded) career. Tomorrow I go up to London to look for houses;
on Saturday I deliver sentence of death upon Nelly and Lottie; at Easter
we leave Hogarth; in June Dadie comes to live with us; and our domestic
establishment is entirely controlled by one woman, a vacuum cleaner, and
electric stoves. Now how much of this is dream, and how much reality? I
should like, very much, to turn to the last page of this virgin volume and
there find my dreams true. It rests with me to substantiate them between
now and then.

Wednesday 9 January
At this very moment, or fifteen minutes ago to be precise, I bought the ten
years' lease of 52 Tavistock Square, London WC1. Subject of course to the
lease, and to Providence, the house is ours; and the basement, and the
billiard room, with the rock garden on top, and the view of the Square in
front and the desolated buildings behind, and Southampton Row, and the
whole of London – London thou art a jewel of jewels, and jasper of
jocunditie – music, talk, friendship, city views, books, publishing, all this is
now within my reach, as it hasn't been since August 1913, when we left
Clifford's Inn for a series of catastrophes which very nearly ended my life,
and would, I'm vain enough to think, have ruined Leonard's. So I ought to
be grateful to Richmond and Hogarth, and indeed, I am grateful. Nowhere
else could we have started the Hogarth Press, whose very awkward
beginning had rise in this very room. Here that strange offspring grew and
throve; it ousted us from the dining room, which is now a dusty coffin; and
crept all over the house. And people have been here, thousands of them it
seems to me. I've sat over this fire many an evening talking, and save for
one fit of the glooms last summer, have never complained of Richmond,
till I shed it, like a loose skin. I've had some very curious visions in this
room too, lying in bed, mad, and seeing the sunlight quivering like gold

water on the wall. I've heard the voices of the dead here. And felt, through it all, exquisitely happy.

Saturday 12 January

Nelly has agreed to stay on alone as a general; and I am to find Lottie a place in Gordon Square. I see difficulty upon difficulty ahead. None of this would much matter if L. were happy; but with him despondent or grim, the wind is taken out of my sails, and I say, what's it all for? Its odd how entirely this house question absorbs one. It is a radical change, though. It means a revision of four lives. Yet for people of our age, which is in full summer, to dread risk and responsibility seems pusillanimous. We have no children to consider. My health is as good as it will be in this world, and a great deal better than it ever has been. The next ten years must see the press into fame or bankruptcy; to loiter on here is a handicap. But I've gone through all these matters time and time again, and wish I could think of something else. I've so much work on hand. Its odd how unimportant my work seems, suddenly, when a practical matter like this blocks the way.

Sunday 20 January

No final news of Tavistock Square yet. Here we are, going through a time of waiting. I shall be happy so soon as my claws are into the move. At present, I feel Oh God another journey? Must I go up by train? Where am I to change before dinner tomorrow, and so on.

Wednesday 23 January

And on Monday if I'd written here I should have had to say 'we have lost Tavistock Square'. It was a very unpleasant shock, and for my part I don't think we could easily have got over it. But my house finding genius was outraged; what's the good of me, it asked, if you let these sharpers trick you? And I warn you, 52 is your house. So, practically not only spiritually speaking it now is. I visited the office with cheque and signature before one today; and then spent a shilling on a plate of beef. Ah well! Now I can sigh contented over my fire, in spite of the rain, and the [rail] strike, and Lady Colefax and Ethel Sands, and all cares and sorrows and perplexities.

I have seen Roger; seen his pictures, which with the irrepressible vanity of the artist, he makes even the blind like me report on, by electric light, in a hurry. But enough of that; in every other way he abounds; cut him wherever you like, and the juice wells up. Lytton has bought his house. But now I am going to write till we move – six weeks straight ahead. A letter from Morgan today saying 'To whom first but you and Virginia should I tell the fact that I've put the last words to my novel [*A Passage to India*]?' He is moved, as I am always on these occasions.

Sunday 3 February

I didn't write however, because L. started the 'flu, the very next day, and gave me an unpleasant day; but there's an odd pleasure too, purely feminine I suppose, in 'looking after', being wanted; giving up my pen, and sitting with an invalid. But he was up in four days or less; and here we are, on the rails again, a very lovely spring day, which, by Heaven's grace, we have spent alone. No servants at the moment; no callers. The sun laid gold leaf over the trees and chimneys today. The willows on the bank were soft, yellow, plumy, like a cloud; like an infinitely fine spray. I reflect that I shan't be walking here again next spring. I am not sentimental about it: Tavistock Square with the pale tower is more beautiful I think, let alone the adorable omnibuses.

Owing to the influenza, I don't think I have seen more than a handful; went to Ethel Sands's; talked to Arnold Bennett, a loveable sea lion, with chocolate eyes, drooping lids, and a protruding tusk. He has an odd accent; a queer manner; is provincial; very much a character. I suspect he minds things, even my pinpricks. He is slow, kind, affectionate, hauls himself along a sofa.

Nelly went to the flat with me, and next day wrote out a time table, to show that by 3 p.m. she would still have to wash up luncheon and do Leonard's boots. Very well, I said, find a place with Lottie. But the end of a week's consideration is, apparently, that Nelly clings to us. The money is paid over, and the house presumably ours tomorrow. So I shall have a room of my own to sit down in, after almost ten years, in London.

Saturday 9 February

We have been measuring the flat. Now the question arises Is it noisy? No need to go into my broodings over that point. Fitzroy Square rubbed a nerve bare which will never sleep again while an omnibus is in the neighbourhood. My feeling about this move is that we're doing the courageous thing.

Morgan was here last night; *A Passage to India* done; and he is much excited, on the boil with it, consulting L. about terms; has been offered £750. So *he's* all right. Marjorie has put earrings in her ears and left Joad. Poor chit! At twenty-four. I was at Fitzroy then, and devilish unhappy too. I'm working at *The Hours*, and think it a very interesting attempt. (And its just as noisy here, if one listens, as it can possibly be in Tavistock Square. One gets into a habit of not listening. Remember this sage advice.) Karin has been confiding. Adrian wants to come back.

Saturday 23 February

Really I've a thousand things to do. I've just said to L. I'm so busy I can't begin, which unfortunately is too true of me. Then I bethink me that with life in its present rush, I may never again write a word of this book at Hogarth House, and so should take a few minutes to lay the sod, or whatever the expression is. Its very cold, barbarous weather. Twice we have meant to go to Rodmell and failed. Warmth is the one need I have. May's will move us on March 13th for fifteen pounds. I am going to force L. into the outrageous extravagance of spending twenty-five pounds on painted panels, by Bell and Grant. We are trying to hook together all the resources of civilisation – telephone, gas, electric light, and, at this distance, naturally find it arduous. The electric light man doesn't turn up. Lottie is going to Karin – I fancy I have forgotten that item. All could not have fallen out better, so far, I say, being by no means ready to bait the deity, who can always show his claws. That reminds me of the celebrated Mr [Bertrand] Russell the other night at Karin's. (She gives her weekly party in the great gay drawing room [at 50 Gordon Square] which is nevertheless a little echoing and lofty and very very chill.) He said "Just as I saw a chance of happiness, the doctors said I had got cancer. My first thought was that was one up to God. When I was getting better – I had very nearly died – the thing I liked was the sun: I thought how nice to feel the sun and the rain still. People came a long way after that. The old poets were right. They made people think of death as going where they could not see the sun. I have become an optimist. I realise now that I like life – I want to live. Before that illness, I thought life was bad." So to Charlie Sanger, who is good all through; and then on to [G. E.] Moore: "When he first came up to Cambridge, he was the most wonderful creature in the whole world. His smile was the most beautiful thing I have ever seen. I said to him once, Moore, have you ever told a lie? 'Yes' he said – which was the only lie he ever told." I asked him, as I ask everyone, to write his life for the press. "But my mind is absolutely relevant. I can't ramble. I stick to facts." "Facts are what we want. Now the colour of your mother's hair?" "She died when I was two – there you are, relevant facts. I remember my grandfather's death, and crying, and then thinking it was over. I saw my brother drive up in the afternoon. Hooray! I cried. They told me I must not say hooray at all that day." He had no one to play with. One does not like him. Yet he is brilliant of course; perfectly outspoken; familiar; talks of his bowels; likes people; and yet and yet – He disapproves of me perhaps? This luminous vigorous mind seems attached to a flimsy little car, like that on a large glinting balloon. And he has no chin, and he is dapper. Nevertheless, I should like the run of his headpiece. We parted at the corner of the Square; no attempt to meet again.

Wednesday 12 March

And I'm now going to write the very last pages ever to be written at Hogarth House. My head is stuffy and heavy. Last night we dined at [Edmund] Blunden's farewell party, thirty-five covers laid, six or seven speeches made. My little drama was provided by Murry, who, as people were going, came and sat beside me. "We're enemies." "Not enemies. We're in different camps. But I've never said a word against you, Virginia." We came into a swift confused wrangle about 'writing well', but here L. came up; said we must go. But I shan't meet Murry for ten years, and I want to finish the argument – "Shall I come to the *Adelphi?*" "Do" he said, yet so oleaginously, with a rolling, lustful, or somehow leering, eye, so that I kept thinking how he'd come down in the world, spiritually, what tenth-rate shillyshallying humbugs he must live among. And we said goodbye for ten years. How honest and trusty and sterling Francis Birrell was in comparison! So home that long cold exhausting journey for the last time. Some odds and ends of ideas came to me at the dinner. For one thing, how pungent people's writing is compared with people's flesh. We were all toothless insignificant amiable nonentities – we distinguished writers; Blunden despairing, drooping, crow-like, rather than Keats-like. And did we really all believe in Blunden's 'genius'? Had we read his poems? How much sincerity was there in the whole thing? The truth is these collective gatherings must be floated by some conventional song, in which all can join, like He's a jolly good fellow, which Squire started. Subtler impressions did occur to me, but I can't place them at the moment. Nor at the moment can I think of any farewell for this beautiful and lovable house, which has done us such a good turn for almost precisely nine years, so that, as I lay in bed last night, I nearly humanised it, and offered it my thanks.

*   *   *

The Woolfs' move from Hogarth House to 52 Tavistock Square, Bloomsbury, took place on 13 and 14 March. They were to inhabit the two top floors of the large four-storey house on the southern side of the square; the sitting tenants, Messrs Dollman & Pritchard, Solicitors, continued their tenure of the ground and first floors; the extensive basement was given over to the Hogarth Press; and a large billiard room built in place of a back garden became both VW's study and the storeroom for Hogarth Press books.

52 Tavistock Square, wc1

Saturday 5 April
Well, I will make a brief beginning – after three weeks' silence. But it has not been silence at all. The noise of bus and taxi has worried me, and the noise of the human tongue has disturbed me, pleasantly and otherwise, and now I'm half asleep. Leonard working as usual. But can I collect any first impressions? My first night in the basement I saw the moon, with drifting clouds, and it was a terrifying and new London moon; dreadful and exciting, as if the Richmond moon had been veiled. Oh the convenience of this place! and the loveliness too. We walk home from theatres, through the entrails of London. Why do I love it so much? ... for it is stony hearted, and callous. The tradespeople don't know one – but these disparaging remarks were interrupted and it is now

Tuesday 15 April
– and L. and I have been having one of those melancholy middle aged summings up of a situation which occur from time to time, but are seldom recorded. Indeed most of life escapes, now I come to think of it; the texture of the ordinary day. L. was desperately gloomy. Not a stroke of work done he says, since we came to London. This is largely imagination, I think, though its true fish keep drifting into the net. Gerald Brenan back; Roger rampant to paint us; Morgan, elflike, mocking, aloof; Nessa and Duncan. Then there was Angelica's accident which, for the psychology of it I should have described. Here was Nessa painting, and I answering the telephone. Louie [nurse] and Angelica have been knocked down by a motor and are in the Middlesex Hospital. I had to repeat it to Nessa: to destroy all that simmering everyday comfort, with the smell of paint in the room, and Tom just coming upstairs to tea. She ran out and away from the telephone instinctively, ran round in an aimless way for a second. Then off they dashed and I after them, and so to the hospital, holding hands in the cab; and then sheer agony, for there was Louie, with her foot bandaged, and no Angelica; only an evasive nurse, parrying enquiries and taking us behind a screen where Angelica lay in bed, still, her face turned away. At last she moved. "She's not dead" Duncan said. They both thought her dead. Then the young doctor came, and seemed silently and considerately but firmly to wish the mother to know that the case was hopeless: very grave; run over across the stomach. Yes there may have to be an operation. The surgeon had been sent for. So Nessa went back to sit there, and I saw again that extraordinary look of anguish, dumb, not complaining, which I saw in Greece, I think, when she was ill. The feelings of the people who don't talk express themselves thus. My feeling was 'a pane of glass shelters me. I'm

only allowed to look on at this.' Its a queer thing to come so close to agony as this, and just to be saved oneself. What I felt was that death and tragedy had once more put down his paw, after letting us run a few paces. People never get over their early impressions of death I think. I always feel pursued. But there's an end of this. Nothing was wrong with Angelica – it was only a joke this time.

It takes a long time to form a habit – the habit of living at 52 Tavistock Square is not quite formed, but doing well. Already I have spent a week without being bothered by noise. One ceases to hear or to see. Dadie has been – a sensitive vain youth, with considerable grit in him, I judge. Sometimes the future appears perilous; problematical rather, the press that is, but always fruitful and interesting.

Monday 5 May
This is the twenty-ninth anniversary of mother's death. I think it happened on a Sunday morning, and I looked out of the nursery window and saw old Dr Seton walking away with his hands behind his back, as if to say It is finished, and then the doves descending, to peck in the road, I suppose, with a fall and descent of infinite peace. I was thirteen, and could fill a whole page and more with my impressions of that day, many of them ill received by me, and hidden from the grown ups, but very memorable on that account: how I laughed, for instance, behind the hand which was meant to hide my tears; and through the fingers saw the nurses sobbing.

But enough of death – its life that matters. London is enchanting. I step out upon a tawny coloured magic carpet, it seems, and get carried into beauty without raising a finger. And people pop in and out, lightly, divertingly, like rabbits; and I look down Southampton Row, wet as a seal's back or red and yellow with sunshine, and watch the omnibuses going and coming, and hear the old crazy organ. One of these days I will write about London. I have left the whole of society unrecorded. Tidmarsh, Cambridge, and now Rodmell. We had a queer little party here the other day – when the sinister and pedagogic Tom cut a queer figure. I cannot wholly free myself from suspicions about him – at the worst they only amount to calling him an American schoolmaster; a very vain man.

Saturday 21 June
I am oh so sleepy; in fact just woken from a hot drowse. If I weren't so sleepy, I would write about the soul. I think its time to cancel that vow against soul description. What was I going to say? Something about the violent moods of my soul. I think I grow more and more poetic. Perhaps I restrained it, and now, like a plant in a pot it begins to crack the earthenware. Often I feel the different aspects of life bursting my mind asunder. Morgan

is too restrained in his new book perhaps. I mean, what's the use of facts at our time of life? Why build these careful cocoons?

I look forward with a little alarm to Dadie coming, chiefly I think that it commits us more seriously. But that will wear off soon. It seems to me the beginning of ten years of very hard work. I don't see how Marjorie will fit in, altogether, and rather anticipate some rearrangement. So far, no gossip and no soul. Yet I've seen – Bob, Desmond, Lytton, Sebastian [Sprott], Dorothy Bussy, Mrs Eliot – this last making me almost vomit, so scented, so powdered, so egotistic, so morbid, so weakly.

I am writing, writing, and see my way clear to the end now, and so shall gallop to it, somehow or other.

Thursday 3 July

This is Dadie's second day. Marjorie is ill, which is all to the good; business is brisk; I sat in the basement two days ago and took five pounds. But I have let Garsington languish like a decaying wreath on my pen. That was last Sunday. And, treading close on Garsington was the enamelled Lady Colefax, actually in this room, like a cheap bunch of artificial cherries, yet loyal, hard, living on a burnished plate of facts; inquisitive; not at all able to sink to the depths; but a superb skimmer of the surface; which is bright, I suppose, and foam tipped. I can't bring myself to despise this gull as I ought. But aristocrats, worldlings, for all their surface polish, are empty, slippery, coat the mind with sugar and butter, and make it slippery too.

Saturday 5 July

Just back, not from the 1917 Club, but from Knole, where indeed I was invited to lunch alone with his Lordship. His Lordship lives in the kernel of a vast nut. You perambulate miles of galleries; skip endless treasures – chairs that Shakespeare might have sat on – tapestries, pictures, floors made of the halves of oaks; and penetrate at length to a round shiny table with a cover laid for one. A dozen glasses form a circle each with a red rose in it. One solitary peer sits lunching by himself, with his napkin folded into the shape of a lotus flower. Knole is a conglomeration of buildings half as big as Cambridge I daresay; if you stuck Trinity, Clare and King's together you might approximate. But the extremities and indeed the inward parts are gone dead. Ropes fence off half the rooms; the chairs and the pictures look preserved; life has left them. Not for a hundred years have the retainers sat down to dinner in the great hall. Then there is Mary Stuart's altar, where she prayed before execution. "An ancestor of ours took her the death warrant" said Vita. All these ancestors and centuries, and silver and gold, have bred a perfect body. She is stag like, or race horse like, save for the face, which pouts, and has no very sharp brain. But as a body hers is perfection. So many rare and curious objects hit one's brain like pellets which perhaps may unfold later. But its the breeding of Vita's that I took away with me as an impression, carrying her and Knole in my eye as I travelled up with the lower middle classes, through slums. There is Knole, capable of housing all the desperate poor of Judd Street, and with only that one solitary earl in the kernel.

MONKS HOUSE, RODMELL

Saturday 2 August
Here we are at Rodmell, and I with twenty minutes to fill in before dinner. A feeling of depression is on me, as if we were old and near the end of all things. It must be the change from London and incessant occupation. Then, being at a low ebb with my book, I begin to count myself a failure. Now the point of the Press is that it entirely prevents brooding, and gives me something solid to fall back on. The country is like a convent. The soul swims to the top.

Julian has just been and gone, a tall young man who, inveterately believing myself to be young as I do, seems to me like a younger brother; anyhow we sit and chatter, as easily as can be. Its all so much the same – his school continues Thoby's school. He tells me about boys and masters as Thoby used to. It interests me just in the same way. He's a sensitive, very quick witted, rather combative boy; full of Wells, and discoveries, and the future of the world. And, being of my own blood, easily understood – going to be very tall, and go to the Bar, I daresay.

Sunday 3 August
L. has been telling me about Germany, and reparations, how money is paid. Lord what a weak brain I have – like an unused muscle. He talks; and the facts come in, and I can't deal with them. But by dint of very painful brain exercises, perhaps I understand a little more than Nelly does of the International situation. And L. understands it all – picks up all these points of the daily paper absolutely instantly, has them connected, ready to produce. Sometimes I think my brain and his are of different orders. Were it not for my flash of imagination, and this turn for books, I should be a very ordinary woman.

Friday 15 August
By the way, why is poetry wholly an elderly taste? When I was twenty I could not for the life of me read Shakespeare for pleasure; now it lights me as I walk to think I have two acts of *King John* tonight, and shall next read

Richard the Second. It is poetry that I want now – long poems. I want the concentration and the romance, and the words all glued together, fused, glowing: have no time to waste any more on prose. When I was twenty I liked Eighteenth Century prose; now its poetry I want, so I repeat like a tipsy sailor in front of a public house.

I don't often trouble now to describe cornfields and groups of harvesting women in loose blues and reds and little staring yellow frocked girls. But that's not my eyes' fault; coming back the other evening from Charleston, again all my nerves stood upright, flushed, electrified (what's the word?) with the sheer beauty – beauty abounding and superabounding, so that one almost resents it, not being capable of catching it all, and holding it all at the moment.

Sunday 7 September

In my last lap of *Mrs Dalloway*. There I am now – at last at the party, which is to begin in the kitchen, and climb slowly upstairs. It is to be a most complicated spirited solid piece, knitting together everything and ending on three notes, at different stages of the staircase, each saying something to sum up Clarissa.

We had Dadie twice to stay; Clive and Mary yesterday; I slept a night at Charleston; L. went to Yorkshire; rather an odd disjointed wet summer, with people dropping in, Nelly rather moping, but loyal. The garden here flourishes.

Monday 15 September

Vita was here for Sunday, gliding down the village in her large new blue Austin car, which she manages consummately. She was dressed in ringed yellow jersey, and large hat, and had a dressing case all full of silver and night gowns wrapped in tissue. Nelly said "If only she weren't an honourable!" and couldn't take her hot water. But I like her being honourable, and she is it; a perfect lady, with all the dash and courage of the aristocracy, and less of its childishness than I expected. She is like an over ripe grape in features, moustached, pouting, will be a little heavy; meanwhile, she strides on fine legs, in a well cut skirt, and though embarrassing at breakfast, has a manly good sense and simplicity about her which both L. and I find satisfactory. Oh yes, I like her; could tack her on to my equipage for all time; and suppose if life allowed, this might be a friendship of a sort. [She] took us to Charleston – and how one's world spins round – it looked all very grey and shabby and loosely cut in the light of her presence. As for Monks House, it became a ruined barn, and we picnicking in the rubbish heap.

Monday 29 September

A fortnight later: writing partly to test my new penkala (professing fountain-pen qualities), partly to exorcise my demon. Only Karin and Ann [aged eight]: only a hole blown in my last chapter. There I was swimming in the highest ether known to me, and thinking I'd finish by Thursday; Lottie suggests to Karin we'd like to have Ann: Karin interprets my polite refusal to her own advantage and comes down herself on Saturday, blowing everything to smithereens. More and more am I solitary; the pain of these upheavals is incalculable; and I can't explain it either. *She* saw nothing. "Disturbing the flow of inspiration?" she said this morning, having shouted outside the door till I had to fetch cotton wool. And its down in ruins my house; my wings broken; and I left on the bare ground. But what cares Karin! She slightly chortles to plant us with some of her burdens and makes off well pleased at having got her way. Here am I with my wrecked week – for how serene and lovely like a Lapland night was our last week together – feeling that I ought to go in and be a good aunt – which I'm not by nature. These wails must now have ending, partly because I cannot see.

And of course children are wonderful and charming creatures. I've had Ann in talking about the white seal, and wanting me to read to her. There's a quality in their minds to me very adorable: to be alone with them, and see them day to day would be an extraordinary experience. They have what no grown up has that directness – chatter, chatter, chatter, on Ann goes, in a world of her own, with its seals and dogs; happy because she's going to have cocoa tonight, and go blackberrying tomorrow; the walls of her mind all hung round with such bright vivid things, and she doesn't see what we see.

52 TAVISTOCK SQUARE, WC1

Friday 17 October

It is disgraceful. I did run upstairs thinking I'd make time to enter that astounding fact – the last words of the last page of *Mrs Dalloway*; but was interrupted. Anyhow I did them a week ago yesterday. 'For there she was.' But in some ways this book is a feat; finished without break from illness, which is an exception; and written really in one year. The only difficulty is to hold myself back from writing others. I see already The Old Man. But enough, enough yet of what should I write here except my writing? Odd how conventional morality always encroaches. One must not talk of oneself, &c; one must not be vain &c. Even in complete privacy these ghosts slip between me and the page.

The thought of Katherine Mansfield comes to me – as usual rather reprehensibly – thinking yes, if she'd lived, she'd have written on, and people would have seen that I was the more gifted. I think of her in this way off and on – that strange ghost, with the eyes far apart, and the drawn mouth, dragging herself across the room. Katherine and I had our relationship; and never again shall I have one like it.

Lytton dined here the other night – a successful evening. Oh I was right to be in love with him twelve or fifteen years ago. It is an exquisite symphony his nature when all the violins get playing as they did the other night; so deep, so fantastic. We rambled easily. We talked of his writing, and I think now he will write another book; of mine: of the School of Proust, he said; then of Maynard: one side of him detestable.

Saturday 1 November

We went to Hamspray on a wet misty day, and saw what the view might be in the sun; a flat meadow with trees in groups like people talking leading to the downs. We walked to the top with Carrington. Carrington was as if recently beaten by Ralph. Is she really rather dull, I asked myself? or merely a sun flower out of the sun? We came home in the rain.

Tuesday 18 November

We were, I was rather, at Mary's party last night, and suffer today. The upper classes pretended to be clever. Duff Cooper, Lady Diana and all that set, as they say; and my chief amusement came from seeing them as a set. That is the only merit of these parties, that individuals compose differently from what they do in private.

Dadie came back yesterday and we had a jolly afternoon – oh infinitely better than a party at River House! lie though I did to Mary on the telephone – I in two jackets, for it is freezing, and hair down; he in shirtsleeves. Thus one gets to know people; not poised on the edge of a chair on the slippery floor, trying to laugh, and being spurred by wine and sugar cakes. Clive of course changes into an upper class man, very loud, familiar, and dashing, at once. Lytton sits in his own green shade, only emerging when the gentle youths come in. I was impressed by Nessa, who went to this party for which we were all titivating and dressing up, in her old red brown dress which I think she made herself.

Saturday 13 December

This diary may die, not of London, but of the Press. For fourteen days we have been in the thick of a long press revolution – Dadie going, Marjorie going, Marjorie staying, Angus Davidson coming. That is the final result, but achieved only at the cost of forty million words. For my own part, I could never see Dadie as a permanent partner, Dadie in his silver grey suits, pink shirts, with his powdered pink and white face, his nerves, his manners, his love of praise. Angus, however, after three days, already seems to me permanent and dependable.

I am now galloping over *Mrs Dalloway*, re-typing it entirely from the start, a good method, I believe, as thus one works with a wet brush over the whole, and joins parts separately composed and gone dry.

Monday 21 December

Really it is a disgrace – the number of blank pages in this book! The effect of London on diaries is decidedly bad. This I fancy is the leanest of them all. Indeed it has been an eventful year, as I prophesied; and the dreamer of January 3rd has dreamt much of her dream true; here we are in London, with Nelly alone, Dadie gone it is true, but Angus to replace him. What emerges is that changing houses is not so cataclysmic as I thought; after all one doesn't change body or brain.

How sharply society brings one out – or rather others out! Roger the other night with Vita for instance. He became the nonconformist undergraduate at once, the obstinate young man (I could see him quite young with his honest uncompromising eyes), who will *not* say what he does not believe to be true. The effect on Vita was disastrous; and pure honesty is a doubtful quality; it means often lack of imagination. It means self assertiveness, being rather better than other people; a queer trait in Roger to unearth after so many years of smooth intercourse. For the most part he is so sympathetic. His Quaker blood protests against Vita's rich winy fluid; and she has the habit of praising and talking indiscriminately about art, which goes down in her set, but not in ours. It was all very thorny until that good fellow Clive came in, and addressed himself to conciliate dear old obtuse, aristocratic, passionate, Grenadier-like Vita.

All our Bloomsbury relationships flourish, grow in lustiness. Suppose our set to survive another twenty years, I tremble to think how thickly knit and grown together it will be. At Christmas I must write and ask Lytton if I may dedicate *The Common Reader* to him. And that's the last of my books to be dedicated, I think. What do we talk about? I wish I could write conversation. We go over the same things, undoubtedly. The press however is always casting up wreckage. People come most days. I enjoy my printing afternoons, and think it the sanest way of life – for if I were always writing, or merely recouping from writing, I should be like an inbreeding rabbit – my progeny becoming weakly albinos. One meets a good many men now. There's a little thrush like creature called Tomlin who wants to sculpt me.

1925

This year Virginia's diary opens on a note – that of petulant exasperation with her resident servant Nelly Boxall – which was to sound again and again until it was finally silenced by Nelly's departure in 1934. In the early months of the year Virginia suffered the usual winter ills, influenza and headaches, while revising and preparing her two books, Mrs Dalloway *and* The Common Reader, *for their publication by the Hogarth Press. Exceptionally, she sent advance proofs of the former to an old pre-war friend with whom she had been corresponding, the painter Jacques Raverat, who was dying in the south of France.*

In April, leaving the Hogarth Press in the nervous care of Angus Davidson, the Woolfs again made what was to become a regular spring excursion, this year to spend ten days by the Mediterranean at Cassis. On their return, while awaiting the publication of her books, Virginia resumed her close-packed intellectual and social life and her involvement in Hogarth Press affairs. One of their authors, the thirty-year-old Robert Graves, burst in on the Woolfs unknown and unannounced at tea-time one day; another evening an emotional T. S. Eliot confided in them the new turn his life was taking and his anxieties about his wife's psychological health. The hostess Lady Colefax sought Virginia's company; the Sitwells asked her to dine; she entertained new and old friends to tea, to dinner, and to after-dinner coffee and conversation at Tavistock Square. Her books were published, and had a mixed reception, the details of which she rather obsessively notes. In fact, a very busy and social summer, and one which exacted its toll soon after their summer migration to Rodmell, when Virginia collapsed at Charleston in the middle of Quentin Bell's birthday dinner, and thereafter had to submit to a period of enforced inactivity. But she was able to make a start on To the Lighthouse, *which had long been germinating in her mind.*

Late in September the newly married Maynard Keynes and Lydia Lopokova came to Monks House and regaled the Woolfs with their observations on conditions in Soviet Russia, where they had spent their honeymoon (Keynes's A Short View of Russia *was published by the Hogarth Press in December). But their visit renewed Virginia's headache, and on returning to Tavistock Square at the beginning of October, she continued her semi-invalid existence under doctor's orders, occasionally allowed out for a walk, able to receive a few visitors. In November, one of the (subsequently tarnished) idols of her youth, Madge Vaughan, died.*

Towards the end of the year the news that Vita Sackville-West was to join her diplomat husband in Persia forced Virginia to examine the nature of her feelings,

188

aroused by a three-day visit to Vita's Kentish home, Long Barn. Builders were at work at Monks House, and the Woolfs spent Christmas with the Bell family at Charleston.

1925

52 TAVISTOCK SQUARE, WC1

Tuesday 6 January
What a flourish I began 1924 with! And today, for the 165th time, Nelly has given notice – Won't be dictated to; must do as other girls do. On the whole, I'm inclined to take her at her word. The nuisance of arranging life to suit her fads, and the pressure of 'other girls' is too much, good cook though she is, and honesty, crusty old maid too, dependable, in the main, affectionate, kindly, but incurably fussy, nervy, unsubstantial.

I spent the morning writing a note on an Elizabethan play; then I went into the printing room to see the time – found Angus [Davidson] and Leonard; Stayed and laughed. L. went off to the [*Nation*] office, when we had dog-walked round the Square; it being a black grained winter day; lengths of the pavement ink black where not lighted. Never shall I describe all the days I have noticed. Rodmell was all gale and flood; these words are exact. The river overflowed. We had seven days rain out of ten. Often I could not face a walk. L. pruned, which needed heroic courage. My heroism was purely literary. I revised *Mrs Dalloway*: the dullest part of the whole business of writing; the most depressing and exacting. L. read it; thinks it my best – but then has he not got to think so? Still I agree. Anyhow it is sent off to Clarks [printers], and proofs will come next week.

I did not see very much at Rodmell, having to keep my eyes on the typewriter. Angus was with us for Christmas, a very quiet, very considerate, unselfish deliberate young man, with a charming sense of humour – colourless, Lytton says: passive. But I think well of him, all the same.

Wednesday 18 March
This disgrace has been already explained – I think: two books to see through the press, mainly between tea and dinner; influenza; and a distaste for the pen.

•   •   •

Wednesday 8 April
Just back from Cassis. Often while I was there I thought how I would write here frequently and so get down some of the myriad impressions which I net every day. But directly we get back, what is it that happens? We strip and dive into the stream, and I am obsessed with a foolish idea that I have no time to stop and write, or that I ought to be doing something serious. Even now, I pelt along feverishly, thinking half the time, But I must stop and take Grizzle out; I must get my American books in order; the truth is, I must try to set aside half an hour in some part of my day, and consecrate it to diary writing. Give it a name and a place, and then perhaps, such is the human mind, I shall come to think it a duty, and disregard other duties for it.

I am under the impression of the moment, which is the complex one of coming back home from the South of France, shot with the accident I saw this morning and a woman crying Oh oh oh faintly, pinned against the railings with a motor car on top of her. All day I have heard that voice. I did not go to her help; but then every baker and flower seller did that. A great sense of the brutality and wildness of the world remains with me – there was this woman in brown walking along the pavement – suddenly a red film car turns a somersault, lands on top of her, and one hears this oh, oh, oh.

Since I wrote, which is these last months, Jacques Raverat has died; after longing to die; and he sent me a letter about *Mrs Dalloway* which gave me one of the happiest days of my life. Jacques died, as I say; and at once the siege of emotions began. I do not any longer feel inclined to doff the cap to death. I like to go out of the room talking, with an unfinished casual sentence on my lips. That is the effect it had on me – no leavetaking, no submission – but someone stepping out into the darkness.

I am waiting to see what form of itself Cassis will finally cast up in my mind. There are the rocks. We used to go out after breakfast and sit on the rocks with the sun on us. Then we would go for a walk in the afternoon, right up over the hill, into the woods. It was stony, steep and very hot. We heard a great chattering birdlike noise once, and I bethought me of the frogs. The ragged red tulips were out in the fields; all the fields were little angular shelves cut out of the hill, and ruled and ribbed with vines. Here and there was an angular white, or yellow or blue washed house, with all its shutters tightly closed; an incomparable cleanness and definiteness everywhere. At La Ciotat great orange ships rose up out of the blue water of the little bay. On the hill, which is stony as a desert, the nets were drying; and then in the streets children and girls gossiped and meandered all in pale bright shawls and cotton frocks, while the men picked up the earth of the main square to make a paved court of it. The Hotel Cendrillon is a white house, with red tiled floors, capable of housing perhaps eight people. The whole hotel atmosphere provided me with many ideas: oh so cold, indifferent, superficially polite, and exhibiting such odd relationships: as if human nature were now reduced to a kind of code, which it has devised to meet these emergencies, where people who do not know each other meet, and claim their rights as members of the same tribe. But L. and I were too too happy, as they say; if it were now to die &c.

Sunday 19 April

I'm out to make £300 this summer by writing, and build a bath and hot water range at Rodmell. But, hush, hush – my books tremble on the verge of coming out, and my future is uncertain.

Lytton came in the other night. He seemed to me autumnal: with that charming rectitude of spirit which no one else attains so perfectly I think. His justice of mind is considerable. But Christ is dismissed, to his disappointment, for he grows more and more fussy about subjects: Christ, he says did not exist: was a figment; and so much is known that really he couldn't pull it all together in one book. We talked of old buggers and their lack of attraction for young men. My anti-bugger revolution has run round the world, as I hoped it would. The pale star of the bugger has been in the ascendant too long. Julian agrees emphatically.

Marjorie and her Tom [Marshall] looked in at the basement this evening, very happy, L. says. She is a nice trusty creature, and if I wished to see anyone, I daresay it would be her.

Monday 20 April

Happiness is to have a little string onto which things will attach themselves. For example, going to my dressmaker, or rather thinking of a dress I could get her to make, and imagining it made – that is the string, which as if it dipped loosely into a wave of treasure brings up pearls sticking to it. And my days are likely to be strung with them. I like this London life in early summer – the street sauntering and square haunting, and then if my books were to be a success; if we could begin building at Monks, and put up wireless for Nelly, and if – if – if. But really what I should like would be to have three pounds to buy a pair of rubber soled boots, and go for country walks on Sundays.

One thing, in considering my state of mind now, seems to me beyond dispute: that I have, at last, bored down into my oil well, and can't scribble fast enough to bring it all to the surface. I have now at least six stories welling up in me, and feel at last that I can coin all my thoughts into words. Now suppose I might become one of the interesting – I will not say great

– but interesting novelists? Oddly, for all my vanity, I have not until now had much faith in my novels.

Monday 27 April
The Common Reader was out on Thursday: this is Monday, and so far I have not heard a word about it, private or public; it is as if one tossed a stone into a pond, and the waters closed without a ripple. And I am perfectly content, and care less than I have ever cared.

I meant to dash off [Robert] Graves before I forget him. Figure a bolt eyed blue shirted shockheaded hatless man in a blue overcoat standing goggling at the door at 4.30 on Friday. "Mrs Woolf?" I dreading and suspecting some *Nation* genius, some young man determined to unbosom himself, rushed him to the basement, where he said "I'm Graves". Everybody stared. He appeared to have been rushing through the air at sixty miles an hour and to have alighted temporarily. So he came up, and, wily as I am, I knew that to advance holding the kettle in a dishclout was precisely the right method, attitude, pose. The poor boy is all emphasis, protestation and pose. He has a crude likeness to Shelley, save that his nose is a switchback and his lines blurred. But the consciousness of genius is bad for people. He stayed till 7.15 (we were going to *Caesar and Cleopatra* – a strange rhetorical romantic early Shaw play) and had at last to say so, for he was so thick in the delight of explaining his way of life to us that no bee stuck faster to honey. He cooks, his wife cleans; four children are brought up in the elementary school; the villagers give them vegetables; they were married in Church; his wife calls herself Nancy Nicholson. Calling herself Nicholson has sorted her friends into sheep and goats. All this to us sounded like the usual self consciousness of young men, especially as he threw in, gratuitously, the information that he descends from Dean, Rector, Bishop, von Ranke, &c &c &c, only in order to say that he despises them. Still, still, he is a nice ingenuous rattle headed young man; but surely once one could live simply without protestations. I tried, perhaps, to curry favour, as my weakness is. L. was adamant. Then we were offered a ticket for the Cup Tie, to see which Graves has come to London after six years; can't travel in a train without being sick; is rather proud of his sensibility. No I don't think he'll write great poetry: but what will you? The sensitive are needed too, the half-baked, stammering, stuttering, who perhaps improve their own quarter of Oxfordshire.

And on Sunday we had our first walk, to Epping.

Wednesday 29 April
Hastily I must record the fact of Tom's long gaslit emotional rather tremulous and excited visit last night, which informed us of his release from

the Bank; some heavensent appointment to take effect next October. He has been thinking over his state these past weeks, being alone, with time on his hands. He has seen his whole life afresh, seen his relations to the world, and to Vivien in particular, become humbler, suppler, more humane – accusing himself of being the American husband, and wishing to tell me privately what store Vivien sets by me, has done nothing but write since last June, because I told her to! He then went into her psychology. Then he said to L. Do you know anything about psycho-analysis? L. said yes, in his responsible way; and Tom then told us the queer story – how Martin the doctor set Vivien off thinking of her childhood terror of loneliness, and now she can't let him, Tom, out of her sight. There he has sat mewed in her room these three months, poor pale creature, or if he has to go out, comes in to find her in a half fainting state. We advised another doctor. But whether its doctors or sense or holiday or travel or some drastic method unknown that's to cure that little nervous self conscious bundle – heaven knows. The upshot was a queer sense of his emotion in coming to tell us all this   something not merely touching to my vanity but to my sense of human worth, I think; his liking for us, affection, trust in Leonard, and being so much at his ease in some subconscious way he said, with me, all making me lay my arm on his shoulder; not a very passionate caress, but the best I can do.

And now I'm a little fidgety about *The Common Reader*, not a single word of it from a soul.

Friday 1 May
The Common Reader came out eight days ago, and so far not a single review has appeared, and nobody has written to me or spoken to me about it or in any way acknowledged the fact of its existence, save Maynard, Lydia and Duncan.

Monday 4 May
Now there's one sneering review in *Country Life*, almost inarticulate with feebleness, trying to say what a Common Reader is, and another, says Angus, in the *Star*, laughing at Nessa's cover.

Saturday 9 May
As for *The Common Reader*, the *TLS* had close on two columns sober and sensible praise – neither one thing nor the other. And Goldie [Goldsworthy Lowes Dickinson] writes that he thinks 'this is the best criticism in English – humorous, witty and profound'. My fate is to be treated to all extremes and all mediocrities. But I never get an enthusiastic review in the *TLS*. And it will be the same for *Dalloway*, which now approaches.

Thursday 14 May

The first day of summer, leaves visibly drawing out of the bud, and the Square almost green. Oh what a country day – and some of my friends are now reading *Mrs Dalloway* in the country. But the odd thing is this: honestly I am scarcely a shade nervous about *Mrs D*. Why is this? The truth is that writing is the profound pleasure and being read the superficial. I'm now all on the strain with desire to stop journalism and get on to *To the Lighthouse*. This is going to be fairly short: to have father's character done complete in it; and mother's; and St Ives; and childhood; and all the usual things I try to put in – life, death, &c. But the centre is father's character, sitting in a boat, reciting We perished each alone, while he crushes a dying mackerel – However, I must refrain.

Yesterday was a terrific chatter day – Desmond on top of Dr Leys, Lord Olivier on top of Desmond, James and Dadie to finish off with, while L. had I forget how many press interviews and committees into the bargain. But I meant to describe my dear old Desmond, whom it rejoiced me to see again, and he held out both his hands, and I set him in his chair and we talked till 7 o'clock. He is rather worn and aged; a little, I think, feeling that here's forty-five on him and nothing achieved, except indeed the children, whom he dotes on. I saw him thinking of his welter of old articles lying dusty in boxes. So I said I would take the thing in hand and see it through, which touched him, for children are not enough, after all; one wants something to be made out of oneself alone – and five boxes of dusty articles are rather raggy and rotten for forty-five years. And he praised *The Common Reader* with enthusiasm; and will write on it; and so we chattered along, when L. came; and then the dinner party, I just having time for a race round the Square; both Dadie and James very easy and affable, indeed for Dadie I feel considerable affection – so sensitive and tender is he, and one of these days will get a pull on himself, and be less of a quicksilver. But what these scholars want is to get at books through writing books, not through reading them.

But I must remember to write about my *clothes* next time I have an impulse to write. My love of clothes interests me profoundly; only it is not love; and what it is I must discover.

Friday 15 May

Two unfavourable reviews of *Mrs Dalloway*: unintelligible, not art &c; and a letter from a young man in Earl's Court: 'This time you have done it – you have caught life and put it in a book ...'

Sunday 17 May

The only judgment on *Mrs Dalloway* I await with trepidation (but that's too strong) is Morgan's. He will say something enlightening.

Just back (all my days here begin with this) from Sutton. Oh it is full summer weather – so hot one can't walk on the sunny side, and all London transmogrified. We came home on top of a bus all the way for a shilling, with the usual glimpses down lanes, into farmyards, at running streams, persisting in between villas, and behind sunbaked yellow or black motor roads. A little girl on the bus asked her mother how many inches are there in a mile. Her mother repeated this to me. I said you must go to school and they'll tell you. But she is at school said her mother. She's seven; and *he* (the baby on her knee) goes to school. He's three. So I gave them two biscuits left over, and the little girl (see my egotism) with her bright excitable eyes, and eagerness to grasp the whole universe reminded me of myself, asking questions of my mother. We saw Lambeth, and I imagined the frolics of clergymen in the boscage, which is very thick; crossed Westminster Bridge; admired the Houses of Parliament and their fretted lacy look; passed the Cenotaph, which L. compromised by sitting with his hat off all the way up Whitehall, and so home.

Wednesday 20 May

Well, Morgan admires. This is a weight off my mind. Better than *Jacob* he says; was sparing of words; kissed my hand, and on going said he was awfully pleased, very happy (or words to that effect) about it. He thinks – but I won't go into detailed criticism; I shall hear more; and this is only about the style being simpler, more like other people's this time.

I dined with the Sitwells last night. Edith is an old maid. I had never conceived this. I thought she was severe, implacable and tremendous; rigid in her own conception. Not a bit of it. She is, I guess, a little fussy, very kind, beautifully mannered, elderly too, almost my age, and timid, and admiring and easy and poor, and I liked her more than admired or was frightened by her. Nevertheless, I do admire her work, and that's what I say of hardly anyone: she has an ear, and not a carpet broom; a satiric vein; and some beauty in her. Nothing could be more conciliatory and less of an eagle than she; odd looking too, with her humorous old maid's smile, her half shut eyes, her lank hair, her delicate hands, wearing a large ring, and fine feet, and her brocade dress, blue and silver. Nothing of the protester or pamphleteer or pioneer seemed in her – rather the well born Victorian spinster. So I must read her afresh. The three Sitwells have considerable breeding about them; I like their long noses, and grotesque faces. As for the house, Osbert is at heart an English Squire, a collector, but of Bristol glass, old fashion plates, Victorian cases of humming birds, and not of foxes' brushes and deers' horns. His rooms are all stuck about with these objects. And I liked him too. But why are they thought daring and clever? Why are they the laughing stocks of the music halls and the penny-a-liners? Not much talk; all easy goodnatured generalities after dinner, Francis [Birrell] bawling, [Arthur] Waley sombre and demure, and I very indulgent with my compliments.

Monday 1 June

Bank holiday, and we are in London. To record my books' fates slightly bores me; but now both are floated, and *Mrs Dalloway* doing surprisingly well.

Tom came in yesterday, rather rockier than last time, not quite so flushed with emotion, and inclined to particularise the state of Vivien's bowels too closely for my taste. What is more to the point is that Tom is to be the editor of a new quarterly, which some old firm is issuing in the autumn, and all his works must go to them – a blow for us. He said nothing of my books. With great dignity, I did not ask for his opinion. People often don't read books for weeks and weeks. And anyhow, for my part, I hate giving an opinion.

Friday 5 June

To work off the intense depression left by Desmond. What does this come from? But I have just made this beautiful image – how he is like a wave that never breaks, but lollops one this way and that way and the sail hangs on one's mast and the sun beats down – And then I was ruffled by Nelly, but got over it, by spending £50 of charm. And we have had Vita, Edith Sitwell, Morgan, Dadie – old Vita presenting me with a whole tree of blue Lupins, and being very uncouth and clumsy, while Edith was like a Roman Empress, so definite, clear cut, magisterial, and yet with something of the humour of a fishwife – a little too commanding about her own poetry and ready to dictate - tremulously pleased by Morgan's compliments (and he never praised Vita, who sat hurt, modest, silent, like a snubbed schoolboy).

Sunday 14 June

A disgraceful confession – this is Sunday morning, and just after ten, and here I am sitting down to write diary and not fiction or reviews, without any excuse, except the state of my mind. After finishing those two books, though, one can't concentrate directly on a new one; and then the letters, the talk, the reviews ... I can't settle in, contract, and shut myself off. I've written six little stories, scrambled them down untidily, and have thought out, perhaps too clearly, *To the Lighthouse*. And both books so far are successful. More of *Dalloway* has been sold this month than of *Jacob* in a year. I think it possible we may sell 2,000.

Waking this morning, rather depressed that *Mrs D.* did not sell yesterday, that we had [a dinner party] last night and not a single compliment vouchsafed me, that I had bought a glass necklace for one pound, that I had a sore throat and a streaming nose, rather under the weather, I say, I snuggled into the core of my life, which is this complete comfort with L., and there found everything so satisfactory and calm that I revived myself, and got a fresh start; feeling entirely immune. The immense success of our life is, I think, that our treasure is hid away; or rather in such common things that nothing can touch it. That is, if one enjoys a bus ride to Richmond, sitting on the Green smoking, taking the letters out of the box, combing Grizzle, making an ice, opening a letter, sitting down after dinner, side by side, and saying 'Are you in your stall, brother?' – well, what can trouble this happiness? And every day is necessarily full of it.

Tuesday 18 June
Old Lytton has fairly passed from our lives. No word about my books; no visits since Easter. I imagine that when he takes a new love, and he has Angus, he gets surly, like a stag; he feels a little ridiculous, uneasy, and does not relish the company of old cynical friends like ourselves.

Thursday 16 June
No, Lytton does not like *Mrs Dalloway*, and, what is odd, I like him all the better for saying so, and don't much mind. What he says is that there is a discrepancy between the ornament (extremely beautiful) and what happens (rather ordinary – or unimportant). So that as a whole, the book does not ring solid; yet, he says, it is a whole; and he says sometimes the writing is of extreme beauty. What can one call it but genius? he said! Fuller of genius, he said, than anything I had done. Perhaps, he said, you should take something wilder and more fantastic, a framework that admits of anything, like *Tristram Shandy*. But he thought me at the beginning, not at the end. And he said *The Common Reader* was divine, a classic; *Mrs D.* being, I fear, a flawed stone. Its odd that when Clive and others (several of them) say it is a masterpiece, I am not much exalted; when Lytton picks holes, I get back into my working fighting mood, which is natural to me.

Saturday 27 June
The first fruit of *The Common Reader* (a book too highly praised now) is a request to write for the *Atlantic Monthly*. So I am getting pushed into criticism. It is a great stand by – this power to make large sums by formulating views on Stendhal and Swift.

Sunday 19 July
By bringing this book down here to the Studio, I have rather stinted it I think, as my mornings have all been spent writing. So a whole tribe of people and parties has gone down the sink to oblivion. A happy summer, very busy; rather overpowered by the need of seeing so many people. I never ask a soul here; but they accumulate. Tonight Ottoline; Tuesday Jack Hutch; Wednesday Edith Sitwell, Friday dine with Raymond. These are my fixed invitations; and all sorts of unforeseen ones will occur. I run out after tea as if pursued. I mean to regulate this better in future. But I don't think of the future, or the past, I feast on the moment. This is the secret of happiness, but only reached now in middle age.

Monday 20 July
I should consider my work list now. I think a little story, perhaps a review, this fortnight; having a superstitious wish to begin *To the Lighthouse* the first day at Monks House. I now think I shall finish it in two months there. But this theme may be sentimental: father and mother and child in the garden; the death; the sail to the lighthouse. (I conceive the book in three parts: 1, at the drawing room window; 2, seven years passed; 3, the voyage.)
   Last night Clive dined with us; and Nelly is rather waspish about it this morning. Ottoline came, in tea kettle taffeta, all looped and scolloped and fringed with silver lace, and talked about Rupert [Brooke] and Jacques [Raverat], and re-told, with emendations, the story of Ka and Henry Lamb and herself. She has been working over these old stories so often, that they hold no likeness to the truth – they are stale, managed, pulled this way and that, as we used to knead and pull the crumb of bread, till it was a damp slab. Then the old motor was heard hooting and there was Philip and Julian [Morrell], at which, at Julian that is, Clive cheered up, and was very brisk and obliging as he knows how. We argued the case of the aristocracy v. the middle class. I rather liked it. I like the sense of other people liking it, as I suppose the Morrells do, for they settle on us like a crowd of crows, once a week now. My vanity as a hostess is flattered. Sometimes a buttery crumb of praise is thrown to me – But enough, enough.

Thursday 30 July
I should here try to sum up the summer, since August ends a season, spiritual as well as temporal. Well; business has been brisk. I don't think I get many idle hours now, the idlest being, oddly enough, in the morning. When the dull sleep of afternoon is on me, I'm always in the shop, printing, dissing, addressing; then it is tea, and Heaven knows we have had enough visitors. Sometimes I sit still and wonder how many people will tumble on me without my lifting a finger.

On Tuesday at 12.30 Maynard retires to St Pancras Registry Office with Lydia, and Duncan to witness (against his will). So that episode is over. But, dear me, I'm too dull to write. Yet I have a thousand things to say.

MONKS HOUSE, RODMELL

Saturday 5 September
And why couldn't I see or feel that all this time I was getting a little used up and riding on a flat tyre? So I was, as it happened; and fell down in a faint at Charleston, in the middle of Quentin's birthday party; and then have lain about here, in that odd amphibious life of headache, for a fortnight. This has rammed a big hole in my eight weeks which were to be stuffed so full. Never mind. I have made a very quick and flourishing attack on *To the Lighthouse* all the same. I am still crawling and easily enfeebled, but if I could once get up steam again, I believe I could spin it off with infinite relish.

Monday 14 September
A disgraceful fact – I am writing this at ten in the morning in bed in the little room looking into the garden, the sun beaming steady, the vine leaves transparent green, and the leaves of the apple trees so brilliant that, as I had my breakfast, I invented a little story about a man who wrote a poem, I think, comparing them with diamonds, and the spiders' webs (which glance and disappear astonishingly) with something or other else. I am writing this partly to test my poor bunch of nerves at the back of my neck – will they hold or give again, as they have done so often; partly to glut my itch ('glut' and 'itch'!) for writing. It is the great solace, and scourge.

Tom has treated us scurvily. On Monday I get a letter that fawns and flatters, implores me to write for his new quarterly; and proposes to discuss Press matters as soon as we get back; on Thursday we read in the *TLS* that his new firm is publishing *The Waste Land* and his other poems – a fact which he dared not confess, but sought to palliate by flattering me.

Tuesday 22 September
How my handwriting goes down hill! Another sacrifice to the Hogarth Press. Yet what I owe the Hogarth Press is barely paid by the whole of my handwriting. Haven't I just written to Herbert Fisher refusing to do a book for the Home University Series – knowing that I can write a book, a better book, a book off my own bat, for the Press if I wish! To think of being battened down in the hold of those University dons fairly makes my

blood run cold. Yet I'm the only woman in England free to write what I like. The others must be thinking of series and editors.

Thursday 24 September
Sad to think a week only left whole of this partially wrecked summer; however, I don't complain, seeing as how I have dipped my head in health again and feel stabilised once more about the spinal cord, which is always the centre of my being. Maynard and Lydia came here yesterday – Maynard in Tolstoy's blouse and Russian cap of black astrakhan – a fair sight, both of them, to meet on the high road! An immense good will and vigour pervades him. She hums in his wake, the great man's wife. But though one could carp, one can also find them very good company, and my heart, in this the autumn of my age, slightly warms to him, whom I've known all these years, so truculently, pugnaciously, and unintimately. We had a very brisk talk of Russia: such a hotch-potch, such a mad jumble, Maynard says, of good and bad. Briefly, spies everywhere, no liberty of speech, greed for money eradicated, people living in common, yet some, Lydia's mother for instance, with servants, peasants contented because they own land, no sign of revolution, aristocrats acting showmen to their possessions, ballet respected, best show of Cézanne and Matisse in existence. Endless processions of communists in top hats, prices exorbitant, yet champagne produced, and the finest cooking in Europe. Then the immense luxury of the old Imperial trains; feeding off the Tsar's plate. One prediction of theirs, to the effect that in ten years' time the standard of living will be higher in Russia than it was before the war, but in all other countries lower, Maynard thought might very well come true. Anyhow they are crammed and packed with sights and talks.

But the Keyneses, I need hardly say, renewed my headache, and when Lytton came, I was drooping over the fire, and could not do much battle with that old serpent. But to tell the truth, I am exacerbated this morning. It is 10.25, on a fine grey still day; the starlings are in the apple trees; Leonard is in London. But why am I exacerbated? By Roger. I told him I had been ill all the summer. His reply is – silence as to that; but plentiful descriptions of his own front teeth. Egotism, egotism – it is the essential ingredient in a clever man's life I believe. It protects; it enhances; it preserves his own vital juices entire by keeping them banked in. Also I cannot help thinking that he suspects me of valetudinarianism and this enrages me; and L. is away and I can't have my thorn picked out by him, so must write it out. There! it is better now; and I think I hear the papers come; and will get them, my woolwork, and a glass of milk.

Wednesday 30 September
This was I suppose successfully accomplished; and it is now Wednesday morning, damp and close and over all the sense already of transmigration, of shedding one habit for another. My autumn coat is grown.

52 TAVISTOCK SQUARE, WCI

Friday 27 November
Oh what a blank! I tumbled into bed on coming back – or rather [Dr] Ellie [Rendel] tumbled me; and keeps me still prostrate half the day. Next week I shall go to the ballet, my first night out. One visitor a day. Till two days ago, bed at 5. On the whole, I have not been unhappy, but not very happy; too much discomfort; sickness (cured by eating instantly); a good deal of rat-gnawing at the back of my head; one or two terrors; then the tiredness of the body – it lay like a workman's coat. Sometimes I felt old, and spent. Madge [Vaughan] died. Rustling among my emotions, I found nothing better than dead leaves. Her letters had eaten away the reality – the brilliancy, the warmth. Oh detestable time, that thus eats out the heart and lets the body go on. They buried a faggot of twigs at Highgate, as far as I am concerned. I drove to the gate, and saw Nessa and Leonard, like a pair of stuffed figures, go in.

Vita has been twice. She is doomed to go to Persia; and I minded the thought so much (thinking to lose sight of her for five years) that I conclude I am genuinely fond of her. Reading and writing go on. Not my novel though. And I can only think of all my faults as a novelist and wonder why I do it – a wonder which Lytton increases, and Morgan decreases. Lytton is off: The Loves of the Famous. Queen Elizabeth &c. I thought him at his most intimate last night; all plumy, incandescent, soft, luminous. Something slightly repels (too strong) Leonard. His character is not so good as Morgan's, he said, walking round the Square in the snow today. "There is something about all Stracheys –." Then, when we talk, L. and I, we rather crab Lytton's writing I observe. But all this vanishes with me when he comes, as yesterday, to talk, and talk, and talk. Nothing, in my sentimental heart, can stand against these old loyalties. If six people died, it is true that my life would cease: by which I mean, it would run so thin that though it might go on, would it have any relish? Imagine Leonard, Nessa Duncan Lytton Clive Morgan, all dead.

Monday 7 December
We shall spend Christmas at Charleston, which I'm afraid Leonard will not like much. We walked at Hampstead on Saturday. It was very cold. It had a foggy winter beauty. We went in to Ken Wood, and it was here that we discussed Lytton, gravely, like married people. But my God – how satisfactory

after, I think, twelve years, to have any human being to whom one can speak so directly as I to L.! He has the faults of a small nature said L. He is ungenerous. He asks, but never gives. But I have always known that – often I have seen the dull eyelid fall over him, if one asked a little too much: some sheath of selfishness that protects him from caring too much, or committing himself uncomfortably. He is cautious. He is a valetudinarian. But – I have known about Lytton's leathern eyelid since I was twenty. But L. said when they were at Cambridge Lytton was not like that to him. Morgan, said Leonard, as we trod back over the slippery hillocks seeing so little as we talked (and yet all this part of Hampstead recalls Katherine to me – that faint ghost, with the steady eyes, the mocking lips, and, at the end, the wreath set on her hair), Morgan has improved. Morgan is I think naturally more congenial to L. than Lytton is. He likes 'Sillies'; he likes the dependent simplicity of Morgan and myself. He likes settling our minds, and our immense relief at this. Well, well.

I am reading *A Passage to India*; but will not expatiate here, as I must elsewhere. (By the way, Robert Bridges likes *Mrs Dalloway*: says no one will read it; but it is beautifully written, and some more, which L. who was told by Morgan cannot remember.) Now, to write a list of Christmas presents. Ethel Sands comes to tea. But no Vita.

Monday 21 December
But no Vita! But Vita for three days at Long Barn, from which L. and I returned yesterday. These Sapphists *love* women; friendship is never untinged with amorosity. I like her and being with her, and the splendour – she shines in the grocer's shop in Sevenoaks with a candle-lit radiance, stalking on legs like beech trees, pink glowing, grape clustered, pearl hung. Anyhow she found me incredibly dowdy, no woman cared less for personal appearance – no one put on things in the way I did. Yet so beautiful, &c. What is the effect of all this on me? Very mixed. There is her maturity and full breastedness: her being so much in full sail on the high tides, where I am coasting down backwaters; her capacity I mean to take the floor in any company, to represent her country, to visit Chatsworth, to control silver, servants, chow dogs; her motherhood (but she is a little cold and offhand with her boys), her being in short (what I have never been) a real woman. In brain and insight she is not as highly organised as I am. But then she is aware of this, and so lavishes on me the maternal protection which, for some reason, is what I have always most wished from everyone. What L. gives me, and Nessa gives me, and Vita, in her more clumsy external way, tries to give me. Anyhow, I am very glad that she is coming to tea today, and I shall ask her, whether she minds my dressing so badly? I think she does.

We go down to Charleston tomorrow, not without some trepidation on my part.

1926

The year again began for Virginia with a period of ill-health and low spirits, the latter intensified by the absence in Persia of Vita Sackville-West, who now engrossed her feelings, and to whom she wrote long letters every few days. Nonetheless she was working on To the Lighthouse *with energy and confidence, though frequently distracted by the claims of the Hogarth Press – manuscripts to be read, parcels to pack, authors to see, etc. In March Leonard decided to resign his literary editorship of the* Nation & Athenaeum, *a decision applauded by Virginia, though in the event he was dissuaded by Maynard Keynes from carrying it out until early in 1930. In April the Woolfs went to Dorset for a few days' holiday, and soon afterwards Virginia finished the first part of* To the Lighthouse; *but then ordinary life was totally disrupted by the General Strike, the effects of which in Tavistock Square she records with a detail she suspects will prove tedious in later years. Vita returned to England in May and, after a first wary reunion, their intimacy quickened and flourished.*

Virginia's growing reputation brought increased social contact with the literary world; she greatly enjoyed meeting George Moore at one dinner party; yet a promising friendship with her contemporary Rose Macaulay received a setback when she and Leonard were her guests at another, unexpectedly formal, 'literary' dinner. She records the lunch-time talk of H. G. Wells and a visit to the Poet Laureate Robert Bridges near Oxford, shepherded by Lady Ottoline Morrell; she again observed the literary establishment with a cynical eye when Vita Sackville-West lectured to the Royal Society of Literature; and in July she and Leonard paid a visit to Thomas Hardy at his home near Dorchester, partly from motives of pure admiration, partly because Virginia had been commissioned by The Times Literary Supplement *to prepare an obituary tribute.*

On retreating to Monks House – where improvements, including the installation of a bath and two WCs had been made – at the end of July, Virginia was for a time prostrated with exhaustion; reviving in the cloudless August weather, she reached the end of To the Lighthouse, *but thereafter fell into a depression, which she analysed as arising from her being idle without being ill. In the autumn she was working on the revision of the first draft of her novel, seeing a great deal of Vita both in London and at Long Barn, being pursued by Lady Colefax, meeting her Bloomsbury familiars, and writing very little in her diary. On 22 December the Woolfs went to Cornwall to spend Christmas with Ka and Will Arnold-Forster at Zennor.*

1926

Tuesday 19 January
Vita having this moment (twenty minutes ago) left me, what are my feelings? Of a dim November fog; the lights dulled and damped. But this will disperse; then I shall want her, clearly and distinctly. Then not – and so on. One wants that atmosphere – to me so rosy and calm. She is not clever; but abundant and fruitful; truthful too. She taps so many sources of life; repose and variety, was her own expression, sitting on the floor this evening in the gaslight. I feel a lack of stimulus, of marked days, now Vita is gone; and some pathos, common to all these partings; and she has four days' journey through the snow.

Monday 8 February
Just back from Rodmell – to use again the stock opening. And I should explain why I've let a month slip perhaps. First, I think, the German measles or influenza; next Vita; then, disinclination for any exertion, so that I never made a book till last week. But undoubtedly this diary is established, and I sometimes look at it and wonder what on earth will be the fate of it. It is to serve the purpose of my memoirs. At sixty I am to sit down and write my life. I am rather tired, a little tired, from having thought too much about *To the Lighthouse*. Never never have I written so easily, imagined so profusely. Murry says my works won't be read in ten years' time.

Tuesday 23 February
Vita is a dumb letter writer, and I miss her. I miss the glow and the flattery and the festival. I miss her, I suppose, not very intimately. Nevertheless I do miss her, and wish it were May 10th.

I am blown like an old flag by my novel. This one is *To the Lighthouse*. I am now writing as fast and freely as I have ever written in the whole of my life; more so – twenty times more so – than any novel yet. Anyhow this goes on all the morning; and I have the devil's own work not to be flogging my brain all the afternoon. I live entirely in it, and come to the surface rather obscurely and am often unable to think what to say when we walk round the Square.

The publishing season is about to begin. Nessa says Why don't you give it up? I say, because I enjoy it. Then I wonder, but do I? What about Rome and Sicily? Am I a fanatical enthusiast for work, like my father? I think I have a strain of that, but I don't relish it. Tonight Francis Birrell and Rose Macaulay dine with us. To celebrate the occasion, I have bought a toast rack and a bedspread, which covers that atrocious chest of drawers which has worried me these two years. I am now so pleased with the colour that I go out and look at it.

Wednesday 24 February
They came last night, Francis and Rose Macaulay – I daresay I shall be calling her Rose one of these days. Rose – too chattery chittery at first go off; lean as a rake, wispy, and frittered. Some flimsy smartness and taint of the flimsy glittery literary about her: but this was partly nerves I think; and she felt us alien and observant doubtless. She has no humbug about her; only [is] frosted and rather cheaply gilt superficially with all that being asked to speak at dinners, to give opinions to newspapers. She is writing an article for an American paper on London after the War. It is this sort of thing that one distrusts in her. Why should she take the field so unnecessarily? But I fancy our 'leading lady novelists' all do as they are asked about this, and I am not quite one of them. I saw my own position a good deal lowered and diminished; and this is part of the value of seeing new people – still more of going to people's houses. One is, if anything, minimised: here in the eternal Bloomsbury, one is apt, without realising it, to expand. I like Francis. I like his laughter; and his random energy. We talked a lot of father, who, said Francis, dominates the Twentieth Century. "A remarkable man; for though he would not believe in God, he was stricter than those who did." Rose Macaulay said her parents called him always 'poor Leslie Stephen' because he had lost his faith. Also they said he was very gentle and charming.

Saturday 27 February
As for the soul: why did I say I would leave it out? I forget. And the truth is, one can't write directly about the soul. Looked at, it vanishes; but look at the ceiling, at Grizzle, at the cheaper beasts at the Zoo which are exposed to walkers in Regent's Park, and the soul slips in. Mrs Webb's book [*My Apprenticeship*] has made me think a little what I could say of my own life. But then there were causes in her life: prayer; principle. None in mine. Great excitability and search after something. Great content – almost always enjoying what I'm at, but with constant change of mood. I don't think I'm

ever bored. Yet I have some restless searcher in me. Why is there not a discovery in life? Something one can lay hands on and say 'This is it'? What is it? And shall I die before I can find it? Then (as I was walking through Russell Square last night) I see mountains in the sky: the great clouds, and the moon which is risen over Persia; I have a great and astonishing sense of something there, which is 'it' – A sense of my own strangeness, walking on the earth is there too. Who am I, what am I, and so on; these questions are always floating about in me. Is that what I meant to say? Not in the least. I was thinking about my own character; not about the universe. Oh and about society again; dining with Lord Berners at Clive's made me think that. How, at a certain moment, I see through what I'm saying; detest myself; and wish for the other side of the moon; reading alone, that is. What did we talk about? Tom and the Sitwells; Eddie Marsh and Lady Colefax, and I felt one could go on saying these things for ever, and they mean nothing.

Tuesday 9 March
Then I was at two parties: Ethel [Sands]'s tea; Mary's dinner. Ethel's was a ghastly frizzly frying pan affair. I chattering in front of the footlights. As for Mary's party, there, save for the usual shyness about powder and paint, shoes and stockings, I was happy, owing to the supremacy of literature. This keeps us sweet and sane, George Moore and me I mean. He has a pink foolish face; blue eyes like hard marbles; a crest of snow white hair; little unmuscular hands; sloping shoulders; a high stomach; neat, purplish well brushed clothes; and perfect manners, as I consider them. That is to say he speaks without fear or dominance; accepting me on my merits; every one on their merits. Still in spite of age uncowed, unbeaten, lively, shrewd. "As for Hardy and Henry James though, what shall one say? I am a fairly modest man; but I admit I think *Esther Waters* a better book than *Tess*. But what is there to be said for that man? He cannot write. He cannot tell a story. The whole art of fiction consists in telling a story. But my good friend (to me – half hesitating to call me this), what have you to say for Hardy? You cannot find anything to say. English fiction is the worst part of English literature. Compare it with the French – with the Russians. Henry James wrote some pretty little stories before he invented his jargon. But they were about rich people. You cannot write stories about rich people," because, I think he said, they have no instincts. But Henry James was enamoured of marble balustrades. There was no passion in any of his people. And Anne Brontë was the greatest of the Brontës and Conrad could not write, and so on.

Saturday 20 March

But what is to become of all these diaries, I asked myself yesterday. If I died, what would Leo make of them? He would be disinclined to burn them; he could not publish them. Well, he should make up a book from them, I think; and then burn the body. I daresay there is a little book in them; if the scraps and scratches were straightened out a little. God knows. This is dictated by a slight melancholia, which comes upon me sometimes now, and makes me think I am old; I am ugly; I am repeating things. Yet, as far as I know, as a writer I am only now writing out my mind.

Wednesday 24 March

"I'm going to hand in my resignation this morning" said L. making the coffee. "To what?" I asked. "The *Nation*." And it is done; and we have six months only before us. I feel ten years younger. It was a temporary makeshift job, amusing at first, then galling, and last night, after an argument of the usual kind about literary articles and space and so on with Maynard and [the editor] Hubert [Henderson], L. came to the decision to resign now. The mercy of having no ties, no proofs, no articles to procure, and all that, is worth a little more exertion elsewhere. I'm amused at my own sense of liberation. To upset everything every three or four years is my notion of a happy life. But I suppose freedom becomes a fetish like any other. These disjointed reflections I scribble on a divine, if gusty, day; being about to dine at a pot-house with Rose Macaulay – not a cheerful entertainment; but an experience perhaps.

Saturday 27 March

We went off on a blowing night to dine at Rose Macaulay's 'pot-house', as I so mistakenly called it. There were ten second rate writers in second rate dress clothes – L. by the way was in his red brown tweed. Then the pitter patter began: the old yard was scratched over by these baldnecked chickens. The truth was that we had no interests private: literature was our common ground; and though I will talk literature with Desmond or Lytton by the hour, when it comes to pecking up grains with these active stringy fowls my gorge rises. What d'you think of the Hawthornden Prize? Why isn't Masefield as good as Chaucer, or Gerhardi as good as Tchekhov? Sylvias and Geralds and Roberts and Roses chimed and tinkled round the table. I said "Holy Ghost?" when Mr O'Donovan said "The whole of the coast." Lodged on a low sofa in Rose's underground cheerful, sane, breezy room I talked to a young cultivated man, mild aesthete, but thank God, not a second rate journalist. All the same I kept saying to myself, Thank God to be out of that; out of the *Nation*; no longer brother in arms with Rose and Robert and Sylvia. It is a thinblooded set; so 'nice', 'kind', respectable, cleverish and in the swim.

Then our set at Nessa's last night was hardly at its best. L. and Adrian silent and satirical; Old Sickert rather toothless and set; I driven to chatter, not well; but Nessa and Duncan don't consolidate and order these parties. L. was off early this morning to Rodmell where Philcox is in the thick of building and drains: so I had no time to uncrease my rose leaf; had to try and work; could not settle; suddenly shook my coat, like a retriever; and pondered where shall I spend the day? decided on Greenwich, arrived there at 1; lunched; everything fell out pat; smoked a cigarette on the pier promenade, saw the ships swinging up, one, two, three, out of the haze; adored it all; yes, even the lavatory keeper's little dog; saw the grey Wren buildings fronting the river; and then another great ship, grey and orange; with a woman walking on deck; and then to the Hospital: first to the Museum where I saw Sir John Franklin's pen and spoons (a spoon asks a good deal of imagination to consecrate it). I played with my mind watching what it would do – and behold if I didn't almost burst into tears over the coat Nelson wore at Trafalgar with the medals which he hid with his hand when they carried him down, dying, lest the sailors might see it was him. There was too his little fuzzy pigtail, of golden greyish hair tied in black; and his long white stockings, one much stained, and his white breeches with the gold buckles, and his stock – all of which I suppose they must have undone and taken off as he lay dying. Kiss me Hardy &c – Anchor, anchor. I read it all when I came in, and could swear I was there on the *Victory*. Then it was raining a little, but I went into the Park, which is all prominences and radiating paths; then back on top of a bus, and so to tea. I think my rose leaf is now uncrumpled. Certainly I shall remember the ships coming up and Nelson's coat long after I have forgotten how silly and uncomfortable I was at Nessa's on Friday.

Sunday 11 April
Mrs Webb's life makes me compare it with mine. The difference is that she is trying to relate all her experiences to history. She is very rational and coherent. She has always thought about her life and the meaning of the world: indeed, she begins this at the age of four. She has studied herself as a phenomenon. Thus her autobiography is part of the history of the Nineteenth Century. She makes herself fit in very persuasively and to my mind very interestingly. She taps a great stream of thought.

Friday 30 April
I have not said anything about Iwerne Minster. Now it would amuse me to see what I remember it by. Cranbourne Chase: the stunted aboriginal

forest trees, scattered, not grouped in cultivations; anemones, bluebells, violets, all pale, sprinkled about, without colour, livid, for the sun hardly shone. Then Blackmore Vale: a vast air dome and the fields dropped to the bottom; the sun striking, there, there; a drench of rain falling, like a veil streaming from the sky, there and there; and the downs rising, very strongly scarped (if that is the word) so that they were ridged and ledged; then an inscription in a church 'sought peace & ensured it', and the question, who wrote these sonorous stylistic epitaphs? And then tea and cream – these I remember; the hot baths; my new leather coat; Shaftesbury, so much lower and less commanding than my imagination, and the drive to Bournemouth, and the dog and the lady behind the rock, and the view of Swanage, and coming home.

And then it was horror: Nelly; faced her going; was firm yet desolated; on Tuesday she said "Please ma'am may I apologise"; and I had enough look into the 'servant question' to be glad to be safe again with Nelly. Now I vow come what may, never never to believe her again. "I am too fond of you ever to be happy with anyone else" she said. Talking of compliments, this is perhaps the greatest I could have.

Yesterday I finished the first part of *To the Lighthouse*, and today began the second. I cannot make it out – here is the most difficult abstract piece of writing – I have to give an empty house, no people's characters, the passage of time, all eyeless and featureless with nothing to cling to: well, I rush at it, and at once scatter out two pages. Is it nonsense, is it brilliance?

Wednesday 5 May
An exact diary of the Strike would be interesting. For instance, it is now a quarter to two; there is a brown fog; nobody is building; it is drizzling. The first thing in the morning we stand at the window and watch the traffic in Southampton Row. This is incessant. Everyone is bicycling; motor cars are huddled up with extra people. There are no buses. No placards. No newspapers. Water, gas and electricity are allowed; but at 11 the light was turned off. I sat in the Press in the brown fog, while L. wrote an article for the *Herald*. Then Clive dropped in, the door being left open. He is offering himself to the Government. Maynard excited, wants the Hogarth Press to bring out a skeleton number of the *Nation*. It is all tedious and depressing, rather like waiting in a train outside a station. One does not know what to do. And nature has laid it on thick today – fog, rain, cold. A voice, rather commonplace and official, wishes us good morning at 10. This is the Voice of Britain, to which we can make no reply. The voice is very trivial, and only tells us that the Prince of Wales is coming back, that the London streets present an unprecedented spectacle.

Thursday 6 May

Everything is the same, but unreasonably, or because of the weather, or habit, we are more cheerful, take less notice, and occasionally think of other things. Clive dines in Mayfair, and everyone is pro-men; I go to Harrison [dentist], and he shouts me down with "Its red rag versus Union Jack, Mrs Woolf". Frankie [Birrell] dines out, and finds everyone pro-government. Bob [Trevelyan] drops in and says Churchill is for peace, but [Prime Minister] Baldwin won't budge. Clive says Churchill is for tear gas bombs, fight to the death, and is at the bottom of it all. So we go on, turning in our cage. It feels like a deadlock, on both sides; as if we could keep fixed like this for weeks. What one prays for is God: the King or God; some impartial person to say kiss and be friends – as apparently we all desire. Just back from a walk to the Strand. One notices lorries full of elderly men and girls standing like passengers in the old third class carriages. Children swarm. The shops are open but empty. Over it all is some odd pale unnatural atmosphere – great activity but no normal life. Business improved today. We sold a few books. Clive calls in to discuss bulletins – indeed, more than anything it is like a house where someone is dangerously ill; and friends drop in to enquire, and one has to wait for doctors' news.

Friday 7 May

No change. 'London calling the British Isles. Good morning everyone.' That is how it begins at 10. The only news is that the archbishops are conferring, and ask our prayers that they may be guided right. Very little work done by either of us today. Leonard went to the [*Nation*] office, I to the British Museum; where all was chill serenity, dignity and severity. Written up are the names of great men; and we all cower like mice nibbling crumbs beneath. I like this dusty bookish atmosphere. Most of the readers seemed to have rubbed their noses off and written their eyes out. Yet they have a life they like – believe in the necessity of making books, I suppose; verify, collate, make up other books for ever. It must be fifteen years since I read here. I came home and found L. and Hubert [Henderson] 'taking a cup of tea', which means an hour and a half's talk about the Strike. L. says if the State wins and smashes the Trades Unions he will devote his life to Labour; if the archbishop succeeds, he will be baptised. Now to dine at the Commercio to meet Clive.

Sunday 9 May

There is no news of the strike. The broadcaster has just said that we are praying today. And L. and I quarrelled last night. I dislike the tub thumper in him; he the irrational Christian in me. Baldwin broadcast last night: he rolls his rs; tries to put more than mortal strength into his words. 'Have faith in me. You elected me eighteen months ago. What have I done to forfeit your confidence? Can you not trust me to see justice done between man and man?' Impressive as it is to hear the very voice of the Prime Minister, descendant of Pitt and Chatham, still I can't heat up my reverence to the right pitch. No I don't trust him: I don't trust any human being, however loud they bellow and roll their rs.

Monday 10 May
Quarrel with L. settled in studio. Oh, but how incessant the arguments and interruptions are! As I write, L. is telephoning to Hubert. We are getting up a petition. There was a distinct thaw (we thought) last night. So we went to bed happy. Today ostensibly the same deadlock; beneath the surface all sorts of currents, of which we get the most contradictory reports. I to the House of Commons this morning with L.'s article to serve as stuffing for Hugh Dalton in the Commons this afternoon. All this humbug of police and marble statues vaguely displeasing. But the Government provided me with buses both ways, and no stones thrown. After lunch to bookshop; to London Library; walk home; Clive; then Maynard ringing up to command us to print the *Nation* as the *New Statesman* is printed; to which I agreed, and L. disagreed; then dinner; more telephones ringing at the moment, 9.5.

Tuesday 11 May
I may as well continue to write while I wait -- here interruptions began which lasted from 12.30 to 3. I believe it is false psychology to think that in after years these details will be interesting. The war is now barren sand after all. But one never knows: and waiting about, writing serves to liberate the mind from the fret and itch of these innumerable details. Events are that the Roneo workers refuse to set up L.'s article in the *Nation*, in which he says that the strike is not illegal or unconstitutional. Presumably this is a little clutch of the Government throttle. Mr Baldwin has been visiting the Zoo. Tonight the names [the petition] are to be handed in; and then perhaps silence will descend upon us. But then everyone rings up -- the most unlikely people. Yesterday Ralph [Partridge] and Frances Marshall were in a railway accident. One man was killed – the result of driving a train without signals, by the efforts of ardent optimistic undergraduates. Day's Library boy was set upon by roughs, had his cycle overturned, but kept his books and was unhurt after calling here.

Wednesday 12 May
Strike settled (ring at bell). The Strike was settled about 1.15 – or it was then broadcast. They told us to stand by and await important news. Then a piano played a tune. Then the solemn broadcaster assuming incredible

pump and gloom and speaking one word to the minute read out: Message from 10 Downing Street. The TUC leaders have agreed that Strike shall be withdrawn. Instantly L. dashed off to telephone to the office; we finished lunch; then I rang up Clive – who proposes that we should have a drink tonight. I saw this morning five or six armoured cars slowly going along Oxford Street; on each two soldiers sat in tin helmets, and one stood with his hand at the gun which was pointed straight ahead ready to fire. But I also noticed on one a policeman smoking a cigarette. Such sights I dare say I shall never see again; and don't in the least wish to.

Thursday 13 May
I suppose all pages devoted to the Strike will be skipped, when I read over this book. Oh that dull old chapter, I shall say. Excitements about what are called real things are always unutterably transitory. Yet it is gloomy – and L. is gloomy, and so am I unintelligibly – today because the Strike continues – no railwaymen back: vindictiveness has now seized our masters. Government shillyshallies. Anyhow it will take a week to get the machinery of England to run again. In short, the strain removed, we all fall out and bicker and backbite. Such is human nature – and really I don't like human nature unless all candied over with art. We dined with a strike party last night and went back to Clive's. A good deal was said about art there.

Thursday 20 May
I think nothing need be said of the Strike. As tends to happen, one's mind slips after the crisis, and what the settlement is, or will be, I know not.
     Vita comes to lunch tomorrow, which will be a great amusement and pleasure. I am amused at my relations with her: left so ardent in January – and now what? Also I like her presence and her beauty. Am I in love with her? But what is love? Her being 'in love' with me, excites and flatters; and interests. What is this 'love'? Oh and then she gratifies my eternal curiosity: who's she seen, what's she done – for I have no enormous opinion of her poetry. I should have been reading her poem tonight.

Tuesday 25 May
Tomorrow we go to Rodmell – to find the bath and the WC and drawing room with the wall pulled down. I have finished – sketchily I admit – the second part of *To the Lighthouse* – and may, then, have it all written over by the end of July. A record – seven months, if it so turns out.
     So Vita came: and I register the shock of meeting after absence; how shy one is; how disillusioned by the actual body; and she was shabbier, come straight off in her travelling clothes; and not so beautiful, as sometimes perhaps; and so we sat talking on the sofa by the window, she rather silent,

I chattering, partly to divert her attention from me; and to prevent her thinking 'Well, is this all?' as she was bound to think, having declared herself so openly in writing. So that we each registered some disillusionment; and perhaps also acquired some grains of additional solidity – This may well be more lasting than the first rhapsody. But I cannot write. Suddenly the word instinct leaves me.

Wednesday 9 June
Then I got the 'flu, last Saturday; so have seen no one. Yes, Rodmell is a perfect triumph, I consider. In particular, our large combined drawing eating· room with its five windows, its beams down the middle, and flowers and leaves nodding in all round us. The bath boils quickly; the water closets gush and surge (not quite sufficiently though). The weather again failed us. We then went to a party at Edith Sitwell's (I in my new dress) 'to meet Miss [Gertrude] Stein', a lady much like Joan Fry, but more massive; in blue sprinkled brocade, rather formidable. Edith distraught; and cherries in handfuls, and barley water.

Wednesday 30 June
This is the last day of June and finds me in black despair because Clive laughed at my new hat, Vita pities me, and I sank to the depths of gloom. This happened at Clive's last night after going to the Sitwells with Vita. Oh dear I was wearing the hat without thinking whether it was good or bad; and it was all very flashing and easy; and [I] sat by Vita and laughed and clubbed. When we got out it was only 10.30 – a soft starry night: it was still too early for her to go. So she said "Shall we go to Clive's and pick him up?" and I was then again so lighthearted, driving through the Park, and finally came to Gordon Square and there was Nessa tripping along in the dark, in her quiet black hat. Then Duncan came, carrying an egg. Come on all of us to Clive's, I said; and they agreed. Well, it was after they had come and we were all sitting round talking that Clive suddenly said, or bawled rather, what an astonishing hat you're wearing! Then he asked where I got it. I pretended a mystery, tried to change the talk, was not allowed, and they pulled me down between them, like a hare; it was very forced and queer and humiliating. So I talked and laughed too much. Duncan prim and acid as ever told me it was utterly impossible to do anything with a hat like that. And Leonard got silent, and I came away deeply chagrined, as unhappy as I have been these ten years; and revolved it in sleep and dreams all night; and today has been ruined.

Thursday 1 July
But all this has obscured Garsington; [Robert] Bridges; and [H. G.] Wells. These great men are so much like the rest of us. Wells remarkable only for a combination of stockishness with acuity: he has a sharp nose, and the cheeks and jowl of a butcher. He likes, I judge, rambling and romancing about the lives of other people; he romanced about the Webbs: said their books were splendid eggs, well and truly laid, but addled. Described Beatrice, as by a gipsy and a Jew: a flashing creature, become Quaker as we all do as we get on. That has nothing to do with Christianity. Are you a Quaker, I asked. Of course I am. One believes that there is a reason for things (I think he said). But he did not rise steadily off the ground for long. Lunch is a hot stodgy hour too. I could see from the plaintive watery look on Mrs Wells' face that he is arrogant lustful and bullying in private life. The virtues he likes are courage and vitality.

As for Bridges: he sprang from a rhododendron bush, a very lean tall old man, with a curly grey hat, and a reddish ravaged face, smoky fierce eyes, with a hazy look in them; very active; rather hoarse, talking incessantly. We sat in his open room and looked past blue spikes of flowers to hills, which were invisible, but when they show, all this goes out he said – his one poetical saying. He is direct and spry, very quick in all his movements, racing me down the garden to look at pinks, then into his library, where I asked to see the Hopkins manuscripts; and sat looking at them with that gigantic grasshopper Aldous [Huxley] folded up in a chair close by. Ottoline undulated and vagulated. I said how much I like his poems – true of the short ones: but was mainly pleased and gratified to find him so obliging and easy and interested.

Sunday 4 July
Then Wells came again; and stayed till 4. He is getting to the drowsy stage: the sixties. He talked about his new book, the thoughts one has at sixty. What other ideas has he? Desmond asked. Well, to do away with Sunday. There should be a holiday once in ten days. That was his own stint. Ten days work, then four or five days off. The present system was wasteful. The shadow of the week-end begins on Friday, is not over till Monday afternoon. He struck me again as an odd mixture of bubble and solidity – likes to blow a phrase now and then. We got him on Hardy – a very simple, subtle old peasant man much impressed by clever people who write; very humble; wrote his early books in chapters as the printers wanted them. Then he got up to go: we asked him to stay and tell us about Henry James. So he sat down. Oh I should be delighted to stay and talk the whole afternoon, he said. Henry James was a formalist. He always thought of clothes. He was never intimate with anyone – not with his brother even:

had never been in love. Wells has learnt nothing from Proust – his book like the British Museum. One knows there are delightful interesting things in it, but one does not go there. One day it may be wet – I shall say God, what am I to do this afternoon? And I shall read Proust as I might go to the British Museum. Would not read Richardson – a man who knows all about feminine psychology – nobody ought to know that. I said on the contrary he knew very little: was conventional. Honour, chastity and so on. Wells said we had changed our ideas completely. That idea of chastity had vanished. Women were even more suggestible than men. He said we are happier perhaps – children are certainly more at ease with their parents. But he thought they were beginning to miss restraints. They were wondering what things were for. Henry James could not describe love – there comes the ahh – laying on of hands. This Wells could do himself. I am a journalist. I pride myself upon being a journalist he said. In all this he showed himself, as Desmond said afterwards, perfectly content to be himself, aware of his powers – aware that he need not take any trouble, since his powers were big enough.

Thursday 22 July

The summer hourglass is running out rapidly and rather sandily. Many nights I wake in a shudder thinking of some atrocity of mine. I bring home minute pinpricks which magnify in the middle of the night into gaping wounds. However I drive my pen through de Quincey of a morning, having put *To the Lighthouse* aside till Rodmell. There all virtue, all good is in retreat. Here nothing but odds and ends – going to the dentist, buying combs; must dine with Osbert Sitwell tonight though, and go to Hardy tomorrow.

Sunday 25 July

At first I thought it was Hardy, and it was the parlourmaid, a small thin girl, wearing a proper cap. She came in with silver cake stands and so on. Mrs Hardy talked to us about her dog. How long ought we to stay? Can Mr Hardy walk much &c I asked, making conversation. She has the large sad lack lustre eyes of a childless woman; great docility and readiness, as if she had learnt her part; not great alacrity, but resignation, in welcoming more visitors; wears a sprigged voile dress, black shoes, and a necklace. We can't go far now, she said, though we do walk every day, because our dog isn't able to walk far. He bites, she told us. She became more natural and animated about the dog, who is evidently the real centre of her thoughts. Then again the door opened, more sprucely, and in trotted a little puffy cheeked cheerful old man, with an atmosphere cheerful and businesslike in addressing us, rather like an old doctor's or solicitor's, saying "Well now –"

or words like that as he shook hands. He was dressed in rough grey with a striped tie. His nose has a joint in it, and the end curves down. A round whitish face, the eyes now faded and rather watery, but the whole aspect cheerful and vigorous. He sat on a three cornered chair at a round table, where there were the cake stands and so on; a chocolate roll; what is called a good tea; but he only drank one cup, sitting on his three cornered chair. He was extremely affable and aware of his duties. He did not let the talk stop or disdain making talk. He talked of father – said he had seen me, or it might have been my sister but he thought it was me, in my cradle. He had been to Hyde Park Place – oh Gate was it. A very quiet street. That was why my father liked it. Odd to think that in all these years he had never been down there again. He went there often. Your father took my novel – *Far from the Madding Crowd*. We stood shoulder to shoulder against the British public about certain matters dealt with in that novel – you may have heard. Some other novel had fallen through that was to appear; and he asked me to send my story. So I sent it in chapter by chapter, and was never late. Wonderful what youth is! I had it in my head doubtless, but I never thought twice about it – it came out every month.

He puts his head down like some old pouter pigeon. He has a very long head; and quizzical bright eyes, for in talk they grow bright. He said when he was in the Strand six years ago he scarcely knew where he was, and he used to know it all intimately. At this rate London would soon be unrecognisable. But I shall never go there again. And he smiled in his queer way, which is fresh and yet sarcastic a little: anyhow shrewd. Indeed, there was no trace to my thinking of the simple peasant. He seemed perfectly aware of everything; in no doubt or hesitation; having made up his mind; and being delivered of all his work; so that he was in no doubt about that either. He was not interested much in his novels, or in anybody's novels. "I never took long with them" he said. Can you write poetry regularly? I asked (being beset with the desire to hear him say something about his books); but the dog kept cropping up. How he bit; how the inspector came out; how he was ill; and they could do nothing for him. Would you mind if I let him in? asked Mrs Hardy, and in came Wessex, a very tousled, rough brown and white mongrel, got to guard the house, so naturally he bites people, said Mrs Hardy. Well, I don't know about that, said Hardy, perfectly natural, and not setting much stock by his poems either it seemed. Did you write poems at the same time as your novels? I asked. No, he said. I wrote a great many poems. I used to send them about, but they were always returned, he chuckled. I wanted him to say one word about his writing before we left and could only ask which of his books he would have chosen, if like me, he had had to choose one to read in the train. I had taken *The Mayor of Casterbridge*. "And did it hold your interest?" he asked. I stammered that I could not stop reading it, which was true, but sounded wrong. Anyhow he was not going to be drawn, and went off about giving a young lady a wedding present. None of my books are fitted to be wedding presents, he said. You must give Mrs Woolf one of your books, said Mrs Hardy, inevitably. Yes I will. But I'm afraid only in the little thin paper edition, he said.

He said to a friend who begged him not to give up poetry, "I'm afraid poetry is giving up me." The truth is he is a very kind man, and sees anyone who wants to see him. He has sixteen people for the day sometimes. Do you think one can't write poetry if one sees people? I asked. "One might be able to - I don't see why not. Its a question of physical strength" said Hardy. But clearly he preferred solitude himself. Always however he said something sensible and sincere; and thus made the obvious business of compliment giving rather unpleasant. He seemed to be free of it all; very active minded; liking to describe people; not to talk in an abstract way.

Now we began to look at the grandfather clock in the corner. We said we must go - tried to confess we were only down for the day. I forgot to say that he offered L. whisky and water, which struck me that he was competent as a host, and in every way. So we got up and signed Mrs Hardy's visitors' books; and Hardy took my *Life's Little Ironies* off, and trotted back with it signed, and Woolf spelt Wolff, which I daresay had given him some anxiety. Then Wessex came in again. I asked if Hardy could stroke him. So he bent down and stroked him, like the master of the house. Wessex went on wheezing away. What impressed me was his freedom, ease, and vitality. He seemed very 'Great Victorian', doing the whole thing with a sweep of his hand and setting no great stock by literature; but somehow, one could imagine, naturally swept off into imagining and creating without a thought of its being difficult or remarkable; becoming obsessed; and living in imagination. Mrs Hardy thrust his old grey hat into his hand and he trotted us out on to the road. And so we left, and he trotted in again.

The whole thing - literature, novels &c - all seemed to him an amusement, far away, too, scarcely to be taken seriously. Yet he had sympathy and pity for those still engaged in it. But what his secret interests and activities are - to what occupation he trotted off when we left him - I do not know.

Monks House, Rodmell

Saturday 31 July
Here is a whole nervous breakdown in miniature. We came on Tuesday. Sank into a chair, could scarcely rise; everything insipid; tasteless, colourless.

Enormous desire for rest. Wednesday – only wish to be alone in the open air. Air delicious – avoided speech; could not read. Thought of my own power of writing with veneration, as of something incredible, belonging to someone else; never again to be enjoyed by me. Mind a blank. Slept in my chair. Thursday. No pleasure in life whatsoever; but felt perhaps more attuned to existence. Character and idiosyncracy as Virginia Woolf completely sunk out. Humble and modest. Difficulty in thinking what to say. Read automatically, like a cow chewing cud. Slept in chair. Friday. Sense of physical tiredness; but slight activity of the brain. Beginning to take notice. Making one or two plans. Saturday (today) much clearer and lighter. Thought I could write, but resisted, or found it impossible. A desire to read poetry set in on Friday. This brings back a sense of my own individuality. But today senses quickening. Curiosity about literature returning.

Friday 3 September
For the rest, Charleston, Tilton, *To the Lighthouse*, Vita, expeditions: the summer dominated by a feeling of washing in boundless warm fresh air – such an August not come my way for years; bicycling; no settled work done, but advantage taken of air for going to the river, or over the downs. The novel is now easily within sight of the end, but this, mysteriously, comes no nearer.

Sunday 5 September
I am frightfully contented these last few days, by the way. I don't quite understand it. Perhaps reason has something to do with it. Charleston and Tilton knocked me off my perch for a moment: Nessa and her children; Maynard and his carpets. My own gifts and shares seemed so moderate in comparison; my own fault too – a little more self control on my part, and we might have had a boy of twelve, a girl of ten. This always rakes me wretched in the early hours. So I said, I am spoiling what I have. And thereupon settled to exploit my own possessions to the full; I can make money and buy carpets; I can increase the pleasure of life enormously by living it carefully. No doubt, this is a rationalisation of a state which is not really of that nature. Probably I am very lucky. Then, I am extremely happy walking on the downs. I like to have space to spread my mind out in. Whatever I think, I can rap out, suddenly, to L. We are somehow very detached, free, harmonious. Hence I come to my moral, which is simply to enjoy what one does enjoy, without teasing oneself oh but Nessa has children, Maynard carpets.

I am almost entirely surrounded by sheep. God knows, I wish we could buy the terrace, and have a garden all round the lodge - but this is not a serious diminution of joy.

Monday 13 September
The blessed thing is coming to an end I say to myself with a groan. Oh the relief of waking and thinking its done – the relief, and the disappointment I suppose. I am talking of *To the Lighthouse*. Morgan said he felt 'This is a failure' as he finished *A Passage to India*. I feel – what? A little stale this last week or two from steady writing. But also a little triumphant.

Wednesday 15 September
A State of Mind. Woke up perhaps at 3. Oh its beginning its coming – the horror – physically like a painful wave swelling about the heart – tossing me up. I'm unhappy unhappy! Down – God, I wish I were dead. Pause. But why am I feeling like this? Let me watch the wave rise. I watch. Vanessa. Children. Failure. Yes, I detect that. Failure failure. (The wave rises). Oh they laughed at my taste in green paint! Wave crashes. I wish I were dead! I've only a few years to live I hope. I can't face this horror any more – (this is the wave spreading out over me). This goes on; several times, with varieties of horror. Then, at the crisis, instead of the pain remaining intense, it becomes rather vague. I doze. I wake with a start. The wave again! The irrational pain: the sense of failure; generally some specific incident, as for example my taste in green paint, or buying a new dress, or asking Dadie for the week-end, tacked on. At last I say, watching as dispassionately as I can, Now take a pull of yourself. No more of this. I reason. I take a census of happy people and unhappy. I brace myself to shove to throw to batter down. I begin to march blindly forward. I feel obstacles go down. I say it doesn't matter. Nothing matters. I become rigid and straight, and sleep again, and half wake and feel the wave beginning and watch the light whitening and wonder how, this time, breakfast and daylight will overcome it; and then hear L. in the passage and simulate, for myself as well as for him, great cheerfulness; and generally am cheerful, by the time breakfast is over. Does everyone go through this state? Why have I so little control? It is the cause of much waste and pain in my life.

Tuesday 28 September
Intense depression: I have to confess that this has overcome me several times since September 6th (or thereabouts). It does not come from something definite, but from nothing. I discovered that, for the first time for many years, I had been idle without being ill. This is a warning then; never to cease the use of the brain. Then, owing to mismanagement, no one came to stay, and I got very few letters; and the high pure hot days went on and on; and this blankness persisted, and I began to suspect my book of the same thing; and there was Nessa humming and booming and flourishing

over the hill; and one night we had a long long argument. Vita started it by coming over, and L. (I say) spoilt the visit by glooming because I said he had been angry. He shut up, and was caustic; but admitted that my habits of describing him and others had this effect often. I saw myself, my brilliancy, genius, charm, beauty (&c &c – the attendants who float me through so many years) diminish and disappear. One is in truth an elderly dowdy fussy ugly incompetent woman, vain, chattering and futile. Then he said our relations had not been so good lately. I admitted that I had been irritated, first by the prevalency of dogs (Grizzle on heat too). Secondly by his assumption that we can afford to saddle ourselves with a whole time gardener, build or buy him a cottage, and take in the terrace to be garden. Then, I said, we shall be tying ourselves to come here; shall never travel; and it will be assumed that Monks House is the hub of the world. This it certainly is not, I said, to me; nor do I wish to spend such a measure of our money on gardens, when we cannot buy rugs, beds or good armchairs. L. was, I think, hurt at this, and I was annoyed at saying it, yet did it, not angrily, but in the interests of freedom. Too many women give way on this point, and secretly grudge their unselfishness in silence – a bad atmosphere. Our atmosphere decidedly cleared, after this, and I am once more full of work, and quite unable, I see, to make plain even to my own eyes, my season of profound despondency.

But it is always a question whether I wish to avoid these glooms. In part they are the result of getting away by oneself. These nine weeks give one a plunge into deep waters; which is a little alarming, but full of interest. One goes down into the well and nothing protects one from the assault of truth. Down there I can't write or read; I exist however. I am. Then I ask myself what I am? and get a closer though less flattering answer than I should on the surface – where, to tell the truth, I get more praise than is right. I am glad to find it on the whole so interesting, though so acutely unpleasant.

Thursday 30 September
I wished to add some remarks to this, on the mystical side of this solitude; how it is not oneself but something in the universe that one's left with. It is this that is frightening and exciting in the midst of my profound gloom, depression, boredom, whatever it is: one sees a fin passing far out. What image can I reach to convey what I mean? Really there is none I think. All I mean to make is a note of a curious state of mind. I hazard the guess that it may be the impulse behind another book.

I was depressed again today because Vita did not come (yet relieved at the same time); had to hold L.'s ladder in the garden, when I wanted to write or to try on Nessa's dress; and slightly afraid that this dress is not very successful. But I am shelving the dress problem on these principles. I am having cheap day clothes; and a good dress from Brooke; and am being less pernickety about keeping to limits, as I have only to write and stir myself to make, I wager, quite £50 extra in the year for my own extravagances. No longer shall I be afraid to lunch out because 'I've no clothes'. Soon, this time next week, I shall have no time for glooming or introspection. It will be "When may I come and see you?"

52 TAVISTOCK SQUARE, WCI

Saturday 30 October
It will be when may I come and see you! – too true a prophecy, though made in the damp and solitude of Rodmell. So the week slips or sticks through my fingers; rage misery joy, dullness elation mix. I am the usual battlefield of emotions; alternately think of buying chairs and clothes; plod with some method revising *To the Lighthouse*; quarrel with Nelly; and so we go on. Among external things, we were at Cambridge for the week-end; kept warm at the Bull – and there's a good subject – the Hotel. A whole life opened to me. Then [Sir Edmund] Gosse introducing Vita at Royal – something [Society of Literature]. I never saw the whole hierarchy of literature so plainly exposed. Gosse the ornament on the tea pot: beneath him file on file of old stout widows whose husbands had been professors, beetle specialists doubtless, meritorious dons; and these good people, reflecting all the depths of the suburbs tinctured with literature, dear Vita told them were 'The Hollow Men'. Her address was read in sad sulky tones like those of a schoolboy; her rich pendulous society face, glowing out under a black hat at the end of the smoky dismal room, looked very ancestral and like a picture under glass in a gallery. She was fawned upon by the little dapper grocer Gosse, who kept spinning round on his heel to address her compliments and to scarify Bolshevists; in an ironical voice which seemed to ward off what might be said of him; and to be drawing round the lot of them thicker and thicker, the red plush curtains of respectability. I don't regret my wildest, foolishest, utterance, if it gave the least crack to this respectability. But needless to say, no word of mine has had any effect whatever. Gosse will survive us all.

Tuesday 23 November
. . . a discussion at tea about Angus. He don't do, L. says: will never make a manager. These difficulties recur. Next year L. thinks we could sell to advantage. It [the Hogarth Press] gives one a full life: but then life is so full already. Colefax complicates the scene – Colefax is the death of

this book. Aren't I always reading her scrawls or answering them. This culminated last week in her dining alone with me, off cold chicken. I found us talking socially, not intimately, she in pearls (shams Vita says) popping up one light after another: like the switch board at the telephone exchange at the mention of names. She is, I maintain, a woman of the world: has all her senses tuned to that pitch. The machine doesn't work in private, though she was very anxious, poor aspiring, slightly suspicious and uneasy woman, that it should. Now, aged fifty, she asks, Is this life? – rushing round, dining and giving dinners; never able to concentrate in a corner, and secretly, in my opinion, not desiring it but pretending it, as she has the habit of pretence. This is all right in her, but wrong in me. So we don't altogether amalgamate; but I have my reservations, she hers. In came Dadie, to our relief, somewhat.

Fame grows. Chances of meeting this person, doing that thing, accumulate. Life is as I've said since I was ten, awfully interesting – if anything, quicker, keener at forty-four than twenty-four – more desperate I suppose, as the river shoots to Niagara – my new vision of death. "The one experience I shall never describe" I said to Vita yesterday. She was sitting on the floor in her velvet jacket and red striped silk shirt, I knotting her pearls into heaps of great lustrous eggs. She had come up to see me – so we go on – a spirited, creditable affair, I think, innocent (spiritually) and all gain, I think; rather a bore for Leonard, but not enough to worry him. The truth is one has room for a good many relationships. Then she goes back again to Persia.

I am re-doing six pages of *Lighthouse* daily. My present opinion is that it is easily the best of my books.

1927

Back in Tavistock Square after a chilly Christmas in Cornwall, Leonard read and approved To the Lighthouse, *which was put into proof, corrected by Virginia, and published in May. In the early months of the year Virginia felt bereft of her intimates; Vanessa and Duncan were at Cassis, where Clive was to join them; Vita, with whom Virginia had spent two nights in January at the Sackvilles' ancestral home, Knole, rejoined her husband in Persia, and again Virginia felt the want of her intensely; and it was the recollection of Vita and a perception of the historical continuity of her forebears at Knole that set off a profusion of ideas which was to result in her fantasy* Orlando.

This year the Hogarth Press published over forty books and pamphlets, and Leonard's doubts about the amiable Angus Davidson's capacity to 'manage' led to the latter's reluctant resignation at the end of the year, after which Leonard himself managed the business until 1931 with what Virginia called 'competent underlings'.

The Woolfs' spring holiday took them via Cassis as far afield as Sicily, with a week in Rome on the return journey. On coming home Nelly the cook was found to be ill; To the Lighthouse *was published and sold well; Vita returned from Persia and again occupied the foreground of Virginia's life. A sharp spell of headache at the end of May gave her the excuse thereafter to fend off unwanted visitors and invitations, but did not prevent her from joining a party with Vita and Harold Nicolson which took an overnight train to Yorkshire to observe the total eclipse of the sun on 29 June. The success of* To the Lighthouse *enabled the Woolfs to buy a motor car in July; Virginia herself took driving lessons but gave up after a while, and it was Leonard who habitually drove.*

Before settling in at Monks House early in August, Virginia crossed the Channel to spend three days near Dieppe with her American painter friends Ethel Sands and Nan Hudson; she then spent a happy summer in Sussex, writing easily, motoring about the countryside, seeing a good deal of Vita, of her family and her friends, observing country life; and, just before leaving, plunging into the 'greatest rapture known to me' – the inspired writing of Orlando. *This kept her absorbed and vigorous during the later months of the year, with little time or inclination to air her discontents in her diary; enjoying her work, enjoying her pleasures, enjoying her success. On Christmas Eve the Woolfs went to Sussex for nine days.*

1927

Sunday 23 January

Well Leonard has read *To the Lighthouse*, and says it is much my best book, and it is a 'masterpiece'. He said this without my asking. I came back from Knole and sat without asking him. He calls it entirely new – 'a psychological poem' is his name for it. Having won this great relief, my mind dismisses the whole thing, as usual; and I forget it, and shall only wake up and be worried again over proofs and then when it appears.

We went to Cornwall. Will [Arnold-Forster] is a water-blooded waspish little man, all on edge, vain, peevish, nervous. Ka is matronly, but substantial. Some views I retain – one of the valley in the evening light – but others were only a dull impression of life suspended and frozen. We came home for these reasons a day early, and next morning I had a letter from the *New York Herald Tribune* asking me to go there, passage paid, £120 in my pocket and, perhaps, expenses, and write four articles. We accepted, on conditions; but have not heard yet. Meanwhile we hesitate, for if Leonard came, we should probably be £150 out of pocket. The adventure is tempting. But the grind of moneymaking is scarcely to be endured unnecessarily. We could go to Greece, or Italy, for less.

At Knole, Vita took me over the four acres of building, which she loves; too little conscious beauty for my taste: smallish rooms looking on to buildings; no views; yet one or two things remain: Vita stalking in her Turkish dress, attended by small boys, down the gallery, wafting them on like some tall sailing ship – a sort of covey of noble English life: dogs walloping, children crowding, all very free and stately; and a cart bringing wood in to be sawn by the great circular saw. They had brought wood in from the Park to replenish the great fires like this for centuries; and her ancestresses had walked so on the snow with their great dogs bounding by them. All the centuries seemed lit up, the past expressive, articulate; not dumb and forgotten; but a crowd of people stood behind, not dead at all; and so we reach the days of Elizabeth quite easily. After tea, looking for letters of Dryden's to show me, she tumbled out a love letter of Lord

Dorset's (Seventeenth Century) with a lock of his soft gold tinted hair which I held in my hand a moment. One had a sense of links fished up into the light which are usually submerged. Otherwise no particular awe or any great sense of difference or distinction. They are not a brilliant race. I came home to Marjorie Strachey, Tom Eliot, Nessa and Roger. A little constricted our society: but how lively and agile compared with the [aristocracy?]

Thursday 3 February
I ask, why another volume? What is the purpose of them? L. taking up a volume the other day said Lord save him if I died first and he had to read through these. And do I say anything interesting? I can always waste an idle hour reading them; and then, oh yes, I shall write my memoirs out of them one of these days.

That reminds me of the Webbs: those thirty-six strenuous hours at Liphook, in an emphatic lodging house, with blue books in the passages; and those entirely devoted – by which I mean those entirely integrated people. Their secret is that they have by nature no divisions of soul to fritter them away: their impact is solid and entire. Without eyes and ears (but Mrs Webb listens in and prefers Mozart to Handel, if I may guess) one can come down with more of a weight upon bread and butter or whatever the substance is before one. On a steely watery morning we swiftly tramped over a heathy common talking, talking. In their efficiency and glibness one traces perfectly adjusted machinery; but talk by machinery does not charm, or suggest: it cuts the grass of the mind close at the roots. I'm too hurried to write. Mrs Webb is far less ornamental than of old: wispy untidy drab, with a stain on her skirt and a key on her watch chain; as if she had cleared the decks and rolled her sleeves and was waiting for the end, but working.

Saturday 12 February
But I am forgetting, after three days, the most important event in my life since marriage – so Clive described it. Mr Cizec has bingled me. I am short haired for life. Having no longer, I think, any claims to beauty, the convenience of this alone makes it desirable. Every morning I go to take up brush and twist that old coil round my finger and fix it with hairpins and then with a start of joy, no I needn't. In front there is no change; behind I'm like the rump of a partridge. This robs dining out of half its terrors. For the rest – its been a gay tropical kind of autumn, with so much Vita and Knole and staying away: we have launched ourselves a little more freely perhaps from work and the Press. But now with Nessa away, Clive away, Duncan away, Vita away, the strenuous time sets in: I'm reading and

writing at a great pace; mean to make all the money we want for Greece and a motor car.

Yesterday rather a flat talk with Angus. L. says he doesn't 'manage'. Angus refuses to budge an inch. He can't see the point of it. As he says, too, what's he to do if he leaves? He doesn't much want to leave. Though sometimes 'fed up' he likes it better than most work. But I'm persuaded we need, the Press needs, a fanatic at the moment; not this quiet easygoing gentlemanliness. I am annoyed at doing cards, and envelopes; and L. does twice the work I do.

Monday 28 February
My brain is rather stale. Do I like *The Lighthouse?* I think I was disappointed. But God knows. I have to read it again.

And now the wind is making the tin screen over the gas fire rattle. How we protect ourselves from the elements! Coming back last night [from Rodmell] I thought, owing to civilisation, I, who am now cold, wet, and hungry, can be warm and satisfied and listening to a Mozart quartet in fifteen minutes. And so I was. That ring may be Tom. No. Tom don't run upstairs – only the lower classes do that.

And I don't think I shall go out in the rain, though I am going to spend this week in long romantic London walks. I have successfully broken the neck of that screaming grey goose – society. There's nothing to be afraid of in dining with Ethel or Sibyl – and I'm shingled now. One spins round for a moment and then settles on one's feet. But about the Soul: the soul has sunk to the bottom. I am empty headed tonight.

Saturday 5 March
Both rather headachy and fatigued. A holiday, without dinner to order, or telephone to answer, or people to talk to, will be a divine miracle. We go to Cassis on the 30th; then to Sicily; so home by Rome. What could be more to my heart. Often I sit and think of looking at things. The greed of my eye is insatiable. To think of seeing a new place fills me with excitement. I now make up pictures of Sicily. Think of the Campagna grey in the evening.

Monday 14 March
Although annoyed that I have not heard from Vita by this post nor yet last week, annoyed sentimentally, and partly from vanity – still I must record the conception last night of a new book. Suddenly between twelve and one I conceived a whole fantasy to be called 'The Jessamy Brides' – why, I wonder? I have rayed round it several scenes. Two women, poor, solitary at the top of a house. One can see anything (for this is all fantasy), the

Tower Bridge, clouds, aeroplanes. Everything is to be tumbled in pell mell. Sapphism is to be suggested. Satire is to be the main note – satire and wildness. The Ladies are to have Constantinople in view. Dreams of golden domes. My own lyric vein is to be satirised. Everything mocked. And it is to end with three dots ... so. For the truth is I feel the need of an escapade after these serious poetic experimental books whose form is always so closely considered. I want to kick up my heels and be off. I think this will be great fun to write; and it will rest my head before starting the very serious, mystical poetical work which I want to come next.

Monday 21 March
Almost in a week now we shall be starting. I dislike the days before going. I went to buy clothes today and was struck by my own ugliness. Like Edith Sitwell I can never look like other people – too broad, tall, flat, with hair hanging. And now my neck is so ugly.

Edith Sitwell came to tea: transparent like some white bone one picks up on a moor, with sea water stones on her long frail hands which slide into yours much narrower than one expects like a folded fan. She has pale gemlike eyes; and is dressed, on a windy March day, in three decker skirts of red spotted cotton. She half shuts her eyes; coos an odd little laugh. All is very tapering and pointed, the nose running on like a mole. She said I was a great writer, which pleased me. So sensitive to everything in people and books she said. She got talking about her mother blaspheming in the nursery, hysterical; terrible; setting Edith to kill bluebottles. She is a curious product, likeable to me: sensitive, etiolated, affectionate, lonely, having to thread her way (there is something ghostlike and angular about her) home to Bayswater to help cook dinner. In other ages she would have been a cloistered nun; or an eccentric secluded country old maid. It is the oddity of our time that has set her on the music hall stage. She trips out into the limelight with all the timidity and hauteur of the aristocratic spinster.

* * *

Sunday 1 May
We came back on Thursday night from Rome; from that other private life which I mean to have for ever now. One is nobody in Italy: one has no name, no calling, no background. Altogether I don't think I've ever enjoyed one month so much. What a faculty of enjoyment one has! I liked everything. I wish I were not so ignorant of Italian, art, literature and so on. However, I cannot now write this out, or go into the great mass of feeling which it composed in me. Nelly was found, at 11.30, when we got back, in bed, with some mysterious affection of the kidney. This was a jar; the coffee was a

jar; everything was a jar. And then I remember how my book is coming out. But I think, honestly, I care very little this time – even for the opinion of my friends.

Thursday 5 May
Book out. We have sold (I think) 1690 before publication – twice *Dalloway*. I write however in the shadow of the damp cloud of the *TLS* review, gentlemanly, kindly, timid and praising beauty, doubting character, and leaving me moderately depressed. I know why I am depressed: a bad habit of making up the review I should like before reading the review I get.

Wednesday 11 May
Vita back; unchanged, though I daresay one's relation changes from day to day. Clive and she together. I think Clive is pretty miserable: his stay at Cassis a failure, so far as writing goes. And then the question rises, has he not gone too far in eating, drinking, love making, to stop dead now? He seemed random and unsettled. He talked (always shifting away from himself yet returning ambiguously to that centre) about going mad: sometimes thought he was going mad.

My book. What is the use of saying one is indifferent to reviews when positive praise, though mingled with blame, gives one such a start on, that instead of feeling dried up, one feels, on the contrary, flooded with ideas? I gather from vague hints, through Marjorie Thomson, through Clive, that some people say it is my best book.

Monday 16 May
The book. Now on its feet so far as praise is concerned. Nessa enthusiastic – a sublime, almost upsetting spectacle. She says it is an amazing portrait of mother; a supreme portrait painter; has lived in it; found the rising of the dead almost painful. Then Ottoline, then Vita, then Charlie [Sanger], then Lord Olivier, then Tommy [Tomlin], then Clive – he came in, ostensibly to praise this 'amazing book – far the best you've ever written', and sat on, but how wandering and unhappy. I have scarcely seen him in this mood ever before. But what is it? Has he lost faith? Has the dancing mist of rhapsody failed him – he who was based so solidly on such beef and beer or champagne rather. Suppose one woke and found oneself a fraud? It was part of my madness – that horror. But then as Clive said, you go mad but you bound up again – the inference being that he was to stay mad.

Monday 6 June (Whit Monday)
I have been in bed a week with a sudden and very sharp headache, and this is written experimentally to test my brain. The *Lighthouse* has sold 2,200

and we are reprinting. And now, with Morgan's morganatic, evasive, elusive letter this morning, the *Lighthouse* is behind me: my headache over; and after a week at Rodmell, my freedom from inspection, my deep dive into my own mind will begin. How odd, it comes into my mind, is Nessa and my jealousy of each other's clothes! I feel her, when I put on my smart black fringed cape, anguished for a second. Then she says she is going to wear earrings: I say at once that I will; this she resents. Yet we are both fundamentally sensible, and so recover from our umbrage. I think, however, I am now almost an established figure – as a writer. They don't laugh at me any longer. Soon they will take me for granted. Possibly I shall be a celebrated writer.

Saturday 18 June
This is a terribly thin diary for some reason: half the year has been spent, and left only these few sheets. Perhaps I have been writing too hard in the morning to write here also. Three weeks wiped out by headache. We had a week at Rodmell, of which I remember various sights, and the immense comfort of lying there lapped in peace. Lay out all day in the new garden, with the terrace. There were blue tits nested in the hollow neck of my Venus. Slowly ideas began trickling in; and then suddenly I rhapsodised and told over the story of the Moths, which I think I will write very quickly: the play poem idea; the idea of some continuous stream, not solely of human thought, but of the ship, the night, &c, all flowing together: intersected by the arrival of the bright moths. A man and a woman are to be sitting at table talking. Or shall they remain silent? It is to be a love story: she is finally to let the last great moth in. Perhaps the man could be left absolutely dim. France: near the sea; at night; a garden under the window. But it needs ripening. I do a little work on it in the evening when the gramophone is playing late Beethoven sonatas. (The windows fidget at their fastenings as if we were at sea.)

   We saw Vita given the Hawthornden [Prize]. A horrid show up, I thought: not of the gentry on the platform – Squire, Drinkwater, Binyon only: of us all: all of us chattering writers. My word! how insignificant we all looked! How can we pretend that we are interesting, that our works matter? The whole business of writing became infinitely distasteful. But there may be a stream of ink in them that matters more than the look of them – so tightly clothed, mild, and decorous – showed. I felt there was no one full grown mind among us. In truth, it was the thick dull middle class of letters that met; not the aristocracy.

Wednesday 22 June
Harold Nicolson and Duncan dined with us, and Nessa came in afterwards, very silent, inscrutable and, perhaps, critical. As a family we distrust anyone outside our set, I think. We too definitely decide that so and so has not the necessary virtues. I daresay Harold has not got them; at the same time, there is a good deal in him I like: he is quick and rash and impulsive; not in our sense very clever; uneasy; seeming young; on the turn from diplomat to intellectual; not Vita's match; but honest and cordial. L. says he's too commonplace. I liked my little duet with him. He wears a green, or blue, shirt and tie; is sunburnt; chubby; pert; vivacious. Talked of politics, but was flimsy compared with Leonard – I thought. Said it was with L. and me that he felt completely at his ease. Told stories which sound rather empty in the bare Bloomsbury rooms.

Thursday 23 June
Never have I spent so quiet a London summer. I have set my standard as an invalid, and no one bothers me. No one asks me to do anything. Quiet brings me cool clear quick mornings, in which I dispose of a good deal of work, and toss my brain into the air when I take a walk.

Vita's book [*The Land*] verberates and reverberates in the press. A prize poem – that's my fling at it – for with some relics of jealousy, or it may be of critical sense, I can't quite take the talk of poetry and even great poetry seriously. Oh and Sibyl [Colefax] has dropped me: and I don't feel the fall. And Adrian came to tea on Sunday, and fairly sparkled. At last I think he has emerged. Even his analysis will be over this year. At the age of forty-three he will be educated and ready to start life. So we Stephens mature late. And our late flowers are rare and splendid. Think of my books, Nessa's pictures – it takes us an age to bring our faculties into play.

Thursday 30 June
Now I must sketch out the Eclipse.

About 10 on Tuesday night several very long trains, accurately filled (ours with civil servants) left King's Cross. In our carriage was Vita and Harold, Quentin, L. and I. Before it got dark we kept looking at the sky: soft fleecy; but there was one star, over Alexandra Park. The Nicolsons got sleepy: Harold curled up with his head on Vita's knee. She looked like Sappho by Leighton, asleep; so we plunged through the midlands; made a very long stay at York. Then at 3 we got our sandwiches. Then we had another doze, or the Nicolsons did; then here was a level crossing, at which were drawn up a long line of motor omnibuses and motors, all burning pale yellow lights. It was getting grey – still a fleecy mottled sky. We got to Richmond about 3.30; it was cold, and the Nicolsons had a quarrel about

Vita's luggage. We went off in the omnibus, saw a vast castle (who does that belong to said Vita, who is interested in castles). All the fields were aburn with June grasses and red tasselled plants, none coloured as yet, all pale. Pale and grey too were the little uncompromising Yorkshire farms. As we passed one, the farmer, and his wife and sister came out, all tightly and tidily dressed in black, as if they were going to church. At another ugly square farm, two women were looking out of the upper windows. These had white blinds drawn down half across them. We were a train of three vast cars, one stopping to let the others go on; all very low and powerful; taking immensely steep hills. The driver once got out and put a small stone behind our wheel – inadequate. There were also many motor cars. These suddenly increased as we crept up to the top of Bardon Fell. Here were people camping beside their cars. We got out, and found ourselves very high, on a moor, boggy, heathery, with butts for grouse shooting. There were grass tracks here and there, and people had already taken up positions. So we joined them, walking out to what seemed the highest point looking over Richmond. One light burnt down there. Vales and moors stretched, slope after slope, round us. It was like the Haworth country. But over Richmond, where the sun was rising, was a soft grey cloud. We could see by a gold spot where the sun was. But it was early yet. We had to wait, stamping to keep warm, Leonard kept looking at his watch. Four great red setters came leaping over the moor. There were sheep feeding behind us. There were thin places in the cloud, and some complete holes. The question was whether the sun would show through a cloud or through one of these hollow places when the time came. We began to get anxious. We saw rays coming through the bottom of the clouds. Then, for a moment, we saw the sun, sweeping – it seemed to be sailing at a great pace and clear in a gap; we had out our smoked glasses; we saw it crescent, burning red; next moment it had sailed fast into the cloud again; only the red streamers came from it; then only a golden haze, such as one has often seen. The moments were passing. We thought we were cheated; we looked at the sheep; they showed no fear; the setters were racing round; everyone was standing in long lines, rather dignified, looking out. I thought how we were like very old people, in the birth of the world – druids on Stonehenge. At the back of us were great blue spaces in the cloud. But now the colour was going out. The clouds were turning pale; a reddish black colour. Down in the valley it was an extraordinary scrumble of red and black; there was the one light burning; all was cloud down there, and very beautiful, so delicately tinted. The 24 seconds were passing. Then one looked back again at the blue: and rapidly, very very quickly, all the colours faded; it became darker and darker as at the beginning of a violent storm; the light sank and sank; we kept saying this is the shadow; and we thought now it is over – this is the shadow; when suddenly the light went out. We had fallen. It was extinct. There was no colour. The earth was dead. That was the astonishing moment: and the next when as if a ball had rebounded, the cloud took colour on itself again; and so the light came back. I had very strongly the feeling as the light went out of some vast obeisance; something kneeling down and suddenly raised up when the colours came. They came back astonishingly lightly and quickly and beautifully in the valley and over the hills, at first with a miraculous glittering and aetheriality. The colour for some moments was of the most lovely kind – fresh, various – here blue, and there brown: all new colours, as if washed over and repainted. It was like recovery. We had been much worse than we had expected. We had seen the world dead. We were bitterly cold. I should say that the cold had increased as the light went down. One felt very livid. Then – it was all over till 1999. What remained was a sense of the comfort which we get used to, of plenty of light and colour. This for some time seemed a definitely welcome thing. Yet when it became established, one rather missed the sense of its being a relief and a respite, which one had had when it came back after the darkness. How can I express the darkness? It was a sudden plunge, when one did not expect it: being at the mercy of the sky; our own nobility; the druids; Stonehenge and the racing red dogs; all that was in one's mind. Also to be picked out of one's London drawing room and set down on the wildest moors in England was impressive. For the rest, I remember trying to keep awake in the gardens at York and falling asleep. Asleep again in the train. It was hot and we were messy. The carriage was full of things. Harold was very kind and attentive. We got home at 8.30 perhaps.

Monday 4 July
Back from Long Barn. Such opulence and freedom, flowers all out, butler, silver, dogs, biscuits, wine, hot water, log fires, Italian cabinets, Persian rugs, books – this was the impression it made: as of stepping into a rolling gay sea, with nicely crested waves. Yet I like this room better perhaps: more effort and life in it, to my mind. Vita very opulent, in her brown velvet coat, pearl necklace, and slightly furred cheeks (they are like Saviour's Flannel). I liked Harold too. He is a spontaneous childlike man; has a mind that bounces when he drops it; an air of immaturity. I should judge him very generous and kind hearted. Vita very free and easy, always giving me great pleasure to watch, and recalling some image of a ship breasting a sea, nobly, magnificently, with all sails spread, and the gold sunlight on them.

Monday 11 July
In a mood of random restlessness – Nelly having for the 125th time 'given notice' this morning. I am sick of the timid spiteful servant mind. But I

have never mentioned the absorbing subject – the subject which has filled our thoughts to the exclusion of Clive and Mary and literature and death and life – motor cars. Every evening we go round with Pinker [dog] for a game in Gordon Square; we sit there in between the sulphur coloured storms; under the shelter of trees with the rain pattering between the leaves. We talk of nothing but cars. Then sometimes, word is brought that Mrs Bell is at the door in her car. I rush out, and find her rather nervously in control of a roomy shabby Renault with Fred beside her. Three times I have been for a little tour with her. And yesterday we commissioned Fred to find us and bring instantly to our door a Singer. We have decided on a Singer. And the reason why I am distracted now is that Fred is going to ring me up and say if I am to have my first lesson this evening. This is a great opening up in our lives. One may go to Bodiam, to Arundel, explore the Chichester downs, expand that curious thing, the map of the world in one's mind. It will I think demolish loneliness, and may of course imperil one's privacy. The Keyneses have one too – a cheap one. Nessa thinks it will break down at once. Nessa takes a very sinister view of the Keyneses. She anticipates ruin of every sort for them, with some pleasure too. Here's Leonard - And now I must quickly dress for Clive's party; there's a plethora of parties this week.

With any luck *The Lighthouse* will reach 3000 this week.

Saturday 23 July
Since making the last entry I have learnt enough to drive a car in the country alone. On the backs of paper I write down instructions for starting cars. We have a nice little shut up car in which we can travel thousands of miles. The world gave me this for writing *The Lighthouse*, I reflect, a book which has now sold 3,160 (perhaps) copies; will sell 3,500 before it dies, and thus far exceeds any other of mine. All images are now tinged with driving a motor. Here I think of letting my engine work, with my clutch out.

It has been, on the whole, a fresh well ordered summer. I am not so parched with talk as usual. My illness in May was a good thing in some ways; for I got control of society at an early stage, and circumvented my headache, without a complete smash. I enjoyed the Eclipse; I enjoyed Long Barn (where I went twice); I enjoyed sitting with Vita at Kew for three or four hours under a cloudy sky, and dining with her: she refreshes me, and solaces me. I have worked very methodically and done my due of articles, so that with luck I shall have made £120 *over* my proper sum by September. That is, I shall have made £320 by journalism, and I suppose at least £300 by my novel this year. The Press is going on. Novels are the great bloodsuckers. I fancy that we don't do as well as we should with novels.

MONKS HOUSE, RODMELL

Monday 8 August
I was to have written here such a brilliant account of my three days at Dieppe, and now shall not, I suppose. We have motored most days. We opened one little window when we bought the gramophone; now another opens with the motor.

Wednesday 10 August
Yes, the motor is turning out the joy of our lives, an additional life, free and mobile and airy, to live alongside our usual stationary industry. We spin off to Falmer, ride over the Downs, drop into Rottingdean, then sweep over to Seaford, call in pouring rain at Charleston, pass the time of day, return for tea, all as light and easy as a hawk in the air. Soon we shall look back at our pre-motor days as we do now at our days in the caves. After a week here, Leonard has become perfectly efficient; I am held back by insufficient lessons, but shall be expert before September is half through. Various little improvements in the house keep me on the thrill with hope and despair. Perhaps if I make an extra sum we might build a bed sitting room for me in the attic, enlarge L.'s study, and so have a desirable, roomy, light house. For if we had £300 every year to spend, it is difficult to think of anything, except this, travel, and pocket money, to spend it on. Here at the age of forty-five are Nessa and I growing little wings again after our lean years.

Sunday 4 September
Many scenes have come and gone unwritten, since it is today 4th September, a cold grey blowy day, made memorable by the sight of a kingfisher, and by my sense, waking early, of being again visited by 'the spirit of delight'. 'Rarely rarely comest thou, spirit of delight' [Shelley]. That was I singing this time last year; and sang so poignantly that I have never forgotten it, or my vision of a fin rising on a wide blank sea. No biographer could possibly guess this important fact about my life in the late summer of 1926: yet biographers pretend they know people.

Tuesday 20 September
A thousand things to be written had I time: had I power. A very little writing uses up my capacity for writing. But I can think of more books than I shall ever be able to write. How many little stories come into my head!
We motored to Long Barn and back yesterday, through suburbs for the most part. All Hampstead, red, sanitary, earnest, view gazing, breeze

requiring, is lodged in the heights of Ashdown Forest. And Quentin came, and the Keyneses came, and Morgan came. Quentin won't let us play him Wagner: prefers Bach. Nessa's children are terrifyingly sophisticated: so Morgan said when Angelica, rigged up in a long black shawl, acted Lady Cornflax and Lady Ottoline at Charleston. They have grown up without any opposition: nothing to twist or stunt. Hence they have reached stages at sixteen or seventeen which I reached only at twenty-six or twenty-seven. But the summer has never burnt; and is now ashes. But we are very happy – seldom more so, I think. Perhaps things are doing rather well – and L. said the other day, "The strange thing is that we always come to the same opinion about things" – which pleased me.

Sunday 25 September

Now let me become the annalist of Rodmell. Thirty-five years ago, there were 160 families living here where there are now no more than eighty. It is a decaying village, which loses its boys to the towns. Not a boy of them, said the Rev. Mr Hawkesford, is being taught to plough. Rich people wanting week-end cottages buy up the old peasants' houses, for fabulous sums. Monks House was offered to Mr Hawkesford for £400: we gave £700. He refused it, saying he didn't wish to own country cottages. Now Mr Allison will pay £1200 for a couple, and we he said might get £2000 for this. He is an old decaying man, run to seed. He is sinking into old age, very shabby, loose limbed, wearing black wool mittens. His life is receding like a tide, slowly; or one figures him as a dying candle, whose wick will soon sink into the warm grease and be extinct. He tumbles into an armchair; and tells over his stock of old village stories, which always have this slightly mocking flavour, as though, completely unambitious, and by no means successful himself, he recouped himself by laughing slyly at the humours of the more energetic. He smokes endless cigarettes, and his fingers are not very clean. Talking of his well, he said "It would be a different thing if one wanted baths" – which for some seventy years, presumably, he has done without. Of his clerical character there is little visible. I asked him if he had work to do: a question which amused him a little. Not work, he said; but a young woman to see. And then he settled into the armchair again, and so sat out a visit of over an hour and a half.

Wednesday 5 October

I write in the sordid doss house atmosphere of approaching departure. Pinker is asleep in one chair; Leonard is signing cheques at the little deal table under the glare of the lamp. The fire is covered with ashes, since we have been burning it all day. Envelopes lie in the grate. I am writing with a pen which is feeble and wispy; and it is a sharp fine evening with a sunset,

I daresay. If my pen allowed, I should now try to make out a work table, having done my last article for the *Tribune*, and now being free again. And instantly the usual exciting devices enter my mind: a biography beginning the year 1500 and continuing to the present day, called *Orlando*: Vita; only with a change about from one sex to another. I think, for a treat, I shall let myself dash this in for a week.

52 TAVISTOCK SQUARE, WC1

Saturday 22 October
'I shall let myself dash this in for a week' – I have done nothing, nothing else for a fortnight; and am launched somewhat furtively but with all the more passion upon *Orlando: A Biography*. It is to be a small book, and written by Christmas. I walk making up phrases; sit, contriving scenes; am in short in the thick of the greatest rapture known to me. Talk of planning a book, or waiting for an idea! This one came in a rush. But the relief of turning my mind that way about was such that I felt happier than for months; as if put in the sun, or laid on cushions; and after two days entirely gave up my time chart and abandoned myself to the pure delight of this farce. I am writing *Orlando* half in a mock style very clear and plain, so that people will understand every word. But the balance between truth and fantasy must be careful. It is based on Vita, Violet Trefusis, Lord Lascelles, Knole, &c.

A great many incidents to record. They come always in a rush together, these bright October days, with everyone just back, fresh from solitude, cheerful, busy, sociable. Nessa has initiated, informally, Sunday evenings; and there Old Bloomsbury is to gather, after dinner – Helen [Anrep], Clive, Roger and so on. Then there's Clive. He has laid his stairs with the vividest green, five inches thick: has every comfort and convenience. I dine there to meet Harold [Nicolson] and Tom [Eliot]: Tom, of course, in white waistcoat, much the man of the world; which sets the key, and off they go telling stories about 'Jean' (Cocteau), about Ada Leverson, Gosse, Valéry, &c &c and L. and I feel a little Bloomsburyish perhaps; no, I think this sort of talk is hardly up to the scratch. Harold does it best.

We saw the pale dove grey coffin of Mrs Wells slide through the gates at Golders Green. It had tassels like bell pulls on it. Wells sat in bottle blue overcoat by [Bernard] Shaw, sobbing. One saw his white handkerchief going in and out of his pocket. Poor Jane! It was desperate to see what a dowdy shabby imperfect lot we looked; how feeble; how ugly for the most part. And yet we were doing our best to say something sincere about our great adventure (as Wells almost called it). And he has been adventurous and plunged about in his bath and splashed the waters, to give him his due. Afterwards we stood about congratulating.

Sunday 20 November
I will now snatch a moment from what Morgan calls 'life' to enter a hurried note. My notes have been few; life a cascade, a glissade, a torrent: all together. I think on the whole this *is* our happiest autumn. So much work; and success now; and life on easy terms. My morning rushes, pell mell, from 10 to 1. I write so quick I can't get it typed before lunch. This I suppose is the main backbone of my autumn – *Orlando*.

Vita comes; Dottie [Wellesley] comes; Clive incessant; Tom; Roger; we have our Bloomsbury evenings; for the first time I have been spending money, on a bed, on a coat (the coat, at the moment, I regret). But the money psychology is odd; and that it doesn't give me enormous pleasure to spend. I doubt that I want anything enough; yet worry about spending wrongly; and must buy an evening dress which worries me too. Domestic life, Nelly, that is, good as gold.

Wednesday 30 November
A very happy autumn this, I repeat. After Christmas discontent will set in no doubt, when I must write criticism. But I will steal a march on that depression. Moreover, aren't I proud at the moment. Ruth Draper admires me: I am to meet her on Friday. So tonight I go to the pit to see Ruth Draper. Lunch with Sibyl; dine with Ethel; and a new dress, made from one a hundred years old. These are the little waves that life makes; which keep us tossing and going up and down on top of them.

Tuesday 20 December
This is almost the shortest day and perhaps the coldest night of the year. We are in the black heart of a terrific frost. The pavement was white with great powdery flakes the other night, walking back with Roger and Helen; this was from Nessa's last Sunday – last, I fear, for many a month. But I have as usual 'no time'. Angus is finally to go: we had another semi-painful interview in the Studio; when he interrupted L.'s dismissal with his own resignation. Not enough money.

Nessa's children's party last night. The little creatures' acting moved my infinitely sentimental throat. And yet oddly enough I scarcely want children of my own now. This insatiable desire to write something before I die, this ravaging sense of the shortness and feverishness of life, make me cling, like a man on a rock, to my one anchor. I don't like the physicalness of having children of one's own. I can dramatise myself as parent, it is true, And perhaps I have killed the feeling instinctively; as perhaps nature does.

I am still writing the third chapter of *Orlando*. I have had of course to give up the fancy of finishing by February and printing this spring. It is drawing out longer than I meant. How extraordinarily unwilled by me but potent in its own right by the way *Orlando* was! as if it shoved everything aside to come into existence.

Yes, I repeat, a very happy, a singularly happy autumn.

Thursday 22 December
I just open this for a moment, being dull of the head, to enter a severe reprimand of myself. I am meretricious; mediocre; a humbug; am getting into the habit of flashy talk. Tinsel it seemed last night at the Keyneses. Dadie says I have no logical power and live and write in an opium dream. And the dream is too often about myself. Now, with middle age drawing on, and age ahead, it is important to be severe on such faults. So easily might I become a harebrained egotistic woman, exacting compliments, arrogant, narrow, withered. To correct this, and to forget one's own sharp absurd little personality, reputation and the rest of it, one should read; see outsiders; think more; write more logically; above all be full of work; and practise anonymity. Silence in company; or the quietest statement, not the showiest, is also 'indicated' as the doctors say. It was an empty party, rather, last night. Very nice here, though.

1928

Thomas Hardy died on 11 January; his ashes were interred in Westminster Abbey, and Leonard and Virginia attended the ceremony in Poets' Corner. Her valedictory article on Hardy's novels, commissioned in 1919, was published in the TLS *on 19 January. Virginia's usual seasonal low spirits were compounded by headaches, by the absence of Vanessa and Duncan who now had a secure winter refuge at Cassis; and by the effect on Vita of her father's death and her consequent sense of being disinherited – Knole and the Sackville estates being entailed on the male heir, her uncle. But Virginia finished writing* Orlando *towards the end of March, and she and Leonard then took three weeks off, driving in their Singer car across France to Cassis and back, before settling to the laborious task of revision. Leonard read the manuscript at the end of May and sent it to press.*

Another death and funeral – that of the respected classical scholar Jane Harrison – again shows Virginia's curiosity about and critical observation of conventional ceremonies; and her ambivalent attitude to public esteem is also evident in her reaction to the award of this year's Femina Vie Heureuse *prize for* To the Lighthouse: *disappointment when she thought she had been passed over; disparagement when she received it at the hands of the best-selling novelist Hugh Walpole (with whom nevertheless she was to strike up an odd friendship).*

At the beginning of the year Virginia had been invited to speak to the Arts Society of Newnham College, and though in the event it was October before she could fulfil this engagement and a similar one at the other Cambridge women's college, Girton, she was gathering ideas for her talk on 'Women and Fiction' throughout the preceding months – talks which were to be expanded and published a year later as A Room of One's Own.

The two summer months at Monks House were animated and sociable; the purchase of an adjoining field gave the Woolfs a greater sense of permanency in the village; the fine weather and the mobility conferred by their motor car enabled them to make day visits to Vita and to her close friend Lady Dorothy Wellesley in Kent. Their own visitors included E. M. Forster, concerned like Leonard about the implications of the forthcoming Bow Street trial of the lesbian novel The Well of Loneliness; *and old Mrs Woolf, Leonard's mother, whose demands on filial consideration both exhausted and discomposed Virginia. The summer ended with Virginia apprehensively setting off to spend a week travelling alone with Vita in Burgundy.*

Orlando *was published on 11 October and, notwithstanding its rather mixed reception, sold better than any of her books, and a third printing was ordered by the end of the year. But apart from her absorption in the preparation of her Cambridge lectures, she had no clear impulse towards another book. Descriptions in a letter from Vanessa of great moths invading her house at Cassis at night hovered in her imagination, and began to take hold; but it was to be many months before these stirrings were to be developed. In the meantime, she was enjoying the social fruits of her success – invitations from the prominent hostess Lady Cunard, dinner parties to meet Max Beerbohm or George Moore, as well as the more familiar pleasures of her own circle.*

1928

Tuesday 17 January
Yesterday we went to Hardy's funeral [in Westminster Abbey]. What did I think of? Of Max Beerbohm's letter, just read; or a lecture to the Newnhamites about women's writing. At intervals some emotion broke in. But I doubt the capacity of the human animal for being dignified in ceremony. One catches a Bishop's frown and twitch; sees his polished shiny nose; suspects the rapt spectacled young priest gazing at the cross he carries of being a humbug; next here is the coffin, an overgrown one; like a stage coffin, covered with a white satin cloth; bearers elderly gentlemen rather red and stiff, holding to the corners; pigeons flying outside; insufficient artificial light; procession to Poets' Corner; dramatic 'in sure and certain hope of immortality' perhaps melodramatic. After dinner at Clive's Lytton protested that the great man's novels are the poorest of poor stuff; and can't read them. Over all this broods for me some uneasy sense, of change, and mortality, and how partings are deaths; and then a sense of my own fame – why should this come over me? – and then of its remoteness; and then the pressure of writing two articles on Meredith and furbishing up the Hardy [for the *TLS*]. And a sense of the futility of it all.

Saturday 11 February
I am so cold I can hardly hold the pen. The futility of it all – so I broke off; and have indeed been feeling that rather persistently, or perhaps I should have written here. Hardy and Meredith together sent me torpid to bed with headache. I know the feeling now, when I can't spin a sentence, and sit mumbling and turning; and nothing flits by my brain which is as a blank window. So I go to bed, stuffing my ears with rubber; and there I lie a day or two. Such 'sensations' spread over my spine and head directly I give them the chance; such anguishes and despairs; and heavenly relief and rest; and then misery again. Never was anyone so tossed up and down by the body as I am, I think. But it is over: and put away.
For some reason, I am hacking rather listlessly at the last chapter of

Orlando, which was to have been the best. Always always the last chapter slips out of my hands. One gets bored. For the rest, Bloomsbury today revives. Clive is back: whereupon Mary asks us to lunch: and so we return to some flicker of the snowdrop pallor of very early spring.

Saturday 18 February
I am happy to say I have still a few pounds in the Bank, and my own cheque book too. This great advance in dignity was made in the autumn. My mind is woolgathering away about Women and Fiction, which I am to read at Newnham in May. The mind is the most capricious of insects – flitting fluttering. I had thought to write the quickest most brilliant pages in *Orlando* yesterday – not a drop came, all, forsooth, for the usual physical reasons, which declared themselves today. It is the oddest feeling: as if a finger stopped the flow of ideas in the brain.

Sunday 18 March
I have lost my writing board; an excuse for the anaemic state of this book. Indeed I only write now, in between letters, to say that *Orlando* was finished yesterday as the clock struck one. Anyhow the canvas is covered. There will be three months of close work needed, imperatively, before it can be printed; for I have scrambled and splashed, and the canvas shows through in a thousand places. But it is a serene, accomplished feeling to write, even provisionally, The End, and we go off on Saturday, with my mind appeased. I have written this book quicker than any: and it is all a joke; and yet gay and quick reading I think; a writer's holiday. So we go motoring across France on Saturday, and shall be back on April 17th for the summer.

Thursday 22 March
Yes it's done – *Orlando* – begun on 8th October, as a joke; and now rather too long for my liking. All this I dismiss from a mind avid only of green fields. The sun; wine; sitting doing nothing. I have been for the last six weeks rather a bucket than a fountain; sitting to be shot into by one person after another. A rabbit that passes across a shooting gallery, and one's friends go pop-pop. Morgan and Desmond were here to tea. Morgan more of the blue butterfly than ever. Unless I talk, he says nothing. And any shadow sends him flitting. Desmond comes in, round as a billiard ball; and this is true of his dear bubbling lazy mind; which has such a glitter and lustre now from mere being at ease in the world that it puts me into a good temper to be with him. Roger and Helen, Ka and Will [Arnold-Forster], the other night. Roger malicious a little, and vain. There is an innocence in this vanity which is likeable; but I am touchy for the reputation of Bloomsbury. I thought I could see Ka and Will comparing us, and being

glad we were not impeccable. They compare us with the political world: we them with our own.

Watery blowy weather; and this time next week we shall be in the middle of France.

*   *   *

Tuesday 17 April

Home again, as foretold, last night, and to settle the dust in my mind, write here. We have been across France and back – every inch of that fertile field traversed by the admirable Singer. And now towns and spires and scenes begin to rise in my mind as the rest sinks. I see Chartres in particular, the snail, with its head straight, marching across the flat country, the most distinguished of churches. The rose window is like a jewel on black velvet. Grey weather dashed all over this; and I remember coming in at night in the wet often, and hearing the rain in hotels. Often I was bobbing up and down on my two glasses of vin du pays. Always some good food and hot bottles at night. And there was Nessa and Clive – Oh and my prize [the *Prix Femina*] – £40 from the French. And Julian. And one or two hot days and the Pont du Gard in the sun; and Les Baux; and mounting all the time steadily was my desire for words, till I envisaged a sheet of paper and pen and ink as something of miraculous desirability. And there was St Rémy and the ruins in the sun. I forget now how it all went – how thing fitted to thing; but the eminences now emerge.

Saturday 21 April

A bitter windy rainy day. There is no blue, no red, no green in this detestable spring. Furs are in the shops. Life is either too empty or too full. Happily, at forty-six I still feel as experimental and on the verge of getting at the truth as ever. Oh and Vita – to take up the burden of facts – has had a stupendous row with her mother – in the course of which she was made to take the pearl necklace from her neck, cut it in two with a pocket knife, deliver over the twelve central pearls, put the relics, all running loose, in an envelope the solicitor gave her. Thief, liar, I hope you'll be killed by an omnibus – so 'my honoured Lady Sackville' addressed her, trembling with rage in the presence of a secretary and a solicitor and a chauffeur. The woman is said to be mad. Vita very gallant and wild and tossing her head.

Dined with Lydia and Maynard: two couples, elderly, childless, distinguished. He and she both urbane and admirable. Grey comes at Maynard's temples. He is finer looking now: not with us pompous or great: simple, with his mind working always, on Russian, Bolshevists, glands, genealogies; always the proof of a remarkable mind when it overflows thus vigorously into bypaths. Lydia is composed and controlled. She says very sensible things.

We went, also, to Jane [Harrison]'s funeral, getting 'there' (somewhere out of the world where buses pass only one every fifteen minutes), just as the service ended. We walked to the grave; the clergyman, a friend, waited for the dismal company to collect; then read some of the lovelier, more rational parts of the Bible; and said, by heart, Abide with me. A bird sang most opportunely; with a gay indifference, and if one liked, hope, that Jane would have enjoyed. Then the incredibly drab female cousins advanced, each with a fat bunch of primroses and dropped them in; and we also advanced and looked down at the coffin at the bottom of a very steep brazen looking grave. But though L. almost cried, I felt very little – only the beauty of the Come unto me all ye that are weary; but as usual the obstacle of not believing dulled and bothered me. Who is 'God' and what the Grace of Christ? and what did they mean to Jane?

Friday 4 May
And now there's the *Femina* Prize to record – an affair of dull stupid horror: a function; not alarming; stupefying. Hugh Walpole saying how much he disliked my books; rather how much he feared for his own. Afterwards there was the horror of having looked ugly in cheap black clothes. I cannot control this complex. I wake at dawn with a start. Also the 'fame' is becoming vulgar and a nuisance. It means nothing; and yet takes one's time. Americans perpetually. We have seen an endless number of people.

Thursday 31 May
It is very quiet at the moment. Whitsun is over. We were at Rodmell and saw the races. The sun is out again; I have half forgotten *Orlando* already, since L. has read it and it has half passed out of my possession. [He] thinks it in some ways better than *The Lighthouse*; about more interesting things, and with more attachment to life, and larger. The truth is I expect I began it as a joke, and went on with it seriously. Hence it lacks some unity. He says it is very original.

June weather. Still, bright, fresh. Owing to the Lighthouse (car) I don't feel so shut in London as usual. Also London itself perpetually attracts, stimulates, gives me a play and a story and a poem, without any trouble save that of moving my legs through the streets. I walked Pinker to Gray's Inn Gardens this afternoon, and saw – Red Lion Square: Morris's house; thought of them on winters' evenings in the 'fifties; thought we are just as interesting; saw Great Ormond Street where a dead girl was found yesterday; saw and heard the Salvation Army making Christianity gay for the people: a great deal of nudging and joking on the part of very unattractive young men and women; making it lively, I suppose; and yet, to be truthful, when I watch them I never laugh or criticise, but only feel how strange and interesting this is: wonder what they mean by 'Come to the Lord'. I daresay exhibitionism accounts for some of it: the applause of the gallery; this lures boys to sing hymns; and kindles shop boys to announce in a loud voice that they are saved. It is what writing for the *Evening Standard* is for Rose Macaulay and I was going to say myself: but so far I have not done it.

Wednesday 20 June
So sick of *Orlando* I can write nothing. I have corrected the proofs in a week; and cannot spin another phrase. I detest my own volubility. Why be always spouting words? Also I have almost lost the power of reading. Correcting proofs five, six or seven hours a day, writing in this and that meticulously, I have bruised my reading faculty severely. Take up Proust after dinner and put him down. This is the worst time of all. It makes me suicidal. All seems insipid and worthless. Mercifully Nessa is back. My earth is watered again. She is a necessity to me – as I am not to her. I run to her as the wallaby runs to the old kangaroo.

Julian dines with us tonight to meet Miss Sylva Norman whom I fetched up from complete nonentity on the telephone last night. Another marvel of science. There she was in ten minutes after we thought of her saying she would LOVE to come. Julian is a vast fat powerful sweet-tempered engaging young man, into whose arms I let myself fall, ·half sister, half mother, and half (but arithmetic denies this) the mocking stirring contemporary friend. Mercifully Julian has his instincts sane and normal: has a wide forehead, and considerable address and competence in the management of life.

Saturday 7 July
All last night I dreamt of Katherine Mansfield and wondered what dreams are; often evoke so much more than thinking does – almost as if she came back in person and was outside one, actively making one feel; instead of a figment called up and recollected, as she is, now, if I think of her. Yet some emotion lingers on the day after a dream; even though I've now almost forgotten what happened in the dream, except that she was lying on a sofa in a room high up, and a great many sad faced women were round her. Yet somehow I got the feel of her, and of her as if alive again, more than by day.

MONKS HOUSE, RODMELL

Wednesday 8 August

I am, as I write, wherever I come to a stop, looking out of the lodge window at our field; and the little cottage boys with the cursed shrill voices playing cricket half way down it; and as usual I am sentimental and worried. Children playing: yes, and interrupting me; yes and I have no children of my own; and Nessa has; and yet I don't want them any more, since my ideas so possess me; and I detest more and more interruption; and the slow heaviness of physical life, and almost dislike people's bodies, I think, as I grow older. I write thus partly in order to slip the burden of writing narrative, as for instance: we came here a fortnight ago. And we lunched at Charleston and Vita came and we were offered the field and we went to see the farm at Lime Kiln. Yet no doubt I shall be more interested, come ten years, in facts; and shall want, as I do when I read, to be told details, details, so that I may look up from the page and arrange them into one of those makings-up which seem so much truer done thus, from heaps of non-assorted facts, than now I can make them, when it is almost immediately being done under my eyes.

Sunday 12 August

Yesterday at Charleston we had tea from bright blue cups under the pink light of the giant hollyhock. We were all a little drugged with the country: a little bucolic I thought. It was lovely enough – made me envious of its country peace: the trees all standing securely – why did my eye catch the trees? The look of things has a great power over me. Even now, I have to watch the rooks beating up against the wind, which is high. And still I say to myself instinctively 'What's the phrase for that?' But what a little I can get down with my pen of what is so vivid to my eye.

Tuesday 14 August

Just back from Long Barn and Dottie [Wellesley]'s new house, Penns in the Rocks. Can one really be in love with a house? Is there not something sterile in these passions? She is too anxious for other people to praise it. And I don't want possessions. I think this is true. I don't want to be Dottie collecting endless settees and armchairs round myself. But then I have now a pressing sense of the flight of time; and if one is so soon to arrive, why pack all these things? More truthfully, if one is so soon to start, why prepare all these impedimenta. I feel on the verge of the world, about to take flight. Dottie on the other hand feels 'I have at least, in spite of every other grudge on the part of fate, ten or fifteen thousand a year; and it is only fair that I should get from my money what I can.'

Friday 31 August
This is the last day of August, and like almost all of them of extraordinary beauty. Morgan was here for the week-end; timid, touchy, infinitely charming. One night we got drunk, and talked of sodomy, and sapphism, with emotion – so much so that next day he said he had been drunk. Morgan said that Dr Head can convert the sodomites. "Would you like to be converted?" Leonard asked. "No" said Morgan, quite definitely. He said he thought Sapphism disgusting: partly from convention, partly because he disliked that women should be independent of men.

Monday 3 September
The Battle of Dunbar, the Battle of Worcester, and the death of Cromwell – how often it seems I said that to my father at St Ives; standing bolt upright in the dining room at Talland House. And it is a perfect 3rd September day. Leonard gave me the blue glass jug today because I was nice to his mother. He went to Brighton to get it for me. Seldom have I felt as tired as I did last night. This shaky ramshackle old lady of seventy-six wore us out. Her talk never stops; never follows a line; is always about people; starts anywhere; at any moment. What makes it difficult is that she divines states of feeling to some extent, and would say pointedly "You must often think of your writing when you are not writing, Virginia," when through exhaustion I became silent. I felt the horror of family life, and the terrible threat to one's liberty that I used to feel with father, Aunt Mary or George [Duckworth, her half-brother]. It is an emotion one never gets from any other human relationship. She had the right to somehow put her claws in me. How strangely she made everything commonplace, ugly, suburban, notwithstanding a charm too. But to be attached to her as a daughter would be so cruel a fate that I can think of nothing worse; and thousands of women might be dying of it in England today: this tyranny of mother over daughter, or father; their right to the due being as powerful as anything in the world. And then, they ask, why women don't write poetry. Short of killing Mrs Woolf nothing could be done. Day after day one's life would be crumpled up like a bill for tenpence three farthings. Nothing has ever been said of this.

Monday 10 September
Desmond, who lunched here with Julian, has just gone. We spent the afternoon – hour after hour wasting away again, or why not say for once turning to gold and silver – coining gold and silver talk then – talk very intimate now, more so than ever: a continuation of our talk in Tavistock Square the other day: there he said he had now twelve years to live; nine to be exact; and here we talked of his work, money, women, children, and

writing; till I took him along the Roman Road; and back to tea. Do you suppose then that we are now coming like the homing rooks back to the tops of our trees? and that all this cawing is the beginning of settling in for the night? I seem to notice in several of my friends some endearing and affecting cordiality; and a pleasure in intimacy; as if the sun were sinking.

This has been a very animated summer: a summer lived almost too much in public. Often down here I have entered into a sanctuary; a nunnery; had a religious retreat; of great agony once; and always some terror: so afraid one is of loneliness: of seeing to the bottom of the vessel.

Monday 17 September
I have precisely five minutes before dinner. Quentin has swallowed those precious two hours in which I was to have read Dorothy Osborne: Quentin grown elegant and self conscious, liking to use French words; very sophisticated, showing in every movement now the shadow of our faults, as a set: uneasy, I doubt not; quick, sensitive; but wanting something of Julian's force and simplicity. So they change parts, growing, changing, turning from fat to thin. The drawing room smells with his paints.

Saturday 22 September
This is written on the verge of my alarming holiday in Burgundy. I am alarmed of seven days alone with Vita; interested; excited, but afraid – she may find me out, I her out. I'm afraid of the morning most; and three o'clock in the afternoon; and wanting something Vita does not want. And I shall spend the money that might have bought a table or a glass.

This has been the finest, and not only finest, but loveliest, summer in the world. Owning the field has given a different orient to my feelings about Rodmell. I begin to dig myself in and take part in it. And I shall build another storey to the house if I make money. But the news of *Orlando* is black. We may sell a third that we sold of *The Lighthouse* before publication. They say this is inevitable. No one wants biography. I doubt therefore that we shall do more than cover expenses – a high price to pay for the fun of calling it a biography. I must write some articles this winter, if we are to have nest eggs at the Bank.

52 TAVISTOCK SQUARE, WC1

Saturday 27 October
A scandal, a scandal, to let so much time slip, and I leaning on the bridge watching it go. Only leaning has not been my pose: running up and down,

irritably, excitedly, restlessly. And the stream viciously eddying. Why do I write these metaphors? Because I have written nothing for an age.

Orlando has been published. I went to Burgundy with Vita. We did not find each other out. It flashed by. Yet I was glad to see Leonard again. How disconnected this is! My ambition is from this very moment, eight minutes to six, on Saturday evening, to attain complete concentration again. I gave up reading and thinking on the 24th September when I went to France. I came back, and we plunged into London and publishing. I am a little sick of *Orlando*. I think I am a little indifferent now what anyone thinks. Joy's life's in the doing – I murder, as usual, a quotation. I mean its the writing, not the being read that excites me. The reception, as they say, surpassed expectations. Sales beyond our record for the first week.

Thank God, my long toil at the women's lecture is this moment ended. I am back from speaking at Girton, in floods of rain. Starved but valiant young women – that's my impression. Intelligent, eager, poor; and destined to become schoolmistresses in shoals. I blandly told them to drink wine and have a room of their own. Why should all the splendour, all the luxury of life be lavished on the Julians and the Francises, and none on the Phares and the Thomases? The corridors of Girton are like vaults in some horrid high church cathedral – on and on they go, cold and shiny – with a light burning. High gothic rooms; acres of bright brown wood; here and there a photograph. And we saw Trinity and King's this morning.

Wednesday 7 November
Since I wrote here I have become two inches and a half higher in the public view. I think I may say that I am now among the well known writers. I had tea with Lady Cunard – might have lunched or dined any day. It was not her atmosphere – this of solitary talk. She is too shrewd to expand, and needs society to make her rash and random which is her point. Ridiculous little parrokeet faced woman; but not quite sufficiently ridiculous. I kept wishing for superlatives; could not get the illusion to flap its wings. Flunkeys, yes; but a little drab and friendly. Marble floors, yes; but no glamour; no tune strumming, for me at least. And the two of us sitting there had almost to be conventional and flat. And then we went up and up to see pictures on stairs, in ballrooms, and finally to Lady Cunard's bedroom, hung entirely with flower pieces. The bed has its triangular canopy of rose red silk; the windows, looking on the [Grosvenor] Square, are hung with green brocade. Her poudreuse, painted and gilt, stood open with gold brushes and looking glasses, and there on her gold slippers were neatly laid gold stockings. All this paraphernalia for one stringy old hop o' my thumb. She set the two great musical boxes playing and I said did she lie in bed and listen to them? But no. She has nothing fantastic in that way

about her. Money is important. But no doubt she has her acuity, her sharp peck at life; only how adorable, I thought, as I tiptoed home in my tight shoes, in the fog, in the chill, could one open one of these doors that I still open so venturously, and find a live interesting real person, a Nessa, a Duncan, a Roger. Some one new, whose mind would begin vibrating. Coarse and usual and dull these Cunards and Colefaxes are – for all their astonishing competence in the commerce of life.

And I cannot think what to 'write next'. I mean the situation is, this *Orlando* is of course a very quick brilliant book. Yes, but I did not try to explore. And must I always explore? Yes I think so still. Because my reaction is not the usual. Yes, but *The Moths?* That was to be an abstract mystical eyeless book: a playpoem. And there may be affectation in being too mystical, too abstract. I rather think the upshot will be books that relieve other books: a variety of styles and subjects: for after all, that is my temperament, I think.

Desmond destroyed our Saturday walk; he is now mouldy and to me depressing. He is perfectly reasonable and charming. Nothing surprises, nothing shocks him. He has been through it all one feels. He has come out rolled, smoothed, rather sodden, rather creased and jumbled, like a man who has sat up all night in a third class railway carriage. His fingers are stained yellow with cigarettes. One tooth in the lower jaw is missing. His hair is dank. His eye more than ever dubious. He has a hole in his blue sock. Yet he is resolute and determined – that's what I find so depressing. He seems to be sure that it is his view that is the right one; ours vagaries, deviations. And if his view is the right one, God knows there is nothing to live for: not a greasy biscuit. And the egotism of men surprises and shocks me even now. Is there a woman of my acquaintance who could sit in my armchair from 3 to 6.30 without the semblance of a suspicion that I may be busy, or tired, or bored; and so sitting could talk, grumbling and grudging, of her difficulties, worries; then eat chocolates, then read a book, and go at last, apparently self-complacent and wrapped in a kind of blubber of misty self satisfaction? Not the girls at Newnham or Girton. They are far too spry; far too disciplined. None of that self-confidence is their lot.

Thursday 8 November

We went to Karin's party last night. The truth is the stimulus is too brisk; one rattles; and only a shout can be heard; and one must stand; and one gets caught, like a bramble on a river by some branch; and hooked up out of the eddy. An emerald green Russian talked to me of seals and then gave me a card; I am to lecture four times a week for eight weeks in America – oh yes – and she will arrange most advantageous terms. But won't mention money in a drawing room: so we lapse upon seals again.

Saturday 10 November
... the [*Well of Loneliness*] trial yesterday at Bow Street. We were all packed in by 10.30; the door at the top of the court opened; in stepped the debonair distinguished magistrate; we all rose; he bowed; took his seat under the lion and the unicorn, and then proceeded. Something like a Harley Street specialist investigating a case. All black and white, tie pin, clean shaven, wax coloured, and carved, in that light, like ivory. He was ironical at first: raised his eyebrows and shrugged. Later I was impressed by the reason of the law, its astuteness, its formality. Here have we evolved a very remarkable fence between us and barbarity; something commonly recognised; half humbug and ceremony therefore – when they pulled out calf bound books and read old phrases I thought this; and the bowing and scraping made me think it; but in these banks runs a live stream. What is obscenity? What is literature? What is the difference between the subject and the treatment? In what cases is evidence allowable? This last, to my relief, was decided against us: we could not be called as experts in obscenity, only in art. So Desmond was only asked his qualifications and then, not allowed to answer the obscene question, was dismissed. After lunch we heard an hour more, and then the magistrate, increasingly deliberate and courteous, said he would read the book again and give judgment next Friday at two, on the pale tepid vapid book which lay damp and slab all about the court. And I lost my little Roman brooch and that is the end of this great day, so far. A curious brown top lighted scene; very stuffy; policemen at the doors; matrons passing through. An atmosphere quite decent and formal, of adult people.

Sunday 25 November
Leonard's 48th birthday. We were at Rodmell, where all has fallen into our hands, rapidly, unexpectedly: on top of the field we get a cottage, and Percy [Bartholomew] is 'our man'.

Wednesday 28 November
Father's birthday. He would have been ninety-six, yes, today; and could have been ninety-six, like other people one has known; but mercifully was not. His life would have entirely ended mine. What would have happened? No writing, no books; – inconceivable. I used to think of him and mother daily; but writing *The Lighthouse* laid them in my mind. (I believe this to be true – that I was obsessed by them both, unhealthily; and writing of them was a necessary act.) He comes back now more as a contemporary. I must read him some day.

Last night was one of our evenings – apparently successful. People enjoyed it. Perhaps I didn't; perhaps I did. Halfway through Lytton vanished, brayed out of the room by Clive's vociferation, L. thinks. Clive makes it all very strident, gaslit, band played.

As for my next book, I am going to hold myself from writing till I have it impending in me: grown heavy in the mind like a ripe pear; pendant, gravid, asking to be cut or it will fall. *The Moths* still haunts me, coming, as they always do, unbidden, between tea and dinner, while L. plays the gramophone. I shape a page or two; and make myself stop.

Sunday 9 December
I have again seen too many people, without much intensity. Christmas impends. And we shall spend it alone here, I think, and go to Rodmell afterwards and plan a new room. And then to Berlin we say. Meanwhile Nessa and I give our Tuesday evenings, and too many people press to come. But why, I ask 'see' people? What's the point? These isolated occasions which come so often. May I come and see you? And what they get, or I get, save the sense of a slide passing on a screen, I can't say.

Tuesday 18 December
Here I should be pegging away at 'Fiction'; rather an interesting little book I think; but I was switched off to write a eulogy of Lady Strachey, burnt yesterday with a bunch of our red and white carnations on top of her. It is odd how little her death means to me – for this reason. About a year ago she was said to be dying; and at once I made up my usual visualisation; felt the whole emotion of Lady Strachey's passing – her memories and so on – that night; and then she did not die; and now when she does die, not a vision, not an emotion comes my way. These little tricks of psychology amuse me.

L. has just been in to consult about a third edition of *Orlando*. This has been ordered; we have sold over 6000 copies; and sales are still amazingly brisk. Anyhow my room is secure. For the first time since I married – 1912-1928 – sixteen years, I have been spending money. The spending muscle does not work naturally yet. I feel guilty; and yet have an agreeable luxurious sense of coins in my pocket beyond my weekly thirteen shillings which was always running out, or being encroached upon. Yesterday I spent fifteen shillings on a steel brooch. I spent three pounds on a mother-of-pearl necklace – and I haven't bought a jewel for twenty years perhaps! I have carpeted the dining room – and so on. I think one's soul is better for this lubrication. The important thing is to spend freely, without fuss or anxiety; and to trust to one's power of making more.

But to return to Max Beerbohm. I met him at Ethel [Sands]'s the other night. As I came in a thick set old man (such was my impression) rose, and I was introduced. No freakishness, no fancy about him. His face is solidified;

has a thick moustache; a red veined skin, heavy lines; but then his eyes are perfectly round, very large, and sky blue. His eyes become dreamy and merry when the rest of him is well groomed and decorous in the extreme. Halfway through dinner he turned to me and we began a 'nice', interesting, flattering, charming kind of talk. I said, as I think, that he is immortal. In a small way, he said; but with complacency. He asked me how I wrote. For he hacks every step with his pen, and therefore never alters. He thought I wrote like this. I told him I had to cut out great chunks. I wish you would send them to me, he said, simply. Indeed, he was nothing if not kind; but looked long and steadily – that queer painter's look, so matching, so considering, apart from human intent; yet with him not entirely. After dinner, he leant on the mantelpiece and Maurice Baring and I flittered round him like a pair of butterflies, praising, laughing, extravagant. But always he had to be led off to talk politely to this person and that; finally disappeared, very dignified, very discreet in his white waistcoat, pressing my hand in his plump firm one long; and saying what a pleasure &c. I own that I don't find much difference between the great and ourselves – indeed they are like us: I mean they don't have the frills and furbelows of the small; come to terms quickly and simply. But we got, of course, very little way.

And we dined last night with the Hutchinsons and met George Moore – like an old silver coin now, so white, so smooth; with his little flipper hands, like a walrus's; and his chubby cheeks, and little knees – yet always saying the thing that comes into his head; fresh, juvenile almost for that reason; and very shrewd. And what it comes to is that the great are very simple; quick to come to terms with; reserved; and don't pay attention to other people's books (Moore throws scorn on them all – Shaw – a shriek of vulgarity – poisoned with vulgarity – never wrote a good sentence in his life – Wells – I spare myself Wells – and Galsworthy –) and live in an atmosphere very serene, bright, and fenced off: for all that they are more to the point than ordinary people; go to the heart of things directly. Moore toddled off and got quickly into a cab, Jack said, for all his look of an old silver coin.

1929

For the Christmas holidays Vita Sackville-West and her two sons had rejoined Harold Nicolson, now Counsellor at the British Embassy in Berlin, and urged the Woolfs to visit them there. Virginia and Leonard crossed from Harwich on 16 January and were joined in Berlin by Vanessa and Quentin Bell and Duncan Grant; they all spent a rather rackety and inharmonious week together, and the Woolfs returned the way they had come, Virginia reaching home in a state of collapse. During the ensuing period of invalidism, she was engrossed by the ideas adumbrated in her Cambridge lectures on 'Women and Fiction', which by the end of June she had written out in the form of a short book entitled A Room of One's Own *and sent to the printer.*

The Hogarth Press was prospering, largely due to the success of Orlando; *it employed a staff of three in the office, under Leonard's authoritative and in the main benevolent direction. Their greater affluence enabled the Woolfs to embark on various improvements to Monks House and, at the end of the summer, to buy a cottage in Rodmell to accommodate a local servant – an alteration in her domestic organisation much to Virginia's liking, uncomfortable as she found her dependence upon and resentment of Nelly's constant presence in her home. When the Labour Party narrowly won the General Election at the end of May, Virginia was disconcerted by the realisation that Nelly, like herself, was now of the ruling party.*

Early in June the Woolfs went by train to Cassis for ten days' holiday, lodging near Duncan and Vanessa. Home again, Virginia suffered from a sense of dejection and aimlessness, but gradually the impulse towards a new work took possession of her mind, and the rather nebulous ideas suggested by Vanessa's description of moths began to take form on paper, developing eventually into The Waves. *The dejection however accompanied her to Monks House at the beginning of their summer stay, and was sustained by a disproportionate sense of grievance at the news that Vita had gone abroad with a new friend, Hilda Matheson, the talks director of the BBC; and by Nelly's provocations and withdrawals. Nonetheless a succession of weekend visitors, including William Plomer, the young writer from South Africa whose first book had been published by the Hogarth Press in 1926, was entertained; visits were made to Charleston, to Vita at Long Barn, to the Labour Party Conference at Brighton; and the proofs of* A Room of One's Own *were corrected and finally despatched. The book was published on 24 October after the Woolfs had returned to London; a few days later it was praised by Vita Sackville-West in what Virginia called a 'flamboyant broadcast', and sales soared: by the end of the year it had gone into a fourth impression. Henceforward the Woolfs were what Leonard considered 'very well off'.*

Two changes in the circumstances of those close to her affected Virginia: Vanessa, whose children were now at Cambridge, in Paris, and at boarding school, gave up her home in Gordon Square and moved into a large studio adjacent to that occupied by Duncan Grant in Fitzroy Street; and Harold Nicolson, encouraged by his wife and both Leonard and Virginia, resigned from the diplomatic service and returned to England and a job on the Beaverbrook Press.

1929

Friday 4 January
Now is life very solid, or very shifting? I am haunted by the two contradictions. This has gone on for ever: will last for ever; goes down to the bottom of the world -- this moment I stand on. Also it is transitory, flying, diaphanous. I shall pass like a cloud on the waves. I am impressed by the transitoriness of human life to such an extent that I am often saying a farewell -- after dining with Roger for instance; or reckoning how many more times I shall see Nessa.

*   *   *

Thursday 28 March
It is a disgrace indeed; no diary has been left so late in the year. The truth was that we went to Berlin on the 16th of January, and then I was in bed for three weeks afterwards, and then could not write, perhaps for another three, and have spent my energy since in one of my excited outbursts of composition -- writing what I made up in bed, a final version of *Women and Fiction*. And as usual I am bored by narrative. I want only to say how I met Nessa in Tottenham Court Road this afternoon, both of us sunk fathoms deep in that wash of reflection in which we both swim about. She will be gone on Wednesday for four months. It is queer how instead of drawing apart, life draws us together. But I was thinking a thousand things as I carried my teapot, gramophone records and stockings under my arm. It is one of those days that I called 'potent' when we lived in Richmond.

I am going to enter a nunnery these next months; and let myself down into my mind; Bloomsbury being done with. It is going to be a time of adventure and attack, rather lonely and painful I think. But solitude will be good for a new book. In old days books were so many sentences absolutely struck with an axe out of crystal; and now my mind is so impatient, so quick, in some ways so desperate. I feel on the verge of some strenuous adventure. So when I wake early, I brace myself out of my terrors by saying that I shall need great courage: after all, I say, I made £1000 all from willing it early one morning. No more poverty I said; and poverty has ceased. I am summoning Philcox next week to plan a room – I have money to build it, money to furnish it. And we have the new car, and we can drive to Edinburgh in June if we like, and go to Cassis.

Nessa has taken a studio and will let 37, thus ending, for ever I suppose, her Gordon Square life. How much I admire this handling of life as if it were a thing one could throw about; this handling of circumstance. Angelica will go to school.

Saturday 13 April
I am sordidly debating within myself the question of Nelly; the perennial question. It is an absurdity, how much time L. and I have wasted in talking about servants. And it can never be done with because the fault lies in the system. How can an uneducated woman let herself in, alone, into our lives? What happens is that she becomes a mongrel; and has no roots anywhere. I could put my theory into practice by getting a daily of a civilised kind, who had her baby in Kentish Town; and treated me as an employer, not friend. Here is a fine rubbish heap left by our parents to be swept.

Hugh Walpole was here the other day, from 4.30 to 7.15, alone over the fire. The same uneasy talk as usual; brisk and breezy, hating war; and then this morbid egotism and desire to scratch the same place over and over again -- his own defects as a writer and how to remedy them, what they spring from; all mixed up with his normal and usual sense of being prosperous and admired – from which, as he admits when I ask him, he gets great pleasure. He starts indeed to protest that he gives pleasure, does good, but can't bring that out in my presence; which is why he seeks my presence – a scratching stone to rid him of the worlds's mud. On the other hand, I like these bustling vigorous characters: I like talk of Russia, and war and great doings and famous people. If I don't see them I romanticise them.

Leonard is upstairs finishing the Hogarth Press accounts. Yesterday he gave the three stall hands a bonus. They sent up a bunch of roses later in the day. For the first time we have made over £400 profit. And seven people now depend on us; and I think with pride that seven people depend, largely, upon my hand writing on a sheet of paper. That is of course a great solace and pride to me. Its not scribbling; its keeping seven people fed and housed. They will be feeding off *Women and Fiction* next year for which I predict some sale. It made itself up and forced itself upon me as I lay in bed after Berlin. I used to make it up at such a rate that when I got pen and paper I was like a water bottle turned upside down.

Monday 29 April
Oh this cold spring! Dry as a bone, though, until today, but with never a blue sky. So that my red coat, which is like haws in winter suits it. I heard the nightingale at Vita's a week or two ago – the one warm night. And we were cold at Rodmell last week, when we went down to see Philcox, who will build two rooms for £320, and take only two months. It was cold; but how silent, how safe from voices and talk! How I resented our coming back; and quickly changed into the social sphere of my soul; and went to lunch with Sibyl; and there had, for my pains, precisely six minutes tolerable talk with Max Beerbohm. But dear me, how little talk with great men now disturbs me.

Poor Tom – a true poet, I think; what they will call in a hundred years a man of genius: and this is his life. I stand for half an hour listening while he says that Vivien can't walk. Her legs have gone. But what's the matter? No one knows. And so she lies in bed – can't put a shoe on. And they have difficulties, humiliations, with servants. And after endless quibbling about visiting – which he can't do these eight weeks, owing to moving house and fifteen first cousins come to England, suddenly he appears overcome, moved, tragic, unhappy, broken down, because I offer to come to tea on Thursday. Oh but we don't dare ask our friends, he said. Would you really come – all this way to see us? Yes I said. But what a vision of misery, imagined, but real too. Vivien with her foot on a stool, in bed all day; Tom hurrying back lest she abuse him; this is our man of genius. This is what I gathered yesterday morning on the telephone.

Sunday 12 May
A wet day, or we should be at Hampton Court with Roger and [Charles] Mauron. And I am glad of the rain, because I have talked too much. We have seen too many people – Sydney Waterlow perhaps the most notable, as a resurrection. A desperate looking pompous sad respectable elderly man; worldly; but quivering as usual in his shell. Any pin pricks him in the unarmoured skin. I liked him. Also we had a party: Roger a little old – to my mind he needs Nessa to fertilise and sweeten him. Some queer rancour often seems to exacerbate him. When his stomach heals his leg aches. And [William] Plomer came – a little rigid I fear; and too much of a gentleman; and little Blunden, the very image of a London house sparrow, that pecks and cheeps and is starved and dirty. And Julian, to me a very satisfactory young man at present; full of ardour, yet clear, precise, and genial too; much more apt to see the good than the bad.

Monday 13 May
... up came Saxon, on his holiday -- going to *The King* of course, and having a day off. For how many years has he done this - strange methodical character that he is. We don't meet for months, and take up the subject again. He took out his cheque book and said he thought the pattern was changed, with the same interest in that minute detail as he had thirty years ago. He has the same umbrella hanging by a hook on his arm; the same gold watch chain; and his pirouetting attitudes; and sprightly bird-like ways. What then has life given you, I asked (myself). Well, he is free to go to the Opera, to read Plato, to play chess. And he will continue doing these things, as if they were the chosen things, till he dies. There is a certain dignity in this steady doing of things which seem chosen. Yet – thus one always ends a comparison of lives – I wouldn't for the whole world live yours.

The reason I dislike dining with Sibyl is that she exacts it; I am to give her a display of intimacy, which she cannot acquire, poor woman, for herself.

Wednesday 15 May
I went to Sibyl's dinner; but Heavens, how little real point there is to these meetings – save indeed that the food is good; and there is wine, and a certain atmosphere of luxury and hospitality. This, on the other hand, tends to drug one; one has been given something, for which one has to pay. And I don't like that feeling. The old white haired baby [George Moore] sat propped up in his high chair; his hair now white like flax, like silk; his cheeks tinted a child's pink; his eyes with their marble hardness; his boneless ineffective hands. For some reason, he paid me compliments, indeed referred to me as an authority on English; and even offered, which I daresay was kindly meant, though nothing has happened, to send me one of his books. What did we discuss? Mostly himself and his books, I think; and how he had known various old dim figures, far away in the past. He talked about Henry James, and a proof sheet which nobody could read; and he said that a sentence ought to form like a cloud at the end of the pen – don't you think so? he said to me.

Tuesday 28 May
It is an odd summer, this one, unexampled in our history. We are going off to Cassis on Tuesday for a week. This is a revolution. We have never been abroad so late in the year I think. The Election will be over. We shall be governed by a Tory or a Labour party – Tory I suppose. And I feel, rather oddly, that this is an important election. Walking down the King's Road with Sydney Waterlow the other night – having been to dine at his

club – talking about the election, Sydney said that human nature has improved. We are all becoming gentler and wiser. Even the dogs are.

Friday 31 May
The oculist said to me this afternoon "Perhaps you're not as young as you were". This is the first time that has been said to me; and it seemed to me an astonishing statement. It means that one now seems to a stranger not a woman, but an elderly woman. Yet, although I felt wrinkled and aged for an hour, and put on a manner of great wisdom and toleration, buying a coat, even so, I forget it soon; and become 'a woman' again.

"We are winning" Nelly said at tea. I was shocked to think that we both desire the Labour Party to win – why? Partly that I don't want to be ruled by Nelly. I think that to be ruled by Nelly and Lottie would be a disaster. Last night at Charleston we heard election results spoken very distinctly in the drawing room. Driving home through Lewes there was not a single light downstairs. No one was even listening in. The streets were perfectly empty. One man was pump shipping against the station wall. I had imagined a crowd, flares, shouts, white sheets – only three black cats, out on business with the mice. So we shall be ruled by Labour.

We went down to Worthing to see Leonard's mother, laid like an old rose – rather lovely this time – in a narrow room; with the sea opposite. And she cried; and was very dismal. Nothing of life, as we see it, remains to her – [she] can't read or sleep, yet anxiously demands, does Leonard think she will get well? We had been saying driving down that one should take poison. She has every reason; and yet demands more life, more life, at seventy-eight. She quarrels; she can't walk; she is alone; she is looked after by nurses; lives in an hotel, but demands more life, more life. I was moved by her; could hardly speak. I suppose human nature, so emotional, so irrational, so instinctive, as it is in her, but not in me, has this beauty; this what they call 'elemental' quality. One may get it too, when one is seventy-eight. One may lie sobbing, and yet cry does doctor think I shall recover? One will not perhaps go to the writing table and write that simple and profound paper upon suicide which I see myself leaving for my friends.

We voted at Rodmell. I saw a white gloved lady helping an old farm couple out of her Daimler.

52 TAVISTOCK SQUARE, WC1

Saturday 15 June
Home last night from Cassis. The hottest holiday I have ever had. And in some ways different from others; partly that it was so hot; then that we

were alone with Nessa and Duncan. I forget what the facts of our stay were. We were there for a week, coming the day before they expected us, oddly enough, as we did last year. I wrote a little article on Cowper, but lifting the words with difficulty in the heat, surrounded by black and white butterflies. And L. and I were very extravagant, for the first time in our lives, buying desks, tables, sideboards, crockery for Rodmell. This gave me pleasure; and set my dander up against Nessa's almost overpowering supremacy.

A sense of nothingness rolls about the house; due to the fact that we came back last night and are not going round in the mill yet. Time flaps on the mast – my own phrase I think. There are things I ought to do. I ought to correct *A Room of One's Own*. I ought to write several dull silly letters. Lytton once said that we can only live if we see through illusion. Now I must somehow brew another decoction of illusion. Well, if the human interest flags, I must not sit thinking about it here. I must make human illusion – ask someone in tomorrow after dinner; and begin that astonishing adventure with the souls of others again – about which I know so little.

Sunday 16 June

As I finished those words, in came Leonard to say that Desmond was coming round in two minutes – which he did, so that the sail filled out again and the ship went on. Desmond was shabby and baggy in grey. He was bubbling and simmering, off to dine at Kettners, and determined to be punctual. A vein of determination lies in him; and he is the most cooked and saturated of us all. Not an atom remains crude; basted richly over a slow fire – an adorable man, a divine man, for all his power of taking the spine out of me. Happily we did not get on to that – writing that is to say.

Sunday 23 June

It was very hot that day, driving to Worthing to see Leonard's mother, my throat hurt me. Next morning I had a headache. So we stayed on at Rodmell till today. At Rodmell I read through *The Common Reader*; I must learn to write more succinctly. I am horrified by my own looseness: the result is a wobble and diffusity and breathlessness which I detest. And so I pitched into my great lake of melancholy. Lord how deep it is! What a born melancholiac I am! The only way I keep afloat is by working. Directly I stop working I feel that I am sinking down, down. And as usual, I feel that if I sink further I shall reach the truth. That is the only mitigation; a kind of nobility. Solemnity. I shall make myself face the fact that there is nothing – nothing for any of us. Work, reading, writing, are all disguises; and relations with other people. Yes, even having children would be useless.

However, I now begin to see *The Moths* rather too clearly; or at least strenuously, for my comfort. I think it will begin like this: dawn; the shells on a beach; I don't know – voices of cock and nightingale; and then all the children at a long table – lessons; the beginning. Could one not get the waves to be heard all through? Or the farmyard noises? Some odd irrelevant noises. Well all this is of course the 'real' life; and nothingness only comes in the absence of this. Everything becomes green and vivified in me when I begin to think of *The Moths*.

Sunday 30 June
My melancholy has been broken, like a lake by oars, since I wrote. I have been so active. We have seen so many people. Last night we dined with Roger, tonight with Clive; Lytton came; Vita came; we had a party. I bought a dress in Shaftesbury Avenue. It was very hot, I think; and is now cold, indeed for the first time for weeks it is, or has been, raining.

This last half year I made over £1800; almost at the rate of £4000 a year; the salary almost of a Cabinet minister; and time was, two years ago, when I toiled to make £200. Now I am overpaid I think for my little articles. Well, after tomorrow I shall close down article writing, and give way to fiction for six or seven months till next March perhaps.

Desmond is being very brilliant about the Byron letters and the Boswell papers. Think! There are eighteen volumes of Boswell's diaries now to be published. With any luck I shall live to read them. I feel as if some dead person were said to be living after all – an odd effect, this disinterment of a mass more of Boswell when one had thought all was known, all settled. And father never knew. These papers were in a cabinet in Ireland.

MONKS HOUSE, RODMELL

Monday 5 August
Yes that is the date, and the last was June 30th – a tribute to the helter skelter random rackety summer I spent. Far the pleasantest memories, standing out like green weed on some civet grey pond, were the week ends here; with the hay cutting and the lights lambent; Leonard's new room, Hedgehog Hall, a-building, and my lodge being made into the palace of comfort which it now is. Yes it was a scattered summer; I felt as if the telephone were strung to my arm and anybody could jerk me who liked. A sense of interruption bothered me. And then I'm cross with Vita: she never told me she was going abroad for a fortnight – didn't dare; till the last moment, when she said it was a sudden plan. Lord Lord! I am half amused though; why do I mind? what do I mind? how much do I mind?

One of the facts is that these Hildas are a chronic case; and, like the damned intellectual snob that I am, I hate to be linked, even by an arm, with Hilda [Matheson]. Her earnest aspiring competent wooden face appears before me. A queer trait in Vita – her passion for the earnest middle-class intellectual, however drab and dreary. You can choose between us, I say, stopping writing; and I get some satisfaction from making up caustic phrases.

Thursday 8 August

This is written to while away one of those stupendous moments – one of those painful, ridiculous, agitating moments which make one half sick and yet I don't know – I'm excited too; and feel free and then sordid; and unsettled; and so on – I've told Nelly to go; after a series of scenes which I won't bore myself to describe. And so at lunch L. and I settled it; and I spoke two words, which she almost pulled out of my mouth in her eagerness to show herself delighted and eager and hard and untouched – a sordid painful scene after fifteen years; but then how many I have had, and how degrading they are. And if we don't break now we drift on endlessly – oh but all these old arguments I know by heart. In truth we never should have gone on, I daresay, if it hadn't been for the war; I don't know. I'm confirmed in my wish to have no resident servants ever again. That is the evil which rots the relationship.

Saturday 10 August

Well, Heaven be praised; it is all over and calm and settled. Nelly – how long ago that seems! – is staying. And I'm too deliciously relieved to have seen Vita this moment and find that her story to me was precisely true. Indeed I was more worried and angry and hurt and caustic about this affair than I let on, even to the blank page; yet afraid too of exaggeration. Of course, one is right about Nelly – right that she is, in bad moods, almost insufferably mean, selfish and spiteful; but – she is in a state of nature; untrained; uneducated, without the power of analysis or logic; but we shan't part now, I think. And I'm half pleased to find that it is harder to part after fifteen years than I thought. And I'm pleased – oh very pleased – about Vita.

Monday 19 August

I opened this book to record the blessed fact that for good or bad I have just set the last correction to *Women and Fiction*, or *A Room of One's Own*. I shall never read it again I suppose. Good or bad? Has an uneasy life in it I think: you feel the creature arching its back and galloping on, though as usual much is watery and flimsy and pitched in too high a voice.

William Plomer has been for the week end and gone. A compressed inarticulate young man, thickly coated with a universal manner fit for all weathers and people: tells a nice dry prim story; but has the wild eyes which I once noticed in Tom, and take to be the true index of what goes on within. Once or twice he almost cracked his crust – sitting on the stones this morning for instance. I think he shows up well against the Raymonds and the Frankies – is somehow solid; to their pinchbeck lustre.

And now, having written my little articles, I must think of that book again, and go down step by step into the well. These are the great events and revolutions in one's life – and then people talk of war and politics. I shall grind very hard; all my brakes will be stiff, my springs rusty. But I have now earned the right to some months of fiction.

Thursday 22 August
I thought on my walk that I would begin at the beginning: I get up at half past eight and walk across the garden. Today it was misty and I had been dreaming of Edith Sitwell. I wash and go into breakfast which is laid on the check tablecloth. With luck I may have an interesting letter; today there was none. And then bath and dress; and come out here and write or correct for three hours, broken at 11 by Leonard with milk, and perhaps newspapers. At one luncheon – rissoles today and chocolate custard. A brief reading and smoking after lunch; and at about two I change into thick shoes, take Pinker's lead and go out – up to Asheham hill this afternoon, where I sat a minute or two, and then home again, along the river. Tea at four, about; and then I come out here and write several letters, interrupted by the post, with another invitation to lecture; and then I read one book of *The Prelude*. And soon the bell will ring, and we shall dine and then we shall have some music, and I shall smoke a cigar; and then we shall read – La Fontaine I think tonight and the papers – and so to bed. But my skeleton day needs reviving with all sorts of different colours. Today it was grey and windy on the walk; yesterday generous and open; a yellow sun on the corn; and heat in the valley. Both days differ greatly; both are among the happiest of my life – I mean among the happy undistinguished days, ripe and sweet and sound; the daily bread; for nothing strange or exalted has happened; only the day has gone rightly and harmoniously.

Monday 16 September
Leonard is having a picnic at Charleston and I am here – 'tired'. But why am I tired? Well I am never alone. This is the beginning of my complaint. I am not physically tired so much as psychologically. I have strained and wrung at journalism and proof correction; and underneath has been forming my *Moths* book. Yes, but it forms very slowly; and what I want is not to write it, but to think it for two or three weeks say. (And they've gone to

some lovely place Hurstmonceux perhaps, in this strange misty evening; and yet when the time came to go, all I wanted was to walk off into the hills by myself. I am now feeling a little lonely and deserted and defrauded, inevitably.) And every time I get into my current of thought I am jerked out of it. We have had the Keyneses; then Vita came; then Angelica and Eve [Younger]; then we went to Worthing, then my head begins throbbing – so here I am not writing – that does not matter, but not thinking, feeling or seeing -- Leonard appeared at the door at this moment; and they didn't go to Hurstmonceux or anywhere; so I missed nothing – one's first egotistical pleasure.

Another reflection – nothing is so tiring as a change of atmosphere. I am more shattered and dissipated by an hour with Leonard's mother than by six hours - no, six days, of Vita. (Nessa don't count.) The tremendous gear changing that has to take place grinds one's machinery to bits.

And then I am forty-seven: yes: and my infirmities will of course increase. To begin with my eyes. Last year, I think, I could read without spectacles; would pick up a paper and read it in a tube; gradually I found I needed spectacles in bed; and now I can't read a line without them. What other infirmities? I can hear, I think, perfectly: I think I could walk as well as ever. But then will there not be the change of life? And may that not be a difficult and even dangerous time? Obviously one can get over it by facing it with common sense – that it is a natural process; that one can lie out here and read; that one's faculties will be the same afterwards; that one has nothing to worry about in one sense – I've written some interesting books, can make money, can afford a holiday. Oh no; one has nothing to bother about; and these curious intervals in life – I've had many – are the most fruitful artistically – one becomes fertilised – think of my madness at Hogarth – and all the little illnesses – that before I wrote *To the Lighthouse* for instance. Six weeks in bed now would make a masterpiece of *Moths*. But that won't be the name. Moths, I suddenly remember, don't fly by day. And there can't be a lighted candle. Altogether, the shape of the book wants considering – and with time I could do it.

Saturday 21 September
Another of those curious plums, things falling unexpectedly in our way, has just happened. Annie the large eyed sad young woman has been to ask us to buy her a cottage, and let her do for us always, in fact be our servant here. She and her baby, aged two, have been turned out at a fortnight's notice to make room for two spinster dog breeders. She would make an ideal servant, I believe; she would be a great standby; one could come here as long as one liked – and poor dear Nelly could be left in London. It needs some thinking – meanwhile Annie is up against this terrific high black

prison wall of poverty – has to manage with a child on fifteen shillings a week.

Sunday 22 September
Though write letters I will and must, I will canter here a moment. It is a fine September morning; the rooks cawing, the shadows very long and shallow on the terrace. The body has gone out of the air. It is thinning itself for winter. An exacting and rather exhausting summer this has been. On the other hand, this is the best appointed summer we have ever had. Never has the garden been so lovely – all ablaze even now; dazzling one's eyes with reds and pinks and purples and mauves; the carnations in great bunches, the roses lit like lamps. Often we go out after dinner to see these sights. And at last I like looking about the drawing room. I like my rug; my carpet; my painted beams. And for some odd reason I have found lovelier walks this year than ever – up into the downs behind Telscombe. Partly it is the weather, perhaps; we have had day after day of cloudless warm sun.

Wednesday 25 September
But what interests me is of course my oil stove. We found it here last night on coming back from Worthing. At this moment it is cooking my dinner in the glass dishes perfectly I hope, without smell, waste, or confusion: one turns handles, there is a thermometer. And so I see myself freer, more independent – able to come down here with a chop in a bag and live on my own. I go over the dishes I shall cook – the rich stews, the sauces – the adventurous strange dishes with dashes of wine in them. Of course Leonard puts a drag on, and I must be very cautious, like a child, not to make too much noise playing.
   Then, old Mrs Woolf – She has come to wear a charm and dignity to me, unknown before, now her old age is crumbling down all the cheerful sentimental small talk – she becomes curiously more human and wise. True she is peevish and bored as a child; but has attained some carelessness of show and pomp and respectability, as if she had washed her hands of most things and were playing on a beach. I must go into the kitchen to see my stove cooking ham now.

Wednesday 2 October
We have just been over Annie's cottage – so I suppose it is. And we therefore own another fair sized house; but the arrangement with Annie seems another of those plums which have dropped into our hands here. She will cook; my oil stove makes hot meals practicable at all hours; but I am dazed with the Brighton [Labour Party] conference (how my days of

reflection have dwindled!). The audience makes an extraordinary baaing noise; and I thought how politics was no longer an affair of great nobles and mystery and diplomacy, but of commonsense, issuing from ordinary men and women of business – not very exalted, but straightforward, like any other business affair.

The light is dying; I hear the village boys kicking footballs; the atmosphere – winter, change, London's imminence – scatter finally my poor efforts at solid concentration. Yet I have, these last days, set my book alight I think – got it going. And all the Americans write and cable for articles. Leonard in the cold windy road is cleaning the car.

52 Tavistock Square, wc i

Friday 11 October
And I snatch at the idea of writing here in order not to write *Waves* or *Moths* or whatever it is to be called. These October days are to me a little strained and surrounded with silence. What I mean by this last word I don't quite know, since I have never stopped 'seeing' people. No; its not physical silence; its some inner loneliness. To give an example – I was walking up Bedford Place this afternon, and I said to myself spontaneously, something like this. How I suffer, and no one knows how I suffer, walking up this street, engaged with my anguish, as I was after Thoby died – alone; fighting something alone. But then I had the devil to fight, and now nothing. And when I come indoors, it is all so silent. Yet I am writing – oh and we are very successful; and it is autumn; and the lights are going up; and Nessa is in Fitzroy Street – in a great misty room, with flaring gas and unsorted plates and glasses on the floor; and the Press is booming; and this celebrity business is quite chronic – and I am richer than I have ever been – and bought a pair of earrings today – and for all this, there is vacancy and silence somewhere in the machine. If I never felt these extraordinarily pervasive strains – of unrest, or rest, or happiness, or discomfort – I should float down into acquiescence. Here is something to fight: and when I wake early I say to myself, Fight, fight.

Its odd, now I come to think of it – I miss Clive.

Wednesday 23 October
I will here sum up my impressions before publishing *A Room of One's Own*. It is a little ominous that Morgan won't review it. It makes me suspect that there is a shrill feminine tone in it which my intimate friends will dislike. I forecast then that I shall get no criticism, except of the evasive jocular kind, from Lytton, Roger and Morgan; that the press will be kind and talk of its

charm and sprightliness; also I shall be attacked for a feminist and hinted at for a sapphist; Sibyl will ask me to luncheon; I shall get a good many letters from young women. I am afraid it will not be taken seriously. I doubt that I mind very much. It is a trifle, I shall say; so it is, but I wrote it with ardour and conviction.

We dined last night with the Webbs. We sit in two lodging house rooms (the dining room had a brass bedstead behind a screen), eat hunks of red beef, and are offered whisky. It is the same enlightened, impersonal, perfectly aware of itself atmosphere. And I compared them with L. and myself, and felt (I daresay for this reason) the pathos, the symbolical quality of the childless couple; standing for something, united.

Saturday 2 November

I dreamt last night that I had a disease of the heart that would kill me in six months. Leonard, after some persuasion, told me. My instincts were all such as I should have, in order, and some very strong: quite voluntary, as they are in dreams, and have thus an authenticity which makes an immense and pervading impression. First, relief – well I've done with life anyhow (I was lying in bed); then horror; then desire to live; then fear of insanity; then (no this came earlier) regret about my writing, and leaving this book unfinished; then a luxurious dwelling upon my friends' sorrow; then a sense of death and being done with at my age; then telling Leonard that he must marry again; seeing our life together; and facing the conviction of going, when other people went on living. Then I woke, coming to the top with all this hanging about me; and found I had sold a great many copies of my book – the odd feeling of these two states of life and death mingling as I ate my breakfast feeling drowsy and heavy.

Tuesday 5 November

Oh but I have done quite well so far with *A Room of One's Own*: and it sells, I think; and I get unexpected letters. But I am more concerned with my *Waves*. I've just typed out my morning's work; and can't feel altogether sure. There's *something* there but I can't get at it squarely.

On Sunday we were at Rodmell; and my room is now about three feet of brick, with the window frames in; rather an eyesore, for it cuts off the garage roof and the downs – both pleasanter sights than I had thought.

Sunday 17 November

A horrid date. Yes, I am feeling a little sick, a little shivery; I can't settle to anything; I am in a twitter; I find myself talking aloud: "After what happened the other morning, I am afraid I must now give you notice . . . After you told me to leave your room I went to Mr Woolf and said that I could not keep you as my maid any longer. I haven't made up my mind in a hurry. But the scenes at Rodmell were worse than ever. And now this is the last. This is the 17th of November. I shall expect you to go on the 17th December." Yes, this is what I have to say to Nelly at 9.30 tomorrow. And I am almost trembling with this nervous anticipation as I write. But it must be done.

Monday 18 November
Well it is over, and much better than I expected – at least for the present. To my question Do you want to give me notice? she replied "I have given you notice –" "Then you wish to go at the end of your month?" As we refused her an hour's extra help when she was ill, yes. But this was said without conviction – which means I'm afraid that she has no more intention of going than I have of taking ship to Siberia. So be it. I shall hope that the dust will be settled now for a week or two.

Sunday 8 December
Dear me; last Monday, as L. advised, I asked Nelly if she wished to go: and so (as I foreboded) she said reasonably no; and proposed solutions. We were landed; not emotionally; rather weariedly and disillusionedly on my part, in a compromise for a month; if the trial is unsatisfactory then to part without further discussion for ever.

Just back from Rodmell. The roof is on; the floors are made; the windows in; giving, it seemed, vast sweeping views of flooded meadows; but there was only a blink of light even at midday; we were engulfed in whirling wet; working up to such a storm on Friday night as I have, I think, never been in. It went round and round; and there was thunder in the crash of the wind; and great zigzags of lightning; and hail drumming on the iron roof outside my room; and such a fury of noise one could not sleep. So at one I went up to L. and looked at the lighted windows in the village; and thought, really with some fear, of being out alone that moment. Dreams were all blown about, elongated, distorted, that night. A tree down in the churchyard. Trees down all the way up today. However, the mind was very still and happy. I read and read and finished I daresay three foot thick of MSS read carefully too; much of it on the border, and so needing thought.

Saturday 14 December
By the way, the sales of *A Room* are unprecedented – have beaten *Orlando*; feels like a line running through one's fingers; orders for 100 taken, as coolly as 12's used to be. We have sold, I think, 5500; and our next year's income is made.

Had I married Lytton I should never have written anything. So I thought at dinner the other night. He checks and inhibits in the most curious way.

L. may be severe; but he stimulates. Anything is possible with him. Lytton was mild and damp, like a wet autumnal leaf. Lonely, and growing elderly.

Sunday 15 December
Last night we went to *The Calendar* (by Edgar Wallace) with Ann [Stephen]; and there was a cheer, and behold a great golden Queen bowing in a very small bow windowed box. Also, when the lights went up, the King, red, grumpy, fidgeting with his hands; well groomed, bluff; heavy looking, with one white flower in his buttonhole, resenting the need, perhaps, of sitting to be looked at between one of the acts – his duty to be done. Once the Duchess of York sat with the Queen; a simple, chattering, sweethearted little roundfaced young woman in pink; but her wrists twinkling with diamonds, her dress held on the shoulder with diamonds. The Queen also like a lit up street with diamonds. An odd feeling came to me of the shop window decorated for the public: these our exhibits, our show pieces. Not very impressive – no romance or mystery – the very best goods.

MONKS HOUSE, RODMELL

Thursday 26 December
And I am sitting in my new room, with curtains, fire, table; and two great views; sometimes sun over the brooks and storm over the church. A violent Christmas; a brilliant serene Boxing day. I find it almost incredibly soothing – a fortnight alone – almost impossible to let oneself have it. Relentlessly we have crushed visitors: we will be alone this once, we say; and really, it seems possible. Then Annie is to me very sympathetic.

Before I went Clive came to tea. He asked me if I had been told that he had criticised *A Room*? I said no. He was a little rasped; said the jokes were lecture jokes. "Girls come round me" – too much of that - little ideas – nothing compared with *Orlando*. But his criticism is founded upon the theory that I can't feel sex: have the purple light cut off. But as always, his own axe wants grinding: that Love is enough – or if love fails, down one goes for ever. And I always feel, how jolly, how much hunting, and talking and carousing there is in you! How long we have known each other – and then Thoby's form looms behind – that queer ghost. I think of death sometimes as the end of an excursion which I went on when he died. As if I should come in and say well, here you are.

Saturday 28 December
Bernard Shaw said the other night at the Keyneses – and the Keyneses have just wrecked my perfect fortnight of silence, have been over in their

Rolls Royce – and L. made them stay, and is a little inclined to think me absurd for not wishing it – Bernard Shaw said to me, "*Heartbreak House* is the best of my plays. I wrote it after staying with you at the Webbs in Sussex – perhaps you inspired it. [George] Moore's an odd man – a very small talent cultivated with the utmost patience. We used to laugh at him in the old days. He was always telling us stories about himself and a lady – a grand lady – and she was always throwing something at his head and just missing it. Nobody was better tempered. But he was our laughing stock. And one day Zola said to me I've discovered your great English novelist! Who's that said I. His name is George Moore. And I burst out laughing – not our little George Moore, with his stories about himself? But it was. A lesson, you see, not to be too quick in judging one's friends."

1930

It was through, and with, Roger Fry that in January Virginia was asked to dine in Bedford Square by Fry's friend Henry ('Bogey') Harris, the wealthy connoisseur and art collector, where their fellow guests were political notables including the Labour Prime Minister, Ramsay MacDonald. Subsequently, while she was semi-immured during her usual winter indispositions, two very disparate visitors, one from the past, the other to loom large in the future, engaged her descriptive powers. Margery Snowden had been a fellow student of Vanessa's at the Royal Academy Schools at the beginning of the century, and remained her lifelong correspondent; Dame Ethel Smyth, the doughty old composer and feminist, fired by reading A Room of One's Own, *was determined to meet its author, and, having met her, threw herself with vigour into what became for her a passionate friendship, and for Virginia an engrossing if demanding new relationship.*

Leonard had finally succeeded in giving up his literary editorship of the Nation & Athenaeum *in mid-February; but the work of the Hogarth Press absorbed more and more of his time, so that by the end of the year he and Virginia decided once again to restrict its operations to the publication of their own books; but, as before, the decision was postponed. Virginia's books were being reissued in a Uniform Edition; Vita Sackville-West's* The Edwardians, *published this year, became a best-seller; manuscripts poured in, the literary ones read by Virginia herself; the Woolfs were glad to escape as often as possible to Rodmell. At the beginning of May they toured south-west England as far as St Ives, travelling their books. Soon after their return, Nelly their servant was admitted to hospital for an operation and, in spite of the inconvenience of organising substitute help, the relief of being free of her perpetual presence determined Virginia to dispense with her altogether and employ only non-resident domestics.*

Despite the distractions of visitors and visits – to Vita at Long Barn, to Ethel Smyth's Surrey home, to Leonard's brother Philip, the Estate Manager to James de Rothschild at Waddesdon Manor in Buckinghamshire – and her rather precarious state of health, Virginia completed her first draft of The Waves *by the end of April, and at once embarked on the second version, which she worked on for the following nine months. At Rodmell during the summer months she varied this work by reading and writing on Hazlitt. At the end of August she fainted in the garden, an alarming experience, but recovered after a week's immobility and resumed her active round of outings and meetings, entertaining Vanessa's family and, less willingly, Leonard's, seeing Vita and Ethel Smyth, inviting friends for weekends or meals. The Woolfs returned to Tavistock Square on 4 October, and Virginia, who had engaged a temporary cook-housekeeper, steeled herself to dismiss the still convalescent Nelly and, having done so, relented. Nelly returned to work at the beginning of 1931.*

Three years earlier Lady Ottoline Morrell had returned to Bloomsbury from Garsington and re-established herself in Gower Street, and it was here, the day after T. S. Eliot and his now seriously deranged wife had been to tea with her, that Virginia encountered the poets W. B. Yeats and Walter de la Mare. She was now much in demand as a guest – so much so that she swore never to dine out again, a vow she signally failed to keep.

The Woolfs drove to Rodmell on Christmas Eve, and Virginia at once took to her bed with a cold and a temperature; but by the end of the year she was again thinking about, if not actually writing, The Waves.

1930

Thursday 9 January
I merely note that I am going to try to keep next week entirely free from 'seeing' people, bating my dinner at Bogey Harris's to meet the Prime Minister, and Angelica's party. I am going to see if I can keep seven days out of the clutch of the seers.

Sunday 12 January
Thanks to my pertinacity and industry, I can now hardly stop making up *The Waves*. Now I feel that I can rush on, after six months hacking, and finish; what is essential is to write fast and not break the mood – no holiday, no interval if possible, till it is done. Then rest. Then re-write. As for keeping a week free – I am now going to visit L.'s mother; then to the Frys after dinner. Marjorie Strachey to tea tomorrow; Duncan, I think, on Tuesday; Vita on Friday; Angelica on Saturday; Bogey Harris Wednesday; one day remains entire – Thursday – and that's the end of my week.

Thursday 16 January
A page of real life. Last night at Bogey Harris's. I came in, flung into the room in my red coat; an oval room, with painted ceiling, and books. "Lady Londonderry will be late; but we won't wait." I have forgotten the Prime Minister [Ramsay MacDonald] – an unimpressive man; eyes disappointing; rather heavy; middle class; no son of the people; sunk; grumpy; self-important; wore a black waistcoat; had some mediocrity of personality. In came Lady Londonderry very late; in ruby velvet, cut to the middle of the back. All went in to dinner, and I was too blind to read Sir Robert Vansittart on the man's card, so had to jumble for my neighbour's pursuit. Never mind. They all called each other Van, Bogey, Ramsay, Edie, across the table; engaged in governing England. And so upstairs, Lady Londonderry running ahead, opening doors, taking us into little rooms to look at majolica, at altarpieces. Then round the fire she started off, fluent, agreeable, hard hitting, telling stories – all indiscreet, open, apparently. We discussed Birth

275

Control. "Dear Edie, you won't let me convert you. But when you see your miners with those terrible illegitimate children – Eight in a room. One bed. What can you expect? Can't do anything else. What would you do? What should we do, if we lived like that?" "But we're not beasts. We can control ourselves. I detest Prohibition for that reason." Swept on, energetically, confidently. Lady Londonderry can do whatever she wishes. She looked like an early Victorian picture – a Lawrence, I thought; a small pinched well cut face; healthy; without paint; very pink, pearls knotted about her wrists. The rooms all set out with cases, chests, pictures, objects. "I never give more than ten pounds: I hunt about in rag and bone shops." Bogey is evidently one of those elderly comfortable men of taste and leisure who make a profession of society; a perfectly instinctive snob. Knows everyone; nothing to say, with all his talk of Lords and Ladies; something of a gorged look, which connoisseurs have; as if he had always just swallowed a bargain. Roger says he has 'flair'; Roger who looks like a ravaged scavenger and lives with sardine tins and linoleum; yes, but Roger's house seems alive, with a living hand in it, manipulated, stretched. I tried, sitting on a priceless settee, picked up in Whitechapel for ten pounds (I never give more) to analyse my sensations. The ladies showed a perfect commercial grasp of the situation. Ramsay was tossed between them like a fish among cormorants. I had the impression that they did not rate this acquisition high; but took it as a part of the day's work. Lady Londonderry had him to herself in a shaded room for an hour.

Sunday 26 January

I am forty-eight; we have been at Rodmell – a wet, windy day again; but on my birthday we walked among the downs, like the folded wings of grey birds; and saw first one fox, very long with his brush stretched; then a second; which had been barking, for the sun was hot over us; it leapt lightly over a fence and entered the furze – a very rare sight. How many foxes are there in England?

I forgot to say that when we made up our six months' accounts, we found I had made about £3,020 last year – the salary of a civil servant; a surprise to me, who was content with £200 for so many years.

Sunday 16 February

To lie on the sofa for a week. If I could stay in bed another fortnight (but there is no chance of that) I believe I should see the whole of *The Waves*. I believe these illnesses are in my case – how shall I express it? – partly mystical. Something happens in my mind. It refuses to go on registering impressions. It shuts itself up. It becomes chrysalis. I lie quite torpid, often with acute physical pain. Then suddenly something springs. Two nights ago, Vita was here; and when she went, I began to feel the quality of the evening – how it was spring coming; a silver light; mixing with the early lamps; the cabs all rushing through the streets; I had a tremendous sense of life beginning; and all the doors opening; and this is I believe the moth shaking its wings in me; ideas rush in me. It is no use trying to write at this stage. I would like to lie down and sleep, but feel ashamed. Leonard brushed off his influenza in one day and went about his business feeling ill. But as I was saying, my mind works in idleness. To do nothing is often my most profitable way.

Thursday 20 February
She [Margery Snowden] came in wrapped in a dark fur coat; which being taken off, she appeared in nondescript gray stockinette and jay blue stripes. Her face is pale, and very small; indeed, has a curious preserved innocency which makes it hard to think that she is fifty. The preserved look seems to indicate lack of experience; as if life had put her in a refrigerator. She brought me a parcel, and this was a book from Ethel Smyth, with a letter. Then we talked – but it was her starved and anguished look that remains, and the attitude of mind. She seemed to be saying inwardly 'I have missed everything. There are Vanessa and Virginia; they have lives full of novels and husbands and exhibitions. I am fifty and it has all slipped by.' I gathered this from the jocose pertinacity with which she kept referring to herself. She said the climate of Cheltenham is so sleepy that she often can't paint; and after lunch they put on the gramophone. Nothing long distracted her from her central concern – I have had no life and life is over. Even clothes suggested the same old theme. In fact I have seldom got a more dismal impression of suffering: call it rather frustration, non-entity; being lifted on a shelf, and seeing things pass. Lord, how I praise God that I had a bent strong enough to coerce every minute of my life since I was born! This fiddling and drifting and not impressing oneself upon anything – this always refraining and fingering and cutting things up into little jokes and facetiousness – that's what's so annihilating. Yet given little money, little looks, no special gift – what can one do? How could one battle? How could one leap on the back of life and wring its scruff?

Friday 21 February
No two women could be more extravagantly contraposed than Margery Snowden and Ethel Smyth. I was lying here at four yesterday when I heard the bell ring, then a brisk tramp up the stairs; and then behold a bluff, military old woman (older than I expected), bounced into the room in a three cornered hat and tailor made suit. "Let me look at you." That over, "Now I have brought a book and pencil. First I want to make out the

genealogy of your mother's family. Old Pattle – have you a picture? No. Well now – the names of his daughters." This lasted out tea. Afterwards, we talked ceaselessly till 7 – when L. came in. We talked – she talked considerably more than I; and she got off: oh about music – "I am said to be an egoist. I am a fighter. I feel for the underdog. Believe me I have to go on coming to London, bullying, badgering – at last they promise me fourteen women in the orchestra. I go and find two. So I begin ringing up." She has a vein, like a large worm, in her temple which swells. Her cheeks redden. Her faded eyes flash. She has a broad rounded forehead. I like to hear her talk of music. She says writing music is like writing novels. One thinks of the sea – naturally one gets a phrase for it. Orchestration is colouring. Rhapsodies about *A Room*. There is something fine and tried and experienced about her besides the rant and the riot and the egotism – and I'm not sure that she is the egotist that people make out. She said she never had anybody to admire her, and therefore might write good music to the end. Has to live in the country because of her passion for games. Plays golf, rides a bicycle; was thrown hunting two years ago. Then fell on her arm and was in despair, because life would be over if she could not play games. "I am very strong" which she proved by talking till 7.30; then eating a biscuit and drinking a glass of vermouth and going off to eat a supper of macaroni when she got to Woking at 9.

Saturday 22 February
I'm not to go down to the studio till Monday; and so must canter my pen amateurishly here. Lytton came in after dinner. Very twinkly, lustrous, easy and even warm. Leonard made cigarettes. I lay on the sofa in the twilight of cushions. Lytton had been sent a book about Columbus and told us the story making it into a fantastic amusing Lytton book – Columbus a mad religious fanatic who sailed west and west because he had read in Isaiah a prophesy; his crew being convicts let out from prison; and they came to Cuba and he made them sign a statement that this was India, because it was too large to be an island; and they picked up gold and gems and went back to Spain and the King and Queen rose as he came in. Here are all the elements of a Lytton concoction, told with great gusto; irony; a sense of the incongruous and dramatic. Then we warbled melodiously about Dadie and Cambridge and so on. He has a new gramophone. He is editing Greville. He is very content too – and very well equipped, and buys books; and likes us; and is going to Cambridge this week-end. Its odd how little one remembers what is actually said.

Saturday 1 March

And then I went for a walk and brought on a headache, and so lay down again till today, when we propose to drive off – oh Thank God a thousand times – to Rodmell and there be at rest. This little affair has taken three weeks, and will land me in four, of non-writing inexpressiveness. Yet I'm not sure that this is not the very thing for *The Waves*.

Tuesday 11 March

My impressions of Margaret [Llewelyn Davies] and Lilian [Harris] at Monks House were of great lumps of grey coat; straggling wisps of hair; hats floppy and home made; thick woollen stockings; black shoes, many wraps, shabby handbags, and shapelessness and shabbiness and dreariness and drabness unspeakable. A tragedy in its way. Margaret at any rate deserved better of life than this dishevelled and undistinguished end. We showed them the garden, gave them tea (and I don't think an iced cake had come Lilian's way this six weeks) and then – oh the dismal sense of people stranded, wanting to be energised; drifting – all woollen and hairy. (It is odd how the visual impression dominates.) Must old age be so shapeless? The only escape is to work the mind. I shall write a history of English literature, I think, in those days. And I shall walk. And I shall buy clothes, and keep my hair tidy, and make myself dine out. Margaret has her tragic past. She is pathetic to me now – conciliatory and nervous, where she used to be trenchant and severe. What I miss is colour, energy, any clear reflection of the moment. I see those thick stockings and grey hairy wraps everywhere.

Friday 28 March

Yes, but this book is a very queer business. I had a day of intoxication when I said Children are nothing to this: when I sat surveying the whole book complete, and quarrelled with L. (about Ethel Smyth) and walked it off, felt the pressure of the form – the splendour and the greatness – as perhaps I have never felt them. How to end I don't know. Yet I think something is there; and I propose to go on pegging it down, arduously, and then re-write, reading much of it aloud like poetry.

Home from tea with Nessa and Angelica. A fine spring day. I walked along Oxford Street. The buses are strung on a chain. People fight and struggle. Knocking each other off the pavement. Old bareheaded men; a motor car accident; &c. To walk alone in London is the greatest rest.

Friday 11 April

Yesterday walked through the Waddesdon greenhouses with [the head gardener] Mr Johnson. There were single red lines taking root in sand.

Cyclamen by the hundred gross. Azaleas massed like military bands. Carnations at different stages. Vines being picked thin by sedulous men. Nothing older than forty years, but now ready made in perfection. A fig tree that had a thousand lean regular branches. The statues tied up, like dead horses, in sheets. The whole thing dead. Made, planted, put into position in the year 1880 or thereabouts. One flower would have given more pleasure than those dozens of grosses. And the heat, and the tidiness and the accuracy and the organisation. Mr Johnson like a nectarine, hard, red, ripe. He was taught all he knew by Miss Alice [de Rothschild], and accepted admiration as his due. Sir he called us.

Tuesday 29 April
And I have just finished, with this very nib-full of ink, the last sentence of *The Waves*. I think I should record this for my own information. But I have never written a book so full of holes and patches; that will need re-building, yes, not only remodelling. This is a reach after that vision I had, the unhappy summer – or three weeks – at Rodmell, after finishing *The Lighthouse*.

PM. And I think to myself, as I walk down Southampton Row, 'and I have given you a new book.'

Thursday 1 May
I have wasted the brilliant first of May which makes my skylight blue and gold; have only a rubbish heap in my head; can't read, and can't write, and can't think. The truth is, of course, I want to be back at *The Waves*. But then we are going touring Devon and Cornwall on Sunday which means a week off.

Sunday 18 May
The thing is now to live with energy and mastery, desperately. To despatch each day high handedly. So not to dawdle and dwindle, contemplating this and that. No more regrets and indecisions. That is the right way to deal with life now that I am forty-eight: and to make it more and more important and vivid as one grows old.

[Undated: late May]
This is all very well; but what if Nelly then gets taken ill with her kidneys, must have an operation. Soberly and seriously a whole fortnight has been blown from my life; because I have had to hang about to see [the doctor], to buy food, to arrange with Taupin [temporary cook], to arrange with the hospital; to go there in an ambulance. My mind in order to work needs to be stretched tight and flat. It has been broken into shivers.

Sunday 15 June

How many skips there are here! Nothing said of our tour through the West; nothing said of Nelly's operation; of Taupin, who lost my key, broke tumblers, and cooked with the faded inspiration of one who had been a good cook; and nothing said of the divine relief of my quiet evenings, without servants; and how we dine out at the Cock; and how we say, can't this last? Leonard is not apt at a crisis. I mean his caution sticks his back up. He foresees obstacles. He has a philanthropic side too, which I distrust. Must be good to dependants.

Monday 16 June

Oh to be rid of servants, for all the emotions they breed – trust, suspicion, benevolence, gratitude, philanthropy – are necessarily bad. And Nelly is now deposited on us for a day; turned out of hospital at a moment's notice. It is odd how those old scenes rankle in my mind – how unwilling I am to have her back. I think with real shrinking of having her in control again.

I don't know why, but I have stinted this book. The summer is in full swing. Its elements this year are Nessa and Duncan, Ethel Smyth, Vita and re-writing *The Waves*. Ethel Smyth drops in; dropped in yesterday for instance. I heard a ring, went up, and saw an old char in her white alpaca coat; sat her down; disburdened her of cardboard boxes: full of white pinks; and looked at her rather monumental old colonel's face (girt round with an inappropriate necklace, for she was going to lunch with [Sir Thomas] Beecham.) I get, generally, two letters daily. I daresay the old fires of Sapphism are blazing for the last time. In her heyday she must have been formidable – ruthless, tenacious, exacting, lightning quick, confident; with something of the directness and singleness of genius, though they say she writes music like an old dryasdust German music master. Her style in writing memoirs though is to her credit – indeed she has ridden post haste through life; and accumulated an astonishing number of observations, with which she qualifies her conversation so as to drive L. almost frantic. One speech of hers lasted twenty minutes unbroken, he says, the other night. She is a game old bird – an old age entirely superior in vitality to Margaret's.

Wednesday 23 July

Edith Sitwell has grown very fat, powders herself thickly, gilds her nails with silver paint, wears a turban and looks like an ivory elephant, like the Emperor Heliogabalus. I have never seen such a change. She is mature, majestic. Her fingers are crusted with white coral. She is altogether composed. A great many people were there – and she presided. But though thus composed, her eyes are sidelong and humorous. The old Empress remembers her scallywag days. We all sat at her feet – cased in slender black slippers, the only remnants of her slipperiness and slenderness. We hardly talked together, and I felt myself gone there rather mistakenly, had she not asked me very affectionately if she might come and see me alone. Her room was crowded with odds and ends of foreigners.

Saturday 26 July
Just back from a night at Long Barn, and am all of a quiver with home coming to L., to two newts in the bathroom, letters (from Ethel, and flowers), books, &c. A very nice homecoming; and makes me a little amazed at my own happiness. I daresay few women are happier – not that I am consistently anything; but feel that I have had a good draught of human life, and find much champagne in it. It has not been dull – my marriage; not at all.

MONKS HOUSE, RODMELL

Wednesday 6 August
This is written at Rodmell; oh yes, and it is the best, the freest, the comfortablest summer we have ever had. Figure to yourself feet swollen in boots. One takes them off – that is my state without poor dear Nelly; with nice bright Annie. The rain pelts – look at it (as the people in *The Waves* are always saying) now. My dinner is cooking. I have so many rooms to sit in, I scarcely know which to choose. And new chairs. And comfort everywhere, and some beginnings of beauty. But it is the freedom from servants that is the groundwork and bedrock of all this expansion. After lunch we are alone till breakfast. I say, as I walk the downs, never again, never again. Cost what it may, I will never put my head into that noose again.

I walk; I read; I write, without terrors and constrictions; I make bread. I cook mushrooms. I wander in and out of the kitchen. I have a resource besides reading. Why we ever suffered that discomfort so long, that presence grumbling, always anyhow (for that's unfair) at a different angle from ours –

Wednesday 20 August
Last night was Quentin's birthday. "Another Quentin birthday over" said Maynard, at the gate after the fireworks, counting perhaps the remaining years. The rockets went roaring up and scattered their gold grain. The willows were lit grey over the pond. The bonfire was forked, like branches in a wind. Nessa, in red, threw on a screen. Angelica, whirring and twirling like an old screaming witch, danced round it. "Childhood – true childhood"

said Lydia. For some minutes everything that was said had the quality of sayings in a Tchekhov play.

Ethel's letters are daily: for we have so much to make up. Should I curtail her and curb them? I think not. If one adventures, adventure wholly. And she is so courageous, remarkable, shrewd, that it would be mere poltroonery for me to hold off for fear of ridicule. So I let that old bonfire rage red and perhaps throw a screen on it.

Monday 25 August

Ethel came for a night on Friday, and let me pelt in a few notes of this curious unnatural friendship. I say unnatural because she is so old, and everything is incongruous. Her head is an enormous size over the temples. Music is there, she said, tapping her temples. That way lies insanity. She cannot refrain from repeating what I guess to be very worn compliments, often repeated to herself at dead of night. For she cannot get over unfortunately her own ill-treatment. A refrain occurs; and it is all the more marked for being in contrast with the generosity, sense, balance, and shrewdness of all else. Off her own music, and the conspiracy against her -- for the Press are determined to burke her, though she fills every hall – that's the line of it – she is an admirable guest. Oh yes and more. I went through some odd vicissitudes, in the way of emotion. Lying in my chair in the firelight she looked eighteen; she looked a young vigorous handsome woman. Suddenly this vanishes; then there is the old crag that has been beaten on by the waves; the humane battered face that makes one respect human nature; or rather feel that it is indomitable and persistent. Then I am conscious, I suppose, of the compliment she pays me. But then she is over seventy. I had some interesting moments. About jealousy for instance. "D'you know, Virginia, I don't like other women being fond of you." "Then you must be in love with me Ethel." "I have never loved anyone so much. Ever since I saw you I have thought of nothing else &c. I had not meant to tell you." But what I like in her is not I think her love, for how difficult it is to make that intelligible -- what I like is the indomitable old crag; and a certain smile, very wide and benignant. But dear me I am not in love with Ethel.

Tuesday 2 September

I was walking down the path with Lydia. If this don't stop, I said, referring to the bitter taste in my mouth and the pressure like a wire cage of sound over my head, then I am ill: yes, very likely I am destroyed, diseased, dead. Damn it! Here I fell down – saying "How strange - flowers". In scraps I felt and knew myself carried into the sitting room by Maynard; saw L. look very frightened; said I will go upstairs. The drumming of my heart, the pain, the effort got violent at the doorstep; overcame me; like gas; I was unconscious; then the wall and the picture returned to my eyes; I saw life again. Strange, I said, and so lay, gradually recovering till 11 when I crept up to bed. Today, Tuesday, I am in the lodge and Ethel comes – valiant old woman! But this brush with death was instructive and odd. Had I woken in the divine presence it would have been with fists clenched and fury on my lips. "I don't want to come here at all!" So I should have exclaimed. I wonder if this is the general state of people who die violently. If so, figure the condition of Heaven after a battle.

I will use these last pages to sum up our circumstances. A map of the world. Leaving out the subject of Nelly, which bores me, we are now much freer and richer than we have ever been. For years I never had a pound extra, a comfortable bed, or a chair that did not want stuffing. This morning Hammond [Lewes furnishers] delivered four perfectly comfortable armchairs – and we think very little of it.

I seldom see Lytton; that is true. The reason is that we don't fit in, I imagine, to his parties nor he to ours; but that if we can meet in solitude, all goes as usual. Yet what do one's friends mean to one, if one only sees them eight times a year? Morgan I keep up with in our chronically spasmodic way. My Bell family relations are young, fertile and intimate. Julian and Quentin change so much. This year Quentin is shabby, easy, natural and gifted; last year he was foppish, finicky and affected. Julian is publishing with Chatto & Windus. As for Nessa and Duncan I am persuaded that nothing can be now destructive of that easy relationship, because it is based on Bohemianism. My bent that way increases – in spite of the prodigious fame. I am more and more attracted by looseness, freedom, and eating one's dinner off a table anywhere, having cooked it previously. Ease and shabbiness and content therefore are all ensured. Adrian I never see. I keep constant with Maynard. I never see Saxon. I am slightly repelled by his lack of generosity; yet would like to write to him. Perhaps I will. George Duckworth, feeling the grave gape, wishes to lunch with Nessa; wishes to feel again the old sentimental emotions. After all, Nessa and I are his only women relations. A queer cawing of homing rooks this is. I daresay the delights of snobbishness somewhat fail in later life – and we have 'made good' – that is his expression.

My map of the world lacks rotundity. There is Vita. Yes – she was here the other day, after her Italian tour, with two boys; a dusty car, sand-shoes and Florentine candlepieces, novels and so on tumbling about on the seats. I use my friends rather as giglamps: there's another field I see; by your light. Over there's a hill. I widen my landscape.

Monday 8 September
I will signalise my return to life – that is writing – by beginning a new book, and it happens to be Thoby's birthday, I remark. He would have been, I think, fifty today. After coming out here I had the usual – oh how usual – headache; and lay, like a fibre of tired muscle, on my bed in the sitting room, till yesterday. Now up again and on again; with one new picture in my mind: my defiance of death in the garden.

But the sentence with which this book was to open ran 'Nobody has ever worked so hard as I do' – exclaimed in driving a paper fastener through the fourteen pages of my Hazlitt just now. Time was when I dashed off these things all in the day's work. Now I spend I daresay a ridiculous amount of time, more of trouble, on them. I began reading Hazlitt in January I think. And I am not sure that I have speared that little eel in the middle – which is one's object in criticism. Never mind; it shall go today; and my appetite for criticism is, oddly, whettened. I have some gift that way, were it not for the grind and the screw and the torture –

Anyhow, this is the happiest summer since we had Monks House; the most satisfactory. The weather is September weather, bright, sunny, cool. We have a project of making my bedroom the sitting room – for the view. To let it waste, day after day, seems a crime: elderly eyes cannot waste.

Wednesday 24 September
I have taken up my staff again; I wish I could say that my book was my staff; but oh dear, how many people have I seen – dashing that support from my hand. Our friends work us very hard – and my two months respite [is] nibbled at by all who choose. I think I will spend August next year in Northumberland.

Monday 29 September
So all those days were completely ruined by the assiduity of our friends. When one has to tidy the table, pick fresh flowers, collect chairs and be ready at four, or at one, to welcome and all the rest of it, the circumjacent parts of the day are ruined. On the whole L.'s family do the trick most thoroughly. Everything is such an effort; so unreal; what I say is so remote from what I feel; their standards are so different from mine; I strain myself perpetually with trying to provide the right cakes, the right jokes, the right affection and inquiries. Naturally it often goes wrong, as on Friday. Mrs Woolf who is the vainest of women, began to pay herself the usual compliments upon her wonderful management of so many fatherless and penniless children. And then of course she will not be satisfied until I have also wondered and exclaimed at her amazing unselfishness and courage. Here of course I begin to see very plainly how ugly, how nosey, how

irreparably middle class they all are. Indeed, my aesthetic sense is the one that protests most obstinately – how they cheapen the house and garden – how they bring in an atmosphere of Earls Court and hotels, how impossibly out of place and stuffy and towny and dressy and dowdy they look on the terrace, among apple trees and vegetables and flowers. But there I am pinned down, as firmly as Prometheus on his rock, to have my day, Friday 26th of September 1930, picked to pieces, and made cheap and ugly and commonplace; for the sting of it is that there is no possible escape – no escape that won't make old Mrs Woolf begin to dab her eyes and feel that she is not being welcomed – she who is so 'painfully sensitive' – so fond of cakes, so incapable of amusing herself, so entirely without any interest in my feelings or friends; so vampire-like and vast in her demand for my entire attention and sympathy. Lord Lord! how many daughters have been murdered by women like this! What a net of falsity they spread over life. How it rots beneath their sweetness – goes brown and soft like a bad pear! At the same time I cannot make out a case for myself as a maltreated person. No, because I have an interest beyond my own nose. But let me note that old age can only be made tolerable by having a firm anchor outside gossip, cakes, and sympathy. Think of imposing even one afternoon of such a burden upon Quentin, Julian and Angelica! I shall spend my day at the British Museum.

The great game of diplomacy is begun with Nelly. I have told [her doctor] that we will pay her wages, but not have her back till she is well.

52 TAVISTOCK SQUARE, WC1

Wednesday 15 October

I say to myself 'But I cannot write another word.' I say 'I will cut adrift – I will go to Roger in France – I will sit on pavements and drink coffee – I will see the Southern hills; I will dream; I will take my mind out of its iron cage and let it swim – this fine October.' I say all this; with energy; but shall I do it? Shan't I peter out here, till the fountain fills again? Oh dear oh dear – for the lassitude of spirit! Rarely rarely comest thou now, spirit of delight. You hide yourself up there behind the hotel windows and the grey clouds. It is dismal to broach October so languidly.

Alas, one day last week Nelly appeared – of course on her best behaviour – very much the old and trusted servant, with, I think, a dash of suspicion. Why did I not have her back and give her help, seeing that she had been with us fifteen years? – that I think was in her mind. But we kept it down; and she is off to Colchester for ten days and then – oh dear, I say again, oh dear.

Thursday 23 October
Ethel came in yesterday evening; rather battered in an old moleskin coat; in the triangular hat which the hotel proprietor at Bath has made into its shape with a few pins. Well, I begin to make note of her, because, among other things – how many others – she said would I like her to leave me some of her letters in her will? Would you like me to write something about you? I said. Oh yes; what fun! So I am to some extent Ethel's literary executor, a post I have always vaguely desired; and so I now make a few notes as she talks, for a portrait. She hopes not to live another seven years; gives me to understand that now that her last barren years have been fructified by knowing me, she can sing her nunc dimittis.

Monday 27 October
How comfortless and uneasy my room is – a table all choked with papers, &c. I'm now grinding out *Waves* again, and have perhaps an hour and a half to spend: a short time on Dante; a short time on MSS; a short time here – with another pen. Yesterday we went to Warlingham and sat in a gravel pit, like a Cézanne. I made this comparison to appease myself for not being in France. And we walked along a bridle path; and saw old quiet farms, and rabbits, and downs, all preserved as by a magic ring from Croydon. Never was the division between London and country so sharp. Home, and made dinner; and read MSS. But rather casually and unanimously we have decided within the last week to stop the Press. Yes; it is to come to an end. That is we are to go on only with my books and L.'s and what we print ourselves. In short, we shall revert next October to what we were in the Hogarth House days – an odd reversal, seeing that we are now financially successful. But what's money if you sell freedom? we say. And what's the point of publishing these innocuous novels and pamphlets that are neither good nor bad? So we make this decision, casually, walking round the Square after lunch and thus slip another shackle from our shoulders. This is what I call living with a pilot in the ship – not mere drifting ahead.

Sunday 2 November
And tonight the final letter to Nelly is to be sent; there it rests in my red bag, but I have great reluctance to read it over, as I had to write it. Yet I don't suppose she will mind acutely. For one thing, she has been prepared, I think, by our readiness to do without her; and then since the famous scene last November I think she has been aware of a change. These five months at any rate have proved that we are freer, easier and no less comfortable, indeed more comfortable, without her, for all her good humour, sense and niceness; which now that I have written the letter, I see once more in their

true proportions. Oh never again to have scenes with servants – that is my ambition.

Wednesday 5 November

The letter is sent; the shock over. And I come in and find the house empty and silent. A slight inaccuracy, if applied to the past few days. Ethel, Lyn [Irvine] and Hugh Walpole to tea on Monday; Vita, Clive and Hilda Matheson to dine; Hugh again later, and his piteous, writhing and wincing and ridiculous and flaying alive story of Willie Maugham's portrait [in *Cakes and Ale*]; Hugh, turning round on his bed of thorns again and yet again, and pressing them further and further in. Clive is home blind of one eye and much in need of society. I thought him, why heaven knows, rather admirable and touching, determined not to be a burden on his friends. And he can't read or write, and has hired a reader. Its the evenings that will be bad he said. Nessa characteristically writes from Cassis that she doesn't think much of it, and supposes that spectacles, 'which we all wear' will put it right.

Saturday 8 November

I pressed his hand when we said goodbye with some emotion: thinking This is to press a famous hand: it was Yeats's, at Ottoline's last night. He was born in 1865 so that he is now a man of sixty-five – and I am forty-eight; and thus he has a right to be so much more vital, supple, high charged and altogether seasoned and generous. He has grown very thick (last time I met him – and I may note that he had never heard of me and I was slightly embarrassed by Ottoline's painstaking efforts to bring me to his notice – was in 1907 or 8 I suppose, at dinner at 46 [Gordon Square]). He is very broad; very thick; like a solid wedge of oak. His face is too fat; but it has its hatchet forehead in profile, under a tangle of grey and brown hair; the eyes are luminous, direct, but obscured under glasses; they have however seen close, the vigilant and yet wondering look of his early portraits. I interrupted a long dream story of [Walter] de la Mare's when I came in: about seeing Napoleon with ruby eyes and so on. Yeats was off, with vehemence even, kindling and stumbling a little, on dreams; those which have colour are rare and mean – I forget what. de la Mare told another very cryptic dream about a book with circles in it; the outermost ring black, the inner blue and so on. Yeats identified this dream at once as the dream of the soul in some particular state – I forget what. And so on to dreaming states, and soul states; as others talk of Beaverbrook and free trade – as if matters of common knowledge. de la Mare had just been to the National Gallery, and had got no pleasure from the pictures. Yeats said he could get nothing from Rembrandt, nothing from El Greco. He then explained our pleasure in pictures, or other works of art, by an elaborate metaphor. Then, discussing what poems we could come back to unsated, I said *Lycidas*; de la Mare said no. Not Milton for him: he could never recognise his own emotions there. Milton's woodbine was not his woodbine, nor Milton's Eve his Eve. Yeats said he could not get satisfaction from Milton; it was Latinised poetry (as somebody said, Milton had (in some way irreparably) damaged the English language). And so to modern poetry, and the question of the spade. Yeats said that 'we', de la Mare and himself, wrote 'thumbnail' poems only because we are at the end of an era. He said that the spade has been embalmed by thirty centuries of association; not so the steam roller. Poets can only write when they have symbols. And steam rollers are not covered in symbolism – perhaps they may be after thirty generations. He and de la Mare can only write small fireside poems. Most of emotion is outside their scope. All left to the novelists I said – but how crude and jaunty my own theories were beside his: indeed I got a tremendous sense of the intricacy of the art; also of its meanings, its seriousness, its importance, which wholly engrosses this large active minded immensely vitalised man. And I was impressed by his directness, his terseness. No fluff or dreaminess. He seemed to live in the centre of an immensely intricate briar bush, from which he could issue at any moment; and then withdraw again. And every twig was real to him. Indeed he seemed in command of all his systems, philosophies, poetics and humanities; not tentative any more. Hence no doubt his urbanity and generosity. Compare him with Tom for instance, who came to tea the day before, and may be, for anything I know, as good a poet. Poor Tom is all suspicion, hesitation and reserve. His face has grown heavier, fatter and whiter. There is a leaden sinister look about him. But oh – Vivien! Was there ever such a torture since life began! – to bear her on one's shoulders, biting, wriggling, raving, scratching, unwholesome, powdered, insane, yet sane to the point of insanity, reading his letters, thrusting herself on us, coming in wavering, trembling – "Does your dog do that to frighten me? Have you visitors? Is it accident? That's what I want to know" (all this suspiciously, cryptically, taking hidden meanings). Have some honey, made by our bees, I say; have you any bees? (and as I say it, I know I am awaking suspicion). "Not bees. Hornets." "But where?" "Under the bed." And so on, until worn out with half an hour of it, we gladly see them go. This bag of ferrets is what Tom wears round his neck.

On second thoughts, Yeats and de la Mare talk too much about dreams to be quite satisfactory. This is what makes de la Mare's stories (lent me by Ottoline) wobbly.

Wednesday 12 November
And I had my talk with Nelly last night. An odd, meandering, contradictory, mainly affectionate and even intimate talk. One of her preoccupations [is]

to establish her own hard lot and innocence of all offence among the [other Bloomsbury] servants. We had treated her badly, turning her off because of ill-health. But Nelly, you gave me notice ten times in the past six years – and more . . . But I always took it back. Yes but that sort of thing gets on the nerves. Oh ma'am I never meant to tire you. But then Nelly you forgot that when you were with us. But then for three years I've been ill. And I shall never like any mistress as much as I like you . . . And so on and so on – all the old tunes, some so moving; so pathetic; some (I'm glad to say) so irrational, hysterical and with that curious senseless reiteration of grievances which used to drive me frantic. The truth – but I could never tell her this – is that that kind of dependency and intimacy wears one down; is a psychological strain. And then the gossip. Oh I won't say how I've heard, but I've heard – And so at last, after every variety of feeling, I was left with the one feeling No I could not have you sleeping here again. [*Later*] And then I let her come back, for three months, from January 1st. How am I ever to apologise to myself sufficiently?

Tuesday 2 December
No I cannot write that very difficult passage in *The Waves* this morning, all because of Arnold Bennett and Ethel [Sands]'s party. I can hardly set one word after another. There I was for two hours, so it seemed, alone with Bennett in Ethel's little back room. And this meeting I am convinced was engineered by Bennett to 'get on good terms with Mrs Woolf' – when heaven knows I don't care a rap if I'm on terms with Bennett or not. Its true, I like the old creature: I do my best, as a writer, to detect signs of genius in his smoky brown eye; I see certain sensuality, power, I suppose; but O, as he cackled out, "What a blundering fool I am – what a baby – compared with Desmond MacCarthy – how clumsy." This innocence is engaging; but would be more so if I felt him, as he infers, a 'creative artist'. "Its the only life" he said (this incessant scribbling, one novel after another, one thousand words daily), "I don't want anything else. I think of nothing but writing." And at last I drew Lord David [Cecil] in. And we taunted the old creature with thinking us refined. He said the gates of Hatfield were shut – "shut away from life." "But open on Thursdays" said Lord David. "I don't want to go on Thursdays" said Bennett. "And you drop your aitches on purpose" I said, "thinking that you possess more 'life' than we do." "I sometimes tease" said Bennett "But I don't think I possess more life than you do. Now I must go home. I have to write one thousand words tomorrow morning." And this left only the scrag end of the evening; and this left me in a state where I can hardly drive my pen across the page.

Friday 12 December
This, I think, is the last day's breathing space I allow myself before I tackle the last lap of *The Waves*. I have had a week off – but I think I have got my breath again and must be off for three or perhaps four weeks more. Then, as I think, I shall make one consecutive writing of the interludes – and then – oh dear, some must be written again; and then corrections; and then send to Mabel [typist]; and then correct the type; and then give to Leonard, perhaps some time late in March. Then put away; then print, perhaps in June.

Tuesday 16 December
I will never dine out again. I will burn my evening dress. I have gone through this door. Nothing exists beyond. I have taken my fence; and now need never whip myself to dine with Colefax, Ethel, Mary again. These reflections were hammered in indelibly last night at Argyll House. The same party: same dresses; same food. To talk to Sir Arthur [Colefax] about Queen Victoria's letters, and the Dyestuff Bill, and – I forget – I sacrificed an evening alone with Vita, an evening alone by myself – an evening of pleasure. And so it goes on perpetually. Forced, dry, sterile infantile conversation. And I am not even excited at going. So the fence is not only leapt, but fallen. Why jump?

Thursday 18 December
Lord David, Lytton and Clive last night. Told them how I had burnt my evening dress in the gas fire – general agreement that parties are a folly. Clive specially emphatic.

Saturday 20 December
And Kingsley Martin lunched with us (sweeping up turkey as a char sweeps feathers) and said that the *Nation* and the *New Statesman* are to amalgamate; and he is to be editor (highly secret, like all nonsense) and would L. be literary editor? No; L. would not.

Monday 22 December
It occurred to me last night while listening to a Beethoven quartet that I would merge all the interjected passages into Bernard's final speech, and end with the words O solitude.

MONKS HOUSE, RODMELL

Saturday 27 December
But what's the use of talking about Bernard's final speech? We came down on Tuesday, and next day my cold was the usual influenza, and I am in bed with the usual temperature, and can't use my wits or form my letters – and so my precious fortnight of exaltation and concentration is snatched; and I shall go back to the racket and Nelly without a thing done. Meanwhile it rains; Annie's child is ill; the dogs next door yap and yap; all the colours are rather dim and the pulse of life dulled. I moon torpidly through book after book.

The *Journal of a Somerset Rector*: the parson – Skinner – who shot himself emerges like a bloody sun in a fog. He shot himself in the beech woods above his house; spent a life digging up stones and reducing all places to Camelodunum; quarrelled, bickered; yet loved his sons; yet turned them out of doors – a clear hard picture of one type of human life – the exasperated, unhappy, struggling, intolerably afflicted. Oh and I've read Queen Victoria's letters; and wonder what would happen had Ellen Terry been born Queen. Complete disaster to the Empire? Queen Victoria was entirely unaesthetic; a kind of Prussian competence and belief in herself her only prominences; material; brutal to Gladstone; like a mistress with a dishonest footman. Knew her own mind. But the mind radically commonplace; only its inherited force and cumulative sense of power making it remarkable.

Monday 29 December
If I can get out, and move about, and yet not get a headache, I daresay in three days I shall be beginning to play gently with the waves. I don't have the temptation here of London. How difficult though to get back into the right mental state: what a queer balance is needed.

Tuesday 30 December
What it wants is presumably unity; but it is I think rather good (I am talking to myself over the fire about *The Waves*). Suppose I could run all the scenes together more? – by rhythm, chiefly – so as to make the blood run like a torrent from end to end. I want to avoid chapters. Now if it could be worked over with heat and currency that's all it wants. And I am getting my blood up (temperature 99).

But all the same I went to Lewes, and the Keyneses came to tea; and having got astride my saddle the whole world falls into shape; it is this writing that gives me my proportions.

1931

At the suggestion of Dadie Rylands, a solution to the heavy demands of the Hogarth Press presented itself in the person of John Lehmann, a Cambridge friend of Julian Bell. He began work at 52 Tavistock Square in January with the prospect of becoming manager after an eight months' apprenticeship. The same day, Virginia and Ethel Smyth, invited by Pippa Strachey, spoke to a meeting of the London Society for Women's Service of which she was Secretary; and this occasion stirred up a ferment of ideas in Virginia's mind on the subject of the relative position of the sexes which led her to envisage a book which in the course of the following years developed into two: The Years *and* Three Guineas. *In the meantime however she was still working on* The Waves, *which she finished in an almost visionary burst of inspiration on 7 February.*

Ethel Smyth's composition for voice and orchestra The Prison *was first performed this year, and Virginia was enticed into attending a rehearsal and, three weeks later, its Queen's Hall performance and Lady Rosebery's party for Ethel afterwards. Vita at this time was engrossed by the creation of her new home and garden at Sissinghurst Castle in Kent, and by a new love affair, and Virginia saw her less often than formerly. The void left by this comparative withdrawal was to some extent filled by Ethel Smyth's persevering ardour, which Virginia was beginning to find rather overpowering, and to which she preferred to respond in long and frequent letters.*

Virginia was much saddened by the death of Arnold Bennett in March; in spite of her criticism of his writing, she respected and liked him, and she and Leonard attended his memorial service at St Clement Dan's. A fortnight later, leaving John Lehmann in charge of the Hogarth Press, they took a rather wet holiday in western France, motoring as far south as the Dordogne, where they visited the birthplace of Montaigne. Virginia derived much imaginative sustenance from such glimpses of artists' chosen habitations.

The summer months in London were dedicated to retyping The Waves *and to trying to limit the time spent 'seeing' people. Leonard read the finished copy at Monks House one weekend in July and declared it to be a masterpiece. In July too Virginia had to endure what was to her a form of torture: being stared at. With Vanessa's connivance, the sculptor Stephen ('Tommy') Tomlin persuaded her to give him six sittings to enable him to model her head, while Vanessa painted her.*

At Rodmell in August Virginia corrected the proofs of The Waves, *which she despatched to the printer only a month after Leonard's approval of the typescript, and for relief occupied herself with writing* Flush, *a fanciful biography of Elizabeth Barrett Browning's spaniel. Besides the usual family and neighbourhood visits and visitors, this year brought Sibyl Colefax, the Kingsley Martins, John Lehmann, George and Lady Margaret Duckworth and Ethel Smyth to Monks House; Vita too came for a night. Politics and economics were meanwhile agitating the country and, inevitably, Maynard Keynes and Leonard. In August, Ramsay MacDonald resigned as Labour Prime Minister and, disowned by his own party, formed a National Government which was then re-elected by a large majority in the General Election on 30 October.*

The Waves *was published early in October, received warm praise from those Virginia most respected, was favourably reviewed, and sold surprisingly well -- in contrast to Leonard's long considered book on the development of democratic psychology* After the Deluge, *a source of great mortification to him. However Virginia relaxed in her success, going to concerts and the theatre, to the motor show, asking people to dinner, spending weekends at Rodmell, and not straining at further writing. But by mid-November she was once again prostrated by debilitating headaches and forced to rest. Just before she and Leonard drove to Monks House for Christmas they learnt that Lytton Strachey was desperately ill, and the rest of the year was spent in a state of acute anxiety on his account, telephoning for news from the neighbouring cottage (whose lady-owners bred dogs, a source of constant aggravation to Virginia).*

1931

Monks House, Rodmell

Friday 2 January
Here are my resolutions for the next three months: the next lap of the year. First, to have none; not to be tied. Second, to be free and kindly with myself, not goading it to parties; to sit rather privately reading in the studio. To make a good job of *The Waves*. To care nothing for making money. As for Nelly, to stop irritation by the assurance that nothing is worth irritation: if it comes back, she must go. Then not to slip this time into the easiness of letting her stay.

52 Tavistock Square, WCI

Wednesday 7 January
Well, we have just got back, had our tea, and there are two hours to dinner. It is very quiet here, not a sound but the hiss of the gas. Oh but the cold was too great at Rodmell. I was frozen like a small sparrow. I looked out at dawn once or twice – a redness, like wood fire cinders, in a frosty sky; frost thick on the fields; the candles alight in some of the cottages, and so back to bed, wrapping my clothes round me. And every morning I took the bellows and chafed up my logs, and made a game of it, and almost always won my blazing fire by the time L. came up.

I shall go down and get the post. Already we are committed to 'see' six people before Monday – the only one of importance is John Lehmann.

Saturday 10 January
Lehmann may do: a tight aquiline boy, pink, with the adorable curls of youth; yes, but persistent, sharp. Shall I be paid if I come as apprentice? Can I have the Hogarth Press books? Not much atmosphere; save perhaps that his eyes are imaginative. Lord knows. And we ask four or five thousand as his share.

Tuesday 20 January

I have this moment, while having my bath, conceived an entire new book – a sequel to *A Room of One's Own* – about the sexual life of women: to be called *Professions for Women* perhaps – Lord how exciting! This sprang out of my paper to be read on Wednesday to Pippa [Strachey]'s society [The London Society for Women's Service]. Now for *The Waves*. Thank God – but I'm very much excited.

Friday 23 January

Too much excited, alas, to get on with *The Waves*. One goes on making up *The Open Door*, or whatever it is to be called. The didactive demonstrative style conflicts with the dramatic: I find it hard to get back inside Bernard again.

The speech took place: L. I think slightly exacerbated. Two hundred people; well dressed, keen, and often beautiful young women. Ethel in her blue kimono and wig. I by her side. Her speech rollicking and direct; mine too compressed and allusive. Never mind.

Monday 26 January

Heaven be praised, I can truthfully say on this first day of being forty-nine that I have shaken off the obsession of *Opening the Door*, and have returned to *The Waves*: and have this instant seen the entire book whole, and how I can finish it – say in under three weeks.

Wednesday 4 February

Today Ethel comes. On Monday I went to hear her rehearse [*The Prison*] at Lady Lewis's. A vast Portland Place house with the cold wedding cake Adam's plaster; shabby red carpets; flat surfaces washed with dull greens. The rehearsal was in a long room with a bow window looking onto other houses – iron staircases, chimneys, roofs – a barren brick outlook. There was a roaring fire in the Adam's grate. Ethel stood at the piano in the window, in her battered felt, in her jersey and short skirt, conducting with a pencil. There was a drop at the end of her nose. Miss [Elsie] Suddaby was singing The Soul, and I observed that she went through precisely the same attitudes of ecstasy and inspiration in the room as in a hall. Ethel's pince-nez rode nearer and nearer the top of her nose. She sang now and then; and once, taking the bass, made a cat squalling sound – but everything she does with such forthrightness, directness, that there is nothing ridiculous. She loses self-consciousness completely. She seems all vitalised; all energised; she knocks her hat from side to side. Strides rhythmically down the room to signify that this is the Greek melody; strides back; Now the furniture moving begins, she said, referring to some supernatural gambols connected with the prisoner's escape, or defiance, or death. I suspect the music is too literary – too stressed – too didactic for my taste. But I am always impressed by the fact that it is music – I mean that she has spun these coherent chords, harmonies, melodies out of her so practical vigorous strident mind. What if she should be a great composer? This fantastic idea is to her the merest commonplace: it is the fabric of her being. As she conducts, she hears music like Beethoven's. As she strides and turns and wheels about to us perched mute on chairs she thinks this is about the most important event now taking place in London. And perhaps it is.

Saturday 7 February
Here in the few minutes that remain, I must record, heaven be praised, the end of *The Waves*. I wrote the words O Death fifteen minutes ago, having reeled across the last ten pages with some moments of such intensity and intoxication that I seemed only to stumble after my own voice, or almost, after some sort of speaker (as when I was mad). I was almost afraid, remembering the voices that used to fly ahead. Anyhow it is done; and I have been sitting these fifteen minutes in a state of glory, and calm, and some tears, thinking of Thoby and if I could write Julian Thoby Stephen 1881–1906 on the first page. I suppose not. How physical the sense of triumph and relief is! Whether good or bad, its done; I mean that I have netted that fin in the waste of waters which appeared to me over the marshes out of my window at Rodmell when I was coming to an end of *To the Lighthouse*.

Tuesday 17 February
And I feel us, compared with Aldous and Maria [Huxley], unsuccessful. They're off today to do mines, factories ... black country; did the docks when they were here; must see England. They are going to the Sex Congress at Moscow, have been in India, will go to America, speak French, visit celebrities, – while here I live like a weevil in a biscuit. Lord, how little I've seen, done, lived, felt, thought, compared with the Huxleys – compared with anyone. Here we toil, reading and writing, year in year out. No adventure, no travel. Here by some invisible rope, we are bound. My ship has sailed on. I toss among empty bottles and bits of toilet paper. All I like is my own capacity for feeling. If I weren't so miserable I could not be happy. Aldous takes life in hand. Whether that damages his writing I don't know ... He is 'modern'. He is endlessly athletic and adventurous. He will be able to say he did not waste his youth. I fancy no one thing gives him the immense satisfaction things give me. That's all the comfort I find.

Monday 9 March
And then I went, more than a week ago, to Lady Rosebery's buffet. Sense of drum and blare; of Ethel's remorseless fangs; her irresistible vanity, and some pang too for her child's craving for a party – how tawdry, how paltry; her facing out the failure of *The Prison*: her desperate good cheer; her one bouquet; her old battered wigged head. How mixed my feelings were – and how exhausted and windswept and disillusioned I was – with my ears ringing, and no warmth, depth, comfort, slippers and ease anywhere; but all effort and strain.

Monday 16 March
These few and rather exacerbated entries show, I think, the backwash of *The Waves*. I am writing little articles of a morning, and should have been sketching the Houses of the Great this morning, but that I have not the material. This afternoon I shall try to see Carlyle's house and Keats's house.

Thursday 19 March
Ethel yesterday, very uneasy about her character; uneasy about her own greatness, requiring assurance, and snatching it rather hastily from such vague remarks as I could make. It seems possible to me that nature gave her everything except the power of expression in music; hence the race and violence and restlessness of her nature; the one outlet is stopped up. And she for ever batters at the door; it remains locked; she flows away over me, Lady Cunard – whoever it may be, with the vehemence of a tortured and baffled spirit. But she would die rather than allow this. Hence her terrific egotism; her insatiable desire for praise, since she is denied the only true satisfaction. An exhausting companion therefore.

Saturday 28 March
Arnold Bennett died last night; which leaves me sadder than I should have supposed. A lovable genuine man; well meaning; ponderous; kindly; coarse; rather dignified; deluded by splendour and success; but naive; much at the mercy of life for all his competence; a shop keeper's view of literature; yet with the rudiments, covered over with fat and prosperity and the desire for hideous Empire furniture, of sensibility. Some real understanding power, as well as a gigantic absorbing power. These are the sort of things that I think by fits and starts this morning; I remember his determination to write 1000 words daily; and how he trotted off to do it that night. Queer how one regrets the dispersal of anybody who seemed – as I say – genuine; who had direct contact with life. An element in life – even in mine that was so remote – taken away. This is what one minds.

Saturday 11 April
Oh I am so tired of correcting my own writing – these eight articles. I have however learnt I think to dash; and not to finick. Its the repulsiveness of correcting that nauseates me. And the cramming in and the cutting out. And articles and more articles are asked for. For ever I could write articles.

On Thursday we have our fortnight in France. I think I shall like La Rochelle best: I shall want to live there. I shall take a house there: I shall dream of walking there when I am old and full of sleep.

* * *

Sunday 3 May
Yes, that's all very well; but how to begin, and why begin? I mean what do these diaries amount to? O merely matter for a book, I think; and to read when I have a headache. After all, Percy could burn the lot in one bonfire. He could burn them at the edge of the field where, so we think, we shall lie buried. That was our conclusion after attending Arnold Bennett's funeral.

We are going to regulate 'seeing' people. There is to be a weekly black hole; a seething mass of people all eating tea together. We shall thus have more evenings free. Two days are to be set aside for reading MSS. These two decisions – the Black Hole, and Hogarth Press MSS, will I think make for an orderly and satisfactory summer.

Wednesday 13 May
Unless I write a few sentences here from time to time I shall, as they say, forget the use of my pen. I am now engaged in typing out from start to finish the 332 pages of that very condensed book *The Waves*. I do seven or eight daily; by which means I hope to have the whole complete by June 16th or thereabouts. This requires some resolution; but I can see no other way to make all the corrections, and keep the lilt, and join up, and expand and do all the other final processes. It is like sweeping over an entire canvas with a wet brush.

Tuesday 19 May
Lytton's book [*Portraits in Miniature*] very good. That's his line. The compressed yet glowing account which requires logic, reason, learning, taste, wit, order and infinite skill – this suits him far better, I think, than the larger scale, needing boldness, originality, sweep. Lytton and Raymond to dinner tonight. Desmond t'other night: much obliterated in the struggle for life.

Thursday 28 May
Soon after this, I started a headache – flashes of light raying round my eyes, and sharp pain; the pain cut into me by Ethel's voice, as she sat telling me – "You've got to listen" – about Adrian Boult, and how he ordered her to leave the room. And then to Rodmell, where the same thing happened – the light round my eyes, but as I could lie still in my bed in my big airy room, the pain was much less. If it were not for the divine goodness of L., how many times I should be thinking of death. At Monks House we had electric light, and the Frigidaire is working. When the electric light fused, we could hardly tolerate Aladdin lamps, so soon is the soul corrupted by comfort. Yesterday men were in the house all day boring holes for electric fires. What more comfort can we acquire? And, though the moralists say when one has a thing one at once finds it hollow, I don't at all agree. I enjoy my luxuries at every turn, and think them wholly good for what I am pleased to call the soul.

Thursday 2 June
Ethel again – All my ills, such as they are, spring from liver: I am a very strong woman, who needs calomel. I think that she wants me to be everlasting; that she dislikes other people's illnesses which interfere with her vitality; that she likes to rationalise everything; that she suspects, on principle, all shrinking, subtlety and sensibility. I don't know.

Monday 8 June
Dreams: I had three lately: one of Katherine Mansfield; how we met, beyond death, and shook hands; saying something by way of explanation and friendship; yet I knew she was dead. A curious summing up, it seemed, of what has passed since she died.

Tuesday 23 June
And yesterday, 22 June – when I think, the days begin to draw in, I finished my re-typing of *The Waves*. Not that it is finished – oh dear no. For then I must correct the re-re-typing. This work I began on May 5th, and no one can say that I have been hasty or careless this time; though I doubt not the lapses and slovenlinesses are innumerable.

A dark kind of summer. In spite of this, my little life has been adventurous and more stable than usual. There was Duncan's show; and considerable content, indeed a kind of bubbling rapture I think, in Fitzroy Street. I must ask Nessa why we are so happy. Clive is in Cassis. Julian has grown a bristling beard like a chimpanzee and is off with volumes of Pope to France. Tonight we go to the Gala Opera with Christabel [McLaren]. Stalls costing twenty-five shillings each.

Wednesday 24 June
Last night we went to the gala opera [Lyceum Theatre]; sat in the stalls, two rows from the stage, with Christabel and [Lady Abingdon], who came in late. Her fortune has been spent on her face. In the interval, old women like Roman matrons, ample, tightly girt; girls wand like; many large clear stoned necklaces and long dresses. I got the feeling of this traditional English life; its garden like quality; flowers all in beds and rows. Between the acts we all stood in the street; a dry brilliant night, with women all opening their cloaks; then came dribbling through us a draggled procession of poor women wheeling perambulators and carrying small, white-haired dazed children; going across Waterloo Bridge. Lady Abingdon stalked off without a good night or glance in our direction. Each of her nails was red, and cut out like a small rose petal. L. who had been reading *The Lady* said that this was considered in bad taste; and that men, according to *The Lady*, don't like it. So home, by cab. Oh and my hair stood the strain very well.

Tuesday 7 July
O to seek relief from this incessant correction and write a few words carelessly. A fine day I think and everything, so the tag runs in my head, handsome about us. L. is now floating on the tide of celebrity: asked to broadcast, asked to go to America, asked to write the Weekly Wayfarer in the *New Statesman*. And I am not jealous. Ethel has been penitent after her fashion. That is she came yesterday, after an intermission of almost a fortnight, and defended and explained herself in a speech which lasted twenty minutes by my watch. She raised her cup of tea six times to her lips but always thought of some new parenthesis or qualification and put it down untouched. Her zeal, sincerity and vitality of course convince; though I'm glad to drive my stake in firmly and so avoid complete overwhelming. I shout obloquies at her like gun shots. She takes them on her solid old body with a thud like that on an elephant's hide. I dominate by silence – a phenomenon to her very formidable. And off she goes at 6.45 subdued.

MONKS HOUSE, RODMELL

Friday 17 July
Yes. This morning I think I may say I have finished. L. will read it tomorrow; and I shall open this book to record his verdict. And I'm nervous, I confess. For one thing he will be honest, more than usually. And it may be a failure. And I can't do any more. As I say, I shall be nervous to hear what L. says when he comes out, say tomorrow night or Sunday morning,

to my garden room, carrying the MS and sits himself down and begins 'Well!'

Sunday 19 July
"It is a masterpiece" said L. coming out to my lodge this morning. "And the best of your books." This note I make; adding that he also thinks the first hundred pages extremely difficult, and is doubtful how far any common reader will follow. But Lord! what a relief! I stumped off in the rain in jubilation.

Friday 7 August
I sat to Tommy [Stephen Tomlin]. Oh dear, what a terrific hemp strong heather root obstinate fountain of furious individuality shoots in me – they tampered with it, Nessa and Tommy – pinning me there from 2 to 4 on six afternoons, to be looked at; and I felt like a piece of whalebone bent. This amused and interested me, at the same time I foamed with rage. And at last, at last, at last, on Thursday 30th we got into the car, slammed the door, and made off. And how satisfactory it has been, is being. I writing *Flush* of a morning, half seriously, to ease my brain, knotted by all that last screw of *The Waves*; L. doing his broadcast and correcting proofs; no one coming, except Bells; no one ringing up; no one to say dinner's ready, or to be stumping about in the kitchen. Annie, composed, neat, nimble, has everything disposed of by 3 – which reminds me I must go and put the pie in the oven, I think.

Monday 10 August
No I will not let this day be a bad one, though it has every sign of so being. First an argument with L. at breakfast about seeing his family; the usual rather embittered argument; and then a headache is incipient; which is caused partly by Charleston; where we were very gay. Now I sit in the lodge this grey pale morning and will not go on with *Flush*, because of my head; and we have a day in London tomorrow; and should begin to correct my first proofs; and perhaps shall when I've done this. No, I say, I will not let this day be a bad one: but by what means? Quiet and control. Eating apples – sleeping this afternoon. And now for *Waves*.

Saturday 15 August
Sibyl [Colefax] came by her own request yesterday; and I wondered after two hours jerking barren gossip, what satisfaction she got from it. Once she looked at the downs. The worst of being Sibyl is that one suspects every action of some motive. 'I am proving myself a woman who loves the country.' One never feels, This is what she likes, as I do when Vita stumbles

over the marsh and hardly has a word to say. Sibyl looks at chairs and tables; sums one up; has a magpie's eye, a larder of facts which she will hand on at her next meeting. Then, as we stood at the door, she tried to make us invite her to stay. And I resisted. As you see, Sibyl's company does not lead to lofty reflections.

A wet wild August, the coldest for fourteen years; and the farmers here burning their hay. Meanwhile the country is in the throes of a crisis. Great events are brewing. Maynard visits Downing Street and spreads sensational rumours.

Sunday 16 August
I should really apologise to this book for using it as I am doing to write off my aimlessness; that is I am doing my proofs – and find that I must stop after an hour, and let my mind spread, after these moments of concentration.

The reason why Colefax is so dull is that she never feels or thinks for herself. That is why I should suffocate of dust if she spent a night here. Also she is forever collecting facts about one, not from interest, but from curiosity. It is a warning not to go to places like Argyll House again, because one is expected to make some return.

It is a good idea I think to write biographies; to make them use my powers of representation, reality, accuracy; and to use my novels simply to express the general, the poetic. *Flush* is serving this purpose.

Monday 17 August
Well now, it being just after 12.30 I have put the last corrections in *The Waves*: done my proofs; and they shall go tomorrow – never, never to be looked at again by me, I imagine.

Wednesday 19 August
My proofs did go: went yesterday; and I shall not see them again.

Tuesday 1 September
And so a few days of bed and headache and overpowering sleep, sleep descending inexorable, as I tried to read.

Thursday 3 September
Oh I was annoyed with Desmond's usual sneer at *Mrs Dalloway* – 'woolgathering'. I was inspired to make up several phrases about Desmond's own processes – none of which, I suppose, will ever be fired off in print. But its true – a snub – even praise – from Desmond, depresses me more than the downright anger of Arnold Bennett – it saps my vitality.

I open this book again to record the fact that this is the 3rd of September. The Battle of Dunbar; the Battle of Worcester; and the death of Cromwell. A heavy flagging windy cloudy day with breadths of sun; not actually raining. Its odd how I always remember father saying that at St Ives on this day, and how I am always writing something in a diary on this day and generally it is crisp and clear.

Tuesday 15 September

I have come up here, trembling under the sense of complete failure – I mean *The Waves* – I mean L. accuses me of sensibility verging on insanity – I mean I am acutely depressed and already feeling rising the hard and horny back of my old friend Fight fight.

Wednesday 16 September

Oh but this morning I'm like a bee in the ivy bloom – can't write for pleasure. John [Lehmann] says "But I loved it, truly loved it, and was deeply impressed and amazed by its achievement in an entirely new method . . . There seems to me only the thinnest wall between such a novel and poetry." And its very difficult he adds; and so on.

Saturday 19 September

And the last few days have been heavenly – at last some heat; and then, with this book done, I'm calm; oh and walk; oh and have to record the horror of two bungalows on the top of the hill. Yes. This iniquity is being inflicted on the downs for ever by our 'prospective Labour candidate'. He shan't have my vote. I swept off into dreams of a house far away in Dorsetshire. But O – again – how happy I am: for the moment how sweet life is with L. here, in its regularity and order, and the garden and the room at night and music and my walks and writing easily and interestedly at Donne of a morning, and poems all about me. I've come to read poetry with intensity.

Monday 21 September

Here I am writing about Donne and we have 'gone off the Gold Standard' this morning. Maynard and [Richard] Kahn like people in the war. We sat talking economics and politics. Guards out: Tower defended (this a joke on Maynard's part). We're off, and I write about Donne. Yes; and what could I do better, if we are ruined; and if everybody had spent their time writing about Donne we should not have gone off the Gold Standard – that's my version of the greatest crisis &c &c &c – gabble gabble go the geese, who can't lay golden eggs.

Wednesday 30 September
I have come up here on this the last evening to clear up papers. All is softly grey: L.'s yellow dahlias are burning on the edge of the terrace. I have been over to Asheham, in the clear pale autumn afternoon, along Mandril walk, which we walked the night of our marriage. So its over, this summer too; and I regret it, and want to stay on, and soothe my mind with Elizabethan poets. Instead we go up tomorrow, and doesn't the lift of my heart tell me that strain, about *The Waves*, friends, reviewers, sales, &c will then begin to make a fiddle string in my side, stretched tight, on which lots of people will carelessly twang this winter. No help for it. So it always is with a book out. And it will be out in one week tomorrow.

52 Tavistock Square, WCI

Monday 5 October
A note, to say I am all trembling with pleasure, because Harold Nicolson has rung up to say *The Waves* is a masterpiece. Ah hah – so it wasn't all wasted then. I mean this vision I had here has some force on other minds. Now for a cigarette, and then a return to sober composition.

Friday 9 October
Really, this unintelligible book is being better 'received' than any of them. And it sells – how unexpected, how odd that people can read that difficult grinding stuff!

Wednesday 14 October
A note. *The Waves* has beaten all my books: sold close on 5,000; we are reprinting. The reviews I think the warmest yet. But Vita found it desperately dull – anyhow for 100 pages. What shall I say to Virginia? I can't get through it.

Saturday 17 October
More notes on *The Waves*. The sales, these past three days, have fallen; after the great flare up when we sold 500 in one day, the brushwood has died down, as I foretold. What has happened is that the library readers can't get through it and are sending their copies back. So, I prophesy, it will now dribble along till we have sold 6000 and then almost die, yet not quite. For it has been received, as I may say, quoting the stock phrases without vanity, with applause. I am in danger, indeed, of becoming our leading novelist, and not with the highbrows only. To show how slow a book it is, not only do Vita and Dotty find the first hundred pages boring

in the extreme, but I have as yet (ten days after publication) had only three letters about it. Nessa's enthusiasm is the brightest spot.

Friday 23 October
Oh but I have been made miserable – damped and disheartened – because the *TLS* only gave half a column of belittlement to [Leonard's] *After the Deluge*. L.. says – and honestly believes – that this puts an end to the book. He says his ten years' work are wasted, and that he sees no use in going on. Oh but the arguments which we have beaten out I daresay for six hours, walking in the Square, sitting over the fire – utterly cloud my mind. Its his curious pessimistic temper: something deeper than reason, that one can't deal with. Influenza has exactly the same effect, liberating the irrational despondency which I see in all Woolves, and connect with centuries of oppression. The world against us &c. How can one laugh off the half-column therefore? And when I say this morning incautiously "I'm reviewed in the *Manchester Guardian*", I.. says 'Is it a long review?" And I say, feeling like a mother to a hurt and miserable little boy, Yes. Lord what human beings are!

Friday 30 October
Happily that morbidity of L.'s is over. Other things have intervened, and praise and some sale. And the General Election which has returned I think twenty-six Labour members to Parliament. Oh – yesterday we made an offer for 47 Gordon Square – a house where we may die; for its a 24-year lease. Strange to anchor there again.

Monday 16 November
But we are not to live and die in 47. The Bedford Estate won't house a publisher; would create a precedent; vans would stop at the door. Though [they] told us that we may stay on here past our term: the side of the Square is to be pulled down; but times are bad for building; and they will treat us with consideration.
　　Here I will give myself the pleasure of copying a sentence or two from Morgan's unsolicited letter on *The Waves*. 'I expect I shall write to you again when I have re-read *The Waves*. Its difficult to express oneself about a work which one feels to be so very important but I've the sort of excitement over it which comes from believing that one's encountered a classic.' I daresay that gives me more substantial pleasure than any letter I've had about any book. Yes, I think it does, coming from Morgan. To be noted, as curiosities of my literary history: I sedulously avoid meeting Roger and Lytton whom I suspect do not like *The Waves*. (*The Waves* has sold more than 7000. *The Deluge* is selling very well.)

Tuesday 17 November
Isn't it odd that I'm really, I believe, ostracised by some of my friends, because of *The Waves*, and lifted to the highest pinnacle by others because of it? But Morgan is the only one, either side, that matters.

MONKS HOUSE, RODMELL

Friday 25 December
(Christmas morning). Lytton is still alive this morning. We thought that he could not live through the night. It was a moonlit night. Nessa rang up at 10 to say that he has taken milk and tea after an injection. He had taken nothing for twenty-four hours and was only half conscious. This may be the turn, or may mean nothing. Now again all one's sense of him flies out and expands and I begin to think of things I shall say to him, so strange is the desire for life – the triumph of life.

After writing the last page, November 16th, I could not go on writing without perpetual headache; and so took a month lying down; have not written a line until the last fourteen days, when I heard about Lytton. He has been ill a month; I have lived through again all grades of feeling; then the telephone; then Angelica coming; then going to see James [Strachey]; then coming here last Tuesday, a dark drive, a tree reminding me of Lytton. Brighton yesterday. All very quiet, misty. Talk to L. last night about death; its stupidity; what he would feel if I died. And the feeling of age coming over us: and the hardship of losing friends.

Sunday 27 December
For forty-eight hours Lytton has been better, and now, Nessa says, realises that he is better, and eats; whatever he is allowed. I am therefore freely imagining a future with my old serpent to talk to, to laugh at, to abuse. I shall read his book on Shakespeare; I shall stay at Ham Spray; I shall tell him how L. and I sobbed on Christmas Eve.

But this page is one of my trials to test my brain. I am cross with Desmond, for talking about dreaming subjectivity and *The Waves*; I have been making phrases about his damnable tepidity – he who neither loves nor hates – in short I'm in a healthy condition. Lunching with the Keyneses, they took Lytton philosophically. "Is he alive?" Lydia asked. They did not go to Ham Spray because Lydia disapproves of the immorality of Carrington. "And what d'you feel about immortality, Maynard?" I asked. "I am an idealist," said Maynard, "and therefore on the whole I suppose I think that something may continue. Clearly the brain is the only exciting thing – matter does not exist. It follows therefore . . . but one is very vague." So, more or less, he said. And L. said death was stupid like a motor accident. And Maynard said he wished one could die at once: there should be death arranged for couples simultaneously, like himself and Lydia, me and Leonard. But he always supposed he would die before Lydia, and I, I said, before Leonard. Then Lydia and Leonard will marry. They will combine all these dogs – (dogs were wandering about). And so home. And I kissed Maynard. And they are coming to tea.

Tuesday 29 December
Lytton is, if anything, better. I need not ring up Nessa today, which is a matter of exquisite relief. It seems as if he were now to be seriously ill with ups and downs for some time. Well, we have lived through every grade of feeling – how strong, how deep – more than I guessed, though that cavern of horror is well known to me. In these acute states emotions are much simplified – there is none of the complexity that I feel this morning about Lytton, when I expect him to recover. I feel annoyance, humour, the desire to laugh with him.

It is a bitter windy morning, and Caburn when I came in was white with snow. Now it is black. Shall I ever 'write' again? Why take to it again? Books come gently surging round me, like icebergs. I could write a book of caricatures. Then there's *Flush*; there's *The Knock on the Door*; there's the appalling novel; there's *The Common Reader* . . . there's my little *Letter to a Poet*. But I'm deficient in excitement.

And L. has sold his 450; and I 9400 – what figures.

1932

The year opened under the shadow of Lytton Strachey's illness. A week before he died on 21 January, the Woolfs drove from London to his Wiltshire home, but were not able to see him. The news of his death reached them in Vanessa's studio during a party given for her thirteen-year-old daughter Angelica. Three weeks later they returned to Ham Spray to offer what support they could to the desolated and suicidal Carrington; she was found next day dying from a shot wound. During this melancholy period and the 'mausoleum talks' the circumstances generated among Lytton's many friends, Roger Fry was lecturing at the Queen's Hall in connection with the great exhibition of French Art at the Royal Academy. And Virginia was invited to give the Clark Lectures at Cambridge (which both T. S. Eliot and E. M. Forster had already done), an exceptionally flattering invitation which she at once refused, and then regretted her resolution. She was still ruminating a sequel to A Room of One's Own, which she now thought of calling A Tap or A Knock at the Door, and had set herself to prepare a sequel to The Common Reader, the volume of essays she had published in 1925, and this involved writing five new pieces and revising some twenty already published in various journals.

On 15 April the Woolfs, feeling they deserved an adventure, set off from Victoria Station with Roger Fry and his sister Margery for a tour in Greece; they were away four weeks. Virginia had been there in 1906 with her brothers and sister, but for her companions it was a new experience and one which, though strenuous, was stimulating and rewarding to all four.

The hot London summer was a very busy time for the Woolfs: innumerable social engagements – lunches, dinners, evening parties; visits to the cinema, the ballet, the Chelsea Flower Show; alternate weekends were spent when possible at Monks House. Virginia was trying to finish off the Common Reader volume, and again her exertions brought on fainting fits. An undercurrent to all this activity was John Lehmann's increasing discontent with his role in the Hogarth Press: he found Leonard a difficult taskmaster, the work too hard, the rewards too little, and Virginia, whom he revered, too aloof. Discussions, proposed rearrangements, interventions by Vanessa, failed to allay his grievances. But the Woolfs were shocked by his sudden decision to quit for good.

One of the Woolfs' first guests after moving to Rodmell for the summer was the prize-winning novelist Stella Benson, who had dined with them in July when visiting London from her home in Indo-China. Two days later the distressing news of the *death of the Cambridge humanist G. L. Dickinson (Goldie) reached them; he was a dear and respected older friend, and a perceptive admirer of Virginia's writings. The country holiday followed its usual course, although Virginia suffered another alarming fainting fit early on, and took things gently, reading a good deal, contentedly writing* Flush, *and despatching her proofs of the second* Common Reader. *There was frequent contact with the Charlestonians and the Keyneses, the Woolf family visit, walks and car expeditions, one to stay a night with the Adrian Stephens in Essex. Unexpected visitors were the Eliots: she apparently more neurotic than ever, he considerate and indulgent of her behaviour, perhaps in the knowledge of his impending departure for a six-month lecture tour in America. It was during their visit that John Lehmann's letter announcing his departure from the Hogarth Press was delivered by the afternoon post.*

Back in London after attending the Labour Party Conference at Leicester, Virginia went to the wedding in St Bartholomew the Great of Desmond MacCarthy's only daughter to Lord David Cecil; and it was on this day that the second Common Reader *was published. Unusually, she seemed remarkably indifferent to its fate, being suddenly engrossed by a wholly new conception for a book, to be called* The Pargiters, *incorporating the ideas she had been turning over for her essay* A Tap on the Door, *but expanded to embody a family chronicle. This excited and absorbed her and she dashed it down at great speed through the autumn months. The effort strained her heart, and again she was advised to be careful, and gladly limited her social activities, mainly seeing people at home at tea-time – though she invited the novelist and journalist Rebecca West to dinner. The Woolfs went to Rodmell for Christmas, and Virginia grudgingly faced the task of polishing off* Flush.

1932

MONKS HOUSE, RODMELL

Friday 1 January
Yesterday we had Keyneses and Bells to tea. Lytton, as I must believe, very slow mending – O these dogs – that's my present curse. This irregular sharp bark is the devil. Nessa's description of the lounge at the Bear [Inn, Hungerford] filled with Stracheys reading detective novels in despair; Carrington moving about scarcely knowing people; Pippa violently self-controlled; Saxon helping by – I forget what; Tommy helping too; and the Stracheys, all grey, all woollen, all red nosed, swollen eyed, logical, quiet, exact, doing crossword puzzles; thinking of Lytton. And that afternoon (Christmas Eve) Lytton said "If its only keeping me alive a little longer, don't." And so they did nothing; but then he drank tea and milk with brandy and enjoyed them, and the Doctor happily had some serum, injected it, and so the turn – if turn they call it – began. This is a scene I can see; and see Lytton too, always reasonable, clear, giving his orders; and dying as he thought; and then, as reasonably, finding some strength returning, deciding to live. And L. and I sobbing here.

During the last days here, they have been putting up a great erection of girders on the bank opposite Asheham. Is this an overhead railway or an engine house? So another view of the downs is lost forever. And Annie repeats vague gossip that there is to be a series of factories between Newhaven and Lewes; are we doomed to go – or to stay on and be worried out of all walks, all views, and become crusted over with villas?

52 TAVISTOCK SQUARE, WC1

Wednesday 13 January
We came back from Rodmell last Sunday afternoon – a wet evening, and comfortable to be back, here high up in the air, beyond barking dogs. "I shall go bankrupt if those dogs bark any more" I said to Annie with some vehemence. John [Lehmann] labours, more nervously, and feels jaded, and

wants a week off, and wants also to be our manager, not partner, but to stay in that capacity. So perhaps, and perchance, the dear old Press to which I owe so much labour – witness the pile of MSS before me – and fun – oh yes, a great deal of variety and oddity – may now settle down for life. For our lives. How long will they be? Can we count on another twenty years? I shall be fifty on 25th, Monday week that is; and sometimes feel that I have lived 250 years already, and sometimes that I am still the youngest person in the omnibus. (Nessa says that she still always thinks this, as she sits down.) And I want to write another four novels; and the *Tap on the Door*; and to go through English literature, like a string through cheese, or rather like some industrious insect, eating its way from book to book, from Chaucer to Lawrence. This is a programme, considering my slowness, to last out my twenty years, if I have them.

Lytton goes on, now better, now not so well.

Monday 18 January

And then we heard that Lytton was very ill again. So down we went to Ham Spray on Thursday. So hot, so fresh. The larks singing over the petrol pumps I remember on the Great West Road as we stopped to fill up. They were strained, silent. Then tears – Pippa sobbing on my shoulder at the Bear after lunch – hopeless almost – he is so ill – how can he get better? Then back to Ham Spray – how lovely, with its flat lawn, and the trees grouped and the down rising; this I noted with envy, thinking of my dogs barking, my downs ruined, as we sat at tea. I long sometimes for this sealed up, silent, remote country; long for its little villages; its muddy roads; its distance from Brighton and Peacehaven. And so home again, leaving them in the frail lovely house, with hospital nurses popping in and out; a light in Lytton's room, the shadow of a screen. Again today Carrington writes he is slightly better.

Thursday 21 January

And last night Lytton was dying – "much worse" Oliver telephoned; and this morning "much better again". So we go to Angelica's party in fancy dress. It is like having the globe of the future perpetually smashed – with Lytton – and then behold, it fills again.

Friday 22 January

Much better was much weaker. Lytton died yesterday morning.

I see him coming along the street, muffled up with his beard resting on his tie; how we should stop: his eyes glow. Now I am too numb with all the emotion yesterday to do more than think thoughts like this. Well, as I know, the pain will soon begin. How queer it was last night at the party –

Duncan, Nessa and I sobbing together in the studio – a sense of something spent, gone; the impoverishment; then the sudden vividness. Nessa said, What would one like if one died oneself? that the party should go on. He is the first of the people one has known since one was grown up to die, she said. It was very hopeless. Yes, twenty years of Lytton lost to us, stupidly; the thing we shall never have again.

Saturday 30 January
Oliver [Strachey] to dinner last night. "Lytton was a great man. Oh the excitement. I came back from India starved, and found – all that. They can't leave Carrington alone. She says she will kill herself – quite reasonable – but better to wait until the first shock is over and see. Suicide seems to me quite sensible." Oliver is a tough old buffer: with one flame inside of him. What the Americans call 'culture'. "*That's* the only thing: to realise the legacy that's been left us. To read. To do nothing from eighteen to twenty-two but read. That's what we did. That's why we shan't grow old – we shan't come to an end. But you can't do it if you don't do it then."

Thursday 4 February
One of the curious things I am now proving – now that I am going through the stages of Lytton's death – is that for us fame has no existence. We say we can't publish Lytton's letters for fifty years, if at all. We can't write about him. He has no funeral. I don't know where his ashes are to be buried. There is no commemoration any more, except when we meet and talk; or in the usual ways, alone at night, walking along the streets. The solid statue that father left – that exists no longer.

Monday 8 February
Why did I ever say I would produce another volume of *Common Reader?* It will take me week after week, month after month. However a year spent in reading through English literature will no doubt do good to my fictitious brain. Rest it anyhow. One day, all of a rush, fiction will burst in. I wake in the night with the sense of being in an empty hall: Lytton dead, and those factories building. What is the point of it; life, when I am not working, suddenly becomes thin, indifferent. Lytton is dead, and nothing definite to mark it. Also they write flimsy articles about him. And we go on – at Rodmell for the week-end; and went over to Caburn, and walked among those primeval downs: bowl shaped shadows; half circles; curves; a deep valley.

Thursday 11 February
My mind is set running upon *A Knock on the Door* (what's its name?) owing largely to reading 'Wells on Woman' – how she must be ancillary and

decorative in the world of the future, because she has been tried, in ten years, and has not proved anything. So in this mood I record Mary [Hutchinson]'s telling me last night how she loved cigars; but Jack refuses to let her smoke them – against his idea of what his wife should do – silly affectation – or to let her dress in a dress cut low at the back. Can't go out with you in that frock. Go and put on another. Its indecent. "He treats us – [their daughter] Barbara and me – as if we were tame leopards – pets belonging to him." As indeed they do, since neither has a penny except of Jack's earning and giving.

Saturday 13 February
I break off from my plain duty which is to read [Donne's] *Anatomy of the World* to record Roger's lecture last night. Roger rather cadaverous in white waistcoat. A vast sheet. Pictures passing. He takes his stick. Gets into trouble with the lanternist. Is completely at his ease. Elucidates, unravels with fascinating ease and subtlety this quality and that; investigates (with his stick) opposing diagonals; emphasises the immediate and instantaneous in French art. Here a Queen about to fling out her fingers; here a mother losing herself in pensive and tender reverie, while her child struggles and she restrains it, unconsciously, with perfect ease and control. So to Nessa's, where the stove was kindled, and there was hot soup and cold meat, and coffee and biscuits – all with the usual skill and organising capacity. There we laughed and exaggerated: about the lecture. And we talked about a new life of Jesus, which offers two proofs of his existence – witness Roger's intellectual vitality after speaking to the Queen's Hall for two hours – really excited about the reality of Jesus.

Tuesday 16 February
I have to dine with Ethel Sands tonight, and must have my hair curled. And I'm quivering and itching to write my – what's it to be called? – *Men are like that?* – no that's too patently feminist: the sequel then, for which I have collected enough powder to blow up St Paul's. It is to have four pictures.

Friday 26 February
And what a mint of people I've seen; dining with Ethel, having Desmond and Lord David and Ottoline and the Keyneses, and going to Monks House – so March-white and lovely, the fields, and the river, that bitter cold day; and then I saw – oh the Keyneses – yes – and talked of Lytton, and how Maynard thought we really carried unconvention too far – no service, no farewell. With Lytton there was no mark to say This is over.
    And Ka shut me in the middle class bedroom effectively last night – so condescending, so self approving, with her docile stories of respectable

lunches with the Cornish aristocracy. "And I do hope you will do more *Common Readers*. I prefer them to –" This little bit of patronage annoyed me more than it should. The day Ka came too we sold the ten thousandth copy of *The Waves*: which thus beats all my novels, unexpectedly.

Monday 29 February
And this morning I opened a letter, and it was from the Master of Trinity [College, Cambridge]: and it was to say that the Council have decided to ask me to deliver the Clark Lectures next year. Six of them. This, I suppose, is the first time a woman has been asked; and so it is a great honour – think of me, the uneducated child reading books in my room at 22 Hyde Park Gate – now advanced to this glory. But I shall refuse: because how could I write six lectures without giving up a year to criticism; without becoming a functionary; without sealing my lips when it comes to tilting at Universities; without putting off my *Knock at the Door*, without perhaps shelving another novel? But I am inclined to smile. Yes; all that reading, I say, has borne this odd fruit. And I am pleased; and still more pleased that I won't do it; and like to think that father would have blushed with pleasure could I have told him thirty years ago, that his daughter – my poor little Ginny – was to be asked to succeed him: the sort of compliment he would have liked.

Thursday 3 March
And now I am rather upset because the devil whispered, all of a sudden, that I have six lectures written in *Phases of Fiction*; and could furbish them up and deliver the Clark Lectures, and win the esteem of my sex, with a few weeks' work. Such is the perversity of my mind, I can now think of nothing else; my mind is swarming with ideas for lectures; things I can only say in lectures; and my refusal seems lazy and cowardly. Yet two days ago I was repugnant to the thought: longed only for freedom in which to write *A Tap at the Door*, and was convinced that I should be a time serving pot hunter if I accepted. Anyhow, I'm thankful that I wrote decidedly in the mood I was then in, before the devil whispered, and I went to my drawer and found that old MS; so well written, so full of thought – all the work done for me.

Saturday 12 March
So we went to Ham Spray – a lovely bright day, and got there at 1.30. "I thought you weren't coming" said Carrington. She came to the door, in her little jacket and socks with a twisted necklace. She was pale, small, suffering silently; very calm. She had hot soup for us. We sat in the cold dining room. "I didn't light the fire" she said. She had cooked us a nice hot lunch, succulent, with her own hands. We talked with effort; did she want us? Did

she resent our coming to spy on her? Then we sat on the verandah. We asked her to make us woodcuts for notepaper. And to do designs for Julia [Strachey]'s book. We tried to gossip; she laughed once or twice: and her eyes seemed to get bluer. Then it got cold and we went and sat in Lytton's study – all beautifully neat, his notepaper laid out – a great fire; all his books exactly fitting the shelves, with the letters over them. We sat on the floor round the fire. Then L. suggested a walk. She said she had some notes to write and would we go by ourselves. We only walked to the bottom of the long low down. Then L. went to do the car, and I wandered in the garden and then back into the sitting room. I was taking out a book when Carrington came in and asked if we would have tea before we went. She had made it. She and I went upstairs, arm in arm; and I said "Let me see the view from the window." We stood looking out – She said "Don't you think one ought to keep a room exactly as it was? I want to keep Lytton's rooms as he had them. But the Stracheys say this is morbid. Am I romantic about it d'you think" "Oh no, I'm romantic too," I said. She burst into tears, and I took her in my arms. She sobbed, and said she had always been a failure. "There is nothing left for me to do. I did everything for Lytton. But I've failed in everything else. People say he was very selfish to me. But he gave me everything. Lytton was like a father to me. He taught me everything I know. He read poetry and French to me." I did not want to lie to her. I said life seemed to me sometimes hopeless, useless, when I woke in the night and thought of Lytton's death. I held her hands. Her wrists seemed very small. She seemed helpless, deserted, like some small animal left. She was very gentle; sometimes laughing; kissing me; saying Lytton had loved his old friends best. She said he had been silly with young men. She had been angry that they had not understood how great he was. I said I had always known that. And this last year Lytton made up his mind to be middle aged. "And we were going to Malaga and then he was going to write about Shakespeare, And he was going to write his memoirs, which would take him ten years. It was ironical, his dying, wasn't it. He thought he was getting better. He said things like Lear when he was ill. I wanted to take you to see him the day you came, but I was afraid to – James and Pippa said one must not run any risk, and it might have upset him." And what else did we say? There was not much time. We had tea and broken biscuits. She stood by the fireplace. Then we said we must go. She was very quiet and showed no desire for us to stay. She kissed me several times. I said "Then you will come and see us next week – or not – just as you like?" "Yes, I will come, or not" she said. And kissed me again, and said Goodbye. Then she went in; and turned and I waved and she waved back and she went into the house.

Next morning at 8.30 the gardener heard a noise in her bedroom. He went in and found she had shot herself through the thigh. She died in three hours.

Thursday 17 March

So Carrington killed herself; and again what L. calls 'these mausoleum talks' begin again. We were the last to talk to her, and thus might have been summoned to the inquest; but they brought it in an accident. She maintained this, even to Ralph. Her foot slipped as she was shooting a rabbit. And we discuss suicide; and I feel, as always, ghosts changing. Lytton's affected by this act. I sometimes dislike him for it. He absorbed her, made her kill herself. Now we have to see Pippa, and James and Alix. Then to Rodmell; then – perhaps – to Greece with Roger and [his sister Margery]. A venture that would be: and I think we're both in the mood for ventures after this morbid time; so much talk of death; and there death is of course.

We went from Cambridge on Saturday to King's Lynn; through the lovely lonely coast that lies between that and Cromer; green meadows against the sea; and trees, and complete solitude, and now and then a line of little old houses; and some village spread out, as in a mediaeval picture, upon the rise of a dune; and lovely stubborn unknown place names; and wild roads; all this jumble somehow shadowed by Carrington's death; the name Partridge of course appearing on tombs and grocer's shops.

MONKS HOUSE, RODMELL

Thursday 24 March

Tomorrow is Good Friday and therefore we are at Rodmell on the loveliest spring day; soft; a blue veil in the air torn by birds' voices. I am glad to be alive and sorry for the dead: can't think why Carrington killed herself and put an end to all this. True, they are building the vast elephant grey sheds at Asheham, but I intend to see them as Greek temples; and Percy says they are building sixty cottages – but we wait to see if this is so. And the country is lovelier and lovelier, still with great empty spaces, where I want to walk, alone, and come to terms with my own head. Another book?

Tuesday 29 March

We went to Sissinghurst, and it was a fine goose grey morning. Harold came out in a torn jacket; Vita in breeches and pink shirt. We went over the grounds. Harold said "I'm getting nobler and nobler as we get poorer. I've refused an offer to write for the American papers. Oh but there are myriads of things to do here." Walls have been built and turf laid. "Yes we want to turn those stables into guest bedrooms; and build a library across the courtyard," said Vita. All is planned. Harold has drawn it in his note book. So we ate cold salmon and raspberries and cream and little variegated chocolates and drank oh lots of drinks; and then climbed Vita's tower; lovely pink brick; but like Knole, not much view, save of stables that are to be guest rooms. So home. And then a very wet Sunday and a prodigious reading and drowsing.

52 Tavistock Square, WC1

Monday 11 April
The eddy of travel – wisps and straws – is already whirling round. I have a list of things to buy on my table. We start at 10 on Friday; shall be sailing down the Dalmatian coast this time next week. It is fiendishly cold, wet, blowing, like last year in France. I like this adventure of Greece all the same; and the fact that we are sociably going with Roger and Margery; and that – intimacy – will be part of our journey. The result of Lytton's death – this desire to be with friends.

As for external facts – it seems likely that our John [Lehmann] will not stay. That is he wishes to work half time in order to write.

Hail now; and camel coloured sky. I am waiting for lunch. Tomorrow we go to Monks House to take Pinker. This is a little girl's writing – like a child's letter.

* * *

Monks House, Rodmell

Sunday 15 May
And now, Whit Sunday, here we are at Monks House, and Greece is perceptibly melting: just for a moment England and Greece stood side by side, each much enlivened by the other. When we landed, the English coast seemed long, low, sweeping, empty. I exclaimed at the extraordinary English green – with its silver mixture; and L. said the earth had an unbaked look – no red in it; and the lines of the hills so sloping. This was Greece still active in our eyes. But its force is waning. Already my mind is hard at work (in my absence) arranging, editing, bringing forward, eliminating, until it will present me, unasked, with visions, as I walk, of Aegina, of Athens – the Acropolis with the incandescent pillars; the view from the goatherd's

hill at Delphi. Last night's gossip at Charleston has further strewn sand over Greece. And my head has settled down; and my body is rapidly using itself to armchairs and soft beds and English meat and jam.

52 TAVISTOCK SQUARE, WC1

Tuesday 17 May
What is the right attitude towards criticism? What ought I to feel and say and do when Miss Bradbrook devotes an article in *Scrutiny* to attacking me? She is young, Cambridge, ardent. And she says I'm a very bad writer. It is perhaps true that my reputation will now decline. I shall be laughed at and pointed at. What should be my attitude? The right way is not to resent; not to . . . be long suffering and Christian and submissive either. Of course, with my odd mixture of extreme rashness and modesty (to analyse roughly) I very soon recover from praise and blame. But I want to find out an attitude. The most important thing is to investigate candidly the charge; but not fussily, not very anxiously.

Wednesday 25 May
Lord how I suffer! What a terrific capacity I possess for feeling with intensity – now, since we came back, I'm screwed up into a ball; can't get into step; can't make things dance; wonder how a year or twenty perhaps is to be endured; the inane pointlessness of all this existence; the old treadmill feeling, of going on and on and on; for no reason: Lytton's death; Carrington's; a longing to speak to him; all that cut away, gone; L.'s goodness, and firmness; and the immense responsibility that rests on him. What to do about the Press; about John; women; my book on professions; shall I write another novel; Nessa's children; society; buying clothes; Rodmell spoilt; all England spoilt; terror at night of things generally wrong in the universe; worst of all is this disjected barrenness. And my eyes hurt; and my hand trembles. A saying of Leonard's comes into my head in this season of complete inanity and boredom. 'Things have gone wrong somehow.' It was the night Carrington killed herself. We were walking along that silent blue street with the scaffolding. I saw all the violence and unreason crossing in the air; ourselves small; a tumult outside; something terrifying: unreason.

Thursday 26 May
And now today suddenly the weight on my head is lifted. I can think, reason, keep to one thing, and concentrate. Perhaps I owe it to my conversation with L. last night. I tried to analyse my depression: how my

brain is jaded with the conflict within of two types of thought, the critical, the creative; how I am harrassed by the strife and jar and uncertainty without.

Wednesday 1 June (Derby Day)
Oh dear, oh dear, I don't like dining with Clive – not altogether. It is true I conquered, at 8, my profound trepidation about my clothes. 'I won't wear my new dress' I said, 'in case I should be laughed at.' This philosophy shivered on the doorstep, when I saw two 20-horse-power cars drawn up, apparently at his door. Again I fluctuated and shivered, like a blown candle flame, when I came in and found only steamy, grubby, inarticulate Rex Whistler. Why have I dressed at all I asked. Then Lord David, then Bea Howe, then Mrs Quennell. That's all. So to dinner. And the boasting! Clive rattling out noble names; but I played my tricks: jumped over the candlestick; and co-operated with Clive in the great business of impressing. No, I don't think I like Clive's parties any more – I pick up too many thorns, one way and another. Anyhow, why not refuse the next party, and rummage on my own? My own pie is full enough.

Thursday 2 June
Lord David's party last night. Half across London. Derby night. Great motors full of men with buttonholes. A rose pink girl tripping across Shaftesbury Avenue hand in hand with a young man: all fluff and roses. Edwardes Square very large, leafy, silent, Georgian, refined; so to No. 41 with its white and green; a butler; an orange cat; Lord David and Elizabeth Bowen talking by the fire; then Puffin [Anthony Asquith], then John Sparrow. Not a good dinner: meagre, exiguous; and I took too many asparagus. All adroit kind nice talk – the note of the Asquiths and Cecils. "How very true" – "Yes, I agree entirely" – so different from Bloomsbury. There's more body to us. Still I don't complain. A little confabulation about Eddy [Sackville-West]; then about crying at crowds, at theatres, at films; what is tragic; about football. Talk about Auden and Naomi Mitchison: her review of Auden read aloud. Then they talked about the German youth movement; about bad people; about Murry; and I wore my new dress, too white and young perhaps; and so came home across London, and must now wash for Maynard's lunch and the Bernard Shaws – oh damn, oh damn – not an idea in my head or a wish to be brilliant.

Friday 3 June
I don't like old ladies who guzzle. My comment upon Ethel Smyth last night – no doubt a harsh one. But she champed and chopped; and squabbled over her duck; and then was over eaten and had to go home.

My comment upon the Shaws: he said "I am not sufficiently fond of myself to wish for immortality. I should like to be different. I should like to be a performer in music, and a mathematician. So I don't keep a diary. I destroy all my letters. Desmond MacCarthy says he's going to write my life – well, he may say so. He comes and talks – I can't tell the truth yet, about myself. The Webbs looked lonely somehow going off to Russia. I've always quarrelled with the Webbs. You see Webb has a gigantic faculty for absorbing information. And so, when I first knew him, I had to overcome an immense amount of useless knowledge. Webb would be much more effective if he'd one drop of the artist. But he has not one. Beatrice is in despair about it. Can't make a good speech therefore. People think my style as speaker is spontaneous, colloquial. It's the most artificial ever known. I've taken long railway journeys and spent them saying the letters of the alphabet aloud so as to make my vowels strike out. Then they forget I'm an Irishman – I think quicker than the English. No I don't mug things up – when I write history I don't read it. I imagine the sort of things people would have done and then I say they did them and then I find out facts – one always can – that prove it. The great pleasure of the Broadcasting to me is that I can sit at home and conduct the *Meistersinger* myself. I sit with the book of the score and conduct and I'm furious when they don't follow me." He is never still a moment – he clenches his fists – he flings himself this way and that; he sprang up to go, as if he were twenty-two, not seventy-four, as L. remarked. What life, what vitality! What immense nervous spring! That perhaps is his genius. Immense vivacity – and why I don't read him for pleasure. His face is bright red; his nose lumpy; his eyes sea green like a sailor's or a cockatoo's. He doesn't much notice who's there.

I heard Maynard say to Mrs Shaw "Well, we're about as bad as we can be. Never been so bad. We may go over the edge – but as its never been like this, nobody knows" – which was uttered in the low tone of a doctor saying a man was dying in the next room; but didn't want to disturb the company. This referred to the state of Europe, while we lunched – very well too.

Saturday 4 June

And last night we stopped the car in Hyde Park and I watched a people on the verge of ruin. How many Rolls Royces, and other low, pink, yellow, very powerful cars weren't booming through the park like giant dorbeetles, with luxurious owners, men and women, lying back, on their way to some party. A Rolls Royce means £5000 a year. Then the children in perambulators with nurses. Then the strollers and saunterers, that cloudy, rainy, thunder yellow evening. So back through the West End – more cars blocked; and we on the edge of a precipice.

Monday 13 June
Back from a good week-end at Rodmell – a week end of no talking, sinking at once into deep safe book reading; and then sleep: with the may tree like a breaking wave outside; and never a person to be seen, never an interruption: the place to ourselves: the long hours. Last week was such a scrimmage: oh so many people. Now Vita rings up: may she and Harold dine tonight; then Ethel; I look ahead to my fortnight's week end.

Saturday 18 June
John stays, on a revised basis, as adviser; and I am to consult and help him more, and not to sit here "with a red.cross on your door, so that I daren't come in". My advice is that he shall be more malleable, and less pernickety. He craves influence and authority, to publish the books of his friends; wishes to start a magazine; is poor; must economise. Am I too aloof – partly so as not to chatter, partly to get to my own work? Ought one to be more sympathetic; but oh so many people to see and things to fit in already; nevertheless I'll try, if the new method is to be tried. He says Leonard is "so deep: and plans things; and never comes out at once with what he means; so that I don't know how to behave". I daresay we've spent ten hours talking about all this.
   Nessa and Duncan's private view, Agnews.

Tuesday 28 June
I am trying to keep pace with the days and deliver the second *Common Reader* done on the last day of June – which I see with dismay is Thursday. It blazes, swoons, the heat. So hot yesterday – so hot.

Wednesday 6 July
Today is Wednesday and the *Common Reader* I confess is not yet quite done. But then – well, I had to re-write the last article, which I had thought so good, entirely. Many many people, too, and parties still to be transacted. These days have been very hot and busy.

Friday 8 July
And so I fainted, at the Ivy [Restaurant]: and had to be led out by Clive. A curious sensation. Feeling it come on; sitting still and fading out; then Clive by my side and a woman with salts. And the odd liberation of emotion in the cab with Clive; and the absolute delight of dark and bed: after that stony rattling and heat and Frankie [Birrell] shouting, and things being churned up, removed.

Monday 11 July
I will take a new pen and a new page to record the fact which is now a fact
that I have slipped a green rubber band round the *Common Reader*, second
series, and there it lies, at 10 minutes to one, ready to take upstairs. There
is no sense of glory; only of drudgery done. Now I'm taking a holiday.

Saturday 16 July
Stella Benson last night: as quiet, as controlled, white, drawn as usual, also
deaf; with steady honest eyes; said she had been to a great many parties.
"I just say nothing. I feel none of these people matters. They say how much
they liked my book [*Tobit Transplanted*] . . . I was given a medal. The old
gentleman couldn't remember what for. He pinned it on. I go back in
August. I hate Hong Kong. They play games. At Government House they
give you a slip of paper with names of games on it: you have to put a cross
next the one you play. Sitting out is one. James and I choose that. So we
sit out together." That was her style in a very weak but persistent voice;
she coughs; and then goes on with a mild persistent patience. The light
faded in the drawing room, and she sat there lying back, telling us in a very
low voice about the slave trade in Hong Kong.

Thursday 21 July
Oh but I'm so tired – I sometimes think people can't know what they do
to me when they ask me to 'see' them: how they hold me in the scorching
light: how I dry and shrivel: how I lie awake at night longing for rest –
this is true. But know that I'm to be pitchforked up into the light and the
glare again next day. Mary [Hutchinson] yesterday; Ethel today; Adrian
tomorrow; and Julia Strachey. Since Monday, Nessa, Angelica, Tom and
Elizabeth Bowen; Katherine [Furse] and [Mary Parker] Follett. And my
head aches; and my back; and I'm sapped; wilted. Never mind. I shall lie
in the cool at Monks House.

Friday 22 July
I do not like Ethel when she is doing the powerful stunt – or whatever
stunt it is: proclaiming that all is over; denouncing me; protesting her love;
whipping up a scene; being august; despairing; melodramatic and wobbly
and weak all at the same time. No I do not like it: and also I am bored.
This is the old fashioned version of an emotional scene – the tactics are to
leave the other person in a hole – where indeed I would willingly have
been left. Its the superficiality of these things that disenchants one: her lust
for emotion. Or so I felt.

Monks House, Rodmell

Friday 5 August

Yesterday L. came in to my room at breakfast and said Goldie is dead. One of those muddles apparently: had an operation, secretly, a week ago; Roger saw him on Tuesday; talked; supposed him to be recovering; he died suddenly that night, of an internal haemorrhage. These are the dismal details of the end of that fine charming spirit. At night L. and I talked of death again the second time this year; we may be like worms crushed by a motor car. There may be a reason; if so not one we, as human beings, can grasp. Goldie had some mystic belief.

And now we have been to Lewes races and seen the fat lady in black with parts of her person spilling over the shooting seat on which her bulk is so insecurely poised: seen the riff raff of sporting society all lined up in their cars with the dickies bulging with picnic baskets; heard the bark of bookies; and seen for a second the pounding straining horses with red faced jockeys lashing them pound by; and beyond, the downs this windy sunny day looked wild and remote; and I could rethink them into uncultivated land again.

So people will go on dying until we die, Leonard said. Lytton, Carrington, Goldie – all last August to be spoken to – or let go, alas, because of the many times one would see them. That is one of my results: not to let friends lapse. But what can one do? One has to follow one's bent – mine often to be moody, irritable, longing for solitude.

Wednesday 17 August

Shall I then describe how I fainted again? – That is the galloping horses got wild in my head last Thursday night as I sat on the terrace with L. We were watching the downs draw back into fine darkness after they had burnt like solid emerald all day. Now that was being softly finely veiled. And the white owl was crossing to fetch mice from the marsh. Then my heart leapt; and stopped; and leapt again; and I tasted that queer bitterness at the back of my throat; and the pulse leapt into my head and beat and beat, more savagely, more quickly. I am going to faint I said and slipped off my chair and lay on the grass. Oh no I was not unconscious. I was alive; but possessed with this struggling team in my head: galloping, pounding. I thought something will burst in my brain if this goes on. Slowly it muffled itself. I pulled myself up, and staggered, with what infinite difficulty and alarm, back back back – how long it seemed – to the house; and gained my room and fell on my bed. Then pain, as of childbirth; and then that too slowly faded; and I lay presiding, like a flickering light, like a most solicitous mother, over the shattered splintered fragments of my body. A very acute and unpleasant experience.

Saturday 20 August

A curious day in London yesterday. I said to myself, standing at L.'s window, 'Look at the present moment because its not been so hot for twenty-one years.' Coming back we had the car shut and the windscreen open – thus sat in a hot rough gale: the coolest place is the front seat of a car going at forty or fifty miles with the windscreen open. For ten days this heat has lasted. After my faint my head soon throbs: or so I think. I think, a little, of dying suddenly. And reflect well then go about eating and drinking and laughing and feeding the fish. Odd – the silliness one attributes to death – the desire one has to belittle it, and be found as Montaigne said, laughing with girls and good fellows.

Friday 2 September

After this the wind blew – but that's long past; and it is a sea fret today, as we had meant to go to Canterbury. As we had meant – but – behold Tom and Vivien [Eliot] – she wild as Ophelia – alas no Hamlet would love her, with her powdered spots, in white satin, L. said; Tom, poor man, all battened down as usual, prim, grey, making his kind jokes with her. Then her chops and changes. Where is my bag? Where – where – then a sudden amorous embrace for me – and so on: trailing about the garden – never settling – seizing the wheel of their car – suddenly telling Tom to drive – all of which he bears with great patience: feeling perhaps that his seven months of freedom draw near. In the middle of their tea the post came with an astonishing letter from John to say that he does not intend to carry out our agreement. He has left the Press. L. says he will send no answer. What could one say indeed? What a blessing! That egotistical young man with all his jealousies and vanities and ambitions, his weakness and changeableness, is no loss. But we – or L. has lost an infinity of time.

A happy lively summer this – and I enjoy my freak of writing *Flush*.

52 TAVISTOCK SQUARE, WCI

Sunday 2 October

Yes. I will allow myself a new nib. Odd how coming back here upsets my writing mood. We are off to Leicester tomorrow, to the Labour Party Conference. Then back to the fever of publishing. My *Common Reader* doesn't cause me a single tremor. I am reading D. H. Lawrence with the usual sense of frustration. I don't escape when I read him; what I want is to be made free of another world. This Proust does. To me Lawrence is airless, confined: I don't want this, I go on saying. And the repetition of one idea. I don't want that either. I don't want 'a philosophy' in the least. I don't believe in other people's reading of riddles. What I enjoy (in his *Letters*) is the sudden visualisation; but I get no satisfaction from his explanations of what he sees. And then its harrowing: this panting effort after something; and 'I have £6.10 left' and then Government hoofing him out, like a toad; and banning his book; the brutality of civilised society to this panting agonised man: and how futile it was. All this makes a sort of gasping in his letters. Then too I don't like strumming with two fingers – and the arrogance. After all English has one million words: why confine yourself to six? and praise yourself for so doing. But its the preaching that rasps me. I mean its so barren; so easy; giving advice on a system. He died though at forty-five. And why does Aldous say he was an 'artist'? Art is being rid of all preaching: things in themselves; whereas Lawrence would only say what proved something. I haven't read him of course. But in the *Letters* he can't listen beyond a point; must give advice; get you in to the system too. Hence his mind's schoolboy tweaking and smacking of anyone offered to him: Lytton, Bertie [Russell], Squire – His ruler coming down and measuring them. Why all this criticism of other people? Why not some system that includes the good?

Thursday 13 October

It was an odd sight – Desmond with Rachel on his arm. Everybody stood up. The white and red procession with the cross in front went ahead. Then very small, smooth, pale and sleek appeared Rachel and Desmond arm in arm. I have never seen him as a father. Now he was that – gentle, kind – leading his daughter. She was a wax work – with her diamond cross; very pale; very small; carrying a white book. Oh but the inadequacy of the service – the sense of its being the entirely obsolete and primitive voice of a defunct tribal magnate, laying down laws for the government of the tribe: and then these civilised sceptical people letting themselves pretend that they obey. That clogged and diluted all the real feeling. And David [Cecil]'s high collar and tails: and their sober decorous backs kneeling there: and the respectability and the wavering watery music: the perpetual compromise. The ceremony went decorously forward in that grey brown church [St Bartholomew the Great]. Now and then one heard a shout from the market. No I don't like the ceremony – oh I wanted some rapture – some precious stone to hold. None. None.

Today *The Common Reader* is out and I haven't given it a thought, being entirely absorbed in my Essay, which I began yesterday. But I still see the two doll figures kneeling – for all the world like a picture -- what do I mean? I'm too sleepy to say. And now for Spender.

Wednesday 2 November
He [Stephen Spender] is a rattle headed bolt eyed young man, raw boned, loose jointed, who thinks himself the greatest poet of all time. I daresay he is – its not a subject that interests me enormously at the moment. What does? My own writing of course. I have entirely remodelled my 'Essay'. Its to be an Essay-Novel, called *The Pargiters* – and its to take in everything, sex, education, life &c; and come, with the most powerful and agile leaps, like a chamois across precipices, from 1880 to here and now. That's the notion anyhow, and I have been in such a haze and dream and intoxication, declaiming phrases, seeing scenes, as I walk up Southampton Row that I can hardly say I have been alive at all, since the 10th October. Everything is running of its own accord into the stream, as with *Orlando*. Then of course, being so excited, all this incandescence led to the galloping horses in my heart the night before last. I lay in bed reasoning that I could not come smash. Death I defy you, &c. But it was a terrific effort, holding on to the reins. So at 2.30 I woke L. and asked, very reasonably, for ice, which he got me. And my horses calmed down – he was so sensible. But Ellie [Dr Rendel] came yesterday and says I am putting a strain on my heart; so I take this as permission not to go to parties, not to do anything I dislike. And that's a great discovery. I think I shall have thus a very reasonable happy winter, writing *The Pargiters*, but for God's sake, I must be careful.

Thursday 10 November
A queer thing that Ott should come, after all these years, old, shabby, tender, to my sofa; and I liked her; its her integrity that's sloppy; that's what we all slipped on. Can't tell the truth about love – but then that's so interesting, and not discreditable, considering her upbringing Welbeck, the young men servants. So she lent me her memoirs, full as they are of love letters, and copulation. I must now write to her.

Saturday 17 December
I have precisely four minutes before luncheon in which to record Rebecca West at dinner – oh yes a very clever woman, rather rubbed about the thorax; with a great supply of worldly talk; and much go and humour; a silky careening society voice; flowers from her afterwards to apologise for staying till 1.30. And then – oh ever so many people; and a wind up with L.'s family and then the Frys to dinner; and so to Rodmell on Tuesday.

Monday 19 December
Yes, today I have written myself to the verge of total extinction. By Heaven, I have written 60,320 words since October 11th. I think this must be far the quickest going of any of my books. But then those 60 thousand will have to be sweated and dried into 30 or 40 thousand – a great grind to come. Never mind. I have secured the outline and fixed a shape for the rest. I feel, for the first time, No I mustn't take risks crossing the road, till the book is done.

A very fruitful, varied and I think successful autumn – thanks partly to my tired heart: so I could impose terms; and I have never lived in such a race, such a dream, such a violent impulsion and compulsion – scarcely seeing anything but *The Pargiters*.

MONKS HOUSE, RODMELL

Friday 23 December
I must write off my dejected rambling misery – having just read over the 30,000 words of *Flush* and come to the conclusion that they won't do. Oh what a waste – what a bore! Four months of work, and heaven knows how much reading – not of an exalted kind either – and I can't see how to make anything of it. L. will be disappointed; and the money loss too – that's a bore. I took it up impetuously after *The Waves* by way of a change: no forethought in me; and so got landed; it would need a month's hard work – and even then I doubt it. And I'm thus led to end the year with a doleful plaint.

Saturday 31 December
I am so tired of polishing off *Flush* that I am taking a morning off, and shall use it here, in my lazy way, to sum up the whole of life. By that phrase I only mean I wish I could deliver myself of a picture of all my friends, thoughts, doings, projects at this moment. Vita is on the high seas, sailing to America. Our new car came, vicariously, yesterday – we are lent one. And I had a long letter from Ottoline, of sheer affection, and one still longer from Ethel Smyth, of dubious jealousy and suppressed temper and love strangled and out-bursting. And [Boris] Anrep wants to put me on the floor of the Bank of England as Clio, and – cards, thanks, catalogues of winter sales. And we shall be here till the 14th of January. And the dew pond is filling; the gold fish are dead; it is a clear pale blue eyed winter's day; and – and – and – my thoughts turn with excitement to *The Pargiters*, for I long to feel my sails blow out, and to be careering with Elvira, Maggie and the rest over the whole of human life.

And indeed I cannot sum this up, being tired in my head. I think of Lytton too. Yes, of course this autumn has been a tremendous revelation. It was a great season of liberation. Well – it is always doubtful how far one human being can be free. However, I secured a season of intoxicating exhilaration. Nor do I intend to let myself pay for it with the usual black despair. I intend to circumvent that supervening ghost – that which always trails its damp wings behind my glories. I shall be very wary. To suppress oneself and run freely out in joy – such is the perfectly infallible and simple prescription. And to use one's hands and eyes; to talk to people; to be a straw on the river, now and then – passive, not striving to say this is this. If one does not lie back and sum up and say to the moment, this very moment, Stay you are so fair, what will be one's gain, dying? No: stay, this moment. No one ever says that enough. I am now going in, to see L. and say Stay this moment.

1933

From January until April Vita Sackville-West and her husband were away on a lecture tour of America; Ethel Smyth's attempts to supplant her in Virginia's affections became increasingly intrusive and, though her visits could not always be evaded, Virginia for the most part fended her off by letter, pleading headache, absence, or other engagements. But for once she was not ill during the early months of the year, and was very fully occupied with her work and a lively social programme – so occupied indeed that she wrote no diary for five weeks in February and March. 'That silly book Flush' was finally polished off, sent to the printer in January, and the proofs corrected after Easter; it was published in October, having already been selected by the Book Society and the Book-of-the-Month-Club in New York, thus ensuring considerable sales. But* The Pargiters was Virginia's chief preoccupation throughout the year, varied by reading and preparing an article on Goldsmith for the* TLS. *In March another academic distinction – an Honorary Degree of Doctor of Letters – was offered to Virginia by Manchester University, and again declined on the grounds that she was opposed to writers accepting honours.*

The celebrated German–Jewish conductor Bruno Walter, introduced by Ethel Smyth, came to see the Woolfs in April; his passionate account, recorded by Virginia, of the evils of the Nazi régime (Hitler had become Chancellor of Germany in January) is her only reference to the growing menace of totalitarianism on the continent. But Fascist Italy held no terrors for the Woolfs; on 5 May they set off in their new car to drive through France to Siena and back, taking three weeks in all, an experience the more enjoyable since Virginia had been learning Italian and was thus able to talk to the people they encountered.

The summer in London was the usual mixture of work, duty (loyalty to Margaret Llewelyn Davies took Virginia to the Jubilee Congress of the Women's Co-operative Guild; family loyalty to visit her ailing half-brother Sir George Duckworth), lunch and dinner parties, 'seeing' people, weekends at Rodmell, to where she and Leonard removed for ten weeks at the end of July. Here it was much the same in a different setting – more people: an American authoress, the family, Vita, Ethel Smyth, E. M. Forster and T. S. Eliot, lately returned from America and separated from his wife; and others. Virginia's response to this country life fluctuated between delight and dejection, energy and exhaustion.

They returned to London and a busy publishing season, and this time Leonard fell ill. Once again Virginia concluded that the Hogarth Press claimed too much of their energies and should be given up; but it survived. Another illness took them to Croydon Airport, when they drove Vanessa and her younger son Quentin to catch an aeroplane, still an exceptional means of travel, for Switzerland where he was to spend months in a clinic for tubercular patients. Dining out with the Hutchinsons, Virginia observed the best-selling author Michael Arlen; and another dinner party, given by Clive Bell for her to meet Walter Sickert, was the outcome of a letter of admiration she wrote him after seeing an exhibition of his pictures; he responded by suggesting she should write about him, which she undertook to do. On 21 December the Woolfs went to Rodmell for Christmas.

1933

MONKS HOUSE, RODMELL

Thursday 5 January

I am so delighted with my own ingenuity in having after only ten years or so made myself, in five minutes, a perfect writing board, with pen tray attached - and besides I'm so glad to be quit of page 100 of *Flush* - that I can't help disporting myself on this free blue page, which thank God in heaven, needs no re-writing. It is a wet misty day; and I daresay we shall drive our new car twenty miles or so this afternoon, by way of a test. It is like travelling first instead of third.

Sunday 15 January

I have come out here, our last morning, to write letters, so, naturally, I write this book. But then I haven't written a line these three weeks - only typed *Flush*, which, Heaven be praised, I 'finished', almost without inverted commas, yesterday. Ah but my writing *Flush* has been gradually shoved out, as by a cuckoo born in the nest, by *The Pargiters*. How odd the mind's functions are! About a week ago, I began the making up of scenes - unconsciously: saying phrases to myself; and so, for a week, I've sat here, staring at the typewriter, and speaking aloud phrases of *The Pargiters*. This becomes more and more maddening. It will however all be run off in a few days, when I let myself write again.

52 TAVISTOCK SQUARE, WC1

Thursday 19 January

We began London briskly. [William] Plomer and Marjorie [Strachey] to dine; and we went to Sadler's Wells and saw *Pomona* with Nessa's designs - dresses, scenery - all very pale and bright - I mean Fra Angelico against a background of Cassis - but dear (said to be from dieu) knows I can't keep my wits at the ballet; can't throw a ring round so many wild horses - music, dancing, decoration; and so hop on my perch, and merely make parrot

332

noises of appreciation – when, at Fitzroy Street [Vanessa's studio], we all had hot sausages. Roger was there – is he older, less volatile? He makes his signal to Helen sooner than of old and drives off in that blind bull of a car – but not before, as I maliciously observed, he had cross-questioned me about his lectures. This insistent egotism has its charm. I never asked him to read my essays.

Saturday 21 January
Well, *Flush* lingers on and I cannot despatch him. That's the sad truth. I always see something I could press tighter, or enwrap more completely. There's no trifling with words – can't be done: not when they're to stand 'for ever'. So I am battening down my *Pargiters* say till Wednesday – it shan't be later, I swear.

Thursday 26 January
Well, *Flush* is, I swear, despatched. Nobody can say I don't take trouble with my little stories. And now, having bent my mind for five weeks sternly this way, I must unbend them the other – the Pargiter way. No critic ever gives full weight to the desire of the mind for change. Now if I ever had the wits to go into the Shakespeare business I believe one would find the same law there – tragedy, comedy, and so on.

I think the Beau Monde has given me up; so I say I will rout further in the bran pie; and go to my Club and meet young working women. I am going to learn Italian.

Thursday 2 February
No we are not deserted by the world – oh dear no. And Galsworthy died two days ago, it suddenly struck me, walking just now by the Serpentine after calling on Mrs Woolf (who's been dying – is recovering). Galsworthy's dead; and Arnold Bennett told me he simply couldn't stick Galsworthy. That stark man lies dead.

Friday 17 February
I steal time from my Italian verbs. Yes I think I know them. I am having two lessons weekly from Bianca; she suggests three; but as I have to get in Ethel &c. Oh yesterday it was like being a snail shell and having a thrush tapping till the beak of her incessant voice broke my skull. And now she goes to Bath for five weeks – yes, to my relief I own. Because I can't bear being a snail shell. And she is so positive, so insistent. Being Ethel is so habitual to her.

I'm launched again in *The Pargiters*, in this blank season of the year – Nessa at Charleston, Clive in Jamaica, Roger in Tangier, Vita in America

– which of my friends is left? But Desmond dined the night before last; Morgan came in last night; [Winifred] Holtby today – so there's no lack of people.

Saturday 25 March

It is an utterly corrupt society I have just remarked, speaking in the person of Elvira Pargiter, and I will take nothing that it can give me &c &c; now, as Virginia Woolf, I have to write – oh dear me what a bore – to the Vice Chancellor of Manchester University and say that I refuse to be made a Doctor of Letters. Lord knows how I'm to put Elvira's language into polite journalese. What an odd coincidence! that real life should provide precisely the situation I was writing about! Nothing would induce me to connive at all that humbug. Nor would it give me, even illicitly, any pleasure. I really believe that Nessa and I are without the publicity sense. Now for the polite letters. Dear Vice Chancellor –

Tuesday 28 March

The polite letters have been sent. So far I have had, nor could have had any answer. No, thank Heaven, I need not emerge from my fiction in July to have a tuft of fur put on my head.

It is the finest spring ever known – soft, hot, blue, misty. Dinner with Lady Rhondda. I felt her a disappointed woman. Should have had ten children perhaps. She was sitting alone, shawled, dowdy, in an old Hampstead flat with a garden with great trees. She is what they call, I expect, 'inhibited' – something tentative, furtive. Discussed *Time & Tide*. She lives for *Time & Tide*. Then on to Clive; back from Jamaica. "The steward came in; and was surprised to find a young lady stark naked brushing her teeth." True Clive.

Thursday 6 April

Oh I'm so tired! I've written myself out over *The Pargiters* this last lap. This is a time of ending. I've ever so many people to see. Ott tomorrow. The people of Manchester have written, very politely, with additional respect for me, because I don't take honours. Nessa and the others at Charleston. Last night Lord Olivier, a jolly old bore, has been a dog in his day, dined here. And Pippa came in later – grown very thick, but looks unhappy.

Thursday 13 April

No I have worked myself too dry this time. There is not one idea left in the orange. But we go [to Rodmell] today, and I shall sun, with only a few books. No I will *not* write; I will *not* see people. But indeed I can't find words – use the wrong ones – that's my state: the familiar state after these three months writing -- what fun that book is to me! And pressing in Italian, and seeing a mint of people - that state I say is quite familiar; and will vanish; yes, and then there's Italy to come. I have my new corduroys. And Ethel is 'cutting the painter' (between us - for the hundredth time).

Tuesday 25 April
No, we didn't see nobody at Rodmell. Lydia and Maynard arrived before we had been there half an hour; and we dined with them. That's all over – our ten days. Yes; I should now be correcting *Flush* proofs - I doubt that little book to some extent: but I'm in a doubting mood: the scrambled mood of transience, for on Friday 5th we go to Siena; so I can't settle.

But *The Pargiters*. I think this will be a terrific affair. I must be bold and adventurous. I want to give the whole of the present society - nothing less: facts, as well as the vision. And to combine them both. I mean, *The Waves* going on simultaneously with *Night and Day*. Is this possible? And there are to be millions of ideas but no preaching - history, politics, feminism, art, literature - in short a summing up of all I know, feel, laugh at, despise, like, admire, hate and so on.

Friday 28 April
We got out of the car last night and began walking down to the Serpentine. A summer evening. Chestnuts in their crinolines, bearing tapers; grey green water and so on. Suddenly L. bore off; and there was Shaw, dwindled shanks, white beard; striding along. We talked, by a railing, for fifteen minutes. He stood with his arms folded, very upright, leaning back; teeth gold tipped. Very friendly. That is his art, to make one think he likes one. A great spurt of ideas. "You forget that an aeroplane is like a car - it bumps - We went over the Great Wall. I caught the Chinese looking at us with horror - that we should be human beings! Of course the tour cost thousands; yet to see us, you'd think we hadn't the price of the fare to Hampton Court. Oh but my publicity! Its terrifying. An hour's bombardment at every port. I found myself on a platform with the whole university round me. They began shouting We want Bernard Shaw. So I told them that every man at twenty-one must be a revolutionary. After that of course the police imprisoned them by dozens. Oh I could only stand the voyage by writing. I've written three or four books. I like to give the public full weight. Books should be sold by the pound. What a nice little dog. But aren't I keeping you and making you cold" (touching my arm). Two men stopped along the path to look. Off he strode again on his dwindled legs. I said Shaw likes us. L. thinks he likes nobody. What will they think of Shaw in fifty years? He is seventy-six he said; too old for the tropics.

Saturday 29 April

Last night – to relieve myself for a moment from correcting that silly book *Flush* – oh what a waste of time – I will record Bruno Walter. He is a swarthy, fattish, man; not at all smart. Not at all the 'great conductor'. He is a little Slav, a little semitic. He is very nearly mad; that is, he can't get 'the poison' as he called it of Hitler out of him. "You must not think of the Jews" he kept on saying; "You must think of this awful reign of intolerance. You must think of the whole state of the world. It is terrible – terrible. That this meanness, that this pettiness, should be possible! Our Germany – which I loved – with our tradition – our culture – We are now a disgrace." Then he told us how you can't talk above a whisper. There are spies everywhere. He had to sit in the window of his hotel in Leipzig a whole day, telephoning. All the time soldiers were marching. They never stop marching. And on the wireless, between the turns, they play military music. Horrible horrible! He hopes for the monarchy as the only hope. He will never go back there. We must band together. We must refuse to meet any German. We must say that they are uncivilised. We will not trade with them or play with them – we must make them feel themselves outcasts – not by fighting them; by ignoring them. Then he swept off to music. He has the intensity – genius? – which makes him live everything he feels. Described conducting: must know every player.

• • •

52 TAVISTOCK SQUARE, WC1

Tuesday 30 May

Yes but of all things coming home from a holiday is undoubtedly the most damned. Never was there such aimlessness, such depression. Can't read, write or think. There's no climax here. Comfort yes: but the coffee's not so good as I expected. And my brain is extinct – literally hasn't the power to lift a pen. What one must do is to set it – my machine I mean – on the rails and give it a push. Lord – how I pushed yesterday to make it start running along Goldsmith again. There's that half finished article. Lord Salisbury said something about dished up speeches being like the cold remains of last night's supper. I see white grease on the pages of my article. Today it's a little warmer – tepid meat: a slab of cold mutton. It occurs to me that this stage, my depressed state, is the state in which most people usually are.

Wednesday 31 May

I think I have now got to the point where I can write for four months straight ahead at *The Pargiters*. Oh the relief – the physical relief! I feel as if I could hardly any longer keep back – that my brain is being tortured by always butting against a blank wall – I mean *Flush*, Goldsmith, motoring through Italy; now, tomorrow, I mean to run it off. And suppose only nonsense comes? I'm disoriented completely after four weeks holiday – no three – but tomorrow we go to Rodmell again.

I thought, driving through Richmond last night, something very profound about the synthesis of my being: how only writing composes it; how nothing makes a whole unless I am writing; now I have forgotten what seemed so profound. Oh the agitation, oh the discomfort of this mood.

Tuesday 20 June
It is a very ugly thing, a ceremony. I detest them more and more. This refers to my waste of a morning at the W[omen's] C[o-operative] G[uild] Jubilee today. Margaret and Lilian, in grey blue and coffee colour – how characteristic! – presented a banner. The great hall full. The women all in pinks and blues. Fine old housekeepers; massive; determined. Now and then a great laugh; and very queer accents. But all was ceremony; and they say things that aren't true: they say we are on the brink of a new world; they talk of the triumph of co-operation. That's why I hate ceremonies – not a word that fits – all wind blown, gaseous, with elementary emotions. Years ago I got something out of the mere conglomeration, the stir, the multitude. But today, I was not annihilated, dispersed; I said to myself *The Pargiters* is more real, truer, harder, more veined with blood than all this, and longed to be back, working. How odd to spend a morning merely vacant, regardant! How many I spend concentrated! Then we shook, and smiled with others intervening, Margaret's, Lilian's hands; and found a back way out.

Monday 26 June
The present moment. 7 o'clock on June 26th: L. printing; hot; thunderous; I after reading *Henry IV Part I* saying what's the use of writing; reading, imperfectly, a poem by Leopardi; the present moment, in my studio. A bucket banged in the mews; dog barks; woman, 'I didn't know if you were out here.' Leaves door open; far away horns; a bee buzzing. King lays stone of London University. Doctors, scarlet, purple, in streets; poor little students in gowns; so to dine, and read; and music; thunder, I daresay; and so to open my windows, and go up: the moment done.

Thursday 6 July
Dinner at Roger's yesterday. Company: Sacheverell Sitwells, [Gerald] Brenans, Oliver [Strachey]. I sat next Georgia [Sitwell] and Roger. Talk of patent medicines. 'And then I found it was an aphrodisiac' Georgia says.

She buys every patent medicine, by way of sedative. Bounds, abounds, halloos dogs on the lawn: brown chocolate eyed; vital as they say, not intellectual. Made the salad with cheese. Mrs Brenan said to be sympathetic and soft and amusing by L. All chatter. Stayed late. Not much satisfaction – yet amusing enough, as such things are.

Also to sit with George [Duckworth] – a solid mound in pink pyjamas: Margaret tender and solicitous; given eau de Cologne; also Roger's show. Two days of misery writing Goldsmith, forced respite from *Pargiters*.

Friday 7 July

Being headachy after *Pargiters* and Goldsmith and ever so many people I have spent the whole morning reading old diaries, and am now (ten to one) much refreshed. This is by way of justifying these many written books. And we have a party tonight – Wests, Hutchinsons, Plomer – so I need rest my head. The diary amuses me.

Monday 10 July

And then I was in 'one of my states' – how violent, how acute, and walked in Regent's Park in black misery and had to summon my cohorts in the old way to see me through, which they have done more or less. A note made to testify to my old ups and downs; many of which go unrecorded though they are less violent I think than they used to be. But how familiar it was – stamping along the road, with gloom and pain constricting my heart; and the desire for death in the old way all for two, I daresay careless words.

It seems possible that Tom has finally deserted Vivien. Jack Hutch came to our frosty sticky party, with the meticulous fish blooded cultivated Andrews – Rebecca [West (Mrs Andrews)] merely a hard painted woman, that night, living in society – and Hutch told us how Vivien has heard by cable that Tom sailed [from America] on 26th and he has not arrived. She has by today worked herself into frenzy – in bed, with a nurse; and then Jack telephoned to Faber [Eliot's publisher] – L.'s idea – and they say mysteriously that they cannot discuss the matter on the telephone, but if Vivien will pull herself together she will realise that there is no reason for anxiety. This we interpret to mean that Tom is back; has told Faber that he is parting from her; but it is kept secret until he gives leave – which he may do today. I should expect that after his six months thought and absence he has decided to make the break here: has warned Vivien and provided for her. But she shuts the letters in the cupboard with the sealed string. L. is made her executor.

Thursday 20 July
This was quite a correct statement of the Eliot position. He has left her 'irrevocably'; and she sits meanwhile in a flat decorated with pictures of him, and altars, and flowers. We dine with the Hutchinsons tonight, and shall I expect found some sort of Vivien fund. It is said that there is a convent next door to Mary in which she might pass her days, praying for Tom.

I am again in full flood with *The Pargiters* after a week of very scanty pages.

MONKS HOUSE, RODMELL

Sunday 30 July
Settled in here again. A question how far places influence one's mood. Certain thoughts I always think: the downs spoilt, could we move, &c, leading to a well known round. Quentin ill with pleurisy; may have to have an operation. This is the first illness at Charleston. We dine there tonight. But I am organising life here, and so far rather well. Reading and walking and swimming into lucid depths, powerfully – that's how I put it. And people impend, but can be shelved for the moment.

Tuesday 8 August
Since we came here I have been twice to Charleston; seen the Keyneses; been to Worthing; had Elizabeth Read (a nice shrewd hard girl with a public mind) to tea; the Easedales and Norman Stewart (a clever, good fellow, scientist) to tea; expect Mrs Nef at three to discuss her scandalous memoirs; we go to London on Friday and Ethel comes on Sunday. Is this peace? I'm heavy brained today – its been so hot; I have read Mrs Nef from 10 to 12.20. Scandals about USA: but I am sworn to secrecy. I imagine a pretty youngish jumpy intellectual-fashionable American, completely disoriented; writes rather well; interesting; but all at sea.

Saturday 12 August
So naturally after Mrs Nef I was so tired – I shivered and shook. I went to bed for two days and slept I daresay seven hours, visiting the silent realms again. It strikes me – what are these sudden fits of complete exhaustion? I come in here to write: can't even finish a sentence; and am pulled under; now is this the sub-conscious pulling me down into her? the refusal of some part of the mechanism? Not quite. Because I'm not evading anything. I long to write *The Pargiters*. No. I think the effort to live in two spheres: the novel; and life; is a strain; Nefs almost break me, because they strain me so far

from the other world; I only want walking and perfectly spontaneous childish life with L. and the accustomed when I'm writing at full tilt; to have to behave with circumspection and decision to strangers wrenches me into another region; hence the collapse.

Thursday 24 August
A week ago, having got my wind again, I dipped into *The Pargiters*, and determined to sweat it bare of flesh before going on, accumulating more scenes. I am rearranging too, all the first part, so as to bring it together. The death happens in the first chapter now. I have just killed Mrs Pargiter and can't shoot ahead to Oxford. For the truth is these little scenes embroil one, just as in life; and one can't switch off to a different mood all in a second. And now I have spent the morning reading the *Confessions* of Arsène Houssaye left here yesterday by Clive. What a vast fertility of pleasure books hold for me! I think I could happily live here and read forever. It is true, we have many interruptions. Yesterday, after knocking against a wild Alsatian that ran into the car – we gave him a great bang – he lay squirming – dead, I thought, then reeled up and went galloping over the field, unhurt, though he broke our lamps and bent the mudguard – after this unpleasant shock, Clive came and Julian and Frances Marshall, and played bowls. Still, we see too many people, to my view: the Kingsley Martins, who are to me mentally and physically unattractive people; she is ugly, stringy, earnest, plain. Kingsley eats so sloppily. And they force themselves upon us. Into the bargain, I have heard from Tom. Tom is all artifice and quips and quirks. A defence. One of these days perhaps he'll give up the trick, with marriage, or perhaps religion. All the same, our quiet days, in between times, are rightly balanced, full of peace, and possibilities. How happy, when people go, to get our dinner, and sit alone, and go to bed in my airy room, where the rising sun on the apples and asparagus wakes me, if I leave the curtain open. A happy day today without visitors.

Sunday 27 August
[Yesterday] morning we went in and found Lewes in festival – the corporation fidgetting about on a doorstep covered in dull red: the local tradesmen habited in blue robes with thin strips of fur, because the troops were coming, on their economy march to Arundel. We ran into them; dirty men in shirtsleeves, marching, with the flaps of their caps let down over their necks, it was so hot. The natives of Lewes stood at the bottom of Station Street waving handkerchiefs, bobbing their umbrellas up and down. Not an inspiring sight – the British army.

And I forgot to say that *Flush* has been chosen by the American Book Society. Lord!

Wednesday 30 August
And two days ago, sitting in the garden at Charleston, Clive in his queer jerky way said he had very bad news of Francis Birrell and brought out a letter from Raymond [Mortimer]. Francis has a tumour on his brain and is to be operated on, perhaps, today. So all night I dreamt of him, my dream giving me, as my dreams often do, the essence of a relationship which in real life will never find expression. I remember sitting beside him on a sofa, and how we kissed and kissed, as friends; though in my dream I do not think that I knew he was ill. I am rather haunted by it. Think of waiting all yesterday, for an operation which may well be fatal. What should I have felt had I been him? And why was I not him? The sense of friends dying is a very terrible one.

Saturday 2 September
With that usual dread of asking for news on the telephone, I rang up Raymond on Thursday and heard to my extreme relief, that Francis's case is not so bad nearly as it seemed. The growth is small, thought to be on the outside, and there seems no reason why he should not recover. Curious how all one's fibres seem to expand and fill with air when anxiety is taken off; curious also to me the intensity of my own feelings: I think imagination, the picture making power, decks up feelings with all kinds of scenes, so that one goes on thinking, instead of localising the event. All very mysterious. But anyhow I expanded, and felt very fond of that dear old rattling milk lorry, and hoped he would see me out. But let us think no more of death. Its life that matters, to quote my quotation from Montaigne.

Suddenly in the night I thought of 'Here and Now' as a title for *The Pargiters*.

L. is having the new pond made, the old one re-grouted, and is going to pave the front garden. *Flush*, I think with some pleasure, has made these extravagances possible.

I am reading with extreme greed a book by Vera Brittain, called *The Testament of Youth*. Not that I much like her. But her story, told in detail, without reserve, of the war, and how she lost lover and brother, and dabbled her hands in entrails, and was forever seeing the dead, and eating scraps, and sitting five on one WC, runs rapidly, vividly across my eyes. A very good book of its sort. The new sort, the hard anguished sort, that the young write; that I could never write. Nor has anyone written that kind of book before. Why now? What urgency is there on them to stand bare in public? She feels that these facts must be made known, in order to help – what? Herself partly I suppose. And she has the social conscience. But I give her credit for having lit up a long passage to me at least. I read and read and read.

Sunday 10 September
Why am I sitting here at 10.30 on a Sunday morning, writing diary, not novel? Because of dear old Tom largely. Twenty-four hours (short interval for sleep) solid conversation, preluded by two hours flimsy conversation with the Hutchinsons. And at 1.30 Rosamond [Lehmann] and Wogan [Philipps, her husband] to lunch; and at 4.30 Charleston to tea. Hence I am sitting here. Tomorrow, in the divine peace of Monday, I shall walk on the downs and think of Tom and my parched lips with some degree of pleasure. He is ten years younger: hard, spry, a glorified boy scout in shorts and yellow shirt. He is enjoying himself very much. He is tight and shiny as a wood louse (I am not writing for publication). But there is well water in him, cold and pure. Yes I like talking to Tom. But his wing sweeps curved and scimitar-like round to the centre, himself. He's settling in with some severity to being a great man. At forty-six he wants to live, to love; he has seen nothing, nobody, for the last ten years. We had it out about Vivien at breakfast. Some asperity on Tom's part. He won't admit the excuse of insanity for her – thinks she puts it on. I thought him a little resentful of all the past waste and exaction. I gather he will see a good deal of us. And we agreed about the infamy of teaching English; the idiocy of lectures; the whole hierarchy of professor, system and so on; at any rate I got him to go some way with me in denouncing Oxford and Cambridge. He learnt (1) self confidence at Oxford; (2) how to write plain English – that's all. I daresay though he will become Professor of Poetry at Oxford one of these days. His father was a brick merchant in St Louis; and they lived in the slums among vacant lots; and his father always gave away money; and died, alas, in 1919 before Tom had become – well, happily his mother lived to see him what she called (and I daresay Tom too) a great man.

Saturday 23 September
This summer, I may say by way of criticism, and as a warning, has been too broken up with people. Next year I intend to be more circumspect. For the past fortnight I have lived, I say, as other people live – that is outwardly. And it is a thorough wet day. The ponds are filling. L.'s new pond and garden are almost done, and surprisingly good, I think. The summer is put away folded up in the drawer with other summers. By God's grace we may get ten or twelve days without visitors before going back, but I say this not with conviction. The truth is, I like it when people actually come; but I love it when they go. Old Ethel came, grown stout. And we go to Brighton today to meet Morgan, and I shall read my memoir tonight, and so consider myself quit of all duties to my friends. Monday begins my holiday.

Tuesday 26 September
I had so much of the most profound interest to write here – a dialogue of
the soul with the soul – and I have let it all slip – why? Because of feeding
the gold fish, of looking at the new pond, of playing bowls. Nothing remains
now. I forget what It was about. Happiness. The perfect day, which was
yesterday. And so on.

Monday 2 October
Yes. I had to write about the Memoir Club. Then they all came over, and
we sat on the terrace; eleven people here. That's all over. Its October now;
and we have to go to Hastings [Labour Party] Conference tomorrow and
Wednesday, to Vita, and then back to London. I opened this book in order
to make one of my self-admonishments previous to publishing a book.
Flush will be out on Thursday and I shall be very much depressed, I think,
by the kind of praise. They'll say its 'charming', delicate, ladylike. And it
will be popular. Well now I must let this slip over me without paying it
any attention. I must concentrate on *The Pargiters*.

Saturday 7 October
And now, letters, packing, going from the lodge to the house; a damp dull
day so far, but it will clear. A very crowded gay summer in its way. Too
crowded; but what happiness, coming back that night from London with
L. for example: the country at midnight. And going up early; and bowls;
and our solitary evenings; and cooking dinner.

52 TAVISTOCK SQUARE, WC1

Monday 9 October
Back again and our burden is on us. Mrs Woolf yesterday; today David
Cecil; tomorrow Nessa Quentin Julian lunch; Hugh Walpole tea; Thursday
Vita and [her sister-in-law] Mrs St Aubyn; and so it begins, with Sibyl and
Rosamond in the background. I'm through the *Flush* wave though. A small
one, compared with others. Desmond praises; *Morning Post* tears me between
the rough, coarse yellow feeble teeth of poor Mr Grigson. So its over.

Friday 20 October
Did I say I was going to write *Here and Now?* Not a word done. L. had
influenza. Up and about in two days of course. But last night I came to the
decision to stop the career of the Hogarth Press; to revert to Richmond
days. What is the use of drudging and sweating and curtailing Siena and
entirely obliterating all Italy England Ireland and Greece for the sake of

publishing Susan Lawrence and bad novels? No. Here we stop and take a fresh course. We go to Rodmell tomorrow and I shall there broach the new scheme. Look, I can't write, can't hold a pen, for all the bother and the worry. Its true we've had the devil's own week. But to me the Press has lost its spring and balance, and could regain it if it now made a constriction to the old ideals. We might start the magazine.

Sunday 29 October
Yesterday the *Granta* said I was now defunct. *Orlando, Waves, Flush* represent the death of a potentially great writer. This is only a rain drop; I mean the snub some little pimpled undergraduate likes to administei, just as he would put a frog in one's bed. But enough. Raymond came yesterday: Francis is still very much paralysed.

Sunday 12 November
I ought to have made a note on Nessa and the aeroplane -- last Friday week – at Croydon. We took them there at 7. Had to be up by moonlight at 6.30. Drove across an empty delicately tinted London; Croydon a great space like a green race course. We stood on the top of the roof; saw the aeroplane whirl, till the propellors were lost to sight – simply evaporated; then the aeroplane takes a slow run, circles and rises. This is death I said, feeling how the human contact was completely severed. Up they went with a sublime air and disappeared like a person dying, the soul going. And we remained. I saw the plane become a little mark on the sky.

Thursday 23 November
Being too tired after dining with the Hutches last night to meet Michael Arlen to produce the finished article in *Here and Now*, perhaps I had better produce the raw. It was a real party – that is I wore my velvet dress. But I took it in my stride. And I had – oh voluminously – all Michael Arlen's confession, as I expected. He made £50,000 out of *The Green Hat*, which money he has perpetually to atone for – as by talking of D. H. Lawrence, and how he escaped his influence, how he made his own life, how he married his own wife, a dumb Greek called Atalanta - silent, he said, but a perfect lady – and has two children and can keep them all, with drains, games, servants – all this is protest and justification. Now he is writing an intelligent novel, from real experience, lacking to highbrows. Yet oh Mrs Woolf how I envy Aldous Huxley his background – his education. I was at a third rate public school, and lived in Earl's Court. His father died of a broken heart when Roumania came into the war. A little scraping dingy porous clammy monkey faced man.

Wednesday 29 November
I think I've got rid of vanity: of Virginia. Oh what a riddance. I've not read an article on me by a man called Peel in the *Criterion*. I feel this is a great liberation. I have cut the string that ties me to that quivering bag of nerves – all its gratifications and acute despair. One sees people lunging and striking at a thing like a straw horse and its not me at all. I sit back in comfort and look round. I wonder if Nessa has always been like this? It is calming. It is dignified. One does not seek uneasily for opinions on oneself.

Thursday 7 December
I was walking through Leicester Square just now when I read Death of Noted Novelist on the poster. And I thought of Hugh Walpole. But it is Stella Benson. Then why write anything immediately? I did not know her, but have a sense of those fine patient eyes; the weak voice; the cough; and sense of oppression. She sat on the terrace with me at Rodmell. And now, so quickly, it is gone, what might have been a friendship. Its like the quenching of something – her death out there in China; and I sitting here, and writing about her. How mournful the afternoon seems, with the newspaper carts dashing up Kingsway – 'Death of Noted Novelist' on the placard. A very fine steady mind; much suffering; suppressed. There seems to be some sort of reproach to me in her death, as in Katherine Mansfield's. I go on, and they cease. Why? Why not my name on the posters? And I have a feeling of the protest each might make: gone with their work unfinished – each so suddenly. Stella was forty-one. A dreary island, she lived on, talking to Colonels.

Sunday 17 December
I finished part 4 of *Here and Now* yesterday – therefore indulge in a contemplative morning. To freshen my memory of the war, I read some old diaries. How close the tears come, again and again; as I read of L. and me at The Green: our quarrels; how he crept into my bed with a little purse, and so on; how we reckoned our income and I was given tea free for a treat. The sense of all that floating away for ever down the stream, unknown for ever: queer sense of the past swallowing so much of oneself. And today we make a loop with the past by going in our grand car to see Margaret and Lilian. Well we are very happy. I think we live very fully, freely, and adventurously. In short, what we made of that strange prelude is good.

I dined with Clive to meet Sickert the other night. Sickert is sunk and old till warmed with wine. He scarcely eats. At last he expanded, and sang a French song and kissed Nessa's hand – spontaneously; mine more formally. I think a difficult old man probably. But the ingrained artist.

Laughter – extravagance. How he was born in Germany, but not German. And lived at Munich till he was eight; and the German maid met the mad King – Sickert branches off. Then he went to Reading, a school kept by a drunken old woman, who beat a boy who had broken his arm. "And we thirty little wretches lay there cowed." How far he wants me to write about him, I don't know. I suspect he is changeable: that he forgets. He gets up at 5 and goes to his garage studio at 7 and has difficulty in lighting his stove. He reads three papers. He wore a pilot's cap with a green brim, but no overcoat, though it was freezing cold. He says one paints – let me see – the canvases galloped towards me. A fine Roman head, crisp hair, thick over the ears. Small dark eyes, broad forehead. "Oh Roger's a darling – but dear me . . ." great jokes about Roger. And so we went on, a little wine-flown, but friendly and communicative, and living on our capital – I mean that we were all artists – free masonry. I can't feel very sure though of any fact or relationship – I've not seen him these ten years, and then only to sing and joke. Yet he's chiselled, severe, has read: was reading Goldoni he said. And Flaubert's letters. And is *Madame Bovary* good? I'm a literary painter, romantic – You are the only person who understands me – kissing my hand. So home in the frost.

Thursday 21 December
This is the relic of a morning when I should tidy, pack, write letters and so on. We lunch at quarter to one, and then go, this yellow cold morning. No longer the great transition that it used to be.

1934

After returning to London from Rodmell in the middle of January, Virginia was at once caught up in a round of social engagements and by the end of the month was forced to rest – rest disturbed by the incursion of workmen carrying out improvements and redecorations to 52 Tavistock Square at the landlord's behest. This activity aggravated the underlying tensions with Nelly and led to rows, which corroded Virginia's peace of mind until she finally dismissed her. Nelly left at Easter after nearly eighteen years with the Woolfs, and was replaced by Mabel Haskins.

Virginia continued working on The Pargiters *(or as she now often called it,* Here and Now*), and finished her essay 'Sickert – A Conversation' after spending Easter at Rodmell (it was published by the Hogarth Press as a one-and-sixpenny pamphlet in October), and at the end of April set off for a fortnight's holiday in Ireland. Virginia had first met the novelist Elizabeth Bowen in 1932; and an invitation to visit her in her Irish home provided the impetus for the Woolfs' tour. They stayed a night at Bowen's Court, drove westwards to County Kerry – where they read in* The Times *of George Duckworth's death – on to Galway City and home by way of Dublin, Holyhead, and Stratford-on-Avon. This holiday was succeeded by a bout of ill-health which lingered off and on through the exceptionally hot summer days, frustrating Virginia's longing to press ahead with* The Pargiters. *At the end of June she was shaken by the horrifying news of the Nazi purge in Germany, when some 1200 people were killed on Hitler's orders.*

At Rodmell too there were domestic changes: Annie vacated the Woolfs' cottage on her marriage and her place was taken by another local girl, Louie Everest, who was to remain their servant until Leonard's death. But their ten weeks' country relaxation was clouded by anxiety over Frankie Birrell's operations, and then shattered by the unexpected death of Roger Fry on 9 September. Despite these distresses and the usual incursions of innumerable visitors, Virginia succeeded in reaching the end of the first draft of her book.

In London again, Virginia was agitated by an attack from Wyndham Lewis in his book Men Without Art, *which it took all her resolution and philosophy to overcome; and Roger Fry's death left a grievous void in her intimate circle. The idea was mooted that Virginia should write his life, a challenge which interested her, though she foresaw that Roger's sister Margery, his literary executor, might impose constraints. Meanwhile she faced up to the task of re-reading and re-writing* The Pargiters. *The sombre year ended with visits to the dying Frankie Birrell before the Woolfs departed before Christmas for three weeks at Monks House.*

1934

Tuesday 16 January

I have let all this time – three weeks at Monks – slip because I was there so divinely happy and pressed with ideas – another full flood of *Pargiters* or *Here and Now*. So I never wrote a word of farewell to the year; and now we are back again. (And have I a touch of the flue?)

Tuesday 30 January

Rather a rush of people; and a dinner to meet Noel Coward at Sibyl's on a cold foggy night. Nessa painting me again. Christmas mercifully over. Nessa very hard up. Question how to make money. Rather an old wives talk. Children, money, education, ways of life. Yesterday rather headachy; sleepy; strange trances in which I make up the last sentence read; to bed; sleep. Today, writing *Here and Now*, which draws out – hence my headache. Lunch with L.; went to the Danish Laundry about his collars. Women ironing. Back room with more women standing. Coppers I daresay downstairs. Looked at flats; L. home to print, I to wander to the Law Courts. Penetrated from end to end. Judge's Chambers: a kind of vault. King's Bench; &c. People scurrying; my sense of guilt at having no business there. So to bus; home.

Wednesday 14 February

But it was rather a bad headache: ten days recumbent, sleeping, dreaming, dipping into oh dear how many different books, how capriciously. And so to Rodmell for the week-end, and the bees buzzing in the hyacinths; the earth emerging very chastened and sharpened from winter under a veil; which became fog as we drove up, and is fog today. In addition, the house rings with the clamour of electricians: the new bath water engine being inserted; and then the Surveyor comes and says we are weighting the floors down with books: a heavy bill threatens; so out to buy ink for my new Waterman, with which I am to take notes for a new *Common Reader*. Now

I have just refused the National Portrait Gallery offer to draw me, thank God, and am very cautiously revising 'Sickert'.

Friday 16 February
Five minutes here before going to lunch with Nessa. A great Nelly row yesterday: which I hereby declare the last. It was about the workmen and her day out, and the end was that we had eggs for lunch and were forced to dine at the Cock, expensively and badly. No more of this, I say, and anticipate many days of ill ease, some violent scenes, and then pray God, after Easter, peace. Finished my Sickert article all the same. I put off *Here and Now* till next week.

Sunday 18 February
And I began *Here and Now* again this morning, Sunday, at the point where I left off all but three weeks ago for my headache. Here I note that from two to three weeks is the right space. It has not gone cold, as after six weeks; I still carry it in my mind.

The new electric boiler in and boiling our bath water this morning. The King of Belgium killed mountaineering. All last week they were fighting in Vienna: this somehow comes closer than usual to our safe London life: the people shot down.

Tuesday 20 February
To note the interesting stages of the duel with Nelly. Today I said, do you want this quarrel to go on? I would like to stop it now; but I shall discuss it later. Whereupon she said she wished it to end, but it was all my fault. So I am indifferent calm and Lord knows if I shan't give her notice tomorrow.

Sunday 4 March
A fine day, no fog; and I'm to sit to Nessa for the last time in ten minutes. Yesterday at Ethel Smyth's Mass [in the Albert Hall]. The Queen in the box: nodding from side to side; Ethel in her three cornered hat beside her; with her hand up. The Queen bowing, doing her duty graciously. So to Lyons [Tea Rooms] – I forget the Mass – where in that sordid crumby room assembled the garish Lady Diana [Cooper], Lady Cunard, and the pensive Lady Lovat and ourselves; amid clerks and shop girls eating cream buns. Lydia's *Doll's House* [Ibsen] tonight; on Wednesday Nessa's Private View. Sickert here to tea: very old – no illusions about his own greatness. "They'll collect it all one of these days" he said, sublimely about his art criticisms.

Wednesday 14 March

I cannot hold out any hope for the next fourteen days. There's the workmen everywhere; there's Nelly gay and garrulous as a lark. Can I do it? I must. I must. If only the fourteen days were over – and I in my bed again!

Monday 19 March

I cannot describe how the Nelly situation weighs on my spirits. I am determined not to discuss it with L. either. I couldn't imagine it would be so hard, and the worst to come. And to think none of this need have happened had I stuck to my guns three years ago! Now I must and will.

To dine with Nessa last night. Clive there. Nessa all ablowing and aglowing with the success of her show, and the money made. Then in came Lydia, all &c too, owing to her success; and I felt so old so cold so dumpish, nothing flowery or fiery glowing in me owing to Nelly, but not jealous: I don't think that. Maynard very flown too, and Duncan too, and Clive quiet.

Monday 26 March

'The worst is to come' – that is with Nelly. Well it is now coming very near – by this time – 3.30 – tomorrow it will be over. And then there'll only be the one dreadful day and we shall be off. I feel executioner and the executed in one. Meanwhile it is a brilliant spring day. Hugh, Stephen, William, Ott, and Vita all coming to tea and so on; I dine with Vita; then must ring up Elizabeth Bowen about our Irish tour, and so the immitigable day passes. I face up to it without any evasion: this has to be lived I say to myself.

Tuesday 27 March

The great scene with Nelly is now over, and of course much less violently than I supposed. She stood by the drawing room door in the full light, white and pink, with her funny rather foolish mulish face puckered up. And I made my speech correctly. She had one outburst, which I cut short and said we had agreed to part on good terms, gave her a cheque for £25 and a £1 note for my mending, and so she went upstairs and I came down here. I suppose some further lamentation and argument, with L. perhaps, is inevitable. But Lord what a relief now.

Wednesday 11 April

I am now back here with Nelly gone, and Mabel [Haskins], declared to be a treasure, coming to see me tomorrow. So this has been definitely accomplished, after all these years. The sense of freedom and calm – no more brooding; no more possessiveness; no more sense of being part of Nelly's world. How dazed and free and quiet I felt driving down to Lewes!

She has taken with her all the cookery books, except too elementary manuals, and the chair cover – a last spasm of possessive spite.

Wednesday 18 April
A curious little fact. Instead of smoking six or seven cigarettes as I write of a morning, I now, for three mornings, make myself smoke only one. And rather enjoy doing without.

Thursday 19 April
Oh but I'm much too sleepy to make even a brief note of the talk. It began at dinner. Tom and Maynard talking about his book [*After Strange Gods*]. You have brought up again one of the primal questions, and nobody has even tried to consider it. No, said Tom, much like a great toad with jewelled eyes. Morality. And Maynard said that he would be inclined not to demolish Christianity if it were proved that without it morality is impossible. "I begin to see that our generation – yours and mine, Virginia, owed a great deal to our fathers' religion. And the young, like Julian, who are brought up without it, will never get so much out of life. We had the best of both worlds. We destroyed Christianity and yet had its benefits." Well the argument was something like that. I pressed Tom to define belief in God; but he sheered off. Then Julian came. How will you live Julian, you who have no moral strictness? We, Julian said, miss your morality which has landed us in psychoanalysis, but I prefer my life in many ways. Maynard accused the young of being anxious to publish too soon. That's to make our names and make money. We want to chip in before the talk has changed, said Julian. Virginia: Its because you have no sense of tradition or continuity. I used to feel that the British Museum Reading Room was going on for ever. I felt I could take fifteen years over a book; I wanted to take longer and longer. Whereas you write and publish at eighteen. Tom agreed. Tom agreed to most of this, but reserved his idea of God. Elizabeth Bowen came in, rayed like a zebra, silent and stuttering. Had also been brought up to repress, by moral ancestors. Is thirty-four. L. said jews with great morality but no religion. Quoted his mother on immortality.

Maynard on becoming a Fellow of King's. The moving nature of the service; how they go to the Chapel and lock the doors and sit in their pews, and then the Provost asks Mr So and So to come up and put his hands in his hands and reads out a statement, about preserving the laws and traditions, and then they all shake hands and he is admitted to the brotherhood, a society for research, religion, and education. And thus he is accepted as a brother whom they will support and sustain. This is a great moment; and there is nothing very ceremonious; religious; only an admittance. I said did this society, this coming together move him, and Maynard said very much.

* * *

MONKS HOUSE, RODMELL

Friday 18 May
I felt I suppose a little shiver. Can't be anything I said to myself after all that holiday; but it was – the flue. So I had to resign all ideas – all flood of *Pargiters*; all was blotted by the damp sponge; and now it is precisely a week since I went to bed, and here we are for Whitsun at Monks. All is calm and profoundly comfortable, owing to the absence for ever even in the background of grumbling Nelly, and her replacement by the steady silent unselfish Mabel.

Tuesday 22 May
At last today, after striking the match on the box despairingly, sterilely, a little flame has come. Perhaps I'm off. I must be very leisurely and patient, and nurse my rather creaking head and dandle it with French and so on as cunningly as possible. We go back this afternoon, and the summer lap therefore now begins in earnest. Out of sheer white mist we drove to Charleston last night and my numbed torpor became slightly incandescent. Clive Nessa Duncan Quentin all talking at once about [Stanley] Spencer's pictures.

52 TAVISTOCK SQUARE, WCI

Monday 11 June
I went back, and again on Friday following shivered, and ached, was stiff as a rod; bed; influenza, and so lay all that week; and then went to Rodmell; and then there was the opera [Glyndebourne], the nightingale singing in the ilex tree; and a very hot concert yesterday, so I cannot, no I cannot write today.

Monday 18 June
Very very hot. A drought over the world. In flood with *Here and Now*, praise be. I forgot we had Aldous [Huxley]: a most admirable cool, antiseptic distempered, but humane and gentle man; has gone about the world, completely sceptical, all the more humane, judging everything, yet nothing. A little theoretical, about religion and sex; not for that reason a novelist; infinitely elongated and bony; his blurred grey eye; his malice and wit. He had spent a weekend at Welwyn with the Sex Reformers; taken off his clothes among the cabbages and read *The Waste Land*. Necessary to say penis and fuck; but that said, no change follows. He uses every instant to

the best advantage but has somehow solved the problem of remaining just, gentle – a very sympathetic mind.

Monday 2 July
Rung up by Osbert Sitwell just now. After hopping and jumping about he comes out with "And can't anything be done about this monstrous affair in Germany?" "One of the few public acts" I said "that makes one miserable." Then trying, how ineffectively, to express the sensation of sitting here and reading, like an act in a play, how Hitler flew to Munich and killed this that and the other man and woman in Germany yesterday. A fine hot summer's day here and we took Philip [Woolf], [his wife] Babs and three children to the Zoo. Meanwhile these brutal bullies go about in hoods and masks, like little boys dressed up, acting this idiotic, meaningless, brutal, bloody pandemonium. In they come while Herr So and So is at lunch: iron boots, they say, grating on the parquet; kill him; and his wife who rushes to the door to prevent them. It is like watching the baboon at the Zoo; only he sucks a paper in which ice has been wrapped, and they fire with revolvers. And here we sit, Osbert and I &c, remarking this is inconceivable. A queer state of society. If there were any idea, any vision behind it: but look at the masks these men wear – the brutal faces of baboons, licking sweet paper. And for the first time I read articles with rage, to find him called a real leader. Worse far than Napoleon. Established for a thousand year says somebody.

Wednesday 11 July
So dazed and dusty: I rather think of marking time till August and Rodmell; where we take Mabel, shall have Louie Everest I think as permanent. We saw her last week end – a merry little brown eyed mongrel who came running to meet us in the road.

Tuesday 17 July
I forgot to put in about the Colefax row, curiously enough. How she wrote me a violent letter – better to break altogether – can no longer have you in my life, because I put off dinner to meet Noel Coward.
 This is one of the dryest and hottest of summers. And heat brings such lassitude; and people swarm. I have let them die out, be extinct: Osbert for instance; with his very sensual Royal Guelf face; his extreme uneasiness; his childish vanity always striking the two notes: rank and genius; so easily touched by praise, so eager. A sensitive man; voluble, august, uneasy; and gushing words. Still I like him – why I don't know.

Tuesday 24 July
Dinner last night at the Hutchinsons. Let me see. Praise of my dress – taken very philosophically. Desmond there and Tom. Dinner: not very good: one element of pleasure lessened. Talk frivolous at first. Mary describes a party: a champagne cocktail. Tom gravely attentive. Talk gets upon whether we frighten or are frightened. Tom said I made him feel I saw through all his foibles; which perhaps I do. Talk of [Coventry] Patmore. Desmond expatiated, praised, all in the *Sunday Times* agreeable manner. Jack robust, rather coarse. Tom remained on the verge; yellow, bony – so much melancholy in his face. Yes, and then, somehow to Hitler. And there was Leonard aquiline and lean; and so Desmond drew on to politics; and then, what with Jack's cross examination, and Tom's intentness, and Desmond burbling general goodwill and human love, and Leonard's special-ised convictions, the argument blazed: how the Labour Party would come in: what it would do. But how can you make any such ridiculous claim Jack boomed. What is it going to do about unemployment, about agriculture? All these questions were put from the view of here and now, capable business men; L. ideal by comparison. How ten sensible men 'round a table', one of his phrases, could so manipulate the supply of locomotives and wheat that one country supplemented another. Oh if we were all men of good will, if we were all ready to be nice about it – Then Desmond as usual praised moderation, tact, the virtues of the defunct Liberal Party: how civilisation runs slowly in a great wide stream, and you must slowly facilitate its course, but by no means introduce whirlpools, cut precipices and so on. They heckled L. between them, and when the argument began to put its tail in its mouth, Mary asked if I would like to withdraw. We went upstairs, and she sat on the fender, and said how, being alone for the week end she had tried to write an ambitious biography. There was to be an outer story, and a second meaning; as far as I could gather. Then the others came; and Tom read [George] Barker's poems, chanting, intoning. He thinks there is some melody, some rhythm, some emotion lacking in the Audens and Spenders. Wants five shillings a week for this young man, who has a wife and child. So home at last.

MONKS HOUSE, RODMELL

Friday 27 July
Rodmell begins again: with this difference, we have Mabel just arrived; and Louie Everest, who is moving in [to the Woolfs' cottage] today. And the usual helter skelter, tidying, and nothing to settle to; must go at once to Worthing, then come back to a meeting.

Wednesday 1 August
Charleston yesterday. This morning, poor old Francis [Birrell] paralysed; another operation tomorrow, under which says Nessa, it is to be hoped he may die, since the cancer has come back. How I hate going through these thoughts again, and what a jumble of meanness and sordidity and the fine, one's feelings are.

Thursday 2 August
Louie's first morning here. A leap in the dark rather. Mabel making currant jam. Vast basins of black currants which she tops and tails. Mabel had a chicken that lived with her fourteen years and was called Old George.

Saturday 4 August
Waiting about to go to Annie's wedding. No signs yet. No bells ringing. So impossible to do anything, and here I am at 11 this hot August morning in full garden party dress. No news of Frankie.

Yesterday just as we had done tea, Adrian's gaunt form appeared; Karin's touseled shape, grown very thick and large. Her inferiority complex takes the form of praising Adrian. Clever old Adrian, she exclaims, if he bowls a good bowl. This is by way of saying – what? My marriage was not so bad after all? He remains perfectly unmoved, quiet, sensible; I suppose curiously immature, though able to go through all the actions correctly of a grown man, father, husband.

Tuesday 7 August
A rather wet Bank Holiday. Tea with Keyneses. Maynard had had teeth out, but was very fertile. "Yes, I've been three weeks in America. An impossible climate. In fact it has collected all the faults of all the climates. This carries out my theory about climate. Nobody could produce a great work in America. One sweats all day and the dirt sticks to one's face. The nights are as hot as the days. Nobody sleeps." So to German politics. "They're doing something very queer with their money. I can't make out what. It may be the Jews are taking away their capital. Let me see, if 2000 Jews were each to take away £2000 – Anyway they can't pay their Lancashire bill. Yet they're buying copper all the time. What's it for? Armaments no doubt. But of course there's something behind it. They're doing something foolish – no Treasury control of the soldiers." (But I am thinking all the time of what is to end *Here and Now*.)

Sunday 12 August
This is Saxon's week end. He is in the house, this windy cold gray day, playing chess with L. He has grown rather pink and chubby in face, and

very mellow and in fact charming in mind. The old eccentricities have been melted in the sun - I cannot guess of what success. Anyhow he is not merely a bundle of dessicated separate remarks about toothbrushes and trains: he is continuous and even suggestive. I have spent an hour or so talking with him about Shakespeare, books in general, then people; and there is some virtue in these old friends: I mean conversationally; they enrich. Thus it was a good idea of mine to ask him. We had the Keyneses over. Old friends again.

News at first, through Julian, extremely optimistic about Francis. Now nothing, but perhaps more doubtful. Oh and the drought has broken; two carp are dead; there is the old ugly grey welter in the sky, which I'm afraid may now become 'weather'. Vita came over very late for dinner, having been kept by a row with her mother who, says Maynard, eats pâté de foie with a shoehorn.

Friday 17 August
Yes. I think owing to the sudden rush of two wakeful nights, making up early mornings rather, I think I see the end of *Here and Now* (or *Music*, or *Dawn* or whatever I shall call it). Its to end with Elvira going out of the house and saying What did I make this knot in my handkerchief for? And all the coppers rolling about –

Thursday 30 August
If I can't even write here, owing to making up the last scenes, how can I possibly read Dante? Impossible. Yesterday I found a new walk, and a new farm, in the fold between Asheham and Tarring Neville. Very lovely, all alone, with the down rising behind. Then I walked back by a rough broad overflowing grey river. The porpoise came up and gulped. It rained. All ugliness was dissolved. An incredibly 18th century landscape. A tremendous hailstorm after tea. Like white ice; broken up; lanced; lashing, like the earth being whipped. This happened several times. Black clouds while we played Brahms.

Sunday 2 September
I don't think I have ever been more excited over a book than I am writing the end of - shall it be *Dawn?* Or is that too emphatic, sentimental. I wrote like a - forget the word - yesterday; my cheeks burn; my hands tremble. I am doing the scene where Peggy listens to them talking and bursts out. It was this outburst that excited me so. Too much perhaps. Another lull; but very slight, caused partly by the great tea table talk yesterday - nine to tea. We arranged lots of little cakes on two tables. And some came early, others late. And they talked (as in my book that morning) about Civilisation.

Wednesday 12 September
Roger died on Sunday. I was walking with Clive on the terrace when Nessa came out. We sat on the seat there for a time. On Monday we went up with Nessa. Tomorrow we go up, following some instinct, to the funeral. I feel dazed: very wooden. Women cry, L. says: but I don't know why I cry – mostly with Nessa. And I'm too stupid to write anything. My head all stiff. I think the poverty of life now is what comes to me, a thin blackish veil over everything. Hot weather. A wind blowing. The substance gone out of everything. I don't think this is exaggerated. It'll come back I suppose. And I can't write to Helen [Anrep], but I must now shut this and try.

I remember turning aside at mother's bed, when she had died, and Stella took us in, to laugh, secretly, at the nurse crying. She's pretending, I said: aged thirteen. And was afraid I was not feeling enough. So now.

Saturday 15 September
I was glad we went to the service on Thursday. It was a very hot summer's day. And all very simple and dignified. Music. Not a word spoken. We sat there, before the open doors that lead into the garden. Flowers and strollers which Roger would have liked. He lay under an old red brocade with two bunches of very bright many-coloured flowers. It is a strong instinct to be with one's friends. I thought of him too, at intervals. Dignified and honest and large – 'large sweet soul' – something ripe and musical about him – and then the fun and the fact that he had lived with such variety and generosity and curiosity. I thought of this. They played Bach. Then the coffin moved slowly through the doors. They shut. They played again – Anon, I think; old music. Yes, I liked the wordlessness; Helen looking very young and blue eyed and quiet and happy. That is much to remember her for. I kissed her on the lips, in the courtyard. Then Desmond came up: said wouldn't it be nice to walk in the garden? "Oh we stand on a little island" he said. But it has been very lovely I said. For the first time I laid my hand on his shoulder, and said don't die yet. Nor you either he said. We have had wonderful friends, he said. We walked a little, but Molly was out of it, with her deafness. So we took them to Wellington Square and had tea. A merry natural talk, about Roger and books and people, all as usual. And it was roasting hot.

Very jaded; can't write. I must take a few days off. Ann and Judith [Stephen] upon us; then Dadie.

Tuesday 18 September
Ann and Judith came, strode in without their box. Great brown naked legged colts. Next day Angelica's party at Charleston. They acted. They acted very beautifully in Chinese clothes by the pond. Well I thought I can

see this through Roger's eyes: its right to enjoy every tint. And yet how can one? This has gone out of the day – that laughter; that energy; and we were all thinned and stunted. So home. And then after Ann and Judith went – and I had begun to fidget because they don't wipe their mouths and eat so much – the Keyneses and Dadie came. We did not exactly repeat the funeral talk: but it loomed over us. Dear old Dadie very charming and affectionate. We talked about Cambridge; about teaching English; I held out a bare pole – I mean I extended my views rashly; he was donnish, serious, very measured; believes in education; in measuring the mind, and sending youth to Africa with 'an improved sense of leisure' and so on. But this rather broke down and he admitted that he means to leave as soon as he can afford it. Teaching without zest a crime.

Wednesday 19 September
I had a notion that I could describe the tremendous feeling at Roger's funeral: but of course I can't. I mean the universal feeling: how we all fought with our brains, loves and so on: and must be vanquished. A fear then came to me, of death. Of course I shall lie there too before that gate, and slide in; and it frightens me. But why? I mean, I felt the vainness of this perpetual fight, with our brains and loving each other, against the other thing; if Roger could die.

Thursday 20 September
But then, next day, the other thing begins to work – the exalted sense of being above time and death which comes from being again in a writing mood. And this is not an illusion, so far as I can tell. Certainly I have a strong sense that Roger would be all on one's side in this excitement.

Sunday 30 September
The last words of the nameless book were written ten minutes ago; quite calmly too. 900 pages: L. says 200,000 words. Lord God what an amount of re-writing that means! But also, how heavenly to have brought the pen to a stop at the last line, even if most of the lines have now to be rubbed out. Anyhow the design is there.

Tuesday 2 October
Yes, but my head will never let me glory sweepingly: always a tumble. Yesterday morning the old rays of light set in; and then the sharp, the very sharp pain over my eyes; so that I sat and lay about till tea; had no walk, had not a single idea of triumph or relief. L. bought me a little travelling ink pot, by way of congratulation. I wish I could think of a name.
So the summer is ended. Until the 9th of September when Nessa came

across the terrace – how I hear that cry He's dead – a very vigorous, happy summer. Oh the joy of walking! I've never felt it so strong in me.

On Sunday we had Bunny [Garnett] and Julian; Bunny so thick and solid, like a beam out of an old tree; Julian rather smaller than usual. Bunny has grey wisps at his temples; talks like a heavy wardrobe; all heavy and angular sentences. I noted how my own rushing pace seemed too rushing, and after ten minutes had adapted itself to Bunny. Then Duncan and Helen came. It was rather fortunate that the first meeting should be among the flowers, vegetables, improvements. Then we went upstairs and talked and laughed about Roger, easily. I felt however the worn out, the used up feeling as if she were now feeling the shallows, after the exaltation; the shingle grating, the sordid – poor Helen.

Thursday 4 October
A violent rain storm on the pond. The pond is covered with little white thorns; bristling with leaping white thorns, like the thorns on a small porcupine; then black waves cross it: black shudders; a helter skelter rain, and the elms tossing it up and down; the pond overflowing on one side. Then completely smooth for a moment. Then prickled: thorns like glass; but leaping up and down incessantly. A rapid smirch of shadow. Now light from the sun: green and red: shining: the pond a sage green: the grass brilliant green: red berries on the hedges: the cows very white: purple over Asheham.

52 TAVISTOCK SQUARE, WCI

Thursday 11 October
A brief note. In today's *TLS* they advertise *Men Without Art* by Wyndham Lewis. Chapters on Eliot, Faulkner, Hemingway, Virginia Woolf ... Now I know by reason and instinct that this is an attack; that I am publicly demolished: nothing is left of me in Oxford and Cambridge and places where the young read Wyndham Lewis. My instinct is, not to read it. Why do I shrink from reading Wyndham Lewis? Why am I sensitive? I think vanity. I dislike the thought of being laughed at, of the glow of satisfaction that A B and C will get from hearing Virginia Woolf demolished: also it will strengthen further attacks. Perhaps I feel uncertain of my own gifts: but then, I know more about them than Wyndham Lewis; and anyhow I intend to go on writing. Already I am feeling the calm that always comes to me with abuse: my back is against the wall. I am writing for the sake of writing: &c. And then there is the queer disreputable pleasure in being abused – in being a figure, in being a martyr. And so on.

Sunday 14 October

This morning I've taken the arrow of Wyndham Lewis to my heart. Well: this gnat has settled and stung; and I think the pain is over. I'm glad that I need not and cannot write, because the danger of being attacked is that it makes one answer back – a perfectly fatal thing to do. I mean, fatal to arrange *The Pargiters* so as to meet his criticisms. If there is truth in Wyndham Lewis, well, face it: I've no doubt I am prudish and peeping, well then live more boldly. But for God's sake don't try to bend my writing one way or the other.

Monday 15 October

Walked with L. all round Serpentine and Kensington Gardens yesterday (a fine blowy day: leaves falling) and asked him these questions: 1) What is the sensible attitude to criticism? Not to read it. 2) What should I do now of a morning – creation flagging? Read. 3) Does he feel I have prevented him from going abroad? No. I have only prevented him from lesser activities (I think this was the answer). We agreed to save up for foreign travel on a large scale, to try to fly over America. Perhaps to go to India and China. I now see us, far far away. A new civilisation &c. Oh and L. was divinely good: so direct: what an immense relief to talk to him! what a simplification. What an egress to open air and cold daylight: how dignified: yes, and I have him every day, as I so often think. So why – &c &c.

Tuesday 16 October

Quite cured today. So the Wyndham Lewis illness lasted two days. Helped by old Ethel's bluff affection and stir yesterday, by buying a blouse; by falling fast asleep after dinner. Writing away this morning.

Wednesday 17 October

I am so sleepy. Is this age? I can't shake it off. And so gloomy. That's the end of the book. I looked up past diaries – a reason for keeping them – and found the same misery after *Waves*. After *Lighthouse* I was I remember nearer suicide, seriously, than since 1913. It is after all natural. I've been galloping now for three months – well, cut that all off – after the first divine relief, of course some terrible blankness must spread. This time Roger makes it harder than usual. We had tea with Nessa yesterday. Yes, his death is worse than Lytton's. Why I wonder? Such a blank wall. Such a silence. Such a poverty. How he reverberated! And I feel it through Nessa. Now there's the dullness, the cold to face and no protection. I'm so ugly. So old. No one writes to me. I'm ... Well: don't think about it, and walk all over London: and see people; and imagine their lives. I can't read seriously. I feel so drowsy, as if my brain were dilated: can't contract: then I suddenly lapse into sleep.

Margery [Fry] is going, Nessa thinks, to ask me to write about Roger. I don't feel ready to. I dread the plunge into the past.

Friday 26 October

Yesterday at Ottoline's. Old [W. B.] Yeats. I'm trying to get the Irish back to the great men of the 18th Century. Swift! But did Swift like Ireland? He started the whole Irish movement – made Irish different from English. Oh the bitterness against England. Must get them back to their own speech. You have always been rich and powerful. You create without hatred. The need of tragedy: some cause: that is what creates literature.

The Occult. That he believes in firmly. All his writing depends on it. Was walking with Robinson Ellis. The words came to him 'The world is the excrement of God': two minutes afterwards Robinson Ellis said them. This convinced Yeats of the existence of another mind. Neither religion nor science explains the world. The occult does explain it. Has seen things. His coat hanger advanced across the room one night. Then a coat on it, illuminated; then a hand in it. Is writing his memoirs. About [George] Moore and Lady Gregory. This went on for one and a half hours, I should say. I was too jaded to whip my brain: but felt Yeats's extreme directness, simplicity, and equality: liked his praise; liked him: but can't unriddle the universe at tea. He is older, less coloured and vigorous. Little burning eyes behind great glasses; ruffled hair; tweeds. Yeats said that in writing his memoirs he had to leave out himself, because no man could tell the truth about the women in his life. Also no man knew about himself.

Monday 29 October

Reading *Antigone*. How powerful that spell is still – Greek. Thank heaven I learnt it young – an emotion different from any other.

Wednesday 31 October

Too tired after dining with Helen last night and talking too much with Oliver [Strachey] about Roger and Bloomsbury – too tired to write. Helen by the way asked me tentatively to write Roger's Life. Julian to collect all the facts, make a skeleton; I to sum and compose. But Margery [Fry] wants to write it. Margery has the documents: is executor. I deferred. Isn't a 'Life' impossible? Yes, said Oliver. All sorts of people should put down recollections. And unprintable. So what's to come of it? I deferred. (What exactly does that word mean?)

Monday 12 November
What is uppermost now, is the question of writing Roger's life. Helen came. Says both she and Margery wish it. So I wait. What do I feel about it? If I could be free, then here's the chance of trying biography: a splendid, difficult chance – better than trying to find a subject – that is, if I *am* free. But Margery hesitates: I have heard nothing from her; and rather suspect she wants to do it herself.

We were at Monks House in a great flood of rain and storm of wind this week-end; which lifted yesterday. Home with the car all acrid and yellow and red with crysanthemums. And so to hear [T. S. Eliot's] *Sweeney Agonistes* at the Group Theatre: an upper attic or studio. I sat by Tom. The acting made more sense than the reading but I doubt that Tom has enough of a body and brain to bring off a whole play: certainly he conveys an emotion, an atmosphere: something peculiar to himself; sordid, emotional, intense – modernity and poetry locked together.

Thursday 15 November
And am now, 10.30 on Thursday morning, November 15th, about to tackle re-reading and re-writing *The Pargiters*. An awful moment.

12.45. Well that horrid plunge has been made, and I've started re-writing *The Pargiters*. Lord Lord! Ten pages a day for ninety days: three months.

Saturday 17 November
A note: despair at the badness of the book: can't think how I ever could write such stuff – and with such excitement: that's yesterday; today I think it good again. A note, by way of advising other Virginias with other books that this is the way of the thing: up down, up down – and Lord knows the truth.

Wednesday 21 November
Margery Fry to tea on Sunday. A long debate about the book on Roger: not very conclusive. She says she wants a study by me, reinforced with chapters on other aspects. I say, well but those books are unreadable. Oh of course I want you to be quite free she says. I should have to say something about his life, I say. The family – Now there of course I'm afraid I should have to ask you to be careful, she says. Agnes is stone deaf; has lived all her life in the family. I couldn't let her be hurt – and so on. The upshot of all of which is that she's to write to the *New Statesman* asking for letters; that I'm to go through them; that we're then to discuss – so it will drag on these many months, I suppose.

Tom's head is very remarkable; such a conflict; so many forces have smashed against him; the wild eye still; but all rocky, yellow, riven, and constricted. Sits very solid – large shoulders – in his chair, and talks easily but with authority. Is a great man, in a way, now: self confident, didactic. But to me, still, a dear old ass: I mean I can't be frozen off with this divine authority any longer. Tom is larger minded than of old. "But that's only human" he said, when I asked him if he still liked seeing his own name in print.

Tuesday 27 November
Poor Francis lies in a hotel bedroom in Russell Square this rainy morning. I went in and sat with him. Quite himself with a lump on his forehead. May die under another operation, or slowly stiffen into complete paralysis. His brain may go. All this he knows; and there it was between us, as we joked. He came to the verge of it once or twice. But I can't feel any more at the moment – not after Roger. I kissed him. "This is the first time – this chaste kiss" he said. So I kissed him again. But I must not cry, I thought, and so went.

Tuesday 18 December
Talk with Francis yesterday. He is dying; but makes no bones about it. He was exactly as usual; no wandering, no incoherence. A credit to atheism. The soul deserves to be immortal, as L. said. We walked back, glad to be alive: numb somehow.

MONKS HOUSE, RODMELL

Sunday 30 December
End the year; with those cursed dogs barking. It has been the wettest Christmas, I should say, on record. I end every morning with a head full of ideas about *The Pargiters*. I am re-writing considerably. My idea is to contrast the scenes; very intense, less so; then drama; then narrative. I think it shall be called *Ordinary People*.

End of the year: and Francis transacting his death at that nursing home. The expression on his face is what I see: as if he were facing a peculiar lonely sorrow. One's own death – think of lying there alone, looking at it, at forty-five or so: with a great desire to live. And here we are, chafed by [Mabel's] lame leg and the dogs: yet as usual very happy I think: ever so full of ideas. L. finishing his *Quack Quack* of a morning. And Roger dead. And am I to write about him?

1935

Virginia's comedy Freshwater *was performed by a family cast before a receptive audience of friends in Vanessa's Fitzroy Street studio in January. Yet there was 'a vast sorrow at the back of life this winter', attributable to the loss of Roger Fry, which depressed her and, even more, Vanessa. The proposal that Virginia should write about him required Margery Fry's endorsement, but not until the summer did she make it clear that she expected a full-scale biography and begin to inundate Virginia with documents, followed by a demand that she speak at a memorial exhibition of Roger's pictures at Bristol.*

In the meantime London life was as demanding as ever; friends and relations, literary and political associates, converged on Tavistock Square. Among the most persistent was the editor of the New Statesman, *Kingsley Martin, constantly seeking Leonard's counsel. Also the indomitable Ethel Smyth, demanding affection, admiration, and attendance at performances of her music.*

Despite their growing awareness of the Nazi threat to European peace and the atrocities of anti-Semitism, on 1 May, avoiding King George V's Silver Jubilee celebrations, the Woolfs set out to drive via Holland, Germany and Austria to join Vanessa in Rome. They prepared for this rash journey by talking to a country neighbour, Ralph Wigram of the Foreign Office; but their best passport proved to be Leonard's pet marmoset Mitz, who bore a striking resemblance to Goebbels and disarmed officials and bystanders. They were away a month, returning through France. While in Rome, Virginia learned that the Prime Minister proposed to recommend she be made a Companion of Honour in the King's Birthday Honours; she declined.

During the summer, both in London and at Rodmell, Virginia's concentration on The Pargiters – *which she now decided to call* The Years – *was repeatedly broken by social distractions, headaches, and the increasing political tension abroad, leading up to Mussolini's invasion of Abyssinia and the imposition by the League of Nations of sanctions against Italy. In England the Conservative Stanley Baldwin succeeded Ramsay MacDonald as Prime Minister, and in November called a General Election which he won with a handsome majority. In October Virginia with Leonard spent a day at the Labour Conference at Brighton. These external concerns roused in her a wish to write a political pamphlet; but she was trying to finish* The Years, *and by the end of the year had embarked on the background reading for the biography of Roger Fry. The Woolfs spent Christmas at Rodmell.*

1935

MONKS HOUSE, RODMELL

Sunday 6 January
Francis died on 2nd. It was a mercy, as we say, that it ended so soon. But a queer thing death. Last night I suddenly thought, how silly and indeed disgusting death, the decomposition of the body, &c. Why think of it as anything noble? We lunched with Maynard and Lydia, the first fine cold day since we came. We talked about Francis: Maynard said he was a case of arrested development; had been a most brilliant undergraduate, and remained one.

Friday 11 January
I have made a very clever arrangement on the new board that L. gave me for Christmas: ink, pen tray &c. I never cease to get pleasure from these clever arrangements. So death will be very dull. There are no letters in the grave, as Dr Johnson said. A very long, rather formal, I mean affected letter from Tom this morning, which I must put away, as it will be so valuable. Did he think that when he was writing it? This spring will be on us all of a clap. Already engagements are piling; and the lap ahead will be full of the usual jerks and strains. Tom suggests a fortnightly tea. And there's Helen . . . I never never invite anyone; but lie like an apron under an apple tree for fruit to drop.

52 TAVISTOCK SQUARE, WC1

Saturday 19 January
The play [*Freshwater*] came off last night, with the result that I am dry-brained this morning, and can only use this book as a pillow. It was said, inevitably, to be a great success; it is good to have an unbuttoned laughing evening once in a way. Angelica ravishing of course, but of course too grown up for my taste. That is, I rather dread Bloomsbury; and rather relish the clumsy directness, the hard fact of the Stephen girls: so clumsy and large.

But they will become workers – in the cause of – how the phrases one has written and listened to so many times run in the head! And Morgan said it was lovely, I mean the play.

Wednesday 23 January
I am taking a fortnight off fiction. My mind became knotted.

Friday 1 February
And again this morning, I'm too tired to go on with *Pargiters*. Why? Talking too much I daresay. I thought I wanted 'society': and saw Helen, Mary, [Louis] Gillet. Ann tonight. I think *The Pargiters* however a promising work. A day off today.

Saturday 2 February
Walked to Chancery Lane in a bitter rain about my spectacles. I wrote in praise of Rebecca's book to Rebecca [West], and have had no answer. This I did because of the talk at Charleston, when they said how much pleasure such letters gave. I expect I have (somehow) given pain. But its no great matter. My conscience, as they say, is clear.

Tuesday 5 February
Why should I mind so much Rebecca not answering my letter? Vanity largely, I suppose. I thought she would be glad &c. Never mind. She is a queer ill bred mind, with all the qualities I lack and fear.

Tom to tea yesterday. An admirable way of seeing him. And how he suffers! Yes: I felt my accursed gift of sympathy rising. He seemed to have got so little joy or satisfaction out of being Tom. A religious soul: an unhappy man: a lonely very sensitive man, all wrapped up in fibres of self torture, doubt, conceit, desire for warmth and intimacy. And I'm very fond of him – like him in some of my reserves and subterfuges. After abusing booksellers yesterday for some time, I said to Tom, do you ever buy a new book? Never, he said. And I said, I sometimes buy poetry, that's all. So this accounts for the problem, it strikes me, why authors don't sell: why booksellers don't stock &c &c.

Wednesday 6 February
I open this book to record the fact, with all its psychological implications – the fact that Rebecca's snub has now worn off. It lasted about four days: gave me a cold goose feather feeling every morning and every evening. It will now gradually fade out; and I shall dismiss her, and all that is implicit in that situation. But I should still be very glad if she did write to me. On

the other hand, the feeling of independence is even better than the feeling of pleasure would be.

Friday 8 February
Dine with Nessa; and oh dear, how the ghost of Roger haunted us. What a dumb misery life is for her. An extraordinary sense of him: of wishing for him; of vacancy. A letter from Margery, who is bringing documents, and wants to see me next week. No letter from Rebecca.

Tuesday 12 February
This should be the coldest day in the year, according to averages. Colefax came half an hour late: and we had it out. Lord what a drubbing you gave me in the summer, I managed to thrust in, after the usual patter about dining last night with somebody who had been dining with Lloyd George. Then her defences crumpled: she flushed and quickened; so did I. She sat on the floor by the way, and pulled down some white undergarment which had become creased. She only wears one undergarment and a small belt, by the way. And she twittered out how what had hurt her had been my thinking, or insinuating, that her dinner was merely a snob dinner to bring celebrities together. The truth was Noel [Coward] adores me; and I could save him from being as clever as a bag of ferrets and as trivial as a perch of canaries. And of course, I rather liked her. And she is so childishly ready to patter about her own simple love of sunsets, comparing herself to the worldly. That I stubbed by saying I admired and loved those who fill their sails with the spice breezes of the great world. So she had to trim and hedge; and admit that parties are a stimulus to the imagination; and that her chief pleasure is to tell herself stories, to make up a life, a picture, as she bustles and flits. This I think was intended to be in my manner – a tribute to the imaginative, artistic life: for indeed what she can't bear is to be rated a hard society woman: as she is, partly; but then we're all curates' eggs, as I was feeling: a mix.

Wednesday 20 February
A row with Clive which spoilt my dinner at the [Herbert] Read's; and sent me parched and throbbing up to that vast comfortless [Hampstead] studio, where none of the charm of Bohemia mitigated the hard chairs, the skimpy wine, and the very nice sensible conversation. Henry Moore, sculptor, and his Russian wife, something like Cordelia Fisher in the old days to look at; but more sympathetic. Respectable Bohemia is a little cheerless. Better have Sybil or the real thing. But all went decorously. Steel chairs, clear pale colours; talk of pots; brainy talk, specialists' talk. Read devitalised: possibly his look – a shop assistant. So this morning I can't write; only correct.

Thursday 21 February

A good party last night with old Hugh [Walpole]. Hugh on Hollywood. What was interesting though and rather horrifying was his account of his own pain: an agony of pain in his arm, like broken bones twittering incessantly. Agony agony agony – hadn't realised there could be such pain. Once he burst into tears and sat up shouting. Was conveyed across America in an aeroplane. And then, just as the pain was coming on at Hampstead, a parcel was delivered: a bottle of quack medicine called Cleano. And he took a dose, and slept; and next day he was better. And has had no pain since. But what was shocking was to see him an old man. All the buoyancy and taut pink skin gone. Something sunk and shuttered in him. I liked him. And I liked his capacity for miraculous rebirth.

A letter of explanation and conciliation from Clive.

Tuesday 26 February

A very fine skyblue day, my windows completely filled with blue for a wonder. And I have been writing and writing and re-writing the scene by the Round Pond. But Lord what a lot of work still to do! It won't be done before August. And here am I plagued by the sudden wish to write an anti-Fascist pamphlet. L. and I, after snarling over my cigarette smoking last night (I'm refraining altogether and without difficulty today) had a long discussion about all the things I might put in my pamphlet. He was extremely reasonable and adorable.

Friday 1 March

First of March: first of spring. Another blue day; and we're off to Walton on Thames.

Monday 4 March

It was a charming grey distinguished expedition too: to Walton; and we walked by the river, and said it was like a French picture. The grey trees, the weir churning, the bridge, the white cupola, and a lion in marble.

Yesterday I did not enjoy. What a guzzler old Ethel has become. She guzzled our very tough chops, till I could not sit still. She is a greedy old woman; I don't like greed when it comes to champing and chawing and sweeping up gravy. And she gets red, drinking. Then the concert. How long, how little music in it that I enjoyed! Beecham's face beaming, ecstatic, like a yellow copper idol: such grimaces, attenuations, dancings, swingings; his collar crumpled. In the artists' room afterwards there was Zélie with the red lips, and another ex prima donna and a dissolute musician, all waiting their turn to plague Beecham. And they hinted and shrugged that poor old Ethel was a well known imposition upon conductors. Out she came in her spotted cat's fur with her hat askew, carrying her brown cardboard despatch box, upon which they – the tight hard old prima donnas, fell on her and larded her with praise. (They had played *The Wreckers* overture). Who are they I said. Haven't an idea, she replied. So we had tea at the Langham, which I don't mind so much as meat and gravy. And then I could stand that stab of a voice emphasising, I don't know what, no longer; and said I must go. It was a Sunday evening drizzle in the street, an 1849 night, as we padded very slowly to the Tube; and thank God, she vanished. I was out of temper.

Monday 11 March

It was the bitterest Sunday for twenty-two years. We went to Sissinghurst: in the bitter wind with the country all lying in its June green and blue outside the window. Now that's an odd observation I have to make. My friendship with Vita is over. Not with a quarrel, not with a bang, but as ripe fruit falls. But her voice saying "Virginia?" outside the tower room was as enchanting as ever. Only then nothing happened. And she has grown very fat, very much the indolent county lady, run to seed, incurious now about books; has written no poetry; only kindles about dogs, flowers, and new buildings. Sissinghurst is to have a new wing; a new garden; a new wall. And there is no bitterness, and no disillusion, only a certain emptiness. In fact – if my hands weren't so cold – I could here analyse my state of mind these past four months, and account for the human emptiness by the defection of Vita; Roger's death; and no-one springing up to take their place; and a certain general slackening of letters and fame, owing to my writing nothing; so that I have more time on my hands, and actually ask people to come here now and again. (But the week fills unbidden mostly.) Coming back in the snowstorm from Vita's: the snow was like long ribbons of paper; whipping, mixing, getting entangled in front of the car.

Saturday 16 March

I have had three severe swingeings lately: Bloomsbury is ridiculed; and I am dismissed with it. And how little I mind, and how much; and how good my novel is; and how tired I am this morning; and how I like praise; and how full of ideas I am; and Tom and Stephen [Spender] came to tea, and Ray [Strachey] and William [Plomer] dine; and I forgot to describe my interesting talk with Nessa about my criticising her children; and I left out – I forget what.

And Rebecca West did answer yesterday, and signs yours ever, and had been ill, and no secretary, so that's done with. Tom's writing a play about Thomas à Becket to be acted in Canterbury Cathedral. In last week's *Time & Tide* St John Ervine called Lytton 'that servile minded man . . . that Pandar' or words to that effect. I'm thinking whether, if I write about Roger,

I shall include a note, a sarcastic note, on the Bloomsbury baiters. No, I suppose not. Write them down – that's the only way.

Wednesday 20 March
Having just written a letter about Bloomsbury I cannot control my mind enough to go on with *The Pargiters*. I woke in the night and thought of it. But whether to send it or not, I don't know.

L. advised me *not* to send the letter. And after two seconds I see he is right. It is better he says to be able to say we don't answer. But we suggest a comic guide to Bloomsbury by Morgan and he nibbles.

Monday 25 March
Last night at Nessa's, talk all very chippy and choppy with Clive oddly inattentive, and a sense of unreality, and a great desire for Roger. Again the sense of him coming in with his great dark eyes, and his tie pin and his brown shoes and how, speaking in that very deep voice, he would have discussed Max Eastman and Epstein. We only flick the surface. And all would have been deepened, and made suggestive. But never mind. This is inevitable, and we must blow on the bellows.

Tuesday 26 March
A very nice dinner at MacCarthys last night. Desmond flung the door open and almost kissed me. But that's not our formula. So glad to see us – He looks firmer and pinker. And we talked of America. Very kind, quite untaught. Desmond never allowed to pay. He had enjoyed himself immensely. Only netted £150 though. Dear me, friendship is a very happy thing.

Wednesday 27 March
Yesterday we went to the Tower, which is an impressive murderous bloody grey raven haunted military barrack prison dungeon place; like the prison of English splendour; the reformatory at the back of history; where we shot and tortured and imprisoned. Prisoners scratched their names, very beautifully, on the walls. And the crown jewels blazed, very tawdry. And we watched the Scots Guards drill; and an officer doing a kind of tiger pace up and down – a wax faced barber's block officer trained to a certain impassive balancing. The sergeant major barked and swore: the men stamped and wheeled like machines: then the officer also barked; all precise, inhuman, showing off – a degrading, a stupefying sight, but in keeping with the grey wall, the cobbles, the executioner's block. People sitting on the river bank among old cannon. Ships &c. Very romantic; a dungeon like feeling.

Thursday 28 March
Spring triumphant. Crocuses going over. Daffodils and hyacinths out. Some chestnut leaves in the bird's claw stage in the park. The country trees and Square trees bare still. Little bushes all green. I want to make vegetable notes for my book. How soft and springy and fresh the air was yesterday – like the sea! And I think of being abroad. But we have not yet decided where to go.

Monday 1 April
We think of three weeks in Holland and France: a week in Rome, flying there. We went to Kew yesterday, and if vegetable notes are needed, this is to signify that yesterday was the prime day for cherry blossom, pear trees, and magnolia. So to walk through Richmond – a long walk by the ponds. I verified certain details. And it was 5.30 when we got back. And Mabel came in and said she had sat for two hours in the Piccadilly [Lyons'] Corner House, watching people and listening to the band. Many people do this, she said. They sit on and on, eating as slowly as possible. She was ashamed how long they had sat. But then they take a long time to bring things she said.

Friday 5 April
L. met James [Strachey] who says he means to set about a very long life of Lytton; and what he wants is that I should write a character of Lytton as introduction. Lytton and Roger – so my work as biographer is cut out – I wonder.

Tuesday 9 April
I met Morgan in the London Library yesterday and flew into a passion. "Virginia, my dear" he said. I was pleased by that little affectionate familiar tag. "Being a good boy and getting books on Bloomsbury?" I said. "Yes. And Virginia, you know I'm on the Committee here" said Morgan. "And we've been discussing whether to allow ladies –"
    It came over me that they were going to put me on: and I was then to refuse: "Oh but they do –" I said, "there was Mrs Green..." "Yes yes – there was Mrs Green. And Sir Leslie Stephen said, never again. She was so troublesome. And I said, haven't ladies improved? But they were all quite determined. No no no, ladies are quite impossible. They wouldn't hear of it."
    See how my hand trembles. I was so angry (also very tired) standing. And I saw the whole slate smeared. I thought how perhaps Morgan had mentioned my name, and they had said no no no: ladies are impossible. And so I quietened down and said nothing and this morning in my bath I

made up a phrase in my book *On Being Despised* which is to run: a friend of mine, who was offered . . . one of those prizes – for her sake the great exception was to be made – who was in short to be given an honour – I forget what . . . she said, And they actually thought I would take it. They were, on my honour, surprised, even at my very modified and humble rejection. You didn't tell them what you thought of them for daring to suggest that you should rub your nose in that pail of offal? I remarked. Not for a hundred years, she observed. Yes, these flares up are very good for my book: for they simmer and become transparent: and I see how I can transmute them into beautiful clear reasonable ironical prose. God damn Morgan for thinking I'd have taken that . . .

The veil of the temple, whether academic or ecclesiastic I forget – was to be raised, and as an exception she was to be allowed to enter in. But for 2,000 years we have done things without being paid for doing them. You can't bribe me now. Pail of offal? No; I said; while very deeply appreciating the hon. . . . In short one must tell lies, and apply every emollient in our power to the swollen skin of our brothers' so terribly inflamed vanity. Truth is only to be spoken by those women whose fathers were pork butchers and left them a share in the pig factory.

Friday 12 April
This little piece of rant won't be very intelligible in a year's time. Yet there are some useful facts and phrases in it. I rather itch to be at that book. But I have been skirmishing round a headache, and can't pull my weight in the morning. It is now almost settled that we shall drive through Holland and Germany, concealing Leonard's nose, to Rome; and so back. A giant tour on our most heroic scale.

Last night I dined with Nessa, L. being at Kingsley's to hear the story of his divided mind. He can't make up his mind, and must display the separated parts, like a heaving oyster, to his friends.

Sunday 14 April
Let me make a note that it would be much wiser not to attempt to sketch a draft of *On Being Despised* until *The Pargiters* is done with. I was vagrant this morning and made a rash attempt, with the interesting discovery that one can't propagate at the same time as write fiction.

Wednesday 17 April
Tomorrow we go to Rodmell, and when [Donald] Brace, at 7, slowly put on his coat, and made some very polite remark about seeing us in New York – when all this happened, I sank back and thought the holiday has begun. I forget I had something in mind to write here, about 'the soul'

perhaps. The soul – the soul – How far could I let myself go in an anti-Fascist pamphlet? I think of dashing off my *Professions for Women*, can I steal a moment between Roger, Lytton and proofs. All this about being so distinguished and cultivated might be knocked on the head.

MONKS HOUSE, RODMELL

Saturday 20 April
The scene has now changed to Rodmell. Good Friday was a complete fraud – rain and more rain. I tried walking along the bank. At the same time through the rain I heard the cuckoo's song. Then I came home and read and read – Stephen Spender [*The Destructive Element*: 'A study of modern writers and beliefs']; too quick to stop and think; shall I stop to think; read it again? But I want to investigate certain questions: why do I always fight shy of my contemporaries? Do I instinctively keep my mind from analysing, which would impede its creativeness? I think there's something in that. No creative writer can swallow another contemporary. But I admire Stephen for trying to grapple with these problems.

In the public world, there are emphatic scares. L. brings home a bunch after every Committee meeting. Its odd how seldom I report them. One of these days they may come true. For instance, [Ernst] Toller says we are on the brink of war. Wants the Allies to declare war on Hitler. Belgium keeps its aeroplanes at active service level, all ready to rise into the air. But as Germany could be on them before they rose this seems useless. There is a dutiful perfunctory stir about the [Royal Silver] Jubilee. We have subscribed £3 towards buns and a bus shelter in Rodmell. The King is said to be almost comatose. Will he get through with his bowings? And – there are incessant conversations – Mussolini, Hitler, MacDonald. All these people incessantly arriving at Croydon, arriving at Berlin, Moscow, Rome; and flying off again – while Stephen and I think how to improve the world.

Monday 22 April
The [Ralph] Wigrams to tea; she something like an old daisy or other simple garden flower; if a flower could look very unhappy. He is very white toothed, blue eyed, lean, red cheeked – a nice rigid honest public school Englishman. Started almost at once telling us about Hitler. He had been at Berlin with [Sir John] Simon [Foreign Secretary]. Hitler very impressive; very frightening. Made speeches lasting twenty minutes without a failure. Very well coached. And all the time a tapping sound. Wigram thought an odd day to have the masons in. But it was the sentry marching up and

373

down the passage. Everything came out. We want ... I want room to move about Hitler said. Must be equal, and so on. A complete reversal to pre-war days. No ideals except equality, superiority, force, possessions. And the passive heavy slaves behind him, and he a great mould coming down on the brown jelly. Talks of himself as the regenerator, the completely equipped and powerful machine. Wigram and the rest frightened. Anything may happen at any moment. Here in England we haven't even bought our gas masks. Nobody takes it seriously. But having seen this mad dog, the thin rigid Englishmen are really afraid. And if we have only nice public schoolboys like Wigram to guide us, there is some reason I suppose to expect that Oxford Street will be flooded with poison gas one of these days. And what then? Germany will get her colonies.

And then we walked them round the garden, and they were, or said they were, envious and impressed. She thinks of cutting the London season and staying at Southease; where, I fear, we shall now be frequently asked, to help with the garden. And then Kingsley [Martin] rang up and is now imminent. So I intend to walk.

Tuesday 23 April

Kingsley coming at eleven of our first fine morning and staying till six has completely taken away any power I may have over the art of fiction. In order to ensure myself two hours of silence and air I went off to Muggery Poke and home by the river. And there was Kingsley eating cold veal and sweeping up his cauliflower on his fork. An effusive slippery mind: always on the fizz: but how without hardness or fineness of texture! And now of course all dissolved by personal anxieties into a chatter of egotism. "Is there anything more we can say about my affairs?" he remarked at three. No, I said to myself, there is nothing more. Should he stay or should he go? I could only amuse myself by probing the depths of his belief in the *New Statesman*. Directly I minimised its importance, he trotted out arguments to prove its immense value to the world. The only paper that tells the truth, the stay and bread of all the serious minded in Britain. Then, directly I'm alone with him, its his arthritis. True, he's not quite in his right mind; but how tiring this shambling through the hot sand is! And how undistinguished, with no ear or eye, no reflective faculty and catching at any straw to float on; garrulous, untidy, slovenly. It is like reading a living newspaper, talking to Kingsley. It is like listening to a perpetual leading article, so admirable, so well meaning, so shallow.

1935

52 TAVISTOCK SQUARE, WC1

Thursday 25 April
Whether it was Kingsley or not, the usual headache wings its way about me, rather like a fowl soaring and settling and giving me a peck in my back: clouding the mind. I think I have earned a headache and a holiday.

Sunday 28 April
Very cold again. A black sky and the paper festoons looking purple and pink across the streets; large paper crowns and roses being delivered. Julian and Alix [Strachey] to dine, James having a cold. Conversation: whether one can give people a substitute for war. Must have the danger emotion: must climb mountains, fight bulls. Julian says all the young are communists in order to gratify their desire to do things together and in order to have some danger. Lust and danger. Can't cut them out at once. Must divert them on to some harmless object. But what? Some fantasy must be provided. I say many people have found life exciting without war and bull fighting. Has war ever won any cause? Alix says our Civil War. No talk of Lytton: all argument; but interesting.

Tuesday 29 April
I should be tidying the room, but I'm not. Everything scattered with winter's soot and cigarette ash. Everything is a little slack now I'm not writing. But I want to experiment with pure external living for a month - looking, sharing, taking in ideas and impressions. And then watch how the old trout at the bottom of the pond rise. I predict that the desire to write will become so frantic by the time we're on the way back that I shall be making up all along the French roads.

A fine spring morning, very quiet, birds chirping, all London busy wrapping up parcels for the Jubilee.

* * *

MONKS HOUSE, RODMELL

Friday 31 May
Home again, and how queer, as we drove up there was Pinker's basket being carried up by Percy, and she had died yesterday: her body was in the basket. Just as we were saying that we should see her in a moment. A very silent breakfast. And I had been saying how she would put out my match and all the usual jokes. And the intensity of the sense of death – even for a dog – our feeling of her character – something pathetic, and the depression, and the, I suppose, fear of sentimentality and so on.

375

The usual tremor and restlessness after coming back, and nothing to settle to. The view as beautiful as any I've seen, by the way, even on a mud coloured day. We drove through Normandy yesterday and it was Bank Holiday owing to Ascension Day, so that all the people were dressed in respectable black coats and fur. A more ugly tribute to the spirit could not be. I am writing to steady the fidgets, to cover over the depression, and it is only eleven, and I can't take up my book. I think that an hour of reading some good author is prescribed. L. very depressed too, about poor dear Pink. Eight years of a dog certainly means something. I suppose – is it part of our life that's buried in the orchard? That eight years in London – our walks – something of our play private life, that's gone?

52 TAVISTOCK SQUARE, WC1

Wednesday 5 June
Back here again, and the grim wooden feeling that has made me think myself dead since we came back is softening slightly. It's beginning this cursed dry hard empty chapter again in part. Also, after the queer interlude, at once life – that is the telephone beginning – starts. So that one is forcibly chafed.

Saturday 15 June
We dined with Clive, and I felt very fond of him. He has great sympathy. Yes, I'm very fond of my old Clive. And L. was charming, genial, affable, urbane. Clive said, I always say you're half cracked (to me). We were saying how many Rogers and Lyttons there are. He said Segonzac thinks Nessa the best painter in England, much better than Duncan. I will not be jealous, but isn't it odd – thinking of gifts in her? I mean when she has everything else.

Thursday 20 June
I am so oppressed by the thought of all the books I have to write that my head is like a bursting boiler. Half an hour ago, Margery Fry rang up to ask me to open an Exhibition of Roger's paintings at Bristol; to speak for fifteen minutes. Oh we should all love it! she said. Then it appeared that they are counting on me to write a life. She is collecting papers. Helen [Anrep] tells me that the Stracheys are hurt that I never offered to write about Lytton. "But I wanted to and they never asked me!" I said. Oh but they didn't like to suggest it – James says they do want it. And here I am wedged – no, buoyant – in a floating storm of scenes at the end of my book. And we are incessantly asked to dine, lunch, and 'see' people.

Tom last night: supple and subtle, simple and charming. Stayed till 12.15. I never felt so much at my ease. He is a dear old fellow: one of 'us': odd: I felt I liked him as I liked Lytton and Roger – with intimacy in spite of God. We made a good dinner. Publishers' gossip. A story about a party to entertain the [Herbert] Reads. Tom bought fireworks; sugar that dissolved and let out small fish; and chocolates that he thought were full of sawdust. "They're very greedy," he said; "and by mistake the chocolates were full of soap. They set on me ... And it was not a success. So much so that I forgot the fireworks, until they were going. I then let them off on the doorstep." This was very amusing, and not as stiff as usual. Tom wants to give me all his works, but thought I didn't read them – would always have given me all his works.

MONKS HOUSE, RODMELL

Saturday 22 June

It has suddenly become full summer: droning, misting, with birds and bees. The cuckoo calling in the elm tree at three or four this morning so that I had to stop my ears. The heat came suddenly as we walked by the river on Friday. Instead of surveying all this in a torpid swoon of pleasure, Mrs Woolf and Harold [Woolf] came to tea. Then there were figures passing the window – Jack and [his son] Jeremy [Hutchinson]; whereupon she lost all interest in life, poor old lady, thinking that no one would listen to her family stories. She cannot stretch to take in any stranger. But they went on to the [Glyndebourne] opera. Harold and Mrs Woolf and I continued our rather burbling conversation: about highbrows, and then about maids, and the hotel. I heard all about L.'s father, and how he did not take silk till he was forty-five, and made his name over – I forget what case; so it comes over and again, the story of her life, with the usual comments. "And I ask myself, what for? And I am now so lonely. I have lived alone so many years now ..." So we droned, sitting on the terrace before this house – very successful as a sitting place on a hot day. Why does this talk smear my mind so that I can't settle in at 6.30 to do anything but march up and down the terrace? Poor old lady.

52 TAVISTOCK SQUARE, WC1

Tuesday 25 June

A curious and rather unpleasant scene with Mabel. She was in tears, because Mr Woolf never believes a word she says. And I think it is true. L. is very hard on people; especially on the servant class. No sympathy with them; exacting; despotic. So I told him yesterday when he'd complained about the coffee. "If I mayn't even say when the coffee is bad &c." His extreme rigidity of mind surprises me; I mean in its relation to others: his severity; not to myself but then I get up and curse him. What does it come from? Not being a gentleman partly: uneasiness in the presence of the lower classes: always suspects them, is never genial with them. His desire, I suppose, to dominate. Love of power. And then he writes against it. It goes with great justice, in some ways; and simplicity too; and doing good things; but it is in private a very difficult characteristic. I must now get rid of Mabel, and find another; but I feel it's unfair on her.

Thursday 27 June
A good thing for old Bloomsbury to be shaken up no doubt: a good thing to dine with Rebecca West and Mr Andrews [her husband] last night in their flat in Portman Square with the view, with the £750 book case, and the fish carved out of a yew branch, and the modern pictures, period furniture, letter box in the wall and which don't work. But the electric light in the coat cupboard does work. And what's wrong? The plumber's nose – the miner's canary, again. I mean scenting out differences, and let us hope inferiorities. Of course its admirable in its way – impersonal, breezy, yes, go ahead, facing life, eating dinner at the Savoy, meeting millionaires, woman and man of the worldly. What's wrong then? Where does the gas escape? I think its the emptiness, the formality, the social strata they live on – the sense of Now we're having a dinner party and must talk till eleven. Nothing said of any naturalness or spontaneity. Yet that's not quite so: that one could go on having dinner every night and never know each other better. No intimacy at the end of that Oxford Street. Rebecca has great vitality; is a broad browed very vigorous, undistinguished woman; but a buffeter and battler: has taken the waves, I suppose; and can talk in any language; why then this sense of her being a lit up modern block, floodlit by electricity?

Friday 28 June
But dinner with the [David] Cecils last night was very good: free and spontaneous; they were all dressed for a party at the Herberts. Origo was there, whom I like. She is young, tremulous, nervous – very – stammers a little – but honest eyed; very blue eyed. Talk spurted. (I hope I did not try to be brilliant?) We talked about: fear of people; parties: they were all afraid. Up in the drawing room, Origo (her name is Iris) sat down on purpose by me. She has read my books, and was of course full of stumbling enthusiasm; so I made a rush, and talked about writing, spilling out ideas, of a kind.

She lives near Siena, in perfect country; they talk of the seasons; harvest; vintage; share with peasants. And we talked about biography and fiction; but with David pricking up his ears across the room. So he had to be drawn in; and I think we have said the same things before - about the relevant facts; biography as an art. And Origo was silent for half an hour, because of going to the party.

L.'s book [*Quack, Quack!*] selling now; and he is cheerful, and very contrite, in his way, about Mabel.

Sunday 30 June
We went to Swakeleys Farm [Ickenham] yesterday and bought a dog - Sally. She has a fine domed head; very globular eyes; a bloodhound's muzzle; very affectionate, thirteen months old, clasps L.'s breast, climbs on his chair, and is afraid of the basement stairs. She cost £18 - dear me. Still as we say, its nice to have a good dog. And we shall breed from her. She has already her own rather whimsical manner, is lighter, more nervous, perhaps less solid a character than Pinker. But so far she has no marked fault. Had her nose been the eighteenth of an inch longer, she would have been a champion like her sister, who fetched £2 or £300.

Monday 15 July
All this time the Bristol speech was weighing on me, and making me unable to get into my swing for the last lap: so I shut down, wrote it, learnt it, and went to Bristol, the hottest day of the year, on Friday and said it, dripping, to a large, but not I think very appropriate audience. It puzzles me why such displays, using up so much nerve power, should be needed. There was Roger's face on the canvas, smiling at me, and them. But oh the heavenly relief when we drove off in the hot evening to Bradford on Avon, and slept the night in an ancient workhouse in the valley; with a disordered garden, a stream with rotting sacks of old clothes, and the usual elderly ladies, retired business men, spaniels, bustling landladies and so on.

Tuesday 16 July
A curious sense of complete failure. Margery hasn't written to me about my speech. And it was for this that I ruined my last pages! I can't write this morning. Can't get into the swing. Innumerable worries, about getting people to dine and so on, afflict me. My head is all jangled. And I have to get that d—d speech printed, or refuse to. The director has written. Never again, oh never again. But oh this anxiety, and the perpetual knocking of the cup out of my hand.

Wednesday 17 July

Last night as I was sitting alone, L. dining with the Noel-Bakers, there were three rings, and I went down and let in Julian, who said "I have been given a professorship in China." He was very much excited, rather alarmed, naturally – it means that he must start in the middle of August and spend three years in China at Wu Jong, or some such place, alone on a flooded river. So we talked – intimately, I mean about the past and our lives, for the first time. I'm very sorry he's to go – the delightful, honest, bubbly yet after all so sympathetic and trusty young man. Still, obviously this is his first real experience. Then he will travel about China in his holidays, and come back a full grown mature man, with a place in the world. He wants to write on politics and philosophy and to enter politics seriously. He says politics have got more and more on his conscience. They're on the conscience of all his generation. So he can't be merely a poet, a writer. I see his dilemma. So he goes, and I'm sorry. Three years. He will be thirty and I fifty-six alas.

Friday 19 July

I go on getting preliminary headaches. It is no good trying to do the last spurt, these last days here. And we have Edith [Sitwell] and Eddie Playfair, and Ottoline and Julian and Quentin tonight.

Saturday 20 July

But it turned out very well last night: headache lifted. Old Edith singular – very, with her great bald face – so beautiful in some lights; and the thin fan shaped hands and their gestures, timid, appealing, attached to this large fat clumsy body in its black rather sack like dress. She has great wit and some sharp edge of character, a gay rambling butterfly mind; and a good deal of sting, and humanity. In came Ottoline, rather garish, and not so quick in the mind as the rest of us. Eddie a very good listener. Then Julian, with his poems, and Quentin. It was all demonstration on Edith's part, done for our amusement, very difficult to recapture. Looks like a Plantagenet tomb said Ott. So she does, with her high nose, in the air, and her thin lips and her little peering eyes – very medieval.

MONKS HOUSE, RODMELL.

Saturday 3 August

So the summer ended; and now opens again here, with Nessa back; Charleston in being, though rather intermittent, with Duncan in Rome still, Clive going to Greece, Julian to China, and Nessa proposing to paint the

[SS] *Queen Mary* in London. And the harvest is positively orange on the hill, and the country divinely coloured, ripe ash coloured and gold.

Friday 16 August
I cannot make a single note here, because I am so terrifically pressed re-writing – yes, typing out again at the rate, if possible, of 100 pages a week, this impossible eternal book. I work without looking up till one: what it now is, and therefore I must go in, leaving a whole heap of things unsaid: so many people, so many scenes, and beauty, and a fox and sudden ideas.

Wednesday 21 August
Margery Fry comes on Friday with her hands full of papers, she says. Another book. Have I the indomitable courage to start on another? Think of the writing and re-writing. Also there will be joys and ecstasies though. Again very hot. I am going to re-paint this room.

Thursday 22 August
Worked in the morning. Went to Lewes, very hot day; and bought stores, also distemper. And went to the County Library; full of books. So hot after tea: walked along the river bank; a game of bowls; beaten; dined with Keyneses. Maynard not well – rather damp talk. Talk of Abyssinia.

Thursday 29 August
I had meant to write one matter of fact note daily, but have never had time. My brain all tossing after the morning's work. Julian is leaving Newhaven at this moment I suppose for three years. Piles of Roger's papers sent by Margery – a whole box. I have now three large boxes, but dare not look in.

Friday 30 August
For a wonder, my head is clear, and my hand does not shake. Now the book seems to me very good.
    Last night they sang the Belgian anthem at the Prom: out of respect for the Queen [of the Belgians]; and after that, the news-reader announced, in his most penetrated with respectful sorrow voice, the death of the Queen in a motor accident. The car ran off the road into a tree, and she was flung out; struck her head. The King kissed her, as she died. "And as I could not do anything, I went on" says the most trustworthy observer, a passer by, this morning. That, in its way is a tragedy. I distempered – the colour is too blue, but better than the green; then we walked to the river, played bowls, and now expect, alas, a teaparty of the most ferocious description, and its a blowing rainy cold day too.

Saturday 31 August

Only the Wolves came however. Torrents and floods and rain and wind. Edgar [Woolf] like a corpse. Yawned behind his hand. Sylvia [his wife] nervous, cat faced, making conversation. Chiefly about gold fish, dogs and cars; I did my usual owl with Mrs Woolf and she said, as my reward, there was no talk she enjoyed more. Angelica did not come. Mercifully, as the party was damp and dismal, sitting till 6.30 in the dining room. How it rains, said Mrs W. Everybody talking about Abysinnia, which I cannot spell, nor can I form letters, though the morning has been fluent – too fluent.

Wednesday 4 September

The most critical day since August 4th 1914. So the papers say. In London yesterday. Writings chalked up all over the walls. 'Don't fight for foreigners. Briton should mind her own business.' Then a circle with a symbol in it. Fascist propaganda. L. said. Mosley again active. The Queen of Belgium's funeral. Flags at half mast. Bought an umbrella for 25 shillings. The first good umbrella I've had for years, with a tassel.

And I think I will call the book 'The Years'.

Thursday 5 September

I've had to give up writing *The Years* – that's what its to be called – this morning. Absolutely floored. Can't pump up a word. Yet I can see, just, that something's there; so I shall wait, a day or two, and let the well fill. I think, psychologically, this is the oddest of my adventures. Half my brain dries completely; but I've only to turn over, and there's the other half, I think, ready, quite happily to write a little article. Oh if only anyone knew anything about the brain. And, even today, when I'm desperate, almost in tears looking at the chapter, unable to add to it, I feel I've only got to fumble and find the end of the ball of string – some start off place – and my head would fill and the tiredness go.

A very sensational voice on the loudspeaker last night. Mussolini closes the door. Deep disappointment. What next? &c. I was also in a stew about war and patriotism last night. And when it comes to my thinking about my country!

Friday 6 September

Violent wind and rain: violent sun and light; and they go on talking, threatening, advancing and retreating at Geneva.

Sunday 15 September

A terrific downpour. Never was such rain, I think, as this year. Autumn showing through. Autumn birds chirping through the rain. I am thinking I will broach the three boxes of Roger; very staidly, merely beginning to drop a few facts into my brain. But I swear I will not let it buzz me into excitement. Shall I ever have time enough to write out all that's in my head? Though suppose what's in my head becomes sillier and feebler? But why should it? Not if I vary it sufficiently: what with pamphlets, criticism, poetry, fiction, and as I think a play perhaps. But then I'm a very slow writer. And *The Years* will have taken me very nearly three years. And I never think, seriously, of dying.

Tuesday 17 September

So they came: I mean all the Bells, and Janie [Bussy], growing a little elderly, but very gayly dressed; Quentin like a large red and white sheep dog. London yesterday: a violent storm of wind all night. Garden a litter of apples and branches.

Friday 20 September

Yes it was a terrific storm; a storm to mark I suppose. We went to Seaford and saw the explosions of white water over the lighthouse. Sea coming over the road. Clive Angelica and Quentin yesterday; I'm ashamed to say I had longed for this week to be all alone; never had a quiet week all this summer, and the balm it would be – and even a tea party means apprehension, breakage. Poor old Clive a little battered I thought. He has a curious antiquity, premature age, sometimes: I suppose when the top doesn't spin. He had been spinning round Greece; enjoyed himself vastly. Clive is writing a letter to the *New Statesman* against war. War's so awful it can't be right anyhow – an argument for which I like him: his genuine humanity. Dislike of being uncomfortable himself: yes; but he dislikes other people's unhappiness too.

Two nights ago I started reading Roger. There's all the schoolboy letters to begin on: whether its wise, I don't know.

Monday 23 September

Reflections on Tom week end: that it is too long. Can't write. That he is more masterly; tells a story like one who has the right; is broader and bonier and more wild eyed – long almond shaped eyes; that he means to write modern verse plays; that he is self confident although going up Charleston Lane in the dark last night, he told me that he has no self confidence. We dined at Charleston. Nessa ordered eleven grouse, having doubled the number, thinking of them halved. Tom is magisterially accepting new experiences. Likes, more than we do, respectability. Went to service at 8 on Sunday: a wet morning. But he did his duty. A very nice man, Tom; I'm very fond of Tom, and at last not much knocked off my perch by him.

Sunday 29 September
Yesterday I saw the kingfisher again on the river. It flies across and across, very near the surface: it has a bright orange chocolate under side. And it is a tropical bird, sitting weighted on the bank. I have also seen a stoat – brown with a white tipped tail.

Wednesday 2 October
Yesterday we went to the Labour Party meeting at Brighton, and of course, though I have refused to go again this morning, I am so thrown out of my stride that I can't hitch on to *The Years* again. Why? The immersion in all that energy and all that striving for something that is quite oblivious of me; making me feel that I am oblivious of it. It was very dramatic: Bevin's attack on Lansbury. Tears came to my eyes as Lansbury spoke. And yet he was posing I felt – acting, unconsciously, the battered Christian man. Then Bevin too acted I suppose. He sank his head in his vast shoulders till he looked like a tortoise. Told Lansbury not to go hawking his conscience round. The women delegates were very thin voiced and insubstantial. On Monday one said, It is time we gave up washing up. A thin frail protest, but genuine. A little reed piping, but what chance against all this weight of roast beef and beer – which she must cook? All very vivid and interesting; but too much rhetoric, and what a partial view: altering the structure of society: yes, but when it is altered? Do I trust Bevin to produce a good world, when he has his equal rights? These are some of the minnows that go round my head, and distract me from what is, after all, my work. A good thing to have a day of disturbance – two days even – but not three. So I didn't go.

52 TAVISTOCK SQUARE, WCI

Tuesday 15 October
Since we came back I have been in such full flush, with *Years* all the morning, Roger between tea and dinner, a walk, and people, that here's a blank. Yes, it has been ten days of calm full complete bliss. London is quiet, dry, comfortable. I find my dinner cooked for me. No children screaming. Three days I got into wild excitement over *The Next War*. Did I say the result of the Labour Party at Brighton was the breaking of that dam between me and the new book, so that I couldn't resist dashing off a chapter: stopped myself; but have all ready to develop – the form found I think – as soon as I get time? And I plan to do this sometime this next spring, while I go on accumulating Roger. This division is by the way perfect, and I wonder I never hit on it before – some book or work for a book that's quite the

other side of the brain between times. Its the only way of stopping the wheels and making them turn the other way, to my great refreshment, and I hope improvement.

Sunday 27 October
Yesterday we walked across Ken Wood to Highgate and looked at the two little old Fry houses. That's where Roger was born and saw the poppy. I think of beginning with that scene. Yes, that book shapes itself. Then there's my *Next War* – which at any moment becomes absolutely wild, like being harnessed to a shark; and I dash off scene after scene. I think I must do it directly *The Years* is done.

Tuesday 5 November
A specimen day, yesterday: a specimen of the year 1935 when we are on the eve of the Duke of Gloucester's wedding; of a general election; of the Fascist revolution in France; and in the thick of the Abyssinian war; it being mild warm November weather. At 2.30 we went to the BBC and listened to some incomparable twaddle – a soliloquy which the BBC requests me to imitate (a good idea, all the same, if one were free) with all the resources of the BBC behind one: real railway trains; real orchestras; noises; waves, lions and tigers, &c; at 3 we reach [the *Sunday Times* Book Exhibition]: a loudspeaker proclaiming the virtues of literature, the Princess Louise having just declared the show open and said that books are our best friends. There we meet old stringy Rose Macaulay, beating about, like a cat a-hawking odds and ends; home; at 5.15 telephone: the Baroness Nostitz has arrived early; up she comes: a monolithic broad faced Hindenburg, bulky; can't get in or out of my chair; says Germany is the better for Hitler – so they say; I want to get some young man to lecture on English poetry; has a rather hard, dominating impassive eye: must have been a beauty; statuesque; aristocratic. Then a card: in comes the Indian; stayed till 7.30. Was turned out of a carriage in Bengal. Liberty. Justice. Hatred of the British rule. Still, its better than the Italian. *You* are our allies. The British will be kicked out. And now Morgan rings up – May I lunch to discuss the French question. And so we go on. Another specimen day.

Sunday 10 November
Then, last night there was [Cecil] Day Lewis at the Book show, a man who makes queer faces; very nervous at first; with blurred eyes; a nice sensitive young man; but I think it would have been better read, his speech. All poets are misfits and therefore want communion with the common people. What exactly is poetry that is part the desire to communicate with the common people? Political poetry? Certainly it's not easy, one word Wordsworth

poetry. Instead of 'The Leech Gatherer' the tank and poison gas. Too much theory: too little gift I think and too much public speaking. But then if he wants to be in touch with the common people he must talk at Book shows. Not very anxious I think to dine with us, for which I liked him. The usual hurry and scramble of literary gents; and Rose again hawking round the area railings for scraps.

Wednesday 27 November

Too many specimen days – so I can't write. Why can't I get quit of it all? Still happiness persists. And now for thirty minutes of Roger's letters to Helen – that vast sparkling dust heap, the best so far; but how to dig out? how to represent? I must read and read and wait on the moment of illumination. Cold frosty weather, dry for a miracle, and very sunny.

Wednesday 4 December

I must take ten – no five -- minutes off before going up, and from reading Roger to Helen. I read and read and the packets hardly lessen, and I think of love, and L. and me; and the different lives. Yesterday Day Lewis wrote that his agent advises him to leave us for a larger firm, as he must make money. This revives the question of the Press – once again, once again. We both said walking at Ken Wood yesterday, we will now decide on a date and stop it. Yes: reading Roger I want to be free to travel as he was: free of MSS. Yet how keep our books? Or shall we try to hand it on to an intelligent youth? I rather doubt if such exist, or able to run it alone, and then we should still be tied.

Tuesday 10 December

I have promised to deliver *The Years* by 15th February. And had a bad morning's work in consequence. But if I want more time, I shall take it. I'm not time's fool -- no. Nessa I thought very sad again, dining with Clive. What thin stuff we talk compared with what we used to talk. And then people say death doesn't matter.

Saturday 14 December

Dinner last night with the [Aldous] Huxleys; not altogether a sparkler. Julian [Huxley] and his wife, whom I did not recognise, but later understood from his eyebrows &c who he was. A very chirpy I don't know why I think dull, man. Full of scraps of information; and the same quickness that Aldous has – the same vivacity – but less sympathetic. Aldous in great flow: enjoys London; is getting on well with his novel; and thus juicy, sympathetic. He has a sense of the suffering, as well as of the infamy of the world.

Tuesday 17 December

How terrified I'm getting of Ethel [Sands]'s dressed dinner tomorrow! It makes a kind of ring round my mind. What I'm to wear: my velvet or chiffon: then my hair. When I'm there it'll be as easy as shelling peas – why this apprehension?

Friday 20 December

"It's because one changes one's values" Nessa said last night, when we discussed why we couldn't paint or write after a dinner party. And that's true. Only artists know how to live. She can't paint after a party. Can't get back into those proportions. Worse for women, because they have to be more active at parties: have to throw themselves into it. She won't go anywhere now where they make her dress.

MONKS HOUSE, RODMELL

Saturday 28 December

Its all very well to write that date in a nice clear hand, but I cannot disguise the fact that I'm almost extinct; like a charwoman's duster; that is my brain: what with the last revision of the last pages of *The Years*. And is it the last revision? And why should I lead the dance of the days with this tipsy little spin? Its only half past eleven on a damp grey morning, and I want a quiet occupation for an hour. That reminds me – I must devise some let down for myself that won't be too sudden when the end is reached. Shall I ever write a long book again – a long novel that has to be held in the brain, at full stretch – for close on three years? Nor do I even attempt to ask if its worth while. There are mornings so congested I can't even copy out Roger. Goldie [Lowes Dickinson] depresses me unspeakably. Always alone on a mountain top asking himself how to live, theorising about life; never living. Roger always down in the succulent valleys, living. But what a thin whistle of hot air Goldie lets out through his front teeth. Always live in the whole, life in the one; always Shelley and Goethe, and then he loses his hot water bottle; and never notices a face, or a cat or a dog or a flower, except in the glow of the universal. This explains why his highminded books are unreadable. Yet he was so charming, intermittently.

Sunday 29 December

I have in fact just put the last words to *The Years* – rolling rolling, though its only Sunday, and I allowed myself till Wednesday. And I am not in such a twitter as usual. But then I meant it to end calmly - a prose work. And is it good? That I cannot possibly tell. Well there still remains a great deal to do. Anyhow the main feeling about this book is vitality, fruitfulness, energy. Never did I enjoy writing a book more, I think.

Monday 30 December

And today, no its no go. I can't write a word; too much headache. Can only look back at *The Years* as an inaccessible Rocky Island, which I can't explore, can't even think of. At Charleston yesterday. The great yellow table with very few places. Reading Roger I become haunted by him. What an odd posthumous friendship – in some ways more intimate than any I had in life. The things I guessed are now revealed; and the actual voice gone. Clive, Quentin, Nessa, Duncan. A little boasting. Some laughter. Politics – but carefully subdued.

A wild wet night – floods out: rain as I go to bed: dogs barking: wind battering. Now I shall slink indoors, I think, and read some remote book.

1936

Virginia had set herself to finish the revision of The Years *by the middle of February for publication in early summer; she restricted her social activities, and devoted the dismal winter days to a task which she found increasingly onerous and which brought on headaches and insomnia. The death of King George V and the manifestations of public mourning diverted her; but she was agitated by what seemed to her the incessant racket at home – the comings and goings, the telephone-ringings, the meetings – resulting from the worsening international situation and Leonard's political involvements. By early March (when Hitler's troops occupied the Rhineland), the decision was taken to have* The Years *set in galleys to accommodate the expectant American publishers, and Virginia began to despatch the typescript to the printers in sections as she finished them, the last batch being sent from Monks House at Easter. Racked by headaches, she was now close to total collapse, alarming Leonard who decided that proof-correction and publication must be postponed until the autumn, and she should have a complete rest. There are no diary entries between 9 April and 11 June. Virginia remained largely recumbent at Monks House, with brief intervals in London and a change of scene when Leonard drove her on a tour of the West Country as far as her beloved Cornwall. After two months she resumed work on the proofs of* The Years, *but again the effort and the pressures of London life threatened her nervous stability. The Woolfs retreated to Rodmell on 9 July and remained there until 11 October, Leonard going up weekly to attend to business at Tavistock Square. Virginia wrote no diary between 23 June and 30 October. At Monks House she rested, read, walked, played bowls in the garden, saw a few familiars, and laboured, an hour at a time, on her galley proofs; but it became apparent that autumn publication would be out of the question. Back in London, much improved in health, she struggled on, alternating between confidence and despair, and in the latter mood finally appealed for Leonard's verdict. He read the heavily worked-over galleys and, fearing the effect of adverse criticism on his overwrought wife, praised her book rather beyond his real opinion of its merit. The relief was immeasurable. She was able to finish the proofs by the end of the year and allow herself to turn eagerly to the writing of her long-simmering political work,* Three Guineas, *and to continue her preparatory reading for the biography of Roger Fry.*

Gradually Virginia picked up the threads of her social life. Events in the outer world also began again to engage her interest and concern (the Spanish Civil War had broken out while she was ill at Rodmell in July), none more so than the drama of King Edward VIII's abdication, which fascinated her. She was interested, and flattered too, when her girlhood friend Nelly's husband Lord Robert Cecil, now Viscount Cecil of Chelwood and President of the League of Nations Union, invited himself to tea at Tavistock Square and confided his opinion of world statesmen.

Curiously enough, throughout this ill-omened year, Virginia was sustained by Ethel Smyth's constant and open-hearted concern, expressed in numerous letters, to which she responded equally: over forty letters from Virginia to Ethel are preserved from this period.

1936

MONKS HOUSE, RODMELL

Friday 3 January
I began the year with three entirely submerged days, headache, head bursting, head so full, racing with ideas; and the rain pouring; the floods out; when we stumbled out yesterday the mud came over my great rubber boots; the water squelched in my soles; so this Christmas has been, as far as country is concerned, a failure, and in spite of what London can do to chafe and annoy I'm glad to go back, and have, rather guiltily, begged not to stay here another week. I am content though because I think that I have recovered enough balance in the head to begin *The Years*, I mean the final revision, on Monday.

Saturday 4 January
The weather has improved, and we have decided to stay till Wednesday. So I have ordered a sirloin and we shall go for a drive. L. is happier: will now do his trees.

Tuesday 7 January
A pouring day. All the angles of the twigs have white drops on them. That's Hardy's gift by the way: minute obstinately individual observations. But how his reputation ever mounted, considering the flatness, tedium, and complete absence of gift of *The Trumpet Major*, I can't say; and would like to discover. I think he had genius and no talent. And the English love genius.

52 TAVISTOCK SQUARE, WC1

Friday 10 January
Back again. A great gale all yesterday and a dusk over everything and rain, so that the comfort I had expected was diminished. Origo to tea, and wants to dine next week. All the same I will keep my hands on the reins. For, to

tell the truth, this six weeks is going to be a most perilous enterprise. How on earth to finish, to get typed, to correct by the end of February?

Monday 13 January

The precious days are ticking over. About thirty now left me, and how much to do! But my new method is working I think: each hour mapped in bed, and kept to, so far.

Thursday 16 January

Seldom have I been more completely miserable than I was about 6.30 last night, reading over the last part of *The Years*. Such feeble twaddle – such twilight gossip it seemed; such a show up of my own decrepitude, and at such huge length. I could only plump it down on the table and rush up stairs with burning cheeks to L. He said This always happens. But I felt, no it has never been so bad as this. Now this morning, dipping in, it seems to me, on the contrary, a full, bustling live book.

Iris Origo to dine alone. At first I thought this too is going to be a wash out. But, chiefly owing to L.'s charm, and making myself a little drunk, we all chattered, and we both liked her. And she is to come again. A genuine woman, I think, honest, intelligent and, to my pleasure, well dressed; also being a snob, I liked her Bird of Paradise flight through the gay world. A long green feather in her hat suggests the image.

Sunday 19 January

I open this, forced by a sense of what is expected by the public, to remark that Kipling died yesterday; and that the King (George 5th) is probably dying today. The death of Kipling has set all the old war horses of the press padding round their stalls; and the papers have to eke out five or six columns with the very bare bulletin – condition causes anxiety – which they supplement with biographies of doctors, of nurses, pictures of Sandringham, remarks of old villagers, gossip about the little Princesses in their cherry coloured coats, a snow man, &c. But the fact remains that all the Princes have gathered together, and I suppose at any moment the butler may come in, just as they're finishing dinner, and say King Edward 8th, upon which – but I need hardly invent that scene having already so many on my hands.

I went up to an elderly stout woman reading the paper at *The Times* Book Club the other day. It was Margery Strachey. What are you doing? I said. 'Nothing!' she replied. 'I've got nowhere to go and nothing to do.' And I left her, sitting reading *The Times*.

Monday 20 January

And the King is not dead, but the same. It is a very fine bright day.

Tuesday 21 January

The King died last night. We were dining [in Pimlico] and drove back past Buckingham Palace. It was a clear dry night, rather windy and rather cold. As we turned the corner and came by the Palace we saw cars drawn up all along the Mall. On the white monument people were standing; there was a cluster like a swarm of bees round the railings. Some people were plastered against the railings, holding on to the bars. There was a discreet frame, like a text, holding a bulletin. We had to drive on past the Monument before the policeman, who spoke with weary politeness, would let us stop. Then we got out, and walked back and tried to shove our way through the crowd. But it was impossible. So I asked a policeman "What is the latest news?" (we had only seen Strength Diminishing on the placards as we drove out) to which he replied "His Majesty's life is drawing to a peaceful close." This he said without conviction, as if he were reciting words put into his mouth, but with a certain official tolerance. There was some agitation and excitement; many foreigners talking German; a large proportion of distinguished looking men, in semi evening dress. As we turned away, a firework – a silver gilt sputtering fizzing torch began bubbling up, like a signal, like a festival, but it was presumably a photographer's light. The crowd clustering on the rails became chalky white for a few seconds; and then we got into the car and drove home. The streets were very empty. But save for the occasional placard – it was now 'The King is Dying' – there was nothing out of the way. What I took for guns booming was only the banging of the loose door in the mews. But at 3 this morning, L. was woken by paper boys shouting in the street. The King had in fact died at 12.05. He was dead when we were outside the Palace.

Most of the men in Southampton Row wear black ties which are brand new, or dark blue ties, which are the nearest they can get. In the stationers' the woman spoke with a subdued kindness as if we were both mourning a great uncle we had never seen. A very fine cold day. Sun shining.

Wednesday 22 January

The people of America are mourning, as if for their own King; and the Japanese are in tears. So it goes on. But as a matter of fact the Prime Minister [Stanley Baldwin] – we are only allowed official announcements on the BBC, and if you turn it on you only hear the ticking of a vast clock – was rather fitting. He gave out the impression that he was a tired country gentleman; the King another; both enjoyed Christmas at home; and the Queen is very lonely; one left the other taken, as must happen to married couples; and the King had seemed to him tired lately, but very kind, and quiet as if ready for a long journey; and had woken once or twice on the last day and had said something Kind ('Kind' was the adjective always) and had said to his Secretary "How is the Empire?" – an odd expression. "The Empire, Sir, is well"; whereupon he fell asleep. And then of course, he ended with God Save the King.

The shops are all black. Mourning is to outlast the London Season. A black Ascot.

Monday 27 January

And I forgot to say we saw the coffin and the Princes come from King's Cross: the coffin with its elongated yellow leopards, the crown glittering and one pale blue stone luminous, a bunch of red and white lilies; after that three undertakers in black coats with astrakhan collars: 'our King' as the woman next me called him, who looks blotched and as if chipped by a stone mason; only his rather set wistful despair marked him from any shop-keeper – not an ingratiating face: bloated, roughened, as if by exposure to drink, life, grief, and as red as a fisherboy's. Then it was over. And I shall not try to see more. But the whole world will be afoot at dawn tomorow.

Tuesday 28 January

The King is at this moment being buried, and if I go up I shall hear the service. A fine mild morning. The sun is out, the streets almost empty. An occasional hoot.

Sunday 9 February

It is now the 9th of February and I have three weeks in which to finish my book. I work three hours in the morning; two often after tea. Then my head swells and I sleep.

Tuesday 25 February

And this will show how hard I work. This is the first moment – this five minutes before lunch – that I've had to write here. I work all the morning: I work from 5 to 7 most days. I have sworn that the script shall be ready, typed and corrected, on the 10th March. L. will then read it.

Saturday 29 February

Leap Year day. In these weeks of solitude, seeing no one, only going round to Nessa, refusing all parties, I become so absorbed in *The Years* that I take the other world as a kind of amplification, variation in another key. Nothing interferes for the moment; and I rush on. It is drizzling. It is a damp dismal day.

All Duncan's pictures have been refused – to give a scrap of upper air news – by the *Queen Mary*. A great Bloomsbury agitation set on foot.

Wednesday 4 March
Well yesterday I sent off 132 pages to Clark [Printers]. We have decided
to take this unusual course – that is to print it in galleys before L. sees it
and send it to America.

I can't help feeling in the subcutaneous way one does feel such things
that we are slightly on the up grade again: old Bloomsbury. Its rather a
nicer feeling than being on the down grade perhaps. The European situation
developed on Saturday. We were at Monks House. Hitler has broken his
word again.

Friday 13 March
We walked round Kensington Gardens yesterday discussing politics. Aldous
refuses to sign the latest manifesto because it approves sanctions. He's a
pacifist. So am I. Ought I to resign? L. says that considering Europe is now
on the verge of the greatest smash for six hundred years, one must sink
private differences and support the League [of Nations]. He's at a special
Labour Party meeting this morning. This is the most feverish overworked
political week we've yet had. Hitler has his army on the Rhine. Meetings
take place in London. Another meeting tomorrow. As usual, I think Oh
this will blow over. But its odd, how near the guns have got to our private
life again. I can quite distinctly see them and hear a roar, even though I go
on, like a doomed mouse, nibbling at my daily page. What else is there
to do – except answer the incessant telephones, and listen to what L. says.
Everything goes by the board. Happily we have put off all dinners and so
on, on account of *The Years*.

Monday 16 March
For my own guidance: I have never suffered, since *The Voyage Out*, such
acute despair on re-reading, as this time. On Saturday for instance: there I
was, faced with complete failure; and yet the book is being printed.
Yesterday I read it again; and I think it may be my best book. However
... A walk down the river and through Richmond Park did more than
anything to pump blood in. Politics have slightly died down.

Tuesday 24 March
I'm so absorbed in *Two Guineas* – that's what I'm going to call it – I must
very nearly verge on insanity I think. I get so deep in this book I don't
know what I'm doing. Find myself walking along the Strand talking aloud.

Wednesday 1 April
I forgot though to make L. an April fool, and he forgot too. We went to
tea with Gerald [Duckworth] yesterday, which was like visiting an alligator

in a tank, an obese and obsolete alligator, lying like our tortoises, half in and half out of the water. I doubt that he much enjoyed seeing us, or has any capacity for enjoying anything left. We talked publishers' shop. And Gerald told me about his diseases, and threw cold water, sensible, business-man's very faded common sense – for he has failed as a business man – on all projects. There's nothing in it – nothing in it, he kept saying. Also, nothing doing, nothing doing whatever. I think felt us perhaps more in the swim than himself. I doubt he has any sentiment about the past. So we went, and walked in the park.

MONKS HOUSE, RODMELL

Thursday 9 April
Now will come the season of depression. The last batch was posted to Clark yesterday. L. is in process of reading. I daresay I'm pessimistic, but I fancy a certain tepidity in his verdict so far; but then its provisional. The horror is that tomorrow, after this one windy day of respite – oh the cold North wind that has blown ravaging daily since we came – after this one day's respite, I say, I must begin at the beginning and go through 600 pages of cold proof. Why oh why? Never again, never again. Dining at Charleston tonight, I'm glad to say.

And then there was Colefax – yes, instantly on us, the first day we arrived, for lunch: in a black beret, and grey tweed coat. Not improved by sorrow. Poor woman, what a hard nature, so that to lose [her husband] only liberates a little misty sentiment. And yet she's brave, I think; but still the hostess, the aspiring, restless, dissatisfied – running, running, like a dog behind a carriage that always goes too fast. We had polite conversation about notables over the fire, and then she left. Rolls Royce.

52 TAVISTOCK SQUARE, WC1

Thursday 11 June
I can only, after two months, make this brief note, to say at last after two months dismal and worse, almost catastrophic illness – never been so near the precipice to my own feeling since 1913 – I'm again on top. I have to re-write, I mean interpolate and rub out most of *The Years* in proof. But I can't go into that. Can only do an hour or so. Oh but the divine joy of being mistress of my mind again! Back from Monks House yesterday. Now I am going to live like a cat stepping on eggs till my 600 pages are done. I think I can – I think I can – but must have immense courage and buoyancy

to compass it. This, as I say, my first voluntary writing since April 9th, after which I pitched into bed: then to Cornwall – no note of that; then back; then to Monks House; home yesterday for a fortnight's trial.

Sunday 21 June
After a week of intense suffering – indeed mornings of torture – and I'm not exaggerating – pain in my head – a feeling of complete despair and failure – a head inside like the nostrils after hay fever – here is a cool quiet morning again, a feeling of relief; respite; hope. I am living so constrainedly; so repressedly; I can't make notes of life. Everything is planned, battened down. I do half an hour down here; go up, often in despair. Lie down; walk round the Square; come back, do another ten lines. I see people lying on sofa between tea and dinner. A very strange, most remarkable summer. I am learning my craft in the most fierce conditions.

Tuesday 23 June
A good day – a bad day – so it goes on. Few people can be so tortured by writing as I am. Yet I think I can bring it off, if I only have courage and patience: take each scene quietly; I think it may be a good book. And then – oh when its finished! My brain is like a scale: one grain pulls it down. Yesterday it balanced: today it dips.

*   *   *

52 TAVISTOCK SQUARE, WC1

Friday 30 October
I do not wish for the moment to write out the story of the months since I made the last mark here. I do not wish, for reasons I cannot now develop, to analyse that extraordinary summer. Can I still 'write'? That is the question, you see.

Tuesday 3 November
Miracles will never cease – L. actually likes *The Years*! He thinks it so far as good as any of my books. I will put down the actual facts. On Sunday I started to read the proofs. When I had read to the end of the first section I was in despair: stony but convinced despair. I made myself yesterday read on to 'Present Time'. When I reached that landmark I said this is happily so bad that there can be no question about it. I must carry the proofs, like a dead cat, to L. and tell him to burn them unread. This I did. And a weight fell off my shoulders. It was cold and dry and very grey and I went out and walked through the graveyard with Cromwell's daughter's tomb down through Gray's Inn along Holborn and so back. Now I was no longer

Virginia, the genius, but only a perfectly insignificant yet content – shall I call it spirit? a body? And very tired. Very old. So we lunched, in a constraint: a grey acceptance. I was not unhappy. And L. said he thought I might be wrong about the book. Then ever so many strange men arrived. Then, after tea, we went to the *Sunday Times* Book Show. How stuffy it was! How dead I felt – Oh how infinitely tired! We went home, and L. read and read and said nothing; I began to feel actively depressed; and I fell into one of my horrid heats and deep slumbers, as if the blood in my head were cut off. Suddenly L. put down his proof and said he thought it extraordinarily good – as good as any of them. And now he is reading on, and tired out with the exertion of writing these pages I'm going up to read the Italian book.

Wednesday 4 November

L. who has now read to the end of '1914' still thinks it extraordinarily good: very strange; very interesting; very sad. But my difficulty is this: I cannot bring myself to believe that he is right. It may be simply that I exaggerated its badness, and therefore he now, finding it not so bad, exaggerates its goodness. If it is to be published, I must at once sit down and correct: but how can I? Every other sentence seemed to me bad. It is one of the most puzzling situations I have ever been in. Of course we might appeal to Morgan.

Thursday 5 November

The miracle is accomplished. L. put down the last sheet about 12 last night; and could not speak. He was in tears. He says it is 'a most remarkable book' – he *likes* it better than *The Waves*; and has not a spark of doubt that it must be published. I hardly know yet if I'm on my heels or head – so amazing is the reversal since Tuesday morning. I have never had such an experience before. Now it is pouring and we go down to Lewes for the fireworks.

Tuesday 10 November

I wonder if anyone has ever suffered so much from a book, as I have from *The Years*. Once out I will never look at it again. Its like a long childbirth. Think of that summer, every morning a headache, and forcing myself into that room in my nightgown; and lying down after a page: and always with the certainty of failure. But now I feel I don't care what anyone says so long as I'm rid of it. Madrid not fallen. Chaos. Slaughter. War surrounding our island.

Tuesday 17 November

Lord [Robert] Cecil to tea. He has grown large, but still has the angular twisting movements of a thin man. His face is moon shaped; brown and pink – it used to be lank and cadaverous. He is more genial, and at his ease. A man of the world. A little frieze of still brown hair, very fine, at the back of his head. Bright merry eyes. In good spirits, in spite of the world. But he said, I think there is more vitality both in men and in institutions, than one expects. "We have failed (the League of Nations); no matter, we must try again. I'm convinced by Winston [Churchill]. An alliance of France, England and Russia. Bertrand Russell insane! Complete insanity! To tell us we are to submit to Hitler! Do what Hitler tells us! What do you think, Sally?" Caressed Sally [dog] with his long pointed fingers. Had been taken to see Mussolini. An absurd fellow. There he sat at the end of a very long room, making eyes at me (he made eyes). That doesn't impress me. Gave the impression of extreme well being: a saucepan gently simmering on the comfort and consideration of seventy years. Best type of English governing class I suppose: the flower of 19th century civilisation: urbane, broadminded, kind and hopeful. Much more cheerful than the intellectuals. Inclined to mock the earnest intellectual. Very nice of him to come of course. I was flattered. And it was raining and he went home in the Tube. Very poor he said. Couldn't afford a car. Anything else? Not much deluded I should say. Winston on side of Franco, because he has friends in that camp. But the people don't respect Winston. He changes his mind and policy. Baldwin a complete failure. That's about all.

Tuesday 24 November
Here I am cleft as usual in my little stick. So free and so cabined. Began *Three Guineas* yesterday. And liked it. Today the old symptoms – time of life: the swollen veins; the tingling; the odd falling; feeling of despair. Brain not fully blooded. Hot and cold. I'm glad, how odd, that I'm lunching with Clive. That I've a new black felt hat, bought yesterday after having Ethel Smyth to lunch. Glad too that Helen Anrep is dining with me: that I shan't be alone; alone I fall into those trances, comas, when I want to be clear and to read. But I've been on the whole vigorous and cheerful since the wonderful revelation of L.'s that night. How I woke from death – or non-being – to life! What an incredible night – what a weight rolled off!

Very cold and dank. We came up on Sunday through the fog. Figures suddenly emerged. Walked by the kerb all through Wimbledon and Wandsworth. The kerb ended. Here I was lost in a trackless mist. And so on and on. A little boy emerged – a street ruffian. People lined the pavement watching the lost cars. Another man led us. Just as we thought we must find a garage and come home by tube a bus driver told us that in two hundred yards it would be clear. So, miraculously, it was. Glass clear – lit up, and so home.

Friday 27 November
L. has a confidential story about the King and Mrs Simpson, told him in secret by Kingsley Martin.

Monday 30 November
There is no need whatever in my opinion to be unhappy about *The Years*. It seems to me to be a taut real strenuous book: with some beauty and poetry too. A full packed book. Just finished it; and feel a little exalted.

Monday 7 December
Now, we are – without a King? With a Queen? What? The Simpson affair is on the surface. It was on Wednesday 2 December that the Bishop [of Bradford] commented on the King's lack of religion. On Thursday all the papers, *The Times* and *Daily Telegraph* very discreetly mentioned some domestic difficulties; others Mrs Simpson. All London was gay and garrulous – not exactly gay, but excited. We can't have a woman Simpson for Queen, that was the sense of it. She's no more royal than you or me, was what the grocer's young woman said. But today we have developed a strong sense of human sympathy: we are saying Hang it all – the age of Victoria is over. Let him marry whom he likes. Harold [Nicolson] is glum as an undertaker, and so are the other nobs. They say Royalty is in Peril. The Empire is divided. In fact never has there been such a crisis. Spain, Germany, Russia – all are elbowed out. Parties are forming. The different interests are queueing up behind Baldwin or Churchill. Mosley is taking advantage of the crisis for his ends. In fact we are all talking nineteen to the dozen; and it looks as if this one little insignificant man had moved a pebble which dislodges an avalanche. Things – empires, hierarchies, moralities – will never be the same again.

Thursday 10 December
Has the King abdicated? I think so. At 3.30 Baldwin will speak. *The Times* reiterates No one has hurried the King. We sympathise but . . . it is for His Majesty to decide. Mrs Simpson at Cannes says she is ready to withdraw from an unhappy and untenable position. Cars, black cars, drive constantly to and from Fort Belvedere where the King is immured, some say drinking. Baldwin goes down constantly: the King is rude and drunk. Last night the Queen and Princess Mary went. A brake laden with luggage was seen to leave the fort. No royal engagements are kept. It is a time of mourning. The Queen visits old curiosity shops and is said to have bought a gold frog. Meanwhile 'the people' have swung round to a kind of sneering contempt. "Ought to be ashamed of himself" the tobacconist's young woman said. Last night Mary [Hutchinson] on the telephone said that to her certain

knowledge the King was entirely possessed, against all friends' advice, of some bourgeois (her word) obsession about marriage: insisted, after two years of license, that the marriage service was essential – though Mrs Simpson did not wish it. She says all his friends think him insane. He could have gone on with Mrs Simpson as mistress till they both cooled: no one objected. Now he has probably lost her, and thrown away the Kingdom and made us all feel slightly yet perceptibly humiliated. Its odd, but so I even feel it. Walking through Whitehall the other day, I thought what a Kingdom! England! and to put it down the sink ... Not a very rational feeling. *The Times* quotes, in its leader this morning, letters which beginning earlier in the week with hysterical sympathy, now say Our sons and brothers gave their wives and lovers and also their lives for the country. And can't even the King do this –? But everything now hardens into the certainty that the King can't do this, and will follow his luggage to Cannes. I am reluctant to end this page, because it is I think the last entry I shall make in this book on the subject of Edward the Eighth. If I write tomorrow, it will be in the reign, I suppose, of Albert the First – and he's not, so Mary says, a popular choice. Let it be. This afternoon I shall go down in the fog to the hub of the universe, and hang about the House of Commons.

[*Later*] This is the first hour, or since it is 5.30, and the abdication was announced at 4, the first hour and a half, of the new reign. Yes, I thought: I will go to Westminster. A bus took me to the top of Whitehall. There traffic was turned off and I dismounted. Whitehall was full of shuffling and trampling. Opposite the Horse Guards there was Ottoline, black, white, red lipped, coming towards me. She intercepted my impulse to escape. We turned and walked on, and on we wandered down the yellow brown avenue. That's the window out of which Charles the First stepped when he had his head cut off said Ottoline, pointing to the great lit up windows [of the Banqueting House] in their frame of white stone. I felt I was walking in the 17th Century with one of the courtiers; and she was lamenting not the abdication of Edward, but the execution of Charles. Its dreadful, dreadful, she kept saying. Poor silly little boy. No one could ever tell him a thing he disliked. But to throw it away ... Still he hadn't yet, so far as we knew, thrown it away. However, she had a tea party: so we hailed a taxi. Have you any news? the man said. No ... What do you think? I say he should. We don't want a woman thats already had two husbands and an American when there are so many good English girls ... We were thus driving and talking when a newspaper car drove by with the word Abdication very large on a placard. It stopped near us; and the first papers in the bale were bought by Ottoline and me.

Sunday 13 December

Then we had the Broadcast. "Prince Edward speaking from Windsor Castle" as the emotional butler announced. Upon which, with slight stammer at first, in a steely strained voice, [he] began: "At long last ... I can speak to you ... The woman I love ... I who have none of those blessings ..." Well, one came in touch with human flesh I suppose. Also with a set pigheaded steely mind ... a very ordinary young man; but the thing had never been done on that scale. One man set up in the Augusta Tower at Windsor addressing the world on behalf of himself and Mrs Simpson. Out in the Square there was complete emptiness. All the life had been withdrawn to listen, to judge. And then Edward went on in his steely way to say the perfectly correct things, about the Constitution, the Prime Minister, Her Majesty my Mother. Finally he wound up, God Save the King with a shout; after which I heard his sigh go up, a kind of whistle. Then silence. Complete silence. Then Mr Hibbert saying: And now we shut down. Good night everybody. Goodnight; and we were tucked up in our beds.

Thursday 30 December

There in front of me lie the proofs – the galleys – to go off today ... a sort of stinging nettle that I cover over. Nor do I wish even to write about it here. A divine relief has possessed me these last days – at being quit of it – good or bad. Now for action and pleasure again and going about.

1937

The millstone of The Years *lifted from her shoulders, Virginia started the new year in a much happier frame of mind, free now to compose* Three Guineas; *and she had need of fortitude: two deaths, that of the sculptor Stephen Tomlin, and that of Miss West, the dependable manager of the Hogarth Press, affected her fairly closely; she endured acute anxiety – happily short-lived – when it seemed that Leonard might have a serious illness; she herself experienced disquieting symptoms which she ascribed to the menopause; her nephew Julian Bell was returning from China determined to fight against the Fascists in Spain; and over all loomed the approaching publication of* The Years *and the dread that it might be condemned. To her relief and some surprise it received very good notices, sold extremely well, and became a bestseller in America.*

Virginia always took pleasure in the company of the younger generation, and besides her nephews and nieces and their friends, liked to entertain young writers such as Christopher Isherwood and Stephen Spender. At this period conversation turned almost inevitably to politics and the Spanish Civil War. The Woolfs took their three-week holiday in May, avoiding the hubbub of the coronation of George VI, driving in Western France as far south as Albi. Not long after their return, Julian, having been dissuaded from joining the International Brigade, departed for Spain as an ambulance driver. Spain was never far from the surface this summer: Virginia saw refugees from Bilbao traversing the streets of Bloomsbury; she sat on the platform at an Albert Hall meeting called to raise funds for Basque children; and on 20 July the blow fell: news of Julian Bell's death reached London, and thenceforward Virginia devoted herself to the care of her stricken sister. The Woolfs drove her to Charleston and settled in at Monks House, Virginia going over almost daily to be with Vanessa. She was able to work at Three Guineas, *defining her ideas on her walks as though in argument with Julian, and reached the end of her first draft soon after returning to Tavistock Square on 10 October, when she at once began the rewriting. Towards the end of the year she had a little bout of temperature, but far worse, there was again a worry about Leonard's health. They went to Monks House for Christmas, but on 29 December his condition so alarmed them that they returned to London to consult his doctor.*

1937

Monks House, Rodmell

Sunday 10 January
Another windless perfectly brilliant day. And Tommy [Stephen Tomlin] is dead and buried yesterday, just as Clive was saying that no one had died lately. But Tommy's death is a queer piece of work. We said on the whole perhaps it was a good thing, because he seemed ravaged by his own misery, couldn't work, had been a failure; tore everyone and everything to bits in a kind of egotistic rage. My own intercourse with him broke over that bust, when I took a shudder at the impact of his neurotic clinging persistency, and perhaps behaved, though I didn't think so at the time, unreasonably, perversely. But the odd thing was that he had, years ago, great sensibility; a human charm, and sympathy. And he had a great gift for making people love him. But there was something twisted, deformed in him: some shudder and profound distaste, and uneasiness. A tragic, wasted life; something wrong in it; and wrong that we shouldn't feel it more.

52 Tavistock Square, WC1

Sunday 17 January
Home again. Poor L. grumbling, making Mabel a peg on which to hang his misery, oh dear. How quiet London is however. Not a sound. I must make up my mind to work. First I must tidy up: throw away all the old *Years* litter, get things clean and fresh. Lunch with Clive tomorrow to meet I don't know who. A great many MSS to read. I shall also go to the National Gallery and to the Zoo.

Thursday 28 January
Sunk once more in the happy tumultuous dream: that is to say began *Three Guineas* this morning, and can't stop thinking it. Dining with Hutchinsons to meet [H. G.] Wells.

Friday 29 January

Wells rather shrunk. Hair still brown, but has the dyed appearance of hair that is brown on an old face. Lines more marked; skin less plumped out. He was very affable. He sat by me, and was a little apprehensive of the highbrow at first I think. We made talk about Scotland; then switched off on to the poverty of authors. Then we got on to Russian politics, so, somehow to Tom Eliot. Tee Ess he called him with a hiss of despite; and then proceeded to say how he, which I think meant we, had been the death of English literature. Afraid of being vulgar, that's what was at the root of it. And Tom's religion. By that we came to the Archbishop. "I wonder – does Cosmo Gordon Lang ever alone at the dead of night face his Trinity? We all have to – But does he ..." and so on. He likes to be listened to; and to chatter on, loosely generally, as he said to me when the gentlemen came upstairs. "We had a loose general kind of talk." Then he lay back in the armchair, put his tiny hands and still tinier feet together, and chirped away. It was old man's talk; mellower than I remembered; mischievous; eyes a little bleared; kindly in his way; merry. He gives the impression that on the whole he is a detached satisfied little man; conscious of his lack of distinction; prone to snap at any pretence; content I think with his position, and immensely interested still. Had one seen him behind a counter he would have seemed the very type of busy little grocer. And I suspect that when he faces his Trinity at dead of night there are a good many books that he thinks, justly, trash; but remembers that he has done a vast mass of work, and thinks it won't all die; and is amused at the place he has made – from Bromley, Kent to Regent's Park; and I suppose the greatest circulation in the whole world. A humane man in some corner; also brutal; also entirely without poetry.

Friday 12 February

Why should I write here? Only that I am devilishly anxious. L. is going to a Harley Street specialist at four today to get a report: whether the sugar means diabetes or prostate gland or nothing serious. And I must face facts: how to keep cool, how to control myself, if it is a bad report. Work is my only help. That is the conclusion I came to last night. Probably it is only a question of treatment. Anyhow we shall soon know, unless he keeps us hanging about. It is a very fine cold day and we are going straight on down to Rodmell where there is a Labour Party meeting and Quentin to dinner. I have been writing hard since January 28th at *Three Guineas*, and must simply keep at it – it is the one support. We had too the anxiety about Julian – he means to enlist for Spain. [Francis] Cornford's son was killed there last week. Nessa was in one of her entirely submerged moods on Monday when we went in. Always that extraordinary depth of despair. But I must fight, that's my instinct: but we are faced with a horrid afternoon. I feel like the man who had to keep dancing on hot bricks. Can't let myself stop. Hence I suppose I write here; which explains why Tolstoy and his wife kept diaries.

Monday 15 February
Oh it was heavenly driving down to Rodmell on Friday evening with that weight off us! I walked Harley Street up and down up and down for an hour. At last just before five L. came in his new light overcoat, and smiled. [Dr] Graham thinks it's only a case of diet: wouldn't even examine him for diabetes; said nothing about prostate gland; found all organs very healthy. So as I say we drove down, in that odd relieved state which seems as much physical as mental. Got to Monks House only at 7.30, had to dine hurriedly; Quentin rang up to say his car had broken down. The meeting. Quentin came at 9.30; in gum boots wet through; had dinner at 10.30; went back over the downs in the rain. And over us brooded the same delicious ease and content, as if another space of life had been granted us.

Thursday 18 February
A kind gentleman has troubled my peace with a copy of the *Saturday Review* (USA) in which I am called a maker of films and laces; a sitter in shaded drawing rooms, and so on. I am quite sure that the next lap of my life will be accompanied with whistlings and catcalls in this strain. The question I have now to settle is what 'attitude' to adopt. This kind of sneer has an inhibiting effect for the moment. But I must be quit of the need even of defending myself. I want to forge ahead, on my own lines. But in London where I am exposed all day and every day to criticism some plating of resolution is absolutely needed. And I think I've got it by the tip of the tail – a new kind of indifference. I experiment with snubs and sneers. How little they matter in the sum! how little they count with other people – how little the goodness or badness of my books affects the world.

Stephen Spender came to tea and dinner the other day. Rather a beautiful if too conventionally poetic young man: sunk cheeks, large blue eyes, skin always burning; great enthusiasm, but now tempered because, having married, his friend, the male, joined the Foreign Legion, is fighting in Spain; [his wife] sits at Brussels studying Spanish MSS in order, should he be killed in Spain, she may have a job to fall back on. A curious interpretation of marriage, dictated by the guns. I like him: told him not to fight. He argued that we cannot let the Fascists overrun Spain: then it'll be France; then us. We must fight. Stephen said the Communist Party which he had that day joined, wanted him to be killed, in order that there might be another Byron. He has a child's vanity about himself. Interesting to me at the moment, as I'm working out the psychology of vanity. Then he went to speak about Spain at the Friends' House, and we to *Uncle Vanya*. A very cold night.

Saturday 20 February
I turn my eyes away from the Press as I go upstairs, because there are all the review copies of *The Years* packed and packing. They go out next week. What do I anticipate with such clammy coldness? I think chiefly that my friends won't mention it, will turn the conversation rather awkwardly. I think I anticipate considerable lukewarmness among the friendly reviewers – respectful tepidity; and a whoop of red Indian delight from the Grig[son]s who will joyfully and loudly announce that this is the long drawn twaddle of a prim prudish bourgeois mind, and say that now no one can take Mrs W. seriously again.

Sunday 21 February
[Christopher] Isherwood and Sally [Chilver] last night. Isherwood rather a find: very small red cheeked nimble and vivacious. He said Morgan and I were the only living novelists the young – he, Auden, Spender I suppose – take seriously. For Morgan's books he has a passion. "I'll come out with it then Mrs Woolf – you see, I feel you're a poetess: he does the thing I want to do . . ." But I was satisfied with my share of the compliment which came very pat in these days of depression. Auden and he are writing away together. He does the prose, Auden the poetry. Auden wants innumerable blankets on his bed; innumerable cups of tea; then shuts the shutters and draws the blinds and writes. Isherwood is a most appreciative merry little bird. A real novelist, I suspect; not a poet; full of acute observations on character and scenes. One of the most vital and observant of the young; and a relief after the mute dismals of the others.

Tuesday 23 February
The doctor says L. is quite normal! So all that might have been spared us.

Wednesday 24 February
I'm off again, after five days lapse, on *Three Guineas*, and hope now to spin ahead. A quiet day for a wonder – no one seen yesterday: so I went to the Caledonian Market, couldn't find spoon shop; bought yellow gloves 3 shillings and stockings 1 shilling and so home.

Sunday 28 February
I'm so entirely imbued in *Three Guineas* that I can hardly jerk myself away to write here (here in fact I again dropped my pen to think about my next

paragraph – universities –). Its a bad habit. Yesterday it was effectively broken by Desmond who came punctually at one, and stayed till 7.15; nor did we stop talking all that time. Nor was I once bored or wished it to stop. A greater tribute to Desmond couldn't be paid. He was well lit – dear old Desmond – as round as a marble: a paunch pendant; but nearly bald; with an odd 18th Century look, as if he had been dining at the Club with Johnson – a kind of Goldsmith or Boswell; a congenial spirit. And as full of human kindness as a ripe grape with juice. I think he had set himself now not to write a great book but to be nice to other people. What can I do for you, was his last remark on the stairs. Alas, he carried off *The Years*, which means – well, never mind.

Monday 1 March

I wish I could write out my sensations at this moment. They are so peculiar and so unpleasant. Partly Time of Life? I wonder. A physical feeling as if I were drumming slightly in the veins: very cold: impotent: and terrified. As if I were exposed on a high ledge in full light. Very lonely. Very useless. No atmosphere round me. No words. Very apprehensive. As if something cold and horrible – a roar of laughter at my expense were about to happen. And I want to burst into tears, but have nothing to cry for. And I cannot unfurl my mind and apply it calmly and unconsciously to a book. And my own little scraps look dried up and derelict. And I know that I must go on doing this dance on hot bricks till I die. Its the 15th March approaching I suppose – the dazzle of that head lamp on my poor little rabbit's body which keeps it dazed in the middle of the road. (I like that phrase. That gives me confidence.)

Tuesday 2 March

I'm going to be beaten, I'm going to be laughed at, I'm going to be held up to scorn and ridicule – I found myself saying those words just now. Anyhow these days of waiting must be a dull cold torture. I shall be happy enough this time next month I've no doubt.

Wednesday 10 March

The fatal day is approaching when my little reputation lies like an old cigarette end. But I'm too jaded with *Three Guineas* to care to find even the right metaphor. In my perhaps cowardly wish to have next week as an empty compartment, I've crammed this too full. On Friday we get off – the doomed discarded ridiculed novelist. What care I? I begin to whistle, but I'm too jaded.

Friday 12 March
Oh the relief! L. brought the *TLS* to me in bed and said Its quite good.
And so it is; and *Time & Tide* says I'm a firstrate novelist and a great lyrical
poet. And I can hardly read through the reviews: but feel a little dazed, to
think then its *not* nonsense; it does make an effect. But now, my dear, after
all that agony, I'm free, whole, round. And so stop this cry of content; sober
joy. Off to Monks House. Julian back today.

MONKS HOUSE, RODMELL

Sunday 14 March
I am in such a twitter owing to two columns in the *Observer* praising *The
Years* that I can't, as I foretold, go on with *Three Guineas*. And when I think
of the agony I went through in this room, just over a year ago ... when
it dawned on me that the whole of three years' work was a complete failure:
and then when I think of the mornings here when I used to stumble out
and cut up those proofs and write three lines, and then go back and lie on
my bed – its no wonder my hand trembles. Now at any rate money is
assured: L. shall have his new car; we will be floated again; and my last
lap – if I've only ten years of life more – should be fruitful. Work – work.
But at the moment, the relief is so great, that I feel myself rocking up and
down, like a bush a huge fowl sat on.
    Dinner at Charleston last night. Julian a grown man – I mean vigorous,
controlled, as I guess embittered, something to me tragic in the sadness
now, his mouth and face much tenser; as if he had been thinking in solitude.
Nessa said he hasn't altogether given up his idea of Spain: all depends on
getting a job here. He comes to tea today.

Monday 15 March
Too much talk – Julian and Bunny – why do we live in such a way that
the sight of our oldest friends and nephews back from China gives us a
little shock of regret – I mean misery for the quiet evening gone? Julian set
and rather self centred. Can only think what he ought to do. Still if what
he ought to do is something for the world at large, one must excuse this
grinding of an iron upon a granite slab.

52 TAVISTOCK SQUARE, WC1

Friday 19 March
Now this is one of the strangest of my experiences – 'they' say almost
universally that *The Years* is a masterpiece. If somebody had told me I

should write this, even a week ago, let alone six months ago, I should have given a jump like a shot hare. How entirely and absolutely incredible it would have been!

Thursday 25 March
Yes, two days lying down, and can't write today. But a divine holiday. No reviews. And sales great. A rush before Easter. 280 sold yesterday. Boat Race at 11.30. Then we go tomorrow.

MONKS HOUSE, RODMELL

Saturday 27 March
Merely scribbling here, over a log fire, on a cold but bright Easter morning; sudden shafts of sun, a scatter of snow on the hills early; sudden storms, ink black, octopus pouring, coming up: and the rooks fidgetting and pecking in the elm trees. As for the beauty, as I always say when I walk the terrace after breakfast, too much for one pair of eyes. We came down on Thursday, packed in the rush in London; cars spinning all along the roads; yesterday at last perfect freedom from telephones and reviews, and no one rang up.

Sunday 28 March
Yesterday a reporter for the *New York Times* rang up: was told he could look at the outside of 52 [Tavistock Square] if he chose. At 4.30 as I was boiling the kettle a huge black Daimler drew up. Then a dapper little man in a tweed coat appeared in the garden. I reached the sitting room – saw him standing there looking round. L. in the orchard with Percy [gardener]. Then I guessed. He had a green note book and stood looking about jotting things down. I ducked my head – he almost caught me. At last L. turned and fronted him. No Mrs Woolf didn't want that kind of publicity. I raged. A bug walking over one's skin – couldn't crush him. The bug taking notes. L. politely led him back to his Daimler and his wife. But they'd had a nice run from London – bugs, to come and steal in and take notes.

Monday 29 March
A man in an overcoat took notes in the field yesterday, and then someone banged on the door. I sat tight. L. was at Charleston. Julian, he says, very depressed.

Sunday 4 April
Another curious idiosyncracy. Maynard thinks *The Years* my best book. L. went to Tilton and had a long quiet cronies' talk. Maynard not well; cramp

in the muscle of the heart. His toes curl up. Lydia anxious. Talk of what to do for Julian, who strikes everyone as depressed. Maynard said that he thought *The Years* very moving; more tender than any of my books; did not puzzle him like *The Waves*; very beautiful; and no more said than was needed.

52 TAVISTOCK SQUARE, WC1

Wednesday 14 April
I'm sunk in privacy, in quiet. How strange! It would be flat, if I were not so active in the head. Not a letter this morning: only ten or eleven perhaps about *The Years* since it came out. Nobody talks to me about it, nobody now writes about it. It seems to have sailed out of sight. Yet it sells – best of all my novels. Sold I think 9,300. Harcourt Brace in America have sold 12,000 before publication – easily my record. Honestly I do not know what to think of this book: is it good or bad? Tonight Kingsley Martin, Stephen Spender and Julian dine.

Thursday 15 April
And Stephen says *The Years* is the best of my books, and Kingsley also – but that don't please me. Stephen does. A long close political argument. Julian, Kingsley, Stephen – all calling each other by Christian names. What is our duty? What is the responsible man like Kingsley Martin to do? Can't be a pacifist; the irresponsible can. I sat there splitting off my own position from theirs, testing what they said, convincing myself of my own integrity and justice. Kingsley Martin very neurotic, dark eyed, melodramatic. Julian peppery and pithy – making his strange faces, suddenly hooting with laughter – uncouth rather, yet honest, yet undisciplined, yet keeping something up his sleeve. Obstinately set on going to Spain – won't argue; tight; hard fisted. Kingsley lives much in the military area: so we discussed hand grenades, bombs, tanks, as if we were military gents in the war again. And I felt flame up in me *Three Guineas*. Stephen runs on too fluent, too formless; but as I say gave me a shock of pleasure. Says *The Years* gives him the sense of time; and is so precise. So that's the young on my side.

Wednesday 21 April
On the whole Monks House was a good week end. Very cold wind. Went to tea at Charleston; and there found the whole family for once. Unfortunately Julian is dog obstinate about driving an ambulance; which casts a shadow over Nessa, and us too. There'll he be keeping us all on the tenterhooks – But it won't be for two months, and what's the use of looking

ahead? Summer time began on Sunday; and I look up and see my clock still an hour late.

Tuesday 27 April

Yes, that'll be nice – to sit out of doors and drink, in some French town, away from all this. Coronation impending. But on the 7th we're off.

Thursday 29 April

Well, we've decided to let the Hogarth Press lapse or change next June. Yes I think that is now definite. Many things have happened – a crowd of little engagements – the pleasantest, indeed a happy one, was the Memoir Club meeting. We dined in a kind of sitting room behind the Etoile [Restaurant] – and soon kindled, though it was a wet night: Duncan had a cold; Bunny the whooping cough. But Desmond was babbling as a nightingale – never have I known him in such jubilant good temper as this year. As if he worked only to enjoy, to radiate. And my thimble of vanity was filled instantly because Maynard praised *The Years* – a lovely book; and Desmond said he is going to write a long essay on me altogether (but he won't). And so round to the Studio. Duncan read a good account of his adventure at Florence, when he misrepresented Maynard. And then old Desmond 'obliged'. That is he had a few notes in his hand, took a comfortable chair, and gave us with perfect ease and fluency and form a character of Wilfred Blunt and his own shooting. And so on to the Trevelyans. Oh but it was beautifully done – and stopped when it might have gone on without boring us. Then Morgan read his condemned introduction to the [T. E.] Lawrence letters, which Bunny is now to do. And then we went off in the rain. Desmond said We're not a day older, and we enjoy our society as much as we ever did. And Morgan said I felt so fond of everyone, I almost wept.

Yesterday oh how Margery Fry snubbed me, by announcing, as she came into the room, that the reviews of *The Years* had been so sniffy she was afraid it must have influenced the sales.

Friday 30 April

So we have reached the last day of this agitating month – far better than I could have foreseen. If it weren't for Julian going to Spain I should be wholly content on our French journey. A very cold grey day; the Busmen threaten to strike tonight; streets laced across; camps and latrines in all the parks, like the Crimea; poles with silver hatchets along the pavements. The Queen told David [Cecil] that she went all ice at the thought of the Coronation; said the monarchy hadn't the same position as in the days of Victoria. All the fiddles are tuning up. The BBC is having a hundred and fifty microphones and observers along the route. I shall try to listen in from some French café. Hugh Walpole is to be knighted. We are giving a youthful party on Monday; and leave on Friday – that is one week, in which I must settle the question of clothes. When I come back I shall instantly pounce on *Three Guineas* and see what I can do.

Tuesday 4 May

The day mother died in 1895 – forty-two years ago: and I remember it – at the moment, watching Dr Seton walk away up Hyde Park Gate in the early morning with his head bowed, his hands behind his back. Also the doves swooping. We had been sent up to the day nursery after she died; and were crying. And I went to the open window and looked out. It must have been very soon after she died, as Seton was then leaving the house. How that early morning picture has stayed with me! What happened immediately afterwards I can't remember.

I'm jaded after our youthful party – they stayed till 12.45. The Bus Strike on, so that they couldn't get buses – had to walk. The streets look odd, all aflutter with banners – white in Bond Street, red at Selfridges; and no omnibuses; a lower level in the streets; all taxis and innumerable private cars; and droves and herds trudging the pavement. The party though – jaded as I am I must refer to the party. Sally [Chilver]; Julian; bell rings: the Spenders; [Richard] Chilver; William [Plomer]. So we were crowded – no fire; a hot spring night. Julian was bitter at dinner against the Bloomsbury habit of education. He had been taught no job; only a vague literary smattering. But I wanted you to go to the Bar, I said. Yes, but you didn't insist upon it to my mother, he remarked, rather forcibly. He now finds himself at twenty-nine without any special training. But then he objected, as I thought, to all professions. The Chilver sat all inhibited and nerve drawn, so I had to give him claret and sit by him and make party talk, about carpentering and bulbs. He would like to leave the Air Ministry and become a carpenter – make good chairs – but of course won't and can't, though Sally urges. Another aspect of the professional question. Air Ministry long hours, hard work; but regular and safe. Julian now all in favour of a settled job. He is learning the mechanics of lorries. Hadn't even been taught that at Cambridge · only the eternal [Alexander] Pope – which I scrambled through as a child. Poor old Julian – rather on a crazy edge of life I feel. And there was some well informed political talk.

Every moment till we go seems now numbered like stones in a building – and that's why I shall be so relieved on Friday – no numbers of any stones for almost three weeks.

*   *   *

MONKS HOUSE, RODMELL

Monday 1 June
I have at last got going with *Three Guineas*. But oh how my heart leaps up to think that never again shall I be harnessed to a long book. No. Always short ones in future. The long book still won't be altogether downed – its reverberations grumble. Did I say that Harcourt Brace wrote and said they were happy to find that *The Years* is the best selling novel in America? They have sold 25,000 – my record, easily. The great desirable is not to have to earn money by writing. 'Gibbon' was rejected by the *New Republic*, so I shall send no more to America. Nor will I write articles at all except for the *TLS*: for whom I am going now to do Congreve.

It has been August hot; Nessa came over and we had a long natural gossip. Maynard has been very ill but is better. Must rest for six months. Duncan in France. We stay here for one week's perfect solitude. Then a London season, very hectic I guess. Mary Hutchinson asks me to dine to meet the Duff Coopers. Courage bids me say Yes. But my hair? and my dress?

52 TAVISTOCK SQUARE, WC1

Friday 11 June
Brain rather dried up after six days strenuous London. Very very hot. Very noisy. And on top, Julian gone to Spain on Monday. So, a strain: which I cannot now go into: and it must last – how long? A year? who knows? Anything to keep talking, inventing, distracting.

Wednesday 16 June
I've seen: the Hutchinsons; Diana [Cooper] beautiful, veiled, easy going. Desmond there. Then Ethel Smyth: with her rough old claws scratching. Sniffing out *Three Guineas*. Then to the Coronation film, bits and bits; some good; others not. Then to Herbert [Woolf]'s on Sunday; oh the ugliness of that perfectly self-satisfied passive stockbroker's life: the orchard, the picture – the coloured photograph – the mats, the maids; unreal, padded, easy . . . and we walked at Staines. Then Adrian after dinner on a visit of friendship. Then the Bowens, Bowras, Butts; then Helen . . . Now lunch.

Sunday 20 June
Last evening Ann Watkins forced her way in: offered me – I could see the bait put on the hook – £1000 and all expenses if I would go to USA and lecture three times weekly for three months. What about, I asked. That

they didn't mind. The more personal the better: for instance, about my experience of publishing, bringing in my marriage – a happy one. At this, your husband, who is sitting in the audience, will cry BOO! Well we declined. I was to repeat the same lecture – not to read it, but to speak it. That was very important. And Aldous and Gerald Heard, those apostles of the inner life and peace and goodness, are touring the States doing this in duet. Lord lord! what an example for the Soul ... and what a good quote for my book. I was amused by her perfectly frank commercialism. Money – money – money. What they want and Donald Brace wants is that I should come over and exhibit my person, and make money for Don and Ann. And what would they spend the proceeds of my personality on? Drink I should say, looking at Ann's cheeks.

Tuesday 22 June
Ann Watkins is now hot on the scent of magazine articles, and wants another talk. But here my gorge rises. No I will not write for the larger paying magazines: in fact, couldn't. In this way I put *Three Guineas* daily into practice.

Wednesday 23 June
I went shopping yesterday, and it grew roasting hot, and I was in black – such astonishing chops and changes this summer – often one's caught in a storm, frozen, or roasted. As I reached 52, a long trail of fugitives – like a caravan in a desert – came through the Square: Spaniards flying from Bilbao, which has fallen, I suppose. Somehow brought tears to my eyes, though no one seemed surprised. Children trudging along; women in cheap jackets with gay handkerchiefs on their heads, young men, and all carrying either cheap cases, and bright enamel kettles and saucepans, filled I suppose with gifts from some Charity – a shuffling trudging procession, flying – impelled by machine guns in Spanish fields to trudge through Tavistock Square, along Gordon Square, then where? – clasping their enamel kettles. A strange spectacle.

Thursday 24 June
A letter from Ott praising my Gibbon article. Now I have observed that any of my friends who disliked *The Years* always praise my articles, by way of urging me to give up fiction, and I suppose to make amends to me for not liking *The Years*. She has been *very* ill; almost thought she would have 'waved us adieu' but is recovering at Tunbridge Wells. Pipsy reads *Emma* to her, and she reads Henry James to herself.

Friday 25 June

To the Albert Hall meeting last night. The last I swear. Oh but I liked being introduced to Auden, a small rough-haired terrier man: slits for eyes; a crude face; interesting, I expect, but wire haired, yellowish white. Then speeches. Then semi jocular money collecting; then an auction of pictures. One by Picasso. All very stagey empty and unreal. The Basque children singing on the gramophone. [Paul] Robeson sang: a sympathetic, malleable nigger, expressive, uninhibited, all warmth and the hot vapours of African forests. I took several snubs and benedictions. Kingsley Martin uneasy – a man I don't like – so voluble, histrionic, and he drove us home, taking a hand off the wheel to gesticulate – a different style of driving from Leonard's. I'm hurrying. Can't analyse. Off to Monks House. Starting my Congreve: going to do it in three days at Monks House. Then back to *Three Guineas* refreshed.

Monday 28 June

Home is the hunter, home from the hill, and the Wolves are back from Monks House. And much refreshed into the bargain. Three solitary nights. Think of that! Not a voice, not a telephone. Only the owl calling; perhaps a clap of thunder, the horses going down to the Brooks, and Mr Botten calling with the milk in the morning. Up at 7.30 this morning, picked a rose, and drove up through Wimbledon, as Wandsworth Bridge is mending, but back by 10.30, and at work on the Second Guinea by 11. It is now started, and if I can drive my pen hard, might have it done by August. But there's a terrible lot of reasoning (for me) and fitting in of the right quotations. *Roger* waiting too.

Sunday 11 July

A gap: not in life, but in comment. I have been in full flood every morning with *Three Guineas*. Whether I shall finish by August becomes doubtful.

Monday 12 July

Alone with Nessa in the studio last night. We are very gingerly in our remarks about Julian, and Madrid, I notice. Always I feel the immeasurable despair just on t'other side of the grass plot on which we walk – on which I'm walking with such energy and delight at the moment. I went to Stoke Newington yesterday and found a study table in white stone on which James Stephen was carved, large and plain, as I suspect he was large and plain. A long inscription about Wilberforce and wife and family neatly filled with green moss on top of the study table. Next door to the old Church, which might be in a hollow under the downs, is Clissold Park, and one of those white pillared houses in which [great] Grandpapa studied *The Times* while She cut roses – now it smelt of Clissold Park mothers; and cakes and tea. I was much refreshed by all this.

Monday 19 July
Just back from Monks House. The kitchen a great success – now green and cool, and the new window shows a square of flowers. Why, all these years, I never thought to lay out £20 on a new cupboard, paint and window, I don't know. On Friday we went to Worthing. Mrs Woolf very plaintive. Then a [Labour Party] meeting at Monks House where the Major, who talks to mice, and holds toads in his hand, treated us to the most drivelling murmured muddle I ever heard – about force, and religion, which is heredity, and may I say with your permission, what I mean is, its all a question of thinking isn't it, and you can't talk to a Spaniard, but you can to a Mahommedan, and that's what I feel, religion's at the back of it, but Sir, if I may say so, its a question of heredity – but I can't reproduce the shell-shock Major; and could only keep from howling by fixing my eyes on a cigarette. L. summed up in a masterly flight; and so concluded. Quentin and I were dumb.

MONKS HOUSE, RODMELL

Friday 6 August
Well but one must make a beginning. Its odd that I can hardly bring myself, with all my verbosity – the expression mania which is inborn in me – to say anything about Julian's death – I mean about that last ten days in London. That was a complete break; almost a blank; like a blow on the head: a shrivelling up. Going round [to Vanessa] that night; and then all the other times, and sitting there. An incredible suffering – to watch it – an accident, and someone bleeding. Then I thought the death of a child is a childbirth again; sitting there listening. No no, I will not go back to those days. The only thing was a kind of comfort in being there with Nessa, Duncan, Quentin and Angelica, and losing completely the isolation, the spectator's attitude, in being wanted. Then we came down here last Thursday; and the pressure being removed, one lived; but without much of a future. That's one of the specific qualities of this death – how it brings close the immense vacancy, and our short little run into inanity. Now this is what I intend to combat. How? Work of course. Directly I am not working, or see the end in sight, then nothingness begins. I have to go over though every other day to Charleston. We sit in the studio door. It is very hot happily. The thought of Julian changing so queerly: now distinct, now close; now of him there in the flesh; and so on. But how it curtails the

417

future: how it reduces one's vision to one's own life – save for Quentin and Angelica.

Well, there's *Three Guineas* to finish: the last chapter; now I suppose its stiff and cold. But I will try that tomorrow; then polish off Congreve; then earn £200, so they say, with a story; and so to *Roger* this autumn. Today we go to Charleston; Nessa is alone today. "I shall be cheerful, but I shall never be happy again."

Wednesday 11 August

Now we are in the worst of the time – I think I can recognise that. We don't talk so freely of Julian. We want to make things go on. Angelica and Quentin come over to play bowls. We beat up talk. We provide amusement, L. and I; this makes us rather quarrelsome when we're alone – the strain I suppose. The unbecoming stage of sorrow. On Monday I went by train to Charleston. Thus I left L. alone: have I the right to leave L. alone, and sit with Nessa? She was again in the submerged mood. An atmosphere of deep grey waters; and I flopping like a dilapidated fish on top. Very hard work. I shall have a long walk this afternoon, to Piddinghoe: walk myself serene; play bowls; read; and not think of little arrangements. Endless unwritten letters – sympathy about Julian who stalks beside me, in many different shapes.

Tuesday 17 August

Not much to say. Its true, the only life this summer is in the brain. I get excited writing. Three hours pass like ten minutes. At Charleston yesterday in the rain. I take the train to Lewes; shop; 4.35 bus; reach Charleston for tea. Its true I cannot write about Nessa; have to keep myself from thinking about her. Now and then she looks like an old woman. How can she ever right herself though? Julian had some queer power over her – the lover as well as the son. He was like her; yet had a vigour, a roughness, a kind of clumsiness, of Cambridge awkwardness, together with his natural gaiety. And that's all lost for the sake of ten minutes in an ambulance. I often argue with him on my walks; abuse his selfishness in going but mostly feel floored by the complete muddle and waste. I think I mean lack of judgement: obstinate and emotional. We should have respected him more if he had stayed in England and faced drudgery.

Sunday 29 August

Yes I am tackling Congreve, because I want to be quit of all articles and ready for *Three Guineas* on the 1st. How far would this energy of mind carry me – could I take this narcotic successfully if Leonard died, if Nessa died? I come out here at 10 and don't wake to anything but Congreve till one.

Go in with my head swaying like a captive balloon. The thing is there's no richness and security when I wake. No depth of happiness to refresh myself in. Considerable agility and gaiety and chatter. A very hot August again. Bowls have become a passion. I gave up a walk to play. But then I'm anxious to vary the day.

Thursday 2 September
Finished my Congreve, the end too crowded, but forced myself to take it to the post. And today's a holiday: letter writing, reading.

Sunday 26 September
Tom [Eliot] and Judith [Stephen] here: therefore I am not writing the end of *Three Guineas*, which has kept me completely submerged from ten to one every morning; and driven me like a motor in the head over the downs to Piddinghoe &c every afternoon from two to four. Then we play bowls from five to six. Then read. Then cook dinner. Then wireless. Then read. Then chocolates. Then bed. And so it begins again. But there have been so many interruptions. We went to Sissinghurst – unrecorded: Vita with that silent goodness, and Harold too, a sense of the human understanding unspoken. Many improvements: men digging: an Elizabethan drain being dug up.

Not a happy summer. That is all the materials for happiness; and nothing behind. If Julian had not died – still an incredible sentence to write – our happiness might have been profound. 'Our' – L.'s and mine, now that *The Years* has sold between 40 and 50,000 in America; now that we are floated financially, and privately as happy and rounded off as can be – but his death – that extraordinary extinction – drains it of substance. I do not let myself think. I cannot face much of the meaning. Shut my mind to anything but work and bowls. Now there's Tom and Judith. Tom is liverish looking, tired; but revives under the effect of Judith's fresh and downright and able but not sophisticated youth. She is a whopper: a strapper; yet with the usual complexities I think, submerged. I should however write a pack of letters.

52 TAVISTOCK SQUARE, WC1

Tuesday 12 October
Yes we are back at Tavistock Square; and I've never written a word since September 27th. That shows how every morning was crammed to the margin with *Three Guineas*. This is the first morning I write, because at 12, ten minutes ago, I wrote what I think is the last page of *Three Guineas*. Oh

how violently I have been galloping through these mornings! It has pressed and spurted out of me, if that's any proof of virtue, like a physical volcano. And my brain feels cool and quiet after the expulsion. So nothing was said here of the last weeks at Monks House. The weather was very fine. That objective statement sounds a little odd.

We have decided, gradually, completely, not to sell the Press; but to let it die off, saving for our own books. This is a good conclusion I think. It keeps the right to adventure; cuts off some money. We could not face writing for publishers.

Friday 22 October
No I didn't go to Paris. This is a note to make. Waking at three I decided I would spend the week end at Paris. Got so far as looking up trains, consulting Nessa about hotel. Then L. said he would rather not. Then I was overcome with happiness. Then we walked round the square love making – after twenty-five years can't bear to separate. Then I walked round the lake in Regent's Park. Then ... you see it is an enormous pleasure, being wanted: a wife. And our marriage so complete. To return to facts (though this 'fiction' is still radiant under my skin): walked to see Roger's Highgate birthplace: suddenly L. developed the idea of making the young Brainies take the Press as a Co-operative company (John [Lehmann]; Isherwood; Auden; Stephen). All are bubbling with discontent and ideas. All want a focus; a manager; a mouthpiece. Would like L. to manage it. Couldn't we sell, and creep out? That's the idea – and yet keep the soul, translated into this on the whole appropriate body? Anyhow, John was heard in the Press: consulted; interested; fights shy of money; £6,000; will lunch with Isherwood and discuss. And now telephones he will come on Monday. So that fat's a frizzling.

Monday 25 October
A terrific gale this week end. We went to Cuckmere, via Seaford. The sea over the front: great spray fountain bursting to my joy over the parade and the lighthouse. Right over the car. Then we walked down to the sea at Cuckmere; the birds came up like shots out of a catapult. We could not stand against the wind, the breath pressed out of us; nor see. We stood behind a shed, and watched the waves: a yellow rough light on them; pounding; a great curled volume roughened of water. Why does one like the frantic, the unmastered? So to Charleston, wet and soaking.

Monday 1 November
Dinner with Clive. I think poor old Clive even a little on the bare wheels; no blown up tyres. That to me is very ominous – if Clive's spirits should

give way – if he were to give up his enjoyment of life! We discussed education; dreams; Nessa and Angelica stitched at some private garment. Angelica alternately silent and decisive. Duncan came in. Not much boasting. An odds and ends evening, neither one thing nor another.

The Co-operative Press hangs: I think the young are eager to bite.

Wednesday 3 November
To Southwark and Lambeth, walking, yesterday. A great autumn for long City walks this.

Tuesday 30 November
Yes, its actually the last day of November, and they've passed like a streak of hounds after a fox because I've been re-writing *Three Guineas* with such intentness, indeed absorption. So I've never even looked at this stout volume. I have left out Cambridge; oh and people innumerable; the Book Show; and buying with some recklessness, fur boots, leather waistcoat, underclothes; for money once more brims the pot. And I'm paid £465 for a handful of old sketches. This a little shames me in comparison with Nessa's sales: but then I reflect, I put my life blood into writing, and she had children.

Wednesday 15 December
And then I had one of my little dips into the underworld – a temperature, sofa, three days recumbent, Monks House in a snowstorm; no walking; Foot and Mouth still dominant; back to our party. Young Newnham, all most free and easy, vigorous and inspiriting, all sitting on the floor; and then – writing, writing; the first chapter taken on Monday to the Chancery Lane typist; cold and rain; visits from Mrs Woolf and Herbert, from John yesterday; the Press question looms and lapses; and our views change: secretly we both wish to fade, not to sell; but John is eager to buy, yet stingy; must consult Isherwood and Stephen; and settle by mid January. Vita, who dined, more matronly and voluptuous than ever, won't go in with them: a parcel of hot headed and ignorant boys; – well, no use trying to pull this five minutes before lunch sentence together so I stop it.

Saturday 18 December
Oh this cursed year 1937 – it will never let us out of its claws. Now its L.'s kidneys: |Dr| Rau says it may be something wrong with the kidneys; possibly the prostate gland – that perennial horror. Its more likely, he says, to be a chill; but can't tell for a fortnight. So we go away with that hanging over us – The great cat is playing with us once more. How much do I mind death? I wondered last night, and concluded that there is a sense in which

the end could be accepted calmly. That's odd, considering that few people are more immensely interested by life: and happy. Its Julian's death that makes one sceptical of life I suppose. Not that I ever think of him as dead: which is queer. Rather as if he were jerked abruptly out of sight, without rhyme or reason: so violent and absurd that one can't fit his death into any scheme. But here we are, on a fine cold day, going to mate Sally at Ickenham: a saner proceeding than to analyse here.

1938

Leonard spent the first ten days of the new year in bed on a strict diet, awaiting the results of X-rays and tests for kidney disease; it was a false alarm and Virginia's relief was intense. She herself suffered her usual winter ailments, but by the beginning of February Three Guineas was ready to be shown to Leonard and sent to press, although she still had a good deal of work to do on the notes. But these months were dominated by discussions about the future management of the Hogarth Press, which on the Woolfs had so often thought of giving up. Now finally it was agreed that John Lehmann should buy Virginia's half-share in the Press and become Leonard's partner, acting also as salaried managing director. Virginia continued to read and advise on manuscripts. This arrangement came into force in April.

In the Soviet Union, Stalin's opponents were being tried and executed; in Europe 11 March Hitler led his troops into Austria and proclaimed the Union (Anschluss) of Austria with Germany. The reverberations of these events were increasingly felt in Tavistock Square, where Leonard was deeply involved in attempts to persuade the Labour Party to agree to conscription and re-armament. Virginia was glad to turn to the past and to her biography of Roger Fry; but at Rodmell at Easter the exciting idea for a new book disturbed her concentration on the facts of his life. This was Pointz Hall, which was to develop during the next years into her last book, Between the Acts.

Two more deaths particularly affected Virginia this spring. Although she had been in poor health for some time, the death of Lady Ottoline Morrell was unexpected; and even more so was that of Ka Arnold-Forster, who was five years younger than Virginia. Both of them had been her friends for nearly thirty years.

Three Guineas was published early in June. Virginia was pleased by the plaudits of several eminent feminists and not unduly upset by the silence of close friends or the censure of detractors. The Woolfs set off on 16 June for a motoring holiday in the North of England and Scotland, crossing to Skye where they spent three days. Home again on 2 July, the remaining three weeks of their London season were exceptionally full and lively, though Virginia persevered in her work on Roger Fry, to which end she invited the painter Sir William Rothenstein – a fellow student of Roger's in Paris in the nineties – to dinner to talk about him.

At Monks House, builders were constructing a new library for Leonard in the roof space, work which continued during the whole of their time there – time during which the international situation grew more and more desperate as Hitler increased his *pressure on Czechoslovakia. Prime Minister Chamberlain's efforts to appease him and avert the imminent outbreak of war were dramatically (if temporarily) concluded by the Munich Settlement of 29 September, which was, for Virginia, deliverance from a nightmare. The Woolfs returned to London on 16 October.*

Virginia Woolf was now a celebrity, which brought both pleasures and pains – the pleasure for instance of Max Beerbohm's flattering attention; the pain of finding that she was now regarded by younger critics as a has-been, rated lower than Forster or Eliot. But she enjoyed a nice old friends' evening with Tom Eliot, and probably ended the year with the feeling that in writing Three Guineas *she had said something that needed saying.*

<u>1938</u>

Sunday 9 January
Yes, I will force myself to begin this cursed year. For one thing I have
'finished' the last chapter of *Three Guineas*, and for the first time since I don't
know when have stopped writing in the middle of the morning. How am
I to describe 'anxiety'? I've battened it down under this incessant writing,
thinking, about *Three Guineas* – as I did in the summer after Julian's death.
[Dr] Rau has just been, and says there is still a trace of blood: if this
continues, L. will have to go next week to a nursing home and be examined.
Probably it is the prostate. This may mean an operation. He was suddenly
worse at Rodmell; we came up on Wednesday [29 December]; since when
its been a perpetual strain of waiting for the telephone to ring. He went to
the hospital to be X rayed; has been, is still, in bed. There is a sense in
which feelings become habitual, dulled; but only laid under a very thin
cover. I walk; work, and so on. Nessa and Angelica and Duncan all at
Cassis, which shuts off that relief, but why should she have this forced on
her? Anyhow they come back in a fortnight, I suppose.

Saturday 15 January
In the five minutes left me before starting for Monks House I can't describe
the relief of hearing at eight on Wednesday: Specimen completely normal.
You can go away – That's where we are at this moment of a wet and windy
January. Definitions, explanations can wait.

Tuesday 1 February
A week at Monks House hard at work. Nessa and Angelica back – dinner
at Charleston. So home: then temperatures; bed; complete submersal, on
the sofa, &c. Now down for final corrections. *Three Guineas* to be shown
up to L. tonight.

Friday 4 February
L. gravely approves *Three Guineas*. Thinks it an extremely clear analysis.
On the whole I'm content. One can't expect emotion, for as he says, its not

425

on a par with the novels. But I'm much more indifferent, that's true: feel it a good piece of donkeywork, and don't think it affects me either way as the novels do.

Monday 7 February
(Mother's birthday). A perfect week end [at Monks House], still, brisk spring: crocuses in the garden; birds rapturous; I was very happy: relieved of my book: and tossing ideas as I walked over the downs.

Thursday 10 March
Relieved of my book? What nonsense. Here am I working five hours a day to finish off those notes, those proofs, and severely warned by L. that unless I send off both in six days from this very Thursday, we must postpone till the autumn. But I've done my due today; and have said nothing here for so long: nothing about the Press; how ten days ago I signed my rights away to John [Lehmann]; how the last week has been June weather; and then all the people. I don't think I can add at this moment; and shall owl round the corner to buy a surreptitious packet of cigarettes.

Saturday 12 March
Hitler has invaded Austria: that is at ten last night his army crossed the frontier, unresisted. The Austrian national anthem was heard on the wireless for the last time. This fact, which combines with the Russian trials, like drops of dirty water mixing, puts its thorn into my morning: a pernickety one spent over notes. Privately I'm, as usual at the proof stage, bored with the book which was like a spine to me all last summer; upheld me in the horror of last August; and whirled me like a top miles upon miles over the downs. How can it all have petered out into diluted drivel? But it remains, morally, a spine: the thing I wished to say, though futile. Three USA papers have rejected it; but the *Atlantic* will pay £120 for 12,000 words. Their cable came when Morgan was here – blown in like thistledown – a very round and voluminous down he is now: but with a breeze behind him. And do I grudge it that *he* should be the best living novelist? He handed me a cutting in which he is thus saluted. And so, jealous as I am, rather mean always about contemporaries, I got my dejection, to run into the dirty drop. But this reminds me that our last Leonard and Virginia season is perhaps our most brilliant. Yes; if there is success in this world, the Hogarth Press has I suppose won what success it could. And money this year will fairly snow us under. In fact we have asked Mr Wicks [Lewes builder] to estimate for a library at Monks House in spite of Hitler.

Tuesday 22 March

The public world very notably invaded the private at Monks House last week end. Almost war: almost expected to hear it announced. And England, as they say, humiliated. And the man in uniform exalted. L. up to his eyes in the usual hectic negotiations. The Labour Party hemming and hawing. And I looked at Quentin and thought They'll take you. And then, just as in private crises, a sudden lull. The tension relaxes. And it was like June.

Now I must ward off the old depression: the book finished, what's the use of it, feeling. So yesterday I went to Wapping Old Stairs, and roamed through Shadwell and Whitechapel; a change, as complete as France or Italy. Then Tom to dinner, and to Stephen's *Trial of a Judge*. A moving play: genuine; simple; sincere.

Saturday 26 March

On Monday the galleys will go. So I can then seriously turn my mind off on to Frys, Highgate, the past. The crisis still shakes our telephone, the voice of Kingsley appealing to L. to have his mind made. But the lull is hushing us; not very profoundly though. When the tiger, i.e.: Hitler, has digested his dinner he will pounce again. I must take up life again on Monday: by which I mean ask Elizabeth Bowen to tea, buy a new dress, arrange one or two parties, and not let myself be submerged in *Roger* quite so completely as in *Three Guineas*.

Tuesday 12 April

Anyhow, on April 1st I think, I started *Roger*. Much of it donkey work; and I suppose to be re-written. Still there is twenty pages put down, after being so long put off. And it is an immense solace to have this sober drudgery to take to instantly and so tide over the horrid anti climax of *Three Guineas*. I didn't get so much praise from L. as I hoped. And I suspect I shall find the page proofs (due tomorrow) a chill bath of disillusionment. But I wanted – how violently – how persistently, pressingly, compulsorily I can't say – to write this book; and have a quiet composed feeling; as if I had said my say: take it or leave it.

Elizabeth Bowen to tea; cut out of coloured cardboard but sterling and sharpedged. Kingsley Martin still rings up, at inordinate length: I've time to change and write a letter while they talk; its about emigrating now from our doomed Europe. "If it weren't that I feel I must stay by the paper –"

Tuesday 26 April

We had our Easter at Monks House; but as for the sun, it never shone; was colder than Christmas; a grudging lead-coloured sky; razor wind; winter clothes; proofs; much acute despair; curbed however, by the aid of divine philosophy. Then Quentin rings up; to warn you: Have you had a letter from Pipsy [Philip Morrell]? Ottoline is dead. They told her Philip might die, and the shock killed her; and he's asking you to write about her. So I had to write. Yet in spite of that here am I sketching out a new book; only please don't impose that huge burden on me again, I implore – not yet awhile. But to amuse myself, let me note: why not Pointz Hall: a rambling capricious but somehow unified whole – a scenic old house – and a terrace where nursemaids walk? and people passing – and a perpetual variety and change from intensity to prose; and facts – and notes; and – but enough. I must read Roger; and go to Ott's memorial service, representing also T. S. Eliot at his absurd command. 2.30 at [St] Martin's in the Fields.

Wednesday 27 April
Ottoline's burial service. Oh dear, oh dear the lack of intensity; the wailing and mumbling, the fumbling with bags; the shuffling; the vast brown mass of respectable old South Kensington ladies. And then the hymns; and the clergyman with a bar of medals across his surplice; and the orange and blue windows; and a toy Union Jack sticking from a cranny. What had all this to do with Ottoline, or our feelings? Save that the address was to the point: a critical study, written presumably by Philip and delivered, very reasonably, by Mr [Robert] Speaight the actor: a sober, and secular speech, which made one at least think of a human being, though the reference to her beautiful voice caused one to think of that queer nasal moan: however that too was to the good in deflating immensities. So to Nessa's where we recounted the story; and yet I'm left fumbling for a house I shan't go to. Odd how the sense of loss takes this quite private form: someone who won't read what I write. No illumination in Gower Street. An intimacy abolished.

Thursday 28 April
Walked in Dulwich yesterday and lost my brooch by way of a freshener when confronted with the final proofs just today done; and to be sent this afternoon: a book I shall never look at again. But I now feel entirely free. No longer famous, no longer on a pedestal; no longer hawked in by societies: on my own, for ever. Well I've done my bit for that cause, and can't be bullied. And then, when they badger me, I can say Refer to *Three Guineas*.

Rain and dark. A lost dog in the Square; political lull. Income Tax up to five shillings and sixpence. Our earnings prodigious. Income last year about £6,000. John much impressed. Press worth £10,000. And all this sprung from that type on the drawing room table at Hogarth House twenty years ago. I can now give all my mind to *Roger*; also blow a few private bubbles of a morning; and don't wait publication day with any expectations. I shall

I feel forget this book completely. Yet I never wrote a book with greater fervour; under such a lash of compulsion. And it stood me in good stead.

Friday 29 April
The difficulty is that I get so absorbed in this fantastic *Pointz Hall* I can't attend to *Roger*. So what am I to do? This is however only my first day of freedom. I'm in a dazed state, hovering between two worlds like a spider's web with nothing to attach the string to.

Tuesday 3 May
My eyes ache with *Roger* and I'm a little appalled at the prospect of the grind this book will be. I must somehow shorten and loosen; I *can't* (remember) stretch out a long painstaking literal book: later I must generalise and let fly. But then, how can one cut loose from facts, when there they are, contradicting my theories? A problem. But I'm convinced I can't physically, strain after a Royal Academy portrait.

We take our treat on Friday now, and went to St Albans, in the grey blizzard; and saw Roman pavements, guarded by men in overcoats, attending upon imbecile sons. Had tea, and heard the local ladies discussing the Empire Day celebrations, which are to include a red white and blue cake decorated with flags. What will they say to *Three Guineas?*

Monday 9 May
This is written to fill up the usual distracted relics of Monday's broken morning: drove up [from Rodmell] in the clear May morning light. A rather patchy week end: bitter cold. Can't settle to my play (*Pointz Hall* is to become in the end a play) or to Roger's Cambridge letters. The truth is we want a holiday; and have to dribble along rather jaded, trying odds and ends to keep moving, till June 8th or so, when we escape. A social week ahead: lunch Clive; to Philip [Morrell] to choose a ring and emotionalise; two plays of Angelica's and God damn it, Saturday at Ray [Strachey]'s. L. rather on edge about that.

Thursday 12 May
Lunch Clive (balderdash, respectability rampant; hard superficiality); to Philip after tea. He pressed things on me. I felt rather uncomfortable: a vulture feeling; didn't want to take so much. But took the big green ring and pearl earrings, shawl and fan. Philip rather battered – simple, cheerful, with a vast black satin cravat. Had a bad heart, from an old rowing strain. The specialist thinking Ott an ordinary wife said "Do you want the truth?" Yes. "Well any shock will kill you. How old?" Sixty-seven. "You won't see sixty-eight – except you live like a potato." She burst into tears, which she seldom

did. Then he recovered, she got ill – paralysed – some nerve affection. They then told her of the Doctor's death: she was sick all night; recovered; and suddenly died in the early morning. A lovely thrush egg blue evening; domes and chimneys very pure and sharp walking home with my green shagreen box, the shawl and the fan. Ott's last gifts.

Friday 20 May

Time and again I have meant to write down my expectations, dreads, and so on, waiting the publication of *Three Guineas* – but haven't. What I'm afraid of is the taunt Charm and emptiness. The book I wrote with such violent feelings to relieve that immense pressure will not dimple the surface. That is my fear. But the fears are entirely outbalanced by the immense relief and peace I have gained, and enjoy this moment. Now I am quit of that poison and excitement. I am an outsider. I can take my way: experiment with my own imagination in my own way. The pack may howl, but it shall never catch me.

Tuesday 24 May

I'm pleased this morning because Lady Rhondda writes that she is 'profoundly excited and moved by *Three Guineas*'. A good omen; because this shows that certain people will be stirred; will think; will discuss; it won't altogether be frittered away. But as the whole of Europe may be in flames – its on the cards. One more shot at a policeman and the Germans, Czechs, French will begin the old horror. The 4th of August [1914] may come next week. At the moment there is a lull. L. says Kingsley Martin says we say (the Prime Minister) that we will fight this time. Hitler therefore is chewing his little bristling moustache. But the whole thing trembles: and my book may be like a moth dancing over a bonfire – consumed in less than one second. Now for the [Chelsea] Flower Show; dinner at the Hutch. What am I to wear? Aeroplanes growling overhead in the cloudy blue sky. They look like sharks, seen through our wavy window.

Wednesday 25 May

Ka [Arnold-Forster] is dead. I read it by chance in the *News Chronicle* yesterday before going to the flower show. No flowers, no mourning. Why did she die? And what do I feel? Oh that one could feel more for the deaths of one's friends! But it comes and goes, feeling. Always at first visual – Ka lying drawn and white, there with the flat sea underneath – the ships passing. Her own identical life ended when Rupert [Brooke] died. So I think. After that she was acting a part very carefully and deliberately chosen. Maternity, Will [her husband], public life. Hence some squint; she was never natural, never with me at least. And I was self-conscious; remembering how she had seen me mad. She used to come to Asheham: condescending, patronising, giving up her own pleasures to tend me and help L. I don't think I was ever at my ease with her. Yet we had an old affection; remembered things – Rupert &c – that we never spoke of. She had that irritating Quack Quack in her voice; as if she always must be impressing me with her busyness, her social standing; her responsibilities: how she was a J P on some Education Committee; doing actual things with important real people, while we frittered our time away writing books in London. In her house – a singularly ugly house in some ways – she was too much the hostess who keeps open house. But at the same time that was her role: to help; to lift lame dogs; to entertain, to arrange; manage; receive confidences. And what was wrong with all that? Only that after Rupert's death she was playing a part. Yet this is superficial. For there was a trustiness in her; a stable goodness; and a good deal of fortitude, patience, a determination to oar her way. I wonder, did she know she was dying? And what did she think of it all? And why? As usual, I regret: that she sent me cream at Christmas, and in the flurry of L.'s illness I never wrote and thanked; that she suggested coming, and absorbed in Nessa last autumn, I did not arrange it. But this is always so; and can't be helped. And I am thinking of her with affection – old Ka.

Thursday 26 May
Ka had a seizure and died without regaining consciousness. This is from a typed form sent by [her brother-in-law] this morning. She is buried today – rainy and dark: and I shall not go to the service. Will is in Canada.

Saturday 28 May
A pouring wet day as dark as November. May – this spring has been blotted from the calendar. The Buzz is beginning, though the little gadfly only emerges from its shell next Thursday. I can foretell that those who dislike will sneer at me for a well to do aesthete; and those who approve will echo Rhondda's 'most exciting, profoundly moving'. All reviews and letters will ring changes on those notes.

Monday 30 May
Nessa's birthday – the fifty-eighth I think it must be. She is at Charleston with Angelica and Quentin. Oh dear – Julian not there. And it rains hard – she says she is glad to be away. The Robson children and Tom at tea. A great spread; mostly eaten. The little boy crammed his mouth with sweets, and added one that Sally had already sucked. Tom came, most respectable; swallow tails and grey silk tie, having he explained to slip into his evening service in time to take round the plate – a churchwarden in South Kensington. Very friendly.
L. says I must expect some very angry reviews from men. I add, From

women too. Then there'll be the clergy. But I think I can sit calm as a toad in an oak at the centre of the storm.

Tuesday 31 May
A letter from Pippa [Strachey]. She is enthusiastic. She says its the very thing for which they have panted. Now I can face the music, or donkey's bray or geese's cackle. Never have I faced reviews so composedly. Maynard may have a gibe; but what care I? And I shan't send copies to my family, and so they need say nothing.

MONKS HOUSE, RODMELL

Friday 3 June
This is the coming out day of *Three Guineas*. And the *TLS* has two columns and a leader; and the *Referee* a great black bar Woman Declares Sex War; or some such caption. Its true I have a sense of quiet and relief. But no wish to read reviews, or hear opinions. Oh it pleased me that the *TLS* says I'm the most brilliant pamphleteer in England. Also that this book may mark an epoch if taken seriously.
   I talked to Nessa about Julian on Wednesday. She can hardly speak. What matters compared with that? Yet I was always thinking of Julian when I wrote.

Whit Sunday 5 June
Walked on the racecourse: bought cakes in Lewes. Charleston and Bunny to tea today, yesterday the first hot summer day. People in tails and white shirts tripping about Lewes. Glyndebourne in full flower. Windy today, but still fine, and the sun still active – after I suppose two months drought and darkness. The ugliest spring on record. So we were wise to save our holiday, though I'm so rested now. We shall attempt Skye, for if we don't now we never shall. L. says we are old. I say we are middle aged.

Saturday 11 June
On the whole *Three Guineas* is taken seriously: many high compliments; some snarls but generally kind, rather surprised, and its over – Off we can go to Scotland for a holiday that I don't really need, but still a freshener before *Roger* won't come amiss. No book ever slid from me so secretly and smoothly. Quit of all this, I've written an article on Walpole, very fast and free, for America. Walked several good walks. We go up this evening after

tea. Bowls. Bells. And the garden being planted by L. with some little help from me. And I must go in to cold mutton.

*   *   *

52 TAVISTOCK SQUARE, WC1

Tuesday 5 July
A thunderstorm, still further to distract my already distracted brain. How am I to calm and contract back again to *Roger?* We returned on Saturday.

Thursday 7 July
Oh the appalling grind of getting back to *Roger*, after these violent oscillations: *Three Guineas* and *Pointz Hall*. How can I concentrate upon minute facts in letters? But Gumbo [Marjorie Strachey] last night threw cold water on the whole idea of biography of those who have no lives. Roger had, she says, no life that can be written. I daresay this is true. And here am I sweating over minute facts. Is it to be done on this scale? I think I will go on doggedly till I meet him myself – 1909 – and then attempt something more fictitious. But must plod on through all these letters till then. Meanwhile I'm so raddled and raked with people, noise, telephones – have endless letters to write, long for peace.

Tuesday 19 July
What about yesterday as a specimen day? Work at *Roger* – fearful niggling drudgery to quarter to one. Robson to lunch. Isherwood wants to see me at three. I slip out; buy flowers, pâté de foie. Back at 3.15. Peep in at Stephen Spender, Chris [Isherwood] and John and L. all talking in John's room. Sit down upstairs. Visit Adrian. Tea on balcony. Dog playing, cars passing – Judith there. Ann to marry on Thursday. No invitations. Karin in and out. Look at house. Gossip and home. Will Rothenstein to dine. A respectable, suppressed, but I don't think quite such a snake as Duncan makes out. Only dimmed, tamed, I think on his guard. No enthusiasm for life – too much high nobility. Only . . . compared with Roger, how blunted, tolerant, and a little plausible. Gave me letters. Nothing vivid about Roger and Paris. All dim now. Fetched by a chauffeur and car.

Mercifully no one – I repeat *no one* – today. Today Julian was killed last year. And its hot again. I shan't say anything to Nessa. Oh dear – We go – this is an event for us – to the Ballet at Drury Lane in proper seats tonight. *Three Guineas* selling very slowly. Abusive or sneering letters the last two days.

Friday 22 July

Weather steamy but no longer blue. Sat in Gordon Square last night and Duncan and Vanessa were we thought unreasonable about Roger and Will Rothenstein and the Grafton [2nd Post-Impressionist Exhibition, 1911]. What a kettle of fish! And *Three Guineas* is once more selling; has now broached the six thousand. Ann was married yesterday. I gave her £15; L. £10.

Tuesday 26 July

Its very true that I have no time. I have simply dedicated the last fortnight to people – seeing people – not a day free from it. Always an engagement. If you let it fill your sails there's something to be said for it.

MONKS HOUSE, RODMELL

Thursday 4 August

Came down on Thursday; almost mute with botheration: six from Charleston on Sunday; then Vita on Tuesday for the night and yesterday; Mrs Woolf, Edgar and Sylvia today. Yet we are very happy. I should add that we found a new gable thrown out in the roof, workmen hammering, Mr Wicks started work, without warning, and says he will be here three weeks which means five. It has been very hot with a strong hot wind. And I'm taking a gallop in fiction, after bringing Roger to his marriage. Rather a jerk and an effort, my work at the moment. Switching from assiduous truth to wild ideas. But I liked seeing Vita, so free and easy again. We sat out here and discussed her loves; death; Ben [her son]'s tears, on being scolded by Vita; Willy Maugham; Clive, who's writing a book, secretly, on war; Julian; Nessa; looking so ill; so many women have lost sons and lovers; I forget how it went. Also she brought a basket of peaches and half a bottle of Château Yquem from her mother's cellar. And off she went in her great black car that impresses Mrs Bartholomew so. She was much like old times.

Saturday 7 August

Yesterday I saw six tanks with gun carriages come clambering down the hill and assemble like black beetles at Rat Farm. Small boys playing idiotic games for which I pay. Harold [Nicolson] is very dismal, Vita says: predicts war, but not this week. A lull at the moment. And terrifically hot. A great purple black cloud massed itself behind Mrs Woolf, Sylvia and Edgar as they sat out here; then thunder; then rain, at last. And we had lights lit. Why they so rub the country bloom off – these family Woolves – I don't know. Always a dusty feeling of Earl's Court and offices. Oh and the commonplaceness of the talk – mostly about [Woolf family] furniture: lovely silver mirrors, most artistic overmantels, suites of dining room chairs, coffee cups. She lies awake counting them, deciding who's to have what, and so falls asleep. Workmen tapping. Yesterday the men about the wireless. Too many gadgets and dodges perhaps in this house. And the children shrieking. But we go to Charleston for tea.

Wednesday 17 August
The old woman who lived up at Mount Misery drowned herself three days ago. The body was found near Piddinghoe – my usual walk. Her son died; she turned queer; had been a midwife in Brighton; lived in the broken windowed half of Mr Bradfield's house. She used to moon over the downs with a dog. Once she came to the shop late on Sunday to beg twopennyworth of paraffin – she was alone in the dark. They threatened to turn her out – farm wanted. She had killed her dog. So at last off she goes, on Monday perhaps when the tide was high in the afternoon, and jumps in. Louie says her brother found a drowned woman the other day at Barcombe Mills – a horrid sight. So I order dinner hastily and come out here to brew more *Roger*.
   So, at supper, we discussed our generation: and the prospects of war. Hitler has his million men now under arms. Is it only summer manoeuvres or –? Harold [Nicolson] broadcasting in his man of the world manner hints it may be war. That is the complete ruin not only of civilisation, in Europe, but of our last lap. Quentin conscripted &c. One ceases to think about it – that's all. Goes on discussing the new room, new chair, new books. What else can a gnat on a blade of grass do? And I would like to write *Pointz Hall*; and other things; and have half a mind one of these days to explain what my intention is in writing these continual diaries. Not publication. Revision? a memoir of my own life? Perhaps. Only other things crop up.

Monday 22 August
I am in the wars, or shall be. Maynard sends for us on Wednesday; is said by Lydia to be very critical of *Three Guineas*. Now the thing to remember is that I'm an independent and perfectly established human being: no one can bully me: and at the same time nothing shall make me shrivel into a martyr or a bitter persecution maniac.

Tuesday 23 August
Its odd to be as nervous as I am at the idea of seeing Maynard tomorrow, and his heckling: dear old Hitler. But I won't be nervous.

Sunday 28 August

By the way Maynard never said a word. Some were unsaid. As for instance, Lydia: we all put up with you Virginia, said significantly, kissing me at parting. Maynard tired, extended, rather grim. Sunday is the devil's own day at Monks House. Dogs, children, bells ... there they go for evensong. I can't settle anywhere. Beaten after three hard fights at bowls. Bowls is our mania. Reading rather scamped. Ding dong bell ... ding dong – why did we settle in a village? And how deliberately we are digging ourselves in! And at any moment the guns may go off and explode us. L. is very black. Hitler has his hounds only very lightly held. A single step – in Czechoslovakia – like the Austrian Archduke in 1914 and again its 1914. Ding dong ding dong.

The autumn mists assemble. And I'm irritable with work and noise. We dine at Charleston. Now its as quiet as the grave ... all grey; the chestnut leaves hanging heavy; birds on the telegraph posts. Letters fret me. Never one that's disinterested. Requests always to speak, write, lecture, see people. That's fame – dogs again. Yap Yap.

Wednesday 31 August

War seemed round the corner again. Question what Hitler will do, when he'll do it. Cabinet Ministers summoned. And, of course, Kingsley Martin ringing up, and annoyed that L. isn't in London to hold his hand, and make it write an article. We were in London yesterday. Kingsley Martin to lunch. Three possibilities. One of them European war. But not at once. A game of bluff on Hitler's part, possibly. If there's war "my own solution is suicidal" – while he munches mutton chops, and sweeps up fragments, scraping his knife and fork round in a way I hate. So he burbled on: with his own article, and his own figure, histrionically arrayed, in the centre. I walked off, bought a pewter plate, a scissors, and a lustre globe, encouraged by a letter from Brace [USA] reporting enthusiasm for *Three Guineas*, good advance orders, and great praise.

Thursday 1 September

Politics marking time. A violent attack on *Three Guineas* in *Scrutiny* by Q. Leavis. And I didn't read it through. But I read enough to see that it was all personal – about Queenie's own grievances and retorts to my snubs. Why I don't care more for praise or wigging I don't know. Yet its true.

Monday 5 September

Its odd to be sitting here, looking up little facts about Roger and the Metropolitan Museum in New York, with a sparrow tapping on my roof this fine September morning when it may be the 3rd August 1914 ... What would war mean? Darkness, strain: I suppose conceivably death. And all the horror of friends: and Quentin ... All that lies over the water in the brain of that ridiculous little man. Why ridiculous? Because none of it fits. Death and war and darkness representing nothing that any human being from the Pork Butcher to the Prime Minister cares one straw about. Not liberty, not life ... merely a housemaid's dream. And we woke from that dream and have the Cenotaph to remind us of the fruits. We may hear his mad voice vociferating tonight. Nuremberg rally begun: but it goes on for another week. And what will be happening this time ten days?

Saturday 10 September
I don't feel that the crisis is real – not so real as Roger in 1910 at Gordon Square, about which I've just been writing. Of course we may be at war this time next week. Seven ships are mobilised today. Meanwhile the aeroplanes are on the prowl, crossing the downs. Every preparation is made. Sirens will hoot in a particular way when there's the first hint of a raid. L. and I no longer talk about it. Much better to play bowls and pick dahlias. Today Morgan comes, and we have our crowded Memoir Club week-end. It is at Tilton, in the afternoon, to suit Maynard, who is going to read.

Sunday 11 September
Morgan here. He is writing in the garden. A very fine clear spruce blue day. The news as black as possible. Hitler has at any rate cursed, and Goering spat: nothing said till tomorrow. And now in to the house to tidy rooms and hair.

Monday 12 September
Papers all say that we shall know the truth, one way or the other, tonight. So there's nothing to do but wait. Memoir Club meeting had its little sensation. Molly [MacCarthy] and Quentin lunched. After lunch, as she came down stairs, Molly tripped and fell over the loose tile. Lay very white in great pain. Obviously a bad twist. When we had to go, she couldn't move. Ankle swollen. So we took her to [the doctor]; then the X ray; at last to Tilton; carried her in. Maynard read a very packed profound and impressive paper so far as I could follow, about Cambridge youth; their philosophy; its consequences; what it lacked; what it gave; the beauty and unworldliness of it. I was impressed. Then he had to rest; it turned grey and cold. Molly had to be slowly conveyed – a bed made on the ground floor at Charleston. Nevertheless a very human satisfactory meeting. Bunny, Desmond, Quentin and Lydia, ourselves, Morgan, Clive, Nessa (in big hat: much more herself than ever yet).

Tuesday 13 September

No war yet anyhow. Hitler boasted and boomed but shot no solid bolt. Mere violent rant, and then broke off. We listened in to the end. A savage howl like a person excrutiated; then howls from the audience; then a more spaced and measured sentence. Then another bark. Cheering ruled by a stick. Frightening to think of the faces. And the voice was frightening. But as it went on we said anti-climax. This seems to be the general verdict. He daren't cross the line. Comes up to it and stands bawling insults. How can people stand this nonsense? Negotiations to go on, under threat that he will use force if &c. Immense relief last night at Monks House, after a gloomy dinner. Peaceful if depressed: anyhow a week or two without a war.

Wednesday 14 September

Things worse today. Rioting in Prague. It looks as if Hitler meant to slide sideways into war. Raises riots: will say Can't be stopped. But its a hopeless war this – when we know winning means nothing. So we're committed, for the rest of our lives, to public misery. This will be slashed with private too. We – L. and I – can make out I suppose down here: vegetables and fruit. And I've made some money. Needn't cringe. That's about all.

Friday 16 September

Chamberlain has flown to see Hitler. Universal relief and approval. No news yet. They say this means Peace. War staved off for one year. Nessa Duncan Angelica and Quentin start for Cassis tonight, driving across France. We settle in for ten days alone. Dined at Charleston. All seemed agreed that a country life is best. Clive is giving notice to Gordon Square. We hear that Tavistock Square will be pulled down in three years. Shall we not all provide ourselves with single rooms in London and live here? Never make any fixed plans for life – that's my motto. Really, for the ten years that remain, be free of the world.

Saturday 17 September

Chamberlain back. In a hard business man's voice told us, as he stepped out of the plane at Croydon, that he was to meet Hitler again: that Hitler was coming to meet an old man half way (is this symbolical?) and we meanwhile not to believe rumour. No statement today. Cabinet meeting. Just as in violent personal anxiety, the public lapses into complete indifference. One can feel no more at the moment.

Dreamt of Julian one night: how he came back: I implored him not to go to Spain. He promised. Then I saw his wounds. Dreamt of Roger last night. How he had not died. I praised Cézanne. And told him how I admired his writing. Exactly the old relationship. Perhaps easier to get this in dreams, because one has dreamt away the fact of his death, to which I woke as L. came in.

Thursday 22 September
The public fluctuates. Chamberlain flying today to Gotesberg (?). A strong opposition has risen. Eden, Churchill and the Labour Party all denounce serving Czechoslovakia on the altar and bidding it commit suicide. Czechoslovakia very dignified and tragic. The prospect of another glissade after a minor stop into abyss. All Europe in Hitler's keeping. What'll he gobble next? That's the summary of us in Sussex.

Wednesday 28 September
This may be the last day of peace; so why not record it, as I've twenty minutes and nothing to do? A tumultuous week end. Pouring wet Monday. L. came out to say Kingsley Martin begged him to come up, in order to act as liaison between the Labour Party and the Liberals. He was the only person &c. So we decided to go at once and spend the night. Drove up in the rain. Men digging trenches at Turnham Green. London crowded. L. went to see Kingsley, I to buy coffee &c. "Its a miserable day and our thoughts are miserable" the woman said. She said we should win; and that it would not be a long war. "But what is the point of winning?" I said, at which she exclaimed and shrugged her shoulders in agreement. Then Kingsley Martin to dinner; charcoal black round his eyes; as usual something histrionic. Hopelessly restless. Melodramatic in his gestures, perpetually looking at the time and ringing people up. No word of any possible plan or reason for summoning L. Stayed on, drinking, smoking. Then said he was going to walk the streets. Couldn't sleep. So to bed. Telephones all the morning. I went to the London Library. Sat in the basement and looked up *The Times* on [the Post-Impressionist Exhibition] in 1910. Old sweeper gently dusting. Came and said They're telling us to try on our masks. Have you got yours I asked. No not yet. And shall we have war? I fear so, but I still hope not. Oh they've laid in sand bags; the books will be moved; but if a bomb strikes the house ... May I dust under your chair? I looked in at the National Gallery being warned by a sober loud speaker to get my gas mask as I walked down Pall Mall. I looked at Renoir, Cézanne &c: tried to see through Roger's eyes: tried to get some solidity into my mind. So to lunch. Question what to do about the Press. Plans can only be sketched. We must settle into work at any rate. We must drive our pens and keep the Press going that way. We had a rather unpleasant farewell – they staying, we going. Its reasonable of course. But one doesn't like leaving them there: and yet they want to stay, for the money. A violent

rain storm; a great crowd in the streets. It was oddly peaceful and sane, getting out here after London. Mr Perkins brought gas masks about 10.30, and so at last we went to bed.

Thursday 29 September

We listened in yesterday at five expecting to hear that War was declared. Instead Mr Chamberlain made a sensational announcement. He has been invited by Herr Hitler to meet him tomorrow at Munich. Signor Mussolini and Daladier will be present. Mobilisation is postponed for twenty-four hours. It was like coming out of a dark room. Anyhow war for the moment is postponed. Perkins and Janson called last night to say fifty children arrive in Rodmell today and to note numbers of our rooms.

Friday 30 September

L. has just come in, it being 11.15, to say that he overheard a Broadcast when he was in the WC; dashed out: turned on our wireless; and heard that terms are being made at Munich. I can't go into them. But it means peace. They are agreeing to let some Germans into Czechoslovakia today; then English Italian and French are to enter and guarantee; then a three months' pause. Three months in which to settle the question, instead of bombs on London and Paris today! Such a reversal was never known. I will try and describe the reversal; which is soberly and truly life after death. For we, even if we escaped, should have had our noses rubbed in death; ruin; perhaps the end finally of all order. It would have meant our last fifteen years of life spent in battling for a thread of liberty; keeping the Press going among the deaths of the young. And now suddenly we can travel and move and use our normal faculties. No slaughter of the young beneath us. I wonder if we could have faced it even here – entertaining East End children in the hall; writing; getting all the dismal fag ends of things thrown at us; and reading Casualty Lists. Now of course one makes not new resolutions, but attacks the old with some fervour. Possibly – sanguinely – a new view will dominate. Hitler will sink instead of swell. But what a shave! A very fine day.

Saturday 1 October

A violent storm – purple ink clouds. L. is storing apples - finest harvest for perhaps some years. We were to live on apples honey and cabbage. Postman delivered an oration – "just my own thoughts" on War and Dictators. How all will worship Chamberlain now: but in five years' time we may be saying we ought to have put him, Hitler, down now. But now we can't help being glad of peace. Its human nature. Of course there's bound to be a turn against relief, as in violent illness. One turns peevish and has a sense of emptiness.

Sunday 2 October
Yesterday would have been the first day of the proclamation of war. It might be amusing to scribble down pall mall some higgledy piggledy of incidents: as they remain over; and will soon be forgotten. The BBC in a measured trained voice: how the public was to go with warm clothing: no glass: post cards: this interrupted by the Archbishop's prayers; then cold menace: a spaced dictated message from the Admiralty to ships. Obviously we'd sunk mines. Then the afternoon (Wednesday) when all foreign stations were jammed. Then the statement that all poisonous snakes at the Zoo would be killed, and dangerous animals shot – Vision of London ravaged by cobras and tigers. Sense of preparation to the last hair. All this mixture of minute detail; with invocations to God; with Hitler braying and the Germans howling; then the composed and cultured voice breaking in, say about not taking pets. Then over all a feeling of the senselessness, futility, so that there was a dilution of emotion. A child's game. Yet extreme physical relief when peace seemed twenty-four hours longer. Some instinctive self preservation. I felt this most when we drove away from 52 [Tavistock Square]. Some remorse at leaving the clerks exposed. Now rapidly other emotions chase each other; that peace seems dull, solid. Then that we must have a bone to gnaw. Some obliquity: after all we admired Chamberlain in the crisis. Is it fair to abuse him now?

Monday 3 October
The Keynes to tea yesterday. All a put up job between Chamberlain and Hitler, Maynard said. Never had been any chance of war. I wish I could get the ripples of all these complexities to land. Maynard and Lydia very congenial – dear old Maynard so sanguine, so powerful, somehow lovable too, and Lord how brilliant. I kissed him. A life time – what remains – of peace now. Reaction of shame beginning. *Daily Telegraph* decent, and starts a pro-Czech movement. *Times* disgraceful.

Thursday 6 October
Politics now a mere 'I told you so ... You did – I didn't'. I shall cease to read the papers. Sink at last into contemplation. Peace for our life time: why not try to believe it?

Friday 14 October
Two things I mean to do when the long dark evenings come: to write, on the spur of the moment, as now, lots of little poems to go into *Pointz Hall*:

as they may come in handy; to collect, even bind together, my innumerable *TLS* notes: to consider them as material for some kind of critical book: ranging all through English literature as I've read and noted it the past twenty years. In fact I must clear my table, as L. calls it and does it – before we go on Sunday.

52 TAVISTOCK SQUARE, WC1

Sunday 30 October

Words, words, words, so many and so many – That I think is the vocalisation of my little sensation this morning. I am tired of writing. 'Words' refers partly to Vita's new poem, 'Solitude'. Does it jab on the nerve? Is it only sleek eloquence? The words I found on my lips were 'Suave and sumptuous'. I suspect there's a good deal more. But no doubt I'm at an angle. I don't want reflections on God: nor do I altogether forget her superficial view of *Three Guineas*: that she never troubled to think out what I meant. This is partly personal; partly not.

Nessa away slightly rasps me. I have no circumference; only my inviolable centre: L. to wit. A great deal on foot. Words words and now roast beef and apple tart. An evening alone.

Tuesday 1 November

Max [Beerbohm] like a Cheshire cat. Orbicular. Jowled. Blue eyed. Eyes grow vague. What he said was, I've never been in a group. No, not even as a young man. It was a serious fault. When you're a young man you ought to think There's only one right way. And I thought – this is very profound, but you mayn't realise it – 'It takes all sorts to make a world.' I was outside all the groups. Now dear Roger Fry who liked me, was a born leader. No one so 'illuminated'. He looked it. Never saw anyone look it so much. I heard him lecture, on the Aesthetics of Art. I was disappointed. He kept on turning the page – turning the page . . . George Moore never used his eyes. He never knew what men and women think. He got it all out of books. Ah I was afraid you would remind me of *Ave atque Vale*. Yes. That's beautiful. Yes, its true he used his eyes then. Otherwise its like a lovely lake, with no fish in it.

About his own writing: dear Lytton Strachey said to me: first I write one sentence; then I write another. That's how I write. And so I go on. But I have a feeling writing ought to be like running through a field. That's your way. Now how do you go down to your room, after breakfast – what do you feel? I used to look at the clock, and say Oh dear me, its time I began my article . . . No, I'll read the paper first. I never wanted to write. But I used to come home from a dinner party and take my brush and draw caricature after caricature. They seemed to bubble up from here ... he pressed his stomach. That was a kind of inspiration, I suppose. I have a public of about 1500 – Oh I'm famous, largely thanks to you, and people of importance at the top like you. I often read over my own work. And I have a habit of reading it through the eyes of people I respect. I often read it as Virginia Woolf would read it – picking out the kind of things you would like. You never do that? Oh you should try it.

Willie Maugham came in: like a dead man whose beard or moustache has grown a little grisly bristle after death. And his lips are drawn back like a dead man's. He has small ferret eyes. A look of suffering and malignity and meanness and suspicion. A mechanical voice as if he had to raise a lever at each word – stiffens talk into something hard cut, measured. Sat like an animal in a trap. And I could not say anything that loosed his dead man's jaw. Isherwood and I met on the doorstep. He is a slip of a wild boy: with quicksilver eyes. Nipped. Jockey like. "That young man," said W. Maugham "holds the future of the English novel in his hands." Very enthusiastic. In spite of Max's brilliance, and idiosyncracy, which he completely realises, and does not overstep, this was a surface evening. All kept to the same surface level by Sybil's hostesscraft.

Monday 14 November
So many pages, I see, about the Colefax party, and none about the incessant stream here. I use my old image. Trying to drink a cup of tea, and having it knocked out of one's hand.

A letter from Duncan. Complete bliss at Cassis, has a country life in view. Angelica perfect. So's the weather today. Jews persecuted, only just over the Channel. Here we feel a faint heat under us, like potatoes frying. But no more than that.

Tuesday 22 November
I meant to write Reflections on my position as a writer. Apparently I've been exalted to a very high position, say about ten years ago: then was decapitated by Wyndham Lewis and Miss Stein; am now I think – let me see – out of date, of course; not a patch, with the young, on Morgan; yet wrote *The Waves*; yet am unlikely to write anything good again; am a secondrate, and likely, I think, to be discarded altogether. I think that's my public reputation at the moment. It is based largely on Cyril Connolly's Cocktail criticism: a sheaf of feathers in the wind. How much do I mind? Less than I expected. I mean, I never thought I was so famous; so don't feel the decapitation. Yes I used to be praised by the young and attacked by the elderly. *Three Guineas* has queered the pitch. So my position is

ambiguous. Undoubtedly Morgan's reputation is much higher than my own. So is Tom's. Well? In a way it is a relief. I'm fundamentally, I think, an outsider. I do my best work and feel most braced with my back to the wall. This is not the measured criticism of my position I meant to write. I'm not able to go deeply. For here's the usual stir and bother – Nessa back tomorrow.

Friday 25 November
L.'s birthday – 58? But I open this, to note, at the foot of the last pessimistic page, in two minutes, the fact that pessimism can be routed by getting into the flow: creative writing. So why not, when pessimistic, dandle the brain a little, until it gets into its circuit?

Sunday 11 December
We walked back from *Twelfth Night* (disappointing) on a clear cold night. Talked of death in Russell Square. L. said he had taught himself not to think about it. Two or three years ago fear of death became an obsession. I said I should not wish to live if he died. But until then found life what? exciting? Yes I think so. He agreed. So we don't think of death.

Very long hours of semi-drudgery on *Roger*. The war years. Mrs Woolf has had a heart attack. But her vitality may again pull her over. The Jews obsess her. This autumn reveals plainly our 'celebrity': that is, that we never get a day to ourselves; and attract a constant stream, from all quarters. Political, social, literary. I suppose this is secretly pleasing. I wonder. A month in winter fields will cool me down. The young all swarm, even if they criticise.

Monday 12 December
Rather a debauched Sunday evening at Clive's last night. Was he drunk? He was so quarrelsome and peevish, after dinner. A long tirade against motorists. Suddenly Nessa got quite red and said "This conversation is so foolish we'd better change it." But Clive wouldn't change it. Every change had its head snapped off. I thought of Roger and Lytton and how we used to talk of a Sunday evening. Now all personal gossip and these tedious bickerings.

Thursday 15 December
This is hell's Black Calcutta hole week.

Monday 19 December
I will spend the last morning – for tomorrow will be an odious scramble – in summing up the year. True, there are ten days or so to run; but the

liberty of this book allows these – I was going to say liberties, but my meticulous conscience bids me look for another word. That raises some questions about my concern with the art of writing. On the whole the art becomes absorbing – more? No, I think its been absorbing ever since I was a little creature, scribbling a story in the manner of Hawthorne on the green plush sofa in the drawing room at St Ives while the grown ups dined.

The last dinner of the year was to Tom Eliot last night. Physically he is a little muffin faced: sallow and shadowed; but intent (as I am) on the art of writing. His play – *Family Reunion* – was the staple of the very bitter cold evening. (The snow is now falling: flakes come through my skylight.) It has taken him off and on two years to write, is an advance upon *Murder [in the Cathedral]*: in poetry. When the crisis came, his only thought was annoyance that now his play would not be acted. And he hurried up the revision. Tom said the young don't take art or politics seriously enough. Disappointed in the Auden–Isherwood. A subtle, splitting mind: a man of simple integrity, and the artist's ingenuous egotism. Dines out and goes to musical teas; reads poems at Londonderry House; has a humorous sardonic gift which mitigates his egotism; and is on the side of authority. A nice old friends' evening.

This year I have worked at *Three Guineas*; and began, about April 1st, *Roger*: whom I have brought to the year 1919. I have also written 'Walpole'; 'Lappin and Lapinova', and 'The Art of Biography'. John says two cabinet ministers are in favour of giving me the OM. The reception of *Three Guineas* has been interesting, unexpected – only I'm not sure what I expected. 8,000 sold. Not one of my friends has mentioned it. I've written too 120 pages of *Pointz Hall*. I think of making it a 220 page book. A medley. I rush to it for relief after a long pressure of Fry facts. To be written for pleasure.

We shall find the new window in at Monks House. And its the coldest day for five years. Snow steadily falling. John temperamental. Another boil over on Saturday. A very bad season. Probable loss. Two years more of 52. The new flats going up in Southampton Row. Clive leaving 50 [Gordon Square]. Deaths this year: Ottoline, Ka. Mrs Woolf recovering.

1939

After spending nearly four weeks at Monks House over Christmas, in extremes of weather, the Woolfs returned to London on 15 January. At the end of the month they paid a courtesy visit to one of the Hogarth Press's most distinguished authors, Sigmund Freud, now a refugee living in Hampstead. The Spanish Civil War was coming to its end, and on 27 February General Franco's government was recognised by Great Britain and France, although Madrid did not fall until a month later. Virginia was working on Roger Fry, the first draft of which she finished in March, sometimes allowing herself the indulgence of writing her fiction Pointz Hall and thinking of a book encompassing the whole of literature. On 16 March Hitler marched into Prague, and in April Mussolini invaded Albania. European war now seemed inevitable. The Woolfs were at Monks House for almost the whole of April, and Virginia had days of extreme depression. A few days before her return to London, at Vanessa's prompting she began to write her memoirs, which she continued intermittently until January 1941.

Although the Woolfs' lease of 52 Tavistock Square ran until 1941, large-scale demolitions were proceeding all around them. The noise and dirt became insupportable. They found an alternative in 37 Mecklenburgh Square, some half a mile to the east, and negotiated a lease. But apart from four weeks from the end of May when they escaped to Rodmell and then across to Normandy and Brittany, they spent the high summer in their old London flat – and it was here that Virginia was subjected to the discomfort of being photographed by Gisèle Freund, a protégée of her wealthy and overbearing admirer, the Argentinian intellectual Victoria Ocampo. The London season ended with more deaths: Mark Gertler the painter committed suicide; and Leonard's mother, after another fall, died on 2 July, aged eighty-eight. The remaining days of July, before the Woolfs went to Monks House on the 25th, were intensely busy and sociable.

At Charleston, the prospect of war had prompted Vanessa to undertake various improvements. Clive Bell contributed the contents of his London flat, and the house was henceforward his, Duncan Grant's, Vanessa's and the children's main home, though the painters kept their studios in Fitzroy Street. In August the Woolfs went up from Rodmell on two successive weeks to supervise the removal first of the Hogarth Press and then of their own furniture and effects to their new home at 37 Mecklenburgh Square. The political crisis intensified with the signing of the German–Soviet Pact on 23 August; and on 1 September Hitler's forces seized Danzig and began their attack on Poland. On 3 September the Prime Minister announced that Great Britain was at war with Germany.

The Woolfs settled in at Rodmell, going up to London from time to time to discuss the business of the Hogarth Press with John Lehmann, to try and make their new flat habitable, and to keep in touch with friends. Virginia's response to the anticipated privations of wartime was to take on more journalism to augment their diminishing income, and to offer weekend respites at Monks House to friends and to the staff of the Hogarth Press. It was the period of what came to be called the 'phoney' war, when, while Poland was overrun and partitioned between Germany and Russia, England waited uneasily and prepared for air bombardment; but action was confined to naval encounters. Petrol rationing had been introduced in September, and the Woolfs bicycled to Charleston for Christmas dinner.

1939

Monks House, Rodmell

Thursday 5 January

So I take a new nib, and spend my last five minutes, this very fine January morning, in writing the first page of the New Year. We came down fourteen or fifteen days ago and found all pipes frozen. There was snow for five days – bitter cold; wind. We staggered for one hour through the blizzard. Chains were on our wheels. We ground over to Charleston and Tilton on Christmas Day. Then, two days later, woke to find green grass everywhere. The long spikes of ice that hung down the kitchen window had drops on their noses. They melted. The pipes thawed. Now its a June morning with an east wind.

Monday 9 January

Now that I have brought my brain to the state of an old washerwoman's flannel over *Roger*, I must expand, first on this irresponsible page, and then for four days I swear, before we go back on Sunday, in fiction. Though I've ground out most wish to write, even fiction. Rodmell is a grind on the brain: in winter especially. I write three solid hours; walk two; then we read, with intervals for cooking dinner, music, news, till 11.30. Weather now broken. Floods and gales; marsh under water. Charleston broken up. Maynard's father dying. And that reminds me of two obituaries I should have written, had I not been immersed: Jack Hills and Mitz [LW's pet marmoset]. Mitz was found dead on Boxing Day I think: her white old woman's face puckered; eyes shut; tail wrapped round her neck. L. buried her in the snow under the wall. Jack died the same day about – no Xmas Eve; and if I had a brain (but haven't) I could retell his life; as it affected ours, thirty years ago. Who he saw, where he lived even had long been lost to me. Yet of all our youthful directors he was the most open minded, least repressive, could best have fitted in with later developments, had we not gone our ways – he to politics and sport, we to Bloomsbury.

Tuesday 17 January
London on Sunday. Five minutes left of the morning. I wish I could distil some thoughts about 'the situation' into nuggets. The Spanish war is being won yesterday today tomorrow by Franco. I dreamt of Julian. A sniping article on him – 'The limitations of Bloomsbury' – by Janet Adam Smith. She advises life in a mining village as a remedy: what is her practice? At Clive's on Sunday. A good discussion of painting and music. Angelica sang a song. L. talked. So did Nessa. I'm taking four days holiday from *Roger*, writing *Pointz Hall*.

Wednesday 18 January
I am going walking and adventuring, going to see pictures of an afternoon; and often come face to face, after tea, at odd moments, with the idea of death and age. Why not change the idea of death into an exciting experience? – as one did marriage in youth? Age is baffled today by my creative gift – still abubble. And then the steady passion with which I now read ... A rainy day. Rain real wet drops: white splashing from the road. I must somehow ease my way back to *Roger* – shut *Pointz Hall* firmly.

Tuesday 24 January
On the placards this afternoon: Franco at the gate of Barcelona. Measures for Defence. This refers to our new voluntary service. The one is the cause of the other. And on the bus coming back from the Flower Show I described my new 'novel'; and we planned the books we should write, if we could live another thirty years.

Sunday 29 January
Yes, Barcelona has fallen: Hitler speaks tomorrow; the next dress rehearsal begins. I have seen Marie Stopes, Princesse de Polignac, Philip and Pippin [Woolf], and Dr Freud in the last three days. Also had Tom to dinner and to the Stephens' party. Dr Freud gave me a narcissus. Was sitting in a great library with little statues at a large scrupulously tidy shiny table. We like patients on chairs. A screwed up shrunk very old man: with a monkey's light eyes, paralysed spasmodic movements, inarticulate: but alert. On Hitler. Generation before the poison will be worked out. About his books. Fame? I was infamous rather than famous; didn't make £50 by his first book. Difficult talk. An interview. Daughter [Anna] and Martin [son] helped. Immense potential, I mean an old fire now flickering. When we left he took up the stand What are *you* going to do? The English – war.

Monday 30 January
Freud said It would have been worse if you had *not* won the war. I said we often felt guilty; if we had failed, perhaps Hitler would have not been. No, he said, with great emphasis; he would have been infinitely worse.

Last night Yeats's death announced. That great thick long jowled poet, whom I last met at Ottoline's. And we are all on tiptoe, waiting Hitler's speech tonight.

Tuesday 31 January
A very sensible day yesterday. Saw no one. Took the bus to Southwark Bridge. Walked along Thames Street; saw a flight of steps down to the river. I climbed down -- a rope at the bottom. Found the strand of the Thames, under the warehouses – strewn with stones, bits of wire, slippery; ships lying off the bridge. Very slippery; warehouse walls crusted, weedy, worn. The river must cover them at high tide. It was now low. People on the Bridge stared. Difficult walking. A rat haunted, riverine place, great chains, wooden pillars, green slime, bricks corroded, a button hook thrown up by the tide. A bitter cold wind. Thought of the refugees from Barcelona walking forty miles, one with a baby in a parcel. So to Tower. Made a circuit: discovered St Olave's, Hart Street: Pepys's Church; too cold to explore; wandered about Fenchurch alleys, Billingsgate; walked through Leadenhall Market; so back by omnibus; the street and shops the product of this factory world; so home; left the kettle on; it blew out its connection; read Michelet; wrote to Desmond; L. out at Fabians; played gramophone; listened to Our Master's Voice, Hitler less truculent than expected; read; and so to bed.

Friday 17 February
Jangled with talk – nine hours solid, frothy, talk; varied by buying Michelet and [H. G. Wells's] *The Country of the Blind*. A hammer and a drill this morning exacerbate still further: they're pulling down Tavistock Square and building offices. So out in the brisk cold to buy note books. I'm starting my grand tour of literature. That is I'm going to write a book of discovery, reading as one pulls a string out; and must follow my trail through Sévigné, Michelet, Somerset Maugham &c. That's the idea; encouraged by that vast marsupial Margery Strachey, who implored me to do criticism; as indeed I've long wanted.

Tuesday 28 February
Yesterday, Franco was recognised. And Julian killed for this. Nessa though I suppose making herself live: succeeding: very busy.

Saturday 11 March
Yesterday I set the last word to the first sketch of *Roger*. And now I have
to begin – well not even to begin, but to revise and revise. A terrible grind
to come: and innumerable doubts, of myself as biographer: of the possibility
of doing it at all; all the same I've carried through to the end; and may
allow myself one moment's mild gratification. There are the facts more or
less extracted.

Thursday 16 March
Jack [Hills] I see in this morning's paper left £3,000 only. I see too that
Hitler has marched into Prague. This, says the Prime Minister 'is not in the
spirit of the Munich meeting'. My comment anyhow is superfluous. We sit
and watch.

Wednesday 22 March
Tom sent me his play, *Family Reunion*. No, it don't do. I read it over the
week end. It starts theories. But no . . . You see the experiment with stylised
chatter isn't successful. He's a lyric not a dramatic. But here there's no free
lyricism: is caught back by the character: as stiff as pokers. And the chief
poker is Tom. A cold upright poker. A clever beginning, and some ideas;
but they spin out; and nothing grips: all mist. A failure: a proof he's not a
dramatist. This is stated very politely by the papers this morning. We go
on Thursday. I'm of course for reasons I can't go into, selfishly relieved:
why? A mixture of motives. No, I can't write here. Politics lulled: but
Kingsley [Martin] vocal on the phone.

Wednesday 29 March
There can be no doubt that Tom knew that his play was a failure. He was
very yellow and heavy lidded. We talked about his cold, and I noted that
he said his lectures, on Church and State, were 'very bad', a proof, I think,
that all his work now seems so. But the evening was oddly successful.
Kingsley Martin invited himself, and privately told L. that German aeroplanes have been flying over London. Madrid surrendered. Kingsley says
war is inevitable.

Thursday 30 March
No, it was a good idea having Hugh [Walpole] alone. He gave me a
full account of his sexual life, of which I retain these facts. He only
loves men who don't love men. Tried to drown himself once over
[Lauritz] Melchior. Jumped into a river; stuck in mud; seized a carving
knife; saw himself in the glass; all became absurd. Reconciliation. Told
me too of the Baths at the Elephant & Castle. How the men go there.

Has had a married life with Harold for fifteen years without intercourse. All this piles up a rich life of which I have no knowledge; and he can't use it in his novels. They are therefore about lives he hasn't lived which explains their badness. Hasn't the courage to write about his real life. Would shock people he likes. Told me how he had had a father and son simultaneously. Copulation removes barriers. Class barriers fade. Lives at Hampstead with Harold's family and friends completely naturally. All this is a great deal better than his literary talk. Saw, at any rate, another Hugh. This lasted from 4.30 to 7.30; without a break. And I liked him and enjoyed it, though crushed in the head.

Friday 31 March
Yes I made a phrase last night about bearing the panoply of life, and being glad to lay it down. I wonder if its true. After a worried domestic day; then L. had a temperature and went to bed; the Memoir Club was imminent. I felt I was bearing up the panoply of life and would be glad to let it sink. I said to myself, Remember, this is the description of age coming. I'm on the qui vive to describe age: to note it. I often think of things in this way, but forget them. And as L. is normal and up and as its a fine morning, I'm not conscious of holding up my panoply, only distracted rather and can't settle in.

Monks House, Rodmell

Tuesday 11 April
Yesterday at Tilton; and Tilton's comfort, and quiet, all seem to make it harder for me to get on with revising *Roger*. Revising *Roger* at the rate of two weeks to a chapter will take me three months. Then there's the war. The finest Easter possible has this purple background. We wait like obedient children to hear what we shall be told when Parliament meets on Thursday. At Tilton we talked first medicine; Maynard's drastic cure; then politics; five minutes left for Tom's play. Maynard, even Maynard, can't find much that's hopeful now that Italy has nipped off Albania save that there's a unity of hatred. The men women children dogs &c are solid for war if war comes. But privately – how one rockets between private and public – his eyes are bluer, his skin pinker, and he can walk without pain. Lydia has devoted herself to the treatment.

Roasting hot: birds achirp: butterflies. I am reading Dickens; by way of a refresher. Also I'm reading Rochefoucauld. Chaucer I take at need. So if I had any time – but perhaps next week will be more solitudinous – I should, if it weren't for the war – glide my way up and up in to that exciting layer so rarely lived in: where my mind works so quick it seems asleep; like the aeroplane propellors.

Thursday 13 April
Two days of influenza. Now politics impend. Chamberlain's statement in the House today. War I suppose not tomorrow, but nearer.

Saturday 15 April
Its odd what extreme depression a little influenza and a cold in the head produces. Happily I'm interested in depression; and make myself play a game of assembling the fractured pieces – I mean I light a fire, and somehow dandle myself over it. Cooking is helpful. Oh but I was very down and dismal yesterday. And then noises and houses abuilding oppress: and there's always our dear old war – now postponed for a month.

52 TAVISTOCK SQUARE, WC1

Friday 28 April
Very much screwed in the head by trying to get Roger's marriage chapter into shape; and also warmed by L. saying last night that he was fonder of me than I of him. A discussion as to which would mind the other's death most. He said he depended more upon our common life than I did. He gave the garden as an instance. He said I live more in a world of my own. I go for long walks alone. So we argued. I was very happy to think I was so much needed. Its strange how seldom one feels this: yet 'life in common' is an immense reality.

Oh such a dismal tea with Mrs Woolf yesterday. She is completely lifeless – like an old weed on a rock. And always recurring to the complaints. That was how, by the way, we came to discuss our deaths. L. said he hoped he would predecease me. Her lonely old age is so intolerable. But its lonely, he said, because she had adopted an unreal attitude. Lives in a sentimental make believe. Sees herself as the adored matriarch, and forces the children to adopt her attitude. This obsession of hers has also shut her off from all other interests: doesn't care for any impersonal thing – art, music, books. Won't have a companion or reader; must depend on her sons. Constant innuendoes therefore about the goodness of Herbert and Harold; inference that L. neglects her; hints that I have taken him away from his family; absorbed him in mine. So in that crowded pink hot room we sat for two hours trying to beat up subjects for conversation. And there were awful silences, and our heads filled with wool; and all was dusty, dreary, old, and hopeless.

Saturday 29 April

But what are the interesting things? I'm thinking of what I should like to read here in ten years time. And I'm all at sea. Perhaps literal facts. The annal, not the novel. Yesterday I went out in a fur coat, for it was bitter cold, to walk in London. I stopped by the Savoy Church; there were photographers. Soon the Bride arrived. The car glided on. Old sitters in the sun watching. Camera men. A little procession – rather skimpy and cold and not very rich I thought. Then I walked along the Embankment, up into the fur quarter behind Blackfriars. A smell of fur. Found some old City Company houses. So into Cannon Street. Bought a paper with Hitler's speech. Read it on top of Bus. Inconclusive. Everyone reading it – even newspaper sellers, a great proof of interest. So to Kingsway. Bought some folders. L. had four gents to discuss a memo. Read Chaucer. Enjoyed it. Was warm and happy. Nessa rang up. Bed.

Monday 1 May

A bad morning, because I'm dried up about *Roger*. I'm determined though to plod through and make a good job, not a work of art. That's the only way. To force myself on – But there's no blinking the fact that it is drudgery and must be; and I must go through with it.

Sunday 14 May

Its a fortnight I see since I had my few minutes margin between *Roger* and lunch. My head is a tight wound ball of string. To unwind it, I lie on my Heal chair bed and doze of an evening. But the noise worries me. The two houses next door are down; we are shored up. There are patches of wall paper where there used to be hotel bedrooms. Thus the Southampton Row traffic gets at me; and I long for 37 Mecklenburgh Square, but doubt if we shall get it. A talk about the future with John [Lehmann]. He is harrassed by the lean year. 37 is a large seeming and oh so quiet house, where I could sleep anywhere. But it don't do to dwell on it. And there would be the horror of the move in August. We are going to Brittany by the way after Whitsun. A whole two weeks rambling. Now that'll fill my dry cistern of a head.

Thursday 25 May

A queer little note to run off in a hurry: L. is bargaining for 37 Mecklenburgh Square upstairs; I'm packing. We're off: and very likely I shan't write much more in this now so tidy studio. I must pack upstairs. Brittany and Rodmell for three weeks.

Interrupted by parties come to see the house. The first day its in the agents' hands. Shall we end our lives looking in that great peaceful garden; in the sun? I hope so.

*   *   *

Friday 23 June
Back to London again after four weeks. Two spent driving about Brittany. The London uproar at once rushes in. We have 37 Mecklenburgh Square; and this is still unlet.

Saturday 24 June
Yes, London broke in fairly vigorously yesterday. [Victoria] Ocampo bringing Gisèle Freund and all her apparatus, which was set up in the drawing room. And the upshot is, a sitting – oh curse this petty vulgar photography-advertising stunt – at 3. No getting out of it, with Ocampo on the sofa, and Freund there in the flesh. So my afternoon is gone in the way to me most detestable and upsetting of all. A life sized coloured animated photograph – however L. is drawn in.

Monday 26 June
Talk at Nessa's last night. Much about [Mark] Gertler's suicide. He gassed himself two nights ago in his studio. He had got through to a new stage as a painter. This was true, Nessa and Duncan said; his last show, just over, was a great advance and very remarkable. So why did he turn on the gas, when his model left him? A most resolute serious man: intellectual; fanatical about painting, even if a fanatical egotist. And he seemed established. Poor of course, and forced to teach; and fundamentally perhaps too rigid, too self centred, too honest and narrow, to be content and happy. But with his intellect and interest, why did the personal life become too painful? His wife? We know no more.

Wednesday 28 June
Vita came to a late lunch; Mrs Woolf fell down and broke two ribs. L. to the nursing home after dinner. She will not die, so I assume. There is a terrible passive resistance to death in these old women. They have the immortality of the vampire. This is I suppose a cruel remark to make. But honestly, everyone would be relieved if she could make an end of it. Its so exhausting, and she has contrived to falsify all emotions, till the end is the only thing the family who are forced to be so devoted by her fantasy honestly wish for.

Thursday 29 June
A dismal day yesterday; shoe hunting in the Hall of Humbug, Fortnums. A Sale; but only of the unsaleable. And the atmosphere – British upper

classes: all tight and red nailed; myself a figure of fun, whips my skin. Noise here very great. Even if we lose our rent, no doubt its worth it – 37 will be heavenly quiet.

Monday 3 July

L.'s mother died last night. And its been jading and somehow very depressing – watching her die. She gradually ceased to breathe. It was like watching an animal die, L. said. It was a bright showery day. We walked in Regent's Park, after giving Kingsley Martin lunch. I always notice the weather in which people die, as if the soul would notice if its wet or windy. But I cannot do my article, and have a regret for that spirited old lady, whom it was such a bore to visit. Still she was somebody: sitting on her high backed chair with the pink cushion, all the flowers round her, a cigar always for Leonard, and plates of cakes which she pressed us to eat. But these feelings are mixed, scrappy, and I'm in the scraped state when writing don't work.

Thursday 6 July

[Mrs Woolf] was buried yesterday; and there was a service in the Synagogue. Women admitted, so I went. But its a compromise; and had nothing whatever to do with [her]. What was she like then? Let me see – She was small, narrow shouldered, and rather heavy. Her head nodded. She had stiff curled grey black hair. She would say as we came in "And Virginia?" My joke was, Conceal your disappointment at sight of me. Then she would laugh, kiss me, and give me a little pat. We were on friendly laughing terms, always at the same stock joke, which carried us through those two hour teas. "And tell me what you have been doing?" I would have some story ready. It was trumped up mostly. Yet there was something spontaneous about her. A great joy in family; in society. All was personal. She attaches to nothing in my own life. The truth was, age had taken everything that was real, I think: only age left the pathetic animal, the body that wanted to live. I know nothing of any interest about her now that I come to write, only little anecdotes; nothing that makes her a real person – save Is Virginia coming? which touches me.

Wednesday 12 July

For the first time for weeks, after being so damnably down in the mouth yesterday, I've worked with some pleasure at *Roger*. Yet how dumpish we were – starting off to the Movies, after dinner – L. asking me what I wanted to see, I not wanting to see anything – the crowds of deformed and stunted and vicious and sweating and ugly hooligans and harridans in the Tottenham Court Road – the sticky heat – all this brooded, till I was saying, step out, on, on, in my usual desperate way. Then instead we went to Nessa's. Angelica in bed. Clive there; Duncan bubbling; and we had a good laugh and gossip. Vanessa very silent, worried I suppose: yet 'cheerful' too. She will laugh and take part, even if she sinks again. Julian in the background. Oh dear. But a jovial sunny evening that rolled off my glooms effectively; perhaps L.'s. Its not a nice season in London.

Thursday 13 July
Two hours at Mecklenburgh Square planning, electric light, kitchen &c. The practical difficulty appals – all of our books carpets furniture and L. gloomy. A grim thought struck me: which of these rooms shall I die in? Which is going to be the scene of some – oh no, I won't write out the tragedy that has to be acted there.

Tuesday 25 July
On this page I should sum up reflections on leaving 52 Tavistock Square. But – Interruption.

MONKS HOUSE, RODMELL

Friday 28 July
I forget that we came down; and its been fine, rather; lovely on the marsh. Hay cutting. Figures spaced on the marsh. Reading Gide's diaries, recommended by poor death mask Eddie [Sackville-West]. An interesting knotted book. Its queer that diaries now pullulate. No one can settle to a work of art.

Sunday 30 July
Its fine; and our day's varied with what we enjoy. Such an expansion after the London pressure. I take my brain out, fill it with books, as a sponge with water – couldn't read a word in London. Taking a day or two with *Pointz Hall* to rest myself from *Roger*.

Monday 31 July
Human voices wake us and we drown – quotation on hearing the telephone yesterday asking us to Charleston. Bunny [Garnett] there; Angelica moody; conversation however well beaten up. Duncan's 480 canvases; new studio; Nessa's bedroom on the garden; Quentin's potting shed. Talk about rumours of war. Next Memoir meeting discussed. So home. Very cold and cloudy – yet the downs aglow with corn much to my liking. My poor old head very feeble – though why? Trying it on *Pointz Hall*. Age is it? or *Roger?*

Monday 7 August [Bank Holiday]
I have been thinking about Censors. How visionary figures admonish us. If I say this So and So will think me sentimental. If that ... will think me Bourgeois. All books now seem to me surrounded by a circle of invisible censors. Hence their self-consciousness, their restlessness. A child crying in the field brings poverty: my comfort: to mind. Ought I to go to the village sports? Ought thus breaks into my contemplation.

Oh and I thought, as I was dressing, how interesting it would be to describe the approach of age, and the gradual coming of death. As people describe love. To note every symptom of failure: but why failure? To treat age as an experience that is different from the others; and to detect every one of the gradual stages towards death which is a tremendous experience, and not as unconscious, at least in its approaches, as birth is.

Friday 25 August
Perhaps it is more interesting to describe 'The Crisis' than Roger's love affairs. Yes we are in the very thick of it. Are we at war? At 1 I'm going to listen in. Its very different, emotionally, from last September. In London yesterday, there was indifference almost. No crowd in the train – we went by train. No stir in the streets. One of the removers called up. Its Fate, as the foreman said. What can you do against fate? Complete chaos at 37 [Mecklenburgh Square]. Museums shut. Search light on Rodmell Hill. Chamberlain says danger imminent. The Russian pact a disagreeable and unforeseen surprise. Rather like a herd of sheep we are. No enthusiasm. Patient bewilderment. I suspect some desire 'to get on with it'. Order double supplies and some coal. Unreal. Whiffs of despair. Difficult to work. Aeroplanes. One touch on the switch and we shall be at war. Underneath of course wells of pessimism. Young men torn to bits: Mothers like Nessa two years ago. The common feeling covers the private, then recedes. Discomfort and distraction. And all mixed with the mess at 37.

Monday 28 August
I stay out here, after bowls, to say – what? on this possibly last night of peace. Will the 9 o'clock bulletin end it all? – our lives, oh yes, and everything for the next fifty years? Everyone's writing I suppose about this last day. I walked on the downs; lay under a cornstack and looked at the empty land and the pinkish clouds in a perfect blue summer afternoon sky. Not a sound. Workmen discussing war on the road – one for it, one against. For us its like being on a small island. Neither of us has any physical fear. Why should we? But there's a vast calm cold gloom. And the strain. Like waiting a doctor's verdict. And the young – young men smashed up. But the point is one is too numbed to think. Old Clive sitting on the terrace,

says 'I don't want to live through it.' Explains that his life recedes. Has had the best. We privately are so content. Bliss day after day. So happy cooking dinner, reading, playing bowls. No feeling of patriotism. How to go on, through war? – that's the question. Yes, its a lovely still summer evening; not a sound. A swallow came into the sitting room.

Wednesday 30 August
Not at war yet. Negotiations. L. pessimistic more than I am this morning. He thinks that Hitler is making up his mind to spring. Raging voices began again last night in German. Last year's mad voice heard again, as if he were lashing himself up. Now I must listen to the 1 o'clock.

Red faced boys in khaki guarding Rodmell Hill. The soldiers in the village. Otherwise quiet and usual enough...

Friday 1 September
War is on us this morning. Hitler has taken Danzig: has attacked – or is attacking – Poland. This after a day in London, submerged doubts and hopes. Now at 1 I go in to listen I suppose to the declaration of war. A dull hot day. I don't know why I write this, or what I feel, or shall feel. All is hovering over us.

Sunday 3 September
This is I suppose certainly the last hour of peace. The time limit is out at 11. Prime Minister to broadcast at 11.15. L. and I 'stood by' ten minutes ago. We argued. If we win – then what? L. said its better to win. I suppose the bombs are falling on rooms like this in Warsaw. No children yet come. Maynard has given Quentin a job as tractor driver. This is a relief. No one knows how we're to fight. Rumours beginning. A flurry of people shopping in Lewes yesterday. Shops rather empty. People buying stuff for windows. Little girl says If we have a chink they'll spy us out. Two hours sewing [black-out] curtains. An anodyne: pleasure to do something: but so tepid and insipid. One's too tired, emotionally, to read a page.

Its now about 10.33. Of course I shall have to work to make money. That's a comfort. Write articles for America. Keep the Press going. So far plenty of petrol. Sugar rationed. So I shall now go in.

Wednesday 6 September
Our first air raid warning at 8.30 this morning. A warbling that gradually insinuates itself as I lay in bed. So dressed and walked on the terrace with L. Sky clear. All cottages shut. Breakfast. All clear.

All meaning has run out of everything. Scarcely worth reading papers. The BBC gives any news the day before. Emptiness. Inefficiency. I may as well record these things. My plan is to force my brain to work on *Roger*. But Lord this is the worst of all my life's experiences. Endless interruptions. We have done the curtains. We have carried coals &c into the cottage for the eight Battersea women and children. The expectant mothers are all quarrelling. Some went back yesterday. Yes, its an empty meaningless world now. Am I a coward? Physically I expect I am. Going to London tomorrow I expect frightens me. This war has begun in cold blood. One merely feels that the killing machine has to be set in action. So far, the *Athena* has been sunk. It seems entirely meaningless – a perfunctory slaughter, like taking a jar in one hand, a hammer in the other. No movies or theatres allowed. No friends write or ring up. Yes, a long sea voyage, with strangers making conversation, and lots of small bothers and arrangements seems the closest I can get. Of course all creative power is cut off. And for the hundredth time I repeat – any idea is more real than any amount of war misery. And what one's made for. And the only contribution one can make – This little pitter patter of ideas is my whiff of shot in the cause of freedom.

Monday 11 September
To London on Thursday. Pitiless fine weather. Over London a light spotted veil – the balloons. Very empty streets. A curious strained silence. At the Press, listening for sirens. Cases all empty but piled up. Mabel and I laid carpets. Sandwiches with John [Lehmann]. Stephen [Spender] came in. His great joints seemed to crack. Eyes stared. Is writing reams about himself. Can't settle to poetry. London after sunset a mediaeval city of darkness and brigandage. The darkness they say is the worst of it. No one can control their nerves. So I was glad to be on the road home. Poland being conquered, and then – we shall be attended to.

Saturday 23 September
Meanwhile Poland has been gobbled up. Russia and Germany divide it. An aircraft carrier has been sunk. But there have been no raids. And I – having said impulsively that I would write for the *New Statesman* by way of using my faculties patriotically – have written two and used up every morning to the margin. Also people have been staying here . . . oh such a fritter and agitation – solid weekends with Mrs Nicholls, Miss Perkins, Miss Woodward [Hogarth Press staff] – So distracted I've scudded over the surface of the days. And now Stephen is on us alone; and so we shall be lip sore and addle headed. Then there's John on Monday.

Civilisation has shrunk. The amenities are wilting. There's no petrol today: so we are back again with our bicycles at Asheham in 1915. And once more L. and I calculate our income. How much must we both earn?

Once more we are journalists. Then one begins stinting paper, sugar, butter, buying little hoards of matches. The elm tree that fell has been cut up. This will see us through two winters. They say the war will last three years. We had an SOS from Kingsley. He came for the night. What was it he couldn't say on the telephone? Nothing. Should he come out in favour of peace? Chamberlain has the terms in his pocket. All in the know say we are beaten. Nothing of the least importance is said though in his article.

I forget who else has been. Nessa painting L. Many games of bowls. No reading.

Sunday 24 September

Stephen scribbling diary – no, reading Proust in English in the drawing room. I've talked miles since last night, in spite of Stephen's colic. A loose jointed mind – misty, clouded, suffusive. Nothing has outline. Very sensitive, tremulous, receptive and striding; and walking the terrace, we plunged and skimmed and hopped – from sodomy and women and writing and anonymity and – I forget. At last I said I must write – and he must write; and so ordered boiled potatoes for his lunch; and sit in semi-retreat out here.

Freud is dead, the stop press says. Only these little facts interrupt the monotonous boom of the war.

Monday 25 September

The week end was sheer drudgery and has left me out of temper, out of mood. *Roger* seems hopeless. Yet if one can't write, as Duncan said yesterday, one may as well kill oneself. Such despair comes over me – waking early. And we're fretted and tormented with people.

Friday 6 October

Well I have succeeded in despite of distractions in copying out again the whole of *Roger*. Needless to say, its still to be revised, compacted, vitalised. And can I ever do it? The distractions are so incessant. Also there's the war: or rather the non-war. Nothing happens. All is held up. Nightly we're served out with a few facts, or a childstory of the adventures of a submarine. Hitler is said to make peace terms today. London is all agog; and also all aquiver. Here its distracted weather – hailstorms and gales and sun. Nessa is painting L. I have composed myself by tidying my room.

Saturday 7 October

Its odd how those first days of complete nullity when war broke out have given place to such a pressure of ideas and work that I feel the old throb and spin in my head more of a drain than ever. The result partly of taking up journalism. A good move, I daresay; for it compacts; and forces me to organise. I'm masterfully pulling together those diffuse chapters of *Roger* because I know I must stop and do an article. Ideas for articles obsess me. Why not try one for *The Times?* No sooner said than I'm ravaged by ideas. Have to hold the *Roger* fort – for I will have the whole book typed and in Nessa's hands by Xmas – by force.

We have a fortnight its said to consider Hitler's terms. If rejected, all the guns boom. So we may get a last safe week in London. And I don't much want to go.

Sunday 22 October

We have spent a week in London. The poster read, at Wimbledon: 'The War begins . . . Hitler says, Now its on'. So as we drove to Mecklenburgh Square I said "Its foolish to come to London the first day of the war." It seemed as if we were driving open eyed into a trap. The flat was oh in such a mess – very small, very crowded. Whistles sounded. The dark was thick as Hell. One seemed cut off. No wireless. There we sat. And people came running in and out. We lunched with the [Sidney] Webbs. The old woman, wearing a white spotted headdress, was as alive as a leaf on an autumn bonfire: burning, skeletonised. I was so harassed and distracted that I could not expand my mind to receive impressions.

You never escape the war in London. People are all thinking the same thing. All set on getting the day's work done. Hitches and difficulties hold one up. Very few buses. Tubes closed. No children. No loitering. Everyone humped with a gas mask. Strain and grimness. At night its so verdurous and gloomy that one expects a badger or a fox to prowl along the pavement. A reversion to the middle ages with all the space and the silence of the country set in this forest of black houses. A torch blinks. An old gentleman revealed. He vanishes. That red light may be a taxi or a lampost. People grope their way to each other's lairs. We were talking in our lair about six hours daily. Great caterpillars dug up the Square. Gradually the sense of siege being normal replaced the fear – the individual fear. One's temper was rubbed by the sheer discomfort and perpetual need for clearing drawers, arranging furniture. The kitchen very small. Everything too large. Stairs bad. No carpets. The clerks scream like parrots. Rain poured – profuse unbridled mediaeval rain. Did nothing – was indeed in fretful useless distraction. So we came down and the world rises out of dark squalor into this divine natural peace. Alone today and for many days. It was an odd morbid week of many disagreeable sensations.

Wednesday 25 October

"The war begins today." So Ribbentrop said or rather howled last night. For so far its sporadic and halfhearted. How then can I say anything about it here? Here it peters out. I rode my cycle to Lewes yesterday. Now Nessa's come and is painting L. And its a blowy but sunny autumn day. And I'm screwed like a vice to the re-composing of the last chapter. Temptations to write other things fret me. As a journalist I'm in demand (not with the *TLS* though). To relax I read *Little Dorrit* and think of going on with my Autobiography. Never have I been so set on my own spinning.

Wednesday 1 November
It strikes me that Morgan probably keeps an admirable diary. I'd like to ask Morgan down. Our week ends are now taking the place of our dinners. Rather a laborious extension. But here we are settling in, very steadily, to a country life, and there's much to be said for it. The space, the concentration, the freedom. Every day on my walk I get a colour bath: the greens dying, the winter colours burnishing. Society too is fairly brisk. Tom comes for the week end. Eddie Sackville invites himself for next week. London and 37 recede. Dim voices reach us. No war news.

Thursday 9 November
Oh yes, Tom for the week end: more supple, less caked and rigid than of old. His teaching he told me, is that one improves with age. I suppose the working of the divine spirit which as usual he adored at 8 on Sunday morning. Last night we listened to the ravings, the strangled hysterical sobbing swearing ranting of Hitler at the Beer Hall. Today they say there was an explosion after he'd left. Is it true? There's no getting at truth now all the loud speakers are contradicting each other.

Monday 27 November
Since I wrote here, we have been in London, had a party, Adrian and Karin and Rose Macaulay; seen Colefax; and come back. It is all storm and rain now. Many ships sunk. Men out in boats. The magnetic mine active. Chamberlain speaking like a military shopwalker.

Wednesday 29 November
A nice dine and sleep visit from John [Lehmann], who pans out well under familiar scrutiny – dining in the kitchen &c – and things aren't doing badly: in fact stirring under the blanket of war. Ideas sprout. For a Bloomsbury Book Club ... for 'our' new magazine. Yes, the young do manage to pull along. And a long gossip ... bed wetting at Eton; its disastrous consequences. Repressions – homosexuality: this explains, I suppose, John's dash. John gets garrulous after wine.

Thursday 30 November

Very jaded and tired and depressed and cross, and so take the liberty of expressing my feelings here. *Roger* a failure – and what a grind . . . no more of that. I'm brain fagged and must resist the desire to tear up and cross out – must fill my mind with air and light, and walk and blanket it in fog. Rubber boots help – I can flounder over the marsh.

Saturday 2 December

Tiredness and dejection give way if one day off is taken instantly. I went in and did my cushion. In the evening my pain in my head calmed. Ideas came back. This is a hint to be remembered. Always turn the pillow. Began reading Freud last night; to enlarge the circumference, to give my brain a wider scope; thus defeat the shrinkage of age. Always take on new things.

I saw a Kingfisher and a cormorant the other day's walk in rubber boots. Planes very active. Russia attacking Finland. Nothing happens in England. There's no reason anywhere. Brutes merely rampant. Its like being in a temporary shelter with a violent storm raging outside. We wait.

Friday 8 December

Two days in London: a great distraction; leaving my mind in a torn state. Shopping – tempted to buy jerseys and so on. I dislike this excitement: yet enjoy it. Ambivalence as Freud calls it. Then Ethel [Smyth] and [William] Gillies. That upset me – Ethel's wig – five incongruous curls, that made her look babyish and foolish. Also she has gone downhill. She is now shut up quite alone in her old age – talks to herself, about herself. I felt this pathetic; also somehow ugly; humiliating; watching the old baby sucking its corals; compliments; the old story of her genius and its non-recognition. How hideous to be reduced to that kind of feeblemindedness – at eighty-four. I think it was pity more than anything that I felt; and all her clothes were undone; shaggy; untidy – like King Lear only without any tragedy or poetry. And the old charm in abeyance.

Saturday 9 December

It is a Saturday morning, and looks fine and still, after the broken whirlpool of weather yesterday. We took Louie to Lewes to have teeth out, and it was blackout driving for the first time. Like fog driving, one can't see people. All the cars have small red eyes. The margins of the road are lost. But I'm thinking of a dozen things as usual. Ideas pullulate, but escape when I try to catch them here. Freud is upsetting: reducing one to whirlpool; and I daresay truly. If we're all instinct, the unconscious, what's all this about civilisation, the whole man, freedom &c? His savagery against God good.

Saturday 16 December

The litter in this room is so appalling that it takes me five minutes to find my pen. *Roger* all unsewn in bits. And I must take fifty pages, should be a hundred, up on Monday. Can't get the marriage chapter right. But its true I don't fuss quite so much as over a novel. I learned a lesson in re-writing *The Years* which I shall never forget.

Horizon out; small; trivial; dull. So I think from not reading it. And now – oh now must I tidy up? London &c looms. And I've promised to lecture the WEA at Brighton.

Sunday 17 December

What the point of making these notes is I don't know; save that it becomes a necessity to uncramp, and some of it may interest me later. But what? For I never reach the depths; I'm too surface blown. Yes, ten minutes left – what can I say. Nothing that needs thought: which is provoking; for I often think. And think the very thought I could write here.

Oh the *Graf Spee* is going to steam out of Monte Video today into the jaws of death. And journalists and rich people are hiring aeroplanes from which to see the sight. This seems to me to bring war into a new angle; and our psychology. No time to work out. Anyhow the eyes of the whole world (BBC) are on the game; and several people will lie dead tonight, or in agony. And we shall have it served up for us as we sit over our logs this bitter winter night.

1940

On Twelfth Night Angelica's twenty-first birthday was celebrated with some flourish by a lively party at Charleston (at which Virginia obliged with a song), and for a time the eddies of social life reached Monks House. But gradually the privations and inconveniences of wartime – the black-out, food and petrol rationing, shortages and rising prices – became more evident. Virginia was polishing her Roger Fry, writing articles, mostly for the New Statesman, and preparing a lecture (later published as 'The Leaning Tower') for the Brighton Workers' Education Association, for which Leonard was already giving a series of twelve talks on 'Causes and Issues of War'. Every other week they drove to London and spent a few days in their Mecklenburgh Square flat dealing with Hogarth Press matters, Leonard's political concerns, and seeing friends. During most of March Virginia was laid low with influenza, but by 1 April was able to send Roger Fry to be printed; she finished correcting the proofs on 13 May and the book was published towards the end of July.

On 13 April the war suddenly erupted again, with the German invasion of Denmark and Norway; and from then onwards, with their assault on Holland and Belgium, their rapid advance across France to the Channel, the evacuation of British troops from Dunkirk, the occupation of Paris and the Franco-German Armistice of 22 June, Virginia observed and noted the unfolding military and political calamities with fatalistic clarity. She and Leonard had obtained the wherewithal to commit suicide should the Nazis invade England, as they had no doubt they would be marked down as Jewish anti-Fascists. Yet Virginia had no wish to die; she was again engrossed in writing Pointz Hall and, despite the day-to-day horrors of the war, was in good health and spirits. Inevitably, if in Virginia's case reluctantly, the Woolfs found themselves drawn further into Rodmell village life, Virginia helping to write and rehearse a play for the Women's Institute and even becoming its Treasurer, while Leonard, already a School Governor, undertook fire-watching duties.

As a prelude to the expected invasion, air attacks on Southern England (the Battle of Britain) began in earnest at the end of June, reaching a climax towards the end of August when they were redirected to the night-bombing of London. Rodmell was in the front line; the skies above were filled with warplanes. In September the Woolfs' London house was first made inaccessible and then uninhabitable by bombs; the Hogarth Press and its staff were moved to Letchworth in Hertfordshire; the Woolfs collected some of their more valued possessions, including Virginia's diaries, and at the end of the year had the damp and dirty remainder brought to Rodmell and piled into Monks House and rented village store-rooms.

In the autumn, still anticipating invasion, the Woolfs relinquished Mabel their live-in servant, and resigned themselves to their isolated country life with their daily help Louie. Virginia was working with confidence on Pointz Hall, continuing her memoirs, reading, and, as always, delighting in the beauty of the countryside on her long daily walks, particularly when a bomb breached the riverbank and the entire Ouse Valley between Newhaven and Lewes became an inland sea. Vita came for a night; Kingsley Martin for another; some contact with Charleston and Tilton was maintained. Helen Anrep was lodging in the district; and so were David Garnett and Angelica, who were now living together to the dismay of some of her relations.

When Virginia finished her first writing of Pointz Hall at the end of November she was well pleased with her work but thereafter began to feel restless and dispirited, a condition she recognised from previous experience, and determined to counteract; but with diminishing success.

1940

Monks House, Rodmell

Wednesday 3 January

This very large sheet begins a new year, on a new system. Evening over the fire writing, instead of end of the morning scrambling. Thus I hope to write a better hand, and more solidly. For unless I can put a little weight into this book, it'll have no interest, even for an old woman, turning the pages.

We have been out looking for skating. Its a long bitter winter frost – I forget how many degrees of a night – I think 22 below freezing. Figure an Italian sun yesterday; and hard white snow; and the street like glass; the butcher saying he'd had enough of it, which, as he has to be in the shop cutting joints at 6, I can follow.

I am oppressed and distracted with all my ideas. All the little cuckoos shoving the old bird – *Roger* – out of the nest. And here's L.

Saturday 6 January

Which of our friends will interest posterity most? Maynard? So that if I had any regard for the future I would use this hour to record what he said. Lying extended on the sofa the other night with the two fog lamps burning, and Lydia a sort of fairy tale elf in her fur cap. He is now supreme, mounted on his sick throne, a successful man – farmer, bursar, man of business, he called himself, applying for petrol. A heavy man with a thick moustache. A moralist. As interested in Patsy the black dog with the bald patch as in Europe. He was saying – odd how hard it is to remember – he was telling us about salt; water; heat and cold and their effect on the urine. About Roger. "Can I mention erection?" I asked Lydia. "What?" Maynard: "Stiff" (their private word). "No you can't. I should mind your saying it. Such revelations have to be in key with their time. The time not come yet." Is he right, or only public school? All is now so ordered, so royally arranged, that we had to go that Wednesday [27 December], because otherwise – "No Maynard says it is not convenient" Lydia on the telephone. But words are soon lost.

Mr Gwynne caught me at Piddinghoe on the down yesterday – a nobleman: lean, sporting, dried, with little wet pebble eyes; a severe man. I smiled; I was scrambling under the barbed wire in my wool helmet. "Where d'you come from?" "Only taking a walk." "This is private." "Hope I'm not spoiling your sport?" "Not at all. You can go on ..." He'll ask his wife, what odd looking woman lives at Rodmell. She'll guess, Mrs Woolf. He'll say ... Louie says he'll say he don't hold with the Labour Party. He had a row about the wood on his down. The villagers mustn't steal it.

Friday 19 January
I can't say that this after tea system has been good for this large page. But Sussex has been sociable. Angelica's twenty-first birthday party, and its legacy; then London, from which we came back this afternoon to frozen pipes. My London technique is improving. A concert at National Gallery; Hugh [Walpole] and William Plomer to dinner, Sybil [Colefax] to tea – all accomplished. And last night *The Importance of Being Earnest*, a thinnish play, but a work of art; I mean, its bubble don't break. Hugh is rather like the winter sun – his ruddy edges slightly blurred. He wore a red flower. William in a buff waistcoat, but sharpened, disappointed – life unsatisfactory; embittered. I diagnose some sense of defeat and strain, part private, part war. We talked – if I could face the labour of inverted commas – about *Horizon*: and about Humbert Wolfe; dead of overwork; and then Hugh told us the story of the [Joseph] Conrads, told it very well; so to diaries, and so to Dickens; and the Victorian hypocrisy, Thackeray hailing a prostitute in the street opposite the Garrick; Dickens and his mistress; (all spoken as if they were old friends – so they are – if you're in the Hugh tradition, but William and I aren't) – so to Trollope; and defamation of Wells; a mere scribbler; compare him with Conrad. A bitter cold night and they stayed till 12.30: then went into the moonlight, and left the door open.

Saturday 20 January
Smoking cigarettes over the fire and feeling – just because the rent of 37 is so high – that we were, for once, foolish. L. went and skated and I walked on the bank and home over the marsh. The beauty was etherial, unreal, empty. All silent, as if offered from another world. No birds, no carts, men shooting. This specimen against the war. This heartless and perfect beauty. The willows ruby red, no rust red; plumed; soft; and all the roofs orange and red; and the hills white. But some emptiness in me – in my life – because L. said the rent was so high. And then the silence, the pure disembodied silence, seemed to correspond to my own vacancy, walking muffled with the sun in my eyes. The men were waiting for widgeon – the quickest birds. Come down like an express. We sat in the sun on the bank.

All looked very distant, and picked out – the little stems of smoke – the wild duck – the horses huddled and still. No thoughts populated; I was somehow held in a pair of pincers, and came home to cook crumpets, to revise my article.

A fire at Charleston. Fire Engines called out on Wednesday night. No letters. A child crying in the school. What do I do to help?

Friday 26 January
These moments of despair – I mean glacial suspense – a painted fly in a glass case - have given way as they so often do to ecstasy. Is it that I have thrown off those two dead pigeons – my story, my 'Gas at Abbotsford' (printed today)? And so ideas rush in. I began one night, absolutely submerged, throttled, to read Julian. And off winged my mind along those wild uplands. A hint for the future. Always relieve pressure by a flight: hack an outlet. Often a trifle does.

What was I going to say? The thaw has set in, and rain and wind, and the marsh is soggy, and patched with white, and two very small lambs were staggering in the east wind. One old ewe was being carted off; and shirking the horror I crept back by the hanger.

Tuesday 30 January
Unable to go to London because of the worst of all frosts. A sudden return. Everything glass glazed. Each blade is coated, has a rim of pure glass. Walking is like treading on stubble. The stiles and gates have a shiny green varnish of ice. Ink frozen. On Sunday no cars could move. On Monday the electric light failed. Cooked breakfast on dining room fire. Came on at 12.30. Today all idea of travel impossible. Trains hours late or lost. No buses running. Walked to Lewes and back. Met snow plough; two or three cars; no walkers. Lewes very empty. Home by the short cut; which was painful. A great flight of wild geese. The grass is brittle, all the twigs are cased in clear brown cases, and look crystallised. Now and then the wireless reports a ship sunk in the North Sea. Almost out of meat, but at last the Co-op sent. Very still tonight. More snow? No papers till the afternoon.

Wednesday 31 January
It is thawing. There's a rush, like a mattress falling, as the snow slides off the roof. We walked on the marsh, and saw a half devoured hare. Dabs of blood on the snow, and such a scrape of a wind, and such hobbling and tumbling over frozen tussocks into the snow that I cut the walk, and came home to type out my ten guinea Corelli. Vita is offered £1,850 for a 25,000 word story. My righteous backbone stiffens. I wouldn't for any money write 25,000 words. A little quick article I enjoy. Settled in for another

two weeks, and only village meetings and books; which are however very 'real'.

Friday 2 February
The snow remains, slightly pocked, but the road is clear. I forget to make extracts from the papers, which boom, echoing, emptily, the BBC. Hitler's speech – Churchill's – a ship sunk – no survivors – a raft capsized – men rowing for ten or twelve or thirty hours. How little one can explode now, as perhaps one would have done, had it been a single death. But the Black Out is far more murderous than the war. Prices rise by twopence then threepence. So the screw tightens gradually; and I can't even imagine London in peace – the lit nights, the buses roaring past Tavistock Square, the telephone ringing, and I scooping together with the utmost difficulty one night or afternoon alone. Only the fire sets me dreaming – of all the things I mean to write: the break in our lives from London to country is a far more complete one than any change of house. Odd how often I think with what is love I suppose of the City: of the walk to the Tower: that is my England; I mean, if a bomb destroyed one of those little alleys with the brass bound curtains and the river smell and the old woman reading I should feel – well, what the patriots feel.

Wednesday 7 February
(Mother's birthday; Nessa's wedding day.) Oh I had such a profound reflection on the tip of my tongue. It was to the effect that now, no longer in the movement, and remote in this water sogged country, now's the time to see if the art, or life, creed, the belief in something existing independently of myself, will hold good. Well, if it don't stand like a flagstaff, then its been a washout (word chosen in deference to the new movement). John for the night; and he plunges us in new this and that. Very nice – so eager and 'boyish' as the old women say. We had the Gardners to tea. The old wispy red veined blue eyed pussy purring Major. Very courteous, rather rambling. The children [Diana and Paul] bolt eyed and transfixed, partly in fear of what Papa might say. John obviously bored, but chivalrous. And then out with his documents, and his plans. Radiant hope for the *New Writing*, for the young. Clearly his metier to go on ringing his cowbell in advance. Oh and all the doings of the boys. The sink of buggery.

Thursday 8 February
Frau – Dr – yes she wasn't Frau though she looked it – [Rita] Hinden has just gone. She has gone back to London, to her house with its lounge and its modern Swedish furniture, in Hampstead Garden Suburb. Lunch lasted till 2.30. After that she and L. retired to the Library to discuss a Fabian

treatise on South Africa, and I in rubbers and great coat plunged into the marsh, which was veiling, oh very effectively, for the wind blew, our unopened spring. Here I stop to insert a remark often occurring: how we're being led to the altar this spring: its flowers will I suppose nod and yellow and redden the garden with the bombs falling – oh its a queer sense of suspense, being led up to the spring of 1940. So I came back, and had to offer tea. Now at tea she shrivelled into the common, the lemon on steel acid vulgarity of the obvious, the cheap hard Jewess, which at lunch I hadn't seen. Confronted with Nessa's carpet, Duncan's table, she could only remember her Hampstead lounge; a transition which made me think of the future: and what'll it be, ruled and guided by these active and ambitious and after all competent, and I suppose, able Fabians – oh why don't they any of them embrace something – but what? Poetry, I suppose, the sensuous, the musical. Why must they always stress the ugliness of life; and yet be themselves so vital?

Friday 9 February

For some reason hope has revived. I've polished off, to the last gaiter button, the three d—d chapters for London on Monday; and though of course I shall get the black shivers when I reread let alone submit to Nessa and Margery [Fry], I can't help thinking I've caught a good deal of that irridescent man in my oh so laborious butterfly net. I daresay I've written every page – certainly the last – ten or fifteen times over. And I don't think I've killed: I think I've brisked. Hence an evening glow. Yet the wind cuts like a scythe: the dining room carpet is turning to mould. Now the wind rises; something rattles, and thank God I'm not on the North Sea, nor taking off to raid Heligoland. Now I'm going to read Freud.

Friday 16 February

This diary might be divided into London diary and Country. Just back from the London chapter. Bitter cold. This shortened my walk, which I meant to be through crowded streets. Then the dark – no lighted windows, depressed me. How silent it is there – London silent; a great dumb ox lying couchant. Dinner party: Tom and Saxon [Sydney-Turner]; Clive in afterwards. Tom's great yellow bronze mask all draped upon an iron framework. An inhibited, nerve drawn, dropped face – as if hung on a scaffold of heavy private brooding; and thought. A very serious face. And broken by the flicker of relief, when other people interrupt. But our talk? – it was about Civilisation. All the gents against me. Said very likely, more likely than not, this war means that the barbarian will gradually freeze out culture. Tom and Saxon said the Greeks were more thoroughly civilised. The slave was not so much a slave as ours are. Clive also pessimised – saw the light going out gradually. So I flung some rather crazy theories into the air. Saxon emitted some scholar's facts. It lasted till 12 I suppose. Then I suffered from my clothes complex acutely buying two new sets of clothes, and being persuaded into a blue striped coat by an astute and human woman at Lewises. "But I want you to have this – I don't want you just because you're in the country, to fling on anything. You've got to think of others" ... as if she guessed all my private life – queer: she seemed genuine. Of course I looked a shaggy dowdy old woman. Then to *Desire Under the Elms* [Eugene O'Neill]: disappointing; flat; elemental situation bare of words; like a scaffold. And Beatrix Lehmann not exciting: and the streets tunnels of gloom.

Monday 19 February
The snow came down on Saturday: thick white cake sugar all over the garden, blowing into my room in the night: door hinge frozen. Now the thaw has come: L. has his barometer: explains it to me. Walk over Mount Misery. Snow still thick, but the cart tracks run with rivulets. Oh and my new coat, the blue striped one, came, and its not too loud: I'm pleased.

Thursday 7 March
A fortnight – well on Saturday it will be a fortnight – with influenza. Up today for the first time. So it shows my inveterate – what's the word for love of writing? – that I open this. Head a white vapour: legs bent candles. All hope abandoned. Oh its the spring that's come while I was ill – birds chirping; Percy spraying apple trees; blue crocuses with snowdrops.

Wednesday 20 March
Yes, another attack – in fact two other attacks. What they call recurring with slight bronchitis. Yes. And the book [*Roger Fry*] read. One Sunday L. gave me a very severe lecture on the first half. We walked in the meadows. It was like being pecked by a very hard strong beak. The more he pecked the deeper, as always happens. At last he was almost angry that I'd chosen "what seems to me the wrong method". His theme was that you can't treat a life like that: must be seen from the writer's angle, unless the liver is himself a seer, which Roger wasn't. It was a curious example of L. at his most rational and impersonal: rather impressive; yet so definite, so emphatic, that I felt convinced: I mean of failure; save for one odd gleam, that he was himself on the wrong tack, and persisting for some deep reason – dissympathy with Roger? lack of interest in personality? Lord knows. Then Nessa came; disagreed; Margery's letter: 'very alive and interesting'. Then Nessa's note 'I'm crying can't thank you' – then Nessa and Duncan to tea up here; forbid me to alter anything; then Margery's final letter – 'Its *him*

... unbounded admiration.' There I pause. Well, I think I re-write certain passages, have even in bed sketched them, but how in time for this spring? That I shelve till tomorrow. Great relief all the same. And Lord to be quit of it and free – and Lord to have given Nessa back her Roger, lost since Julian died.

Easter Sunday 24 March

A curious sub-life has set in, rather spacious, rather leisured, and secluded and content. Still sleep in L.'s room; then I slowly bath and dress and sit in the sitting room, quietly, entering Margery's corrections. Not much bothered really, though I've so short a time. I can't help thinking, in spite of L., that its interesting. This is an egg shell life – so gingerly do I step to avoid rousing my temperature, which was 99 pt 4 and is again a little up. Wobbly like one of the spring lambs in my legs. And its refreshing and rejuvenating to see the gold thick clumps of crocuses, and the unopened green daffodils, and to hear my Asheham rooks dropping their husky caws through the gummy air. The twig carrying has begun, and this goes on while all the guns are pointed and charged and no one dares pull the trigger. Not a sound this evening to bring in the human tears. I remember the sudden profuse shower one night just before war which made me think of all men and women weeping.

Tuesday 26 March

A curious letter from Hugh [Walpole] this afternoon: 'As to my writing you and I are the opposite ends of the bloody stick. You are the supreme example of the aesthetic-conscience – there has never been such another in English fiction. But you *don't* write novels. What you write needs a new name. I am the *true* novelist – a minor one but a true one.'

Yesterday old Botten faded out under the eyes of Mrs West who's layer out and night watcher to the village. A frail old man; the last of the old villagers, talking the melodious Sussex, sprinkled with words like 'nard' for shoulder, wily and sly and grasping; yet poetic too. And a bore. Bringing the milk he'd stay talking, so we always cut at the sight of him.

Friday 29 March

What shall I think of that's liberating and freshening? I'm in the mood when I open my window at night and look at the stars. Unfortunately its 12.15 on a grey dull day, the aeroplanes are active, Botten is to be buried at 3. Well I recur what shall I think of? The river. Say the Thames at London Bridge; and buying a notebook; and then walking along the Strand and letting each face give me a buffet. For we're up in London on Monday. Then back here I'll saunter ... oh yes and we'll travel our books round the Coast – and have tea in a shop – and look at antiques, and there'll be a lovely farmhouse – or a new lane – and flowers – and bowls with L. and May coming and asparagus, and butterflies. Perhaps I'll garden a little oh and print, and change my bedroom furniture. I'm inducing a state of peace and sensation feeling – not an idea feeling. The truth is we've not seen spring in the country since I was ill at Asheham – 1914 – and that had its holiness in spite of the depression. I think I'll also dream a poet-prose book, perhaps make a cake now and then. Now, now – never any more future skirmishing or past regretting – for in God's name I've done my share, with pen and talk, for the human race.

Saturday 13 April

'The first crunch of the war' that's how Winston [Churchill] puts it. The Germans have invaded Norway. Battles are going on. News leaks out. Some say this is Hitler's downfall. A fine spring day in front; daffodils luminous groups along the terrace. Aeroplanes overhead. Mine fields laid, apparently to let us land our army. I write, because it is a crunch; after the long lapse; also that I'm maggoty with lecture writing. Must ease my head. Herbert Fisher was knocked senseless, had arm and ribs and skull fractured two days ago by a lorry. On Tuesday, London: perhaps Sibyl Tom and Desmond. No letters. Dinner in the oven. Meat bad and scarce. Eggs for dinner. Fish for L.; maccaroni. And its time

Saturday 20 April

Desmond to dinner; London week. And we had Sibyl and Herbert [Woolf] to tea. And came back yesterday. I remember Clive saying how he was the only person who felt uncomfortable when a singer had a flybutton undone. I had meant to note some such fragments. A stuffy evening. News suspended. Herbert Fisher dead. Sibyl saw him the day before – of course.

Thursday 25 April

Herbert Fisher as a young man was almost ungainly: with his prominent cheekbones and adam's apple. He had innocent blue eyes: a wisp of hair. Much improved in dignity and distinction as he aged. Finally the very type of culture and distinction. Composed, benevolent, wary. A crane like man. Much like Adrian.

Butterflies ball day three days ago. Cuckoo heard. Swallows come.

Monday 6 May

Nessa has just been and told us a "very tiresome piece of family news" A.'s affair with B. (I keep to the discretion of initials). A most astonishing piece of news. Today they set off for two months alone in Yorkshire. Pray

God she may tire of that rusty surly old dog with his amorous ways and his primitive mind. It makes one feel oddly old: even to me comes the emptiness that Nessa feels, as I can guess. This blocks the way to my crowded London diary, and reduces it to fribble and patter. Clive's night; the police; and Mary's visit; Clive's unshaven cheeks; Desmond next day – all this I leave like torn scraps in a waste paper basket. Item my tea with Hugh; the sulphurous vista of the Green Park; the traffic; Hugh's sodomitic confession of affection; my lecture ['The Leaning Tower' at Brighton WEA]; two hundred about there; no fear on my part – and so home, last Friday, jaded and jangled, with my proofs – and this evening's work blown up, by this explosion of love; and the dream of the Yorkshire moors, and those two setting the supper in order, and retiring to the couch. Nothing will induce her to marry.

And we have withdrawn from Norway. The first defeat of the war. Compare Maynard's optimism three weeks ago. War practically over . . . Kingsley of course croaks in triumph. Another lull.

The worst year we've ever had in the Press I gather. Its odd how much I thought of that lecture, and now its all forgotten – the agony and the sweat.

Monday 13 May

I admit to some content, some closing of a chapter, and peace that comes with it, from posting my proofs today: I admit – because we're in the third day of 'the greatest battle in history'. It began (here) with the 8 o'clock wireless announcing, as I lay half asleep, the invasion of Holland and Belgium. Apple blossom snowing in the garden. Churchill exhorting all men to stand together. "I have nothing to offer but blood and tears and sweat." Duncan saw an air battle over Charleston – a silver pencil and a puff of smoke. Percy has seen the wounded arriving in their boots. So my little moment of peace comes in a yawning hollow. But though L. says he has petrol in the garage for suicide should Hitler win, we go on. Its the vastness, and the smallness, that make this possible.

Tuesday 14 May

Yes, we are being led up garlanded to the altar. A soldier with his rifle. The Dutch Government and Court here. Warned of clergymen in parachutes. War war – a great battle – this hot day, with the blossom on the grass. A plane goes over –

Wednesday 15 May

An appeal last night for home defence – against parachutists. L. says he'll join. An acid conversation. Our nerves are harassed – mine at least: L. evidently relieved by the chance of doing something. Gun and uniform to me slightly ridiculous. Behind that the strain: this morning we discussed suicide if Hitler lands. Jews beaten up. What point in waiting? Better shut the garage doors. This a sensible, rather matter of fact talk. A thunderous hot day. Dutch laid down arms last night. The great battle now raging. Ten days, we say, will settle it. I guess we hold: then dig in: about November the USA comes in as arbitrator. On the other hand – No, I don't want the garage to see the end of me. I've a wish for ten years more, and to write my book which as usual darts into my brain. L. finished his [*The War for Peace*] yesterday. So we've cleared up our book accounts – though its doubtful if we shall publish this June. Hospital trains go by. A hot day to be wounded. Anyhow, it can't last, this intensity – so we think – more than ten days.

This idea struck me: the army is the body: I am the brain. Thinking is my fighting.

Monday 20 May

This idea was meant to be more impressive. It bobbed up in one of the sentient moments. The war is like a desperate illness. For a day it entirely obsesses; then the feeling faculty gives out. Then the battery is re-charged, and again – what? Well, the bomb terror. Going to London to be bombed. And the catastrophe – if they break through: Channel this morning said to be their objective.

Desmond and [G. E.] Moore are at this moment reading – i.e. talking under the apple trees. Moore has a thatch of soft unattached hair: red rimmed eyes, very steady; but less force and mass to him than I remembered. Less drive behind his integrity which is unalloyed, but a little weakened in thrust by the sense of age (sixty-five). So that our reverence is now what one might call retrospective. At tea yesterday with Nessa and Quentin we *remembered* his great influence: his silences. "I didn't want to be silent. I couldn't think of anything to say" he said, rebutting our charge that he had silenced his generation. Hence his dependence on Desmond; who started talking, to the towel horse, to the cat, when he was a baby, and was sent to school to silence him. Many old memories. These spin a kind of gauze over the war, which is broken by papers and at listening-in time. Moore munches like a chaff cutter; I guess has not a liberal table at home: takes a logical view of food; eats philosophically to the end: while Desmond sprinkles sugar and cream, also liberally but erratically. So the housekeeper in me rises into being, in this miserable life of detail and bombast.

Saturday 25 May

Then we went up to what has been so far the worst week in the war. And so remains. On Tuesday evening the BBC announced the taking of Amiens and Arras. On Monday they broke through. It seems they raid with tanks and parachutists: roads crammed with refugees can't be bombed. They crash on. Now are at Boulogne. What are the great armies doing to let this 25 mile hole stay open? The feeling is we're outwitted. They're agile and fearless and up to any new dodge. The French forgot to blow up bridges. The Germans seem youthful, fresh, inventive. We plod behind. This went on the three London days. Rodmell burns with rumours. Are we to be bombed, evacuated? Guns that shake the windows. Hospital ships sunk. So it comes our way. Today's rumour is the Nun in the bus who pays her fare with a man's hand.

Tuesday 28 May
And today at 8, the French Prime Minister broadcast the treachery of the Belgian King. The Belgians have capitulated. The Government is not capitulating. Churchill to broadcast at 4. A wet dull day.

Wednesday 29 May
But hope revives – I don't know why. A desperate battle. The Allies holding. L. has been in London. A great thunderstorm. I was walking on the marsh and thought it was the guns on the channel ports. We had our First Aid meeting. The [Women's Institute] plays rehearsed here yesterday. My contribution to the war is the sacrifice of pleasure: I'm bored: bored and appalled by the readymade commonplaceness of these plays: which they can't act unless we help. I mean, the minds so cheap, compared with ours, like a bad novel – that's my contribution – to have my mind smeared by the village mind; and to endure it, and the simper. So, if Margaret Llewelyn Davies says, how insolent we middleclass women are, I argue, why can't the workers then reject us? What's wrong is the conventionality – not the coarseness. So that its all lulled and dulled. The very opposite of 'common' or working class.

Began *Pointz Hall* again today, and threshed and threshed till perhaps a little grain can be collected.

Thursday 30 May
Walking today (Nessa's birthday) by Kingfisher Pool saw my first hospital train – laden, not funereal, but weighty, as if not to shake bones. Something grieving and tender and heavy laden and private – bringing our wounded back carefully through the green fields at which I suppose some looked. And the faculty for seeing in imagination always leaves me so suffused with something partly visual, partly emotional – the slowness, cadaverousness, grief of the long heavy train, taking its burden through the fields. Very quietly it slid into the cutting at Lewes. Instantly wild duck flights of

aeroplanes came over head; manoeuvred; took up positions and passed over Caburn. No news today. Holding the line – heroism – all the usual perorations, in the usual highflown tense voice. Oh for a speaking voice, once in a way. And being beaten at bowls irritates me; and I'm strained writing *Pointz Hall* – so much more of a strain than *Roger*. And no meat today. And weeded this morning. And was very happy – the moment can be that: only there's no support in the fabric, there's no healthy tissue round the moment. Its blown out. But for a moment, on the terrace, no one coming, alone with L., one's certainly happy.

Friday 31 May
Raid, said to be warned, last night. All the searchlights in extreme antennal vibration. They have blots of light, like beads of dew on a stalk. Desperate fighting. The same perorations.

Monday 3 June
Leonard said, after Miss Griffiths [Hogarth Press clerk] went, "If it gives them so much happiness, we ought to put up with it from time to time." I said, But how, seeing she never spoke and was as unresponsive as a fish, could it have given her pleasure? "She leads such an awful life in Acton. She likes the food and sitting in the garden." This fairly sums up a very laboured week end: when we drew bucket up after bucket and nothing happened. But we made her sing, Monteverdi: and she sang quite simply. Will she marry? or fade? Again I'm struck with the helplessness of the lower orders. All of us on top. What can they get at –?

Four-fifths of the army over here now. A respite, a pause, perhaps. Perhaps Italy comes in . . . We have now been hard at it hero-making. The laughing, heroic Tommy – how can we be worthy of such men? – every paper, every BBC rises to that dreary false cheery hero-making strain. Will they be grinding organs in the street in six months? Its the emotional falsity; not all false, yet inspired with some eye to the main chance. Its the myth making stage of the war we're in.

Friday 7 June
Just back [from London] this roasting hot evening. The great battle which decides our life or death goes on. Up till 1.30 this morning, Kingsley diffusing his soft charcoal gloom. Question of suicide seriously debated among the four of us – Rose Macaulay the other – in the gradually darkening room. At last no light at all. This was symbolic. French are to be beaten; invasion here; fifth column active; a German pro-Consul; English Government in Canada; we in concentration camps, or taking sleeping draughts. The menace now is Ireland. Kingsley gives us about five weeks before the

great attack on England begins. I will continue tomorrow when less sleepy. Saw Stephen, Sibyl, John, Morgan, Judith, Raymond [Mortimer], Kingsley, Rose Macaulay, finally W. Robson – but can't discriminate.

Sunday 9 June
I will continue – but can I? The pressure of this battle wipes out London pretty quick. As sample of my present mood, I reflect: capitulation will mean all Jews to be given up. Concentration camps. So to our garage. That's behind correcting *Roger*, playing bowls. Another reflection: I don't want to go to bed at midday: this refers to the garage. What we dread (its no exaggeration) is the news that the French Government have left Paris. A kind of growl behind the cuckoo and t'other birds: a furnace behind the sky. It struck me that one curious feeling is, that the writing 'I' has vanished. No audience. No echo. That's part of one's death.

Monday 10 June
A day off. I mean one of those odd lapses of anxiety which may be false. Anyhow they said this morning that the line is unbroken – save at certain points. Anyhow its a day off – a coal gritty day. And cool mercifully after the furnace. Today, too, I sent off my page proofs, and thus have read my *Roger* for the last time. The Index remains. And I'm in the doldrums. The after book stage is on me.

Tuesday 11 June
Today or yesterday Italy came in: French said to be holding most lines; Government offices leaving Paris. Plays rehearsed, working till eyes blind at Index.

Wednesday 12 June
Black news. French apparently withdrawing but only guarded news. Percy says the little boats all summoned again, as if to fetch off more troops.

Thursday 13 June
If it weren't for – oh dear the retreat – Paris now almost besieged – 20,000 of our men cut off – still the French have gained five miles somewhere – if it weren't for this, today would have been a happy day. My Index sent off – so that's the very final full stop to all that drudgery. Up and down – up and down. No petrol at the pumps – providing for Invasion, only served a dribble, the man said.

Friday 14 June
Paris is in the hands of the Germans. Battle continues. We spent the day seeing Penshurst with Vita – picnicked in the park. Very fine and hot. The

house of yellowish Oxford stone. Banqueting hall: disappointing furniture, like heavy and over ornamental Tottenham Court Road, only made 1314. Queen Elizabeth dancing. Elizabeth herself in another picture, delicate skinned, red haired, aquiline. Then the shell of Lady Pembroke's lute – like half a fig. Then some very ugly tables . . . a long panelled room with soft veined panels. Out into the garden, which has certain trim lawns, and long grass walks, then lapses into wilderness. Sidneys very poor – given up weeding. A great lily pond; the goldfish making an odd subacqueous tapping as they moved among reeds. Then through old pink courtyards to the car: but the butler came and said his Lordship wanted to see us. Vita went – we stayed. Then were summoned. Lord de L'Isle and Dudley is like a very old liver and white Sussex spaniel – heavy pouched, both eyes with cataract, eighty-seven but looks younger, waistcoat undone. Glad of company. Padded us into a small room; made us look at pictures said to be good. Can only keep a few rooms open. And those like seaside lodging rooms. Vita said he'd told her he was so poor he couldn't have people to stay: whole place run by two maids and a boy and butler; is alone – but d'you mind being alone? she asked. "Hate it" he said. Twice a week he goes to Tonbridge and plays Bridge. There this old snail sits in the corner of his tremendous shell. Odd to have seen this Elizabethan great house the first day that invasion becomes serious. But I like Monks House better.

Thursday 20 June
London diary: just back; and dinner so close and events so crowded that I must abstract. Monday lunch: John. The French stopped fighting; Kingsley Martin after dinner. Tuesday, dine with Adrian. They both off to air raid rehearsal at Middlesex Hospital. Adrian promises us a prescription. Churchill broadcasts. Reassuring about defence of England; not all claptrap. Now we're fighting alone with our back to the wall. Bombs first, then invasion. Ethel Smyth tea. Oh of *course* we shall fight and win. Monday ended in charcoal gloom. Kingsley Martin says we must and shall be beaten. He says perhaps four more numbers of the *New Statesman* will come out.

Here, as soon as we begin bowls, Louie comes agog. Harry [West, her brother] came back on Monday. It pours out – how he hadn't boots off for three days; the beach at Dunkirk – the bombers as low as trees – the bullets like moth holes in his coat – how no English aeroplanes fought; how the officer told them to take their shoes off and go past a pill box on all fours. Then went himself with a grenade and blasted it. At Dunkirk many men shot themselves as the planes swooped. Harry swam off, a boat neared. Say Chum, can you row? Yes, he said, hauled in, rowed for five hours, saw England, landed – didn't know if it were day or night or what town – didn't ask – couldn't write to his mother – so was despatched to his regiment.

Harry has had enough war, and is certain of our defeat – got no arms and no aeroplanes – how can we do anything?

Saturday 22 June
And the fighting goes on in France; and the terms aren't yet public; and its a heavy grey day, and I've been beaten at bowls, feel depressed and irritated, and vow I'll play no more, but read my book. I would like to find one book and stick to it. But I can't. I feel, if this is my last lap, oughtn't I to read Shakespeare? But can't. I feel oughtn't I to finish off *Pointz Hall*: oughtn't I to finish something by way of an end? The end gives its vividness, even its gaiety and recklessness to the random daily life. This, I thought yesterday, may be my last walk. The corn was flowing with poppies in it. And I read my Shelley at night.

Nightly raids on the east and south coast. Six, three, twelve people killed nightly.

Thursday 27 June
How difficult to make oneself a centre after all the rings a visitor stirs in one – in this case Elizabeth Bowen. These rough rapid twinkling ripples spread out and out – for some hours after Elizabeth is in the train. It is a disagreeable after-visit feeling. It has its connection too with too many cigarettes, with incessant knitting. Then a visit to Charleston threw another stone into the pond. And at the moment, with *Pointz Hall* only to fix upon, I'm loosely anchored. Further, the war – our waiting while the knives sharpen for the operation – has taken away the outer wall of security. No echo comes back. I have no surroundings. We pour to the edge of a precipice ... and then? I can't conceive that there will be a 27th June 1941.

Elizabeth's stammer also had a disintegrating effect: like a moth buzzing round a flower – her whirr of voice as she can't alight on a word – a whirr of sound that makes the word quiver and seem blurred. We talked however – and very on the whole congenially. A very honourable horse faced, upper class, hard constricted mind.

Thursday 4 July
Again, back from London. But its here that the events take place. Louie, toothless, but all agog: yesterday at 5pm. pop, pop pop out over the marshes. She was picking fruit. Backfiring she thought. Told by someone it was a raid. So she went in. They bombed the train at Newhaven: the driver died this morning. Passengers lay under seats. Rails wrecked. Today a plane – ours – crashed at Southease. So, the Germans are nibbling at my afternoon walks. The French fleet has been seized and sunk. All Lewes listening to the wireless. In London, Kingsley Martin decreed that Tuesday,

or today, Thursday, was fixed for invasion. London very safe and solid in feeling. Pink brick fortresses – for ammunition? – in main streets. Wire mazes in Whitehall &c. We passed strings of ambulances coming down tagged with boughs. Canadians swarm – want to see Buckingham Palace.

Friday 5 July
Rumour, via Percy, has it that the streets of Newhaven were machine gunned. L. gets annoyed with Percy. I see the imagination – that should have turned a wheel, running to waste and foam instead. The French Fleet fought: Pétain cuts off diplomatic relations. So shall we be at war with our ally? Last month indissolubly determined to fight to the end.

Friday 12 July
How the grass shone pale emerald green when I walked off my temper on the marsh after dinner. The passages of colour, over Asheham, like the green backgrounds in Vermeer and then the little rusty grey church, and the cows, sun beaded, fringed with sun. We quarrelled about our communal feeling ... but we made it up. L. has given all our saucepans to Mrs Ebbs [the vicar's wife] to make aeroplanes with. I don't like any of the feelings war breeds: patriotism; communal &c; all sentimental and emotional parodies of our real feelings. But then, we're in for it. Every day we have our raids: at night the bloodhounds are out. I open my window when I hear the Germans, and the broad stalks of light rise all over the meadow feeling for them – a strange early morning spectacle. Then the drone buzz booms away, rather like a dentist's drill. No invasion so far.

Wednesday 24 July
I want at the moment, the eve of publication moment, to discover my emotions. They are fitful: thus not very strong – nothing like so strong as before *The Years* – oh dear nothing like. Still they twinge. Two strains, as usual, will develop: fascinating; dull; life-like; dead. So why do I twinge? knowing it almost by heart. But not quite. I shall of course be sneered at by those who sniff at Bloomsbury. I'd forgotten that. But as L. is combing Sally I can't concentrate. No room of my own.

Thursday 25 July
I'm not very nervous at the moment: indeed at worst its only a skin deep nervousness; for after all, the main people approve. What a curious relation is mine with Roger at this moment – I who have given him a kind of shape after his death – Was he like that? I feel very much in his presence at the moment: as if I were intimately connected with him; as if we together had

given birth to this vision of him: a child born of us. Yet he had no power to alter it. And yet for some years it will represent him.

Friday 26 July

I think I have taken, say a good second, judging from the *TLS* review. *Times* says it takes a very high place indeed among biographies. *Times* intelligent, but not room for more. By the way, I'm rather proud of having done a solid work. I am content, somehow. But its an incredibly lovely – yes lovely is the word – transient, changing, warm, capricious summer evening. Also I won two games.

When the twelve planes went over, out to sea, to fight, last evening, I had I think an individual, not communal BBC dictated feeling. I almost instinctively wished them luck. I should like to be able to take scientific notes of reactions. Invasion may be tonight or not at all. And – I had something else to say. But what? And dinner to get ready.

Sunday 28 July

Why do I mind being beaten at bowls? I think I connect it with Hitler. Yet I played very well. Such a curious peace; a satisfactory quiet. I shall see no one in London. Yes for a moment I believe that I can compass a season of calm weather. Yet 'they' say the invasion is fixed for August 16th. Yesterday at Charleston; Angelica there: I diagnose strain; a little defiance, restlessness. And feel in Quentin something heavy, mature, depressed. Almost a year he's been in the fields: all corn coloured and red poppied with his blue eyes for convolvulus.

Waiting for the Sunday papers in which *Roger Fry* will, or may, be disposed of by Desmond. I know that Desmond (who very likely won't do it) will if he does, gently hum and haw something about Mrs Woolf's charm and sympathy and then proceed to give his own version of Roger which will probably be more amusing than mine; and that'll fill his short column.

Friday 2 August

Complete silence surrounds that book. It might have sailed into the blue and been lost. 'One of our books did not return' as the BBC puts it. No review by Morgan, no review at all. No letter. Still I remain – yes honestly – quiet minded, and prepared to face a complete, a lasting silence. I'm so jaded after Philip Morrell, Pippa, and the London uproar – but with a sense of things forming, and freedom.

Sunday 4 August

Just time to record oh a great relief – Desmond's review really says all I wanted said. The book delights friends and the younger generation say

Yes, yes we know him; and its not only delightful but important. That's enough. And it gave me a very calm rewarded feeling – not the old triumph, as over a novel; but the feeling I've done what was asked of me, given my friends what they wanted. Now I can be content.

Tuesday 6 August
Yes I was very happy again when I saw Clive's blue envelope at breakfast this morning. Its Clive almost – what? – devout – no quiet, serious, completely without sneer approving. As good in its way as the best of my books – the best biography for years. So I'm really and truly immune, and feel, if only Louie's father hadn't died, and Mabel's lover hadn't gone to hospital so that I've all the cooking and washing up to do today, that I could go on to the next thing – to many next things. Is it an illusion that I'm freer and stronger, as a writer, than ever?

Men excavating gun emplacements in the bank. They look like swarms of busy ants, as I walk. Cementing floors; sandbagging walls. Great lorries of material go bursting down the Roman Road. No one pays any attention – so blasé are we. Guns along the river, boughs for camouflage, excite no one. *Roger* sells well. Talk of reprint.

Friday 16 August
They came very close. We lay down under the tree. The sound was like someone sawing in the air just above us. We lay flat on our faces, hands behind head. Don't close your teeth said L. They seemed to be sawing at something stationary. Bombs shook the windows of my lodge. I thought, I think, of nothingness – flatness, my mood being flat. Some fear I suppose. Then another came from Newhaven. Hum and saw and buzz all round us. A horse neighed on the marsh. Very sultry. Is it thunder? I said. No guns, said L., from Ringmer, from Charleston way. Then slowly the sound lessened. Mabel in kitchen said the windows shook. The All Clear, 5 to 7. 144 down last night.

Monday 19 August
Yesterday, Sunday, there was a roar. Right on top of us they came. I looked at the plane, like a minnow at a roaring shark. Over they flashed – three, I think. Olive green. Then pop pop pop – German? Again pop pop pop over Kingston. Said to be five bombers hedge hopping on their way to London. The closest shave so far. 144 brought down – no that was last time. And no raid (so far) today.

Friday 23 August
Book flopped. Sales down to fifteen a day since air raid on London. Is that the reason? Will it pick up? But I'm ravaged by Ann [Stephen] in house,

Judith Leslie Eleanor Camilla in and out of house. L. says he has a moral feeling of duty to young.

Wednesday 28 August

But well it taught me, that week of unintermittent interruptions, bowls, tea parties and droppings in, what public school is like – no privacy. A good rub with a coarse towel for my old mind no doubt. I should say, to placate VW when she wishes to know what was happening in August 1940 – that the air raids are now at their prelude. Invasion, if it comes, must come within three weeks. The harrying of the public is now in full swing. The air saws; the wasps drone; the siren – its now Weeping Willie in the papers – is as punctual as the vespers. We've not had our raid yet, we say. Two in London. One caught me in the London Library. Sales a little better.

Saturday 31 August

Now we are in the war. England is being attacked. I got this feeling for the first time completely yesterday. The feeling of pressure, danger, horror. Vita rang up at 6 to say she couldn't come. She was sitting at Sissinghurst, the bombs were falling round the house. I'm too jaded to give the feeling – of talking to someone who might be killed any moment. Can you hear that? she said. No, I couldn't. That's another. That's another. She repeated the same thing – about staying in order to drive the ambulance – time after time, like a person who can't think. It was very difficult talking. She broke off – Oh how I do mind this, and put the telephone down. I went and played bowls. A perfect quiet hot evening. Later the planes began zooming. Explosions. Planes very close. A great raid on London last night. Today quiet here. When I rang up Sissinghurst after dinner, someone cut in with "Restricted service. Things very bad there just now." Of course this may be the beginning of invasion. A sense of pressure. Endless local stories. No – its no good trying to capture the feeling of England being in a battle. L. sleeps sound all through it every night.

Monday 2 September

There might be no war, the past two days. A lull after the attacks on London. At Charleston yesterday a skeleton Memoir Club. We sat in the sun. It was hot. The apples hung red. Not a sound. Maynard what I call unredeemed Maynard, rather severe, snubbing, truculent. Talk about lives. Mine of Roger I gather is called by Maynard 'The official life'. I read my Dreadnought notes, not very well. Lydia wouldn't come. "She feels this is not the time for brains" said Maynard. Yet talk is interesting.

Thursday 5 September

Hot, hot, hot. Record heat wave, record summer if we kept records this summer. At 2.30 a plane zooms; ten minutes later air raid sounds; twenty later, all clear. Hot, I repeat; and doubt if I'm a poet. An idea. All writers are unhappy. The picture of the world in books is thus too dark. The wordless are the happy: women in cottage gardens. Now, in my nightgown, to walk on the marshes.

Saturday 7 September

An air raid in progress. Planes zooming. No, that one's gone over very quick and loud. Couldn't see if it were English. More planes over the house, going I suppose to London, which is raided every night.

Tuesday 10 September

Back from half a day in London – perhaps our strangest visit. Mecklenburgh Square roped off. Wardens there, not allowed in. The house about thirty yards from ours struck at one this morning by a bomb. Completely ruined. Another bomb in the Square still unexploded. We walked round the back. The house was still smouldering. That is a great pile of bricks. Underneath all the people who had gone down to their shelter. Scraps of cloth hanging to the bare walls at the side still standing. A looking glass I think swinging. Like a tooth knocked out – a clean cut. Our house undamaged. The garage man at the back – blear eyed and jerky – told us he had been blown out of his bed by the explosion; made to take shelter in a church. He said the Jerrys had been over for three nights trying to bomb King's Cross. So we went on to Gray's Inn. Left the car and saw Holborn. A vast gap at the top of Chancery Lane. Smoking still. Some great shop entirely destroyed: the hotel opposite like a shell. Heaps of blue green glass in the road at Chancery Lane. Men breaking off fragments left in the frames. Then to the *New Statesman* office: windows broken, but house untouched. We went over it. Deserted. Wet passages. Glass on stairs. Doors locked. So back to the car. A great block of traffic. The cinema behind Mme Tussaud's torn open: the stage visible; some decoration swinging. All the Regent's Park houses with broken windows, but undamaged. And then miles and miles of ordinary streets – all Bayswater – as usual. Streets empty. Faces set and eyes bleared. Then at Wimbledon a siren – people began running. We drove, through almost empty streets, as fast as possible. Horses taken out of the shafts. Cars pulled up. The people I think of now are the very grimy [Bloomsbury] lodging house keepers; with another night to face: old wretched women standing at their doors; dirty, miserable. Well – as Nessa said on the phone, its coming very near.

Wednesday 11 September

Churchill has just spoken. A clear, measured, robust speech Says the invasion is being prepared. Its for the next two weeks apparently if at all. Ships and barges massing at French ports. The bombing of London of course preparation to invasion. Our majestic city – &c, which touches me, for I feel London majestic. Another raid last night on London. Time bomb struck the Palace. John rang up. Wants the Press moved at once. L. is to go up on Friday. Our windows are broken John says. Mecklenburgh Square evacuated.

We count now on an air raid about 8.30. Anyhow, whether or not, we hear the sinister sawing noise about then, which loudens and fades; then a pause; then another comes. "They're at it again" we say as we sit, I doing my work, L. making cigarettes. Now and then there's a thud. The windows shake. So we know London is raided again.

Thursday 12 September

A gale has risen. Weather broken. Terrific air traffic last night. But the raid beaten off by new London barrage. This is cheering. If we can hold out this week – next week – week after – if the weather's turned – if the force of the raids on London is broken – We go up tomorrow to see John about moving Press; to patch the windows, rescue valuables, and get letters – if that is we're allowed in the Square.

Friday 13 September

Just back from half day in London. Raid, unheard by us, started outside Wimbledon. Saw a pink brick shelter. Twice we left. More guns. Came back. At last started, keeping an eye on shelters and people's behaviour. Reached Russell Hotel. Loud gunfire. We sheltered. Started for Mecklenburgh Square: met John, who said the Square still closed; so lunched in the hotel. Decided the Press emergency – to employ Garden City Press [Letchworth] – in twenty minutes. Raid still on. Walked to Mecklenburgh Square. Refused admittance. John told us the story of Monday night. He rather white and shaky. Left him with distant guns firing. Started back. All clear in Marylebone High Street.

Saturday 14 September

A sense of invasion – that is lorries of soldiers and machines – like cranes – walloping along to Newhaven. An air raid is on. A little pop rattle which I take to be machine guns, just gone off. Planes soaring and roaring. Mabel comes out and looks. Asks if we want fish fried or boiled. As the result of a friendly cool talk it's settled, I think, that she leaves here. A great relief. I like being alone in our little boat. I like provisioning and seeing all's shipshape and not having dependants.

The great advantage of this page is that it gives me a fidget ground. Fidgets: caused by losing at bowls and invasion; caused by another howling banshee, by having no book I must read; and so on. I think I will begin my new book by reading Ifor Evans' sixpenny Penguin [*A Short History of English Literature*]. And whatever happens I will settle and sun on the moment. Fifty-eight – not so many more. I sometimes think about violent death. Who's whistling in the churchyard? Keep out the war from this page, now and then.

Sunday 15 September
No invasion yet. Rumours that it was attempted, but barges sunk with great loss. Raids over Brighton this afternoon. Mabel goes tomorrow; so pray God the Church Bells don't ring tonight. Now we go to our last Cook cooked dinner for I don't know how long. Could it be the end of resident servants for ever? This I pray this lovely fitful evening, as well as the usual Damn Hitler prayer.

Monday 16 September
Well, we're alone in our ship. Mabel stumped off, with her bunions, carrying her bags, at 10. Thank you for all your kindness, she said the same to us both. "I hope we shall meet again" I said. She said Oh no doubt – thinking I referred to death. So that five years' uneasy mute but very passive and calm relation is over.

To Charleston this afternoon, after provisioning for our siege in Lewes. Great air traffic all night – some loud explosions. I listened for Church Bells, thinking largely I admit, of finding ourselves prisoned here with Mabel. She thought the same. Said that if one is to be killed one will be killed. Prefers death in a Holloway shelter playing cards – naturally – to death here.

Tuesday 17 September
No invasion. High wind. Yesterday in the Public Library I took down a book of Peter Lucas's criticism. This turned me against writing my book. Turned me against all Lit. crit.; these so clever, so airless, so fleshless ingenuities and attempts to prove – that T. S. Eliot for example is a worse critic than F. L. Lucas. I dipped for five minutes and put the book back depressed. The man asked What do you want Mrs Woolf? I said a history of English Literature. But was sickened, I couldn't look. There were so many.

Wednesday 18 September
'We have need of all our courage' are the words that come to the surface this morning; on hearing that all our windows are broken, ceilings down,

and most of our china smashed at Mecklenburgh Square. The bomb exploded. Why did we ever leave Tavistock? – what's the good of thinking that? The Press – what remains – is to be moved to Letchworth. A grim morning. But I did forge ahead with *Pointz Hall* all the same.

Thursday 19 September

Another loud night. Another bad raid. Oxford Street now smashed. John Lewis, Selfridge, Bourne & Hollingsworth, all my old haunts. Also British Museum forecourt. A gale and rain here.

Saturday 21 September

We've just bottled our honey. Very still and warm today. So invasion becomes possible. The river high; all softly blue and milky; autumn quiet – twelve planes in perfect order, back from the fight, pass overhead.

Wednesday 25 September

All day – Monday – in London, in the flat; dark; carpets nailed to windows; ceilings down in patches; heaps of grey dust and china under kitchen table; back rooms untouched. A lovely September day – tender – three days of tender weather. John came. We are moved to Letchworth. *Roger* surprisingly sells. Invasion again withdraws.

Thursday 26 September

A talk on the phone with Nessa. [She] held the trump card. "Both our studios have been destroyed. The roofs fallen in. Still burning. Pictures burnt." So I had to pipe low. My fallen ceilings a trifle. Gathering apples all the afternoon. German raider comes over. Shots fired at Asheham. Bombs towards Seaford. Writing I remain unmoved. Only a German bomber? Oh that's all – No I didn't look out – Consider this remark last year – still more, ten years, still more fifty years ago. In flush with *Pointz Hall* thank God.

Saturday 29 September

A bomb dropped so close I cursed L. for slamming the window. I was writing to Hugh, and the pen jumped from my fingers. I was thinking (among other things): that this is a lazy life. Breakfast in bed. Read in bed. Bath. Order dinner. Out to Lodge. After rearranging my room (turning table to get the sun: Church on right; window left; a new very lovely view) tune up, with cigarette: write till 12; stop; visit L.; look at papers; return; type till 1. Listen in. Lunch. Read papers. Walk to Southease. Back 3. Gather and arrange apples. Tea. Write a letter. Bowls. Type again. Read Michelet and write here. Cook dinner. Music. Embroidery. 9.30 read (or sleep) till 11.30. Bed. Compare with the old London day. Three afternoons someone coming. One night, dinner party. Saturday a walk. Thursday shopping. Tuesday going to tea with Nessa. One City walk. Telephone ringing. L. to meetings. Kingsley Martin or Robson bothering – that was an average week; with Friday to Monday here.

I think, now we're marooned, I ought to cram in a little more reading. Yet why? A happy, a very free, and disengaged – a life that rings from one simple melody to another. Yes; why not enjoy this after all those years of the other?

Nessa rang up. A statue and frigidaire alone salved.

Wednesday 2 October

Ought I not to look at the sunset rather than write this? A flush of red in the blue; the haystack in the marsh catches the glow. Now a plume of smoke goes from the train under Caburn. And all the air a solemn stillness holds; till 8.30 when the cadaverous twanging in the sky begins; the planes going to London. Well its an hour still to that. Why try again to make the familiar catalogue, from which something escapes. Should I think of death? Last night a great heavy plunge of bomb under the window. So near we both started. A plane had passed dropping this fruit. We went on the terrace. Trinkets of stars sprinkled and glittering. All quiet. The bombs dropped on Itford Hill. There are two by the river, marked with white wooden crosses, still unburst. I said to L.: I don't want to die yet. Oh I try to imagine how one's killed by a bomb. I've got it fairly vivid – the sensation: but can't see anything but suffocating nonentity following after. I shall think – oh I wanted another ten years – not this – and shan't, for once, be able to describe it. It – I mean death; no, the scrunching and scrambling, the crushing of my bone shade in on my very active eye and brain: the process of putting out the light – painful? Yes. Terrifying. I suppose so – Then a swoon; a drum; two or three gulps attempting consciousness – and then, dot dot dot

Sunday 6 October

Never had a better writing season. *Pointz Hall* in fact pleases me; and so little to do now. Many letters to write.

Thursday 10 October

Rather flush of ideas, because I have had an idle day, a non-writing day – what a relief once in a way – a Vita talking day. About what? Oh the war; bombs; which house hit, which not; then our books – all very ample easy and satisfying. She has a hold on life, knows plants and their minds and bodies; [is] large and tolerant and modest, with her hands loosely upon so many reins: sons; Harold; garden; farm. Humorous too, and deeply, I mean awkwardly, dumbly affectionate. I'm glad that our love has weathered so well.

Saturday 12 October

If it were not treasonable to say so, a day like this is almost too – I won't say happy: but amenable. I can't stop looking: October blooms; brown plough; and the fading and freshening of the marsh. Now the mist comes up. And one thing's 'pleasant' after another: breakfast, writing, walking, tea, bowls, reading, sweets, bed. But I was thinking I must intensify. In London, now, or two years ago, I'd be owling through the streets. More pack and thrill than here. So I must supply that – how? I think book inventing. Scraps of memoirs come so coolingly to my mind. Wound up by those three little articles (one sent today) I unwound a page about Thoby.

But I want to look back on these war years as years of positive something or other. Queer the contraction of life to the village radius. All our friends are isolated over winter fires. No cars. No petrol. Trains uncertain. And we on our lovely free autumn island. But I will read Dante.

Thursday 17 October

Our private luck has turned. John says Tavistock Square is no more. If that's so, I need no longer wake in the night thinking the Wolves luck has taken a downward turn. A perfect day – a red admiral feasting on an apple day. The light is now fading. Soon the Siren; then the twang of plucked strings ... But its almost forgettable still; the nightly operation on the tortured London. We go up tomorrow. I must black out – the Siren, just as I had drawn the curtains. Now the unpleasant part begins. Who'll be killed tonight? Not us, I suppose. One doesn't think of that – save as a quickener. Indeed I often think our Indian summer was deserved: after all those London years. I mean, this quickens it. Every day seen against a very faint shade of bodily risk.

Sunday 20 October

The most – what? – impressive, no that's not it – sight in London on Friday was the queue, mostly children with suitcases, outside Warren Street tube. This was about 11.30. We thought they were evacuees, waiting for a bus. But there they were, in a much longer line, with women, men, more bags and blankets, sitting still at 3. Lining up for the shelter in the night's raid – which came of course. To Tavistock Square. With a sigh of relief saw a heap of ruins. Three houses, I should say, gone. Basement all rubble. Only relics an old basket chair (bought in Fitzroy Square days) and Penman's board TO LET. Otherwise bricks and wood splinters. I could just see a piece of my studio wall standing: otherwise rubble where I wrote so many books. Open air where we sat so many nights, gave so many parties. So to Meck. All again litter, glass, black soft dust, plaster and powder. Books all over dining room floor. Only the drawing room with windows almost whole. A wind blowing through. I began to hunt out diaries. What could we salvage in this little car? Darwin, and the silver, and some glass and china. Then lunch off tongue, in the drawing room. John came. I forgot *The Voyage of the Beagle.* No raid the whole day. So about 2.30 drove home. Cheered on the whole by London. Damage in Bloomsbury considerable; but miles and miles of Hyde Park and Queen's Gate untouched. Now we seem quit of London. Exhilaration at losing possessions – save at times I want my books and chairs and carpets and beds – how I worked to buy them – one by one – And the pictures. But to be free of Meck. would now be a relief. But its odd – the relief at losing possessions. I should like to start life, in peace, almost bare – free to go anywhere.

I must add that today is as hot as August: walked on downs; heard gunfire at Dover? – shelling Calais; summer clothes. Too hot for fire. Mist rising, must black out.

Tuesday 22 October
The vast ideas that float are never caught. I thought: how L. sees people in the mass: I singly. I thought, I will write supports and additions for my old *TLS* articles; a good deal about manners, and our class; about my rug; about a prayer for the Victorian scene in *Pointz Hall*; if I wait the thought may return. A lovely almost a red admiral and apple day; twenty-four volumes of diary salved; a great mass for my memoirs.

Wednesday 23 October
Heard the whistle of bombs for the first time today. About 5 – windy, cloudy: playing bowls. Suddenly heard a plane: suddenly heard a whistle. Like a toy pig escaping – rather; then I saw smoke, over the field path. Then four separate thuds – said to be at Iford. Went into village. Then Annie and two children appeared. In the bus from Lewes they had seen the bombs fall near. No one hurt – as far as known.

Tuesday 29 October
Today I cycled to Newhaven – city of the Dead. Sepulchred shops empty; silent, dour men. Baker boasted of the raid – at 5.30 yesterday twenty-five Germans descended: dropped twenty-five bombs – houses ruined – little girl killed. "And not a Spitfire anywhere near..." The gloomy self-consequence of the newly bombed. Home by Tarring Neville. The loveliest of low views.

Friday 1 November
A gloomy evening, spiritually: alone over the fire – L. in bed with influenza cold: caught off Percy. So I am alone; and by way of conversation, apply

to this too stout volume. The relics of my distracted morning were spent tightening the wretched £150 story, 'The Legacy'. Well, I combed and tidied it – so far as 'it' has any hair on its head. Then dipped into my memoirs: too circuitous and unrelated. All the same, I can weave a very thick pattern, one of these days, out of that pattern of detail. Early in the morning Annie came, asked me to stand for the Women's Institute Committee. "No" I cried too violently. The poor don't understand humour. I repented; went round later and found her in the sunny parlour and said I would. Then I carried L.'s lunch. Then I pumped my bicycle. Then I rode to Lewes.

Sunday 3 November

Yesterday the river burst its banks. The marsh is now a sea with gulls on it. L. (recovered) and I walked down to the hanger. Water broken, white, roaring, pouring down through the gap by the pill box. Today the rain is tremendous. Flood deeper and fuller. Bridge cut off. Water made road impassable by the farm. So all my marsh walks are gone – until?

Tuesday 5 November

The haystack in the floods is of such incredible beauty . . . When I look up I see all the marsh water. In the sun deep blue, gulls caraway seeds; yellow islands; leafless trees; red cottage roofs. Oh may the flood last for ever – a virgin lip; no bungalows; as it was in the beginning. Now its lead grey with the red leaves in front, our island sea. Caburn is become a cliff.

I was thinking: the University fills shells like H. A. L. Fisher and [G. M.] Trevelyan. They are their product. Also: never have I been so fertile. Also: the old hunger for books is on me; the childish passion. So that I am very 'happy' as the saying is; and excited by *Pointz Hall*.

Thursday 7 November

Morgan asks if he may propose me for the London Library Committee. Rather to my pleasure I answered No. I don't want to be a sop – a face saver. This was a nice little finish to a meeting with Morgan years ago in the London Library. He sniffed about women on the Committee. One of these days I'll refuse I said silently. And now I have. Bad bombing last night – four thuds at 7 – said to be Glyndebourne. London tomorrow.

Tuesday 12 November

Chamberlain is dead: and if we hold on till March we have broken the back (or whatever the phrase is). These two facts sum up the papers. I could add about Greece . . . Hitler's speech . . . no: time goes so heavy and slow, that nothing marks the days. A bomb fell at lunch yesterday. There is nothing new. Eastbourne bombed. London.

Friday 15 November
As I cannot write if anyone is in the room, as L. sits here when we light the fire, this book remains shut. A natural slimming process. A screw over the end of *Pointz Hall* made me rather sink into the disillusions yesterday. We have been a bit pressed. Michael MacCarthy to lunch; L.'s lecture; Nessa to lunch – two hard shopping days, in one of which I bought blue serge slacks – all this has rattled my head; so I plunged into the past this morning, wrote about father; and then we walked in top boots and trousers through the flood. Increased again. Lewes this evening with two lights showing looks like a harbour – like a French town spreading its skirts round a bay. Coventry almost destroyed. The usual traffic last night. All the hounds on their road to London. A bad raid there. When I am not writing fiction this fact seeps in.

Sunday 17 November
Butter stolen yesterday; Louie says "You are too well liked for any villager to take it." This flatters us. The butter disappeared when we were playing bowls. A man's voice heard, and the card of St Dunstan's found in the door. Assumption then that the voluntary Collector took it.

Saturday 23 November
Having this moment finished *The Pageant* – or *Pointz Hall?* – (begun perhaps April 1938) my thoughts turn, well up, to write the first chapter of the next book (nameless). *Anon*, it will be called. The exact narrative of this last morning should refer to Louie's interruption, holding a glass jar, in whose thin milk was a pat of butter. This was a moment of great household triumph. I am a little triumphant about the book. I think its an interesting attempt in a new method. I think its more quintessential than the others. More milk skimmed off. A richer pat, certainly a fresher than that misery *The Years*, I've enjoyed writing almost every page.

The flood is less today. Yesterday a raider came popping over the hill; L. saw smoke rise. In fact it was shot down at Tarring Neville.

Friday 29 November
Many many deep thoughts have visited me. And fled. The pen puts salt on their tails; they see the shadow and fly. I was thinking about vampires. Leeches. Anyone with £500 a year and education, is at once sucked by the leeches. Put L. and me into Rodmell pool and we are sucked – sucked – sucked. I see the reason for those who suck guineas. But life – ideas – that's a bit thick. We've exchanged the clever for the simple. The simple envy us our life.

John has written – wobbly: wants limelight and bouquets. Third impression of *Roger*: and I not told.

Friday 6 December

And then what they call real life broke in. Vans arrived in a deluge. Oh, we unpacked standing in the rain. Monks House gorged with old jugs and lidless pots. And the [rented store] room laden with four tons of old damp books. Real life is a helter skelter, healthy for the mind doubtless. I see what a working woman's life is. No time to think. No silence. I cannot concentrate on Ellen Terry. Rather depressing – old papers, letters, note-books: I'm going to bind the survivors tonight; and in coloured paper they may refresh my eye. All this writing – what a deluge of words I've let loose – on paper only: I mean not printed.

Sunday 8 December

I have only five minutes after a struggle with Ellen Terry to say that the war – yes I have only five minutes to fill in that omission – the war goes on. In ten years I shall ask, what was happening to the war? It is better. The Greeks are driving the Italians out of Albania. Perhaps this is the turning point in the war. But it dribbles out in such little drops. One can't always catch them. The war slowly enacts itself on a great scene: round our little scene. We spend fifty-nine minutes here; one minute there.

Monday 16 December

Exhausted with the long struggle of writing 2,000 words about Ellen Terry – interrupted by four days of furniture moving – distracted by the chaotic state of our possessions – oh the huddle and hideousness of untidiness – oh that Hitler had obliterated all our books tables carpets and pictures – oh that we were empty and bare and unpossessed – I take my pen to drawl and drowse a little. The year draws to an end; and I am harassed, damp: but I will take the matter in hand: scrub and polish and discard; and make our life here as taut and bright and vigorous as it can be. Its rather a hard lap: the winter lap. So cold often. And so much work to do. And so little fat to cook with. And so much shopping to do. And one has to weigh and measure. Then Kingsley comes and devours sugar and butter. I will write memoirs, I think: then *Reading at Random*. Measure, order, precision are now my gods. Even my hand shakes. One day last week we lunched at King's Cross with John. He was polite, impersonal – the Prince Consort. A ceremonious lunch. Why are we hooked to that large, rather pretentious livid-bellied shark? And must I spend my last years feeding his double row of teeth? I forget. I forget what I wished to say.

Kingsley Martin effusive but less distasteful. He ruined two days, now I come to think of it. Yes, its like going to the films – the film of December 1940 talking to Kingsley. I sit with my eyes dazed. Then at meals he scrapes and sops. I cook in the damp kitchen. And the village keeps tugging and jogging. The Women's Institute party tomorrow. My old dislike of the village bites at me. I envy houses alone in the fields.

Thursday 19 December

1940 is undoubtedly coming to an end. The shortest day comes this week: then the days draw out. It would be interesting if I could take today, Thursday, and say exactly how the war changes it. It changes it when I order dinner. Our ration of margarine is so small that I can't think of any pudding save milk pudding. We have no sugar to make sugar puddings: no pastry, unless I buy it ready made. The shops don't fill till midday. Things are bought fast. In the afternoon they are often gone. Meat ration diminishes this week. Milk is so cut that we have to consider even the cat's saucer. I spent an hour making butter from our skim of cream – a week's takings provides about half a pound. Petrol changes the day too. Nessa can only come here when she goes to Lewes shopping. All prices rise steadily. The screw is much increased since the summer. We buy no clothes but make do with the old. These are inconveniences rather than hardships. We don't go hungry or cold. But luxury is nipped off, and hospitality. It takes thought and trouble to feed one extra. The post is the most obvious inconvenience perhaps. It takes two days to get a London letter; four to get a parcel. I bicycle to Lewes instead of driving. Then the black out – that's half an hour daily drudgery. We can't use the dining room after dark. We are of course marooned here by the bombs in London. This last week the raids are so few that we forget to listen for a siren. That used to come at 6.30 punctually. What's Hitler got up his sleeve next – we ask? A certain old age feeling sometimes makes me think I can't spend force as I used. And my hand shakes. Otherwise we draw breath as usual. And its a day when every bough is bright green and the sun dazzles me.

Friday 20 December

We have been shopping in Brighton. It is a raw cold day, with the wind rising now. We bought a duck for our Christmas luncheon. We bought some buns and a wedge of cheese. Yesterday we went to the village school. They make things. I sat beside the flushed and cushioned Mrs Janson; and invited Mrs Ebbs to tea.

Sunday 22 December

How beautiful they were, those old people – I mean father and mother – how simple, how clear, how untroubled. I have been dipping into old letters and father's memoirs. He loved her – oh and was so candid and reasonable and transparent – and had such a fastidious delicate mind, educated, and transparent. How serene and gay even their life reads to me: no mud: no whirlpools. And so human – with the children and the little hum and song of the nursery. Nothing turbulent; nothing involved; no introspection.

Tuesday 24 December

I note with some dismay that my hand is becoming palsied. Why I can't say. Can I make clear straight lines any more? It seems not.

We lunched with Helen [Anrep, at Alciston]; and again 'I could have fancied living there.' An incredible loveliness. The downs breaking their wave, yet one pale quarry; and all the barns and stacks either a broken pink, or a verdurous green; and then the walk by the wall; and the church; and the great tithe barn. How England consoles and warms one, in these deep hollows, where the past stands almost stagnant. And the little spire across the fields ... L. is now cutting logs, and after my rush of love and envy for Alciston farm house, we concluded this is the perfect place. L. says it is exactly right, for we needn't be cumbered with possessions here. Which reminds me. We are very poor; so I must write. Yes, our old age is not going to be sunny orchard drowse. By shutting down the fire curtain, though, I find I can live in the moment; which is good; why yield a moment to regret or envy or worry? Why indeed?

Sunday 29 December

There are moments when the sail flaps. Then I ride across the downs to the cliffs. A roll of barbed wire is hooped on the edge. I rubbed my mind brisk along the Newhaven road. Shabby old maids buying groceries, in that desert road with the villas, in the wet. And Newhaven gashed. But tire the body and the mind sleeps. All desire to write diary here has flagged. What is the right antidote? I must sniff round. I detest the hardness of old age – I feel it. I rasp. I'm tart.

> The foot less prompt to meet the morning dew,
> The heart less bounding at emotion new,
> And hope, once crush'd, less quick to spring again.

I actually opened Matthew Arnold and copied these lines. While doing so, the idea came to me that why I dislike, and like, so many things idiosyncratically now, is because of my growing detachment from the hierarchy, the patriarchy. When Desmond praises *East Coker* [T. S. Eliot], and I am jealous, I walk over the marsh saying, I am I; and must follow that furrow, not copy another. That is the only justification for my writing and living.

How one enjoys food now: I make up imaginary meals.

1941

The year began with snow and bitter cold. Virginia felt harassed by the straits and exigencies of wartime and generally dejected. She was copying the manuscript of Pointz Hall and reading for her projected work – a survey of the whole of literature. She enjoined herself to take pleasure in her writing; but her diary-writing became more laconic, less fluent, and less frequent.

Octavia Wilberforce, a Brighton doctor and a distant relative, drew on the connection to make fairly regular visits to Monks House with offerings of milk and cream from her Sussex farm, with which Virginia made butter. Every ten days or so Leonard would go by train to London for the day, sometimes accompanied by Virginia, who would wander, forlornly, among her bomb-devastated haunts. In February they made an expedition to Cambridge, dining one night with Pernel Strachey, the retiring Principal of Newnham, the next with Dadie Rylands in King's, spending the intervening day at Letchworth where their Hogarth Press was now accommodated. Elizabeth Bowen came to stay a night at Monks House on their return, followed by Vita Sackville-West, whom Virginia had persuaded to lecture to the Women's Institute.

On 26 February Virginia notes that she has finished Pointz Hall – now to be called Between the Acts – which she gave Leonard to read. She was désoeuvré; she attempted to spring-clean and tidy up the house; one day she and Leonard bicycled to Brighton; another they went there by car when he had to lecture. There was still a great deal of enemy air-activity over Sussex, and solemn warnings were being given to prepare for the German invasion before Easter. Virginia was irritable and depressed. On 14 March she and Leonard met John Lehmann in London. He was told of Virginia's new book, about which she was clearly worried. But she sent him the typescript with a deprecatory note, asking him to judge whether it was fit to be published. He had no hesitations about it; but she subsequently wrote to tell him she could not publish it as it stood, and that she would revise it and try and pull it together before the autumn. Leonard was now seriously alarmed by her state of mind and health, and took her to see Octavia Wilberforce as a doctor. But Virginia was convinced that she was now so far down the remembered road to madness there would be no getting over it, and next day, leaving notes for Vanessa and Leonard, she walked across the water-meadows to the river Ouse and threw herself in. Her body was not retrieved until three weeks later. Leonard buried her ashes beneath the great elms which stood at the edge of Monks House garden and which they had called Leonard and Virginia.

1941

Wednesday 1 January

On Sunday night, as I was reading about the Great Fire in a very accurate detailed book, London was burning. Eight of my city churches destroyed, and the Guildhall. This belongs to last year. This first day of the new year has a slice of a wind -- like a circular saw. Leslie H[umphrey]. came to lunch; said um-um so often I nearly goggled; he was discussing the foundations of communism, having come chiefly to pick L.'s brain. Then old Octavia [Wilberforce] came, with her market woman's basket. Great white bottles of milk and cream. L. looking at the comet. Rather a strong moon, and so can't identify the constellation. And now its close on cooking time. A psychologist would see that the above was written with someone, and a dog, in the room. To add in private: I think I will be less verbose here perhaps – but what does it matter, writing too many pages. No printer to consider, no public.

Thursday 9 January

A blank. All frost. Still frost. Burning white. Burning blue. The elms red. I did not mean to describe, once more, the downs in snow; but it came. And I can't help even now turning to look at Asheham down, red, purple, dove blue grey, with the cross so melodramatically against it. What is the phrase I always remember – or forget. Look your last on all things lovely.

Yesterday Mrs Dedman was buried upside down. A mishap. Such a heavy woman, as Louie put it, feasting spontaneously upon the grave. And today she buries the aunt whose husband saw the vision at Seaford. Their house was bombed by the bomb we heard early one morning last week. And L. is lecturing and arranging the room. Are these the things that are interesting? that recall; that say Stop you are so fair? Well, all life is so fair, at my age. I mean, without much more of it I suppose to follow. And t'other side of the hill there'll be no rosy blue red snow. I am copying *Pointz Hall*. I am economising. I am to spend nothing. Is it difficult now to string tight? The great change isn't that but the change to the country.

Miss Gardner instead of Elizabeth Bowen. Small beer. But space, silence; and time.

Wednesday 15 January

Parsimony may be the end of this book. Also shame at my own verbosity, which comes over me when I see the twenty is it – books shuffled together in my room. Who am I ashamed of? Myself reading them.

Then Joyce is dead – Joyce about a fortnight younger than I am. I remember Miss Weaver, in wool gloves, bringing *Ulysses* in typescript to our tea table at Hogarth House. Roger I think sent her. Would we devote our lives to printing it? The indecent pages looked so incongruous: she was spinsterly, buttoned up. And the pages reeled with indecency. I put it in the drawer of the inlaid cabinet. One day Katherine Mansfield came, and I had it out. She began to read, ridiculing: then suddenly said, But there's something in this: a scene that should figure I suppose in the history of literature. He was about the place, but I never saw him. I bought the blue paper book, and read it here one summer I think with spasms of wonder, of discovery, and then again with long lapses of intense boredom. This goes back to a pre-historic world. And now all the gents are furbishing up opinions, and the books, I suppose, take their place in the long procession.

We were in London on Monday. I went to London Bridge. I looked at the river; very misty; some tufts of smoke, perhaps from burning houses. There was another fire on Saturday. Then I saw a cliff of wall, eaten out, at one corner; a great corner all smashed; a Bank; the Monument erect; tried to get a Bus; but such a block I dismounted. A complete jam of traffic; for streets were being blown up. So by tube to the Temple; and there wandered in the desolate ruins of my old squares: gashed; dismantled; the old red bricks all white powder. Grey dirt and broken windows; sightseers; all that completeness ravished and demolished.

Monday 20 January

I will be curt, compressed. A mood like another. Back from a damp, perhaps rather strained, visit to Charleston. Nessa and Quentin; Adrian has almost died of pneumonia. Visit from Oliver Strachey. All stocky gloom. Civilisation over for 500 years. I say to Nessa, Do you find painting gets slower? Yes. And money? Never think of it. And Helen? She does nothing. How can one do nothing? All the same Monks House is somehow cheerful. I am reading – oh all lit. for my book.

Sunday 26 January

A battle against depression, routed today (I hope) by clearing out kitchen; and by breaking into *Pointz Hall* two days, I think, of memoir writing. This trough of despair shall not, I swear, engulf me. The solitude is great. Rodmell life is very small beer. The house is damp. The house is untidy. But there is no alternative. What I need is the old spurt. "Your true life, like mine, is in ideas." Desmond said to me once. But one must remember one can't pump ideas. I begin to dislike introspection.

We are going to Cambridge for two days. There's a lull in the war. Six nights without raids. But Garvin says [in *The Observer*] the greatest struggle is about to come – say in three weeks – and every man, woman dog cat even weevil must girt their arms, their faith – and so on. Yes, I was thinking; we live without a future. That's what's queer, with our noses pressed to a closed door.

Friday 7 February

Why was I depressed? I cannot remember. A week of broken water impends. Cambridge; then Elizabeth Bowen; then Vita and Enid [Bagnold]. The snow came back. Marshes in the thaw a swamp. We were in London, and had to come home, owing to a bomb, by Dorking. London streets are very empty – Oxford Street a wide grey ribbon. At Charleston Clive was stockish, like a Bell. I said "What a risk Nessa ran in marrying him!" The third week in March is fixed for invasion. Now black out.

Sunday 16 February

In the wild grey water after last week's turmoil. I liked the dinner with Dadie best. All very lit up and confidential. Then Letchworth – the slaves chained to their typewriters, and their drawn set faces and the machines – the incessant more and more competent machines, folding, pressing, glueing and issuing perfect books. They can stamp cloth to imitate leather. Our Press is up in a glass case. Very long train journeys. Food skimpy. No butter. No jam. Elizabeth Bowen arrived two hours after we got back, and went yesterday; and tomorrow Vita.

Wednesday 26 February

Finished *Pointz Hall, The Pageant: The Play* – finally *Between the Acts* this morning.

Yesterday in the ladies lavatory at the Sussex Grill at Brighton I heard: She's a little simpering thing. I don't like her. But then he never did care for big women. He has wonderful white teeth. He always had. Its fun having the boys ... If he don't look out he'll be court martialled. They were powdering and painting, these common little tarts, while I sat, behind a thin door, p—ing as quietly as I could. Then at Fuller's. A fat, smart woman, in red hunting cap, pearls, check skirt, consuming rich cakes. Her shabby dependant also stuffing. They ate and ate. Something scented, shoddy, parasitic about them. Where does the money come to feed these fat white slugs? Brighton a love corner for slugs. The powdered, the pampered, the mildly improper. We cycled. Irritated as usual by the blasphemy of Peacehaven. No walks for ever so long. People daily. And rather a churn in my mind. And some blank spaces. Food becomes an obsession. I grudge giving away a spice bun. Curious – age, or the war? Never mind. Adventure. Make solid. But shall I ever write again one of those sentences that gives me intense pleasure? There is no echo in Rodmell – only waste air. No life; and so they cling to us. This is my conclusion. We pay the penalty for our rung in society by infernal boredom.

Saturday 8 March

No: I intend no introspection. I mark Henry James's sentence: Observe perpetually. Observe the oncome of age. Observe greed. Observe my own despondency. By that means it becomes serviceable. Or so I hope. I insist upon spending this time to the best advantage. I will go down with my colours flying. This I see verges on introspection; but doesn't quite fall in. Occupation is essential. And now with some pleasure I find that its seven; and must cook dinner. Haddock and sausage meat. I think it is true that one gains a certain hold on sausage and haddock by writing them down.

Oh dear yes, I shall conquer this mood. Its a question of letting things come one after another. Now to cook the haddock.

Monday 24 March

When we came in she was sitting perched on a three cornered chair with knitting in her hands. An arrow fastened her collar. And before five minutes had passed she had told us that two of her sons had been killed in the war. This, one felt, was to her credit. Sitting there I tried to coin a few compliments. But they perished in the icy sea between us. And then there was nothing.

A curious seaside feeling in the air today. It reminds me of lodgings on a parade at Easter. Everyone leaning against the wind, nipped and silenced. All pulp removed.

This windy corner. And Nessa is at Brighton, and I am imagining how it would be if we could infuse souls.

Octavia's story. Could I englobe it somehow? English youth in 1900.

L. is doing the rhododendrons . . .

INDEX

Index

Made in the USA
Lexington, KY
19 September 2010